ADVANCE PRAISE FOR *USES OF*

Roll up your sleeves and get ready for action: this book has s̲_ _ _ _ _ _ _ _ _ _ _
plan your part of the movement.
—The Yes Men

Arm your mind and fuel your spirit with the wide range of perspectives, case studies, and multi-layered insights captured in this great anthology of grassroots dreamers, thinkers, and doers. *Uses of a Whirlwind* lives up to its name by tossing our political imaginations around a bit and then harnessing some of the gale force inspiration with pragmatic approaches to building bigger, stronger, and smarter movements for fundamental social change. Don't let this essential resource blow by you without checking it out!
—Patrick Reinsborough | Co-founder SmartMeme Strategy & Training Project; Co-author with Doyle Canning of *Re:Imagining Change: How to Use Story-based Strategy to Win Campaigns, Build Movements and Change the World* (PM Press, 2010)

The gift of the whirlwind metaphor is that it allows us to see ostensibly disparate movements as a concentrated force of energy. What it speaks to is the interconnectedness of all struggles for basic dignity and respect. We can more readily see every moment then as an opportunity to make real connections with each other in the process of fighting against injustice and modeling the society we want. Care work in particular is singled out as providing a distinct site for facilitating this possibility. The book then implicitly and quite rightly challenges us to rebuild a system that doesn't just shift the balance of power but fundamentally transform social relations by holding our interdependence as human beings as a core value.
—Priscilla Gonzalez | Domestic Workers United

Uses of a Whirlwind is vitally important to radical community organizing in the United States today because the collection captures the spirit of the radical pedagogical theories of the Brazilian educator Paulo Freire. His "Popular Education" is based on the conviction that every human being is capable of looking critically at their world in a dialogical encounter with others, and can gradually perceive their own personal and social reality, and can then deal critically with it themselves. Oppressed people have no need of outside "experts" who lecture to them about their situation. These articles remind us that if we want to create a society based upon direct democracy, then the organizing that we employ must be based on democratic practice that creates the conditions for full and equal participation in discussion, debate, and decision-making by those who are oppressed, trusting them to change the power relations in society.
—Carlos Canales | Workplace Project & Bob Lepley | Freeport Community Worklink Center

Organizations and organizers mix up *in Uses of Whirlwind*—to get to know each other, to learn from each other—in order to build more effective movements for radical change. Such cross-fertilizations are essential if a better world is ever to blossom.
—John M. Miller | National Coordinator of the East Timor and Indonesia Action Network and member of the National Committee of the War Resisters League

It is no accident that all genuine revolutionary movements have emerged from activists unafraid to confront the limits of previous struggles, worn down by the necessary compromises of the epoch in which they worked. What's bracing about this book is the willingness of its writers to engage in a genuine critique of previous movements while remaining within the struggle of the concrete, everyday work of the 21st century. The praxis they seek is thus embedded in both the ideas they analyze and the actions they undertake. Anyone wanting to organize in ways that carry within them the prospect of societal transformation would do well to read this book.

   —Steve Burghardt | Professor of Community Organizing, Hunter College School of Social Work

Uses of a Whirlwind is an important contribution to an emergent, yet still sparse body of literature working to critically engage and rethink what it means to make political interventions today, in a world characterized by crises, uncertainties, and complexities. Not only is it one of the few collections of texts to do so grounded explicitly in the United States, it also brings crucial topics and perspectives often excluded from political and activist analyses to the fore. It argues that care and cultivating durable and holistic activist practices and communities are vitally important parts of any truly radical political project.

   —Michal Osterweil | Turbulence Collective

Uses of a Whirlwind offers a detailed assessment of the grassroots left in the United States—its recent developments, present limitations, and future possibilities. Leaving aside the formulae and dogmatism characteristic of so much political writing, the contributors focus their attention instead on messy, dynamic, unpredictable reality. The result is a book that inspires hope, demands engagement, and does not flinch from the hard work ahead.

   —Kristian Williams | Author of *Our Enemies in Blue: Police and Power in America* (South End Press, 2007)

Those who would like to hold sway over our lives seek to convince us that the constraints of our current situation are inescapable. In any case, they tell us, we cannot do anything about them. This book is a testimony to the fragility of those constraints. It documents a variety of current struggles against intolerable forms of power, offering both inspiration and strategy for everyone who, in one way or another, is subject to exploitation and oppression—that is to say, nearly everyone.

   —Todd May | Author of *The Political Philosophy of Poststructuralist Anarchism* (Pennsylvania State University Press, 2004)

The Zapatistas have a saying: "Walking, we ask questions." *Uses of a Whirlwind* follows this adage, serving not only as a crash course in today's most prominent political issues and movements but also raising important, rarely-asked questions about the subjects and organizing that have grabbed headlines and sparked our imaginations. *Uses* is not only a start to examining these movements and connecting them with each other, but is also an invitation to investigate and identify other, less prominent struggles for liberation and to develop connections between these movements and organizations to build a better world.

   —Victoria Law | Co-founder of Books Through Bars-NYC, Author of *Resistance Behind Bars: The Struggles of Incarcerated Women* (PM Press, 2009)

In 1925, Pan Africanist leader Marcus Garvey penned his "First Message" from Atlanta prison, proclaiming: "When I am dead wrap the mantle of the Red, Black and Green around me, for in the new life I shall rise with God's grace and blessing to lead the millions up the heights of triumph with the colors that you well know. Look for me in the whirlwind … I shall come and bring with me countless millions of Black slaves who have died in America and the West Indies and the millions in Africa to aid you in the fight for Liberty, Freedom and Life." Close to fifty years later, the militant members of New York City's Black Panther Party—on trial in the infamous Panther 21 case—they titled their collective autobiography "Look for me in the Whirlwind." It was not surprising, therefore, that Muhammad Ahmad called his recent review of Black Radical Organizations (1960–1975) "We Shall Return in the Whirlwind." To be sure, Team Color's *Uses of a Whirlwind* addresses different colors and different winds than those described by Garvey, Ahmad, and the Panthers. Yet the multiplicity of voices they have assembled, and the analysis they begin to develop out of their "militant inquiries" and "interventions" into the struggles and resistances of everyday life, provide real gifts to the left. They challenge us to look with fresh eyes at the assumptions too often made about the legacy of past decades. They incite us to take action based on new compositions of strategy, tactics, and organization. And they invite us to join them, in dialogue and in resistance, as we rebuild our revolutionary movements. If we are to mold our many whirlwinds into winds of truly lasting change, we would do well to listen, and to take up their call.

    —Matt Meyer | Editor of *Let Freedom Ring: A Collection of Documents from the Movements to Free U.S. Political Prisoners* (PM Press, 2009) & Founding member Resistance in Brooklyn

This is an important book. Distilling the lessons of the past and traversing the distance from today's struggles to the movements of the future, Team Colors has created a vital resource for anyone concerned with struggles for justice and liberation. Taking inspiration from the most exciting organizing happening in the U.S. today, and avoiding pitfalls such as the nonprofit industrial complex and vanguard leadership, they have created a document of resistance and hope. The voices in this book span movement elders and young revolutionaries, scholars and organizers, farmworkers and homeless activists. What they all have in common is that they have challenged the systems of patriarchy, white supremacy and economic exploitation that have held us back and helped create the whirlwinds that will bring a new world.

    —Jordan Flaherty | Author of *Floodlines: Community and Resistance from Katrina to the Jena Six* (Haymarket Books, 2010) & Editor of *Left Turn* Magazine

A keeper of knowledge on the Medicine Wheel for movement activists, *Uses of a Whirlwind* reaps vital stories of contemporary struggles and avails the next revolution of movement builders with critical seeds of insight—ones that might otherwise have been left fallow amongst a tangled dérive of impassioned memories and competing perspectives. It prepares a possibility space from which to strategize for the whirlwinds yet to come.

    —J. Cookson | SmartMeme Studios

If you think there's anything glaringly missing from this collection: get together with some likeminded people and start doing it yourselves.

    —David Graeber | Author, most recently, of *Direct Action: An Ethnography* (AK Press, 2009)

USES OF A WHIRLWIND

Movement, Movements, and Contemporary
Radical Currents in the United States

Edited by Craig Hughes, Stevie Peace, and Kevin Van Meter

for the Team Colors Collective

AK
PRESS
EDINBURGH · OAKLAND · BALTIMORE

Uses of a Whirlwind:
Movement, Movements, and Contemporary Radical Currents in the United States
Edited by Craig Hughes, Stevie Peace, and Kevin Van Meter
for the Team Colors Collective

All articles © by their respective authors

This edition © 2010 AK Press (Edinburgh, Oakland, Baltimore)

ISBN-13: 978–1–84935–016–7
Library of Congress Control Number: 2010925766

AK Press	AK Press UK
674–A 23rd Street	PO Box 12766
Oakland, CA 94612	Edinburgh EH8 9YE
USA	Scotland
www.akpress.org	www.akuk.com
akpress@akpress.org	ak@akdin.demon.co.uk

The above addresses would be delighted to provide you with the latest AK Press distribution catalog, which features several thousand books, pamphlets, zines, audio and video recordings, and gear, all published or distributed by AK Press. Alternately, visit our websites to browse the catalog and find out the latest news from the world of anarchist publishing:
www.akpress.org | www.akuk.com
revolutionbythebook.akpress.org

Printed in Canada on 100% recycled, acid-free paper with union labor.

Cover design by Josh MacPhee | www.justseeds.org
Interior by Margaret Killjoy | www.birdsbeforethestorm.net

Cover photograph by Rene Brochu
Cover art by Kristine Virsis | www.justseeds.org

TABLE OF CONTENTS

ORGANIZATION CASE STUDIES

MOVEMENT STRATEGIES 109

THEORETICAL ANALYSES 223

ACKNOWLEDGMENTS

As a COLLECTIVELY CONCEIVED AND executed project, *Uses of a Whirlwind: Movement, Movements, and Contemporary Radical Currents in the United States* came together from concentric circles of activity. Though compiled and edited by three members of the Team Colors Collective, *Whirlwinds* was also constructed through the tasks and active support of fellow collective member Conor Cash and close friend and comrade, Benjamin Holtzman. The influence of Holtzman and Cash on this project and on us personally cannot possibly be reflected upon in such a small space nor in the printed word.

The Journal of Aesthetics and Protest Press (Marc Herbst, Robby Herbst, and Christine Ukle) was among the first to believe in our fledgling research collective and responded by publishing a similarly envisioned online journal entitled *In the Middle of a Whirlwind: 2008 Convention Protests, Movement and Movements* in May of 2008. The Icarus Project, Philly's Pissed / Philly Stands Up (Philadelphia), Jen Angel, Brett Bloom, the anonymous "Smalltown U.S.A. Workers Center," Emmanuelle Cosse of ACT UP Paris and Regards (France), Brian Holmes, "I Want to Do This All Day" Audio Documentary Group, SmartMeme, CrimethInc., Daniel McGowan, and Ultra-Red (International) all joined Team Colors in the online project, and we very much look forward to working with each of these authors/groups again. Additionally, Jim Fleming and Stevphen Shukaitis of Autonomedia, Maia Ipp of City Lights, and Alexander Dwinell of South End Press deserve special recognition for their early support of the book, as do Joe Biel of Microcosm Publishing and Ramsey Kanaan of PM Press for their advice.

Kate Khatib, our editor at AK Press, has been dedicated to the *Whirlwinds* project even before it was conceived in book form. Throughout this process she has provided supportive words and useful criticism when necessary to produce the volume you have before you. We also want to acknowledge the important work of the AK Press collective on behalf of this volume and the betterment of radical politics and anarchist literature in general.

No collection of this sort is possible without the tireless efforts of our contributors, preface authors, and interviewees. Each of those included have taken much needed energy away from organizing campaigns, writing projects of their own, and their communities to participate in *Whirlwinds* and further the circulation of struggles in the United States. We couldn't be more honored to have them included among these pages.

The contents of the introduction to *Whirlwinds* were reviewed and greatly improved through the assistance of Chris Dixon, Ryan Fletcher, Farah Fosse, Juliana Hu Pegues, Eric Laursen, Kristyn Leach, Claudia Leung, Lize Mogel, Todd May, Amanda Plumb,

Anita Rapone, Tim Sarrantonio, Dvera Saxton, Charles Simpson, Spencer Sunshine, Tracy Serdjenian, Kristian Williams, and Eddie Yuen. While we took much of the brilliant advice offered, we did not take all of it, and any errors in judgment, fact, or argument are entirely our responsibility.

Team Colors, in no particular order, would like to acknowledge the contributions of the following: Rick Feldman and the Boggs Center for their assistance in setting up the interview with Grace Lee Boggs; Charles Overbeck of Eberhardt Press for printing our stunning promotional materials; Rene Brochu, who devoted considerable time and effort towards locating the photograph for the book's cover; Kristine Virsis of Justseeds, whose engaging art work and design accompany this cover's imagery; Frank Richards, Joseph B. Keady, and Alexis Bhagat for help with copy editing; and Paul Cash for assisting with transcription. We would also like to thank the following collectives and publications: Midnight Notes Collective (U.S.), Turbulence: Ideas for Movement (U.K./U.S./Europe), *The Commoner* (UK), Arranca! (Germany), Edu-Factory Collective (International), Precarias a la Deriva (Spain), Colectivo Situaciones (Argentina), *Upping the Anti* (Canada), the Institute for Anarchist Studies (U.S.), the editors of *An Atlas of Radical Cartography* (U.S.), Temporary Services (U.S.), *The Indypendent Reader* (U.S.), Groundswell Collective (U.S.) and all the militant/co-research collectives across the planet, who have lent their support and influence to Team Colors. Bluestocking Books (NYC), Red Emma's (Baltimore), Red and Black Café (Portland), Boxcar Books (Bloomington), Lucy Parsons Center (Boston), Dry River Collective (Tucson), Brian Mackenzie Center (now closed, DC), and Wooden Shoe (Philadelphia) have all hosted Team Colors events over the past two years, and we are greatly appreciative.

Finally, Craig Hughes would like to express deep thanks to his immediate family and friends, particularly Faline Hughes and Michael Fotis; Stevie Peace thanks his immediate family, friends, and Twin Cities communities, especially Marissa Steen for her gracious support and the crew of local libraries for being so accommodating; Kevin Van Meter appreciates all the time and attention that was lost to his partner Sarah Hughes, their dog Sissy, friends, and family while he was busily huddled over his computer working.

These circles widen to our other friends, colleagues, comrades, and communities, all too numerous to mention; they need not see their names in print to know who they are. But we will mention one: Jodi Tilton. Surrounded by a community of friends who loved her dearly and miss her terribly, she passed into the unknown one July evening in 2007 at the age of twenty-three.

Uses of a Whirlwind: Movement, Movements, and Contemporary Radical Currents in the United States *is dedicated to all those who occupy the small, imperceptible moments. For it is their collectivized refusals, transgressions, everyday resistances, inquiries, creative expressions, and desires that will create a new world, one in which many worlds fit.*

PREFACE

IN THE WIND

Roxanne Dunbar-Ortiz and Andrej Grubacic[1]

TEAM COLORS HAVE CREATED THIS indispensable book—the purpose of which is to inquire into current organizing in the United States—under the assumption that there needs to be much more organizing and that it must be consciously directed toward the working class and its relationship with capitalism and the state. The essays and interviews that make up the collection respond to the perceived desperate need of current radical movements for processes of inquiry, that is, investigations into the strengths of contemporary organizing and processes that involve dialogue and communications in relation to the realities and experiences of oppressed peoples. At the same time, Team Colors has been meticulous in assuring that the inquiries and dialogue herein reflect a requisite humility—that we do not have all the answers but will begin a journey to find them as we walk together.

As authors of this Preface, we have taken up the challenge of contributing our shared perspective to the project. As an inter-generational duo of historians, we have been collaborating on a number of writing and organizing projects during the past three years. At the same time, we are each writing books attempting to re-imagine a radical grand narrative of the U.S. *Uses of a Whirlwind* commanded our immediate interest, as we believe it will have the same effect on the readers of the collection.

This book arrives at a time of grave crisis for poor and working people and oppressed and Indigenous peoples all over the world. It appropriately focuses on social movements and their relative weakness within the U.S. As the carrier of advanced capitalism and imperialism, inherited from the massive European empires that ruled the world for centuries, the residents of the U.S. enjoy vast privileges and over-consumption of the world's resources. At the same time, the U.S. working class is burdened with paying for the maintenance of empire, with little financial security and with deteriorating infrastructure, particularly public education. The rampage of industrial capitalism has also for the past several centuries degraded the earth's ecological balance to the edge of disaster.

This Preface's title, "In the Wind," is police jargon for a suspect not captured, a fugitive. In the context of our work, we may imagine it signifying that the state has not yet consumed some of us. But that would make us simply outlaws, not revolutionaries. How we may go from being in the wind, grouped in whirlwinds, to making a revolution, is what we wish to figure out. To do that, we have to come to grips with U.S. history, which is itself a fugitive, having been held hostage to the master narrative of exceptional morality and manifest destiny. It is a history now up for grabs, looking to be told and fiercely contested. A grand narrative, not a counter-narrative, is needed to displace the one that persists in forming the ideology of Americanism.

A parable and an explication are called for.

PARABLE

THE YEAR OF THE GREEN Corn Rebellion, 1917, was a tumultuous year.[2] The war among the imperialist European states had been raging for three years when President Woodrow Wilson ordered U.S. troops to join the fray in April 1917. After nearly four decades of increasingly militant labor struggles in the U.S. with the Socialist Party and the Industrial Workers of the World (IWW) gaining members daily, it is not far-fetched to conclude that Wilson saw entry into the war as an effort to unite U.S. citizens around a patriotic cause, while simultaneously defusing the social revolution he was determined to crush.

U.S. socialists and anarcho-syndicalists had a strong sense of connection with like efforts elsewhere. Revolution in Mexico, fundamentally agrarian in nature, was followed closely. Anarchists Ricardo and Enrique Flores Magón, Mexican brothers in San Diego, organized on both sides of the border, and with the IWW in the U.S.; Ricardo was incarcerated and died in Ft. Leavenworth federal prison, having been jailed for speaking against U.S. entry into the European war. In the spring of 1916, the northern Mexico revolutionary leader, Pancho Villa, led his army across the U.S.-Mexico border into the small border town of Columbus, New Mexico. Eighteen U.S. citizens were killed along with ninety members of Villa's army. Wilson sent his top general John J. Pershing—a veteran of U.S. wars against the Lakota, Puerto Rico, Cuba, and many other nations—with 10,000 troops to capture Villa, employing the new technology of aerial surveillance. After a year of failure, the troops withdrew, and Pershing led U.S. forces in Europe. 1917 was also the year of triumph of the Russian Revolution. It was also the year of extreme U.S. government repression against any person or organization that opposed entering the European war, which meant repression of Socialists and anarchists.

In the summer of that year, the low, hard hills and wooded creek bottoms of eastern Oklahoma were the scene of an organized rebellion by some 1,500 Anglo, African, and Muskogee tenant farmers. Trouble had been brewing since the U.S. entered World War I in April. The Working Class Union's (WCU) local lodges in Oklahoma had lain dormant for six months, but stimulated by the IWW, they began a new organizing campaign. The little red membership card was once again a common sight along the South Canadian River Valley. Lights from kerosene lamps flickered at late hours through the windows of little rural schoolhouses throughout the countryside as secret meetings laid plans and set deadlines. All spring there were vivid indications of a discontent of some more than ordinary gravity. Rumors that riots would break out on registration day, June 5, did not materialize. But the deep rumbling continued while the tenants were working the crops. Then in August the lightning flashed and the storm broke.

Within two weeks, civil authorities restored order, with 450 men arrested and held for trial, charged with resistance to the draft and seditious conspiracy. The rest were bonded as government witnesses or freed through pity or a lack of conclusive evidence. At first consideration, the rebellion was a simple political protest against the draft law, quickly crushed.

Newspapers referred to the rebels as "draft-dodgers," "slackers," or "anti-draft resisters," when in fact they were antiwar and anti-capitalist radicals. The rebels were certainly not alone in their resistance. More or less organized antagonism to the draft appeared all over the country, including in other agrarian settings. Yet, this largely political explanation of the Oklahoma rebellion is superficial, for it never really makes clear why these particular tenant farmers were the ones to follow the agitators, to organize, and finally to break into conscious, headlong defiance of the recognized government of the U.S.; after all, they did announce their intention of overthrowing the government in Washington and replacing it with the Socialist Commonwealth. They also believed their action would embolden the four Railroad Brotherhoods and the IWW and the Socialist Party, with their hundreds of thousands of militants, to join them.

Undoubtedly, there were hundreds, if not thousands, of Green Corn Rebellion uprisings around the world during this revolutionary era, rebellions that flared and were crushed. Stories, especially among Indigenous peoples, are passed down through the generations, but they don't make it into the history books. The Green Corn Rebellion does not make it into many history books, except for a few studies of agrarian socialism, and then often negatively, even with ridicule. Or when lauded, it is placed in the master narrative of settler agrarian uprisings, most often pressuring the government to seize Indigenous lands, as was the case with Bacon's Rebellion and others. Or, it is tarred as "populist." But the Green Corn Rebellion was animated by a class-consciousness that sought to overcome race, which is significant in that it wasn't until the late 1920s that even the Communist Party began to embrace racial equality. The Green Corn Rebellion took the form of a multi-racial armed struggle, a political anti-war movement, against conscription and against U.S. entrance into the European war ("the rich man's war" as they called it), against capitalism and imperialism.

Between 1906 and 1917, the IWW and the Socialist Party won converts on a mass scale in small towns and the countryside of Oklahoma, as well in the camps of the coal mining and oil workers. There had never been anything like it in the rural U.S. The Socialists adopted the religious evangelists' technique of holding huge week-long encampments with charismatic speakers, male and female, usually near small towns. Many Protestant Christian evangelists were themselves converts to the gospel of socialism, which took the teachings inside the main—and sometimes only—community institution. Socialists were elected as local officials and the lampposts of many towns were hung with red flags. In 1915 alone, 205 mass encampments were held in Oklahoma. This was the seething social cauldron in the region and the country when the Green Corn Rebellion exploded in the summer of 1917. It is the story of the power of grievance meeting vision.

The racial question is central, as always in the U.S. It is amazing that white, black, and brown rural poor people, in that part of the country then, in the Age of Jim Crow and Lynching, of state-sponsored (both states and federal government) violence against African-American, were willing and able to come together and think of themselves together overthrowing the government. They were not seeking to become individual yeoman farmers of Jefferson's fantasy, but together to build the socialist commonwealth where they could raise food, and no one would go hungry, with no rich man's army to take their sons away. This indisputable fact is the heart of the story.

One condition is fundamental and essential in accounting for the situation in southeastern Oklahoma at the time of the rebellion: namely, the fact that Oklahoma had been Indian Territory, promised by the government to remain so "as long as water shall run, as long as grass shall grow." This was the territory carved out of the Louisiana Purchase to be a dumping ground for Indigenous farmers forced out of their homelands east of the Mississippi, the best known of them the "five civilized tribes," the Cherokees, Creeks, Choctaws, Chickasaws, and Seminoles, who had for thousands of years farmed the rich land that now makes up the southern states of the U.S. During the presidency of Andrew Jackson, they were forcibly removed to Indian Territory in what they remember as the "Trail of Tears."

Despite the uprooting and hardships, the displaced peoples, representing dozens of Indigenous nations, rebuilt their institutions and adopted many European technologies, such as the printing press and written language, formal orphanages and schools. As the U.S. military moved to annex western and southwestern Indian lands following the Civil War, the refugees of those wars were also forced onto reservations in Indian Territory, on top of the buffalo hunting communities already there—the Kiowas, Comanches, Wichitas, Poncas, and Caddos. Then, in 1889, following legislation to divide and allot the communal Indigenous holdings, Indian Territory was opened to non-Indigenous settlement, as the federal government abrogated every treaty previously entered into with the Indigenous nations.

From the beginning of establishing Indian Territory, Anglo-American men had slowly filtered in, sometimes illegally, often as missionaries and traders; soon after the Civil War, Anglo- and African-American families began to enter the region in increasing numbers. Some married into the tribes and became legal members and landholders. By 1880, these numbered several thousand. Indian Territory was also a haven for African-Americans escaping from slavery before the Civil War, and for free blacks afterwards, due to the autonomy of living in a territory governed by sovereign Indigenous nations. Others came as businessmen, merchants, or railroad employees on the Atlantic and Pacific, MKT, or Santa Fe lines that now crisscrossed the territory. Still others came as coal miners, imported under permits granted by the tribal governments, who brought with them European working class radicalism that meshed with the rising agrarian radicalism. Several thousand more white men arrived illegally, many of them outlaws who fled there and lived under protection of the tribes, including the infamous former Confederate guerrillas such as Jesse James and Belle Starr. The Cherokee and other southeastern tribal elites had owned enslaved Africans in their original southeastern homeland, and they brought the Africans with them to Indian Territory. Freed after the Civil War, a significant population of Freedmen also became renters in the industrialization of agriculture in eastern Oklahoma, as did a mass of poor Indians, after the federal government divided their common lands into allotments in the 1890s. As the tenant system grew more entrenched, "full blood" Indians soon held only a few acres of good land; most of it had drifted into the clutches of intermarried white men.

With a history of chaos, Indian Territory developed a system of cultivating land where the worker was an industrial wage-hand, and an atmosphere of violence and poverty prevailed. Cotton became the single cash crop, binding tightly the lives of most of the people of that part of the state to its rise or fall. By 1910, the oil industry was firmly established in eastern Oklahoma as well. This setting provided both the basic foundation and deepest explanation of the situation in eastern Oklahoma in the summer of 1917.

For a decade before the Green Corn Rebellion, the most popular and powerful vehicle for protest by the tenant farmers was the Socialist Party. Oklahoma Socialism developed a hybrid religious appeal. Eugene Debs, head of the Socialist Party at the national level, could give gathered tenants a speech in the Holiness Tabernacle at Durant, and they would sing Socialist songs that were themselves the tunes of traditional hymns. The large Socialist camp meetings of those days suggest the evangelical flavor of the movement. An encampment lasted a week or ten days and attracted crowds of thousands. Many came for miles in wagons. The program included music, history, and economics classes, as well as a great deal of oratory. The Socialists also published the *Appeal to Reason* and the *National Rip-Saw* that got out to every community. The Socialist Party supported not only women's right to vote, but also the full equality of women. Women leaders and encampment speakers provided living examples of women's public role.

The Socialist Party platform contained attractive proposals for the support of the debtor-renters, advocating laws setting maximum legal interest rates and invalidating all contracts that charged more than the legal rate. They called for state-owned elevators and warehouses, and demanded tax exemptions for farm dwellings, tools, livestock, and improvement, as well as state insurance against natural disasters. However, the Socialists were unable to produce results and lost the trust of the tenants who sought more radical solutions in the direct action they found in the WCU, which was founded in 1914. Like the IWW, the WCU advocated the abolition of rent, interest, profits, and the wage system.

Many blacks and Indians joined with whites in the WCU, but this fact should not be taken as a sign of lack of intolerance. The poor Scots-Irish settlers who came to eastern Oklahoma came from a tradition of settling and squatting on stolen Indian lands, dreaming of becoming plantation owners and buying enslaved Africans. To see the WCU and the Green Corn Rebellion as a movement for the brotherhood of races is misleading. The fact that these groups who did not like each other united due to their common situation—their class interests—makes the Green Corn Rebellion a first in the history of the U.S. Similarly, the challenge to male supremacy in their programs and actions did not create a paradise for women, but did bring whole families into the struggles, out of which extraordinary women's leadership emerged. The rebellion failed, and the descendants of the white rebels may have later joined the Klan or voted for proud racist George Wallace in 1968, and their descendants may now be in patriot militias or the very recent Tea Party activities, but the fact of their unity with other oppressed neighbors at the time cannot help but hold promise for the unity of the oppressed and exploited.

But this is more than an uplifting, if tragic, story. It reveals both the secrets to success as well as the seemingly impenetrable barriers to assembling local movements into a revolutionary movement. We could have presented dozens, even hundreds of narratives about Indigenous resistance and liberated territories throughout colonial and U.S. history, but the Green Corn Rebellion is one of the few examples of an organic inter-racial movement based in the working class, the least mobilized of the working class at that. There are lessons in the winds of our past, histories of the fugitives who came before us. But there are other places, hidden both from the wind and learned theorists, where surprising glimpses of possibility may be found. Allow us another, more recent parable.

From April 11 to 21, 1993, what appears to have been the longest prison rebellion in U.S. history took place in Lucasville, Ohio. Not many on the Left paid attention to this rebellion, despite the fact that more than four hundred prisoners were involved. Nine prisoners and a guard were killed. After a negotiated surrender, five prisoners in the rebellion were sentenced to death.

This rebellion is still largely unknown outside of Ohio.[3] Just like with insurgent Oklahoma, the single most remarkable thing about Lucasville is that white and black prisoners formed a common front against the authorities. When the authorities came into the occupied cell block after the surrender they found slogans written on the walls of the corridor and in the gymnasium that read: "Convict unity," "Convict race," "Black and whites together." The five prisoners from the rebellion on death row—the Lucasville Five—are a microcosm of the rebellion's united front and its politics of "convict race." Two of the blacks are Sunni Muslims. Both of the whites were, at the time of the rebellion, members of the Aryan Brotherhood. What can be learned from this? The self-organized resistance and inter-racial solidarity of prisoners can become a model for the rest of us in overcoming racism and building an organic inter-racial working class movement. In Lucasville, as in Oklahoma, solidarity was not constructed in the university library: it can only be built on the basis of action that is in the common interest, where experience runs ahead of ideology and program. Actions speak louder than organizational labels, a radical praxis that is already existent and resides not in theory but practice.

So what do these parables suggest? *What kind of revolution can occur in the middle of the whirlwinds?* Wobblies and Oklahoma socialists offered an image of a constructive revolution, built on the positives of a socialist commonwealth emerging from existing creations improvised from below. The preamble to the IWW Constitution gives us an illustration of this perspective, declaring, "We are forming the structure of the new society within the shell of the old." One choice that exists today in the U.S. is to revive this experience, to infuse it with new energy, new passion and new insights; in the process to discover a *revolutionary praxis for the twenty-first century*; to rekindle dreams of a "socialist commonwealth"; and to bring socialism, that "forbidden word," into a new and contemporary meaning.

EXPLICATION

THIS BOOK INTENDS TO ASK questions. The Zapatistas have a word for it: asking questions while walking (*Caminar Preguntando*), maintaining humility in listening and being open to other people's perspectives and experiences in the world, rather than claiming superiority. Another important principle of Zapatismo is to propose, and not impose (*Proponer, y No Imponer*). In this spirit, we would like to propose that the contemporary reading of past revolutionary experiences—from Wobblies and Oklahoma socialists to Lucasville prisoners—could be organized around the following elements:

1. *Opposition to imperialism and militarization*: This was the dynamic aspect of the radical Socialist Party—local working class and rural organizing along with opposition to capitalism and imperialism—driven even more that way after the founding of the IWW in 1905. But when the grassroots took these revolutionary ideas to heart, devised their own demands and program, and rose up, the Socialist Party leadership in Oklahoma denounced them and abandoned them, instead of organizing to build upon the audacious actions and program of the Green Corn organization. There is a knee-jerk fear of 'the people' becoming a mob, more in the U.S. than elsewhere, and it has severely limited revolutionary development. When John Brown attacked the army base at Harper's Ferry with a guerrilla unit—made up mostly of African-American fugitives from slavery—with the goal of sparking a massive slave uprising, the great majority of Abolitionist organizations and wealthy donors distanced themselves from him.

The most difficult and seemingly impossible task in building a revolutionary movement within the working class in the U.S. is introducing anti-imperialism and anti-capitalism, to question the military occupations, wars of aggression and coups, as well as the more nuanced but just as destructive "humanitarian interventions," such as those that took place in the Balkans. But a way must be found, because therein lies the heart of U.S. nationalism and arguments for citizen unity and sacrifice. We have before us a European settler state forged in nearly four centuries of wars, occupations, and genocides against the Indigenous nations of what now constitutes the United States. Through study, observation, discussion, and experience, it may be possible to assess the quality of U.S. patriotism, its sources and content. A commonwealth cannot be built upon lies.

Yet none of this can be presented or argued abstractly, as is often done by most of the radical groups that do include U.S. imperialism in their organizing; still others simply avoid the subject. It is important to figure out how U.S. imperialism and militarism affect communities, not in isolation, but *with* communities. For instance, there may be a military base nearby, and projects to organize in the military and in military communities are much needed. Indeed, with this country involved in major wars, occupations, and military operations raging on every continent along with the maintenance of over a thousand military bases, there are active and returning or soon to be recruited young people in nearly every poor community in the country, and the military has become a major job opportunity in a time of capitalist economic crisis. Also, nearly every community in the U.S., even rural areas, now have members of immigrant communities from Africa, Asia, the Caribbean, and Latin America, especially from Mexico and Central America, who can provide their uninformed neighbors with testimonies. Above all, in every inch of U.S. claimed territory are found the remnants of Indigenous nations and some thriving Indigenous communities and nations. One way to introduce the history of U.S. conquest and genocide of the Indigenous where there are no descendants still living there is to conduct research of the specific community's history, determining which Indigenous people were killed or forced out. This kind of research has been done by radicals in communities throughout Germany regarding the absence of Jews where once there were thriving communities.

2. *Self-activity*: In creating a new revolutionary praxis, it is possible to rely on self-activity expressed through organizations at the base. Industrial Workers of the World organizing is an example of "solidarity unionism." Unlike relentlessly vertical, mainstream trade unionism, always beyond the arena of the local union, solidarity unionism, premised on direct action, is local, horizontal, and unmediated—a social vision for working people and no job hierarchy for organizing. Older labor models had a social vision for creating a post-capitalist society, but that disappeared following World War II, with the Taft-Hartley purge of labor movement radicals. Looking at solidarity unions in Toledo, Minneapolis, and San Francisco in the early 1930s, or today at the Starbucks Workers Union, it's encouraging to find that these are all *horizontal* gatherings of all kinds of workers in a given *locality*, who then form regional and national networks with counterpart bodies elsewhere. This form of self-activity closely corresponds to the Mayan idea of *mandar obediciendo* that informs the contemporary practice of the Zapatistas. What the Zapatistas and also the Bolivian revolutionaries mean by this is an active effort to create and maintain a horizontal network of self-governing communities, connected through countless linkages: socializing power rather than taking state power.

3. *Local institution*: The Green Corn Rebellion was short-lived; this is not unusual. Every generation of revolutionaries—every experiment of "government from below"—has been haunted by what we might call "Michelet's problem." Michelet, a famous French

historian, wrote the following words about the French revolution: "That day everything was possible, the future was the present and time but a glimmer of eternity." But as Cornelius Castoriadis used to say, if all that is created is just a glimmer of hope, the bureaucrats will inevitably show up and turn off the light. The history of revolutions is, on the one hand, a history of tension between brief moments of revolutionary creativity and the making of long-lasting institutions. On the other hand, the history of revolutions often reads like a history of *revolutionary alienation*, when the revolutionary was, more than anything else, ultimately and almost inevitably alienated from his or her own creations. Michelet's problem is about resolving this tension between brief epiphanies of revolutionary hope and the long-term institutionalization of revolutionary change.

The crucial question, then, is how to create such lasting institutions, or better yet, an ongoing culture of *constructive* struggle that financially can sustain itself beyond donors and individual contributions. So what is missing? How to approach the answer to Michelet's problem? We would like to suggest here the importance of local institutions. A local institution is, first and foremost, a place where people conduct their own affairs—an immigrant center or local union, for example—that expands in time of crisis to take on new powers and responsibilities, and then, after the revolutionary tide ebbs, continues to represent, in institutionalized form, an expanded version of what existed to begin with. In U.S. labor history, the most important meetings and organizations—including the ones that led to the formation of the Congress of Industrial Organizations in the 1930s—took place in pre-existing local institutions, such as fraternal societies, credit unions, burial associations, singing clubs, churches, and newspapers. One cannot hope to understand what happened in the South and in the Civil Rights Movement without understanding that student action emerged from pre-existing institutions such as African-American churches and college campuses. The Zapatistas provide perhaps the clearest example of all: hundreds if not thousands of years of life in pre-existing *asembleas*, and a decade of organizing by a group of Marxist-Leninists from the universities of Mexico.

Revolutionaries can often light a spark, but whether or not a fire will catch hold depends on the response of people in their pre-existing local unions, factory committees, benefit associations, and other local institutions. Some of the self-governing institutions are old entities that have taken on new powers and objectives. In Chiapas, Mayan *asembleas* play this role. In the hills of Oklahoma, evangelical encampments served this purpose. In Russia, soviets were the heart of the revolution. The nature of a revolutionary process is such that the distinction between old and new local institutions becomes blurred. The role of new revolutionaries is above all to nurture the creation, spread, and authority of local institutions to defend the existence, legitimacy, and autonomy of such formations. Following the Zapatistas, we invite our readers to construct, and not destroy (*Construir, y No Destruir*).

4. *Solidarity*: More than a movement, a community of radical transformation and a culture of resistance are possible. We offer a form of radical community activism in the process of "accompaniment." Accompaniment is simply the idea of walking side by side with another on a common journey. When an activist walks beside someone rich in experience but lacking formal skills, each contributes something vital to the process. Accompaniment thus understood presupposes, not uncritical deference, but equality. Most importantly, an individual can join a movement without being 'politically correct,' without theory, at the same time that the organizers will share theory and analysis that avoids mere rhetoric.

Revolutionaries may choose to accompany people in struggle in the creation and maintenance of popular self-governing institutions, walking beside people in struggle just as we are, hopefully providing support and certain useful skills. "I do not organize you; I accompany you, you accompany me, or, more precisely, we accompany each other." Implicit in this practice is the understanding that neither of us has a complete map of where our path will lead. In the words of Antonio Machado: "*Caminante, no hay camino. Se hace camino al andar.*" ("Seeker, there is no road. We make the road by walking.")

One of the authors of this Preface, Andrej, experienced this vision of accompaniment while he was still living in Yugoslavia. A few students from Belgrade University recognized that the only organized resistance to the encroaching tide of privatization and neoliberalism was coming from a group of workers in the Serbian countryside. They decided to go to northern Serbia, to a city called Zrenjanin, and approach the workers. These workers were very different from the students. Some of them had fought in the recent Yugoslav wars. Most of them were very conservative, patriarchal, and traditional. The students went there and offered their skills: they spoke foreign languages; they had internet access and know-how in a country where only two percent of the people used this service; they had connections with workers and movements outside Serbia; still others were good writers, and a few had legal expertise. The workers were grateful but understandably quite skeptical, as were the students. Soon, however, something like a friendship emerged. Students and workers started working together and learning from each other. In the process of struggle against the boss, the private armies he sent to the factory, and the state authorities, trust formed. Both workers and students changed. Today, after ten years of accompaniment, the same group of students plays an important role in the Coordinating Committee for Workers Protests in Serbia, where five Strike Committees represent workers from three cities and five branches of industry.

Roxanne had a similar experience following the Wounded Knee uprising in the Lakota Nation at Pine Ridge in 1973. It had started from many sparks, mostly very local grievances, but with the backdrop of the biggest grievance of all, the century-old illegal taking of the sacred Black Hills and the break-up of Lakota territory into small reservations, all contradicting the 1868 peace treaty between the Lakota and the U.S. The Lakota elders had invited the American Indian Movement (AIM) to assist them. AIM was founded in 1968 by 'urban' Indians from many different Indian communities, most of whom were relocated through a 1950s federal program that placed them in the poorest neighborhoods of major industrial centers, living in poor housing. Two of the AIM founders were recently released from prison; a few were Vietnam veterans. AIM had played a role in the seizure and occupation of Alcatraz in 1969–1971, then led the November 1972 "Trail of Broken Treaties" to Washington DC where they occupied the Bureau of Indian Affairs Building, renaming it the "Native American Embassy" with a huge banner strung up outside the building. Those experiences had honed their skills as militant activists, but not until they went to Pine Ridge did they begin a process of accompaniment. Following the end of the Wounded Knee occupation, there were more than a hundred Indians and some non-Indians charged with crimes and misdemeanors, miring AIM in legal nightmares while a reign of terror against AIM families took place at Pine Ridge and all over Indian country. The Indigenous elders of AIM wanted to go to the World Court and the United Nations to challenge the U.S. regarding the treaty, insisting that nothing would change until they could regain freedom and the sovereignty of their nations. They suggested that the involved Indigenous lawyers and scholars do research and find a way to internationalize the Sioux Treaty and all Indian treaties. Only a few began this work, but the numbers grew during the next twenty years. The international Indigenous movement exploded in the public eye in 1992, when the young Mayan leader, Rigoberta Menchú Tun, received the Nobel Peace Prize in the midst of a huge continental Indigenous movement against celebrating the 500–year anniversary of Columbus. After years of Indigenous lobbying at the U.N., an official study of Indigenous treaties was completed, and the U.N. General Assembly approved the *Declaration on the Rights of Indigenous Peoples*. Then, to the amazement of the world, Evo Morales, of the Andean Aymara community, emerged from a grassroots rural labor movement, Movement Toward Socialism, to become President of Bolivia. But we must remember that an element of this miracle had its roots in the tiny, impoverished hamlet of Pine Ridge, South Dakota.[4]

In this project of accompaniment, there are accessible models to emulate, such as the IWW, as well as those Mexican intellectuals, students, and professors, who went to live in the jungle, and after ten years, came forth as protagonists of a revolution from below. The Zapatistas were not footloose: they went to a particular place and stayed there, in what must have been incredibly challenging and difficult circumstances, for a decade of accompaniment. The central component of accompaniment is to be rooted in particular places, so that when crises come, the revolutionary will already be a trusted friend and member of the community.

A NEW LIBERTARIAN-SOCIALIST, INTER-RACIAL movement is possible only in the context of practical, lived solidarity that transcends differences while learning from and respecting difference, and avoiding the corrosiveness of "white guilt." A new movement, emerging from the whirlwinds, will be built on the understanding that the only movement worthy of that name is inter-racial, with the full participation of women, rooted in the struggles of working class people, built in the process of walking while asking questions, of accompaniment, as a specific form of radical community organizing. Proceeding in a way that builds community—not only organizing skills, but also conduct toward one another—engenders a sense of truly being brothers and sisters. We must try to convince and not defeat, to practice comradeship and keep our networks, our social centers, our collectives, and our affinity groups alive. If we are to find our place in the middle of the whirlwind, our communities of struggle must become affective communities—places where we practice direct dialogue and prefigurative relationships.

The new generation of revolutionaries has a huge responsibility today, most of all in the current crisis of capitalist civilization. It will take imagination, creativity, and flexibility to demonstrate that radical transformation of society is indeed possible, that another world is conceivable. It will take a new kind of praxis informed by history, a reinvented and solidarity-centered libertarian socialist praxis that combines direct democracy with solidarity unionism. It will take the creation of a strategy with a program, accompaniment with local institutions, anti-imperialism with anti-militarism, structural analysis with prefigurative theory arising from practice, and a stubborn belief in the possibility of overcoming racism with affective anti-sectarianism.

Team Colors' process of creating this collection, as well as its intent and spirit, furthers and creates inquiry and dialogue in interpreting contemporary political realities. Its purpose is to launch dialogue processes, inquiring into current struggles, their composition, and their strengths and challenges. We have attempted to contribute to that endeavor here. The following texts come together as a many-faceted model of such processes, which, it is hoped, will provoke and inspire conversations, moving toward these ends and ideals.

NOTES

1   The authors wish to thank Matt Bokovoy, Rachel Jackson, Margaret Randall, and members of Radical Writers—Unite! (Raj Patel, Amy Sonnie, and James Tracy) for reading this Preface at an early stage of writing and for making useful suggestions.

2   John Womack, Jr. contributed much of the material and analysis on the Green Corn Rebellion in an article he co-authored with Roxanne Dunbar-Ortiz, "Revolution in the Air: The Historical Significance of the Green Corn Rebellion," published in *The Oklahoma Revelator: A People's Almanac and Cultural Quarterly* 1:2 (Winter 2009), from which this narrative is taken. He is the author of the classic biography, *Zapata and the Mexican Revolution*.

3   Staughton Lynd has written about the Lucasville rebellion in "Black and White and Dead All Over," *Race Traitor*, no. 8 (Winter 1998), which can also be found online at: HTTP://RACETRAI-TOR.ORG; "Lessons from Lucasville," *The Catholic Worker*, v. LXV, no. 7 (Dec. 1998); and "The Lucasville Trials," *Prison Legal News*, v. 10, no. 6 (June 1999). This work is gathered together in his book *Lucasville: The Untold Story of a Prison Uprising* (Philadelphia: Temple University Press, 2004). Staughton has also contributed to a play by Gary Anderson about the Lucasville events.

4   For a brief history of the development of the international Indigenous movement, see Roxanne Dunbar-Ortiz's article, "What Brought Evo Morales to Power? The Role of the International Indigenous Movement and What the Left is Missing," HTTP://MRZINE.MONTHLYREVIEW.ORG/2006/DUNBARORTIZ060206.HTML.

FOREWORD

THE WHIRLWINDS PROJECT IN CONTEXT

Marc Herbst for **The Journal of Aesthetics and Protest Press**

I N CONTRAST TO THE UNIFORM and paranoid mainstream reporting on the potential for radical collective action, and despite the equally rhetorical statements on the potential of activist practice by Leftist agitators, *Uses of a Whirlwind* comes across as simultaneously passionate and realistic, idealistic and critical—all while maintaining a balanced appeal for the full potential of politically engaged cultural work. We are very excited to see this collection in print.

Two years ago, we published an early online incarnation of this effort, entitled *In the Middle of a Whirlwind: 2008 Convention Protests, Movement and Movements*. That collection asked readers to comprehend the potentials and difficulties, as well as strategies, of contemporary radical efforts in context of the short-lived media-fueled moment of the protests against the Democratic and Republican conventions in 2008.[1] This substantially revised print edition again creates an important space for reflection and discussion of contemporary radical struggle. Though the project is released at the time of the 2010 U.S. Social Forum, it is less oriented toward a particular event and instead seeks to comprehend the particulars of contemporary radical movement building in context of the current crises of capitalism and the movements against it.

The initial 2008 online collection, framed as a "strategic intervention," assumed legitimacy for its editorial decisions not because of the esteem of the writers included (although some were quite esteemed), and not because of the legitimacy of its publisher (they approached us, an outlier in the world of activist publishing), but because Team Colors believes that their ethically engaged approach to dialogue *assumes* meaningful conversation between a multitude of actors. Team Colors' strategy for engagement went deeper than collecting and editing essays. As one example, in launching the project they aimed to create posters that did more than advertise—they wanted a poster that was part of the conversation. Cognizant of both the digital divide and the fact that people can be visual thinkers, Team Colors wanted a conceptual work that placed viewers in the thought patterns of the broader project. The posters were then sent to infoshops, cultural spaces, and workers' centers throughout the States. They realized that these were already open dialogical spaces that they needed to reach in order to make the collection useful. The aim was to, in light of the 2008 anti-convention protests, generate a broad critical cadre to push the longevity and scope of the two convention mobilizations beyond their momentary spectacles. Similarly, in this volume Team Colors seeks to deepen discussion of current organizing at a critical juncture.

The initial project in 2008, much like this one, sought to compose a readership—gluing a diverse pool of subjects together, knowing that the gathered all might talk together. Importantly, in 2008 and in 2010, Team Colors critically includes voices they may disagree with within the discussions they frame—not for some fake "balance," but because these voices provide important insights into organizing and help to assist dynamic conversations of the multitude at the table.

We assumed that it was for the goal of composing a broader critical movement that Team Colors approached us about the first incarnation of *Whirlwinds* in the fall of 2008. Coming out of the anti-globalization movement, we have nurtured a culturally-minded and politically-engaged readership of artists and do-it-yourself community organizers. Innately, our hybrid place is an odd perch. Readers of the journal we have published for a decade, *The Journal of Aesthetics and Protest*, are making things happen between people —as teachers, cultural organizers, musicians, fashion designers, and graphic designers. Our journal communicates and activates ideas with multiple publics, and the initial *Whirlwinds* collection, with its intent of bringing together a wide diversity of voices, was something we were very sympathetic to.

Our magazine and broader project was borne out of the anti-globalization movement of the Clinton years, and our pages have been pressed through the Bush era. As Brian Holmes recently wrote, "1999 was our 1968."[2] The protests in Seattle against the WTO and the anti-globalization organizing surrounding those demonstrations set out ideals and presented a realm for imagining the possibilities for growing movements. For us, these were primarily the terrain of the social potential of networks. Seattle showed how networked organizing, in the underbelly of networked global capital and through the digital activist networks of the seemingly limitless internet, can be successful. By the time 2008 rolled around, this movement was more than stalled. Corporate web 2.0 and lifestyle development had cashed in on the liberatory networking of the 1990s and created an even more unequal space, which continues to make horizontal organizing increasingly difficult.

The initial online journal represented for us and our readership a needed theoretical rupture. Team Colors, along with the UK-based Turbulence: Ideas for Movement and others, are part of a trend to critically re-engage in protest movements, so as to take stock of what has occurred since Seattle. It becomes clear that much of the late nineties' protests were based on activism as a global dance party. By the 2005 Gleneagles actions in Scotland against the Group of 8, the party had been badly co-opted.

Refusing then to imagine a nonexistent wind at their backs, the 2008 *Whirlwinds* brought to the table influences of the Italian autonomous struggles of the 1970s and its more studied analysis of how movements are borne. The autonomous network of struggles in Italy during the 1970s looked at movements as smart organisms, growing in relationship to the society around them. The theoretical framework Team Colors attempted to enact in their 2008 collection contributed greatly to our Aesthetics & Protest collective. Since then we have been able to ask aesthetic questions in ways that would not have been previously possible.

As Team Colors, their readers, and the broader movements generate more responses to the questions that spring from the *Whirlwinds* collections, we will all undoubtedly participate in the rise of another clearly articulated praxis linked to a broadly successful movement. In this sense, *Uses of a Whirlwind* articulates not only the messages of its contents, but the desires of a broader populace that is keen on making a revolution possible.

NOTES

1   The initial collection was entitled, *In the Middle of a Whirlwind: 2008 Convention Protests, Movement and Movements*, and is available online at HTTP://WWW.JOAAP.ORG.

2   Brian Holmes, "Decipher the Future. Experimental work in mobile territories" in *Springerin*, Issue 3 (2009); HTTP://WWW.SPRINGERIN.AT/DYN/HEFT.PHP?POS=0&LANG=EN.

INTRODUCTION

SOWING RADICAL CURRENTS IN THE ASHES OF YESTERYEAR:

The Many Uses of a Whirlwind

Team Colors Collective

> *When earthquakes, floods, droughts and volcanic eruptions strike where*
> *we live, they are usually considered instances of crisis and unmitigated*
> *natural disaster. Yet, recently I have had opportunities to witness how the*
> *meaning of crisis depends entirely on one's point of view.*
> —Harry Cleaver, "The Uses of an Earthquake"[1]

> *For they have sown the wind, and they shall reap the whirlwind...*
> —Hosea 8:7

A BOOK ON MOVEMENTS IN THE United States today: the areas of focus are endless; the history of past organizing, rich in new revelations; the implications, potentially seismic, yet mostly uncertain. And as with any project of broad scope, there are dangers. Omit too much, and incur the wrath of shunned organizations as well as accusations of hunt-and-peck selection in support of hidden agendas. Take the other route—massive, fully parsed, comprehensive analysis—and risk becoming mere compilers of lists, heavy in documentation but short on substance. Gaps and open seams strain as the book stretches further out; research only uncovers more gaps. This is the sort of project that cannot, with any sense of honor and satisfaction, end with one book—or even end at all.

We knew all this going in, weathering through the predicaments and limitations as best we could. But for us, the challenge of a project like this one was not our primary motivation, nor was it the beginning premise. Rather, we came to the project after years of quiet listening, sharing, dialog, and organizing. It was an organic development that started from the simplest of places: the questions and flows of our everyday lives.

WE STARTED WITH THE QUESTIONS of where we were at, what we saw, where we were coming from. Irresistibly, we found connections. All of us were too young to have personal memories of the struggles of forty years ago; instead, our personal radicalizations came about through participation in strands of the alter-globalization movement at the tail end of the twentieth century. Each of us had burgeoning radical communities that supported us in our growth, from do-it-yourself (DIY) and punk culture in suburban New York to anarchist relief workers in post-Katrina New Orleans. We got involved in local organizing that was informed by our immediate terrains, but as our participation in activity deepened and became more complex, and as we engaged in dialogue with others, we began to discern how the larger regional, national, and planetary landscape was being shaped and transformed. We located the monstrous forces of capital and state as well as its opposing working class struggles as agents of this transformation, and never took our finger off of that pulse. Yet this attention confounded us more than it clarified, as we uncovered worrisome shifts that were intimate to our organizing and our lives: social services, non-profits, foundations, bizarre alliances, and questionable 'community organizing,' many of which seemed more complicit in the social order than resistant to it. Our criticisms frequently fell on ears that refused to listen; our stores of energy, once fully tapped, devolved into burn-out and exhaustion. We took a step back, feeling the need to reflect on what had happened and understand what *is* happening. *Uses of a Whirlwind* is part of that process.

Besides our initiations and experiences of organizing, there was something else we had in common, not necessarily distinctive except for how centrally placed it was in our lives: trauma. Each of us had experienced unexpected events that shook us to our core: the devastating loss of a partner and dear friend; a near-fatal racially-charged assault committed by a stranger; bogus "domestic terrorism" charges and a draining judicial trial, both of which were intended to break our organizing and our communities. We didn't know it at the time, but these experiences of loss, harm, and trauma would transform our politics greatly. As we attempted to recover and heal, we saw more clearly how important relationship processes are in our lives and struggles, though these processes were rarely examined. We asked questions about how movements renew themselves around care, sustaining over many years in the midst of turmoil. And we drew more critical stances on the individuals and communities surrounding us who, we came to realize, often sported radical politics as though it were a favorite shirt—comfortable yet disposable, rather than bound up in life's intimacies. Our knowledges of trauma told us that these 'politics,' though prevalent and important in their own ways, were inadequate to the present reality.

So we came together as the Team Colors Collective, moved by desire and frustration. We wanted what many radicals want: new worlds and new ways of living, the abolition of the controlling forces that had made us damaged and cynical. We wanted to fully express our desires and construct ourselves and our relations accordingly, drawing particular inspiration from an image offered by Gilles Deleuze and Felix Guattari in *A Thousand Plateaus*, that of the wasp and the orchid.[2] Many orchids have evolved to resemble species of wasps; wasps, in turn, pollinate their respective orchids out of desire, attraction, and pleasure. The wasp and orchid don't really "need" each other in this relationship; rather, they *become* each other, less motivated by end goals than the boundless possibilities of living in common, through intimate, corporeal, and desirous processes. We wanted to move as wasps and orchids do, towards a new kind of politics. Or to paraphrase those famous words of Marx and Engels, we wanted to "rid ourselves of the muck" of capitalism, state repression, and mechanisms of control, all of which paralyzed us in our walk to different worlds and different politics.[3]

Yet we were also motivated to clear away a great deal of intransigent muck on the Left as well—the activist pitfalls, baffling strategies, and politically unconscionable positions that continue to raise impasses in our organizing and movement building, if not outright pushing us backward. Witnessing this pervasive "stuckness" amongst radicals, activists, and organizers—the *immobilizing* kind of inertia—has been dismaying, to put it mildly. We saw an unsettling shift away from questions of power, organizing, and movement building that needed rectification.

We were also tired of the tendencies and perspectives amongst the Left that refused to abandon their seats in radical discourse, tendencies that never seemed to lack for invested adherents despite their clear insufficiencies. There was the moral high ground and ideological purism circulating among anarchists; there was the let's-all-work-together syndrome of liberals and 'progressives,' still intent on swaying the Democratic Party; there was the obsession with struggles everywhere *but* inside the United States. Equally unsettling was the seeming pervasiveness of Activist-identity organizing, one that prized insular counterculture activity, self-referential knowledge, individual conviction, and a sense of condescension toward many everyday struggles that are often pivotal to working class life. Here was a politics of narcissism, insisting on differentiation from the masses, positioning self-identified revolutionaries as *the* primary agents of change. It was also a politics that often resented, refused, and downright *discouraged* intellectual engagement. Philosopher and movement elder Grace Lee Boggs puts it best in her interview that closes this collection, namely, that *practice* (specifically, the most 'correct' or ideologically sound practice) "has become so fixed in the minds of radicals, and in the practice of radicals, that they *look down* on thinking." Perhaps we can find comfort in Grace's recollection that this anti-intellectualism isn't new, as she encountered it when she first became a movement activist—*in the early 1940s*. If she could manage her despair that whole time, surely we could too, but we needed a new engine, a way to engage with the activities surrounding us and flowing through us, a form of intellectual *activity* more than *practice*.

Out of this miasma we arrived at our purpose: intervention into the struggles and resistances of everyday life. From here we began a series of inquiries, intended to provide the grist of our "militant research"—that is, research by invested militant activists for the purpose of clarifying and amplifying struggle. We aren't the first to go down this route, as we drew from long traditions and histories of militant and co-research, including projects and groups that are still active today. But this approach is more fully developed in Europe and South America than in the United States, and we felt that our perspectives and activities, while not necessarily 'filling a gap,' could at least shed light on the absences in movement discourse: the imperceptible moments of the everyday, the processes and relations of care, the honest assessments of roadblocks in our way, the desires waiting to be announced, all constituting the engines of radical community organizing. We sought to bring these aspects to the foreground, and as we did so, we realized that the struggles on the ground illustrated a multitude of radical community organizing approaches—not a model, nor a set of examples to be copied, but a series of interlocking characteristics, which seek to build upon and amplify the forms of organization and resistance already taking place every day, around conditions that motivated struggles everywhere.[4]

As an example, when we heard about workers organizing in one of the most difficult places—Starbucks, one of the emblematic corporate chains—we asked the organizers to join us in an inquiry into the place, function, and motivation of their efforts. What they pulled together was not a trumpeting press release of an essay, nor a bland, corporate-style accounting of its committees, meetings, and decision-making processes; instead, they offered a remarkable exposé on the historical development of "precarity" (the expendability, insecurity, and violently fluctuating conditions of the working class) and the challenges and successes of organizing from this reality. Their essay, included in this collection, illustrates the simple effectiveness of inquiry: not a research activity from the 'outside' or a frantic grasping at theories to explain one's lot, but a strategic reflection on the everyday questions of where we are at, what we are seeing, and where we come from.

Many others joined in the intervention. Julie Perini inquired into radical and "interventionist" art by arranging dialogues with many organizations, from the Yes Men to the 16 Beaver Group, uncovering a multifaceted democratization in art that can build new social relations. Peter Linebaugh based his inquiry in hidden histories, revealing tools and weapons of popular sovereignty wielded by common people against encroaching enclosures, the likes of which demand re-examination as we try to understand the value and uses of the commons and what is common among us. Michael Hardt and El Kilombo Intergaláctico approached their inquiry into political encounters through long-running conversation. Dorothy Kidd, in her examination of media struggles, emphasized community empowerment, radical communication efforts, and the dangers of co-optation. Malav Kanuga explored the potentials and limitations of Left spaces through an analysis of Bluestockings, the radical bookstore that has been central to his activity and life. And Marina Karides examined the inspiring and complex development of the United States Social Forum from her position as a participant and researcher. Their inquiries have all made their way into this collection.

As the inquiries amassed, we arranged opportunities for some of them to encounter and amplify each other, beginning with the online journal *In the Middle of a Whirlwind: 2008 Convention Protests, Movement and Movements*—using the protests against the Party conventions as a strategic point of intervention—and extending through workshops and presentations across the country. *Uses of a Whirlwind* is a counterpart to that effort, drawing together many of these interventions.[5]

WHIRLWINDS

THESE INQUIRIES YIELDED MANY INSIGHTS, but more importantly, they converged on and illuminated a reality that grew increasingly difficult to ignore: that today's movements are substantially different from those that blossomed in the 1960s and 1970s.

This revelation—"things are different now"—seems obvious, but it jars with more pervasive movement mythologies in the United States. Mainstream discourse is inundated with assertions that the Civil Rights movement, anti-war movement, feminist movement, and ecological movement, among others, destroyed themselves in short order; thus, the logic goes, today's movements are working hard to revive themselves to their former glory. Other accounts suggest that the fizzle was a natural consequence of winning, as equal rights legislation and crucial reforms rendered these movements irrelevant and unnecessary today—a very incomplete perspective, though not without its kernel of truth about the real danger of demobilization that movements face. Of course, mythologies circulating on the Left and in radical circles are more hard-hitting; they note the backlashes against hard-won victories and the brutal success of new mechanisms like the FBI's Counter Intelligence Program (COINTELPRO) in destroying radical organizations. The seriousness of the ongoing resistance through the 1970s and the repression that accompanied (and sought to destroy) it certainly cannot be overstated; Ashanti Omowali Alston powerfully recounts these many moments of incredible possibility and terror in his interview in this collection. But the conclusions drawn from these developments often do not reflect anything different we should consider about our position today. Instead there is a widespread understanding on the Left that "the struggle continues" (*a luta continua!*), that movements underwent a downturn in the 1970s but are still very much alive, manifesting in new forms like climate change organizing, ecological defense, student upheavals, and alter-globalization protests.[6]

Running through all these mythologies is a persistent undertone: "The world really isn't *different* today so much as it's *changed*, as all things do over time." What holds water in the 1960s and 1970s should still hold water forty years later, as we are led to believe. The oppressors are the same, the oppressed are the same, our goals and strategies (and even, unfortunately, our tactics) from back then are, presumably, equally valid now. Yet this explanation did not sync up with what we saw, what we felt in our deepest thoughts; we understood that something—or rather, a great many things—had fundamentally shifted.

During the Great Depression and New Deal era of the 1930s, the early days of industrial mass production, when factories in the U.S. were at the core of the economy, workers' struggles were surging out of basic refusals: refusals to work such long hours, at such low wages, with so few means of security. They were encouraged by the passage of the National Industrial Recovery Act in 1933 (declared unconstitutional in 1935) and by the Wagner Act in 1935, which allowed collective bargaining in many industries (though, crucially, not all of them). Facing a paralyzing crisis of profitability—a massive intensification of workers' struggles, and with the Russian Revolution's impact, influence, and legacy still fresh in the historical memory—the capitalist classes knew they could not continue fighting back against resurgent worker organizing through traditional methods of strike-breakers, militias, and violent repression. So they began to broker deals. Unions presented demands for higher wages, adequate protection, and social supports; each of these would be answered, to some degree, as long as they increased their productivity and output. This arrangement of negotiation in replacement of class struggle rapidly permeated the industries, as unions—largely declawed by the suppressive 1947 Taft-Hartley Act that limited the ability to strike, and purged of radicals by the early 1950s—were increasingly incorporated into the structure of capital itself. The markets hummed happily with the fruits of maximal profits, and many workers received some comfort and security, in both the monetary wages of their labor and new "social wages"—pensions, health insurance, and unemployment insurance. Yet mass-production workers did not have control of the factories; there were concessions to workers' demands, but determination over the means of production was not one of them.

This was the Keynesian economic model, derived from the ideas of British economist John Maynard Keynes: a capitalist strategy of channeling and preventing struggle, predicated on state protection of workers, whose "productivity deal" would in turn maintain markets.[7] The deal didn't benefit everyone equally; it deliberately deepened and solidified divisions within the working class through New Deal-era reforms that privileged whites, unions that supported the privilege of white and male factory workers, and the many rank-and-file workers that banked on whiteness as its own wage. Gendered divisions within the class were also reinforced through the continued imposition of housework—the unpaid work of housewives and women care-givers, hidden behind the male wage and couched in the enforcement of the heterosexual nuclear family.[8]

Even with these mechanisms in place against worker struggles, Keynesianism wasn't free from resistance, found in small, everyday moments (sabotage, for example) as well as collective confrontations, from sit-down strikes during the 1930s to wildcat strikes in the 1940s, which escalated the class struggle beyond bureaucratic control. There were also the 1950s struggles of blacks against Jim Crow in the South, actions that, unbeknownst to many, were premonitions of a more massive resistance on the horizon. Overall, though, Keynesianism, launched as an attempt to 'save' capitalism from the Depression's crisis of falling profits and threat of workers' struggles, thrived as the dominant economic model in the post-war decades. And its legacy remains, especially the divisions it fostered around racism, patriarchy, and the kinds of labor seen as 'valid' spaces for struggle—divisions that are still central to understanding working class struggle today.

But Keynesianism seems a somewhat distant memory nowadays because a "cycle of struggles" brought the Keynesian deal into profound crisis. What was this "cycle," and how did it achieve such an impact?[9]

The notion of the "cycle" finds parallels in other descriptions we have for historical movements—that they come in 'waves,' undergoing periods of perpetual rising and falling. Yet "cycles" may be a more useful frame of understanding, especially in relation to Keynesianism; the measure of cycles of struggle lies in *political composition* as much as the energy and intensity of resistance. The political composition of the working class—its power-building processes, its amplification, the intensity of its communication and activity, all of which become its sources of strength—was very high during the 1930s and 1940s. Upon the success of Keynesianism, paired with codified limitations on workers' organizing and the political uses of anti-Communism, the class began to decompose as labor unrest turned notably quiet during the late 1950s and early 1960s.

But this did not mean class conflict disappeared. Rather, other actors—namely, those offered the rawest end of the Keynesian deal and reaping next to none of its benefits—undertook a new series of struggles. Starting in small actions—black students holding sit-ins at Woolworth's, women's councils calling for a boycott of the Montgomery bus lines—the working class quickly began recomposing, and in so doing acquired new dimensions, articulations, and formulations that were substantially different from those expressed by the class thirty years previously. The *political* composition of the working class—the level of its collective power to make demands on, against, and beyond capital—is recomposed *in struggle* in relation to the technical composition of capitalism, the particular ways in which work *for capital* is organized. Capital, in turn, seeks to decompose the class when its political composition is high. This constitutes the full cycle of struggle. Thus the working class confronts state and capital as they are technically composed all the while, but it often achieves its greatest potential for rupture at the peak of recomposition.[10]

This peak was witnessed by billions across the planet in the late 1960s and early 1970s, as people of color, women, youth, peasants, farmworkers, and many others burst onto the landscape of struggle, disrupting the relative inactivity of organized (and largely white male) labor's "golden age." One apt description of this cycle of struggles was captured perfectly in writer James Baldwin's prophetic warning shot to the world, pulled from an old spiritual:

> God gave Noah the rainbow sign
> No more water, the fire next time![11]

And when the "fire" emerged, its worldwide raging led to unprecedented devastation of the social order. A spirit of active rebellion and desire captured the times as increasing numbers of people organized. Here in the United States, these struggles achieved substantial victories: bringing forth a "Second Reconstruction," forcing open many social and political structures that had previously excluded those who had suffered immense historical oppression, and increasing both monetary and social wages to unprecedented levels. The movements of fire squeezed profits to the breaking point, as wage increases, welfare transfers, environmental regulation, diffuse emergent cultures of rebellion, and a class (nationally and internationally) that was seemingly uncontrollable brought unbearable demands on the Keynesian deal. Fires went beyond metaphor, too, as many people of color set their cities aflame in the mid-to-late 1960s.

Compositely, these struggles fundamentally changed the relations of power, refusing the attempts at mediation and negotiation that capital and state had erstwhile used as its primary mechanism. Echoing a history and predicting a future of working class internationalism, movements went well beyond borders as struggles shared knowledge, tactics, and attacks on capitalist accumulation and state power. Pervading the 1950s through the 1970s, fires erupted in the decolonization movement, moving to the spread of national liberation struggles, the student uprisings in Prague and Japan, the workers struggles in the Middle East, the waves of rebellions that defined Mexico's 1968, France's 1968, Italy's 1969 and 1977; these constitute a small illustration of the immense contention capital faced. This was an unparalleled level of circulation among struggles; all it took to start a fire, it seemed, was a mere spark.

Make no mistake: these planetary movements of fire, at their peak in the cycle of struggle, had spawned a crisis—the relinquishing of authority, the breaking of tenuous deals, the mass refusals in countless areas of life, the announcement of new desires. From the point of view of the multifaceted working class in the United States, this rupture was welcome and demanded further rending. Harvard political scientist Samuel Huntington called it the "crisis of democracy" in 1975; that is, there was *too much democracy* at work.[12] As capitalism's proponents watched their carefully crafted Keynesian model fall into shambles, they knew that the times required extraordinary measures, dramatic and powerful enough to defuse this threat—violently if necessary.

So capital and state reorganized themselves again, just as they had done in the 1930s, tossing out the old model and boldly taking on a new one. Starting by the early 1970s and bulldozing its way through the 1980s, neoliberalism, the abandonment of state protection of the class in favor of protection of free trade and the full function of markets, became the new order. As historian Robin D.G. Kelley notes in this collection's interview, "The move from the so-called Great Society to extreme *laissez-faire* capitalism was a revolution ... for the worse." It was a mean and terrible process, attacking the areas of highest composition as well as the most vulnerable populations. Deindustrialization and the dismantling and outsourcing of factories left millions flailing without employment, while capital continued its exploitative trajectory in other parts of the world. The state cemented its neoliberal protection of markets through devastating withdrawals and abandonment of communities. Social wages underwent welfare cuts and safety net slashes; urban space met with disinvestment, austerity, and privatization. The United States went through a blatant program of structural adjustment, echoing similar developments in the "Third World." New industries of discipline and control skyrocketed, particularly the prison industrial complex, which served as state and capital's primary solution to 'problems' (in this case, discontented and potentially unruly populations). Capital became increasingly footloose, diverse in investment, and global in scale, intent on escaping recalcitrant workers. The combined result of these developments, along with many others, made for a seismic shift on the political landscape, reorganizing space and fundamentally altering all forms of sociality, including the ways collective resistance functioned.

Central to this process was the development of the "non-profit industrial complex," through which capital and the state apparatus increasingly captured and channeled oppositional organizing by sponsorship of its development toward codification, the use of less confrontational tactics, and less radical positions.[13] From the perspective of the ruling class, the kind of access-based politics that non-profits usually promote is a welcome development that can be accommodated. Illustrative here are the words of John D. Rockefeller's "Commission on Foundation and Private Philanthropy," in 1970:

> The spirit of dissent has spread its contagion across our student population and from there to other sectors of American life.... If they are not to reach their climax in a war of all against all, we are summoned by this turmoil to carefully consider the ways in which we can convert dissent into a force for constructive action and civil peace....We must evolve more responsive processes through which our young and disenfranchised can secure a fair piece of the social action, whether or not they can acquire a piece of the affluent *economic* action.[14]

Radical groups that raised questions of wealth and power fell to mechanisms of disruption, violence, and repression during the late 1960s and early 1970s. So-called "advocacy" organizations more committed to institutional channels and accepted forms of political action substantially increased, raising funds and organizing for less radical demands. Organizing and organizers became more professionalized. Adolph Reed, Jr.'s comments in the context of black struggles haunt us here. He argues against trivializing the important outcomes of reform movements, while simultaneously holding an important tension: "Insofar as the nongovernmental organizations and their elites carry the historical sediment of adversarial, protest politics, their integration into the new regime further ratifies its protocols as the only thinkable politics."[15] In our view, this tension expands across the social field; one danger, as Max Rameau from Take Back the Land puts it in this collection, is that a professional class of organizers has developed, increasingly separate from the masses of people capable of bringing about revolution.

So it is that capital and the state have *more successfully* defined the terms of oppositional engagement since the Keynesian crisis. Demobilization has relied on sheer violence, but also the capture and enclosure of struggle: turning away from community control and a redistribution of power and wealth in exchange for some crumbs. For complex reasons, many on the Left have actively helped this process along, oftentimes committed to a middle-class, *anti-revolutionary* politics, whether explicit or implicit. In a way that matters deeply to all those suffering oppression and exploitation, getting *something* is always better than getting *nothing* when it comes to basic resources, and it would be wrong not to see many (though limited) reforms as anything but the outcome of difficult and important struggle. Yet Reed's comments echo painfully here: where *is* our imagination of what struggle can achieve? Our discourse is now plagued with non-profit and professional thinking, to the point where the betterment of *struggle* takes a backseat to the betterment of *organizations*. In this scheme, a wealth of 'strong' organizations is supposed to usher in fundamental change on a sea of 'consciousness' shifting instead of power shifting. Thus the Left generally endorses and upholds mechanisms of capture that are hard-wired to avoid radical struggle—that is, struggle that gets to the *roots* of problems; yet as each year has passed since the 1970s, pervasive devastation has only worsened. Many of us persist in the midst of these contradictions, hoping for shifts on the landscape without actually moving ourselves, focusing on the questions of consciousness rather than composition.

The immersion within these tensions and the desire to escape them has led to a new cycle of struggles. This cycle does not function as the fires of the 1960s and 1970s once did in the Keynesian structures of power. Its struggles face substantial difficulty in helping to create a generalization of social struggle and political recomposition of the working class. Yet the cycle is here, and it is real; it has demonstrated many times its capacity for damage and disruption. We call this cycle of struggle a period of *whirlwinds*. They are dissimilar to fires that erupt out of a definable mix of elements with specific targets and accurate generalities; rather, winds are caused by pressures that vary in different locales, constructed from particularities and, at times, incommunicable singularities. Fires burn until the oxygen or fuel runs out, whereas winds are fluid, open, and constantly shifting across the terrain. Fires carry a creative and destructive urge, extinguishing what exists to make way for something new; winds search for what is common and articulate the common in new ways as they circulate. Winds have come in many forms, including environmental justice movements, anti-apartheid solidarity, AIDS activism, new cultural expressions such as rave music, hip-hop, and punk, and the "movement of movements" that have solidified vividly at mass summit demonstrations throughout the world. This book includes even more contemporary examples: Harmony Goldberg's exploration of domestic worker organizing, John Peck's analysis of the booming efforts around food sovereignty, and Student/Farmworker Alliance's description of the victorious campaigns of migrant workers.

Whirlwinds face a multitude of difficulties in building radical struggles, which many of these chapters depict. They range from the intra-movement conflicts Ben Shepard documents in his examination of contemporary queer struggles, to the challenges of a largely liberal and badly focused anti-war movement that Direct Action to Stop the War discusses. They have to reckon with globalization and the harsh new terrain it has created, as Basav Sen illustrates in his account of local struggles based in a global justice context. The threat of state repression still looms large, apparent in Roadblock Earth First!'s account of organizing against capitalist infrastructure in Indiana. And the flow of whirlwinds also incurs the risk that these flows will be directed into sophisticated captures, enclosures, channels, and other avenues of co-optation and benign activity, as Stevie Peace describes in his chapter on the restorative justice movement's worrisome directions into the non-profit industrial complex and academia.

Yet winds continue to circulate, teasing out the potential for revolution. True, they cannot be translated as simply as sparks to a fire; there is nothing universal about them, nor can they readily be distinguished from each other. But where they come into encounter, intersection, and nodes of contact, they amplify and strengthen into whirlwinds, powerful enough to threaten and disrupt the technical composition of capital and its protective neoliberal state. They can converge around seemingly insurmountable challenges such as climate change, where Brian Tokar's chapter tracks alliances and networks forming out of indigenous groups, urban environmental justice organizing, and struggles against mountaintop removal in Appalachia. And the whirlwinds can potentially be much more than a metaphor for this cycle of struggles, transcending into theoretical and strategic reflection that can inform new understandings of today's movements. We are heartened by the potential and possibility in the whirlwinds, despite the dangers they face. Oppressive forces continue to sow new seeds of violence, discipline, and control; whirlwinds remind us that these seeds, destructive as they are, reap harvests of unabashed resistance and desires that refuse to be quelled.

USES OF A WHIRLWIND

THUS WE ARRIVE AT THE present moment. It is 2010, and capitalism and state apparatuses are once again in crisis—not entirely of their own making, as both Brian Marks and George Caffentzis remind us in their contributions. We've been down this road before, back when Keynesianism was the banner; the cycle of fire forced it into cataclysm. Similarly, we suggest that the winds and whirlwinds of the last few decades—fomenting from radical community organizing, autonomous struggle, and 'hidden' everyday resistance—have been responsible, in various ways, for the punctures and ruptures in the neoliberal order.

Does this suggest that "we" are "winning," as many radicals pronounced after the Seattle WTO protests ten years ago? Even the most casual glance about us indicates otherwise. The whirlwinds of this current cycle of struggle have certainly built power and caused damage, but we would do well to remember that they are part of a *cycle*, stirring up battles and new fronts even as they have ebbed to a point of harrowing decomposition. Though oppressive agents are reeling in crisis, they can take some comfort (momentarily) from the position of the working class, who has entered into the crisis heavily weakened and co-opted, devoted to institutions more than movements. Our knowledges of despair are not innate; they flow out of memories of ruin, of neoliberal havoc, of a Left that has generally found it easier to invest in capitalism's 'benefits' than to resist them.

We in Team Colors have a strong desire to see the current cycle continue into recomposition; as we read and assess the new fronts of struggle opened by today's whirlwinds, we believe this is an emergent possibility. But if we are not careful, movements will continue to languish in the dregs of decomposition for some time to come, unsure of the first steps to take. From our own experiences, as well as the knowledges we've gained from our inquiries into everyday resistance and struggle, we thus offer a few areas for increased attention and development within movements.[16]

Firstly, we assert that any serious attempt at movement building and recomposition requires a return to radical community organizing. We aren't suggesting that this kind of organizing has been abandoned; we *do* suggest that it needs to be pulled out of the sky and formed on the ground. Movements share common desires for engaged, substantive, continuously open, and concrete processes; for cooperative institutions of care and support that can sustain and reproduce movement work; for mechanisms of ongoing dialog, coordination of struggles, and direct action that is open to a diversity of tactics. Reflected here is a deeper desire of radical community organizing: to deploy mechanisms that will create resonances and encounters between oppressed and struggling peoples, in particular and situated locales, as we create what the Zapatistas call "a world in which many worlds fit." Crucial to this vision is the construction of new relationships, replacing commodification with desire, becoming each other more than moving en masse to a different place. In the spirit of Deleuze and Guattari's wasp and orchid, we seek contact, resonance, and dialogue, connecting with the flows of everyday life and lives that flow into one another.

Such a return also necessitates a critique of 'community organizing,' as derived from the Alinsky model of organizing. This model centers on specific gains and getting those in power to bend to people's demands, working towards a delusionary and deeply limited goal of creating "equal *opportunity* for everyone," rather than self-determination, autonomy, and accesses to basic life resources. The serious limitations of this model are manifesting to worrying levels as 'organizing' has been increasingly incorporated into access-based politics, whether in non-profits, electoral campaigns, or other non-confrontational avenues. Undertaking radical community organizing in this environment is vital, as we sharpen our analyses and reflections into a strong framework for launching collective action that proactively complicates and challenges the limits of the Alinsky tendency. Struggles that utilize elements of radical community organizing abound in the United States and throughout the planet, as well as in this collection. Most notable is a roundtable contribution of four poor people's organizations (United Workers, Picture the Homeless, Take Back the Land, and City Life/Vida Urbana) that resist many effects of the crisis through eviction defense, living wage campaigns, and the reclamation and squatting of foreclosed properties.

Secondly, there is a need today for movements that centralize their own reproduction—working from understandings and activity associated with care, support, and needs. If we can't care for one another, construct new forms of life, and address our vast experiences affected by care issues, then our movements won't develop the strength to confront and transcend oppressive structures. We also need to redefine and clarify our structures of support, not only as used in struggle, but also in addressing loss, intimate violence, mental and physical health problems, relationships with those imprisoned and confined, and the needs of youth, children, and the elderly. It is precisely because social reproductive activity sits invisibly on the back burner that struggles undergo sporadic bursts and declines of energy, leading to affirmations that continuous eye-catching protests can keep movement momentum going—a deceit as well as a reification of poorly strategized 'Activism.' But when self-activity and organizing around care and support are prioritized and amplified, momentum can continue building, pushing up against limits imposed by capital and the state apparatus. Thus self-reproduction is not solely inward-looking; at some point, this work must directly confront the forces that capture, enclose, and violently suppress our ability to address these experiences and realities.

We believe this dynamic must change if we wish to sustain movement toward class recomposition; indeed, self-reproduction is bound up in successful radical community organizing. Silvia Federici, who has written at length about the importance of reproduction and whose critical analysis has helped ground Team Colors' own political projects, perhaps sums it up best in her contribution here: "We cannot build an alternative society and a strong self-reproducing movement unless we redefine in a more cooperative way our reproduction and put an end to the separation between the personal and the political, political activism and the reproduction of everyday life." Chris Carlsson rounds out this point in his chapter, arguing for sustainable, joy-filled radicalism that avoids self-marginalization and burnout in order to be effective "over the long haul." Although focus on reproduction alone has its limits, we would do well to remember its importance in grounding struggle as a *process* through time. Revolutionary potential emerges out of people growing and changing through this undertaking, allowing new forms of life to take hold.

What radical community organizing and movement self-reproduction look like will vary, of course, depending on where these efforts are situated and the questions that emerge from them: What is the composition of the class, the community, the movement (keeping in mind that none of these exists prior to their self-constitution, developing instead through activity and struggle)? How do struggles function, build and sustain power, and develop antagonistic ruptures into capital and the state's apparatuses? These questions do not seek 'answers'; they unfold at the barricades, in the streets, in fields, forests, gardens, homes, farms, community centers, workplaces, and neighborhoods, where we struggle everyday to create new worlds and new lives. The contributions of Sebastian Cobarrubias and Maribel Casas-Cortes of Producciones Translocales and Daniel Tucker of AREA Chicago provide useful insights of grounded practices that may help deepen radical struggles based in knowing exactly where we're at. Understanding our current composition is the central goal of *Uses of a Whirlwind*, but we cannot possibly inquire into all activity on the terrain. Still, we believe several small inquiries are important, and the selections offered here, though often disjointed, also weave powerful connections and new understandings that make the collection much more than the sum of its parts.

The contributors to *Uses of a Whirlwind* entered into this project with such a spirit. We didn't ask them to fire at will on whatever they wanted to write, nor did we enforce strict parameters on their words so that they would fit tidily (or politically) with each other or with our perspectives and arguments. Instead we posed a question: "Will you join us in the middle of a whirlwind?" The invitation is not merely poetic; it has a twofold purpose. At its heart, it is an offer to participate in inquiry, to examine the composition of movements, to analyze how they function in different locales, to assess how the terrain informs their development, and to draw out critiques and questions of organizing that can aid us in deploying and projecting movement strategies. And on a more conceptual level, it is an invitation to join the whirlwinds as a current cycle of struggles, a basic recognition of our current period and an intention to develop understandings and knowledges from the framework of class war in the neoliberal era.

Thus we sought in our contributors a merging of these two activities, the inquiries and the whirlwinds. We arrange their chapters into sections that best fit with their sources of inquiry. Our first section, "Organization Case Studies," brings in voices from those at the sites of struggle, as they reveal their respective terrains, the flows and functions of their responses, and the challenges to come. From here enter more thematic perspectives, "Movement Strategies," as these struggles are positioned in the context of emerging movements that confront current realities of capital and state imposition. Tying both of these sections into praxis, the pieces in "Theoretical Analyses" analyze today's predicaments and eruptions with concepts, theories, and knowledges that may prove invaluable as they circulate. We close the book with a final section, "Interviews," where three movement elders share the lessons of their experiences as they help us bring notions of struggle into dialogue with the understandings of those who have come before us. To prepare and assist readers as they flow from chapter to chapter, we have also offered basic signposts at the beginning of each section, which summarize the chapters and tie them into our theoretical approach to whirlwinds and current movements.

Perhaps these words, these writings, these *whirlwinds* will inspire much and activate little; perhaps they will be turned over and over in curious hands, puzzling over how, precisely, to *use* them. Perhaps they become tools and weapons, as we intend them to be. We in Team Colors are both excited about and wary of the ways *Uses of a Whirlwind* will be used. We hope, at the very least, that this is a start, an end, and a continuation; a point of dialog, a position for inquiry, a step in one's own walk; a cue for reflection throughout and a magnifying glass on the small moments of becoming between wasps and orchids. All with an ear to the multiplicity of voices, resonating in many languages of struggle, stirred by the same desires that move today's winds: to make possible a revolution borne not of vanguard leadership nor ideological conformism, but rather of lives that demand new worlds and new ways of being and settle for nothing less.

NOTES

1 Harry Cleaver, "The Uses of an Earthquake" *Midnight Notes* 9 (1988), 10.
2 Gilles Deleuze and Felix Guattari, *A Thousands Plateaus* (Minneapolis: University of Minnesota Press: 2000).
3 Karl Marx and Friedrich Engels, *The German Ideology*, first published by David Riazanov (Moscow: Marx-Engels Institute, 1932).
4 It is essentially activist parlance that organizing 'begins' from nowhere; it is a given that people start out 'unorganized' and 'unresisting,' thus it is up to apparently 'enlightened' activists to catalyze struggle. We work from a different assumption: that there is an ongoing and frequently invisible guerrilla war in everyday life against the imposition of capital and state; thus communities and the working class are already organized in many ways. Indeed, there are no meetings or committees involved when workers mouth off about conditions at lunchtime, public transportation riders request or offer transfers from a common pool, or friends arrange visits to the imprisoned. We suggest that radical community organizing finds sets of practices and characteristics that further existing struggles and organizational forms such as these.
5 *In the Middle of a Whirlwind: 2008 Convention Protests, Movement and Movements* was published online by the *Journal of Aesthetics and Protest*, the author of one of this book's prefaces. The journal can be found at HTTP://WWW.INTHEMIDDLEOFAWHIRLWIND.INFO.
6 "A Luta Continua" is a Portuguese phrase that translates in English as "the struggle continues." The phrase was popularized in the Mozambiquean movement against Portuguese colonization, and has since become a Left catch-phrase of sorts, divorced from the particular conditions from which it initially arose as a movement phrase.
7 An important starting point for a class struggle analysis before and during the Keynesian period can be found in Guido Baldi, "Theses on the Mass Worker and Social Capital," *Radical America* Vol. 6 #1 (1972), 3–21.
8 Our use of the notion of "class deals" is inspired and informed by the Midnight Notes Collective. See Midnight Notes Collective, "A Conceptualization of the Law in the Manifold of Work," *Midnight Notes* 8: 1–8.
9 A useful synopsis of the notion of 'cycles of struggle' can be found in: Nick Dyer-Witheford, *Cyber-Marx: Cycles and Circuits of Struggle in High-Technology Capitalism* (Urbana and Chicago: University of Illinois Press, 1999), 62–90. Also very useful is Zerowork Collective, *Zerowork: Political Materials 1* (Brooklyn: Zerowork), 1975.

10 Zerowork explains the process of composition in 1975: "By political recomposition we mean the level of unity and homogeneity that the working class reaches during a cycle of struggle in the process of going from one composition to another. Essentially, it involves the overthrow of capitalist divisions, the creation of new unities between different sectors of the class, and an expansion of the boundaries of what the 'working class' comes to include." Zerowork, *Political Materials 1*, 1–6. Also see: Harry Cleaver, *Reading Capital Politically* (Oakland, California: AK Press, 2000).

11 James Baldwin, *The Fire Next Time* (Dial Press, 1963).

12 Samuel Huntington, "The United States," in Michel Crozier, Samuel Huntington, and Joji Watanuki (eds.) *The Crisis of Democracy: Report on the Governability of Democracies to the Trilateral Commission* (New York: New York University Press, 1975), p. 59–118.

13 The "non-profit industrial complex" was given its name by INCITE! Women of Color Against Violence, in their book *The Revolution Will Not Be Funded: Beyond the Non-Profit Industrial Complex* (Cambridge: South End Press, 2007).

14 Commission on Foundations and Private Philanthropy, "The Role of Philanthropy in a Changing Society," in *America's Voluntary Spirit: A Book of Readings*, ed. Brian O'Connell (New York: Foundation Center, 1970), 293.

15 Adolph Reed, Jr., "Demobilization in the New Black Political Regime: Ideological Capitulation and Radical Failure in the Postsegregation Era," in *The Bubbling Cauldron: Race, Ethnicity, and the Urban Crisis*, eds. Michael Peter Smith & Joe R. Feagin (Minneapolis: University of Minnesota Press, 1995), 184.

16 These areas are merely introduced here; their theoretical and practical dimensions are explored more fully in the Team Colors Collective pamphlet, "Wind(s) from Below: Radical Community Organizing to Make a Revolution Possible" (Portland, OR: Eberhardt Press, 2010, in association with the Team Colors Collective); visit HTTP://WWW.WARMACHINES.INFO for more information and to obtain a copy. See as well Team Colors Collective, "Of Whirlwinds and Wind Chimes (or ways of listening): Movement Building and Militant Research in the United States," *The Commoner* (February 4, 2009), available at HTTP://WWW.COMMONER.ORG.UK/?P=76 (accessed January 31, 2010); Team Colors Collective, "To Show the Fire and the Tenderness: Self-Reproducing Movements and Struggles In, Around, and Against the Current Economic Crisis in the United States," *Indypendent Reader* 12 (Spring/Summer 2009), available at HTTP://INDYREADER.ORG/CONTENT/TO-SHOW-FIRE-AND-TENDERNESS-BY-TEAMS-COLORS-COLLECTIVE-CONOR-CASH-CRAIG-HUGHES-STEVIE-PEACE- (accessed January 31, 2010).

ORGANIZATION CASE STUDIES

SECTION SUMMARY

Winds and inquiries, in their most basic forms, begin with small moments and initiatives that arise out of everyday life. Organizational forms come into being as expressions and amplifications of the daily struggles and desires of their participants. We want to understand how a set of projects function and seek to recompose the political environs in which they find themselves. These sample case studies cycle through the political landscape, covering many areas, themes, and movements that are sometimes interrelated but seemingly disconnected. These struggles reflect the desire to confront neoliberal capital and the state apparatus, as well as the need for substantive radical community organizing efforts.

As we discussed in the introduction to this volume, capital's response to the movements of "fire" in the 1960s and 1970s was brutal in its discipline of the working class through what equated to the structural adjustment of the United States. Waged work and unwaged reproductive work have become increasingly precarious in the subsequent decades. In response, precarious workers have created organizational forms to reconstruct their working and everyday lives. The following chapters describe some of these developments, including the Starbucks Workers Union, Student/Farmworker Alliance, and the National Domestic Workers Alliance.

Confronting capitalist planning has become more important as neoliberal capital seeks to expand its reach. Direct Action to Stop the War, Roadblock Earth First!, Right to the City Alliance, City Life/Vida Urbana, Take Back the Land, and Picture the Homeless have engaged in struggles that address, respectively, wars of discipline and resource extraction, the construction of a massive neoliberal highway system in the United States, processes of gentrification and privatization, and crisis-induced waves of foreclosure, evictions, wage declines, and homelessness.

Throughout the history of working-class struggle, the circulation of knowledges and of struggles themselves in sites of "encounter" has amplified, strengthened, and coordinated movements. Recent developments include the proliferation of infoshops, such as Bluestockings in New York City, and the creation of a U.S.-based counterpart to the World Social Forum, where the circulation of struggles finds important expression.

It is in these areas, where case studies have begun to be mapped and situated within the winds, that the possibilities of magnifying and expanding current struggles can be found.

In **"Bluestockings Bookstore and New Institutions of Self-Organized Work: The Space Between Common Notions and Common Institutions,"** Bluestockings co-owner and collective member Malav Kanuga discusses the importance and difficulties of a radical space in the context of post-fiscal crisis New York City. Kanuga addresses the challenges of a radical space in a gentrifying city, the complexities of intersecting politics, the benefits and pitfalls of collective ownership, and the role space can potentially have in increasing class composition.

Direct Action to Stop the War (DASW) is one of the few prominent anti-war groups to use direct action. In **"Anti-Authoritarian Organizing in Practice,"** DASW organizers in the San Francisco Bay Area track the development and implementation of a series of actions in 2008 marking the fifth anniversary of the Iraq War. The authors examine the predicaments that many struggles face currently including questions of sustainability, larger movement strategy, and engagement with the Left.

At a point when Earth First! was waning nationally, the organizing efforts of Roadblock Earth First!—based in Bloomington, Indiana and focused on stopping construction of Interstate-69, part of the NAFTA superhighway—helped to spur new energy. Rather than continue increasingly futile summit hopping, Roadblock aims to directly target capitalist infrastructure, as explained in their contribution, **"A Look at Resistance to Interstate 69: Past, Present, and Future."** The addendum written by one Roadblock organizer discusses some of the weaknesses and strengths encountered in their work, as well as the benefits of using direct action.

The Starbucks Workers Union formed out of difficult circumstances: a deflated and tightly managed labor movement, a boom in corporate chains, and an immense growth in the "precarious class" of workers—easily disposable, seemingly unorganizable. **"The Precarious Economy and its Discontents: Struggling Against the Corporate Chains Through Workplace Organizing"** discusses the extent of the precarious conditions from which their organizing emerged, campaigns they have launched, and new challenges in light of the economic crisis.

In the wake of the 1990s victories of the Coalition of Immokalee Workers, an alter-globalization organization known for waging high-level campaigns against fast food industry giants such as Taco Bell, a loose network of Florida students formed the Student/Farmworker Alliance (SFA), which has provided strategic support and solidarity for the CIW. In **"Harvesting Solidarity: Farmworkers, Allies, and the Fight for Fair Food,"** SFA enumerates on the function and composition of their work, consistently emphasizing the importance of popular education as a tool in struggle.

In 2009, organizations and activists convened in Baltimore for the City From Below Conference, intended as a site of encounter among struggles in the cities. **"A Conversation on Organizing Models for Social Justice Struggles in the City"** was one conversation that resulted. Moderated by veteran organizer Betty Robinson, this roundtable with the organizations Take Back the Land, City Life/Vida Urbana, Picture the Homeless, and the United Workers explores a variety of approaches and strategies deployed in current poor people's organizing, particularly focused on the effects of the economic crisis.

The U.S. Social Forum serves as a site of encounter, discussion, and the sharing of knowledges and struggles. Marina Karides of the U.S. Social Forum Documentation Committee lays bare the skeleton of the U.S. Social Forum process as well as the issues, concerns, and experiences that connect with it in her chapter, **"What's Going On? The United States Social Forum, Grassroots Activism, and Situated Knowledge,"** Karides demonstrates that the "U.S. Yet to Come" begins to take shape from a myriad of struggles, organizations, experiences, and realities circulating across the country.

The Right to the City Alliance and the National Domestic Workers Alliance have emerged as new urban-centered struggles against neoliberalism. In **"Building Power in the City: Reflections on the Emergence of the Right to the City Alliance and the National Domestic Workers Alliance,"** Harmony Goldberg analyzes these movements' form and function, their challenges on both local and national levels, and their potential as oppressed people's organizing that learns how to navigate nonprofits and political campaigns without being trapped by them.

This closing chapter reminds us of the interconnected elements of neoliberal capital and the organizational responses needed to address these elements. From these case studies and other countless initiatives on the social field, we turn to movement strategies, where we find connections and relations among these initiatives.

BLUESTOCKINGS BOOKSTORE AND NEW INSTITUTIONS OF SELF-ORGANIZED WORK:

The Space Between Common Notions and Common Institutions

Malav Kanuga | **Bluestockings Bookstore and Activist Center**

INTRODUCTION

TENSION: A STRETCHED CONDITION BETWEEN two or more forces. Contradiction: to speak against. Antinomy: against, but within, a law. These three words describe the conditions from which we attempt to organize *space* in our movements. Here I present some ideas about these conditions as they manifest in one struggle to organize an autonomous space in the heart of a capitalist city. I write from the perspective of my participation in a small workers' collective that daily organizes Bluestockings, a bookstore, café, and event space on the Lower East Side of Manhattan. We collaborate weekly with nearly seventy-five volunteers and interact annually with tens of thousands of people that come through our space. I explore the tension between two forces that propel us: the need to end capitalist work and the wage-unwaged relation that constitutes capital's dividing powers, and the desire for a type of 'free activity' that self-organizes nomadically, recoding and decoding social cooperation in a manner that simultaneously reorganizes the work relation as it flees it. This tension exists within another: our ambition to organize a *common space* that inverts the commodity relation, while restrained by the logic of rent and the broader attacks afflicting working classes since the 1970s that have been characterized, variously, as 'neoliberalism,' 'gentrification,' 'globalization,' and 'urban development.'

My central assertion is simple and verifiable across so many other movement spaces: the self-organization of space facilitates the experimentation and multiplication of new relationships, compositions, and struggles against and beyond capitalism.[1] I describe Bluestockings as an autonomous space inscribed within many tensions, contradictions, and antinomies, which signal both its limitations and potentialities. Nevertheless, its many organizers and collaborators evince the desire, will, and ability to organize increasingly collective exits from capitalist relations, produce new subjectivities and forms of life, and seek to dehierarchize their relationships.[2]

Bluestockings exists within many vicissitudes of urban movements that have arisen in the last ten years, since the cycle of protests during the alter-globalization movement waned after the Seattle mobilizations against the World Trade Organization in 1999, and as new initiatives in mass organizing within migrant and people of color communities emerged. Our history must also be understood in the terms that unfolded across New York City since the global capitalist crises of the 1970s, specifically the 1975 fiscal crisis in New York, reoriented the balance of class forces.[3] This is crucial if we are to understand how spaces like Bluestockings can aid in setting the terms for a reversal of class powers in our present context.

Bluestockings is situated within a compromised rent relation that affords us great visibility and accessibility but also disciplines our labor by allowing the money-form to become central to the dialectic of our space. While collective self-organization has consolidated relative power, our workers' collective does not have the capacity to emancipate our daily lives from wage labor or exploitation. Greater financial solvency has allowed us to increase our project's consistency and further build community, but it has also undermined our project through questions of financial management that obscure and overshadow political and social ambitions of the space. As a collectively organized worker and volunteer space, we encounter challenges of specialization of knowledges, experiences, and labor, at the same time as our activities decode and reinvent the meaning and relations of work.

As a feminist space, Bluestockings has invented a multiplicity of anti-hierarchical practices that facilitate the construction of new social selves, yet these have not adequately addressed the pervasiveness of patriarchy and other hierarchies as they are reproduced in other aspects of our lives. The experience of organizing a *local* space upon feminist democratic practices has been remarkably empowering but has yet to solve the problems of patriarchy which seem to construct "everyday life" and "planetary class forces" as opposite political scales.[4] Our experience alerts us to how easy it might be to fall into an attitude of localism when the conditions of reproducing our space are so demanding. Still, participants recognize that the space is an important precondition for encountering others and constructing common languages of struggle.

Throughout these tensions, contradictions, and antinomies, Bluestockings remains a powerful laboratory for testing the hypothesis that autonomous space facilitates the production of new social relations in the struggle against capitalism. Relations and cooperative activities that proliferate in our space hold great promise yet have hitherto remained limited in their approach. Bluestockings' future and the future organization of radical community efforts to transform global power relations depend on inquiring into these experiences and lessons and posing them in the form of *common notions* that seek to answer a basic question: to what extent are our needs and desires, forms of life, and current expressions combining with others? An inquiry into this theme and subsequent common notions has aided our ability to recompose within substantial and transformative movements, and it will continue to do so if we can draw out political lessons from our experiences, potentials, and limits. Likewise, we need to think about how to organize our common notions into *common institutions* that can endure and facilitate recompositions. The organization of both common notions and common institutions form the potential horizon of Bluestockings' political attempts to organize space in anti-capitalist directions.

Infoshops, radical bookstores, and other spaces similar to Bluestockings have existed in the U.S. for decades through community organizing efforts in a wide variety of contexts.[5] The particular forms that have operated since the 1990s are as much a part of contemporary national and international anti-authoritarian networks as they are linked to a generation of place-based community initiatives associated with European squatted social centers of the 1970s and 1980s.[6] Generally, these radical spaces have also taken on various forms, including cafés, alternative media centers, artist spaces, and pirate universities. In the New York City of this generation, a variety of collective experiments have utilized autonomous space in the movement against capital, such as Blackout Books, Brecht Forum, and Times Up! Each adds to our collective history and knowledge of autonomous urban struggle, otherwise abrogated by gentrification, fragmentation, and the imposition of precarity across the social fabric of the city.

One common understanding of bookstores and infoshops such as Bluestockings is that they aim to distribute literature and thus organize within a mode of circulation. The prevailing assumption is that access to information efficiently correlates to political consciousness and therefore to political action. This type of circulation is important but often remains an untested proposition in many Left milieus. Empty phrases like "knowledge is power" elide the political potential of these movement spaces. While they can become important locations and means through which our power combines along the expansive capillary forms of common life, it is not *primarily* a matter of changing one's consciousness. Common life is seeded in social terrain that can recompose people's existences, their livelihoods, and their relations with others—and certainly therefore also their consciousness. However, this ability relies on certain *modes of production* that are the real potential of these spaces: *the production of common subjectivities, common knowledges,* and *common struggles.*

A HISTORY OF BLUESTOCKINGS

BLUESTOCKINGS WAS FOUNDED IN 1999 as a women's bookstore, with an emphasis on gay and lesbian culture and politics. Its mission was in many ways faithful to the 1970s women's movement, specifically the political urgencies that situated women-run bookstores and publishers as important mechanisms through which the movement could circulate their ideas.[7] For just over three and a half years, Bluestockings Women's Bookstore operated as an informal collective project comprised entirely of women. While there were two or three paid staffers, there were also approximately twenty volunteers, a traditional component of most women's bookstores and community-run spaces. It was a small but important place for predominantly queer women to produce a social, literary, and political community in common, meet and discuss issues, and also collectively recover the power of women. The few monthly events the space hosted included poetry readings as well as forums on incarcerated women, immigration, food, midwifery, and other issues.

Despite being the city's only feminist bookstore, the business succumbed to the declining trend of women's bookstores nationally, as well as the impact of 9/11, which devastated so much of downtown life. By the end of 2002, the informal collective was disbanded, and debts had mounted. In March 2003, these debts (and relatively few assets) were sold to an assemblage of new members and old volunteers. Bluestockings Women's Bookstore now became Bluestockings Radical Bookstore, continuing but expanding the social justice mission of the original space, and now with a greater interest in relating to direct-action organizing in the anti-globalization movement. Over the following months, a new and smaller collective emerged, with refined structures and processes in place. Before long, the last of the loan and debt repayments, as well as ongoing expenses and an expanding inventory, were being financed from book sales. In June 2005, we undertook a second loan and expanded into an adjacent storefront, enabling us to stock more books and host more people during our increasingly regular programming. Since 2003, we have fully organized as a self-managed worker-owned business, with collective members participating as equal owners and equal decision-makers.

This workers' collective has had as many as six members and as few as three, and has always been majority women-identified (and for a certain time, also majority people of color as well). Since our re-founding in 2003, our collective ownership structure has been pooled from our volunteer base, which has grown considerably. Although our location in Manhattan's Lower East Side has greatly aided in our visibility and accessibility, it also pits us against powerful real estate forces and expanding rent cycles, and so has increasingly put concern about overhead and expenses at the forefront of our existence. It has taken steadfast commitment and a high level of organization to sustain our financial needs entirely from sales and activity generated within the store. In this time we have transitioned from unpaid, to variously paid, to equally salaried collective positions. Year after year, we increased the power to entwine the best decisions for both the project and our livelihoods, but we never fully escaped the deeply rooted precarity in our lives, with its many symptomatic financial, social, and psychological effects. Our growing solvency was also a harbinger of increasingly difficult decisions about how we would self-manage the financial foundations of the entire project. More success meant more work and greater ambition but also greater responsibility. Fortunately, it has also signaled an expanding community that has daily relied on the space that Bluestockings fosters, and to which we have become increasingly accountable.

These tensions have only exacerbated since the economic crisis hit in 2008. On the one hand, it broke the spell of our sense of workers' power and pitted the project's well-being against our own, eventually requiring us to work harder while foregoing remuneration in order to pay our overhead expenses despite lagging sales. On the other hand, we have also seen our space grow in social significance, with overwhelming interest and support coming from a vast community, swelling our volunteer ranks and sharing in the wealth of mutual aid and community-directed initiatives (such as a Bluestockings CSA called "Foodstockings") that help keep the space going. A delirious, energizing, surprising, and disorienting multitude of experiences—the product of our struggle to self-organize and work out kinks in our collective process—have slowly shaped Bluestockings.

One question in particular lies at the heart of our experience of organizing a radical bookstore: how can feminist relations and practices rooted in autonomous spaces work to de-neoliberalize our lives and reorganize our powers?[8] As a continuation and updating of our origins as a women's bookstore, our collective asserts the need to be a predominantly women-run movement space that is nonetheless open to all. This is something that has brought us great strength, specifically in highlighting the anti-patriarchal practices that undergird direct democracy. Chandra Mohanty reminds us that "many of the democratic practices and process-oriented aspects of feminism appear to be institutionalized into the decision-making processes of some of [the anti-globalization] movements."[9] Our challenge has been to affirm a multiplicity of feminist perspectives that enable all of us to further our liberatory tendencies within both the space of Bluestockings and our daily lives.

It is important to root this process in everyday experience in order to focus on the potentialities that emerge when we shift power relations on a micro-scale. Our ground is the basis for the many particularized analyses that inform, identify, and re-imagine the collective practices that we enact in our many different communities. Our challenge is to engender a direct and lived space for feminist practices to experiment, confront problems, and pose community solutions while creating loops to a politics without representations. We recognize the stalemate of mediations, of substituting equivalence for real differences, or allowing contradictions that exist in our global movements to simply pass along in some higher form or for some higher purpose. We know these issues cannot live in the apparatuses of representation because they are manifest; they rely on lived experience as the register for struggling against these dominations. In the context of decomposition of movements throughout the world, what are the techniques a space like Bluestockings can invent to expand the scales from which we understand domination? How can we move ourselves through the political distance Mohanty describes as ranging from "the micropolitics of context, subjectivity and struggle [to] the macropolitics of global economic and political systems and processes?"[10] These are questions to which further inquiry, experimentation, and organization must be devoted.

FROM SELF-ACTIVITY TO FREE ACTION: THE SELF-ORGANIZATION OF WORK

As a WORKER-OWNED BOOKSTORE, THE collective self-organizes within the principles of cooperation, mutualism, autonomy, and participation. While worker control does not inherently emancipate daily life, decoding the work relation nevertheless amounts to quite a bit organizationally. Without collective control and autonomy, it would not be possible for us to expand our vision and determine for ourselves the product of our labors and the direction of the space. The relative autonomy afforded to us by being a worker-owned business is not a goal, but a necessary precursor and premise.[11]

Being a self-managed worker project requires us to rearticulate a new dynamic and ethic of work within the space and our daily lives. Nevertheless, just because no structural position is left for a boss does not mean that we have not all internalized the boss in our modes of behavior and interaction, nor does it mean that we've been able to successfully eradicate all the potential indignities that soft hierarchies sometimes rear.

One enduring challenge is sustaining the perpetual democratizing machine of worker's autonomy in such a way that it extends into all other facets of our lives. Since collective members tend to have multiple jobs, we are forced to transition from the horizontalism of our workplace to more alienated work where we become isolated individuals dealing as best we can with precarious psychological and structural forces that command our labor.

It seems like our collective can sometimes recompose and be decomposed within the length of the working day, spread out as it often is across various workplaces. Such dispersal often creates fissures, tensions, and exhaustions in our collective that are difficult to understand or guard against. Increasing the time we work together, as well as bringing in issues of care into our collective work both unseats some of this tension and reveals to us the promise of our collective power, but we nevertheless find ourselves profoundly limited in our ability to assert more than a temporary autonomy inscribed within larger and more profound processes of command.

Another decoded work relation runs diagonally across our self-organization in the activities of the volunteers. This type of work highlights the differences, tensions, as well as co-articulation of those whose waged work is carefully delinked from their free-activities, technical know-hows, and social-creative desires. Outside of their time at Bluestockings, many volunteers are students, communication, education, and information workers, and young precariats of all types, especially in the service industries. Some are professionals, non-profit staffers and researchers, and some are employed in the arts. Many are women, gender-queer, or gender-non-conforming; are working class white youth, or people of color; are first or second generation migrants; speak a number of languages; and have lived in vastly different social geographies.

There are more than seventy active volunteers who participate in the running of the space during weekly three-hour shifts. Many hundreds of past volunteers continue to participate in one way or another. The combination of collective workers and weekly (and more provisional) volunteers run the entire project each day. In the process, we reproduce the skills and knowledge of how to organize a collectively-run social space, as well as manage a worker-owned business. The process of combining also enables us to make real connections across economic circumstance, education, work life, conceptions of time, know-how, notions of self and different experiences of race, gender, and sexuality, and the meaning of urban life.

Collective members and volunteers combine in a fluid model that resists any overcoding of 'collective power' and 'volunteer power,' as both manifest the regime of capitalist- and state-defined work. Gilles Deleuze and Felix Guattari describe this model of combination as *free action* in relation to the code of work and the code of creation: "Regardless of the effort or toil they imply, they are of the order of free action, related to pure mobility, and not of the order of work with its conditions of gravity, resistance, and expenditure."[12] It is certainly true that collective work retains the character of gravity, resistance, and expenditure. But what happens when we combine these conditions with the condition of "pure mobility," of free action, of unencumbered (volunteer) power? New relationships organize our space and invent a value-system that tests and builds our potential to collectively decode the work relation and set it free.[13]

FROM SUBVERSION OF COMMUNITY TO ARTICULATING IN COMMON

SINCE 2003, WE HAVE BECOME highly visible as a 'Leftist' bookstore, fair-trade cafe, and free event space. Such institutions, however much they exist within anti-capitalist cultures, are still 'alternates' within a capitalist web of relations. They say nothing of their desire, will, or ability to organize their exit from capitalist relations. Autonomous institutions, on the other hand, root their anti-capitalism not in stances, but in the ability to create new social relations and subjectivities that are linked to each other in circuits of struggles that create new forms of life and collective flight lines from domination and control. The latter institutional form is most significant to Bluestockings; it is this form that constitutes the transformative role our space has across an ephemeral network of autonomous community practices locally, nationally, and internationally.

That is why the immediate, formally visible notion of our 'politics' is inadequate, since it merely seeks to codify our powers in the services and labors we perform: selling Leftist books and hosting activist-oriented discussions, with its corresponding ties to the money-form and the forced differential inclusion of spaces with finite resources. The most significant aspect lost in this immediate codification is the role that Bluestockings plays in another register of social struggle, one that is outside the locus of most politics. While the practices that constitute our self-organization are rooted in an historical array of traditions and expressions of resistance and movement organizing, ours is a politics organized around a "refusal to constitute [ourselves] as frontal opponents," as Colectivo Situaciones have described similar autonomous practices.[14] The collective and volunteers organize a space that does not put sole emphasis on achieving oppositional stances to current political orderings. We start with our daily lives and attempt to invest in practices and encounters that reconstitute political power within us based on the desire to affirm and build communal life. This long and slow process affords very few visible markers of success or defeat. But it does reorient our understanding of the plane of politics as corresponding with the plane of our lives; it organizes our experiences into increasingly common notions, a becoming-aware that we live within and against capitalist planning. While we struggle to achieve this reorientation, we must confront an implicit problem of this plane: how to link separate experiences of daily life across the vast geographic differences of degree and scale. This can range from the challenge of connecting communities that inhabit the same fragmented city, to the ability to correlate experiences that arise from differences within planetary class hierarchies.

As a space that seeks to dehierarchize relationships while still encountering each other through authentic differences, we must ensure Bluestockings remains transparent and open to participation. This is challenging given the pressures that the command of money imposes on our current configuration as a rent-paying space, and which ceaselessly discipline our labor and promote increased specialization of tasks. Nevertheless, by linking the openness of our space with the dynamic of direct participation and the need for collaboration and mutual co-articulation of ideas and visions, Bluestockings gathers multiple and fluid singularities who continually invest their energy as an emergent, rooted, and self-constituted community.

All of this openness occurs, paradoxically, somewhat underground. While autonomous relationships, encounters, and common labors are the significant logics of the space, Bluestockings is never closed to those who do not know or seek these things. Our open character includes being affable and inviting to anyone and involves inquiring about people's needs and desires for new experiences of space beyond those self-initiated in radical milieus. Accordingly, there operate concentric circles (etymologically, centered and in common) within the Bluestockings community that only make sense in relation to what each does, and then in relation to the others. A very large and variegated community, comprising many tens of thousands of people a year, comes to the shop and participates in the economy we have set up as a bookstore and cafe. A smaller but similarly striated community intersects or integrates into the fabric of our space through our programming, where they attend study and reading groups, meet people, propose and organize events, or participate in discussions, readings, and screenings. This circle actualizes the inestimable imagined network of people who are sympathetic and interested in our activities but participate only when already-existing paths converge (etymologically, to bend in common). Each level, as concentric circles tend toward a center, is increasingly intimate—there are those friends, comrades, volunteers, organizers, conspirators, or challengers, who at each level choose to what degree their experiences and involvements will enable them to become-common with others.

This vast community, with its many circles centering nearer or further from the autonomous production of new social selves at the core of our project, is not defined by any outside, but merely what it seeks to become and seeks to do *next*.[15] This community remains nomadic and faithful to its own needs, but suspicious of institutions. Therefore, it chooses to interpret the significance of the space Bluestockings organizes, as well as its own orientation to the multiple participant-created economies propagating at any given time—money economies, knowledge economies, alternative value practices, mutual aid and just negotiation, and mental, spiritual and emotional support, to name a few.

Nevertheless, we must remember to constantly bring forward the notion of discipline and control as it permeates all facets of the social factory.[16] There are two major points here. First, our community cannot pretend to exist apart from larger capitalist relations or society that threaten to further entrench and subsume our being. Remembering this merely makes clear the necessity of inscribing our autonomous spaces within the struggle *against* capital, the 'refusal' to be productive for capital while simultaneously being productive of ourselves. As Selma James has stated, "Once we see the community as a productive center and thus a center of subversion, the whole perspective for generalized struggle and revolutionary organization is re-opened."[17]

Second, this same community seems to enact its refusals not through confrontation or opposition but through elusion. Our community is formed in relation to desire (whatever you want) and not identity (the conditions of belonging). In this formation, we decode claims of belonging that are based on properties (being queer, being young, and being fearless are the qualities that most predominate our space) while simultaneously attempting to dismantle the power of identity as organized racially, through gender and sexuality, and through the differential inclusions of nationality and ethnicity. What takes the place of identity is activity: the orientation, values, and practices that emerge from encounters with others. The precursor is an ethics that is constantly opening up the space for perpetual transformation.

This community takes shape as an unrepresentable "multiple common place," a dynamic that raises the scale of antagonism by traversing the limits of both individuality and state and capitalist institutions.[18] Giorgio Agamben's discussion of this aspect of community (what he calls the gathering of 'singularities') is important here:

> In the final instance the State can recognize any claim for identity. What the state cannot tolerate in any way, however, is that singularities form a community without affirming an identity, that humans co-belong without any representable condition for belonging. For the State, what is important is never the singularity as such, but only its inclusion in some identity, whatever-identity. A being radically devoid of any representable identity would be absolutely irrelevant to the State. [This being] rejects all identity and every condition of belonging, [and is thus] the principal enemy of the State."[19]

The political potential of this community is something that remains to be seen in the relations that proliferate around Bluestockings. Our self-organization subverts community in the sense that the space facilitates a singular community defined by conditions of capacity, not by conditions of belonging. To understand the coming-to-be of this kind of community is to sense the vitality that is infused in a space like Bluestockings, one that provokes the constant reorganization of what it means to work, that encourages us to associate and collaborate freely toward productive and antagonistic ends. However, in moving from bodily terms of new social relations and encounters to describing an abstract community, one can perceive the tensions, contradictions, and antinomies prevalent in the organization of autonomous spaces: they always require links to larger and more abstract worlds than the ones they seek to concretize, and, therefore, attempts to define it are inevitably disorienting. Nevertheless, if we return to the bodies and the labors of self-organization, we see that the reorganization of time, space, and relations produces a critical *moment* in the process of recomposition: the act of encounter at the center of community.

In one sense, this encounter is at the singular level of newly forming relations, borne from the co-articulation of desires, experiences, and modes of acting. There is, however, another level to the encounter that we facilitate. Nightly, Bluestockings serves as a venue for movement thinking, visioning, and collaborating. We host authors, filmmakers, writers, poets, musicians, visionaries, travelers, and storytellers in an effort to construct new knowledges about our daily lives and the larger (and often equally obscured) world.

We do not simply seek a catalog of injustices against gender, racial, national, and class formations in different communities, but what Mohanty calls the "mutuality and co-implication" of struggles, "which suggests attentiveness to the interweaving of the histories of these communities."[20] We address not just the connections of domination, but primarily those of struggle and resistance. Our starting point is the articulation of a better world in common; at the heart of this yearning is the question of knowledge and value production. The attempt to bring people together to co-produce and expand local knowledges into the register of larger ecologies begins with the realization that knowledge itself is a terrain of struggle. The facilitation of local and global productions of knowledge is not a static phenomenon, nor are there 'neutral subjects.' Our resources and capacity to engage in this struggle must necessarily be attuned to linkages, strategic navigation around conceptual blockages, and the ability to recognize practical inertias. In this way, inquiries, discussions, and debates themselves become adversarial spaces of knowledge.

COMMON NOTIONS

We have to distinguish between ghetto and autonomy. The ghetto is completely functional to the governance regime: it is a particular form of differential inclusion. Autonomy is the liberation of collective power. It is struggles and exodus, resistance and flight lines, the refusal of dominant knowledge and the production of antagonistic living knowledge.
—Alberto De Nicola & Gigi Roggero[21]

AT THE END OF 1995, in a now-defunct heterodox Marxist journal called *Common Sense*, Ed Emory called for a militant class composition study project that would be the basis of future political organization, declaring, "No politics without Inquiry!"[22] Emory's intention was to get closer to an understanding of international and historical developments in social struggles, to the circulation of subterranean movements that many did not recognize and therefore could not understand, connect to, valorize, and draw strength from. Indeed, a new class formation was emerging from the class defeats of its previous formations and combining into new compositions. His simple assertion: we do not yet know the conditions of our new class composition (because it is in the process of formation), and so we must analyze it through a process of *inquiry*.

Then as now, this inquiry relies on *composition analysis*.[23] We can discern within the concept both the various procedures associated with it as well as its objectives. Its 'object' is to explicate the "structure of needs, behaviors and antagonist practices, sedimented through a long history of different struggles."[24] The methods and procedures of such an analysis come into existence in particular contexts in the accumulation of knowledge and class conditions; they are by no means static, and are available and adaptable to new contours and needs.

This process of collective research simultaneously allows us to better understand our own experiences organizing Bluestockings as well as posit new directions as we seek to connect to movement-building efforts. This political organizing has yet to take on a sustained commitment within our organization. Inquiry would assist us in learning what tools of research were explored and utilized within various movements that empowered them to understand the terrain of struggle upon which they were pitched and subsequently develop strategies that enabled them to take initiative in their struggles.

This is increasingly urgent political work when so much of what we experience as contemporary metropolitan life seems dictated to us in terms of an historic class defeat. Inquiry into our struggles reveals the strategy embedded in this defeat—a continuous and reactionary response from capital's local, national, and global planners to destabilize communities that they deem potential threats. Over the past few decades, unemployment, lack of affordable housing, limited access to public transportation and healthy food, slack or falling wages, and other conditions adding to urban instability have not been problems for capitalist planners *per se*, so long as these elements were extended over destabilized working classes that are isolated from other similarly affected communities, their struggles, and from the general accumulation of the history of these many experiences.

In 1975, Donna Demac and Phil Mattera inquired into the reorganization of class powers during the New York City fiscal crisis and uncovered the political significance of the above realization. This so-called crisis signaled the intensity of capital's counteroffensive after a cycle of struggle had subverted and undermined capitalist planning and accumulation. Their lesson was that "*no longer do the autonomous struggles of the different sectors of the class in the city result in more power for each vis-à-vis capital.*"[25]

This is exactly the condition that autonomous spaces in the city seeking to recompose a broad base of power must face. The limits of Bluestockings' political strategy of instituting a *space of relative autonomy* derives from the neoliberal period of struggle in New York City that followed in the wake of the fiscal crisis. Our experience verifies that spaces of *relative autonomy* can become quite significant but remain vulnerable to attack precisely because they are partial. This is why it is crucial for the context of our present movement efforts to be understood genealogically through the history of struggles over space that have preceded it. Then, just as now, "the outright manipulation of money [was planned] to accomplish perhaps the most decisive defeat of working class power in the world today."[26] Since then, movements and working class communities have sustained themselves despite a "circulation of defeat" in the last three decades of urban struggles in New York City, where enervating counter-measures have *decomposed* and disintegrated working class power to the advantage of capital.

The first step in addressing this profound limitation is to pose these spaces as essential resources in the act of inquiry. Bluestockings, as a place for encounters between peoples' struggles, can contribute to collective efforts to regain connection, knowledge, initiative, and power to resist and move beyond these conditions, through the production and circulation of common notions that facilitate necessary alliances within our movements.

In both a moment of capitalist crisis and the crisis of movements, we ought to formulate our politics on the basis of inquiries into the nature of class struggle and the reorganization of social relationships of work in our current time. Because militant practices of *inquiry* must always include a process of investigating the conditions of our everyday lives, open and autonomous self-organized spaces like Bluestockings have a vital role to play in aggregating experiences and formulating common inquiries. We must study ourselves, never taking for granted that our understanding of the world we live and produce is conditioned by being in it. Who are we, how are we constituted, what is our shared history, what are our various histories, how do hierarchies and commonalities both intersect, inspire, and interrupt us constantly? These are political questions that set us on the road to recover the knowledges necessary to grapple with social defeats and develop strategies to organize ourselves within more powerful compositional bodies.

Infoshops, bookstores, and other common places in our movements are significant articulations of collectively-organized spaces of encounter and inquiry. Within these spaces, the production of rebellious subjectivities becomes the same process as the production of rebellious knowledges. These powers are in excess to the forms of control, exploitation, and hierarchization that operate in our lives. The point is to *organize* this excess—to understand these powers as arising from our lived common conditions but requiring significant recomposition before they are able to transform the material, historical, and subjective foundations of our lives.[27] There are an infinite array of rebellious bodies engaged in subversive acts and everyday resistance. We must inquire about these, understand their basis in the needs and urgencies they express, and pose the question of organization into common institutions.

Here, radical social spaces allow us to gather our different experiences and various analyses of: (1) capitalist planning, in the strategies of austerity, underdevelopment, and the financial powers of money-capital as well as the wage-form; (2) the organization of much of the Left, in the variety of ways it fails to understand its own privileges and interests as often aligned with capital and against other sectors; and (3) working class struggles, the expressions of their needs and desires that are not contained by the two preceding functions. Combined, we may understand the stakes, limits, and compositional contours of class power.

As significant sites for research and inquiry, which are also sites for the production of common subjectivities, we must be careful to recognize the technical and political composition of our spaces as they relate to the composition of capitalist space, as well as the needs and desires of other movements as they traverse this same space. Without this recognition, it would be possible to organize a significant space of encounter that is antagonistic to those who share the neighborhood. This is an enormously difficult tension and contradiction to analyze and resolve, one that adds to the litany of challenges Bluestockings faces on a daily basis.

One possible solution comes from Madrid, where the collective researchers of *Observatorio Metropolitano* approach a political understanding of complex urban processes, such as gentrification, displacement, access to food, housing, and social wealth by distinguishing between knowledge-from-us and knowledge-with-others.[28] The first resonates with the discussion above of a knowledge-subjectivity that arises from collective encounters, that starts from our *position*. The second alludes to the desire to weave these subjectivities and knowledge alongside others, who are experts in their own situations. Their practice pushes to the moment of research-from-us and with-others, or *co-research*, where practices, knowledges, subjectivities, and powers all change, and thus emerge the first strategic bases of social transformation.

In this process, it will often be necessary to return to a question at the root of these desires: where does the power to change social relations in our lives stem from? Surely it lies in our ability to resist forces: capitalist exploitation and the money-form, integration as well as exclusion based on racialized class and gender hierarchies, the state structures of the police and prisons, the enervating representations of party and many non-profit organizations, the corruption of direct culture by spectacular separation, the enclosure of our social wealth, the infinite array of the same consumer choices. These are some of the many forces from which subjectivities must *subtract*. But the root power also stems from our ability to *construct* subjectivities that *combine*, that combine in order to confront capital with the whole of our lives: solidarities rooted in a tradition of mutual aid, livelihoods and forms of support reproduced in common, struggles that improve instead of expend life, reclamations of our deep histories that vivify the manners in which commonalities preempt national, racial, and gendered divisions. Common notions stem from these conditions and allow us to link relations of support to build power through common forms that simultaneously attack institutional control.

COMMON INSTITUTIONS

Every space initially obtained by subversion has instead to be filled by us with something 'new,' something 'constructive.' Construction has to be combined with subversion into one process: substruction. Construction should never be a pretext to renounce on subversion. Subversion alone creates only straw fires, historical dates and 'heroes,' but it doesn't leave concrete results.
—(p.m.)[29]

IT IS WITHIN THE TENSIONS described in the beginning of the chapter—of both recoding and exiting work relations while determining the social wealth we need to reproduce ourselves—that the issue of the commons enters our movement thinking. Our common spaces are the sites where we can subtract from the forces that produce subjectivities codified in processes of exploitation, domination, and oppression, and begin producing other kinds of subjectivities. What is 'common,' then, needs to be understood from our class perspective, that is, as the historical, material, and continual site of our collective power against capital. Those who have the commons struggle to defend it. Those who do not have the commons struggle to produce it. These commons require encounters, antagonisms, and intelligences, and therefore require institutions of the common to endure, such as autonomous organizations that are able to refuse the capture of their energies by capitalist command. As much as common institutions consolidate power, they can only succeed if they extend across divisions and hierarchies, gendered and racialized, as articulated in the state-space of borders and international divisions of labor. Thus, common institutions, just as struggles, need to circulate, to complete "strange loops" that connect lives not directly encountered.[30]

In 1985, the Zurich-based writer p.m. began conceptualizing these questions. He spoke then of a "planetary work machine" that constructed for its functioning three types of workers, each characterized by the "worlds" they lived in, and the specific ways each are blackmailed by capitalist "deals." There was A, Informational, Technical, and Intellectual workers; B, Industrial and Agricultural workers; and C, Reproductive workers responsible for maintaining the planetary working class.[31] These three worlds are always present in every city or metropolitan region, and while there is often an extremely policed and rigid separation amongst them, they share proximity as their lives overlap in certain lived spaces. p.m. writes:

> The power of the Machine, its control mechanism, is based on playing off the different types of workers against each other. The three types of workers learn to be afraid of each other. They're kept divided by prejudices, racism, jealousy, political ideologies, economic interests. The planetary work machine is a machinery consisting of people put up against each other; we all guarantee its functioning.[32]

How this composition has changed in our organizing contexts is an important question for collective research. How are we variously composed, technically in our relation to the work-deal-machine, but also in terms that can cross-circuit these separate but stitched "worlds"? A second important question is how the deals that each type of worker makes are renewed, shifted, executed, and refused on the terrain of class struggle that cuts across each worker and their experiences.

Moreover, if the machine is *us*, then dismantling it requires careful effort not to destroy others or ourselves. What must happen, p.m. states, is that different sectors need to develop "strange loops" within their struggles, in an effort to combine their unique potential within a shared commo(tio)n: disinformation, disproduction, and disruption (A-, B-, and C-, accordingly) across struggles. What is necessary is "a kind of communication that's not adequate to the design of the Machine."[33] Since the work machine separates our lives according to its needs and functions, this kind of communication will need to emerge beyond the realm of work—in spaces, for example, that can construct themselves for these communications. Can we transform our collectively organized autonomous spaces into these institutions?

Because these spaces seek to overcome the organized divisions of capitalist life, they can become important common sites of aggregation. But taking as a challenge the construction of non-hierarchical spaces is not the same as being equipped to deal with the accumulative effects of these divisions over our lifetimes and over generations. Most self-organized spaces are severely squeezed by the pervasive power of money and weakened by institutionalized and internalized forms of oppression. In our everyday lives, just struggling to create breathing room while being choked by these things can be disorienting; so spaces begin dealing with their perceived scarcity and the threat of blackmailed oppression everywhere by orienting inward, toward a familiarly constituted community that can begin to breathe together, and so conspire together.

Where are the time, courage, and other resources to learn how to authentically combine with others across hierarchies? This is a question for our spatial contexts, but is also an especially grave concern given that "purely local, regional, or even national dysco knots [the word used for *substructive* dis-communication loops across struggles] will never be sufficient to paralyze the Work-Machine as a whole."[34] Our common institutions need to build knots of power and intelligence across our class divisions, as well as our racial and sexual hierarchies, along and beyond the circuits that currently connect us all. We must learn how to address ourselves and our recompositions to the problems of spatial hierarchies across international (territorial, political, economic, and cultural) divisions.

We need an adequate manner of speaking about who we are and who we (can) become together—to speak of the common without being reduced to its least denominator. This requires that we understand how we produce radical subjectivity. Marta Malo reminds us that "the promoters of consciousness-raising groups were certain that the only way to build a radical movement was starting *from the self*" and relating it to the general conditions of others.[35] But where to from here? No one would be satisfied with an introspective self-study. Regardless, capital has ways of rewarding our self-consciousness, so long as it stays local and diverts itself from class struggle—as in the ethical self-satisfaction of living "compassionately" through our life "choices." A revolutionary current can only emerge from our self-inquiries if we are able to connect our compositions to the story of class and political compositions on a planetary level.

Inquiry into current compositions of our class and movement experiences must be done collectively. It is not just a matter of knowing what we once did not know, however potentially useful that is. It is a process of recovering our powers to act collectively, not based on shared ideologies, but because we are composed within and with each other. These are encounters that produce insurgent subjectivities capable of producing action from their very occurrences.

Indeed, the processes blur; collective thought becomes collective action and self-organization. The aim has to be made explicit. By starting with a collectivity or organization with certain contours, a self-inquiry into one's collective context pushes questions about the social picture of struggle beyond the self and aims toward a greater political organization that can both dehierarchize relations within the group and break down divisions preventing it from jumping tracks toward another, larger social composition. Are other compositions recognized in the field of struggle simply by their representations, the medium of images and distortions that are necessarily part of struggling through the spectacular limits of capital? Or rather, are others recognized through an encounter of shared experience and action, beyond and against these representations? In an historical sense, this work extends our feminist roots, which simultaneously entwines anti-patriarchal and anti-racist roots. The class implications become commonalities as we discover how our relations to each other, the city, and work are mediated through the balance of powers between capital and our circulating refusals.

Radical spaces such as Bluestockings have a powerful role to fulfill within these wagers. Our first step was to self-organize a bookstore that could collectively reinvent practices of work and community forms of organization. Our experiences have traversed many tensions, contradictions, and antinomies in ways that continue to produce space, community, and insurgent knowledge—the core of radical subjectivities. Through common notions of our organizing potential vis-à-vis other sectors, formations, and expressions of the class, we can now begin to articulate the potential role of common institutions in our movements. An aggregation of different networks of militancy that can share the flows of rebellious subjectivity and knowledge would go a long way in discovering the possibilities inherent in these claims for generalized social cooperation, in our communal lives as well as in our collective struggles against and beyond capitalism. Through the weight of our experiences and desires for self-transformation, perhaps we can find out what a body like this can do.

NOTES

1   On class composition and the related political concepts of 'recomposition' and 'decomposition,' see the introduction to this volume by Team Colors collective. This discussion is historically informed by a variegated tradition of compositional analysis arising from militants in Italian autonomist struggles of the 1970s (see for example Sergio Bologna, "Class composition and the Theory of the Party," 1972) as well as U.S.-based Zerowork collective's use of the concept in their *Political Materials*, 1975 and 1977 and Midnight Notes Collective, 1979–present.

2   The term "exit" links to the notion of "exodus," a concept that signifies many practices seeking power not to construct a state, but to enhance sociality, productive relations, and affects through an inventiveness across a generalized horizontal cooperation that changes the rules of power against the state. See Paolo Virno, *Grammar of the Multitude* (New York: Semiotext(e), 2004).

3   The 1975 Fiscal Crisis signaled an intense assault by capital on various sectors of the working class in New York City. This crisis, coupled with the oil and food crises of the same period, functioned as an essential component in the broader attacks worldwide. For more on this, see Eric Lichten, *Class, Power and Austerity: The New York City Fiscal Crisis* (New York: Bergin and Garvey, 1986); Midnight Notes Collective (eds), *Midnight Oil* (Brooklyn: Autonomedia, 1992); David Harvey, *A Brief History of Neoliberalism* (Oxford: Oxford University Press, 2007).

4   The tension between the 'scales' of everyday life and planetary relations have long been part of the challenge of understanding social transformation. For more on this, see Henri Lefebvre, *Production of Space* (Oxford: Blackwell, 1992); Neil Smith, *Uneven Development* (Athens: University of Georgia, 1984); Maria Mies, *Patriarchy and Accumulation on a World Scale* (London: Zed Books, 1986).

5   For more on infoshops, see: Antonios Vradis' "Infoshops" in *The International Encyclopedia of Revolution and Protest* (Blackwell 2009); Joel Olson, "Between Infoshops and Insurrection: U.S. Anarchism, Movement Building, and the Racial Order," in *Contemporary Anarchist Studies*, ed. Randall Amster, Luis Fernandez, et. al. (New York: Routledge, 2009).

6   For contemporary analyses of these European counterparts, see the *Transversal* issue on this: HTTP://TRANSFORM.EIPCP.NET/TRANSVERSAL/0406 (accessed January 15, 2010).

7   For more on feminist movement culture and organizing, see Melissa Kesler Gilbert and Catherine Sameh, "Building Feminist Educational Alliances in an Urban Community," in *Teaching Feminist Activism: Strategies from the Field*, ed. Nancy A. Naples and Karen Bojar (New York: Routledge, 2002), 185–206; Deborah Yaffe, "Feminism in Principle and in Practice: Everywomans Books," *Atlantis: A Women's Studies Journal. Special Issue: Connecting Practices, Doing Theory* (Fall 1996): 154–157.

8   See Anita Lacey's "Forging Spaces of Liberty" for more on the creation of space that links patriarchy and neoliberalism, in *Constituent Imagination: Militant Investigations, Collective Theorizations*, eds. Stevphen Shukaitis & David Graeber (Oakland: AK Press, 2007), 242–250.

9   Chandra Talpade Mohanty, *Feminism Without Borders: Decolonizing Theory, Practicing Solidarity*, (Durham: Duke University, 2003), 250.

10 Mohanty, *Feminism without Borders*, 223, 225.

11 Todd Hamilton and Nate Holdren eloquently describe a model of workplace organizing that fits with our own: "It's more like a scale or key in music [than a model], it provides the framework within which we improvise the affective, immaterial, flexible processes of organizing and building organization." Todd Hamilton and Nate Holdren, "Compositional Power," in *Turbulence: Ideas for Movement*, June 2007: 20–21.

12 Gilles Deleuze and Felix Guattari, *A Thousand Plateaus* (Minneapolis: University of Minnesota Press, 1987), 401.

13 Gilles Deleuze and Felix Guattari, *A Thousand Plateaus*, 402.

14 Colectivio Situaciones is a militant research formation in Buenos Aires, Argentina. See "On the Researcher-Militant," translated by Sebastian Touza. *Transform*, 2003, HTTP://TRANSFORM. EIPCP.NET/TRANSVERSAL/0406/COLECTIVOSITUACIONES/EN (accessed January 15, 2010).

15 This community-being "is not … an essence or an existence but a *manner of rising forth*; not a being that is *in* this or that mode, but a being that is *its* mode of being, and thus, while remaining singular and not indifferent, is multiple and valid for all." Giorgio Agamben, *The Coming Community* (Minneapolis: University of Minnesota Press, 1993), 28.

16 The concept of the social factory conveys the historic transformations and reorganization of work in increasing metropolitan territories due to the form of class struggles in the factory that have (to a greater or lesser degree) been resolved by dissolving the site of the factory into all elements of social life. This is related to the thesis put forth by Italian workerists that we have entered a period of "real subsumption" of life under capital. While there are many references to this body of work, two substantial overviews are Jason Read's *The Micro-Politics of Capital* (Albany: SUNY Press, 2003) and Nicholas Thoburn, *Deleuze, Marx and Politics* (New York: Routledge, 2003).

17 Selma James, introduction to Mariarosa Dalla Costa and Selma James, *The Power of Women and the Subversion of the Community* (Brighton, UK: Falling Walls Press, 1972), 17.

18 Giorgio Agamben, *The Coming Community*, 28.

19 Giorgio Agamben, *The Coming Community*, 86–87.

20 Chandra Mohanty, *Feminism Without Borders*, 242.

21 Alberto De Nicola and Gigi Roggero, "Eight Theses on the University, Hierarchization and Institutions of the Common," *Edu-Factory*, HTTP://WWW.EDU-FACTORY.ORG/INDEX.PHP?OPTION=COM_C ONTENT&TASK=CATEGORY&SECTIONID=7&ID=18&ITEMID=41 (accessed December 20, 2009).

22 Ed Emory, "No Politics without Inquiry! A Proposal for a Class Composition Inquiry Project 1996–7," *Common Sense*: no. 18, December 1995.

23 For a further discussion of "class composition," please see: Steve Wright, *Storming Heaven* (London: Pluto, 2002), Harry Cleaver, *Reading Capital Politically* (Oakland: AK Press, 2000).

24 Marta Malo, "Common Notions, Part 1: workers-inquiry, co-research, consciousness-raising," Spanish original in *Nociones Comunes* (Traficantes de Sueños: Madrid, 2004).

25 Donna Demac and Philip Mattera, "Developing and Underdeveloping New York," *Zerowork Political Materials #2* (Zerowork: New York, Fall 1977), 136.

26 Donna Demac & Philip Mattera, "Developing and Underdeveloping New York," 113.

27 This is one of many provocative organizing lessons coming out of the Anomalous Wave, specifically in Bologna. I thank Andrea Ghelfi for pointing this out to me.

28 Observatorio Metropolitano, "How Research Became Militant," (email correspondence).

29 p.m., *bolo'bolo* (Brooklyn: Autonomedia, 1985).

30 The concept of "strange loops" can be found in an article of the same name, in Midnight Notes Collective (eds), "Space Notes," *Midnight Notes* 4 (1981).

31 For more on these distinctions, see *bolo bolo*.
32 p.m., *bolo bolo*, 12.
33 p.m., *bolo bolo*, 44.
34 p.m., *bolo bolo*, 52.
35 Marta Malo, "Common Notions," and "Common Notions, Part 2: Institutional Analysis, Participatory Action-Research, Militant Research," Spanish original in *Nociones Comunes* (Traficantes de Sueños: Madrid, 2004).

ANTI-AUTHORITARIAN ORGANIZING IN PRACTICE

Anonymous | **Direct Action to Stop the War**[1]

IN MARCH OF 2008, DIRECT Action to Stop the War (DASW) was re-formed in the San Francisco Bay Area to coordinate actions protesting the five-year anniversary of the war in Iraq. This essay intends to provide a case study memory and assessment of the implementation of anti-authoritarian organizational practices within a diverse anti-war coalition. It is our hope that this candid description proves useful to others organizing in struggle. These structures are not rigid, and the assessments are not universal. Take what you want, leave the rest, and apply it to the organizing you are most passionate about.

"Anti-Authoritarian Organizing in Practice" traces a brief history of the rise and fall of the original DASW, leading to the rebirth of DASW in 2008. Included here is an outline and critique of the organizational structures and methods used to build momentum and coordinate mass action. Organizational structures are described at the point when the re-born DASW was at its largest in March of 2008. The essay concludes with an account of the 2008 actions, the history of the group's decline, and assessments of DASW's efforts.

THE RISE AND FALL OF DIRECT ACTION TO STOP THE WAR

THE ATTACKS OF SEPTEMBER 11, 2001 opened the door for the United States to justify an aggressive foreign policy geared toward the consolidation of global energy resources and the expansion of the U.S. empire. Labeling this policy as the "War on Terror," the U.S. invaded and occupied Afghanistan in October of that year, then immediately turned its focus to Iraq, Afghanistan's uninvolved but oil-rich neighbor. With the assistance of the corporate media, the Bush administration and Congressional representatives began a massive propaganda campaign advocating the invasion of Iraq. As anti-authoritarians, we saw right through their "weapons of mass destruction" fear tactics. We were having none of it.

Momentum spread quickly in building resistance to the government's imminent war, and soon it became clear that the anti-war struggle was emerging both nationally and internationally. Locally, much of the energy came from anti-authoritarians, many of whom were radicalized in the anti-globalization struggles of the 1990s. We had learned long ago to see this move towards invasion for what it really was: a naked power grab, an expansion of empire, and further grist for the military-industrial complex.

The new anti-war movement was unique in that its premise was the prevention of invasion entirely, as the majority of demonstrations were held during the build-up. It also reached historic numbers, including the largest single coordinated protest in recorded history on February 15, 2003.[2] But for such an enormous movement, its impact on policy was generally very weak. Nationally, most anti-war demonstrations were permitted marches and rallies; there were very few attempts to truly disrupt 'business as usual' for the government or profiteers behind the war. Organizers focused on drawing large numbers to events, but there was little strategy behind them. The growing movement became a sideshow, literally laughed at by the government, and President Bush himself referred to protestors as mere "focus groups." This was infuriating to many involved and was a clear sign that these tactics were not working. However, largely because much of the organizing was done by national 'big name' groups (which, due to their size and prominence, repeatedly avoided any kind of militant action), the general tone and tactics underwent few changes, and the movement remained stagnant.

It was in this environment that Direct Action to Stop the War was created in its first incarnation in 2003. The organization was formed with a specific purpose: to coordinate mass action in San Francisco in response to the impending bombing and invasion of Iraq. But it was very different from other anti-war groups. It was anti-authoritarian in principle and in practice; it organized direct action instead of permitted demonstrations, out of the understanding that disruption was tactically more effective, creative, and threatening to 'business as usual.'

On March 20, 2003, the day after the U.S. started bombing Iraq, the original DASW succeeded in uniting the San Francisco Bay Area anti-war movement to shut down the city's financial district. As San Francisco Police Department officer Drew Cohen put it, "They succeeded this morning; they shut the city down. They're highly organized but they are totally spontaneous. The protesters are always one step ahead of us."[3] This was one of the largest and most successful direct actions in recent history. However, this effort, along with the protests of millions in cities across the globe, did not stop the invasion.

Over the next two years, there was continued momentum in the Bay Area anti-war movement, including several large actions over the three months following the invasion. Organizers led a successful campaign against Bechtel Corporation and mobilized significant numbers to send to the Free Trade Area of the Americas actions in Miami in 2003 as well as the Republican National Convention in New York City in 2004. Yet there lingered a feeling of powerlessness to make a true difference in ending the war. DASW's organizing fizzled over these years, much like the rest of the anti-war movement. This, combined with the decline of the anti-globalization movement, led to a general deflation in West Coast anti-authoritarian mass mobilizing that prevailed until the rebirth of DASW in late 2007.

THE REBIRTH

AS THE FIVE-YEAR ANNIVERSARY OF the war in Iraq approached, a call-out for broad-based anti-authoritarian action was created and distributed in pamphlet and email form. A few affinity groups and individuals responded, who then met to discuss laying a foundation for mass direct action. Many of these participants lacked time, resources, and experience, so they developed and distributed a communiqué to every affinity group, anti-war group, anti-authoritarian co-op, bookstore, and working space they knew of. They hit the streets hard, running pamphlets oriented toward the public to every worker's cooperative, living cooperative, coffee shop, artist space, and bike shop around, then typed it into email form and repeated the process. Once a critical momentum was reached, things began moving fast, and word spread quickly. The first spokescouncil was called for December of 2007, leading to the rebirth of Direct Action to Stop the War.

ORGANIZATIONAL STRUCTURES OF DASW, 2008

THE RE-BORN DIRECT ACTION TO Stop the War operates very similarly to its predecessor. It is a decentralized, anti-authoritarian network and coalition of individuals, affinity groups, and organizations from throughout the San Francisco Bay Area, which uses a spokescouncil organizing structure to coordinate mass action affinity groups comprised of four to twenty people who work together autonomously on their chosen projects. Not all organizations involved are explicitly anti-authoritarian, but they all agree to work in an anti-authoritarian manner within the spokescouncil structure. Each affinity group or organization empowers a spoke (representative) to attend spokescouncil meetings to decide on important issues. There are no established leadership positions in the organization, and group decisions are made by consensus. Meeting facilitators are changed for each spokescouncil meeting on an open and voluntary basis. This horizontal framework facilitates equality, autonomy, and productivity, and protects against domination, co-opting, and oppression.

DASW uses a working group structure to facilitate decision-making and work on specific tasks, and members are encouraged to join a working group which interests them. Working groups include those planning specific days of action as well as overarching groups such as outreach, financing, medical support, legal support, media, and communications. The working groups meet and work independently and then report back to the spokescouncil. Only very important discussions that absolutely require the input of all affinity groups are conducted at spokescouncil meetings.

For major group decisions, a proposal is brought before the council and discussed, and the proposal is reformulated with the input of the discussion. When the group is ready, everyone present votes in agreement, as a stand-aside, or in objection (a block). Decisions reach consensus when most people vote in agreement and one or zero persons has blocked the proposal. If there are a number of stand-asides, these persons are asked if they wish to express the reasons for their reservations. If there are two or more blocks, the reasoning behind blocking is discussed, and the proposal may be voted on again or dropped.

DASW continually strives to employ internal anti-authoritarian dynamics in its work. For example, as mentioned above, there are no established leadership roles in DASW (although some people may lead by effort or example, or temporarily lead groups as part of an empowered tactical team during actions). Each individual or affinity group gets involved at whatever level they are comfortable with and no one is told what to do. The organization encourages a 'step up' work ethic within the network, meaning that any suggestions for what an individual feels needs to be done or would like to be done are at least initially led by that person. These methods allow members to feel comfortable in their involvement and empower people to work on projects that are most important to them.

Maintaining efficient internal communication is particularly important for DASW, due to the group's broad-based nature and commitment to working around a variety of perspectives and organizational relationships. Routine internal communication is generally internet-based. The group began with an initial email listserv for communication. Once the group size reached a certain point, the list became cluttered, so a discussion list was created for those who were more involved or more interested in the day-to-day chatter. The original listserv became a moderated announcement list to keep clutter down and content relevant. When the group was at its largest, we set up emails for each working group, but this was difficult to manage since people switched working groups often. Also, DASW's website has resources and a main email address that is checked frequently.

DASW embraces two main tactical methods in struggling toward ending the wars in Iraq and Afghanistan. First, direct action is used to actively confront the economic and political interests behind war. The use of direct action circumvents our flawed electoral political system to directly affect the business of those responsible for the continuation of the war. Secondly, all DASW actions are nonviolent, in order to broaden the base of support for the organization and its goals.

FIVE-YEAR ANNIVERSARY ACTIONS

March 15, 2008

As a lead-up action, Direct Action to Stop the War took action against the Chevron refinery in Richmond, California. This facility refines over one million barrels of Iraqi oil every month and serves as a busy central refueling station for tanker trucks of all types (Shell, Exxon Mobil, etc.) for a large portion of the Bay Area. DASW coordinated a rally with community-based environmental justice groups and environmental non-profits, followed by a march to the refinery to take direct action. Several affinity groups locked together across the entrance of the truck refueling station, and the street was reclaimed in a festival spirit with bands, dance, and street theater. Once it was clear that the police were blocking the Chevron refinery entrances regardless of the lockdown, people calmly unlocked and simultaneously stormed the police barricades protecting the facility. Twenty-five people were arrested.

The direct action was a success in several ways. The lockdown shut down Chevron's truck refueling station for most of the day. The actions also brought media coverage linking Chevron to the war in Iraq. Further, the event linked domestic issues (local community struggle against an oil refinery) concretely with foreign policy (the war in Iraq). In combining a peaceful rally with an effective direct action, DASW was also able to expose local individuals, community-based environmental justice groups, and members of environmental non-profits to more radical forms of protest. DASW members have made a point of supporting the community since then, and some have maintained relationships to assist in the anti-Chevron refinery campaign still active in 2009. In truth, there were difficulties and tensions in organizing such a diverse coalition. However, the ability to bridge the divide between anarchists, community groups, and liberal non-profits proved to be a major strength of this coalition-organizing effort.

March 19, 2008

On March 19th (M19), the fifth anniversary of the war, DASW called for direct actions against the economic and political interests behind the war in the Financial District of downtown San Francisco. The main short-term goals of the day's actions were to bring attention to the fifth anniversary of the war and to disrupt the normal operations of war profiteers and government facilities in San Francisco. A variety of tactics were employed including a snake march, bike bloc, paint-bombings, poetry readings, U-locks on building entrances, and most notably, sit-ins, lock-downs, and die-ins. Targets included the San Francisco Federal Reserve building, downtown Chevron offices, the University of California Regents meeting, and the intersection of Montgomery and Market streets. Legal, medical, media, and communications teams coordinated support for the day of action. Organizationally, the day went off with varied success.

The media working group had spent considerable time beforehand giving interviews, alerting national media outlets, and making press kits. On the day of M19, they scouted action sites to directly engage the media upon arrival. The events made local, national, and international media in many forms. Some messaging was picked up in the coverage. However, much of it had a condescending and paternal tone, patting protesters on the back for not causing too much trouble or making note of low turnout. Of course, due to the debilitating structure of the corporate media, it was only possible to have a minor influence on the tone of the coverage. This raises a question as to whether the amount of energy and resources the network used to engage the corporate media was worth it. Opinions vary widely on this issue.

The legal team, in conjunction with the National Lawyers Guild, provided a great deal of support for those risking arrest, and thus aided in the goal of business disruption. An arrestee hotline was set to track those arrested into the jail and through the process until release. Legal observers were stationed at major meeting points and places of public direct action. The legal team also set up a support system for actions that relied on the elements of surprise and secrecy. In this system, action teams could call the hotline to request the dispatch of legal observers to the secret location a half-hour before the action was to take place. Having a legal support structure aided the actions in immediate capacity and movement sustainability. By its very existence, the legal support team helped encourage action by providing a sense of support, confidence, rumor control, and concrete information about where the legal limits of action lay. The legal team provided a feeling and reality of solidarity for those who were arrested, continuing all the way through trial.

The medical working group was not widely utilized on this day of action because the police did not engage in large-scale brutality (though there were incidents of police aggression). Regardless, the presence of medics was important for the safety, well-being, and perceptions of those attending the actions. Although the medics did not physically treat anyone, they did monitor crowds for dehydration and signs of mental distress associated with long days of action. In doing this, their visual presence showed those attending that DASW considered their safety while organizing these actions. Further, their presence demonstrated that public support systems can be organized in the absence of hierarchy or the state apparatus. The event provided an opportunity to train new medics and for more experienced medics to hone their skills. The medic team contributed to the day's action by creating the perception and actuality of physical and psychological support, work that is integral to longer-term sustainability.

The communications team (comms) was very successful in many aspects but did have some troubles. Each affinity group had a designated comms person to contact a central comms team to disperse information. A text mob was set up so that anyone who signed up would get immediate notifications of where events were occurring in the city. Because of the relatively low number of subscribers (hundreds not thousands) and the purposeful limitation of the volume of messages, the text mob worked without much time lag. A pirate radio station also broadcast updates in downtown. Minute-by-minute updates were posted online at regional and national Indymedia sites. However, there was one comms incident that illuminated a larger problem with DASW's planning. At one point, an affinity group called in a paint-bombing action to comms and the dispatcher refused to relay the action over the text loop. Some interpreted this refusal as a rejection of the tactic being a departure from the nonviolent direct action agreement. The incident caused tension within the group in the days following. This could have been avoided if the spokescouncil had discussed the group's definition of 'violence.' However, a discussion of this sort would have doubtless been very long and had the potential to rip the coalition apart.

Critiques and Lessons

There are many critiques and lessons to be learned from this organizing effort. Of course, there are many people deeply involved in the effort and opinions vary widely, so this essay will focus on more widely agreed upon critiques from an anti-authoritarian perspective.

First, uniting persons with a wide spectrum of opinions toward a common goal is a daunting task for anti-authoritarians engaged in coalition building. Considering the urgency of the organizing effort and the amount of work that needed to be done, it was decided early on to only sketch out points of unity and avoid long theoretical debates at meetings unless absolutely necessary. This allowed the coalition to grow quickly, but led to problems which contributed to the group's decline once the 2008 actions were over.

Secondly, the commitment to the tactic of nonviolent direct action should be discussed. Persons involved in the group range in their opinions on this issue, but it was decided early on to embrace this tactic as a whole. Many existing organizations refused to join DASW unless this tactic was embraced, and the group agreed in order to broaden the coalition. While effective in gaining support from a broader base, this decision alienated much of the anarchist and anti-authoritarian base committed to a 'diversity of tactics' approach.

The group lost many new possible allies in the beginning because of its assumption that people had organizing experience and understood organizing structures and language. As anti-authoritarians, we often have a great deal of experience organizing and rarely have large influxes of new persons interested in joining our groups. We could have done a better job of explaining how things worked in order to be more inclusive.

Related to this issue, the consensus process across a broad coalition is more difficult than in other anti-authoritarian organizing contexts. Within a diverse coalition there is a variability of experience with the consensus process, so it takes more patience and tolerance. DASW was able to use consensus fairly successfully because it explained the process at meetings often.

DASW could have done more to encourage the formation of affinity groups at spokescouncil meetings for individuals interested in planning actions. Closer to the anniversary, we realized there were very few solid affinity groups, so more experienced activists began explaining the basics to those interested in starting temporary affinity groups, and then severed their connection to allow the groups to develop as independent organizing bodies. Once formed, these affinity groups decided their own level of action. This effort proved successful but could have been employed earlier on.

Finally, more involved members could have been more inclusive. It is easy to forget how intimidating it can be to walk into a bustling room of activists for the first time.

Taking more time to show new people around and explain to them how things work could have strengthened DASW and helped with member retention.

Five-Year Anniversary Actions Assessment
DASW succeeded in organizing one of the largest five-year anniversary actions in the U.S. The actions undoubtedly succeeded in bringing local and national attention to the anniversary of the war in Iraq in an anti-war context. However, all things considered, DASW did not succeed in disrupting the normal operations of war profiteers and government facilities in San Francisco. Constraining the assessment to organizational aspects of the actions, we identify four main reasons: 1) lack of inclusivity led to smaller overall numbers than hoped, despite a broad coalition; 2) too much secrecy around actions, a surprising development considering they were nonviolent direct actions; 3) lack of affinity group formation to plug new people into specific direct actions; and 4) the position of the March 15 lead-up action so close to the main action, dividing DASW's energy and resources.

THE STEADY DECLINE

THE M19 ACTIONS WERE FOLLOWED closely by a very sharp decline in overall membership from which the organization has not recovered. The lack of inclusiveness toward new members left much of the organizing to a core group. This core experienced an extreme level of burn-out; however, a solid group remained for several months, hoping to continue the organizing effort.

In the first month after M19, Direct Action to Stop the War focused on evaluation and long-term strategy discussions. On May 1, DASW took action in solidarity with the International Longshore and Warehouse Union by trying to close the Port of Oakland's main train terminal as part of a greater plan to shut down all West Coast ports. Later, DASW led an unpermitted march to the U.S. Military Recruiting Center and U.S. Immigration and Customs Enforcement buildings in San Francisco, shutting down both office entrances for short periods. In the early summer, the group initiated a campaign against a U.S. Army-sponsored recruitment video game as well.

During these months, DASW attempted to reform the organization into a vehicle for long-term organizing by continuing broad strategy discussions while engaging in progressively smaller direct and symbolic actions. Attendance eventually waned to a small core in the fall of 2008. This core endures in 2009, meeting sporadically as a skeleton hub for coordination, communication, and some action planning.

Reasons for the Decline
There are several possibilities to explain DASW's steady decline. First, it is possible that the longer-term strategy discussions exposed the divisions that the coalition had initially been able to ignore, driving individuals, affinity groups, and organizations to steadily leave. While the coalition was very strong and came together well in support of the M19 actions—a feat in itself in a time when Left resistance is very weak—the means of sustaining it after the actions passed were much less clear, and as unity was found lacking, divisions surfaced in its place. Some of this could be mitigated through more organizational coalition-building, a direct contrast from our experience of individuals from different organizations participating rather than the entire organizations themselves; however, this

would require more long-term relationship-building that requires a full reckoning with different perspectives and disagreements that exist.

Second, many liberals and anti-authoritarians were swept up in presidential candidate Barack Obama's campaign of "Hope" and placated by the possibility that the war would come to an end through the outcome of the presidential election. Of course there was real desire and excitement to finally get rid of the eight years of the Bush Doctrine, and to do that in a momentous way—by electing our first black president—could be additionally symbolic. But Obama has no intention of changing the status quo, even hypocritically accepting the Nobel Peace Prize in 2009 just days after announcing new deployments to Afghanistan. The Left's decision to put all their eggs in one basket and move forward with blinders on is disappointing, even more now that we have seen how few changes have occurred in Obama's first year in office; perhaps this disillusionment will remind people once again that true change does not happen with a ballot box, but through taking to the streets and using direct action. The massive decline of the anti-war movement, combined with the failure of mass voting, should tell us that it is time to re-think everything.

Third, the organization's original impetus for working together was a single date. Once that day was over, successful or not, people focused their attention elsewhere. Organizing around one event is very powerful because we can concretely confront oppression in our everyday lives by converging on one moment, with one goal, facing police and agents of the state without the façade of politeness. But these events cannot sustain a movement alone; we need long-term work. What does that look like? For one, it comes out of recognizing that war and oppression are everyday realities; they do not just happen at the next big political party convention or mass demonstration. There are probably many ways of organizing that focus less on big events and more on what is constant. Military recruiters work every day to bring in young, mostly people-of-color recruits to join in the devastation. Half of our tax dollars go to building the war and defense machinery. Veterans and their families are facing huge health crises, trauma, and shock; many are also homeless. Thinking hard about these realities and figuring out long-term organizing around them may not be as energizing or as eye-catching as the big events. But without this foundation to work from, we will keep thinking about events as the only places to take action against oppressive forces, and so movements will keep going through sporadic heights and declines like what we have experienced in DASW.

CONCLUSION

IN RETROSPECT, IT IS DIFFICULT to assess what difference the rebirth of Direct Action to Stop the War made toward actually ending the wars. It is possible that media coverage of these actions contributed to the strict anti-war rhetoric of Democratic Party candidates during the 2008 election cycle (although this did not materialize into policy once Obama was elected). The media images of resistance reached the eyes of many viewers that week, and coverage, at the very least, must have reinforced anti-war sentiments within some people. It is our hope that those engaged in struggle were inspired by the actions, but this is difficult to gauge. For those directly involved, the effort led to individual empowerment, organizing experience, radical exposure, and new interpersonal relationships. Whether or not this growth leads to more effective organizing in the future is yet to be seen. What is clear is that our organizing did not immediately lead to the end of the war in Iraq. At this moment, at the end of 2009, the occupation of Iraq continues, and the war in Afghanistan is escalating. However, moments of change often come as the result of tension built from the sustained long-term efforts of many. We can only hope that our organizing played a role in the cumulative efforts that will eventually bring this war of empire to an end.

NOTES

1   This essay was originally written in May 2008 and later updated in October 2009.

2   It is estimated that anywhere between six to ten million people participated in anti-war demonstrations throughout the world on this day. See BBC News online article, "Millions join global anti-war protests" (February 17, 2003). HTTP://NEWS.BBC.CO.UK/2/HI/EUROPE/2765215.STM.

3   Joe Garofoli and Jim Herron Zamora, "S.F. police play catch-up; Protesters roam in small, swift groups to stall city traffic," *San Francisco Chronicle* (March 21, 2003).

A LOOK AT RESISTANCE TO INTERSTATE 69:

Past, Present, and Future

Roadblock Earth First!

Editor's Note: The Earth First! Campaign against I-69 in Indiana has substantially slowed since 2008, when much of this piece was first written. This article provides important lessons about the uses of anarchist organizing in contemporary struggle. It also illuminates some frightening experiences of repression by corporations and the state of the direct action-oriented strands of environmental struggles, anarchist organizing, and the animal liberation movement. Finally, the piece also discusses an important part of recent radical history and current radical organizing. The original essay is largely untouched since the time of its writing, but this version includes a significant addendum by one organizer from Roadblock Earth First! (RBEF!), who was also involved in writing the initial essay. Significant changes in the struggle have also occurred since the addendum was written in January 2010; such changes are not addressed here.

HOW I-69 AND THE LIVES OF INDIANA ECO-ANARCHISTS BECAME INTERTWINED

IN THE EARLY 2000S, ONE of the main anarchist projects in Indiana—outside of maintaining infoshops and developing local anarchist infrastructure—was summit hopping. We traveled all over the country simply to attend a weekend-long mass mobilization against this-or-that arm of capital. Attempting to intervene in the decision-making process of free trade agreements, we took the demonstrations and our involvement in them seriously:

planning "effective" strategies, attending all the necessary planning meetings, anything and everything. After a few years of these mass mobilizations constituting the majority of our action, it became apparent that we were not, in fact, intervening; rather, we were only pawns in the spectacle created by the State. Reading the press after the summits was one of the things that tipped us off to this.

We realized that no matter how large our movement was, how effective our strategies, or how many meetings we attended, the agenda of exploitation and destruction would be carried out by the International Monetary Fund (IMF), World Bank, and free trade agreements regardless of demonstrations. Our involvement in them largely served to perpetuate divisions of class and the farces of representative democracy and liberal ideology.

The summits had less and less to do with the experiences of our daily lives and our longing for worlds worth living in. Accordingly, we decided it was time to look elsewhere for meaningful resistance and intervention, since we were unable to find our desires reflected in these mass mobilizations.

At the time, a good portion of our crew had come out of environmental circles and still had many connections and ties to those communities. Through this, word was passed along that there was a North American Free Trade Agreement (NAFTA) superhighway, called Interstate 69 (I-69), in the works and intended to go through Indiana, our state of residence. When we found out that I-69 would rip through our homes and destroy a good portion of our state, we decided to look deeper into this road-building project.

I-69 is directly linked to many infrastructure projects that span from Nova Scotia to Argentina; all of these projects are necessary to implement the free trade agreements that are the subjects of massive global protest. It is these projects—dams, roads, deep-water ports, dry canals, security agreements— that are physical manifestations of the war being waged against us by capital in the name of "free trade." In order for our resistance and opposition to free trade to be effective, we had to fight against the economic and environmental devastation these free trade agreements were causing in our own communities; our intervention had to be fighting to stop I-69.

THE POTENTIAL HAVOC OF I-69

IN INDIANA, PLANNERS FOR I-69 have explicitly stated that the road will uproot nearly 500 families, 1,500 acres of forests, 400 acres of wetlands, and many more communities. With over 94% of the population of Indiana opposed to this road-building project, it is ludicrous to think that the state believes resistance will be low enough to go through with their plans.[1]

These statistics are only the beginning for I-69. After the road is built, the state intends to implement projects to open up the entire area of southwestern Indiana—which the Environmental Protection Authority designated a "non-attainment area" due to extremely high levels of pollution—for corporations that will further the demolition of our bioregion. There are plans for many biomass incineration ethanol plants, low-employment factories, and coal-fired power plants. The way that the road is laid out also opens up huge sections of farmland to corporations like Monsanto to come and buy up the leftover acreage, which would be combined into huge agri-business monocrop fields and genetic engineering testing grounds. Black Beauty coal, a Peabody subsidiary, is also involved in insidious attempts to buy mining rights from landowners that are facing eviction. The whole gamut of corporations is trying to make a grab for a piece of the I-69 pie.[2]

Unfortunately, the exploitation and development plans that are being proposed for southwestern Indiana are the norm in the furthering of capital's plans. The arms of development and corporations are far-reaching: to the north there are plans for Atlantica and the Security and Prosperity Partnership; to the west there are plans for Pacifica; across the states there are projects like the Corridors of the Future, the expanding of Interstate-5, dam projects, natural gas pipelines, and many others; and to the south, I-69 directly links up to the remains of Plan Puebla Panama (PPP), the massive neoliberal development project intended to slash through Latin America.

In South America, an almost identical infrastructure project is being proposed: the Regional Integration Initiative of South America (IIRSA). IIRSA and PPP have been fiercely fought over the years, and as a result they have been forced to diminish in scope. In order for us to survive or have anything left in the future, it is not just I-69 that has to be stopped, but all of the infrastructure projects. It is only then that we can start undoing the existing concrete and industrialized fortresses and realize our possibilities.

A HISTORY OF RESISTANCE TO INTERSTATE 69

WHEN WE BECAME INVOLVED IN organizing against I-69, we inherited a long legacy of resistance that runs deep in southern Indiana; for those people that have not been co-opted by liberal environmentalism and confined to the cages of wage, it runs in their veins. For nearly twenty years, landowners and those directly affected by the road have engaged in blocking roads with tractors, harassing surveyors and planners, shouting down local politicians, and taking over meetings.

Some of the more exciting and inspiring actions have occurred over the past five years. 2002 was a particularly abundant year of resistance, during which some key actions took place in Bloomington. For example, when the planners of the highway hosted a required "public" meeting, the room where it was hosted was stuffed full of folks speaking in opposition to the highway. The meeting eventually erupted into a mini-riot of sorts, resulting in Indiana State Police escorting out two proponents of the highway—"for reasons of safety."

Later that year, an event happened that highlighted the breadth of the resistance: farmers along the proposed route harvested food which they shared at a Thanksgiving dinner in Indianapolis with opponents of I-69. The dinner was a place for folks to meet and strategize. From the dinner, a majority of the people present staged a march to the governor's mansion. Upon arriving at the mansion, it became obvious that people had already started construction of I-69, but not along the proposed route; rather, this construction began in the governor's lawn, adding another face to the I-69 opposition. There have been many other actions and events that have served to motivate and encourage resistance.

Roadblock Earth First!'s point of entry was admittedly late in the game. From this point, however, we have attempted to create frameworks that honestly express our intentions and motivations. We have tried to recognize our limitations, both socially and politically, and are trying to work within them, as discussed below.

STRUGGLES THAT INSPIRE AND INFORM OUR RESISTANCE

HERE WE PROVIDE A SMALL handful of salient examples that provide a point of reference for our organizing.

Anti-nuclear Struggle in Comiso, Italy: In Comiso, opponents of the missile base went door-to-door, communicating openly as insurrectionary anarchists, and seeking connection with local people on the basis of the common goal of rebellion against the base.

U.K. Anti-Roads Movement: In this struggle, raging throughout the 1990s and which eventually grew to include much larger critiques of institutions and programs such as car culture, ports, the criminal justice bill, and mining, people from various subcultures and backgrounds came together to destroy 400 out of the 500 proposed roads projects. Their resistance included defense of wild and urban areas, merging of party and protest, and intensely beautiful blockades.

Obviously the above examples are just two of many points of reference. Other inspirational resistance projects continue to give us a broader view: the Treno Alta Velocità (TAV) struggle against high-speed rail tracks in Italy; the San Salvador Atenco airport stoppage and resistance to the La Parota dam, both in Mexico; and the Minnehaha Free State, an important anti-road struggle and road occupation in Minnesota during the 1990s. We could name many others.[3]

The resistance we hear of on our travels, and that which we read about, continue to build and sustain our struggle. When we continue to share these stories and weave together a collective historical context, we start to see how endless the possibilities are.

THE ACTIVITY OF ROADBLOCK EARTH FIRST!

WHEN WE BECAME INVOLVED IN resistance to I-69, a number of our crew came out of ecological groups, which played a major role in our decision to identify with Earth First! (EF!), a national group that is largely known for its use of direct action against eco-destruction since the 1980s. Our identification with EF! became cemented as a result of our desire to expand theoretical perspectives, learn skills, and find affinity and friends. EF! is now at a point that is more or less anarchist-dominated and insurrectionary in direction, which has not always been the case; it has grown to include a much wider perspective than that of an exclusively ecological ideology. These shifts have allowed us to plug into EF! at a optimal juncture.

Building on (or continuing from) these points of reference, one of our primary intentions is to connect in open ways with landowners, ways that validate and encourage their forms of struggle. These relations have been tenuous at times and have proven difficult to form and maintain. However, they are one of the concrete ways that we have been able to broaden our vantage point and figure out how to move forward. The landowners have continually shared the experiences of contesting the road with us, and they have provided grounding in areas along the proposed route that are less familiar to us.

Another of our intentions is to clearly show the links between I-69 and the larger infrastructure networks that are being built. This is largely based on our efforts to orient I-69 as a solidarity project with people resisting (and defeating) infrastructure projects in Mexico, Central America, and South America. As the Arizona-based group Root Force has repeatedly and more eloquently stated, we also view infrastructure as a solid point of attack.[4] In the U.S., there is a major focus on plans like the massive road extension project Corridors of the Future, and it is clear that such projects are necessary for the completion of the capitalist free trade projects.

Since I-69 was first proposed more than twenty years ago, resistance has fluctuated frequently in relation to what the state is doing. For this reason, a large part of our focus has been on creating networks and forming affinity with folks from all over Indiana and from multiple groups and subcultures. Some common activities in this regard have been potlucks, public assemblies, meetings, benefit shows, and tabling at the Farmers Market. This has proven extremely helpful in decentralizing specific tasks, as well as broadening and incorporating more voices into the resistance. However, this method and framework pushes us further into an inescapably activist framework, and compromises have been made in order to "grow numbers" and become "more relevant."

We have also focused a good deal of energy on knowing intimately the land that we're defending. Some of the activities that have encouraged this include bike tours, walking tours, plotting out maps, studying GIS systems, having research parties, and spending time at people's houses along the route. While we have become much more knowledge-able about the land—in many cases, an intense connection is felt with the land that is proposed for clearing—we have been unable to spend as much time on the route as would be beneficial. Although there are few remedies for this at such a late point, attempts have been made to increase comfort with the land. Bike tours have proven to be one of the best ways for folks to get acquainted with the route; they have allowed activists to spend time with people on the route and learn from them about their homes and land.

As is to be expected, another focal point has been action. Early on, a lot of energy was placed on home and office demonstrations, or demos, against those responsible for implementing and planning the road. There were waves of these throughout the summer of 2005, which continued into 2007. The demos had some successes but mainly just led to increased security at the most targeted offices. The increased security, repression, and lack of any substantial successes resulting from these demos made continuing them inef-fectual. Another reason for the shift away from office and home demos was the inability to focus in on one particular area, as we felt the need to target everyone equally. Although office demos still happen, they are no longer a main activity.

Public meetings hosted by the Indiana Department of Transportation (INDOT) have been a significant source of energy and resistance, with a lot of effort going into them on both our side and that of the enemy. These meetings have brought out people from along the route who are directly affected by the road, as well as a huge amount of general op-position. Nearly all of these meetings wound up with INDOT having to scramble around, trying to regain control of the meetings—a rare accomplishment.

WHERE RESISTANCE IS CURRENTLY: A 2010 POSTSCRIPT BY ONE EARTH FIRST! ORGANIZER

A CONSIDERABLE AMOUNT OF TIME has passed since the original publication of our essay in *In the Middle of a Whirlwind* in the summer of 2008. It seemed apt to include updates and reflections since much has changed; most centrally, Roadblock Earth First!'s campaign against I-69 has slowed. Not only has the center of gravity in Indiana shifted, but the national climate has as well, leading to a different situation for organizing that brings new complexities and, hopefully, new lessons on building resistance movements.

When the most recent attempts at anarchist intervention in the construction of In-terstate 69 were initiated, it was at a time when the anti-globalization movement was waning, yet energy was still at a relatively high point. Various ideas and projects sprang forth—RBEF!, Root Force, and others—with the intent of attacking the "concrete manifestations" of global capitalism and free trade while expanding upon the desire for international solidarity. From the early 2000s until recently, these attempts were sound and seemed to resonate much farther than any of us had expected. Currently, though, with economic crises, a rise in insurrectionary theory within the anarchist milieu, our own experiences with internal group difficulties, and a variety of other components, it is time to reflect, refocus, and continue on the quest for relevance and liberation in the context of RBEF!.

In December of 2007, liberal groups—including the Hoosier Environmental Council, Citizens for Appropriate Rural Roads (CARR), and others—lost a lawsuit that they had hoped would halt the road's construction. At the very beginning of April in 2008, the road's construction began. One of those evicted was an elderly woman whose spectacular eviction by the Indiana Department of Transportation was clearly utilized to scare others along the proposed construction route. This kind of intimidation has prevented many rural folks from engaging in substantial resistance against the project; people fear that INDOT will assess their home at a very low value or target them in other ways. In some cases, those who have been outspoken against the road have seen the plans for the road's development change to include their homes, when it had not previously. In Bloomington, the base of RBEF!, uniformed and undercover police have been present over the last several years at every community meeting about the road. The repression is pervasive and deep.

In mid-May of 2008, the first tree-sits began, and on June 20, 2008, the treesitters were forcibly removed by more than two dozen police. There were eight arrests at that point, all of which catalyzed an increase in solidarity actions throughout the country that June and July.[5] In Bloomington, supply and government offices were targeted for disruption; in Maryland, contractors' homes faced demos; on Long Island, locks were glued and windows painted; in Washington, DC, the right-wing CATO institute was briefly invaded by activists who covered their doors in anti-I-69 stickers.

The occupations and road blockades—with a tree-sit component—were a major element of our organizing, but they were driven largely by one affinity group. It was clear that the campaign had stretched itself too thin. With many avenues of attack and a lack of consensus on a unified direction, the campaign was substantially weakened.

Two organizers involved in RBEF! have been charged with racketeering and are facing significant amounts of jail time in relation to fighting I-69. Their arrests are intended—as other arrests of perceived direct action organizers have been in recent years—to quell dissent.[6] A number of other activists are facing Strategic Lawsuit Against Public Participation (SLAPP) suits, civil charges that are direct attempts to limit dissent, as well as criminal charges. There are many families facing evictions up and down the route of I-69. In the midst of this, CARR, the long-standing liberal membership-based organization that continues its lobbying efforts, celebrated its twenty-year anniversary this year. One main CARR organizer stated, "We think we're on a roll now, because the cost of the project is just getting out of hand."[7] Another organization, Bloomington Against I-69 (largely university-based), continues to organize protests and indirect, symbolic actions against the road.

In addition, there was a rather comical argument between the Monroe County government and the Indiana Department of Transportation in relation to I-69, centered on Monroe's attempts to block the road coming through the county. The argument was settled, and funding has been freed up to continue the road's construction. The Governor predicts that the first half of I-69 will be completed by 2012.[8]

REFLECTING

A NUMBER OF STUMBLING BLOCKS arose in Indiana for resistance to I-69. Below is a brief discussion of the stumbling blocks we have encountered, as well as a brief discussion of some of the positive lessons learned.

One stumbling block has developed from our reliance on college students and other anarchists coming into Indiana from out of town/state, which left us little time to build more substantial relationships with those along the route and made it difficult to continue actions and resistance when people left town. Some people along the proposed I-69 route have disliked folks coming in from outside, which has created further difficulties.

A major lesson we have learned is about healthy functioning and communication. If this is lacking among those involved in organizing, the campaign will reflect that. Another set of difficulties came from our lack of processing internal interpersonal dynamics, which harmed us too many times to count. Struggling to hoist barricades in the middle of a field is no time or place for arguments to arise.[9] Any campaign that includes a core set of organizers who work together over many years will have difficulties with interpersonal dynamics, and this campaign has been no different.

Another stumbling block was a lack of confidence in our ability to actually stop the highway. As anarchists and activists, we are perpetually used to failure; we often adjust to the idea that we are going to organize a project for a couple of years, fail, and move on. In Roadblock's case, we have not had enough courage to think that we could win. And we have not had enough courage to be honest about our intentions; this played a major role in our reliance on the anarchist scene, because at times it felt safer to do this than attempt to create lasting relationships with folks along the route.

Yet in our view, a benefit of explicitly anarchist organizing has been our up-front clarity about what we could bring to the table of resistance efforts, which also made clear the ways we could approach resistance. The differing groups involved in the anti-I-69 campaign all had their own approaches, overwhelmingly relying on lobbying and other institutional-ized tactics. While the majority of Indiana is against the road, none of the campaigns have substantially changed the direction of the road's plans. Roadblock's willingness to utilize surprise, support of direct action, and ability to build a network of activists willing to confront elements of I-69 around the country have been very important for building resistance to I-69. This also positively impacted the national Earth First! movement at a point when it was waning, by directing attention toward the local manifestations of global capital, increasing discourse on Indiana's highway project, and bringing a new generation of Earth First! into being.

CARR, the central mainstream group involved in fighting I-69, has used their two decades worth of activism to engage in activities like monitoring public meetings, or-ganizing rural people, lobbying legislators, and filing lawsuits, all intended not to stop the highway, but rather to support "The Common Sense Alternative," a reroute of I-69 through another existing road. This type of organizing, while valuable in some regards, is not one that RBEF! identifies with tactically or politically. Throughout this, however, a number of working relationships have formed. CARR has a history of condemning more radical actions, but after the theatrical actions that took place at the planning offices and the subsequent public support around them, CARR stopped condemning actions and provided support to the road occupation in 2008.

The state and the media shared a similar disdain for both CARR and RBEF!, so pressure from the media and the state for the two groups to disassociate was not overwhelming. While the feeling between the state and media and RBEF! has been mutual dislike, CARR has consistently tried to pander to the media and state in order to get a seat at the table. This created some internal tension as CARR pressured folks not to be so militant, but when CARR lost much of its relevancy with the loss of the lawsuit, this tension died down significantly.

What RBEF! was able to bring to the table in the fight against I-69 were tactics that strove to take away the power from the state and put it back in the hands of the people in the form of direct action. Roadblock has never applied for a permit, sought permission from any government officials, or supported any political figures running on an anti-I-69 ballot. We prepared for direct action—knowing that the state was not going to voluntarily stop the road—and went from there. One very important and concrete contribution that anarchists and RBEF! brought to the larger coalition fighting I-69 was the resistance to paid work on the part of anarchists; we set up our lives in order to have large amounts of unstructured time that could be dedicated to fighting the highway development process. Resource procurement for things such as banners, food, and flyers was also an important contribution.

While reflecting, it is important to address the benefits and limitations of the different types of organizing against I-69, which may provide a useful addition to discussions of tactics more generally.

Limits of lobbying: Lobbying puts the power back in the hands of the state; the schedule and time frame for action are dictated by the state, and so are the rules of engagement. Activists have to avoid burning bridges. This kind of work normally seeks concessions rather than concrete changes. Furthermore, lobbying-oriented work often relies on the mainstream media to relay messages, leaving the choice and tone of information to corporate reporters.

Limits of anarchist organizing: One difficulty with anarchist organizing, in our experience, can be that many anarchists do not identify primarily with their employment, which sometimes led to suspicion by people along the route. Sometimes anarchists are also off-putting to folks due to judgments upon basic appearance (certain kinds of dress, outsider-ness). State repression against anarchists caused many not to use last names. All of this means that it takes a lot longer to form ties with people, especially when the starting point is such a grandiose idea like a new society.

Benefits of a direct action focus for I-69 resistance: Direct action was largely responsible for delaying construction of I-69 until the spring of 2008. The economic crisis then postponed construction longer. Direct action also made it easier for people to speak out against the highway; it showed that people were not simply full of rhetoric. This opened up channels for liberal groups to say, "See, we're reasonable, we're not like them." Our approach also kept the "no-build option" around, opening a forum for contesting the chosen route. Direct actions cost large sums of money for the state and invested companies, money that could have otherwise been used on the road itself. Confrontational approaches kept road construction in the spotlight, making I-69 more of a household name in Indiana as well as across the country. Finally, confrontational actions showed that younger people were actually capable of offering real solidarity.

Benefits of direct action for people in the campaign: Direct action provided a way to continue *acting* without waiting for the state's permission or in a strictly reactionary manner. The direct action approach has also been a morale booster, providing "cred" for folks involved in RBEF! that made talking with landowners along the route easier.

On one hand, organizing explicitly as anarchists in small towns and rural areas in Indiana has allowed us to proceed honestly in solidarity and coalitions with other people, but it can also be an extremely isolating and challenging feat. The state's wrath is felt greatly and there is less of a buffer since, overall, there are fewer anarchists here than in many major towns or cities. Long drives, little money, and nervousness led to rural organizing not going as well as planned.

REFOCUSING

As FOLKS DESIRING SO MUCH more out of life, it is terribly important that we look with a certain amount of clarity on the world and the events that are happening. Because of the current economic crisis, we are, for the first time in a decade, in a position where the ideas of capitalism and neoliberalism can be called into question. People far outside the small groupings of radicals are doing the questioning; in some cases, they are in positions of revolt. Given this, do we continue attacking global infrastructure, utilize mass mobilizations, or strategize to go after the whole system? These are questions that we struggle with everyday.

If we are serious about attacking global capitalism and finally bringing eco-destroyers to their knees, we must reflect and familiarize ourselves with the details of struggles like these and so many others, learn what we can from them, and figure out how to go forward. "We will never let them build this road!" was one of the mottoes of anarchist resistance to I-69, and that sentiment continues. Since the state was courteous enough to temporarily stop road-building, it has provided people with some time to refocus and support those going through legal troubles.

On a larger level, Earth First! exists to defend the earth, taking a no-compromise stance and employing direct action tactics. Practically, this often includes activities such as tree-sits, blockades, banner drops, and theatrical actions. More often than not, these tactics are successful in halting destructive projects. When these tactics and other community organizing efforts become unsuccessful, EF! ceases to be relevant, in a similar fashion to CARR's legal strategy. The increasing failures of certain tactics that EF! employs in recent campaigns has led to significant conversations taking place within the EF! community. Luckily, these are occurring simultaneously with an upswing in involvement about what directions EF! should head in and what the next decades will look like.

NOTES

1   "94% of the comments submitted to INDOT on the DEIS opposed the new terrain I-69 plan favoring no build or I-70/US41." From online fact sheet "Why oppose new terrain I-69," HTTP://WWW.169TOUR.ORG/OPPOSE.HTML.

2   Both Monsanto and Black Beauty have a long history in southern Indiana, and both currently operate there. It is common knowledge that Black Beauty has solicited folks along the I-69 route for years.

3   On the Treno Alta Velocità, see Portland Indymedia, "Popular uprising against high-speed train (TAV) in Italy" (May 24, 2006), HTTP://PUBLISH.PORTLAND.INDYMEDIA.ORG/ EN/2006/05/339925.SHTML. On San Salvador Atenco, see Narco News, "How the Victory at Atenco Was Won" (August 20, 2002), HTTP://WWW.NARCONEWS.COM/ISSUE38/ARTICLE1395. HTML. On La Parota, see International Rivers website, "Victory: Mexico's La Parota Dam

Delayed Until 2018" (September 14, 2009), HTTP://WWW.INTERNATIONALRIVERS.ORG/ NODE/4652. On the Minnehaha Free State, see one account of the struggle written by Elli King, *Listen: The Story of the People at Taku Wakan Tipi and the Reroute of Highway 55; or, the Minnehaha Free State* (Los Angeles: Feral Press, 2006).

4   "A major focus of *every* American government is expanding the infrastructure of "trade" to ac-celerate the extraction and transport of resources to the wealthy north…. The unstated reason for the push behind these projects is that as resources continue to run out around the globe, the US will need to import an ever-increasing volume of raw materials just to sustain its consumer lifestyle. As forests in the US Northwest and Southeast shrink, for example, imports from Asia and Latin America must increase concurrently. Prevent this from happening, and we are not just defending this hemisphere's most important reservoirs of cultural and ecological diversity; we are undermining the foundations of the whole system." From Root Force's description of their strategy, HTTP://WWW.ROOTFORCE.ORG/WHAT-IS-ROOT-FORCE/STRATEGY/.

5   For a brief summary of these actions, see: Roadblock EF!, "Roundup of Actions Against I-69," HTTP://WWW.EARTHFIRSTJOURNAL.ORG/ARTICLE.PHP?ID=405 (accessed January 21, 2010).

6   For more information see the website HTTP://WWW.MOSTLYEVERYTHING.NET (accessed January 21, 2010).

7   Michael Mallik, "CARR Marks 20th Year of Fighting I-69 Plan," *Herald Times*, Novem-ber 2, 2009.

8   "Ind. Governor: Half of I-69 Will be Done by 2012," *The Associated Press State & Local Wire*, October 21, 2009 (accessed January 21, 2010).

9   An important article on this issue is Jezzabell, "Toward Stronger Communities and Direct Ac-tion," HTTP://EARTHFIRSTJOURNAL.ORG/ARTICLE.PHP?ID=426 (accessed January 21, 2010).

THE PRECARIOUS ECONOMY AND ITS DISCONTENTS:

Struggling Against the Corporate Chains Through Workplace Organizing

The Starbucks Workers Union

IF YOU DRIVE DOWN THE highway outside of any major city in the United States, you will pass countless glowing signs for corporate food and retail chains. From coast to coast, McDonald's follows Starbucks, follows Walmart, follows Target, follows Taco Bell, on and on, ad nauseam. Lost in a forest of fluorescent consumerism, social revolution is probably the furthest thing from your mind. Indeed, many activists are dismissive not only of the corporations that monopolize our landscape, but of the radical potential of those who toil inside the big boxes and fast food chains as well. This tendency results in a problematic conclusion: surely, the Revolution will not start at a Starbucks.

As members of the Industrial Workers of the World (IWW) Starbucks Workers Union, we believe that the need for workplace organizing is greater than ever before. Behind each shiny logo lies a potential struggle, particularly as corporations seize on the current economic crisis as an excuse to slash benefits, lay off workers, impose stricter discipline, and demand increased productivity from workers.

This most recent attack on the working class is a continuation of a shift that began in the 1970s. For four decades, bosses have been on the offensive: battering workers with inflation, union busting, outsourcing, industrial restructuring, and the destruction of the last shreds of the social safety net. In unionized sectors, the defeats came hard and fast: the mass firing of striking Professional Air Traffic Controllers Organization workers in 1981; the defeat of Local P-9 in the 1985–86 strike at Hormel in Austin, Minnesota; the defeat at International Paper in 1987; the lost strike battles in the Decatur, Illinois "War Zone" in the mid-1990s. The list of labor's defeats goes on. At the same time as labor lost battles in its traditional stronghold, corporate bosses built a brave new world in their own image, rapidly constructing a non-unionized, low-wage, unskilled food and retail service sector where they could reign unchallenged by organized workers.

The combination of the rollback of gains in the industrial sectors and the growth of a low-wage, non-unionized service industry was a one-two punch that left the working class staggering as the world spun out of control beneath our feet. "Precarity" became a defining fact of life for an ever-growing section of the waged working class. Make no mistake: workers have put up resistance to the bosses' offensive every step of the way, but the correlation of forces was clearly not in our favor. Over the years, resistance in the workplace became more and more hopeless. Now, as bosses use the economic crisis as pretext for a new "Shock Doctrine" of attacks on our class, the need for a working-class counter-attack has assumed renewed urgency.[1]

As shop floor militants who have been on the front lines of struggle against corporate capitalism, first in the age of globalization and now at the dawn of an era of profound global capitalist crisis, we feel that our experience may be instructive for workers who want to fight back. We will discuss the roots of precarity and of the Starbucks Workers Union, as well as how the bosses have again reshaped the terrain of struggle in the economic crisis.

THE PRECARIAT: AN IMPOSSIBLE CLASS

LIFE IN THE CORPORATE CHAINS has always been "precarious." Even during the boom years of globalization, before the crisis, it was very hard to make a life for oneself working in the corporate service sector. Because of the lack of union organization in these industries, we are almost all legally classified as "At Will" employees. This means that under U.S. labor law, we can be fired for no reason. The threat of firing, however, is only the least subtle of many mechanisms management uses to control us.

At Starbucks, many workers have difficulty budgeting or planning ahead because our work hours fluctuate wildly from week to week. The company uses a computer system to determine staffing levels for the stores based on past sales. Starbucks' "Automated Labor Scheduling" software displaces the risk of the vagaries of the market onto individual workers. Bosses order 'labor' exactly like they order coffee beans or other inputs. When workers challenge the arbitrary authority of the boss, they often face punitive measures, such as cuts in hours.

With the aid of computerized labor scheduling systems, bosses are able to split what would be one full-time job into three or four part-time jobs. They would rather have forty workers each working ten hours per week than ten workers working forty hours per week. They want us to consider our jobs something we do 'on the side' or even 'for fun.' But living precariously is anything but fun. As a result of our unstable schedules, many workers take on two or three 'part-time' jobs, working double and triple shifts at wages hovering near minimum in order to make ends meet. Unable to save money for emergencies, medical expenses, or major purchases like tuition or a car, workers often end up buried beneath thousands of dollars in credit card, medical, and student loan debts.

Aside from the stress of never having enough money and never being able to plan ahead, our jobs themselves are intensely exploitative. Through careful engineering of each task we perform, management makes sure to squeeze as much labor from us as possible while we are on the clock. On each shift, a supervisor or manager assigns workers to one or a few of several repetitive tasks that our job consists of. At Starbucks, these tasks include operating the cash register, stocking milk and other supplies on the espresso bar, making drinks at the espresso "hot bar," making drinks at the Frappuccino "cold bar," "expediting" (asking customers for orders and writing the order on a cup), or cleaning the lobby and bathrooms. Management seeks to exert total control over the shop floor, refusing even to allow workers to self-manage their rotation between task stations. After all, in this situation, a little democracy is a dangerous thing.

On top of micro-management, we have to deal with understaffing. There are never enough workers scheduled to take care of all the tasks. As a result, we sometimes never stop moving for hours at a time while at work. In statements reminiscent of the words of workers in industrial production, Starbucks workers complain that by the time they punch out for the day and stagger off the shop floor, they feel like they have been physically beaten up. Work is not 'fun.' Work is the coercive extraction of labor from workers.

The corporate chains have proven almost as difficult to organize as they are hellish to work in. This is no accident. Since the 1970s, the industry has been restructured with the explicit goal of reducing workers' power on the shop floor. Workers are broken into small groups at numerous, networked production sites, which are all monitored closely for signs of subversion. There are very few 'chokehold' points where industrial action can shut down a corporate chain. But it rarely even gets that far; in a move paralleling the evolution of U.S. military counterinsurgency strategy, union busting is now fully integrated into the day-to-day operations of 'Human Resources' departments. Rather than fight a union drive once it has been initiated, corporations spend billions on "union avoidance" programs to prevent workers from being able to organize in the first place.

The corporate chains will not even settle for short-circuiting workers' struggle; they seek to stamp out the potential of revolt once and for all by destroying the historical subject of the working class itself. Thus there are no 'workers' in the corporate chains: at Starbucks we are "partners," at IKEA we are "coworkers," and at Walmart we are "associates." Once everyone is assumed to be on the same team, workers are encouraged to compete with each other for advancement within the company, which in turn is supposed to advance the company on the market. In the mythology of free market capitalism, corporate success is supposed to 'trickle down' to workers on the lowest level of the food chain.

Accordingly, under the guise of corporate 'partnership' or 'teamwork,' the culture of solidarity built by the working-class movements of the nineteenth and twentieth centuries is being undermined by an ethos of class collaborationism with the boss and mutual suspicion, snitching, and cutthroat competition amongst workers. Most workers are unable to even think of uniting to fight the bosses. The bosses want us to think that the only way out of precarity is by becoming a boss ourselves.

The bosses' offensive on the shop floor has been complemented by the bosses' cultural offensive in mainstream media and culture. Since the 1970s, pundits and opinion-makers have engaged in a concerted and long-term campaign to undermine solidarity by reviving the acceptability of selfishness and greed in mainstream culture. The media retouched the mirage of the American Dream for a new generation of workers that came of age after the revolts of the 1960s and 1970s, seeking to lure workers away from collective action.

They promised us consumer goods bought on easily available credit. They told us that we would have fantastic high-paying jobs, that the economy needed a "creative class," that racism was a thing of the past, that hierarchy in the workplace was obsolete, that we can all get rich as day-traders or start our own businesses, that work could be fun and part-time. They told us that we did not need to organize to take control over our own lives; the benevolent dictatorship of corporate capitalism had a place for everyone. In the new galaxy of neoliberal global corporations, Starbucks was the brightest light. For many, Starbucks symbolized the capitalist dream of frictionless accumulation, growth without limits, a world without a working class where capital could move freely between cosmopolitan markets, a world where labor unions or any criticism of the right to profit would be rendered unnecessary by the fig leaf of promised capitalist self-regulation and adherence to ethics—"corporate social responsibility."

Workers were thrust onto this new terrain of global capitalism: under attack in the workplace by a new regime of constant competition and surveillance, underpaid, overworked, in debt, flung across networked production sites on multiple continents, always on the move, desperate, scrambling for the next foothold, tempted to sacrifice solidarity for a favor from the boss, undermined in the public sphere by a mass media bombardment trumpeting the values of selfishness and greed, forced to worship the false god of corporate "social responsibility." This may not seem to be fertile ground for the growth of worker solidarity. Yet, as organizers, it is here we have begun to learn to walk.

THE BEGINNING

THE STARBUCKS WORKERS UNION was founded by baristas in May 2004 at a single store in New York City. With the help of a website and the extensive network of the Industrial Workers of the World, organizing has since gone public in Chicago, Maryland, Grand Rapids, Minneapolis, Fort Worth, and now Quebec City and Chile. Baristas continue to self-organize under the radar across the world.

From the outset, it became clear that the typical bureaucracy-dependent weapons of the business unions would be of no avail against the Starbucks Goliath. The government-sponsored system of union elections that most unions rely on simply would not work in a corporate chain environment. When baristas at the 36th and Madison Starbucks in New York City filed for a National Labor Relations Board election, Starbucks reacted by using its political clout to gerrymander the bargaining unit from one pro-union store to every store in midtown and downtown Manhattan. Seeing the writing on the wall, IWW baristas pulled their election petition and have eschewed the election tactic ever since.

For the American Federation of Labor and Congress of Industrial Organizations or "Change to Win" unions, this would have been the end of the campaign; for the IWW, this was just the beginning. Our subsequent organizing approach can be described as a combination of two strategies: the "Ground War" and the "Air War."

THE GROUND WAR: SOLIDARITY UNIONISM

WHAT DOES IT TAKE TO fan the flames of discontent in any corporate workplace into a fire hot enough to withstand the union busting, high turnover rates, and manipulative socio-psychological techniques of retail management? In the Starbucks Workers Union, we have adopted an approach known as Solidarity Unionism.[2] The essence of this organizing model is its underlying power analysis. We believe workers' power is greatest where the bosses need us most: on the shop floor.

Instead of relying solely on the inadequate provisions of the National Labor Relations Act, we encourage workers to build solidarity with their coworkers and take direct action on the job. This takes the form of confrontations with managers in the stores, petitions, picket lines, slowdowns, walkouts, work stoppages, and blocking drive-thrus, amongst other tactics.

While the above tactics are powerful, developing solidarity among Starbucks workers is hard work. Because of constant turnover, building a memory of struggle amongst an informal work group is nearly impossible. When conditions deteriorate, most workers simply move on to another low-wage job. Constant surveillance prevents open discussion of workplace issues or past action. Even if a committee is successfully organized in one shop, there remains the challenge of reaching out to workers in other locations who are frequently beyond contact. In the face of these odds, the IWW Starbucks Workers Union has still successfully organized numerous job actions where we have a presence. These actions have resulted in critical health and safety improvements, reinstatement of fired workers, and a 25% pay raise in the New York City market.[3]

However, the above list of victories does not touch on the most valuable result of our struggle. The primary goal of direct action is to win concrete gains and build industrial power, but for many of us, the most inspiring result of solidarity unionism is its transformative effect on workers.

Through organizing, we catch a glimpse of the world we would like to create. Workers who once watched the world pass them by from behind a cash register begin taking control over their surroundings. People who once turned a blind eye to their fellow workers' suffering break the silence and speak out for justice. Workers make nationalism obsolete through organizing down the supply chain to coffee farmers, and through direct support from sympathetic organizations and individuals worldwide. For example, the French National Confederation of Labour occupied the lobbies of several Paris Starbucks to protest the illegal firing of Starbucks worker Daniel Gross in 2006. In 2007, a delegation of New York City baristas traveled to Ethiopia to make contact with hyper-exploited coffee farmers. Through tireless organizing and outreach, our resistance is as local as the coffee shop next door, and it is becoming as global as capital.

THE AIR WAR: CORPORATE CAMPAIGNING

THE STARBUCKS WORKERS UNION HAS augmented shop floor organizing with an extensive effort to reveal the truth behind the brand. Widespread popular misconceptions about the working conditions at Starbucks mean that we must constantly explain the necessity of organizing a union at this 100% part-time poverty-wage employer. We are eager to engage in public debate on this subject. The management-promoted neoliberal discourse of "social responsibility" has undermined support for the workers' movement in general. By winning the debate on the necessity of organizing at Starbucks, we hope to open the door to a much broader social awareness of the need for workers to organize everywhere, not just at Walmart or another vilified exploiter *du jour*.

From our perspective, Starbucks' brand image is an enormous asset to our union campaign. Because the company has cultivated such a high awareness of their brand, we are able to piggyback on their own public relations efforts to broaden awareness of our union and union organizing in general. By organizing a highly visible industry leader, we are able to lay the foundations for a much broader working-class offensive.

Indeed, by bringing the workers movement into the heart of one of the leading symbols of global capitalism, we have put working-class solidarity back on the map. As the economic crisis each day brings fresh revelations of corporate greed, Ponzi schemes, and general malfeasance among the capitalist class, it is becoming clear that the capitalist system is both fiscally and morally bankrupt. Our campaign's successful use of the capitalist media to raise the profile of worker solidarity means that as workers lose faith in the bosses, they may well be inspired by our example to take direct action themselves. As attacks on our class intensify, this is a source of hope.

FROM BAD TO WORSE: THE SHOCK DOCTRINE AT STARBUCKS

IN THE FIRST FIVE YEARS of organizing at Starbucks, we developed a model of organizing that works, even on the shaky ground of precarity at the corporate chains. We walked slowly, learning as we went and building power one class-conscious worker at a time.

The bosses' attack during the economic crisis has lent a new sense of urgency to our work. We need to pick up the pace.

Since the financial meltdown of 2008, corporate bosses have nullified any past promises of privileges or benefits made in exchange for our subservience. We have watched as our bosses have torn down the façade of fairness at Starbucks. In the biggest layoff in fast food history, Starbucks shuttered over 600 store locations in 2008, many of them profitable, in order to touch up their profit margin figures for Wall Street.[4] With the threat of unemployment looming, Starbucks bosses sought to lay off all but the most docile workers. Those who survived the massacre face intensified exploitation.

Starbucks cut staffing in all the stores, decimating the skeleton crew staffing that already left us scrambling to get our jobs done. They imposed new availability requirements under the Orwellian moniker "Optimal Scheduling." Under the new requirements, workers were required to be available almost around the clock in order to have any hope of getting anything approaching full-time hours. With fewer workers on the floor, Starbucks actually sought to implement Lean production methods to get more work from fewer workers. Lean is a production system initially developed in the Japanese auto industry. It seeks to discover the shortcuts workers develop to complete a job task, and then imposes these shortcuts as the standard for workers across the company in order to be able to cut staffing and hours, managing every motion workers make. In effect, Lean was another backdoor layoff. As a result of Lean at Starbucks, workers now have only fifteen minutes to open the store, where previously we had thirty or forty-five minutes to go through the same tasks and routines. We are also now required to brew coffee exactly every eight minutes. Lean has left workers with even less autonomy, fewer hours, and less staffing than before.

The list of attacks goes on. Starbucks doubled our health care premiums and switched to a lower-quality plan. Bosses have begun to restrict our ability to take a bathroom break, talk to other workers, or give away a free drink now and then. As consumers restrict their spending, competition between retailers for market share sharpens. The result for workers is intense pressure to 'upsell,' to ask every single customer if they want to try the most recent promotional product, nudging corporate profits higher while the workers themselves get no security or rest.

As the euphoria over Obama's election has worn off, and the possibility of social democratic reform in the U.S. recedes under a pile of rotting campaign promises, workers clock in every day to a work environment that feels more and more like fascism. In the boom years of globalization—the dot.com bubble, the housing bubble—class conflict could be hidden by a few token benefits and the fig leaf of social responsibility. It was always a lie, but more people believed it. The fig leaf has now fallen. The bosses make their demands with no apologies and no promises. Workers are asked to accept cutbacks so that the corporations can maintain boom-era profitability. One day it is healthcare, the next day they are cutting hours. Under a new Shock Doctrine of emergency cutbacks, even the farce of "social responsibility" seems to be too extravagant to waste money on. The bosses have no reason to put on a show for an audience of workers held hostage by the threat of unemployment. Our new reality is class war. Until now, the war has been mostly one-sided… but it will not stay that way much longer.

TWO, THREE, MANY STARBUCKS WORKERS UNIONS!

WILL THE REVOLUTION START AT a Starbucks? In a sense, it already has. The IWW Starbucks Workers Union receives a steady flow of new members through our website and from the shop floors where we have a presence. These members are trained by IWW organizers to reach out to their coworkers and begin building power on the job. Every job action, every organizing meeting, every discussion between angry workers on a cigarette break, every group confrontation with the boss: these are the first tremors of the next cycle of workers' struggle.

The tremors are now multiplying. As the economic crisis rocks the world, even the few shaky footholds we have established as precarious workers—individually and collectively—have come loose, bringing new layers of the working class into the struggle.

What would happen if workers organized at every Starbucks in the world? What if workers organized at every corporate chain in the world? What kind of world would the millions of our sisters and brothers create? As our ranks deepen and our power grows, we are confident that some day we will find out the answers to these questions.

NOTES

1 "Shock Doctrine" refers to the Naomi Klein book of the same name: *The Shock Doctrine: The Rise of Disaster Capitalism* (New York: Picador, 2007).

2 For the origins of this concept see, Staughton Lynd, *Solidarity Unionism: Rebuilding the Labor Movement from Below* (Chicago: Charles H. Kerr Publishing, 1992).

3 The Starbucks Workers Union has documented these victories as well as others on their website, HTTP://WWW.STARBUCKSUNION.ORG.

4 Michael J. de la Merced, "Starbucks Announces It Will Close 600 Stores," *New York Times* (July 2, 2008). An additional 300 stores were closed in 2009. See Janet Adamy, "At Starbucks, A Tall Order For New Cuts, Store Closures," *Wall Street Journal* (January 29, 2009).

HARVESTING SOLIDARITY:

Farmworkers, Allies, and the Fight for Fair Food

Student/Farmworker Alliance

O<small>N</small> M<small>AY</small> 23, 2008, <small>FARMWORKERS</small> and student activists gathered with corporate executives, United States Senator Bernie Sanders, and dozens of members of the local and national media for a standing room-only press conference at the U.S. Capitol announcing an accord between Burger King and a Florida farmworker organization, the Coalition of Immokalee Workers (CIW). Weeks earlier, Burger King made headlines when a spate of malicious internet postings defaming the CIW and its supporters were traced back to a company executive, and news surfaced that the company hired an unlicensed private investigator to infiltrate and spy on the CIW's key ally organization, the Student/Farmworker Alliance (SFA).[1]

Established in 2000 as a loose network of college students in Florida, SFA evolved through a program of intense education and action into a diverse, formidable national organization. SFA played no small part in forcing Burger King to pivot from a position of antagonism to partnership with the CIW and the thousands of tomato pickers it represents, and has similarly played a key role in other victories in the CIW's national Campaign for Fair Food.

According to industry figures, "Florida tomatoes account for 95% of all U.S. grown tomatoes eaten by Americans October to June ... [and] 45% of all tomatoes consumed in the U.S. year-round are Florida tomatoes."[2] Largely sold to major food retailers and distributors, these tomatoes are harvested under conditions that amount to a human rights crisis. Florida tomato harvesters toil from dawn to dusk for sub-poverty wages at a per-bucket harvesting piece rate that has not changed significantly in over thirty years. They perform this grueling work without fundamental labor and human rights protections, a direct legacy of racially-motivated exclusions of farmworkers and domestic workers from key New Deal-era reforms. In the resulting climate of poverty, desperation, and powerlessness, forced labor has continued to take root. Since 1997, the CIW has been involved in the investigation and successful prosecution of seven separate cases of modern-day slavery in which a total of over 1,000 farmworkers (including U.S. citizens) were held against their will and forced to labor for little or no pay.[3]

Responding to this crisis, workers in Immokalee—a hardscrabble epicenter of the Florida tomato industry, just forty miles inland from the beach resorts of Southwest Florida—formed the CIW in the early 1990s. The group then embarked on years of intense community-based organizing and education including work stoppages, hunger strikes, marches, and other actions directed at local farm labor bosses and growers who, despite the workers' efforts, made few major concessions.

Parallel to this impasse, however, developments were unfolding that would create an opening for farmworkers under a broader umbrella of *food justice*. The agricultural industry was undergoing a major shift as consumers demanded the sale of pesticide-free produce at a premium price under organic standards and, to a lesser extent, fair trade certification. Meanwhile, students across the country launched a formidable anti-sweatshop movement, aiming to reshape the international garment industry. These forces resulted in a drive by major corporations to make new claims to social and ecological responsibility. This fertile terrain provided the chance for the struggle of Immokalee's workers to go beyond the farm gate and align itself with these broader movements. That moment would come in early 2001.

WORKERS AND STUDENTS UNITED

IN 2000 AND 2001, RESPECTIVELY, the Coalition of Immokalee Workers held two major, multi-day marches across the State of Florida. These actions brought the harsh reality of life in Immokalee to the public consciousness. Students at several campuses dotting the march route hit the streets alongside workers and hosted them at on-campus events. These students coalesced into a network that would later become the Student/Farmworker Alliance.

Realizing that localized struggle alone would not bring about the systemic changes in the agricultural industry they sought, by the end of the 1990s, workers in Immokalee began to look towards more powerful forces behind their exploitation. The CIW began to analyze the role of the high-volume, low-cost tomato purchasing practices of large food retailers in funneling wealth away from communities like Immokalee.

In April 2001, the CIW launched the first-ever farmworker boycott of a fast-food corporation: Taco Bell. Facing a growing whirlwind of resistance—by boycott's end, students at twenty-five high schools, colleges, and universities had successfully organized to remove Taco Bell restaurants or sponsorships on campus—Taco Bell's parent company, Yum Brands, agreed to the workers' demands in the spring of 2005. In the years since the victory against Yum Brands, several other corporations—McDonald's (2007), Burger King (2008), Whole Foods Market (2008), Subway (2008), as well as food-service providers Bon Appetit Management (2009) and Compass Group (2009)—have also agreed to major concessions to the farmworkers, including wage increases, enforceable labor and human rights standards, and a voice for workers in the industry.

The logic behind the Taco Bell boycott and what would become known as the "Campaign for Fair Food" is simple. Farmworkers and consumers work together to organize

intensive pressure on the major corporate purchasers of tomatoes, who in turn are compelled to yield to reforms, changing their purchasing practices to demand (and to help
enforce) better wages and human rights standards in their tomato suppliers' operations.
Through this process, consumers—particularly young consumers—are moved from a position of complicity to one of agents of change.

As the Taco Bell boycott progressed, workers and their student allies came to a mutual
realization: in order for the boycott to work, strong alliances would have to be formed
with people outside of Immokalee, and in order to sustain the movement, workers would
have to take the lead. Thus was born a critical challenge to the food industry's status quo,
as students and other young consumers—themselves objectified and exploited by the corporate food industry—began working in solidarity "*with*, and not *for*, farmworkers ... for
collective liberation."[4]

This application of solidarity has been critical to the movement and its victories of
much-needed reforms. It reflects the unique interplay between farmworkers and their
allies in SFA, who have been influenced by the CIW's organizing model rooted in Latin
American and Caribbean notions of popular education, leadership development, and
critical consciousness. Indeed, the Freirean concept of *conscientização*—the process of
consciousness-raising—is a cornerstone of the movement.[5] The techniques of popular
education were developed by Paulo Freire while he was engaged in literacy education
with rural workers in Northeastern Brazil.[6] Central to this style of education is the use of
'codes,' along with an understanding that change can be made through a nonlinear, three-
step educational process, focusing on critical questioning, group reflection, and action.[7]
Due to its effectiveness in consciousness-raising and community self-empowerment, this
process has been translated from a technique of literacy education to more widespread
use by social movements throughout Latin America.[8] Today, popular education plays an
integral role in the transformation of an impoverished corner of Florida and its population of young immigrant workers into the nexus of a broad-based, exciting, effective social
movement. SFA has been heavily influenced by the CIW's motto of "Consciousness +
Commitment = Change," and their success together is indebted to the translated techniques of popular education.

While the reformation of Florida agribusiness is a clear primary objective, the movement also desires a societal shift in consciousness, one that affirms the dignity of all people.
The struggle of the CIW has changed the lives of thousands, yet it is more difficult to grasp
how this struggle touches and teaches those not directly involved, such as people who
witness small pieces of this campaign via picket lines and media coverage. One cannot
decisively track such changes, but there are tools at our disposal to aid in the effort, like
public pedagogy.[9] Examples of this can be found in SFA's organizing model, such as the
use of "brand-busting" (retooled corporate images that convey campaign messages), drawings and music converted into popular education 'codes,' and the style of workshops used
during conferences and convergences. Educational techniques, adapted to various organizing tactics and philosophies, have made their way from communities in rural Haiti,
Mexico, and Guatemala to immigrant farmworkers who have fought against exploitation
in Florida. Subsequently, students and young people in the U.S. have adopted these philosophies and educational practices in their local organizing efforts.

How does the CIW's model influence SFA's work? How has SFA used critical consciousness, grassroots education, and its own program—rooted in solidarity, education,
and action—to build a movement of successful social change? We will examine these

questions through examples of SFA work in Santa Ana, California; Chicago, Illinois; and the Río Grande Valley, Texas.

SANTA ANA AND THE MUSIC OF SON JAROCHO

The room was filled to capacity with CIW workers and SFA student allies dancing and laughing, strumming along to the syncopated rhythms of *son jarocho*, a traditional music of Veracruz, México. The gathering was in Santa Ana, California, in the middle of conservative Orange County, but the space, El Centro Cultural de México, was full of people with a vision for a better world. Most of the crowd just finished a forty-four-mile march from East Los Angeles to Irvine, home to fast food giant Taco Bell. Everyone in the room was glowing from the long day and positive energy that only comes from marching alongside hundreds of people exploding in enthusiasm with music, inspired chants, enormous tomato signs, and even larger puppets. The whole day, we marched, played, and danced on call, improvising melodic verses as Centro volunteers helped with the Spanish-English translation. It was refreshing; when some of the organizers got tired, the music pumped them up; when we'd get tired, the example of the Immokalee workers pushed us too. It was the first of many celebrations between the CIW and their allies in Santa Ana.[10]

WHEN THE COALITION OF IMMOKALEE Workers first came to Orange County in 2004, looking to secure office space to plan a major mobilization against Irvine-based Taco Bell, they found not only a small room to work out of, but also a welcoming community of would-be allies at Santa Ana's El Centro Cultural de México. This volunteer-run organization creates space for the Santa Ana community's cultural activities, ranging from *danza azteca* and adult education to punk shows and *paisano* fundraisers. Since then, students, activists, workers, and families from Santa Ana have joined with the CIW and Student/ Farmworker Alliance in an effort to transform the U.S. food industry.

The bonding that resulted from sharing space at El Centro began a long-lasting relationship, empowering Centro volunteers and affirming the plausibility of CIW's long-term efforts to build broad-based alliances. It was a primer in network-style community organizing and collaboration for young people in Orange County, a taste of what it meant to belong to an extensive social justice movement, one that extends throughout the U.S. and beyond. In Santa Ana, as in many cities, the Campaign for Fair Food was an opportunity to see activism and education through the lens of the workers' personal narratives, ultimately leading to a deeper analysis of power, a real understanding of solidarity, and the long-term involvement of Centro volunteers.

Son del Centro is a music program based out of El Centro Cultural that encompasses free music workshops of traditional *son jarocho*, an active performance group, and transnational collaborations with cooperatives and projects in southern Mexico. The project uses music as a vehicle to both educate and encourage action, supporting popular movements across the U.S. and Mexico (see Appendix A for *son jarocho* verses). As part of the Campaign for Fair Food, many of the members of Son del Centro have received organizing trainings and participated in SFA, translating this experience to challenge injustices in Santa Ana and Orange County. Conversely, many of the members of the CIW and SFA have since learned to play *son jarocho* and now use it to support their communities in struggle on this side of the U.S./Mexico border. The music has spread with the SFA, as both a powerful medium to make our voices heard, but also as powerful art that has brought people together and encouraged their growth, not only as activists and organizers, but as social beings. The CIW and SFA found in Santa Ana a community that not only shares their sense of urgency to transform society, but also a vision to do this through very basic, fundamental aspects of our lives: education, art, culture, and food.

Beyond bringing allies together (as in the regular music workshops in Santa Ana, Madison, and Austin), *son jarocho* also provides a basic (heart)beat for actions. After years of live performance at rallies and alongside the farmworkers in marches, Son del Centro has become the soundtrack of the CIW in motion. Although a march in and of itself does much to convene supporters under one banner, the inclusion of art, in this case folk music, imbues participants with a sense of belonging and ownership of the message through song. For the young *jaraneros*[11] of Santa Ana during the years of the Taco Bell Boycott, playing alongside protesters at rallies was their calling to continue the legacy of such *cantores* as Pete Seeger and Víctor Jara. With guitar in hand, one can communicate not only problematic conditions through song, but also reinforce the humanity and dignity of people through their engagement with art. Like the iconic machete, the *jarana* is also rooted in rural life, and thus *son jarocho* is both a relevant music form and symbol of the dignified aspects of *campesino* communities, of an honest day's work of laboring in the fields.

ORGANIZING IN CHICAGO

AFTER THE SUCCESSFUL TACO BELL Boycott, the campaign surged forward, seeking to reform the tomato industry as a whole. The workers chose McDonald's as the next campaign target. Seeking to deflect worker and consumer pressure, McDonald's took a page from the anti-activist playbook, teaming up with growers—and one of the company's own public relations firms—to create a toothless 'code of conduct' for its tomato suppliers. The code of conduct, dubbed SAFE (Socially Accountable Farm Employers), excluded many aspects that were critical to the Coalition of Immokalee Workers-Taco Bell deal, including transparency, worker participation, and independent verification.[12] It was clear that McDonald's would not come to the table and do the right thing willingly. So a team of CIW, Student/Farmworker Alliance, and Interfaith Action members were dispatched to live and organize in Chicago—whose suburbs are home to McDonald's global headquarters—from the fall of 2006 through the spring of 2007, while national efforts were coordinated from Immokalee.[13]

From the beginning, organizing in Chicago was aided by several factors. Since the CIW had been to Chicago for several cross-country education/action-packed "Taco Bell Truth Tours," many in the area already knew about the campaign and considered themselves to be allies of the CIW. Chicago also has a proud and strong history of labor and immigrant struggles and is home to a plethora of active social justice organizations. In addition, the timing of the organizing team's presence in Chicago was impeccable; just a week after the team's arrival in the spring of 2006, the first wave of massive immigrant rights mobilizations took place against the Sensenbrenner Bill, a Congressional proposal to increase draconian measures of detention and deportation against undocumented immigrants. It was in this climate that student allies of the CIW began organizing in the greater Chicago community against McDonald's.

In a major urban center such as the city of Chicago, what goes on in rural, agricultural communities is not at the forefront of popular consciousness; at best, what exists is a distorted view of the small farmer with a tractor and a few heads of livestock down on the family farm. This posed a challenge for SFA's education-based approach. For many of the students and community members the Immokalee organizers spoke with, it was their first time hearing or thinking about how food is actually produced. Nevertheless, there were many in the immigrant community who had been farmers or farmworkers in their home countries as well as in the Midwest, and the struggle immediately resonated with them.

SFA's efforts have always connected the CIW's struggle to other mobilizations, from other labor struggles and immigrant rights to the anti-war movement and efforts against gentrification and the criminalization of youth. A great deal of time was spent in the early stages of the Chicago campaign attending other organizations' meetings and events to develop relationships and demonstrate genuine solidarity with the groups who were being asked to support the drive against McDonald's. The Immokalee team even lent its experience to the planning of local campaigns and actions in a grassroots exchange of education and movement consciousness. Through networking and intentional outreach, the Immokalee team cultivated a strong "fair food" committee of active local allies (including people of faith, students, members of community-based organizations, and labor and international solidarity organizers) that met frequently, planned McDonald's actions, and worked to spread the campaign. The campaign also helped to broaden SFA's organizing efforts with students; McDonald's, after all, targets a wide swath of youth under a 'family-friendly' marketing rubric. SFA organizers realized that in order to get the messages of farmworker exploitation and resistance to children as young as five, they needed to stick to the popular education tools and codes they had been developing for years.

Drawings and theater, for example, conveyed a clear message to children and adults alike. Younger children especially enjoyed and understood skits depicting a stingy, unfair Ronald McDonald (oftentimes portrayed by their teacher), farmworkers (portrayed by the students), and one of the presenters from Immokalee as the farm labor boss, telling the 'workers' to work harder and faster. In one presentation in a suburban Chicago classroom, the six–year-old students—including the child of a McDonald's executive—reached the end of the presentation tremendously excited to go home and talk about the issue with their parents. Kindergarteners from Pilsen, a predominantly Mexican neighborhood in the city, produced drawings of people marching to McDonald's holding signs; many students had just participated in the walkouts of the immigrant rights mobilizations and received early exposure to the use of marching as a viable form of protest. (We were later invited back to the budding young artists' school to hold a presentation with the students' parents, who wanted to learn more about the campaign after hearing about it from their children.) Many middle and high school students were also energized to become involved and took the initiative to flier local McDonald's restaurants in their free time. The art used on fliers was designed to be appealing to young consumers. These experiences show popular education is boundless.

As plans began to materialize for a national mobilization on Chicago in the spring of 2007 (to culminate in a boycott declaration against McDonald's), it was clear that the action would have to excite young people and the diverse communities of allies in Chicago. With this in mind, organizers decided to hold a Latin American-style *carnaval* that would sweep through the streets of Chicago. Festivities would kick off from a popular downtown park and continue to the original McDonald's restaurant several miles away. Young people from across the country contributed ideas and Chicagoans planned floats and blocks for the *carnaval* representing different organizations and constituencies. The action, infused with art and music, would have a celebratory yet defiant spirit. SFA'ers in Chicago and beyond organized a Midwest Encuentro, bringing together people from the broader region to strategize around the campaign and the upcoming convergence. Many of the educational and consciousness-raising techniques forged in Immokalee were used at that Encuentro and in a variety of different cities across the nation in the build-up to the massive action.

The excitement and energy for the *carnaval* was palpable as 100 workers from Immokalee and thousands of CIW allies from across the U.S. (largely coordinated by SFA) were set to descend on Chicago. But just days before the action, the organizers were hit with an abrupt development: McDonald's, sensing the impending buildup, agreed to the workers' demands. CIW and SFA had another big victory in their campaign, albeit anticlimactically, and as a result, the *carnaval* never took place.

But the organizers found an outlet for their festive plans, and they quickly pulled together a massive celebratory concert, featuring local and national artists interspersed with declarations from prominent human rights, labor, community, and faith leaders, as well as SFA members. Piled into Chicago's House of Blues, the 2,000-person crowd pumped their fists in unison with CIW members and Zack de la Rocha and Tom Morello of political rock group Rage Against the Machine, whose performance capped an hours-long event. CIW members used the opportunity to declare an open campaign against a new target, Burger King, promising a major mobilization near that company's headquarters in Miami by the end of the year if Burger King had not caved by then.[14] The event was a great showcase of the melding of popular art, education, and culture so vital to the work of CIW and SFA.

Although it lasted only half as long as the Taco Bell boycott, the McDonald's campaign and the experiences in Chicago provided many lessons and raised many questions. As soon as the celebration ended, buses were packed up and workers and their allies—including the Chicago organizing team from Immokalee—returned home to tackle the urgent work in the next phase of the campaign. Melody González, a member of SFA and the Chicago organizing team, recalls:

> In many ways, the victory was bittersweet. We had built great relationships with a lot of people in Chicago and to some extent felt a part of the community. There were also a lot of ideas already in progress…. I often wonder what else we could have done and built together with our allies in Chicago if the campaign had lasted longer and had been a boycott—not only for the campaign, but other social justice work in Chicago. At the same time, it was great to have won the campaign against McDonald's and build on the gains that started with Yum Brands/Taco Bell. At the end of the day, our commitment and accountability is to the CIW, with an understanding of our solidarity with and involvement in the broader movement for social justice.[15]

LIFE IN THE RIO GRANDE VALLEY

LOCATED ACROSS THE BORDER FROM Tamaulipas, México, the Río Grande Valley (RGV) is recognized globally for its prolific agricultural production. A legacy of migration and exploitation in the RGV and Florida has imparted a similar history to the two regions. In recent years, participation in the Campaign for Fair Food has become a new part of that shared history. One of the main conduits for bringing youth together in the Valley to engage in Student/Farmworker Alliance's work has been the World Peace Alliance (WPA), a youth-administrated group organizing mainly around issues of immigration, peace, and economic justice. WPA members know the issues of Immokalee well; within their circle of working-class community organizers are many migrant children and children of farmworkers. The WPA's first major effort was participation in the Coalition of Immokalee Workers' McDonald's campaign in 2006. From the beginning, the group has used popular education—rooted in and strengthened by the Valley's own rich history of farm labor—to develop critical consciousness around the campaign. One of the main tasks at hand of the WPA was to connect that preexisting context to the CIW struggle by illustrating that farmworker poverty is born of a particular model of food production.

Methods for raising awareness have grown from the difficult circumstances faced by organizers in the RGV. The majority of Valley households, for example, do not have computers. Online communication, therefore, is supplemented by other media and educational tactics in order to effectively educate and update people on the campaign. Dependence on printed materials alone, written primarily in English, is not an effective choice either, given that so many Valley residents grow up speaking Spanish as a first language and go to schools with few resources to focus on literacy. More effective means for raising consciousness, including presentations and discussions that emphasize dialogue and imagination, are deployed to overcome these constraints. These interactive methods, similar to tactics employed by the CIW with the farmworker community in Immokalee, are based on visuals and allow for questions and interaction.

Preexisting ties to agriculture also aid the process of getting people involved. WPA member Marina Sáenz-Luna observes, "While I myself am a daughter of a farmworker, I only learned of the harsh realities for *familias migrantes* in my adulthood. I quickly learned that stories of my father picking fruit throughout the West Coast were much like the conditions I was reading about in Florida's fields."[16] Marina soon began organizing discussions about the campaign in her living room for her friends and family.

By analyzing their own experiences and those of the people around them, WPA members have successfully raised consciousness around the Campaign for Fair Food. Translating this into action, however, has often been extremely challenging, given that the RGV is one of the poorest areas in the U.S. In that context, successful organizing in the Valley looks quite different from most other parts of the country, in everything from underlying motivations to the structure of meetings. For folks in the Valley, organizing a successful campaign means not only raising awareness and planning strategic actions, but also making house visits, coordinating rides, and providing for basic needs.

WPA member Héctor Guzmán knows this well. During his time organizing with the WPA he was able to bring friends in his *barrio* into action by staying in constant contact through visits to their homes. He made sure to see them every day since many lacked email, phones, or cars. Héctor personally invited people to meetings, discussions, and demonstrations, giving them rides when necessary. WPA members have also grown accustomed to sharing of themselves or finding the resources to facilitate the involvement of others, a thriftiness that has been useful for pulling together movie screenings, art for protests, food at meetings, and short campaign videos.

Valley organizers have learned that in order to create effective plans of action, their organizing methods must grow out of the specific experiences and challenges of their communities. One WPA member shares their story of returning to the Valley after some time in a coastal urban area:

> I had just decided that I would take a break from work in Baltimore, where I was having a hard time adjusting to alternative communities and had only been exposed to a few projects, most of which were led by mostly white, middle-upper class folks who grew up in the suburbs and were trying to create autonomous spaces. They used a consensus decision-making process with specific hand gestures and clearly as-signed roles. I thought I'd use what I had learned and try it out at one of our upcoming meetings in the Valley.

> As the meeting commenced, we knew there was an important action that needed to be planned in a week; we were feeling the pressure to get some concrete goals in place to make sure it happened. In the next hour, another eight people showed up and we needed to go over again the litany of hand signals and roles for the meeting. I tried to jump back into the agenda, since the "time keeper" let me know that we had two more minutes left to talk about the event. Panicking, I started speaking faster and listing our 'to-do' list, trying to move people to a vote on priorities, even though there had been no discussion about doing so. One of the newcomers said, "I don't even know what we're talking about." Another, frustrated, blurted out, "Do we even need to vote. I mean it's obvious, right?" I realized that people were speaking out of turn, and so looked to the "stack people," both of which had lost count. I tried to get back on topic. What was the topic again? I stared down at our 'to-do' list and felt like tearing it up. We didn't come to any concrete decisions that night, except, of course, that we needed another meeting.[17]

Valley youth found that the consensus-based decision-making process simply did not work in their community; the code proved to be more work than it was worth. Because the core group is always changing and it is unclear who can come to any given meeting, they realized that using such a formal and pre-defined process was tantamount to holding the meeting in a foreign language. Such formalities limited participation for those whose hearts were in the movement but could only be at meetings occasionally. The process also seemed unnatural; groups of friends were accustomed to joking around with each other, going in and out of Spanglish, yet the formal process blocked the built-in ability to break things down in a clear way.

In contrast, another member discusses her experience of a much more productive and inclusive meeting:

> I headed to the front yard for a round of hugs and kisses, making sure I didn't miss anyone, introducing myself to two new people. Even

though it was a potluck, I was worried there wouldn't be enough food and people would be hungry for the meeting. I felt relieved when I saw everyone with small Tupperware and a big can of grapefruit juice!

"So, do we have an agenda?" someone asked.

"Nah. What's the most important thing that we can actually get through tonight?" another voice responded.

"Well, the last email from the SFA listserv made me think we still don't know what kind of research we need to do, so let's start there."

About an hour late, or rather right on time, after eating, talking about research, and coordinating and delegating tasks, we start to make art and signs for the upcoming action. Quirky one-liners followed by sleep-deprived laughter fill the darkness on this humid night as we push the envelope with our signs, just enough that we don't lose the integrity of our message. These are the times when avid readers and those who don't have Internet access mix, when we, the 'well schooled' and the "pochas and pochos," think together about the kind of messages we want to share with the world.[18][19]

This informal meeting featured key elements that make WPA's particular organizing successful. Food at meetings is especially important when many refrigerators at home are empty; also, it does not make sense to organize around issues of food and poverty in faraway places when members themselves are hungry. Additionally, this convivial meeting format allowed participants to use their own voices and language, which creates space for education. Recognizing that the Valley is largely composed of working-class folks with little formal education, this style of organizing is as much about educating oneself as educating others. Every aspect of this work must allow space for questions and discussion, allowing for *real* consensus, one based on self-education, collective growth, and confidence in each decided plan of action. In this way, meetings become tools for popular education just as much as presentations and trainings.

THE BEGINNING OF THE END

COALITION OF IMMOKALEE WORKERS MEMBER Gerardo Reyes writes, "It is our hope that today's farmworker movement will serve as one of many points on the horizon that inspires young people to believe in the possibility of a better world—a world where we all have space to realize our dreams."[20] While the struggle of Immokalee's farmworkers continues to inspire scores of young organizers across the U.S., it also presents a particular avenue for achieving social change against long odds. The campaigns of the CIW and the Student/Farmworker Alliance have successfully managed to utilize popular education and leadership development in a framework of collective action that continues to generate victories.

The significance of these victories—the agreements established between the CIW and Yum Brands, McDonald's, Burger King, Whole Foods, Subway, Bon Appetit, and Compass—is hard to overstate. They have established enforceable, long-term changes in the wages and rights of workers in Florida agribusiness that may well signal "the beginning of the end of the harvest of shame that has existed for far too long in Florida's tomato fields," as Senator Sanders noted in the wake of the deal reached between the CIW, Compass Group, and major Florida tomato grower East Coast Packers in late 2009.[21] This accord prompted *The Nation* editor Katrina vanden Heuvel to proclaim that "the vision that CIW has pursued and is beginning to see come to fruition is an inspiring one, and a model for the nation,"[22] and investigative journalist and food system activist Eric Schlosser to declare, "There's no question that this is the greatest victory for farmworkers since Cesar Chavez in the 1970s."[23]

Far from stale or symbolic gestures, these hard-fought, living agreements include important stipulations. Major food corporations have to pay at least one penny more per pound for the tomatoes that they purchase, directly increasing farmworker wages. They agree to work together with the CIW to develop and implement an enforceable, human-rights-based code of conduct (including zero tolerance for modern-day slavery) in their supply chains, reversing decades of inhumane treatment of workers in the agricultural industry. They also guarantee that workers themselves are involved in the development, verification, and monitoring of all aspects of these agreements. This participation—a permanent seat at the negotiating table for farmworkers—is crucial to both the CIW and SFA because farmworkers have their *own* voices and must be genuine partners in the process of changing the agricultural industry. SFA's role as an ally is important for helping to actualize such a change.

The leadership of the worker community in Immokalee and the confluence of a network of wide-ranging allies committed to respecting that leadership has helped the Campaign for Fair Food avoid some of the pitfalls that have plagued other recent movements on the Left. In its own way, with its own tools, the campaign has opened, sustained, and widened cracks in the structure of exploitation. For many SFA members, the lessons learned from front-lines immersion in this organizing model have forever altered their perceptions of themselves and the social world. In the years ahead, it will be well worth monitoring these developments and community impacts on the terrain of political organizing in the U.S., as the struggle yields harvests that can potentially inform other movements in their work toward radical change.

Appendix A

Examples of Son Jarocho versada (verses) written by youth from Santa Ana, Immokalee, Madison, and Texas:

Education in Santa Ana

Viendo yo la educación	As I see the kind of education offered
en mi escuela, me encabrona	in my school, I am angered.
que coraje me ocasiona	What sadness it brings to me
y causa desilución	and disillusion it causes.
se me gasta el corazón	It tires my heart
aguantando pendejadas	to put up with their nonsense
ya no quiero de ellos nada	I don't want anything more from them.
sólo mentiras enseñan	All they teach us are lies.
prefiero pueblos que sueñan	I prefer the common people that dream
con ideas liberadas.	thoughts of liberation.

CIW Victory (Taco Bell)

Hoy les contaré una historia	Today I will tell you a story
de los campos de Florida	about the fields of Florida
que a una gente afligida	where upon its wounded people
les llovió agua de victoria	rained the waters of victory
y les dió esperanza y vida	giving them hope and life.
la esperanza no se pierde	Hope is never lost
si es un árbol bien sembrado	if it is a well planted tree
y desde el martes pasado	and since last Tuesday
el mundo se ve mas verde	the whole world looks greener.
el que dude, que se acuerde	He who doubts it should remember
de Immokalee, y su memoria	Immokalee and its memory.
trabajadores de historia	Workers who have made history,
que en los campos encendidos	who from the blazing fields
piscaron, bien merecido	plucked, very-well deserved,
el fruto de la Victoria.	*the fruit of victory.*

NOTES

1   Ęric Schlosser, "Burger With a Side of Spies," *New York Times* (May 7, 2008).

2   Florida Tomato Committee. HTTP://WWW.FLORIDATOMATOES.ORG/BITSANDPIECES.HTML.

3   Katrina vanden Heuvel, "In the Trenches and Fighting Slavery," article for online blog *Editor's Cut* (December 28, 2008). HTTP://WWW.THENATION.COM/BLOGS/EDCUT/391546/IN_THE_TRENCHES_AND_FIGHTING_SLAVERY.

4   Student/Farmworker Alliance, "Organizing Philosophy." HTTP://WWW.SFALLIANCE.ORG/ORG-PHILOSOPHY.HTML.

5   Popular education is a term used most often in social movements within the U.S. and Latin America; in academia it is often referred to as critical pedagogy. This form of pedagogy stems primarily from the work of Brazilian educator Paulo Freire. In the 1970s, Freire began using a process of critical reflection as part of a literacy education program with peasant communities to 'unpack' and act upon problematic realities. Freire's literacy education practices spread throughout Latin America and have been adopted worldwide to teach on a range of subjects. They are also widely used within social movements to collectively build analyses and to problem-solve. Critical pedagogy is rooted in an analysis of power, and ultimately a strong understanding of the role of solidarity in working for justice. In the words of one CIW member, "It is education for action, and as such its effectiveness must ultimately be measured by the degree to which it moves the community to take action, fight for change, and win a degree of control over its collective destiny" (Greg Asbed, Coalition of Immokalee Workers: "¡Golpear a Uno Es Golpear a Todos!," *In Bringing Human Rights Home*, v. 3; Cynthia Soohoo, Cathereine Albisa, and Martha Davis, eds. (Santa Barbara, CA: Greenwood, 2008), 1–23. See also Paulo Freire, *Pedagogy of Freedom: Ethics, Democracy, and Civic Courage* (Lanham, MD: Rowman & Littlefield, 2000), 45.

6   Paulo Freire, *Education for Critical Consciousness* (New York: Seabury Press, 1973).

7   One CIW member helpfully provides some context: "At [popular education's] heart is the use of 'codes'—drawings, theater, song, video, stories, and so on—designed to capture a piece of community reality and to present that reality for reflection in a group" (Greg Asbed, note 4).

8   Greg Asbed, "Pigs, Peasants, and Politics in Haiti: Migdal's Theory of Peasant Participation in National Politics and the Fall of Jean-Claude Duvalier," *Journal of Public and International Affairs* 2:2 (1991): 67–83.

9   The concept of public pedagogy asks us to acknowledge how we educate and learn in social spaces, highlighting the idea that the world around us—and the actions and interactions we witness and take part in—are all sites of pedagogy. Henry Giroux argues for a radical public pedagogy that harnesses the counter-hegemonic possibilities when public pedagogy is used as a conceptual tool to create change, asserting that we ought to make "the notion of public pedagogy central to the struggle against neoliberalism…. Such action depends on various groups … within and across national boundaries to form alliances in which matters of global justice, community, and solidarity provide a common symbolic space and multiple public spheres where … an attempt to develop a new political language, culture, and set of relations is undertaken." See Henry Giroux, *Against the Terror of Neoliberalism: Politics Beyond the Age of Greed* (Boulder, CO: Paradigm Publishers, 2008), 12.

10   Account of a post-demonstration *son jarocho* celebration by one of the article's authors.

11   *Jaraneros* play the small percussive guitar of *son jarocho*, the *jarana*. The term is used to refer to the resurgence of the folk tradition, since the instrument is the central element of the genre.

12   SAFE is a non-profit independent auditor and reviewer for the agriculture industry. The advent of independent auditors in lieu of government regulation coincides with the development of "corporate social responsibility," that is, corporate promises to monitor their own actions in accordance with particular standards and ethics. Such practices have been widely characterized as toothless, a façade of accountability that ignores a company's more egregious injustices.

13   Interfaith Action of Southwest Florida is a faith-based ally organization that also works closely with the CIW.

14   2,000 farmworkers and supporters marched on Burger King in November 2007. Burger King agreed to the workers' demands by May 2008.

15   Account from personal communication with the authors.

16   Account from personal communication with the authors.

17   Account from personal communication with the authors.

18   *Pocha* (f) and *pocho* (m) are derived from the Spanish word *pocho*, used to describe fruit that has become rotten or discolored. It refers mostly to Mexican-Americans and/or Chicana(o)s who are identified by their use of poorly spoken Spanish. They are often thought to be *maleducados*, or uneducated.

19   Account from personal communication with the authors.

20   Dan Berger, Chesa Boudin, and Kenyon Farrow, *Letters from Young Activists: Today's Rebels Speak Out* (New York: Nation Books, 2005), 204.

21   Bernie Sanders, email communication to the CIW, September 24, 2009.

22   Katrina vanden Heuvel, "A Compass for Fair Food," article for online blog *Editor's Cut* (September 27, 2009). HTTP://WWW.THENATION.COM/BLOGS/EDCUT/477927/A_COMPASS_FOR_FAIR_FOOD.

23   Quoted in "Tomato workers win new pay deal" by Amy Bennett Williams, *Ft. Myers News-Press* (September 26, 2009).

A CONVERSATION ON ORGANIZING MODELS FOR SOCIAL JUSTICE STRUGGLES IN THE CITY

Moderated by Betty Robinson | Introduction by John Duda

Participant Organizations: City Life/Vida Urbana | Picture the Homeless | Take Back the Land | United Workers

INTRODUCTION

THE CITY FROM BELOW CONFERENCE was a project initially conceived by Red Emma's, a collectively-managed and worker-owned bookstore and coffeehouse in Baltimore, MD.[1] Very early on in the organizing process, we were joined by the Baltimore *Indypendent Reader*, a free quarterly social justice newspaper project, and the Baltimore Development Cooperative, a collective of artist-activists responsible for, among other things, an occupied urban farm in East Baltimore. All of the projects worked toward building infrastructure for what we called the 'project of urban democracy.' For its part, the *Indypendent Reader*, in each of its thematic issues, attempts to take stock of the composition of a particular sector of Baltimore social justice organizing and offer back the resulting paper as a resource for that same work. The Baltimore Development Cooperative starts with design practices and reinserts these strategies and skills into projects aimed at concretely reconstructing urban space in a more participatory and anti-capitalist fashion. Red Emma's storefront, beyond the obvious goals of distributing radical information and running a cafe collectively, exists to provide a nodal point for the flows of Baltimore's social movements, a place for building and solidifying often informal connections and alliances essential to movement building.

So just within the three groups that made up most of the conference's organizing committee, there was a realization, grounded in our own practices as activists, that 'the city,' understood as a shared horizon, a terrain of struggle and a scope of action, was essential to the way we were thinking and doing our own politics, and especially to the way our own separate projects could enter into productive conjunctions against the background of a shared urban fabric. We wanted to think this dynamic of a network of struggles in and for the city on a larger scale: against the city envisioned by neoliberalism—a space of exclusion, displacement, and control—we wanted to convene a gathering to explore a "city from below." At our disposal was 2640, a large-scale community events venue and center for political organizing that had been started as a side project of Red Emma's a few years prior, capable of hosting an event of the scale we were envisioning without having to worry about the constraints of funding or institutional support.

At least from the perspective of someone working primarily with Red Emma's and within the anarchist milieu, the idea here was a departure from most of the radical conferences and bookfairs we had as models (including our own previous efforts). Rather than trying to cram every single issue of note into one weekend, we wanted to organize something more focused, with an emphasis on a common overarching framework knitting the various strands of the event together. Beyond that, we also wanted to ensure that we did not fall into the trap of merely convening a conference on urban social justice only to recite the litany of all the things wrong with the city. We wanted to focus on bringing together people who were not just interested in critique, but rather were involved in concrete urban organizing projects, shared our vision of the city, and were already working to bring it about.

The panel on organizing models, a portion of which has been transcribed and reproduced below, was one of the many highlights of the conference. We are exceptionally grateful to the moderator, Baltimore social justice veteran Betty Robinson, whose vision guided and shaped the conversation from the beginning. On the panel, one of Baltimore's most inspiring social justice organizations, the United Workers (who work for human rights at the intersections of poverty, precarious labor, and urban development), would be joined by organizers from Right to the City Alliance member organizations Picture the Homeless (a homeless-led advocacy and action group from NYC) and City Life/Vida Urbana (a Boston-based multi-issue urban justice organization, one of the first groups to organize foreclosure blockades at the onset of the subprime mortgage crisis), as well as Max Rameau, from Take Back the Land, which had been successfully moving homeless families into empty foreclosed homes in Miami. The panelists here are not talking to raise awareness about the issues surrounding urban poverty; rather, they are talking, primarily to each other, about what kinds of models and strategies they use in their own work—not (just) about what is wrong in the city, but about how we are going to organize ourselves to fix it.[2]

Betty Robinson began the discussion with some very important questions:

> •How do we create, build, and nurture organizations that can be in the forefront of our new social justice movement?
> •How do such organizations build capacity and leadership?
> •What does their strategic thinking look like?

ORGANIZING FROM BELOW: GETTING PEOPLE INVOLVED, BUILDING LEADERSHIP

Betty Robinson: My sense is that we don't just need one type of organization, we need many, but most of them need to be where the people affected by the crisis are in the leadership and moving the agenda forward.

Steve Meachem (City Life/Vida Urbana): We certainly have been involved in struggles and with organizations trying to recruit people who are sympathetic to a struggle, to recruit people who are morally opposed to gentrification, to recruit people who don't like the foreclosure crisis, but we emphasize recruiting the people directly affected by the crisis—folks who are getting the rent increases, the folks who are getting foreclosed on, the folks who are getting evicted after foreclosure. Additionally, I would also emphasize the importance of creating a culture of resistance. Most of the people who come to City Life come by word of mouth, which happens as a result of a growing culture of resistance in the city. That in turn comes about because of all the media attention to the work and by word of mouth.

We want to decentralize decision making as much as possible to those directly affected by the struggle. So we organize tenants' associations all around the city of Boston—in an average year we have maybe 150 meetings of tenants' associations across the city—and all of those meetings are making the decisions about their struggle. We are there to give advice, we are there to provide political perspective, we are there to link that struggle to other struggles, but when it comes down to whether or not you're going to pay that rent increase or not, how long you are willing to fight, when you want to give up, when you want to push forward, all those decisions have to be made by those people directly affected.

Greg Rosenthal (United Workers): The mission of United Workers is to build a movement to end poverty. There's a reason you see Harriet Tubman on all our posters—Harriet Tubman was a leader in the movement to end slavery. We're building leadership to end another form of slavery, which is poverty. Within that, we have a focal point campaign, which is how we build leadership, how we build political power and bring resources and allies into the work that we do. So we started out with the day laborers at the baseball stadium, Camden Yards, and the process was organizers just going in and meeting workers. We organize through home visits. We meet people at their workplace and then go to their home and go through a process of what we call 'reflective action' which is our form of human rights education. You understand that this one conversation, it could be someone who is the next leader of this movement—anyone could be a leader.

We had a victory at the stadium; we won living wages after a three and a half year campaign. It was a really concrete win—workers going from $4.50 an hour as day laborers to having direct employment and making $11.30 an hour. Everywhere along the way, people said, you're not going to do it. But workers said, no, this is our lives, poverty can end, and we're going to be a part of a process that does this. It's not just a process of changing your workplace. This is the difference between transformative values and transactional values, having the understanding that it's not just about me, and whether or not I'm going to get a wage increase if I participate in this organization. That's not what it's about. A wage increase is something needed to survive, and of course that's really important. But the transformative value is believing that every person should have human dignity, should be able to live with dignity and basic human rights. And realizing that that's the process that I want to be a part of. Not because I pay a union due, and so therefore you're going to help me out. That's transactional—and if that kind of approach, the kind of approach unions use, worked, things would be different, things would be getting better. It's not working. The greatest victory of the stadium campaign wasn't the wage increase, it was that there was 30 committed leaders in this movement who came out of the campaign and are moving on with the understanding they've gained to new campaigns, like the one we're working on in the Inner Harbor.

Veronica Dorsey (United Workers): We know that every low wage worker isn't at the same place. So we like to meet people where they are. There are a number of different projects we have going on simultaneously, and wherever the people are at the time in their lives is the project that the staff helps them to get into to develop the skills that they already have, and once they develop them and they gain more self-esteem, then they'll ask questions, like we did this, what they can do next? We have retreats where we sit down and discuss our strategies, the problems at the work site so we know what to do next. They allow us to broaden our own horizons, they allow us to come up with our own solutions because we got tired of band-aid solutions people were giving us, because every time we went to the medic and got a band-aid, the next day that band-aid was dirty and we had to go right back to the same medic for the same kind of band-aid: we got tired of that. So United Workers helped us stop using band-aid solutions and use our own brains and come up with our own solutions.

Jean Rice (Picture the Homeless): We believe in participatory democracy at Picture the Homeless. We are led and directed by homeless New Yorkers. We believe in participatory democracy and transparency in government. Until that fails, we're not going to sign on to any centralized form.

Rob Robertson (Picture the Homeless): We don't have a hard time building membership because a lot of folks are angry. They're angry because you're keeping me in a shelter every night. They're angry because you won't give me a rent subsidy that will give me permanent housing. You give me a rent subsidy that has no sustainable waged job training attached to it, and I wind up in the shelter system again because after the year when that subsidy is over, I have nowhere to turn.

Our mayor in New York has an ambitious plan that in five years he's going to end homelessness, but we find that his numbers decrease by small percentages, and when he started that plan almost five years ago—this June will be 5 years—there were 38,000 people in the shelters. If we were to take a look at that number today, I guarantee it's 35,000 in the shelters. So his system is failing miserably; we recruit membership based on that position. Folks are angry. We go to soup kitchens to do outreach. Folks are standing in line, they can't afford to get a meal. We do a soup kitchen called Holy Apostle in New York City which is probably one of the largest groups of homeless people who get together on a daily basis. There are some 1,600 meals served at this particular soup kitchen on a daily basis so it's pretty easy for us to find homeless people that are angry. You stand there, you start to have some conversations; before you know it, you're recruiting new members.

We retain membership and recruit membership by a combination of things. We have regularly scheduled meetings. We do this because it's difficult for members who don't have phones, who don't have a permanent place to stay, to be contacted. So the one thing they know is that that meeting will be there, and if they're hungry there will be meals supplied for them there, they'll have metro cards, transportation.

Our membership is involved in the decision-making process. We're a membership organization, all the members decide on the issues we vote on. The staff is there to support, to show a way how, and create processes. We select issues to work on basically by talking to homeless people, and we do that outreach. "What are you angry about?" "What bothers you the most?"

Max Rameau (Take Back the Land): Something we don't talk about enough as organizer types: because of material conditions and particularly now, exaggerated with the rise of the 501(c)3 industrial complex there's a growing split between organizers and the masses. Right now we have a professional class of political organizers and it makes it very difficult for grassroots groups, native grassroots groups, to rise and compete in a real way with professional grassroots organizers who are trained in college, and who have particular political ideologies and are clearer on certain things because they have access to study those things. So there's times, as organizers, when we're thinking about the movement going in one direction or going at a particular speed or rate, and the masses aren't keeping up. But there's other times when the masses are far surpassing us. In 1992, after the not guilty verdict in the case of the police officers who beat Rodney King in Los Angeles, the people—without any planning, without any organizers getting there and saying let's have a meeting, let's discuss this—got up, rose together, and burned the city down. Without any level of organizing or planning, they took action on what they saw was an issue which directly impacted their interests. Organizers were not prepared for that, organizers were not leading that, and organizers were struggling to catch up to the people.

TAKING ON THE SYSTEM: WHAT KIND OF POLITICS?

Max Rameau: Material conditions need to be taken into account in choosing organizing tactics: the fact there was this so-called housing boom, which turned out to be a big bubble and a bust, and the level of gentrification in our community changed things. We could not have gone, say, five or six years ago, and tried to take over vacant houses, even though that's a great and exciting campaign—it's a great and exciting campaign that could only work when the conditions were right. You can't force a really cool idea into inappropriate conditions; the campaign not only has to be right, but right for the conditions that exist.

Given these material conditions, Take Back the Land tries to think about power in terms of how a community develops its own power rather than how the community holds power in relation to elected officials or other people. We don't think about power in the sense of how to meet with elected officials or get elected officials to concede to certain demands. We think about the capacity of our community and how we can maximize and then expand that capacity. So we don't think in terms of what we can get them to do for us; we think in terms of what we can do for us. What we could do was take over a plot of land and build the city that we could run ourselves and we were in fact able to do that.[3] We never thought about, never wanted to turn that into demands from the system or demands from the city or developers.

Rob Robertson: I've been struggling with Max's refusal to deal with elected officials. In the work we do with Picture the Homeless, we have to constantly confront elected officials.

And a lot of our work is adversarial with elected officials, because as Max so eloquently put it, they're the ones who got you in the positions you're in. His reasoning for not wanting to deal with it, I love it—I think it's great, but unfortunately we *have* to deal with them—and we have to deal with them sometimes at a pretty high level. With homelessness in New York City, its shelter system has become a quasi-industry. The department of homeless services which runs homelessness in NYC has a budget of $750 million a year. This is to keep people temporarily housed—it makes absolutely no sense. And so often our work is directed at them.

Steve Meachem: I would describe City Life's role as that of an organizing collective— we don't simply staff tenants' associations, we bring our organizing philosophy and our politics into it. There's this debate among organizers about whether an organizer should bring his or her politics into the work, we don't think that's the right question. We think an organizer always brings their politics into their work; it's just a question of what politics it is. When City Life goes to a meeting of people being affected by rent increases or foreclosures, our political perspective which we lay out at the beginning creates the moral space that allows certain options to be chosen that weren't even on the table before.

These new options help in linking individual struggles to the big picture. It's certainly true in our experience that individuals' defensive action on a really local scale can have offensive system-challenging consequences depending on how they are conducted. To give an example: when we're doing an eviction blockade of families in buildings that have been foreclosed on, these are defensive struggles to save the home of an individual or a couple of families. And they're powerful in part because the personal story of that individual or those families is on the table juxtaposed against the interests of the bank. But beyond that, the blockade has system-challenging properties. First, we're taking a clearly collective response to those individual struggles—it's not that one person or one family plus a lawyer, it's that person or family plus a whole lot of other tenants who are willing to defend them. Second, it challenges the system because people are taking direct action; they're not simply going through legal channels, but are going outside of legal channels to defend an individual or a family's home, and insisting on their moral right to take those actions. And finally, it's a challenge to the system because when we bring publicity to these struggles, we're pointing out the contradiction between banks getting giant bailouts and this person who is simply willing to pay rent or buy the building back at a real value and instead is going to be evicted from their home.

NOTES

1   For more information on The City From Below (including video and audio from the conference), visit HTTP://WWW.CITYFROMBELOW.ORG; for information on Red Emma's visit HTTP://WWW.REDEMMAS.ORG.

2   The Baltimore Indypendent Reader's publication on the conference, which includes the roundtable re-printed here, can be found at: HTTP://WWW.INDYREADER.ORG/CONTENT/SPRINGSUMMER-2009-ISSUE-12.

3   Rameau is referencing the Ujoma Village Shantytown. For more information on this effort, see: Max Rameau, *Take Back The Land: Land, Gentrification and The Umoja Village Shantytown* (Miami: NIA Interactive Press, 2008).

WHAT'S GOING ON?

THE USSF, GRASSROOTS ACTIVISM, AND SITUATED KNOWLEDGE

Marina Karides | **U.S. Social Forum Documentation Committee**

Originally written in the spring of 2008 during the presidential campaigns, and leading up to the protests at the site of the Democratic and Republication Convention, "What's Going On?" was revised and updated with a new postscript to address the current climate in January of 2010. The postscript addresses the organizing process for the 2010 USSF, questioning the analysis presented in the original essay and the election of Barack Obama.

> *You look at the course of the world and we're heading toward an oligarchy.*
> *The primary reason to have this forum is to return society back to the people.*
> —Anonymous Member of the USSF National Planning Committee,
> September 2007

T HE FIRST UNITED STATES SOCIAL Forum (USSF) was a milestone in social forum organizing, opening a new chapter for U.S. movements. Those who attended were mobilized, demonstrating how the forums are processes more than events. Months and years before the five-day event that took place in early summer of 2007 in Atlanta, groups and organizations around the U.S. were learning about this new planetary space of social justice and the forums that were occurring around the world, deciding whether it was fruitful to participate and how it may or may not connect to their struggles on the ground. The USSF is part of a lineage of hundreds, maybe thousands, of national, regional, and local social forums that began with the 2001 World Social Forum (WSF) in Brazil. The social forum reached the U.S. as a concrete national project around 2004 and materialized in 2007 after several regional and city level forums.

What made the forum process so striking was its participatory democracy style of politics. The National Planning Committee (NPC), composed of fifty different groups, facilitated the organizing process; the events, sessions, tents, and workshops were sponsored by groups that attended the USSF. This is unique in the U.S. context, where gatherings of activists that cut across movement-building sectors are often dictated by funding organizations. The USSF was determinedly grassroots, not only because of the participatory control over programming developed through the first World Social Forum, but also because of who was there.

The lion's share of energy, time, and resources for USSF organizing was provided by Grassroots Global Justice Alliance (GGJ) and Project South. Grounded in base-building organizations across the nation, GGJ is largely responsible for the unique character of U.S. engagement in the forum process. Working-class people of color dominated the event, a broad swath of U.S. society that communicates with a variety of identities—indigenous, Chicana, queer, Korean-American, low-income, Haitian, feminist, domestic worker, housing activist, black, brown, and poor, to start. This diversity was previously unseen in the U.S. history of political mobilizations. There was a palpable power gained from it, a seizure of control from the white middle class that has in recent decades dominated the U.S. Left's ideological landscape and public meaning of 'activism,' 'organizing,' and 'social justice.'

Despite the diversity and all the rave reviews of the USSF, there has been concern that the process of organizing was *too* intentional. That is, given the commitment of the forum to providing an open space where expression of all ideologies and forms of organizing that oppose neoliberalism can come together and dialogue, the USSF was driven by base-building organizations with a particular agenda.

For many organizations that work for liberation and justice, most on a shoestring budget in their small corner of the U.S., participating in the USSF was a decision of committing limited time and resources. That 1,000 organizations did register and more than 15,000 people participated tells us not only that the mobilizing efforts of the NPC were successful and savvy, but also that a collective meeting of U.S. groups in struggle against the severity of the current capitalist moment was in demand.

DEBATE

THE WORLD SOCIAL FORUM HAS been under study and debate by a growing cadre of scholars and activists who participate in attending and organizing events that discuss the future of the forum. There are several centers around the world (i.e. the India Institute for Critical Action: Centre in Movement and the Centre for Civil Society in South Africa) that have built up around studying and participating in the social forums and working with local mass movements. Many of the current theoreticians who examine the WSF address important questions in locating (or dislocating) the WSF in the history of the Left (such as Boaventura de Sousa Santos) and in debating the forum's current crossroads push for more-or-less political unity and declarations (including Chico Whitaker and Walden Bello). With concerns being raised as to the utility of the forums, the USSF was a major boost to forum promoters, confirming its necessity as an organizing vehicle and place for political exchange.

Chico Whitaker, an early founder of the WSF, supports the social forum as a space for activist exchanges of ideas, strategies, and deepening movements that understand the neoliberal context. Articulación Feminista Marcusor, a Latin American feminist network with early involvement in the WSF, also emphasizes the forums as a location for dialogue about definitions of democracy, the political meaning of the forum, and methods for successfully challenging and altering globalization. These sorts of discussions were evident throughout the USSF: in coffeehouses, around and in the Atlanta Civic Center, in programmed sessions, informally in the streets, in open rooms provided for impromptu or follow-up meetings, and even in the corporate hotels.

At the forum, disparate participants and organizations fighting capital's decrepitude in their cities and towns expressed appreciation that their ongoing grassroots struggles were similar and met with similar disinterest by governments and corporations. The recognition of the systematic inequality perpetrated across the nation could have caused groups to flounder at the size of the neoliberal project: its depth of racism and gender abuse, weakness of labor rights, environmental injustices, and disingenuous government policies. But that is not what happened. Despite years of sectarianism, many involved had the sense that social movements came away more united, with a greater consciousness of the interrelationship of their struggles.

Yet the USSF was also a highly charged program of action. In the larger debates of the forum process, the Whitaker position that calls for maintaining the social forum process as an open space of collective exchange contrasts with Walden Bello's position that calls for a more concentrated action or voice from the WSF. The USSF has been described as a 'movement' rather than a 'space,' intent on moving towards concrete steps for political action. There certainly were all kinds of movement happening at the USSF: a national alliance of domestic workers formed, indigenous tribes from various regions met and joined together, urban organizing groups moved forward as the Right to the City Alliance, and the Women's Caucus continued as a node for U.S. women's groups to share and promote actions. But the debates occurring on a global level centralize a tension in purpose that will have important impacts for the future.

A GLOBAL DAY OF ACTION

The desire for action following the first United States Social Forum was reflected in the internationally coordinated Global Day of Action (GDA). Coming on the heels of the USSF, the International Committee of the WSF decided that coordinated events throughout the world at the end of January 2008 would help ground the global organizing of the social forum process in local context.[1]

A national self-recognition of the grassroots and its place in world activism emerged from the Atlanta forum. The actions on January 26th proved that U.S. social movements are able to coordinate nationally and in concert with a global struggle. Tom Goldtooth of Indigenous Environmental Network and member of Grassroots Global Justice Alliance explained:

> As the base-building groups in the belly of the beast, we are the local voice and struggle against globalization; by taking action on January 26, we are raising the consciousness in our communities to help them understand how to link our struggles with our brothers and sisters in the Global South.[2]

The national GDA events demonstrate even further that the U.S. grassroots and their communities have taken the WSF process to heart. Numerous events grounded in community issues took place in the U.S. during the week of the GDA. The actions were as wide and diverse as the U.S. itself, from Boston Jobs with Justice's teach-in on the Colombia Free Trade Agreement and funeral procession to the Colombian Consulate, to the Southwest Workers Union's march to the Alamo calling for "human rights for all," to Indigenous Environmental Network affiliates organizing a number of actions for climate justice. In the city of the first USSF, the Georgia Citizens' Coalition on Hunger and Project South organized a poor people's caravan through historic sites in Atlanta that ended with a Poor People's Assembly. In New York City, Domestic Workers United launched a state legislative campaign for the Domestic Workers Bill of Rights.

The right to safe housing and land figured centrally in several GDA events in the U.S.; many of them focused on the crises in New Orleans and the U.S. Gulf Coast. At their GDA event, Direct Action for Rights and Equality presented performance art at a flea market in Providence, Rhode Island to protest gentrification and express solidarity to stop the demolition of public housing in New Orleans. In San Francisco, several groups convened—including People Organized for Westside Renewal, St. Peter's Housing Committee, and Just Cause—to hold a vigil at Senator Dianne Feinstein's home in solidarity with the people of the New Orleans on housing issues. And in the city of New Orleans, the New Orleans Folks and Black Workers for Justice targeted Louisiana Senator David Vitter of the Senate Banking Committee to stop the destruction of public housing and demand passage of the Gulf Coast Recovery Act.

THE GLOBAL MEANING OF RESISTANCE IN MIAMI

AFFORDABLE HOUSING, SAFE HOMES, AND community and neighborhood control over development are all at an unprecedented low. One place that captures the convergence of hotbed issues in the U.S.—including migration, housing, and land rights—is Miami, Florida. Indeed, the global connectedness of Miami is hard to miss: a majority migrant population, the nexus for financial transactions between North and South America, and inescapable effects of Cuban politics on the city's culture. As Denise Perry, Power U's co-founder and director states, "Miami is a unique place politically around race, class, and global perspectives."[3]

The city government's current eagerness to expand Miami's global reach and define it as a "world class global city" or a center of neoliberalism is destroying the lives and homes of low-income people and workers, as well as neighborhoods like Overtown, an historic African American community in Miami. City leaders embraced the worst architectural practices, constructing tall monotonous structures that give no consideration to street life, community facilities, and the cultural vitality of its neighborhoods. According to a 2007 report by the Research Institute on Social and Economic Policy, housing prices in Miami grew twenty percent higher than wages between 2002 and 2006[4].

In the last decade, several grassroots groups—including Take Back the Land, the Miami Workers Center, and Power U Center for Social Change—have responded to the gentrification of neighborhoods and removal of families and communities (primarily African American and Latino) from their homes to make way for large corporate development. Organized by Power U, the Global Day of Action in Miami was a celebratory event attended by numerous local groups. After three years in struggle, Power U won its battle against city commissioners and Crosswinds, a development group that had planned to build up-scale condominiums on a large sector of land in Overtown.

Overtown, like many lively and historic black communities in the U.S., suffered greatly with the large interstate highways that 'incidentally' divided thriving black neighborhoods.

Formed during the era of segregation, when African Americans were pulled and pushed to Miami to work on the construction of the railroad, Overtown is well known for hosting the African American entertainers that would play in the elite hotels of Miami Beach.

Towners, as members of Overtown refer to themselves, were immersed in global struggles when the ministerial meetings of the Free Trade Area of the Americas (FTAA) came to town in November 2003. Working together with two other major grassroots organizations in the South Florida region, the Coalition of Immokolee Workers and Miami Workers Center, they formed Root Cause to lead the FTAA fight in Miami. Perry sees this event as "a critical moment and opportunity" for poor and low-income African Americans that built the organization's connections to a global justice movement.[5] Not only did it reorient how they understood the struggles they face in Miami, but organizing for and participating in the FTAA protests helped them to appreciate themselves as a movement among movements, as they hosted the national and international groups and organizations that arrived to Miami to join in the protests. The People's Tribunal, which put the FTAA on trial—with numerous international guests attesting to the intensification of poverty and injustices it would render in each of their nations and communities—was a particularly internationalizing experience for Power U. In addition, both the thirty-four mile march completed by Root Cause to represent the thirty-four countries that would have been subject to trade agreements, and the community impact report collectively produced by groups, effectively supported a global political education of and for the community.

A second turning point for Power U and the grassroots organizations of Miami was the United States Social Forum. Perry explains:

> The USSF was the first time we participated in the social forum; it was a huge eye opening for our staff, humbling and inspiring, and caused us to reflect on how we can be more a part of making another world possible. Meeting other organizations and looking at our work, how do we move into the space of being more deliberate around our youth organizing and member political education?[6]

Power U's experience shows how participation in the USSF supports grassroots organizations, even though it meant a huge expenditure of time and resources. It also suggests that listening to other organizations' concerns and struggles, and dialogue and exchange with them, are beneficial for future movement building. The organization's location in Miami and a site of the FTAA struggles accents an appreciation of the global context, but one of the key themes in Perry's discussion is the recognition that their efforts in long-neglected Overtown are part of a global struggle against neoliberalism.[7]

Further, Power U's experiences at the USSF and the GDA capture what groups like it are beginning to create in the U.S. While many reviews of U.S. activism saw it splintering into identity-based politics and formations throughout the 1980s, another aspect to consider is how activists had to engage locally to weather the waves of neoliberalism. The USSF has helped these organizations "lift their ear from the ground" and hear the connections that exist between their struggles.

Finally, Power U's lessons from the USSF certainly suggest the benefit of dialogue and the value of sharing thoughts in an open space not dictated by a particular political mission, other than having the U.S. grassroots meet collectively by their own programming. But underlying the USSF was a need to proceed where there was no particular direction, socialist, anarchist, or even anti-capitalist; movement forward was what many groups came seeking.

SITUATED KNOWLEDGE AND COLLECTIVE MEMORY

FOR SOME, THE USSF COMPROMISED the tenant of open space. Several have argued that the emphasis given to the leadership of base-building organizations or working-class people of color within the USSF proceedings shadowed the organizing process of the USSF from groups that otherwise would have joined. As many have pointed out, the open space promise of the WSF to ensure inclusiveness often leads to more participation by the privileged, as long-term and institutionalized social inequalities continue to replicate themselves. Many forums, particularly in the U.S., have been white and middle class. Yet as Thomas Ponniah expresses, the USSF was one of the most racially and ethnically diverse forums thus far.

So what happened in the organizing process of the USSF that resulted in this highly diverse but grassroots-dominated social forum, that a process that was exclusionary overall was inclusive of many who are typically excluded? Was it a deliberate outreach strategy on the part of USSF organizers? Turning to the National Planning Committee's collective timeline that was constructed in the first face-to-face NPC meeting after the USSF, this allows us to consider the process of planning the USSF from the perspectives of the organizers, rather than try to make truth claims about what happened.

It was somewhere between October 2006 and January 2007 that the organizing committee of the USSF came together. Of the organizations listed as members of the NPC, approximately fifteen put in the time, resources, and commitment to make the USSF happen. The behind-the-scenes process seems to demonstrate that there was a lot less intentionality in organizing the forum and more of a will and practice towards getting tasks accomplished that brought groups *in* rather than push them *out*.

While the USSF organizers may have strategized to gain grassroots involvement, the process to get engaged "was a work under construction." It was elusive to all. Many of the active grassroots organizations involved initially had difficulty becoming engaged. In pasting together this process through the collective memory, it was understood that the process was not haphazard; it was pieced together step by step, with repeated meetings on structure. While organizations signed on to the USSF, it was a different job to have members *act*. As an NPC member states:

> How do we get folks to have more ownership? We went through that special period, we were trying to figure structure. We don't know how to tell groups how to get on board. A lot of it was us holding things down, how people became chairs. It was not political.[8]

While many of these were base-building organizations, they came from various regions, worked in different sectors, and had scarcely organized collaboratively. The formation of the NPC as a decision-making body that was also responsible for carrying out tasks only came after months of debate. Rather than organizing a forum, the early organizers of the USSF spent extensive time debating structure. One of the NPC representatives explained that her organization implored her not to dare come back from another NPC meeting "and tell us that all you talked about was structure."[9]

Interestingly, the time taken to engage in political dialogue regarding hierarchy and organizational structure shows that grounding the USSF was a space for vetting political positions. Long discussions over structure speak volumes on the importance of space for talking about political meanings, which clearly had their worth in creating a backbone for moving forward. As an NPC member reflected:

> It became an issue of communications, and gatekeeping. We did not have personal and political trust, and this is an outcome of what the discussion over structure was to me. There was a volunteeristic will for things to happen, to work, and it was out of the sheer—we had to get it done. The stakes and exhaustion were high. And we did not treat each other in camaraderie. We were trying to figure it out. It was a huge learning curve. We were asked to work with each other and feel ourselves in the process.[10]

It is significant that, although the process of garnering strength for a U.S. social forum had started almost four years ago, it was not until March 2007, three months prior to the event, that "the spirit in the room, in March, is when people left with a greater belief that the forum might happen."[11]

This is just a sketch for thinking about what it meant to organize the USSF. The struggle over structure had to do with finding a way to meet the criteria set out by the World Social Forum as an egalitarian and open space that can create a situation to provoke collective action. It also had to do with which groups were putting in the work and staying on top of the communication. Finally, the local organizing committee in Atlanta and the NPC also had its share of tension, which from Atlanta's perspective was connected to the negative stereotypes of the South that brought doubt on the local infrastructure. Yet all social movements in the U.S. that have fomented national change started in the South.

AFRICAN CITIES AND THE USSF

WORKING ACROSS SECTORS TO SECURE an event that had no precedent in the U.S. but required significant resources and time makes the success of the USSF particularly curious. How does trust get built when there are no formal structures or past practices to assure it?

Abdoul Malik Simone's study of life and survival in African cities can be applied to understanding this success.[12] Granted, comparing social-economic relations in urban Africa to relationships among organizers and activist sectors in the U.S. is a stretch. Yet both sets of relations are shaped outside the traditional structures of government and capital and may be the basis of future forms of associations "for the city yet to come" and for a U.S. yet to come.

In most African nations where there is a limited state, or a state stripped by neoliberalism and International Monetary Fund structural adjustment policies, urban residents create spaces for livelihoods outside the government and the limitations of capitalist production. First, as Simone points out, the Africanization of the urban is reflected in the imagination of the population to develop informal forms of housing, services, and education that both provide political form and sustain urbanites economically. Second, their independent economic forms are based on their networks of informal exchange. In other words, if urban residents engaged only with others in their quarter of the city, they could not sustain livelihoods on the risk of waning local resources. Instead they gain by moving throughout the city and region and expanding their associations. With no formal system to safeguard economic exchange, the networks of connection are based on extended family systems (or invented as such) based on history and memory. Mostly, the networks and associations formed and continually forming rely on repeated successful transactions that eventually confirm trust and permit growth.

The establishment of the USSF process similarly relied on repeated transaction—tasks accomplished by various members of the NPC—that started the process of establishing trust. And this trust developed beyond traditional activist sectors, extending networks outside of their 'quarters' or issues. The future of building a program of collaborative social justice in the U.S. will rely on groups and organizations extending beyond their usual body politics and building alliances with other sectors and political leanings. Yet in the case of African cities, Simone argues that urban residents could draw from long-held practices of associations, independent networking, and collective resistance to colonization. On what could the organizers of the USSF build?

Here I draw on black feminist thought and its articulation of situated knowledge as discussed by Patricia Hill Collins.[13] The National Planning Committee of the USSF was almost all people of color; with the exception of a few white women and a white man, those present and doing the work were Indigenous, African American, Latinas/Latinos, Asian and South Asian American, Chicana/Chicano, and Pacific Islander. At least six percent were queer, gay, or lesbian. More than half were women and therefore situated at the margins of U.S. society in terms of race, gender, and class.

Those who heralded the success of the USSF or criticized it for too much intentionality pointed to the domination of base-building organizations or working-class people of color. The people active in organizing the USSF and the power behind it are women of color—an analysis absent in both criticisms and applause for the USSF. Feminists active in the forum have brought attention to the gender bias and neglect of feminist perspectives in the social forums. The USSF is unique among the world's forums because it is probably the only forum where women of color have been the primary organizers. Illustratively, analyses of the European Social Forum suggest that, even when women of color are present, their voices are not heard, nor are their concerns visible in the programming. This does not discount or underestimate the enormous efforts of the men involved in the USSF, nor does this nose-dive into politics of identity, but as one of the central male organizers states, "It was the leadership of the young women, it has been a long time coming. It exceeded expectation."[14]

The situated knowledge of these women who deeply understand intersectionality—"the connections between various types of oppression"—provided the foundation to build networks of trust and organize across sectors and regions.[15] Although these women's experiences and thoughts are not monolithic, varying based on class, ethnicity, education, demographic area, sexual orientation, and age, what they do have in common is their situations within oppressive locations that generate common experiences.

Hill Collins explains that, while black women live and work inside the mainstream system, they are not fully accepted in that system, and this gives them an outsider-within perspective on oppression, a space where resistance and agency is enacted. Their location in a society that is organized by racism, gender discrimination, and class inequality situates them in social and economic locations where new knowledges can be produced.[16]

THE U.S. YET TO COME

THE MARGINALIZATION OF WOMEN IN larger Left struggles should be hackneyed information; their experiences as significant actors and leaders in a host of social justice movements have been unappreciated, under-appreciated, or invisible to many of the men who have dominated movements and those who write about them. The same holds true for efforts and experiences of women of color who are often 'left out' by feminist movements in this country.

That is why the large presence of women of color mattered in the USSF organizing process. There may have been a tendency to privilege attendance by base-building organizations such as Power U in the USSF outreach strategy, but this was clearly due to many of the organizers' situated knowledge. Living at the margins of privilege, they recognized that white middle class organizations would dominate the process, had the grassroots not made efforts to maintain some control. In one National Planning Committee preparatory meeting, we sketched out the worst-case scenarios for the USSF; one of the common themes in these sketches was the concern that an organized forum with sufficient infrastructure could not be created, to the chagrin of the grassroots and the pompousness of well-funded U.S. organizations.

More than intentionality, the organizing process of the USSF was a pieced-together process, built on a common location and practice of trust that permits particular insights into hierarchical power and ways to beat the system. While the space for dialogue and the discursive meaning of 'global democracy' were less visible than at that the global level, the USSF opened space for discussion between activist sectors and across U.S. regions that did not exist before. With a foundation of grassroots established, future U.S. social forums may have an even broader representation of U.S. society, including the white working class and poor, rural folks and agricultural sectors, traditional academics and scholars, and larger social justice organizations.

POSTSCRIPT: BACKTRACK—WHOSE SITUATED KNOWLEDGE?

THE INTENSE ECONOMIC CRISIS OF the current moment has shaped the planning of the USSF and also the urgency for building a movement around it. The huge bailout of corporations, itself problematic, was never matched with a bailout of indebted families and workers. In our context, a bailout for workers—such as those received by corporations— would be magical, but real increases in social welfare programs, more money in public education, and the creation of public employment opportunities would be quite ordinary, given the historical precedents of U.S. policy during the New Deal era and the Great Society. The social forum process is a response to neoliberalism at large, but the next USSF will be directed towards a response to its recent catastrophic results.

This economic crisis occurs within the neoliberal framework, the same that was 'supposed' to solve previous crises. It is unclear if Obama's actions as President are situated in his experiences as a black or bi-racial man in the U.S. Although he documents his experience of marginalization in his autobiography,[17] the lack of policies designated for urban America, migrants, African-Americans, and the poor suggests he is operating under the constraints of his current position of privilege and power. The social forum being organized for June 2010 may be a platform for grassroots organizations to hold the Obama administration to its promises and make even further demands.

At the 2009 World Social Forum in Nairobi, Kenya, a session organized by Network Institute for Global Democracy on the implications of the Obama presidency drew mixed commentary. Some were confident in his ability to support the grassroots, at least if the grassroots organized successfully. Others, especially those not from the U.S., were not optimistic at all. The latter were particularly concerned with the continuation of U.S. military expansion, a concern that has been proven well-founded. Several Latin American participants warned U.S. attendees and speakers not to relax in their political activism after Obama's victory. They referred to the example of Lula's victory of the Brazilian presidency earlier in the decade, suggesting that many who were engaged in grassroots activism and supported Lula were less engaged politically after his election. Many felt that this change permitted Lula to swing somewhat toward the right. They encouraged the U.S. political activists to stay on top of the Obama administration.

Strategically located in Detroit, the 2010 USSF is happening three years to the day from the first USSF. Reflections on the past process have altered some of the dynamics for the next USSF. Several of these changes are discussed here, including the programming format, the relationship between the national and local planning committees, and the creation of the Gender Justice Working Group (GJWG).

The programming of the USSF reflects momentum towards convergence. Rather than each organization having the opportunity to organize two or three events, each will be permitted one. This is in part due to the increase in organizations participating in the forum. Along with the urgency of the current moment, word has spread over the success of the USSF in building relations. Rather than leading their own events, organizations will be asked to converge, that is, communicate with each other prior to the USSF and join together as second and third sponsors of events.

The structure of the National Planning Committee and its relationship with the local organizing committee and various 'constituencies' has also gone through considerable review and revision. Negotiation between the NPC and the Local Organizing Committee (LOC) in Detroit is more intentional, so that the *de facto* hierarchy that occurred between the NPC and the Atlanta LOC would not repeat. The local organizing committee participates on the NPC, not relegated to the nuts and bolts of hosting a major national event, but still participating in the political decision-making process.

The Gender Justice Working Group has formed out the Women's Working Group (WWG). For the 2007 USSF, the Women, Indigenous, and Youth working groups were incorporated into the NPC decision-making structure. In the process of redeveloping the NPC structure for the 2010 USSF, these groups were defined as 'constituencies,' and would not be part of the newly formed Organizing Committee, where decisions about process were executed. Members of the WWG challenged being relegated to a 'constituency,' arguing that the process of being defined as such was not transparent or participatory, and so did not keep with social forum practice.

The WWG had raised concerns over gender representation and the inclusion of women-centered issues in the 2007 USSF. Some of the WWG leaders expressed that women—as a constructed gender category—as well as issues such as gender violence, harassment, and control over women's bodies were being neglected in the forum planning, despite the fact that the majority of NPC members represented as women.

In revisiting the organizing process, the analysis presented in the article above (written just after the 2007 USSF) now seems questionable. Although the first USSF was able to have a racially diverse conference with class diversity, it seems that gender concerns did not hold the same centrality as race and class. Why? The strange old story that gender oppression is either less economically pertinent or does need to be directly addressed continues to plague the forum process in the U.S. and around the world. While it appeared that the first USSF was able to circumvent this absence due to the makeup of its organizing body, the results were consistent with the forum process globally: feminist concerns were neglected, and events dealing with gender inequity were attended largely by women.

Around the world and in the U.S., women are poorer, work more, are paid less and own less, and subject to more violence, harassment, and neglect. Yet the global justice movement, as reflected in the social forums, has not embraced the centrality of gender in communities, families, and individuals. The marginalization of gender in the forum process also overlooks how gender subordination is a potent force of neoliberal exploitation and expansion. Without the construction of women (especially as it intersects with race and class) as a group that labors for free in a household and for less money outside of it, the momentum of corporate capital and the global assembly line could not have so quickly reached every nook and cranny of the globe. Further, the centrality of hegemonic masculinity that resides in the pursuit of power, manipulation, and deceit was clearly displayed in the downfall of the financial industries.

Although a focus on gender issues and women is being falsely relegated as a privileged liberal pursuit, a number of young activists, new to the social forum process, took charge of clarifying the importance of gender justice. In a face-to-face planning meeting for the 2010 USSF, the planning committee of the WWG directly addressed the marginalized location of the group in the NPC structure. Through fruitful debate and discussion, the group reformed itself into the Gender Justice Working Group with several positive effects. First, in bringing its case to the NPC, the GJWG emerged as a working group with a mission to assure that the forum process would be gender equitable. Much like any other working group—technology, language access, and international solidarity, defined by the work they must complete for the forum to succeed—the GJWG also has its projects to accomplish. It states that "the goal of the Gender Justice Working Group is to ensure that gender, transgender justice and LGBTQ issues are well-integrated into the planning, implementation and program of the USSF." Further:

> To have a gender analysis is to identify and understand the ways in which gender interacts and intersects with various forms of oppression, including race, class, sexual orientation, migration status, etc. and that people's experiences are defined by the intersection of these oppressions.[18]

Through its transformation, the GJWG highlighted that it does not actually represent a constituency, but challenges a system of inequity imbued in our political economy and in the social forum process as well. That gender justice was not centralized in the first USSF process suggests that it requires a concentrated effort, one that the GJWG has taken up and is organizing for the USSF in 2010.

To its credit, the NPC accepted the understanding that the GJWG introduced. This reflects the effective space for social justice organizing that the social forum provides for organizers and activists worldwide. Unlike other activist histories, the social forum is not mired in institutions, traditions, precedents, or single visions.

Alice Lovelace, lead organizer of the USSF, remarked that a wave of change and activity proceeds after a nation or region holds a social forum. There is no doubt that the U.S. is experiencing such a wave, which can drive the new political movements that we will witness in this nation. The process is alive; it can change, flow, and grow.

NOTES

1   The website HTTP://WWW.WSF2008.NET includes an interactive map of all the GDA events that occurred throughout the world.

2   Global Day of Action (press conference, Atlanta, Georgia, January 2008).

3   Denise Perry, interview with the author, January 2008.

4   Marcos Feldman. "The State of Miami's Housing Crisis: An Updated Look at Housing Affordability Problems in One of the Country's Least Affordable Housing Markets," *Research Institute on Social and Economic Policy* (November 9, 2009); HTTP://WWW.RISEP-FIU.ORG/2007/11/THE-STATE-OF-MIAMIS-HOUSING-CRISIS-AN-UPDATED-LOOK-AT-HOUSING-AFFORDABILITY-PROBLEMS-IN-ONE-OF-THE-COUNTRYS-LEAST-AFFORDABLE-HOUSING-MARKETS/.

5   Interview with Perry (2008).

6   Interview with Perry (2008).

7   Interview with Perry (2008).

8   NPC meeting following the first USSF (September 2007).

9   NPC meeting (2007).

10 NPC meeting (2007).

11 NPC meeting (2007).

12 Adbou Maliq Simone, *For the City Yet to Come* (Chapel Hill: Duke University Press, 2004).

13 Patricia Hill Collins, *Black Feminist Thought* (Sydney: Allyn and Unwin, Ltd., 1990).

14 NPC meeting at the end of the first USSF (July 2007).

15 Collins, 1990.

16 Collins, 1990.

17 Barack Obama, *Dreams from My Father: A Story of Race and Inheritance* (New York: Crown, 2007).

18 Statement (a revision of the WWG original statement for the first USSF) developed at the first face-to-face meeting of the GJWG (October 2009).

BUILDING POWER IN THE CITY:

Reflections on the Emergence of the Right to the City Alliance and the National Domestic Workers Alliance

Harmony Goldberg | **Right to the City Alliance and National Domestic Workers Alliance**[1]

In 2008, for the first time in history, more than half of the world's population will be living in urban areas.
—United Nations Population Fund Report 2007[2]

O N THE EVE OF THE transition to an urban world majority, the struggle in the cities of the United States took two important steps forward. Two national grassroots networks representing different fronts of urban struggle were launched in 2007: the Right to the City Alliance (RTTC), a national network of grassroots organizations fighting against gentrification, and the National Domestic Workers Alliance (NDWA). The formation of these networks represents the maturation of organizing that began in the era of neoliberal globalization. These networks recognize that capitalism has changed, and accordingly, social movements must also change.

Neoliberal globalization has transformed the nature of cities in the world economy. Cities in the U.S. used to serve primarily as the site for industrial production and trade. The globalization of production has meant that corporations have shut down most factories in the U.S. and moved production to the Global South in search of low wages and fewer regulations. Many of the former industrial cities in the U.S., like Detroit and Buffalo, have gone into economic decline, facing high rates of unemployment and fiscal crises. Other cities have transformed into a new kind of city: the "global city." As production has become increasingly decentralized, its management has become increasingly centralized into "global cities" which serve as 'command posts' for the corporate heads that manage the world economy. In the U.S., this includes cities like New York City, Los Angeles, Chicago, and Miami. The cities that have taken on this role are growing and gentrifying at a rapid pace. Large numbers of middle- and upper-class workers have moved into city centers to be close to their corporate jobs. The same urban core communities that were abandoned by the government in the middle of the twentieth century have now become ground zero for gentrification. Although the industrial economy has declined over the past several decades, the service industry has boomed, particularly in big cities where the elite demand labor-intensive personal services to maintain a 'world-class' lifestyle.[3]

The consequences for working-class people and people of color have been devastating. Communities of color have been torn apart by gentrification in order to make space for the new layer of corporate workers. Private developers and banks have made huge profits from land speculation. Well-paid union jobs are disappearing, weakening the labor movement, whose strongest base was the large-scale industries that have moved overseas. The only employment alternatives left to most working-class people are low-wage service jobs without stability or benefits; service industry jobs tend to be underpaid, unregulated, and stigmatized. All of these changes have hit black, Latino, and Asian working class communities the hardest.

David Harvey has pointed out that capitalism simultaneously makes profit through the exploitation of working-class people in the production process (accumulation by exploitation) and through the dispossession of peoples from their land (accumulation by dispossession).[4] We can use this framework to understand capitalism's new urban strategies. The presence of lower-wage labor in the Global South means it is no longer profitable for capitalists to exploit industrial workers in the U.S. They have, however, found new ways to profit from the exploitation of workers in the service industries. This strategy relies on ramped-up exploitation of people of color and women of color in particular; the rise of the domestic work industry is one example of this trend. Similarly, gentrification is one of the most important fronts of accumulation by dispossession in the current period. Echoing back to the original theft of land from Native American people, this new wave of gentrification and land speculation is yielding massive profits to the wealthy off the backs of poor and working-class people of color.

These political-economic processes have changed the terrain of the city, and social movements have had to change to fight on this new terrain. The past decade has seen the emergence of a range of urban struggles in communities across the country, including campaigns against gentrification and intensified policing, urban worker organizing among day laborers and domestic workers, and fights to defend and expand governmental services like welfare and public transportation. The RTTC and the NDWA represent two crucial fronts in this growing urban movement.

THE RIGHT TO THE CITY ALLIANCE

INITIATED BY THE MIAMI WORKERS Center, Strategic Action for a Just Economy, and Tenants and Workers United in 2007, the Right to the City Alliance brought together organizations from across the country that were organizing against gentrification in working-class communities of color, specifically organizations from the "global cities" in the U.S.[5] RTTC member organizations include organizations from: Boston (Alternatives for Community and Environment, City Life/Vida Urbana, Centro Presente, and the Chinese Progressive

Association); Los Angeles (Koreatown Immigrant Workers Association, Strategic Action for a Just Economy, and South Asian Network and Union de Vecinos); Miami (Miami Workers Center, Power U Center, and Vecinos Unidos-Jobs With Justice South Florida), New Orleans (Safe Streets); New York (CAAAV/Organizing Asian Communities, Community Voices Heard, FIERCE/Fabulous Independent Educated Radicals for Community Empowerment, Families United for Racial and Economic Equality, Good Old Lower East Side, Make the Road NY, Mothers on the Move, New York City AIDS Housing Network, Picture the Homeless, Teachers United, and WE ACT for Environmental Justice); Oakland (Just Cause Oakland), Providence (Direct Action for Rights and Equality and the Olneyville Neighborhood Association); San Francisco (Chinese Progressive Association, People Organized to Win Employment Rights, People Organized to Defend Environmental and Economic Rights, St. Peter's Housing Committee, and South of Market Community Action Network); and the Washington DC metropolitan area (Organizing Neighborhood Equity DC and Tenants and Workers United). RTTC also engages researchers, academics, lawyers, and allies to support the work of the base-building organizations.

These groups are not only united because of their shared struggle against gentrification; they also share a deeper vision for urban social change, that their communities have a "right to the city." The French Marxist philosopher Henri Lefebvre first developed the call for the right to the city in 1968.[6] Mirroring the call to expand the liberation project beyond the factory floor (as advanced by the students and workers who led the May 1968 uprisings in France), the "Right to the City" was a call to see the city itself as a central site of struggle. Lefebvre argued that the right to determine the future of the city does not belong to private capital or to the state; instead the right to city belongs to *all* people who live or work in the city. The "Right to the City" banner has been taken up by urban movements around the world. At the Social Forum of the Americas and the Urban Social Forum in 2004, urban movements from around the world developed a World Charter on the Right to the City, which parses this liberation vision into concrete policies that, if enacted, would increase equality, democracy, and self-determination in urban regions. Until the RTTC was founded in 2007, the call for the "Right to the City" had not gained much traction in social justice organizing inside the U.S.

At its founding conference, the RTTC built on this framework and developed principles of unity that reflected their vision for today's cities. "We all have the right to remain and return to our cities, to take back our streets and neighborhoods, and to ensure that they exist to serve people rather than capital. We all have a right to the city. We believe the right to the city is the right for all people to produce the living conditions that meet their needs."[7] Lefebvre's framework spoke to the RTTC's vision for a radical transformation of power relations in the city and for a real practice of democracy. They challenged the market-based approach to urban development, arguing instead for economic justice, environmental justice, immigrant justice, racial justice, and democracy. They do not believe that the fight for the city can be isolated from broader social dynamics. They connect the fight for the city to the struggles of rural people and indigenous people against environmental degradation and economic pressures, and they believe that the struggle for cities in the U.S. is connected to international struggles.

In order to achieve their vision for a city based on the needs and the dreams of their communities, the RTTC believes that the movement against gentrification must go beyond housing. Gentrification transforms much more than just housing; it also reshapes public space, undermines locally-owned businesses, and increases repressive policing. The

Right to the City network includes many organizations like Just Cause Oakland, St. Peter's Housing Committee, and the Miami Workers Center, whose primary work is to defend public housing and low-income renters and homeowners, yet none of these organizations organize narrowly on housing issues. They also incorporate work to preserve and expand community-based businesses and cultural institutions that are crucial to the survival of their communities. Organizations like FIERCE and Picture the Homeless in New York City organize to defend community access to public space, while groups like Safe Streets in New Orleans work against the role that repressive policing plays in gentrifying communities. This movement-building approach shuns narrow definitions of gentrification; instead, they want to foster a resistance that is as complex and wide-ranging as the process of gentrification itself. In fact, over time, the Alliance's self-conception has explicitly grown from an "anti-gentrification" framework to a more expansive "urban justice" frame.

Although the day-to-day organizing work of RTTC organizations continues to focus on local campaigns, the RTTC has provided a national space where grassroots organizations can reflect on their organizing practices, the conditions in their cities, and national patterns (e.g. mapping the projects of national real estate development corporations, whose luxury residential and corporate office development projects have often been the driving force in gentrification in many cities around the world). National conventions have served as sites where groups develop relationships and common analysis. Several workgroups have started to connect organizers working on different fronts of the anti-gentrification struggle: tenant organizing, organizing public housing residents, civic participation, and New Orleans solidarity work. These groups organize regular conference calls to reflect on their local work and to strategize towards shared work.

In its first years, the Alliance focused on relationship-building and analysis development to lay the groundwork for powerful joint organizing and building the capacity of the network. In 2008, the RTTC held its first national actions, as member organizations convened in Miami during the U.S. Conference of Mayors, marching in protest against most mayors' corporate-driven urban policies and holding a shadow "Urban Strategies" conference to develop an alternative vision for urban development. The national alliance also organized commemorations of the Katrina tragedy in cities across the country in 2008, drawing connections between the devastation of New Orleans and the conditions in their communities. In 2009, the RTTC initiated its first national campaign to track the racial and economic justice implications of the federal stimulus program, demanding a "People's Recovery" instead of corporate bail-outs.

NATIONAL DOMESTIC WORKERS ALLIANCE

DOMESTIC WORK IS DEEPLY CONNECTED with the legacy of slavery in this country. Today, the industry remains racially stigmatized and treated as low-value, unskilled 'women's work.' According to Antonia Peña, a domestic worker and a member of CASA de Maryland, "Society does not look at our work as important, but we know how important our work is. We take care of children from early in the morning to late at night. We clean houses from top to bottom. This is hard work, and it takes real skill." Domestic workers are excluded from federal labor protections like the National Labor Relations Act and the Fair Labor Standards Act. This leaves many workers vulnerable to intense exploitation and mistreatment. "Many of us face extreme abuse in the workplace, and it annihilates our souls. Then employers tell us to be grateful for the little that they give us," says Peña.

Most domestic workers have to work long hours for pay below minimum wage, with no overtime, sick leave, or health insurance.

The recent upsurge in the domestic work industry is intertwined with global political-economic dynamics. As global inequality increases, many people are forced to leave their home countries in search of work. Once they arrive here, most of these migrants are tracked into low-wage service jobs, and many female migrants find that domestic work is the only work available to them. According to Antonia Peña, "It's not workers' fault that we were born to poor families in a poor country. For many of us, domestic work was our only option. Now we do this work for some of the richest people in society."

In response to the resurgence of the domestic work industry, a wave of domestic worker organizing has taken root in cities across the country over the past ten years. Building on this groundswell, domestic worker organizations from around the country came together at the first U.S. Social Forum in June of 2007 to found the National Domestic Workers Alliance. The alliance includes organizations from: New York City (including Domestic Workers United, Haitian Women for Haitian Refugees, Damayan, Andolan, CAAAV/ Organizing Asian Communities, the Unity Housecleaners of the Workplace Project, and Las Señoras de Santa Maria); Maryland (CASA de Maryland); San Francisco (including Mujeres Unidas y Activas, People Organized to Win Employment Right's Women Workers Project, and the Women's Collective of the Day Labor Program at La Raza Centro Legal); and Los Angeles (including the Filipino Workers' Center and Coalition for Humane Immigrant Rights of Los Angeles).

While the underlying political vision of the NDWA is not as explicitly articulated as that of the Right to the City Alliance, the organizations share a deep level of political unity, which Ai-jen Poo of Domestic Workers United in New York City described as "working class feminism." This feminism differs from narrow conceptions of women's issues, as defined during the second wave of feminism in the 1960s and 1970s, which mostly reflected the needs and interests of white middle-class women. Instead, working-class feminism incorporates issues of race, class, and nationality, reflecting the needs and interests of working-class immigrant women of color. Instead of working towards women's integration into the U.S. power structure, the Alliance envisions the transformation of power relations on a global scale. Political education and dialogue are weaved into all of their meetings and gatherings, a priority that endures even with the immense demands of organizing. During each of their congresses, workers and allies have led trainings and dialogues on many topics, which have laid a solid foundation of deeper political unity. The Alliance's political vision is also reflected in its willingness to both engage with and challenge the many movements with which its work intersects, including the women's movement, the labor movement, and the racial justice movement. Rather than dismiss the labor movement for its historic marginalization of women workers and workers of color, or denounce the middle-class women's movement because the entry of middle-class women into the professional workforce has often been accomplished on the backs of domestic workers, the organizations in the NDWA have chosen critical engagement with these movements. As a result, they have gained much-needed political support, and they have also helped those movements to develop a more integrative political vision.

The member organizations of the NDWA have many different approaches to organizing. "We've really tried to build an organizational culture that makes room for people who come to the work in different ways. Some groups are building worker cooperatives; others are using a mutual aid approach. There are groups that have a more traditional base-building approach, and there are other organizations that are primarily focused on the international connections," says Ai-jen Poo. "All of these approaches are important in this period. The movement will be stronger if each approach can grow and evolve. It's important to have a space where we can all work together and build long-term relationships." In that spirit, the NDWA started by focusing on relationship-building between its member organizations, including joint political education to develop shared analysis and "organizing exchanges" to give member organizations the space to learn from each other's models.

Since its founding three years ago, the Alliance has initiated several exciting campaigns. In California and New York, NDWA member organizations are pushing their state legislatures to adopt a "Domestic Workers Bill of Rights," which would provide basic worker protections and benefits to domestic workers. These locally-based protections would provide precedents for similar legislation on a federal level. Nationally, NDWA is working to pressure the U.S. Department of Labor to address the exclusion of domestic workers from more federal labor legislation. They are demanding regulation reform in the industry as well as the creation of a Domestic Work Bureau, which would provide domestic workers with a mechanism through which to bring complaints against their employers. On an international level, the NDWA is also working with domestic workers organizations around the world to pressure the International Labor Organization to set a high bar for standards and protections for domestic workers. The ability of the NDWA to grow from its grassroots founding in 2007 to simultaneous work on all these levels demonstrates the vibrancy and dynamism of a growing movement.

BELIEFS UNDERLYING THE WORK

ALTHOUGH THE RIGHT TO THE CITY Alliance and the National Domestic Workers Alliance focus on different fronts of the struggle, both networks are responding to the ways in which working-class people and people of color are being exploited in cities in the neoliberal era. Their purpose is to build the power of the communities who have historically been marginalized by both mainstream society *and* by the Left. The two networks are built on similar underlying political assumptions:

- **The fight is fundamentally a struggle against neoliberal globalization.**
  "The daily issues in our communities—like the experiences of low-wage service workers, or people getting displaced from their homes through gentrification—are expressions of national and international trends, specifically, how neoliberalism has transformed our cities. That's why our local organizations have formed alliances that are national in scale with international analysis," says Rickke Mananzala, Director of FIERCE in New York City and a member of the RTTC Steering Committee. These organizations believe that they need an international analysis in order to do effective local and national organizing, and they believe that their organizing offers important new insights into analyses of global political-economic dynamics. According to Ai-jen Poo, "The people who are at the frontlines of the impact of neoliberalism—sectors like migrant workers, domestic workers, the people who are being displaced from urban centers, unemployed workers in the rust belt—these are the people who really understand neoliberalism. Because of their experiences, they have a lot to say about what kind of movement we need to build." At their founding meetings, both networks incorporated explicit conversations about the way that neoliberalism has shaped the terrain of their work: creating conditions that have led to an upsurge in international migration, driving deindustrialization

and the rise of the gendered and racialized low-wage service economy, and reshaping cities to meet the needs of global capital.

- **The struggle cannot be confined to one system of oppression.** Working-class communities and communities of color face class exploitation, racial and gender oppression, xenophobia, and homophobia; all of these issues have to be addressed in the work. This "intersectional" approach—first developed by women of color feminists—clarifies the intersections between different systems of oppression (e.g. the ways in which gender and racial oppression have played a central role in the capitalist project).[8] This illustrates the need for a more complex understanding of the dynamics of class. The NDWA does not organize narrowly around 'worker' issues; the life experiences of their members make it absolutely clear that, if dynamics of race, gender, and immigration status are ignored in the name of a narrow class analysis, their workplace issues cannot actually be addressed. Similarly, the RTTC has moved beyond a narrow "housing" approach to a broader fight for urban justice, understanding that racist policing practices, the privatization of historic LGBT public spaces, and immigration raids also play central roles in the process of gentrification.

- **The city is a key site for the struggle.** Cities have traditionally been crucial spaces for progressive organizing, and that dynamic is no different in these times. Cities play a central role in the contemporary global economy, housing the majority of the world's people and serving as key nodes for transnational management, consumption, and communication. The particular way that globalization is reshaping cities has opened up new fronts of struggle for working-class communities and communities of color. René Poitevin, a professor at New York University who is affiliated with the RTTC, said, "In the twenty-first century, the city will play the role that the factory did in the twentieth century; it will be the main site for capitalist accumulation, and therefore the main site for class struggle. Figuring out how to build the revolution from the city is the main theoretical and political challenge for our generation today."

  In the wake of the economic crisis, the struggle over conditions in urban areas has intensified. Massive disinvestment in urban regions and increased unemployment has augmented the survival struggles of oppressed communities, while the crisis has also checked the growth of corporate gentrification. This presents unique challenges and opportunities for urban organizers. For example, RTTC organizations in New York City recently launched a campaign to convert private condominiums (now sitting empty in the wake of the economic crisis) into housing for low-income people. Because public subsidies were used to construct these developments, RTTC-NYC argues that these empty buildings should be turned over to meet the needs of working-class urban residents. This demand reflects both a response to the daily needs of their constituents, and, in challenging the supremacy of private property rights over community needs, the deeper transformative vision of the "right to the city."

- **"Organizing oppressed people is the heart and soul of the movement,"** says Ai-jen Poo. "Building lasting institutions in working class communities and communities of color is the most important work that the Left can do; these organizations are the building blocks of a stronger movement." After decades of both a decline in the labor movement and the growth of an organized movement on the Right, these organizations are working to re-build the organized power of the people who are on the front lines of neoliberalism. This is based on the belief that oppressed people have the most interest in changing the system and, if organized, the most power to actually win change. These organizations' commitment to the methodology of grassroots organizing is also based on a commitment to the self-determination of oppressed people. It is in the *method* of their work—building the collective power and leadership of working-class people and people of color to win real changes in the daily lives of their communities—that the RTTC and the NDWA are different from many other Left organizations.

- **We need to combine grassroots organizing with a deep political analysis.** Just as the methodology of these two networks differs from much of the Left, it also differs from traditional community organizing models. Challenging the non-ideological and anti-Left approach of traditional community organizing practices based on the Alinsky model, these organizations incorporate intensive political education with their members and leaders.[9] At the founding meeting of the NDWA, the San Francisco-based Day Labor Program's Women's Collective led a workshop connecting the contemporary domestic work industry with the legacy of slavery, while Domestic Workers United led a workshop on the rise of the domestic work industry under neoliberal globalization. At the U.S. Social Forum, the RTTC held a series of workshops to provoke dialogue on the "Right to the City" framework in a variety of contexts, including gentrification in global cities, urban struggles in the Philippines and South Africa, and race, gender, and nationality. By promoting internationalist analyses and engaging in regular strategic dialogues, these networks break open political spaces that are often closed in the mainstream organizing world.

REFLECTING ON THE SUCCESSES AND THE CHALLENGES

DESPITE THEIR RELATIVELY SHORT EXISTENCE, these two networks of grassroots organizations have been able to make several advances. Perhaps most significantly, they have been able to raise the possibility of building a Left that is deeply rooted in oppressed communities. For the past several decades in the U.S., the Left has overwhelmingly been composed of middle-class activists, many of whom are also privileged along axes of power like race and gender. Without dismissing the important role that middle-class radicals and white activists can play in the Left and in social movements, the Right to the City Alliance and the National Domestic Workers Alliance offer a reminder of a basic principle: that oppressed people have to be the ones to lead the struggle for liberation. This is more than an abstract moral issue or an outdated political idea; it is a real political possibility that challenges the white middle-class Left to consider the strategic implications of its social base and tactical orientation. Assertions like "We are all oppressed by capitalism" or "It's not just about class (or race)" may contain some kernels of truth, but they also radically oversimplify social relations and political strategy. A Left that is committed to democracy and self-determination has to consider the intense level of racial, national, and gender stratification that exists within the broad cross-section of people who are oppressed by capitalism. A Left that is serious about transforming structures of power has to engage with the challenges presented by these emergent grassroots developments.

As essential as this work is, it is not without its difficulties. Any organizer working in a time of relatively low social struggle faces an uphill battle. Many contradictions have emerged in the work of these networks and their member organizations. Rather than defaulting to easy answers, organizers have attempted to struggle through and approach these complications in a balanced and productive way. What follows are some of the most prominent challenges.

Navigating the Non-Profit System

Building member-led organizations of working class people of color to fight for substantive change is incredibly labor-intensive. The day-to-day demands of base-building, leadership development, and campaigns are intense, and many of these organizations have chosen to work in the non-profit system in order to raise the funds necessary to enable people to do this work full-time. This approach presents a host of problems that have been well-explored in INCITE! Women of Color Against Violence's book, *The Revolution Will Not Be Funded*.[10] They raise several relevant issues: full-time organizing can privilege the skills and capacities most often held by middle-class people, pushing organizations to hire people outside of their base; hiring full-time organizers can mean that staff members have a higher level of investment and leadership in an organization than the members themselves; the intensive work it takes to build a non-profit can promote an organization-building or "empire-building" mentality rather than a movement-building approach; and foundations can put the brakes on radical politics and limit how far organizations are willing to push the political envelope. The organizations in the RTTC and the NDWA acknowledge these realities, but for the most part, they still choose non-profit organizational forms to invest more time in the work of building working-class power.

However, organizations in both alliances are intentionally working to address these contradictions and explore alternative models. The political clarity of these alliances demonstrates that they are not limiting their politics out of fear of losing funding. They also challenge narrow approaches to organization-building by prioritizing movement building. Rickke Mananzala reflects on this dynamic, saying, "We have to avoid the trap of getting stuck in building our separate organizations. We definitely need strong organizations to serve as effective anchors for the movement, but we need to do our organization-building in the service of movement building. We see the Right to the City Alliance and the National Domestic Workers Alliance as vehicles for the broader social movement." In addition to building these networks, both alliances invest significant amounts of time in other movement-building initiatives (i.e. the U.S. Social Forum), even when these efforts do not directly benefit the organizations themselves.

Leadership Development

These organizations also work to develop the individual leadership capacity of their member-leaders, preparing them to take on organizing positions as staff. According to Rickke Mananzala, "Developing leadership from within our communities is ultimately the key to building the power that we need." Almost all of the organizations engaged in these networks integrate intensive political education and skills training into their work. In this way, they differ from mainstream community organizing, which tends to focus on developing the practical leadership skills of grassroots leaders. These organizations are not just developing leaders to direct successful reform fights; they are also working to develop working-class organizers who will be able to provide leadership to the Left and to broader social movements.

Many of these organizations also develop collective member leadership bodies to counter the tendency toward staff leadership and control. In describing the success of Domestic Workers United in building its member leadership, Ai-jen Poo says, "We are working to be an organization that is member-driven and truly led by worker leaders. We have built a solid steering committee of domestic workers who provide overall strategic direction for the organization and who coordinate work with other members."

In so doing, organizations have had to confront several hurdles. The leadership development process has to support people in overcoming the social stigmatization they face on a daily basis. Antonia Peña describes this process clearly:

> We face many challenges in our organizing. At first, many domestic workers are scared to fight back. Others are ashamed to stand up and say publicly that they are domestic workers, because society puts such a low value on our work. But we help workers to understand that they do have power. Many people who have been abused or exploited at work have been able to face their employers and say, 'No more!' Their self esteem grows as they challenge their employers, and that is so important.

Member-leaders also face practical challenges, since they often juggle many stresses and responsibilities in their lives. Ai-jen Poo discussed this challenge, saying, "We've made progress, but there's still work to be done. There are particular leadership challenges facing low-wage workers who work long hours. We need to acknowledge those challenges and develop a stronger infrastructure to help us advance members to fully lead the work."

Fighting for Reforms

Although the national campaigns of the RTTC and the NDWA are still too new to have won significant victories, their member organizations have succeeded at local levels. These organizations have pushed back attacks on their communities and succeeded in improving the daily lives of their members by winning affordable housing provisions, gaining remuneration for domestic workers who have been underpaid and abused, stopping the demolition of public housing, and maintaining access to public space. Because these victories are clearly "reforms," radical activists might criticize these organizations for promoting faith in the current system or undermining the possibilities for more revolutionary transformation. But these organizations make a distinction between "fighting for reforms" and "reformism," that is, the belief that reforms can meet the fundamental needs of oppressed people. The fight for reforms can have a role in longer-term struggle, as part of a pedagogical process that can reveal the composition of the power structure and clarify the power that working-class people have to challenge that structure. By combining reform fights with agitation and radical political education, these organizations are working to prevent reform fights from falling into reformism. Instead, organizations use these methods to build their power and capacity to fight, providing concrete mechanisms to build larger bases that can attain the scale necessary to significantly impact the power structure. They strive to grow the constituent base of their member organizations, to increase the intensity and impact of their organizational activities, and to learn to function at local, regional, national, and international levels. According to Rickke Mananzala,

> We don't have the luxury to sit back and stay small. It would take thousands of people to win just the basic reform battles that we need in this country. If our longer-term vision is to reorganize power so that our communities have the right to decide how our cities will operate, we're going to need hundreds of thousands of people to be engaged in the movement. We have no choice but to build our work up to scale. It's going to take a lot of hard work to get out into the public housing projects, into the restaurant kitchens and the parks, to organize the

people who are being hurt by neoliberalism and to get them out into the streets. But that kind of hard work is our responsibility, if we're serious about winning change for our communities.

Building Unity Across Differences

The RTTC and the NDWA are made up of a range of political beliefs and different organizational models—a potentially challenging dynamic, given the tendency in social movements and in the Left for differences to become divisions. Explicit ideological engagement and friendly struggle over differences have often devolved into unproductive organizational splits, debates over long-past historical conflicts, and theoretical hair-splitting. These networks have attempted to handle political and methodological differences differently. Because they are grounded in practical work on concrete issues impacting oppressed communities, political differences can be handled in the context of unity-building, rather than division-making. The concrete work provides a container to hold the differences between Marxists, anarchists, autonomists, nationalists, and a range of other social justice activists. Organizations with different methods of work—workers' cooperatives, traditional base-building organizations, service providers— have a shared interest in winning real changes in the lives of working-class communities and communities of color. According to Rickke Mananzala,

> We need to stop pitting the strategies of 'building alternatives' and 'fighting for reforms' against each other. We need to build alternatives *and* we need to directly challenge the system. It should be both-and, not either-or. Our communities need us to challenge the system through reform fights, whether it's organizing LGBT youth to fight police brutality or fighting to defend public housing. But we also need to build alternative institutions, and we need them on a much larger scale. The Black Panther Party's free breakfast programs weren't just in one community; they were in communities all around the country. We need to be building *all* of our work to that level."

In their external movement relationships, both alliances have experienced an outpouring of support from many areas of the Left, including direct action movements, mainstream labor movements, progressive academics, and radical cultural workers. These experiences demonstrate the possibility of building a more unified Left that could help galvanize a stronger social movement in this period of low social struggle. The fact that these alliances have brought a range of social forces together across historically divisive lines of political difference suggests that Left unity can be built most effectively when it is based in the struggle of working-class communities and communities of color.

MOVING FORWARD

THE WORK OF THE RIGHT to the City Alliance and the National Domestic Workers Alliance demonstrate the power of grounding Left analysis in the practical work of organizing working-class communities and communities of color. These networks reflect a growing tide of resistance against the impact of neoliberalism on urban communities in the U.S. They also represent a more general trend towards the increasing consolidation and strategic clarity of grassroots movements inside the U.S. Other national networks and organizations, including Grassroots Global Justice, the National Day Laborers Organizing Network, the Poor Peoples' Economic Human Right Campaign, Restaurant Organizing Center United, and the Taxi Workers Alliance, have also emerged to consolidate power and analyses in different sectors of working-class communities and communities of color in cities around the country. In 2009, the Right to the City Alliance and the National Domestic Workers Alliance came together with Grassroots Global Justice, Jobs with Justice, the National Day Laborers Organizing Network, and the Pushback Network to build the "Inter-Alliance Dialogue," a space for dialogue and joint work between these national networks that are rooted in different working-class communities of color around the country. As these grassroots networks continue to grow, they may provide a solid foundation for the growth of more powerful and popular social movements and for the regeneration of a strategic Left that is grounded in mass struggle.

NOTES

1   Research for this article included many personal conversations and interviews between the author and organizers working on the ground, including Rickke Mananzala of FIERCE, Ai-jen Poo of Domestic Workers United, Antonia Peña of CASA de Maryland, and René Poitevin, affiliated with the Right to the City Alliance. All of their direct quotations here are taken from these conversations.

2   United Nations Population Fund, "State of the World Population 2007: Unleashing the Potential of Urban Growth," HTTP://WWW.UNFPA.ORG/SWP/2007/ENGLISH/INTRODUCTION.HTML.

3   Saskia Sassen, *The Global City: New York, London, Tokyo* (Princeton: Princeton University Press, 1991).

4   David Harvey, *The New Imperialism* (New York: Oxford University Press, 2003).

5   While the Right to the City Alliance is primarily based in the growing "global cities," other social justice networks, like the Poverty Scholars, are based in the declining former industrial cities. While there are clearly important connections between these two fronts of urban struggle, the unity between them has not yet manifested in an organizational form. This may be an important area of growth over the next several years.

6   Henri Lefebvre, "The Right to the City," in *Writings on Cities by Henri Lefebvre*, Eleonore Kofman and Elizabeth Lebas, eds. (Cambridge: Blackwell Publishing, 1996).

7   These statements are from the Right to the City Alliance 2007 founding points of unity.

8   One of the first groups to articulate this approach was the Combahee River Collective, who throughout the 1970s developed a statement that has since gained national and international recognition. The full text of the Combahee River Collective Statement can be found in *Home Girls: A Black Feminist Anthology*, Barbara Smith, ed. (New York: Kitchen Table Women of Color Press), 1983.

9   Named after Saul Alinsky, this model of community organizing was developed in the 1940s and gained national prominence during the Civil Rights struggles of the 1960s and 1970s. The model uses 'relational meetings,' or one-on-ones, to identify people's motivations and values, with the intent of eventual agitation and mobilization around common self-interest to achieve concrete reforms.

10 INCITE! Women of Color Against Violence, *The Revolution Will Not Be Funded: Beyond the Non-Profit Industrial Complex* (Cambridge: South End Press, 2007).

MOVEMENT STRATEGIES

SECTION SUMMARY

As we move from locally-based organizations to regional and national formations in the previous section, we see how specific and separate struggles uncovered complex relationships between local struggles, regional contexts, and planetary configurations of neoliberal capital. By exploring a selection of current movements in the abstract—how they move, where they meet, where they are located, and what strategies they use—we find areas of resonance among whirlwinds that can assist us in our organizing endeavors.

The points of contact among movements in this section are not easily discernible; in some cases, these points don't exist at all. This is due to the multiplicity of forms struggle has taken in the current period, and we would be remiss to impose artificial links between them in the hope that such struggles can effortlessly translate. Rather, we wish to inquire into the composition of movements, as we contextualize, amplify, and describe them *as they are*, not how they should be. What results is a partial map, as these movement strategies provide lessons without trying to copy their respective landscapes.

Alter-globalization strategies peaked at the turn of the century before giving way to a period of decomposition; they are now undergoing significant shifts, as the climate justice and food sovereignty movements have connected planetary struggles to local contexts. The now-defunct organization Mobilization for Global Justice was at the forefront of such strategies, particularly in its later years when it sought to create linkages between planetary neoliberal phenomena and gentrification processes taking place in Washington, DC.

Looking across the social field, we find another key area for political recomposition and strategic thinking over the past decade, situated in movements around harm reduction, prison abolition, and restorative justice. These relatively new formulations draw from deeper movement histories that engage with harm and healing, but they also intersect with a myriad of projects and areas of life.

Radical queer organizing has also been resurgent as activists reorient around powerful intersections with struggles concerning gentrification, public space, policing and prison, sex work, and immigration. This organizing draws from community-based initiatives as well as creative action infused with play. Here we see attempts to revolt against the imposition of gender binaries and heteronormativity, while simultaneously connecting queerness with the multifaceted and diverse lives, bodies, and affects of queers themselves.

Concluding this section are chapters on radical art, autonomous media, and mapping. Radical artists have sought to engage their environs, create new social relationships, and challenge power dynamics with creative and communicative responses that build movements by moving minds and bodies. Independent and autonomous media have decomposed as radical approaches have been increasingly infused into capitalist practices, but autonomous media forms have continually composed, even through intense corporate efforts to co-opt them, to circulate struggles and provide important encounters. We've also seen the rise of radical mapping projects that research and inquire into radical movements and their locales. *Uses of a Whirlwind* echoes this development, partially mapping current struggles so that they can be "read" and used.

"Local Struggles, Global Contexts: Building Movements in North America in the Age of Globalized Capital" summarizes Basav Sen's reflections on the alter-globalization cycle of struggle and the unsustainability of mass mobilization movements without strong local bases. Sen discusses attempts to clearly attack local manifestations of neoliberalism in cooperation with grassroots community organizing groups. He calls for continued movement building with an international perspective that seriously engages community struggles in the United States.

Rural America has long been a site of rich organizing campaigns as well as violent repression and decomposition; these struggles flow into national and international food systems. John Peck of the Family Farm Defenders argues for food sovereignty—not just food security—in his chapter, **"You Are What You Eat: The Food Sovereignty Struggle within the Global Justice Movement."** Peck illustrates linkages between global justice movements and national developments in the era of globalized food systems, pointing to areas of organizing and movement expansion.

As the planet's climate changes, so turn the American weather systems, in the form of desertification in the Southwest or massive flooding in the Gulf Coast. Brian Tokar explores the rise of the global climate justice movement in **"Toward a Movement for Climate Justice."** Tokar explores both statist and radical approaches to a problem that disproportionately impacts the world's poor and the Global South, noting that the recent failure of the Copenhagen U.N. Summit indicates the need for a climate justice movement that challenges both capital and the state apparatus.

Stevie Peace looks critically at the political terrain of harm in **"The Desire to Heal: Harm Intervention in a Landscape of Restorative Justice and Critical Resistance,"** currently dominated by the prison industrial complex, yet also a landscape of developing forms of harm engagement in struggle. He brings the harm intervention projects Restorative Justice Community Action and Critical Resistance into encounter, exposing their potentials as well as dangers, such as the non-profit industry and academia. He suggests that the memory of harm and trauma may lead to emergent "desires to heal."

In **"DIY Politics and Queer Activism,"** Ben Shepard contrasts the queer organizing of groups like Radical Homosexual Agenda and the Sylvia Rivera Law Project with the assimilationist work of Human Rights Campaign. Shepard emphasizes the passion and creativity of DIY approaches to radical community building and resistance. He sees the creation and development of queer commons, harm reduction, direct action, and zines as important counters to the limits and dangers of assimilationist approaches to organizing.

In **"Art as Intervention: A Guide to Today's Radical Art Practices,"** Julie Perini begins to map current radical and interventionist art practices as a way of building new social relations. Advocates for social change such as The Yes Men flow into interventionist practices like Critical Art Ensemble, connecting further with projects that specifically coordinate resources and dialog. The democratization of radical art practices demonstrates that new social relations and organizing approaches are possible.

The launch of the Independent Media Center in 1999 at the WTO protests in Seattle shook up the media world. Dorothy Kidd assesses the developments and challenges since this eruption in **"Whistling into the Typhoon: A Radical Inquiry into Autonomous Media,"** where she explores autonomous forms of media, efforts at corporate co-optation thereof, and continued efforts by activists for self-determined media that function for the purpose of social justice.

In **"Getting to Know Your City and the Social Movements That Call it Home: The Hybrid Networking and Documentary Work of AREA Chicago,"** Daniel Tucker discusses the development of AREA Chicago, a publication that examines social relations and struggles using a strategy of locally grounded analysis. AREA seeks to understand capital's manifestations and developments in order to clarify how a community responses to this imposition. Tucker calls for local re-engagement in radical organizing and community building.

The more we understand movement strategies on the social field, the more codes, lessons, and motivations we can use in our own locales to create movements and winds. In the next section, we explore the points where winds meet, intersect, and strengthen into whirlwinds, transcending metaphor and moving into political concepts and theories.

LOCAL STRUGGLES, GLOBAL CONTEXTS:
Building Movements in North America in the Age of Globalized Capital

Basav Sen

A GOVERNMENT SUBVERTS DEMOCRACY BY HANDING out large portions of a public school system to private operators. Another government joins forces with big corporations to evict low-income farmers from their land to make way for mining and manufacturing operations. An international agency compels a government to privatize water delivery in major cities, benefiting a major multinational corporation. Large financial institutions speculate recklessly to make astronomical sums of money, and when their bets go bad, governments of wealthy countries (or international institutions that they control) step in to rescue them, using taxpayer funds—without imposing adequate safeguards and controls to make such bailouts unnecessary in the future, but sometimes with onerous conditions imposed on citizens.

What is striking about each of these stories is that they have repeated themselves in different cities, countries, and continents. The first story is true of Washington, DC. It is also true of New Orleans and Dayton, Ohio. The second story is true of India. It is also true of Guatemala and Honduras. The third story could be set in Ghana, Tanzania, Bolivia, Argentina, or the Philippines. Minus the role of the international agency, it could have been New Orleans, Atlanta, or Stockton, California.[1] The last story could, with some differences in detail, refer to the International Monetary Fund bailout of Wall Street banks in 1997–1998 for irresponsible lending in South Korea, Thailand, Indonesia, and elsewhere, or to the bailout of some of these same banks by the governments of the U.S., U.K., and other wealthy countries today.

Why is it that disparate groups of people on different continents are facing similar assaults on their homes, their services, and their livelihoods at the same moment in history? Why is there so much in common between which groups of people are especially targeted as victims of this assault, and what types of entities shape this process and benefit from it? The answer can be found in the rise of "neoliberalism," a hegemonic ideology that informs policy and politics at all levels from the local to the international, in almost every corner of the globe.

Neoliberalism is a belief in the supremacy of private capital, and the private profit motive, over all else. Capital and its priorities take precedence over human needs, over collective aspirations of peoples, over any value system that values anything for any reason other than its potential to generate a profit. Ultimately, neoliberalism is the political ideology of the anti-political, which seeks to depoliticize public spaces and public discourse by claiming, first, that it is not an ideology, and that decisions flowing from it are driven instead by rational choice, and second, that choices dictated by neoliberalism are the only possible rational ones. Margaret Thatcher summed this up in her famous statement: "there is no alternative," to unrestrained free-market capitalism.

In cities across North America, public school systems are being systematically replaced with privately operated (sometimes for-profit) charter schools, unaccountable to the public but nevertheless subsidized with public funds. This process is fundamentally the same as the privatization of water, electricity, and other public utilities across the Global South at the behest of the World Bank and its regional counterparts. In neoliberal ideology, public infrastructure created with public resources is treated as another frontier to extend the reach of the market.

Most major North American cities are being 'redeveloped' for the benefit of the real estate industry and the wealthy elites who work for global capital, displacing long-term low-income residents in a process commonly called "gentrification." Fundamentally, this is the same process by which low-income peasants and fishing communities are displaced across much of the Global South to make way for mining, manufacturing, dams, tourism, and other infrastructure for the benefit of private capital and the wealthy. In both instances, resources are viewed as existing for the benefit of capital, while people who depend on these resources for their livelihood are viewed as expendable. More striking, the people affected in both instances have more in common besides the fact that they are both low income; they are also predominantly people of color. This is not accidental; rather, it stems from racialized global inequalities of wealth and power, a colonial legacy that has been termed "global apartheid," which is a very useful framework to view the commonalities of both neoliberalism and its consequences in the South and the North.

Beneficiaries of neoliberalism also have much in common in the North and South. Capital is globalized and consolidated to the extent that, in most industries, the dominant players are a relatively small number of multinational corporations. Real estate, retail, and hotel corporations benefiting from gentrification of U.S. cities are multinationals, often with interests in the Global South. Private corporations taking over water systems throughout the Global South are also attempting to take over water utilities in the United States. Major U.S. banks embroiled in the mortgage lending crisis are multinationals, holders of the sovereign debt of countries in the Global South. Many of these banks have been involved in previous global financial crises, such as those in East and Southeast Asia in 1998 and Argentina in 2001.

MOVEMENTS AND SOLIDARITY: POTENTIALS AND PITFALLS

THE POTENTIAL FOR BUILDING A cross-border, cross-issue, global solidarity movement against capital is immense. To a large extent, such a movement is already taking shape, with the gathering of worldwide movements at the World Social Forum being just one example. Yet aside from some inspiring exceptions, social movements in the U.S. are isolated from global movements. Conversely, in the U.S and other Northern countries, there are organizations and movements acting in solidarity with people's struggles worldwide, such as the Latin America solidarity movement or the small, relatively new (in the U.S. context) 'global justice' movement, which fights against global financial institutions and trade agreements. However, these movements are often isolated from any real grassroots community base.

While this is a weakness, U.S. movements do not lack the vision or capacity for forming local-global connections. As an organizer who has attempted to build such connections, this author recognizes good reasons why such connections are very hard to build and sustain in meaningful ways beyond mere gestures of verbal solidarity. Further, for reasons too complex to analyze here, the U.S. is a particularly difficult terrain on which to build social movements in general. When it comes to building a local struggle in the U.S. that is truly aware of its global context, or a global solidarity struggle that genuinely connects with local struggles, the difficulties are compounded.

International solidarity activists in the U.S often come from relatively privileged backgrounds. Simply put, with some exceptions, one needs to be fairly privileged to have the luxury to focus activist energies entirely on solidarity with a population halfway across the world, rather than the survival of one's own community.[2] This is not intended as a criticism—given the aggression of U.S. military and economic policy, the world needs a U.S.-based global solidarity movement to resist this foreign policy in its home country. U.S.-based solidarity movements have been important in global struggles, such as the struggle to dismantle apartheid in South Africa. But a privileged background can sometimes act as an impediment, keeping global solidarity activists from seeing the impact of neoliberalism in their own backyard.

Even when solidarity activists can theoretically grasp the impacts of neoliberalism in the U.S., translating this understanding into concrete action entails overcoming another layer of difficulty. Sometimes, the institutions one confronts in one's global work have neither direct impacts on the local community nor local counterparts. Nevertheless, creative and meaningful ways can be found to integrate global work with local solidarity.

Conversely, local struggles for housing, health care, education, and low-income workers' rights in the U.S. do not have the easiest time contextualizing their work globally. The analysis of the assault on low-income and working people in the U.S as a product of neoliberalism, fundamentally connected to similar phenomena elsewhere, is relatively new and not widespread. However, as is illustrated here, the integration of locally-based U.S. struggles with the global context has also found considerable success.

THE IMMIGRANTS' RIGHTS STRUGGLE AS A GLOBAL CROSSROADS

A KEY STRUGGLE IN THE U.S. today—in terms of the urgency of action, the viciousness of the right-wing backlash against it, the popularity and level of participation, and most of all, the maturity and depth of analysis informing the movement—is the immigrants' rights struggle. A movement that unapologetically demands full human rights for all immigrants regardless of their documentation status has been forming and growing for years, but it burst onto the national scene with unprecedented strength from March through May of 2006, capturing the public imagination.

The immigrants' rights movement is by its very nature international. Undocumented immigrants are a population of international origin who have experienced the ravages of neoliberalism in their home countries in the Global South, which usually compelled them to migrate in the first place. In the words of Maria Elena Letona, former director of Centro Presente, an organization of the Latino immigrant community in Massachusetts fighting for the rights of the community as immigrants and as workers, "Migration flows in the 21st century [are] a direct result of corporate globalization."[3] She points out that the displacement of people in the Global South because of neoliberal policies has been "quite radical"; for example, in Mexico, about two million small farmers have been displaced. In the U.S., immigrants face the impacts of neoliberalism as exploited workers living in low-income communities. Often the corporations exploiting their labor are the very same multinational corporations who are pillaging the Global South. Finally, immigrants in the U.S. "are still very connected to their families, communities and native countries," as Letona puts it. Thus the immigrant's experience inevitably creates an internationalist perspective.

An example of internationalism in the U.S. immigrants' rights movement is Centro Presente's work as a founding member of two national networks, the Salvadoran-American Network and the National Alliance of Latin American and Caribbean Communities (NALACC). These networks have organized delegations to El Salvador, Guatemala, Honduras, Mexico, and other countries to network with non-governmental organizations there, promote sustainable community-based development, and lobby national government officials against free trade agreements and in favor of increased government advocacy for the rights of migrant communities in the United States.

Centro Presente, along with many other immigrants' rights organizations from the U.S., have participated in the World Social Forum, the Social Forum of the Americas, and the Social Forum on Migration. In 2007, NALACC organized the first ever Latino Hemispheric Summit on Migration in Michoacan, Mexico. The summit drew leaders of Latino immigrant communities from all over the Americas, as well as Spain and Italy.

In the Washington, DC area, Mexicanos Sin Fronteras, a Mexican immigrant community organization, was very active in solidarity work with the 2006 people's strike and revolt in Oaxaca, Mexico. Internationalism provides immigrants' rights organizations with the benefit of linking up with migrants' rights organizations and other social movement organizations in the Global South, which, according to Letona, "tend to be more creative, out of the box, and radical than in the U.S."

For immigrants' rights organizations, internationalism also represents an adaptation to a changed reality of the world, with globalized flows of capital and goods (endowed with rights) as well as migrants (stripped of their rights). As Letona states, "Corporate globalization, migration flows, and technology are making physical borders obsolete, and the concept of the nation-state as the way to organize ourselves politically and socially is becoming more of an illusion…. It is urgent that we globalize social and economic justice movements. It is urgent that we see our struggles in ways that transcend nation-state borders."

As with most other struggles, attempts to integrate immigrants' rights work in the U.S. into an international context can be tremendously challenging. One major challenge is what Letona calls "the persistent compartmentalization of public policy, especially in the U.S." She gives the example of Centro Presente and allied organizations visiting

Congressional offices to lobby on immigration reform and talk about how the global economy and U.S. foreign policy drive flows of migration: "Invariably we get blank stares, and are told to speak to other aides that deal with this kind of policy."

Another impediment is the lack of a well-developed political consciousness in the U.S.; according to Letona, "The general public in the U.S. has a tough time grasping the complexity of the current global economy and its effects both here and abroad." This makes the required popular education work to build alliances much harder. As Letona says, "We continue to struggle with easier, more accessible ways of talking about the broader context in which migration flows and the subsequent exploitation of migrant workers takes place."

ASSERTING THE RIGHT TO THE CITY ON A GLOBAL LEVEL

WHILE AFFECTED COMMUNITIES HAVE BEEN resisting gentrification processes for decades, in recent years there have been two very positive developments. First, there is increasing coordination between organizations fighting gentrification in different cities across the country. Second, a number of these organizations have coalesced around a proactive agenda—articulating a "Right to the City." Tired of fighting defensive actions to hold on to the limited, shrinking space that low-income communities can still inhabit and access in cities, the Right to the City Alliance (RTTC) states, "We all have the right to remain and return to our cities, to take back our streets and neighborhoods, and to ensure that they exist to serve people rather than capital."[4] RTTC came together in January 2007 and has since grown to include almost forty core member organizations.

The principles that unite RTTC are remarkably broad and inclusive, placing the struggle against gentrification in the wider context of struggles for economic, racial, and gender justice. They make particular reference to "Internationalism," defined as "the right to support and build solidarity between cities across national boundaries, without state intervention."

Thus far, the spirit of internationalism of the Alliance has manifested itself most concretely in the collaboration with urban poor people's movements in Venezuela and the Philippines. Activists from these movements have participated in RTTC workshops at the U.S. Social Forum in 2007, and the Alliance has subsequently provided solidarity for their struggles. Recently, representatives of RTTC have gone to the climate talks in Copenhagen as civil society participants to push for a climate justice agenda that addresses the needs of impoverished urban populations.

Jon Liss of Tenants and Workers United (TWU), an Alliance member organization working for access to housing, healthcare, and democratic rights for the majority of people in Northern Virginia, attributes the emphasis on internationalism in the Alliance's principles to successive waves of immigration, which have resulted in urban working-class communities that have an "organic link with the Global South."[5] Another reason for the internationalist focus, he says, is that "many communities and organizers have radical roots and see domestic issues and global empire as connected."

The internationalist focus is also self-interested. As an example, Liss asserts that the influx of federal "anti-terrorism" funding into Northern Virginia after 9/11 is largely responsible for the recent wave of gentrification there, by creating a boom of high-paying jobs in the security-industrial complex. This shows how U.S. international policy can have a concrete effect on communities' access to housing.

Sometimes, the effect is less direct, but nonetheless devastating. Most local governments in Virginia are dependent on property taxes for revenue, and with the current economic crisis and the fall in property values, property tax receipts are down, resulting in budget cuts of 15 to 35%, according to Liss' estimations. He identifies the structural problems leading to this local crisis as a combination of the de-regulatory philosophy of neoliberalism, which led to the current recession in the first place, and the neoliberal insistence on downsizing any role for government other than defense and law enforcement, which eviscerated state funding for local services. "The current crisis really has its roots in Reaganism," says Liss, "and now that the effects of Reaganism have come down to the local level, local governments are left holding the bag." Thus, Liss sees a clear link between the global ideology of neoliberalism and the cutbacks to education, public libraries, and mass transit in Northern Virginia today.

TWU is responding by building a "fight-back coalition" led by low-income workers and immigrants. On a national level, RTTC has decided on a common message of a "people's recovery" as a solution to the economic crisis, in conjunction with other organizations such as National People's Action and Jobs with Justice. Various member organizations have taken direct action, such as eviction blockades, as well as analyzed the ways that low-income communities and communities of color are being shortchanged in the grab for stimulus dollars. RTTC targeted the financial institutions responsible for the crisis by participating in an action in Chicago at the American Bankers Association meeting in October of 2009 and against Wells Fargo Bank in December 2009.

Liss sees clear benefits of internationalism for RTTC, including learning from advanced struggles in the Global South, which, according to him, "have a high level of political consciousness, and sometimes a deeper analysis of the political economy of the United States than U.S. movements." He gives the example of participatory budgeting in Brazil as a strategy that people in the U.S. can learn from Southern social movements. He also mentions the sweeping political changes across Latin America over the last few years as fertile ground for ideas, a vivid example of an emerging alternative to the neoliberal world order.

Liss believes that the key to fighting back against the effects of the current economic crisis—foreclosures and evictions, budget cuts, handouts to corporate interests—is to fight at "both the ideological and practical level." The neoliberal ideology of trickle-down economics and the rollback of the state from all except its coercive functions has to be directly confronted and challenged in order to build a mass movement in the U.S., according to Liss. To do this effectively requires an internationalist vision of a counter-neoliberal ideology.

Liss cautions, however, that internationalism has its limitations and U.S. social movements have to be "aware of the reality of our political base." He says that there can be a tension between that reality and the demands of solidarity with international movements, which could result in lower prioritization of international work. He gives the example of the recent escalation of the war in Afghanistan as an arena where it is not clear what immediate role, if any, can be played by a mass movement of low-income people in the U.S. who are organizing for racial, gender, and economic justice. Such a movement, according to Liss, "will have the effect of undermining empire eventually, but will not help Afghanistan immediately." However, this dichotomy between the local and the international is somewhat misleading because, as Liss says, "U.S.-based struggles for housing, health care, immigrants' rights, and low-income workers' rights constitute a social movement that is part of, and not different from, the universe of global social movements."

GROWING LOCAL ROOTS FOR GLOBAL JUSTICE

IT IS SOMEWHAT UNDERSTANDABLE THAT a movement focused on foreign policy issues would draw the participation of a privileged demographic who have relatively less at stake in immediate local struggles. But regardless of the more privileged character of a global justice movement in the U.S., it is too important a struggle to dismiss. The world needs a global justice movement in the U.S. to resist neoliberal imperialism in its home base. Since the U.S. government and U.S. business interests are major driving forces behind the unjust global economy, it is imperative that people in the U.S. resist this agenda. We owe this to the rest of the world.

However, this relatively privileged composition of the movement raises concerns about its effectiveness. A major limitation of the U.S. global justice movement has been its small size and lacking base. That the movement lasted as a powerful force for only about four years, from 1999–2003, shows that it lacked sustainable organizing and base-building. By largely failing to connect the struggle against neoliberalism globally with the daily struggle against neoliberalism in communities across North America, the U.S. global justice movement has missed the opportunity to widen and deepen its base, developing staying power as well as political power.

There have, however, been exceptions. Some global justice organizations have attempted, with varying degrees of success, to connect their work locally, and here we look at one example, based on the author's first-hand experience.

Mobilization for Global Justice (MGJ) in Washington, DC functioned in various forms from late 1999 until 2008. It started as an ad-hoc coalition to mobilize for the A16 demonstrations at the International Monetary Fund and World Bank meetings in April 2000, and evolved into more of an organization than a coalition. MGJ disbanded after a decline in membership and participation, closely aligned with the decline of mass demonstrations against the International Financial Institutions (IFIs). Some of its organizers have since moved on to become more involved in locally-rooted and sustained struggles against neoliberalism.

Throughout its history, MGJ made sporadic attempts to integrate its work with local struggles but did not do so consistently until about 2005. In what follows, I examine approximately two years of MGJ's activities, from 2005 through 2007, to identify successes and failures in the attempts to integrate local struggles against neoliberalism with its regular work around the IMF, World Bank, and global trade.

In February 2005, MGJ presented a workshop at the National Conference on Organized Resistance titled "Structurally Adjusting Washington, DC." The workshop was conceived as a one-time popular education effort to frame the onslaught on communities in Washington, DC as the product of neoliberalism. Specifically, the workshop looked at the effective privatization of health care in the District (by closing the only public hospital), the publicly subsidized construction of a baseball stadium, and gentrification in city neighborhoods. The motivation for doing this was a desire on the part MGJ members to connect our work to local struggles.

Interest in this workshop was overwhelming, and a number of the participating organizations, including DC Jobs with Justice, the DC Health Care Coalition, Project South, and MGJ, decided to continue popular education work, linking local and global struggles. This informal coalition put together another popular education teach-in in April 2005, in conjunction with protests planned for the meetings of the IMF and World Bank. What was particularly powerful about this teach-in was that it featured dialogue between visiting activists from the Dominican Republic, South Africa, and the Philippines, as well as activists working for low-income tenants' rights, access to affordable health care, access to education, and environmental justice in Washington, DC. The education went both ways. I vividly remember how one of the activists from the Global South came up to me after the event to say that she had no idea that neoliberalism was ravaging the capital of the U.S. to quite this extent, nor that there was such a vibrant movement here to resist the neoliberal onslaught.

A key lesson to be learned from the experience of the workshop and the teach-in is that there exists a tremendous amount of interest among local organizers in understanding and discussing the global context for their work. The U.S. global justice movement has not done nearly enough to tap into this interest. A clear understanding of neoliberalism and its global nature can help organizers working on local struggles to identify more strongly with the periodic protests against IFIs and trade agreements as part of the same wider struggle, instead of treating them as irrelevant to one's own causes. This addresses a major problem faced by the U.S. global justice movement: relevance. To much of the public, the concerns of the global justice movement have appeared esoteric, bearing no relation to their daily lives, when in fact the concerns of this movement are vital to the daily lives of people everywhere, including those in the United States. It is partly our own fault that we as a movement have not been able to communicate the relevance of the issues we work on in a compelling manner.

Right after this teach-in, the local-global connection-building work of MGJ hit an impasse. Popular education is a great tool, but ultimately, it has to lead to action for it to serve a purpose. At first we could not figure out an obvious way to translate our developing understanding of the local impacts of neoliberalism into a program of action that would seamlessly integrate our work on the global economy with our work on local struggles.

After deliberation, we settled on a course of action: reviving the Tax the Bank Campaign that had been abandoned by an earlier informal coalition. The campaign sought to restore fairness by pressuring the IMF, World Bank, and Inter-American Development Bank to enter into a Payment in Lieu of Taxes (PILOT) agreement with the District of Columbia to make up for their tax-free status. Currently, the three institutions pay neither property taxes on the more than $1 billion of property that they own nor any corporate income taxes, and foreign citizens working for them pay no personal income taxes. The combined total of revenue foregone by the District because of the tax-free status of the institutions is $1 billion.[6]

The campaign model we chose entailed building a broad, diverse coalition of labor, housing rights, women's, environmental justice, and other groups. The level of participation of coalition members would be of their own choosing, with the understanding that many of the organizations were working on other matters of more pressing importance, like preventing evictions or helping communities cope with immigration raids. The model necessitated extensive outreach and popular education targeted at organizations actively engaged in local struggles, communicating the relevance and importance of fighting for PILOTs from the IFIs, as well as communicating an understanding of the imperialist nature of the institutions.

The implementation of the campaign encountered immediate problems. MGJ had built most of its expertise around organizing street demonstrations and direct action. While the organization endorsed the notion of working on Tax the Bank, it soon became clear that there was not a critical mass of members in the group comfortable doing the extensive popular education work and, in the later stages of the campaign, legislative work to bring the effort to fruition. After proceeding for some time with very limited participation by most MGJ members, the campaign fizzled out.

The above example points to a major failing of the U.S. global justice movement, which has built too much of its history and experience around organizing street protests; it is episodic rather than sustainable, living from one major action to another while neglecting the base-building work that needs to happen between major actions. Even from the narrow perspective of the viability and sustainability of the street protests, this approach has been self-defeating.

Another important observation about Tax the Bank, as it applies to the broader question of integrating local and global action by the U.S. global justice movement, is that it is, in many ways, a unique situation. The tax free status of the IFIs has a direct impact on the city of Washington, DC by further constricting the resources of an already impoverished and disenfranchised city. This is a rare example of a direct impact of a global institution on local communities. Tax the Bank afforded MGJ the opportunity to take its understanding of the local impacts of neoliberalism beyond analysis and popular education into action. It is unfortunate that MGJ could not make more of this unique opportunity to engage in local action against a global institution. Other global justice groups in the U.S. may not be in the position to engage in a similar campaign or action.

The next major foray by MGJ into linking with a local struggle produced one of the most unusual and important (if small) actions in the history of the organization. In September 2006, while the IMF and World Bank were meeting in Singapore, MGJ linked up with the Committee to Save Franklin Shelter (CSFS), a local homeless shelter residents' group, for a joint action.

Franklin Shelter was a homeless men's shelter in downtown Washington, DC, housed in a historic school building. The city administration had its eyes on the building, planning to turn it into a luxury hotel. The original plan called for leasing it to a developer at $9 per square foot in an area where properties typically leased for about $45 a square foot (an 80% discount).[7] This corrupt plan brought together many elements of neoliberalism. It was a classic form of gentrification, displacing low-income (in this case, homeless) people to make room for a more profitable use of the prime downtown real estate. It was remarkably similar to the displacement of poor, often indigenous people across the Global South for more 'profitable' uses of land such as mining, logging, plantation agriculture, and dams. It was a huge public subsidy to a private interest, on the lines of much of the World Bank's lending.

A coalition came together to organize a Washington, DC demonstration around the IMF/World Bank meeting in Singapore. CSFS was not one of the organizations initially approached to join the coalition, but they came out of their own interest. There is a sizable homeless population in the park outside the lavish headquarters of the IMF and World Bank in Washington, DC. The irony of destitute homeless people congregating outside institutions who claim to solve the problem of world poverty does not escape the homeless individuals, and so CSFS decided to take action against the IMF and World Bank, linking that action with their own struggle for shelter and dignity.

The small but spirited demonstration made a convincing link between the crisis of displacement of poor people of color in Washington, DC from the Franklin Shelter, as well as from neighborhoods throughout the city, and the worldwide displacement of poor people in the Global South through the neoliberal policies of the IFIs. The attendees were a mix of global justice activists and homeless people, unusual for a demonstration.

It had a popular education impact by handing out hundreds of informational sheets to passers-by.

The most positive thing about the demonstration was that, temporarily, it had an impact: the city dropped its plan to close the shelter. Afterward, unfortunately, a different city administration closed the shelter in search of a more 'profitable' usage. While this demonstration was certainly not the only factor behind the city's temporary decision to keep the shelter open—the residents of the shelter had been campaigning for months on this issue and were demanding improved services for themselves and for all homeless Washingtonians—the spectacle of homeless people joining up with anti-globalization activists must have been frightening to the powers-that-be in the city.

Months later, in 2007, Empower DC, a local low-income people's organization, approached MGJ for help in organizing a joint action with the National Association of HUD Tenants (NAHT). While the Group of 8 wealthy nations (G-8) met in Germany, NAHT and Empower DC planned to target a German bank, Deutsche Bank, for its lending to AIMCO, a real estate investment trust that was actively taking over public housing nationwide and converting it into market-rate housing. Through its lending, Deutsche Bank was financing this process of gentrification. The meeting was an opportunity for global justice activists to take an action that was focused on the impact of global financial capital on low-income people right here in the United States. The action embarrassed Deutsche Bank enough that they agreed to meet with NAHT.

The Franklin Shelter and NAHT examples illustrate the kinds of actions and relationships that global justice activists in the U.S. need to build and regularly participate in if we want our movement to remain viable and relevant. Today's economic crisis, caused by the recklessness of global casino capitalism, provides a unique opportunity for the movement to draw direct connections between the global economy and people's lives here in North America. As a movement, we have to engage with the response of workers and low-income people to this crisis. We need to shed old, more irrelevant ways of doing things and embrace the struggles of the most marginalized people in our own backyards, and not just the struggles of marginalized people halfway across the world.

SEIZING THIS UNIQUE MOMENT

THE NATURE OF THE POLITICAL and economic restructuring of the U.S. is becoming clearer by the day. While the economy is in its deepest recession in decades, and low- to moderate- income homeowners lose their homes to predatory mortgage lenders by the millions, the government bails out the Goldman Sachs and J.P. Morgans of this world— much like the International Monetary Fund bailing out Wall Street bankers while Korea, Thailand, and Indonesia sunk into a recession in 1997–1998. The increasingly regressive tax structure of the U.S. is systematically shifting wealth and income from the majority of the population to a small wealthy minority. The number of workers represented by unions keeps shrinking, as employers mount vicious and often illegal anti-union campaigns while the government looks the other way. Environmental and consumer safety laws and regulations have been gutted to increase corporate profits. At local levels, cities and towns are being taken over by real estate interests, displacing entire communities to make way for luxury condominiums and hotels.

This is why it is imperative for social movements in the U.S. today to place their work in the global context of the neoliberal assault on peoples' rights everywhere. A clear understanding and articulation of neoliberalism will help weave different struggles together by breaking down the barriers between those for housing justice, racial justice, workers' rights, immigrants' rights, and many others. Such an understanding will also demystify the motives and interests behind the powers that we fight, sharpening our insight. As we have seen with the experience of the social movements discussed above, an understanding of the global context of neoliberalism and its domestic manifestations can help us find allies in similar struggles worldwide, rescuing a largely moribund global justice movement in the United States.

NOTES

1   The privatization of the water supply was averted in all three of the U.S. cities, but not before a major struggle. On Atlanta: Douglas Jehl, "As Cities Move to Privatize Water, Atlanta Steps Back," *New York Times*, February 2, 2003; On New Orleans: see WDSU News, "Nagin Nixes Water Privatization, Appoints new Director," August 18, 2004, from: HTTP://WWW.WDSU.COM/NEWS/3664128/DETAIL.HTML; On Stockton, California: Democracy Now!, "Stockton, California City Reverses Water Privatization it Passed Over Widepsread Local Opposition," August 1, 2007, from: HTTP://WWW.DEMOCRACYNOW.ORG/2007/8/1/STOCKTON_CALIFORNIA_CITY_COUNCIL_REVERSES_WATER.

2   The exception to the phenomenon of relative privilege of international solidarity activists often consists of immigrant communities, including low-income people, acting in solidarity with movements in their home countries.

3   Maria Elena Letona, interview by the author, Spring 2008.

4   This statement is from the Right to the City Alliance 2007 founding points of unity.

5   John Liss, interview by the author, December 17, 2009.

6   Chidozie Ugwumba, "Freeloading Bankers: How the Global Economy's Rulemakers Thrive on Subsidies from an Impoverished and Disenfranchised City," 50 Years is Enough Network, HTTP://WWW.50YEARS.ORG/ISSUES/TAXTHEBANK/REPORT.HTML.

7   Theola S. Labbe, "Legality of Deal to Turn Shelter Into Hotel Questioned," *The Washington Post*, Metro Section, June 10, 2006.

YOU ARE WHAT YOU EAT:

The Food Sovereignty Struggle within the Global Justice Movement

John E. Peck | **Family Farm Defenders**

HAVE A BUTTON ON MY backpack that says: "If You Are What You Eat, Then I'm Fast, Cheap, and Easy." Thankfully, this quip is sarcastic in my case, but for many people, including many of those working for global justice, it is all too true. Whether due to marketing hype or sheer convenience, ordinarily smart folks can fall down when it comes to what they put in their mouths. The personal is political, and this is reflected each time someone votes for "business as usual" by giving their money to a fast-food chain or big box retailer. The result is a broken food/farm system that is systematically abusing animals, exploiting workers, perverting biodiversity, undermining democracy, jeopardizing health, and destroying the planet. If we believe that another world is possible, then we need to radically transform how we eat, and this means incorporating food sovereignty into our thinking and organizing.

I grew up in central Minnesota, on a small farm straight out of Garrison Keillor's Lake Wobegon, surrounded by grazing dairy cows and century old farms homesteaded by immigrants from Germany and Scandinavia. Sadly, I'm no longer looking forward to my high school reunions since so many of my classmates have seen their family farm sold on the auction block to the highest bidder. The "unsettling of America," described by Wendell Berry decades ago, has actually been the order of the day for centuries.[1] Whether it was the conquistadors outlawing quinoa cultivation by the Inca, pioneers wiping out bison as a form of bio-warfare against the tribes of the Great Plains, or the death squads in Colombia now liquidating peasants who stand in the way of agrofuel plantations, these policies end up benefiting global agribusiness cartels and the current empire they sustain.

Since so few people are now physically connected with the land, it might be worth sharing some rude rural realities. The United States now has more prisoners than farmers.

In fact, some of the prisoners are farmers! I know of at least one farm family that is behind bars for writing bad checks simply to keep the electricity on so they could milk their cows. Close to half of U.S. farmers do not even own the land they now cultivate.[2] When I'm asked which nation needs land reform the most, the U.S. is always at the top of my list. Despite their best efforts to be productive and efficient, the majority of farmers in the U.S. do not even get parity (i.e. a fair price to cover their costs, plus a living wage). Consequently, rural people usually have to send someone off-farm to earn enough to make ends meet, and—if they are lucky—also get some healthcare benefits. This sorry scenario is not just limited to family farmers; it goes all the way up the food chain from the undocumented farmworker, to the non-unionized meatpacker, to the part-time minimum wage fast-food cook or grocery clerk. For every dollar spent on an apple at Walmart, only four cents goes to the apple picker and seven cents to the apple farmer, compared to sixty- eight cents for the mega retailer. Walmart alone now sells 20% of all U.S. conventional groceries and is the largest organic retailer, as well.[3]

It was not always like this. Many of the European settlers who first came to the U.S. were landless peasants themselves, fleeing persecution by wealthy abusive landlords. In their hope for a better life in the New World, they often found solidarity with indigenous communities of hunters, gatherers, fishers, and farmers who were already here. This is why the democratic egalitarian principles of the Iroquois Confederacy resonated so well amongst the authors of the U.S. Declaration of Independence, though they hardly went far enough in actual practice. Like the Diggers defending the Commons from Enclosure, in 1776 colonial America, the right to life, liberty, and the pursuit of happiness also meant access to land, and the capacity to grow food. If the state violated this agreement, then it was the right of the people to abolish it and create another government that would promote the general welfare.

Thus, one finds numerous episodes of popular rural resistance throughout U.S. history: the Whiskey Rebellion of the late 18th century in New England; the post-Civil War Grange Movement followed by the Populists who took on the robber barons and railroad monopolies in the latter half of the 19th century; the Industrial Workers of the World members who agitated amongst harvest stiffs across the Great Plains in the early 20th century through the Agricultural Workers Organization; the founding of the United Farm Workers under the leadership of Cesar Chavez and Dolores Huerta to fight slavery in the fields in California; and the creation of the Federation of Southern Cooperatives to defend African American farmers in the South. Both of these later struggles were critical facets of the broader 1960s Civil Rights movement. The Coalition of Immokalee Workers (CIW) in Florida is still waging this fight today to win fair wages and human rights for tomato pickers.

Growing up in the Midwest during the 1970s farm crisis, I watched many 'tractor-cades' of family farmers departing for St. Paul to Washington, DC in the vague hope of influencing politicians. I also had farmer friends who chose suicide rather than face foreclosure—a situation that is repeating itself across the U.S. with the latest corporate-induced financial meltdown.

Far more inspirational as a child was to hear tales of the "Bolt Weevils," chronicled in a folksong by Dana Lyons as well as the book, *Powerline*, co-authored by the late Senator Paul Wellstone.[4] This homegrown resistance movement turned out thousands of farmers and their allies across west-central Minnesota against the energy giants, who were seizing prize farm land and threatening public health for the sake of a high voltage line. When petitions and lawsuits proved useless, the midnight toppling of towers and other acts of sabotage ensued. Despite dozens of attempted arrests and a massive FBI operation, no Bolt Weevil ever went to jail. On one occasion when a few farmers were singled out as lead conspirators, the judge still had to release them as hundreds of agitated supporters surrounded the courthouse. There are valuable lessons to be learned from this example of solidarity, direct action, and non-cooperation today, particularly in relation to the ongoing Green Scare that has targeted radical environmentalists.[5]

In the early 1990s, I went off to study agricultural economics at one of the many land grant colleges established under the 1862 Morrill Act "in order to promote the liberal and practical education of the industrial classes."[6] Of course, this noble mission was forgotten long ago as corporate agribusiness corrupted university curriculum and hijacked the public research agenda. I recall one patenting seminar for graduate students and researchers where an administrator from the Office of University and Industry Relations bluntly told us that the University of Wisconsin was no longer interested in the scientific value of our work, merely its commercial value. It was while struggling to get through my PhD dissertation that I first met John Kinsman, an organic dairy farmer, who had been protesting the selling of experimental dairy products from University of Wisconsin at Madison's test herds to unsuspecting students, staff, and visitors since the mid 1980s.

Kinsman, who was hospitalized after toxic pesticide exposure, is one of the U.S. pioneers of the sustainable agriculture movement and current president of Family Farm Defenders (FFD). In 1993, the Food and Drug Administration (FDA) had finally ruled that recombinant Bovine Growth Hormone (rBGH) was "safe" for humans, but this was only after President Clinton had installed former Monsanto employee, Michael Taylor, at the FDA to rubberstamp its approval. Taylor is now back at the FDA under President Obama, serving as a go-between for Monsanto, the Gates Foundation, and United States Agency for International Development (USAID) to push through biotech as part of the new "Gene Revolution" for Africa.

FARMER RESISTANCE: NATIONAL AND INTERNATIONAL

UNLIKE MANY OTHER "FARMER" ORGANIZATIONS that are just a front for agribusiness giants and commodity groups, Family Farm Defenders welcomes anyone who cares about sustainable agriculture, farm worker rights, animal welfare, consumer safety, fair trade, and food sovereignty. This inclusive perception of who is part of the global food/farm system aligns well with that of La Via Campesina, the largest umbrella organization for farmers, farmworkers, gatherers, hunters, fishers, herders, and foresters in the world. Thanks to this affiliation, FFD is often invited to send food/farm activists to international conferences, such as the February 2007 Nyéléni Food Sovereignty Forum held in Sélingué, Mali, which drew over 600 participants from ninety countries, as well as the Fifth International Conference of La Via Campesina held in October 2008 in Matola, Mozambique.[7]

At the U.N. Climate Change Conference (COP15) held in Copenhagen, Denmark in December 2009, La Via Campesina had by far the strongest contingent of rural activists from across the globe, hosting several panels exposing the "false solutions" to climate change—such as agrofuels and biotech crops—as well as coordinating protests that targeted those responsible for greenhouse gas emissions, such as the export factory farm industry.[8]

Joining others in a unified call for climate justice, La Via Campesina was instrumental in reminding official delegates that "one can't eat carbon," and that "cap and trade" proposals pushed by corporate agribusiness and the Obama Administration are only going to make climate change worse by marginalizing those family farmers and indigenous communities that are now doing the lion's share of mitigating emissions.

La Via Campesina's stance had been confirmed in 2008 by a 2500–page report authored by 400 scientists for the United Nations' International Assessment of Agricultural Science and Technology for Development (IAASTD). The report concluded that small-scale organic agriculture is not only the best means to feed the world, but also the best response to climate change.[9] Ultimately, the COP15 negotiations collapsed under the hypocritical weight of a few in the Global North who refused to take responsibility for their own pollution and tried to shift their clean-up obligations onto the Global South. If Miami was already drowning due to rising sea levels rather than the Maldives, the "what, me worry?" attitude of the U.S. in Copenhagen would have been much less tenable.

Grassroots solidarity delegations are another great organizing tool that bypasses powerful elites and breaks down artificial barriers. At the invitation of our Via Campesina allies, FFD took eighteen members to Oaxaca, Mexico in January 2008, to strategize with pro-democracy activists, strengthen ties with fair trade coffee co-ops, and condemn the Mexican regime for its political repression. Thanks to such cross-border pressure, one prominent Oaxacan prisoner, Flavio Sosa, was released a few months later. In return, FFD often hosts visits to the U.S. by farmers from elsewhere: Brazil, Venezuela, Timor-Leste, Uganda, and Kenya. Our experience is that when U.S. farmers see and hear for themselves the horrible economic conditions that force other farmers off their lands and across borders, they are much less likely to believe xenophobic rhetoric that scapegoats immigrants and instead focus their energy on the common enemy: corporate globalization.

Here in the U.S., we bear particular responsibility for this "race to the bottom" situation, since we provide the legal 'casino' for much of the runaway commodity speculation that manipulates world food prices to the detriment of farmers and consumers alike. This is why for several years now FFD and others have been staging protests to expose the corruption and demand federal anti-trust action on the steps of the Chicago Mercantile Exchange, now subsumed within the Chicago Board of Trade. It is in Chicago that prices are set worldwide for everything from corn to wheat, from pork bellies to fertilizer. Unless you buy directly from a farmer, the free market is a myth today in agriculture, since most producers have been reduced to taking whatever they are told by the middlemen working for the food giants. For example, just three biotech outfits (Syngenta, Monsanto, and Dupont) now control over half of the seeds on earth.[10]

The current global dairy crisis is a particularly poignant illustration of all that is wrong in our food farm system. Just one firm, Dean Foods, now controls a third of the fluid milk market in the U.S., including 80% of the organic milk market via its Horizon subsidiary.

On the other hand, we have less than 75,000 dairy farmers left in the entire U.S.— 90% of them having gone extinct since I was a child.[11] Some states have lost so many dairy farmers they are now importing a third to half of their milk from thousands of miles away. Each morning I bike by semi-loads of milk that have arrived overnight to Wisconsin courtesy of a "cheap" oil policy from taxpayer subsidized factory farms in New Mexico destined to become "Wisconsin" butter. Worse yet, those U.S. dairy farmers still clinging onto life are now receiving just half the price for milk that they got a year ago, while consumers are still paying about the same per gallon at the store and the dairy giants are laughing all the way to the bank in the midst of a worldwide recession.

Some misguided economic pundits would counter that these low prices are due to oversupply, conveniently forgetting the shenanigans happening in the "block cheddar market" at the Chicago Mercantile Exchange or that under global free trade, it is much cheaper to import low-grade milk protein concentrate than to bother using fresh domestic milk to manufacture the likes of Velveeta, Singles, or Mac 'n Cheese. With the FDA once again asleep at the wheel, there is also no worry about pesky food safety enforcement, even though milk protein concentrate is classified as an industrial ingredient to make adhesives and is not approved for human consumption (hence Kraft's label makeover from "cheese food" to "cheese product").

Contrary to popular stereotypes, the U.S. is not feeding the world, and the typical farmer is not some old white guy on a tractor in the Dakotas. Over 85% of the world's harvest never crosses a border, and in fact, most food is consumed within the bioregion where it was grown. The U.S. has been a 'food deficit nation' for years now—we currently import 13% of our total diet, including 22% of our fresh fruit, 25% of our fresh vegetables, 50% of our fruit juice, and 80% of our honey. Half of U.S. cropland is now devoted to just two crops—corn and soybeans—and much of that does not even go to feeding people directly, but instead becomes feedstock for factory farms, junk food makers, and agrofuel refineries. Even in a farm-rich state like Wisconsin, over 90% of our food is imported from other states or abroad. In order to keep such globetrotting food "fresh," corporate agribusiness must resort to all sorts of dubious technological fixes— from ethyln dioxide to nitrates to irradiation to carbon monoxide. Nonetheless, food contamination and food poisoning are skyrocketing, which is not surprising given that imported produce has three times as much salmonella as produce grown in the United States.

When South Korean farmer Lee Kyung-Hae stabbed himself to death on September 10, 2003 on the barricade outside the World Trade Organization (WTO) meeting in Cancun—in protest of U.S. taxpayer-subsidized rice dumping—he was hardly the first victim of corporate globalization. Indeed, many other names come to mind: Chico Mendes, Judi Bari, and Ken Saro-Wiwa, among others. On October 21, 2007 Valmir Mota de Oliveira was shot to death by security guards hired by Syngenta in the western Brazilian state of Paraná state. Hundreds of activists with the Movimento dos Trabalhadores Rurais Sem Terra (MST) had been occupying Syngenta's research facility for over a year in order to block illegal cultivation of biotech crops. In India, as a result of Monsanto's promises of prosperity through biotech cotton that later failed miserably, thousands of farmers have committed suicide. Other farmers, from France to the Philippines, have burned and uprooted these noxious biotech weeds instead.[12] Here in the U.S. such an action would be deemed a federal felony—as well as an act of "eco-terrorism" post 9/11—and Monsanto has a vast war chest and army of patent lawyers devoted to suing contaminated farmers for "theft" of their biotechnologies.

"FOOD SECURITY" VERSUS FOOD SOVEREIGNTY

According to the U.S. Department of Agriculture, there are no longer any hungry people in the U.S., just an estimated thirty-six million people who are "food insecure." The term "food security" was first invoked by Henry Kissinger before the Food and Agriculture Organization (FAO) at the height of the Cold War and basically considers hunger a technical problem of how to get food to those who need it. It thus evades the deeper global justice debate about why hunger exists at all in a world that has plentiful food.

Following Naomi Klein's analysis of "disaster capitalism," "food security" also functions as a Trojan Horse for market penetration and commodity dumping. For instance, in the context of Hurricane Katrina and the government's response, there was little debate about whether displaced people would be eating "donated" irradiated foods or whether toxic FEMA trailers would be parked atop former community gardens.

In contrast to "food security," most people in the world are more likely to talk about, and act upon, their local vision for food sovereignty. First elaborated back in 1996 by La Via Campesina, food sovereignty valorizes common sense principles of community autonomy, cultural integrity, and environmental stewardship—in other words, local people determining for themselves just what seeds they plant, what animals they raise, what type of farming occurs, and what they will ultimately eat for dinner. Food sovereignty is a term used by those who see food as a basic human right, not just another weapon or commodity, and who treat farmers with respect and dignity, rather than dismissing them as backward and anachronistic. In fact, one could argue that the Boston Tea Party which helped spark the American Revolution was a classic struggle, pitting food sovereignty against corporate profit.

Since the 1999 protests against the WTO in Seattle, FFD has been planting the seeds of food sovereignty across the U.S. as a grassroots alternative to corporate globalization. Through this popular education campaign, we hope to bring U.S. global justice activists into a deeper solidarity with their counterparts abroad and bridge the divide that often exists between farmers and eaters, as well as between rural and urban communities here at home. The National Family Farm Coalition, Grassroots International, Rural Coalition, Community Food Security Coalition and Food First!, amongst others, have since joined FFD in this effort. One of our major challenges has been trying to bring the often-disparate struggles for fair trade, buying local, slow food, sustainable agriculture, and farmworker rights together under a broader food sovereignty umbrella. Another has been resisting efforts by the state to "criminalize" local agriculture, whether it is by outlawing the sale of raw milk, branding Food not Bombs a "terrorist" organization, hunting down "unlicensed" backyard chickens, or mandating the registration, RFID chipping, and tracking of all U.S. livestock through the National Animal Identification System.

Adopting internationally-recognized principles of food sovereignty would have sweeping implications in a setting such as the U.S., which is most likely the reason corporate agribusiness and their political supporters have so fiercely resisted them. For instance, preemption legislation that takes away local control over the regulation of factory farms grossly undermines food sovereignty, as does lack of comprehensive country of origin labeling that would allow consumers to actually know where their food comes from. This even applies to organic foods, as corporate agribusiness scours the planet for the cheapest suppliers with bottom of the barrel standards. How a consumer could trust the integrity of Whole Foods "organics" imported from China is quite beyond me. Similarly, the corporate patenting of life forms, expropriation of indigenous knowledge, and subsidized dumping of commodity crops are all flagrant violations of food sovereignty.

The food sovereignty struggle is particularly relevant today, as a global food shortage spawned by agrofuel expansion and commodity speculation triggered food rioting in the Global South and food rationing in the Global North. Close to half of the U.S. corn harvest in 2008 was diverted into making fuel—it takes as much grain to fill a twenty-five gallon SUV tank once as it does to feed a person all year. Given the taxpayer subsidies and federal mandates behind the boom, many farmers jumped on the agrofuel bandwagon, shifting land out of conservation programs and even away from other staple food crops. The result was cascading price hikes: eggs increased 36% in the U.S., cornmeal up 60% in Mexico, flour up 100% in Pakistan, and rice up 130% in Haiti. Meanwhile, the food giants posted record earnings; Cargill alone saw its profits climb by 50% to $4 billion in 2007 thanks to the global food crisis.[13]

Adding insult to injury, the corporate response to the global food crisis has been to outsource even more commodity production under contract, create new agricultural hedge funds for wannabe speculators, and try to corner the global market in farmland. Since 2008, over 180 such land grab schemes across the Global South have been exposed. Former AIG trader and current CEO of NY-based Jarch Capital, Philippe Heilberg, recently signed a deal with a Sudanese warlord to establish four thousand square kilometers worth of plantations. Another brazen attempt by the South Korean company Daewoo to purchase 1.3 million hectares in Madagascar—half of the country's cropland—mostly to grow corn for export only fell apart after massive public outrage.[14] Other land grabs are proceeding forward more quietly, often with the support of the World Bank, Gates Foundation, International Fund for Agricultural Development, and others eager to push biotech crops and agrofuel plantations for carbon offset credits.

ORGANIZING FOR FOOD SOVEREIGNTY

THANKFULLY, THERE ARE POSITIVE EXAMPLES of food sovereignty in action all around us to counter such "agribusiness as usual." Though these grassroots initiatives often don't make splashy headlines, they do capture some of the best aspects of intentional community, mutual aid, reciprocity, and cross border solidarity that global justice activists would espouse. To give but a few examples: there are now more than 3,700 farmers' markets in the U.S., having doubled in number since 1994; over nine million acres of land are now protected from development through 1,500 community landtrusts; there are over 2,000 community-supported agriculture (CSA) operations in the U.S. directly providing fresh food from farmers to eaters each week throughout the growing season; there are over 400 farm-to-school projects getting healthy local food back into cafeterias, as well as over 30 local and state food policy councils that are reclaiming democratic control over agriculture.[15] From community gardens and local currencies to permaculture and seedsaving, there are countless opportunities to reclaim our local food/farm systems.

The Great Lakes bioregion has become a hotbed of such activity. For instance, the Oneida Tsyunhekwa Project near Green Bay, Wisconsin is reasserting indigenous food sovereignty through "Three Sisters," squash, corn, and bean gardens and a community-processing kitchen open to everyone. Similarly, the White Earth Land Recovery Project in northern Minnesota is defending the cultural integrity of "manoomin" (wild rice) from corporate bio-piracy and promoting other traditional foods as a form of preventative medicine. Dane County boasts the largest farmers' market in the U.S., with over 15,000 people converging each Saturday during the growing season around the State Capitol in Madison, WI, to support hundreds of vendors and keep millions of dollars in the local economy. Over a third of U.S. organic dairy products now come from Wisconsin, where the fastest growing farm sector is small-scale and grass-based.[16] In Milwaukee and Chicago, Growing Power has seen incredible amounts of success in bringing the joy of urban agriculture and delicious food to those who have been marginalized by the forces of gentrification.

FOOD SOVEREIGNTY—NOT JUST FOR BREAKFAST ANYMORE

WHILE SOME GLOBAL JUSTICE ACTIVISTS find building coalitions with U.S. family farmers and farmworkers to be daunting, the resulting creative synergy makes the effort more than worthwhile. Just like in the Global South, the "digital divide" is very real in rural America; mass emails often garner few responses. Many FFD members don't have computers, and then there are thousands of Amish farmers who don't even have phones! When we try to reach folks, it is often better to send an action alert around with the milk truck or to post fliers in small town cafes, feed mills, and public libraries.

Talk radio is another venue that is often underestimated by activists. One half-hour radio interview on a consumer's right to know and a farmer's right to label can generate hundreds of phone calls to a governor who previously thought it would be easy to just make everyone drink rBGH-induced milk. Depending upon the issue and publicity, one should also be ready for a diverse audience. We have hosted rural town hall style meetings with farmers and immigrant farmworkers from a dozen countries and speaking half a dozen languages, and this requires not only multilingual literature and volunteer translators, but also culturally respectful food and a family friendly format. Progressive faith-based communities are another important outreach mechanism, whether it is a Catholic parish rural justice committee or the eco-halal buying club for an urban Muslim center.

Food sovereignty work should be part of the standard tool kit for any global justice activist. If we truly wish to build a new world from the ashes of the old, as the slogan of the IWW suggests, then we cannot be trapped in a purely reactive mode. No one needs to suffer from chronic hunger in a food desert. We have the right and the capacity to reclaim the land, the seeds, our health, and our food as a common treasury for all. To paraphrase Anishinabe activist Winona LaDuke, we don't want a bigger slice, we want a whole new pie!

NOTES

1   Wendell Berry, *The Unsettling of America: Culture and Agriculture* (San Francisco: Sierra Club Books, 1977).
2   Economic Research Service / USDA, *Agricultural Outlook* (May 1998); HTTP://WWW.ERS.USDA.GOV/PUBLICATIONS/AGOUTLOOK/MAY1998/AO251D.PDF.
3   Conventional Groceries: Jon Ortiz, "Can Kroger slow Wal-Mart?" in *Desert City News* (Salt Lake City, October 25, 2005); Organic Groceries: Richard A. Levins, "Walmart Comes Calling: New Challenges, New Strategies for OFARM" in *OFARM Quarterly* (November 2006).
4   Casper Berry and Paul Wellstone, *Powerline: The First Battle of America's Energy War* (Minneapolis: University of Minnesota Press, 2003).
5   On the Green Scare see Will Potter's, "Green is the New Red" blog at: HTTP://WWW.GREENISTHENEWRED.COM.
6   U.S. Congress. *Morrell Act of 1862*, (7 U.S.C. § 301 et seq.).
7   Nyéléni.org, HTTP://WWW.NYELENI.ORG/.
8   John Peck, "Corporate Agribusiness Helps Scuttle Climate Justice" in *Capital Times* (Madison, WI) Dec. 29th, 2009; also republished on Common Dreams, 29 December 2009, available at: HTTP://WWW.COMMONDREAMS.ORG/VIEW/2009/12/29 (accessed January 30, 2010).
9   HTTP://WWW.AGASSESSSMENT.ORG.
10 GM Watch, "The world's top 10 seed companies," HTTP://WWW.GMWATCH.ORG/GM-FIRMS/10558—THE-WORLDS-TOP-TEN-SEED-COMPANIES-WHO-OWNS-NATURE.

11   Family Farm Defenders, "Know Your Dairy Giants—Dean Foods", HTTP://WWW.FAMILYFARM-DEFENDERS.ORG/PMWIKI.PHP/MAIN/KNOWYOURDAIRYGIANTS-DEANFOODS.

12   Brian Tokar (Ed.), *Redesigning Life: The Worldwide Challenge to Genetic Engineering* (New York and London: Zed Books, 2001).

13   Eric Holt-Giménez and Raj Patel with Annie Shattuck, *Food Rebellions: Crisis and the Hunger for Justice* (Oakland: Food First Books, 2009).

14   GRAIN, "Korean women farmers on the Daewoo/Madagascar land deal," HTTP://WWW.GRAIN.ORG/VIDEOS/?ID=194; GRAIN, "Land grabbing and the global food crisis" (November 2009), HTTP://WWW.GRAIN.ORG/O_FILES/LANDGRABBING-PRESENTATION-11–2009.PDF.

15   U.S. Department of Agriculture, "Number of Farmers Markets Continues to Rise in U.S." (September 19, 2008), HTTP://WWW.AMS.USDA.GOV/AMSV1.0/AMS.FETCHTEMPLATEDATA.DO?TEMPLATE=TEMPLATEU&NAVID=&PAGE=NEWSROOM&RESULTTYPF=DETAILS&DDOCNAME=ST ELPRDC5072471&DID=100574&WF=FALSE&DESCRIPTION=NUMBER+OF+FARMERS+MARKET S+CONTINUES+TO+RISE+IN+U.S.+&TOPNAV=NEWSROOM&LEFTNAV=&RIGHT.

16   Bradford L. Barham, Caroline Brock and Jeremy Foltz, "Organic Dairy Farms in Wisconsin: Prosperous, Modern, and Expansive," *PATS Research Report No. 16* (June 2006), HTTP://FUTURE.AAE.WISC.EDU/PUBLICATIONS/ORGANIC_DAIRY_FARMS_IN_WISCONSIN.PDF;   Land Trust Alliance, "2005 Land Trust Census," HTTP://WWW.LANDTRUSTALLIANCE.ORG/ABOUT-US/LAND-TRUST-CENSUS; Local Harvest, "Community Supported Agriculture," HTTP://WWW.LOCALHARVEST.ORG/CSA/; Farm to School, "Statistics," HTTP://WWW.FARMTOSCHOOL.ORG/.

TOWARD A MOVEMENT FOR CLIMATE JUSTICE

Brian Tokar

COMPLAINING ABOUT THE WEATHER IS about as American as apple pie, sitcoms, and rock and roll. But while the rest of the world has been noticing for years that our increasingly unstable weather is a first sign of potentially devastating global climate changes, North Americans' collective heads have mostly remained in the sand. Over the past few years, political awareness of the magnitude of the climate crisis has begun to emerge from hiding.

It helps, of course, that weather changes in recent years have become so severe that it is virtually impossible not to notice. The upper Midwestern plains survived two recent years of unprecedented drought; in much of the Southeast, the situation has been even more severe, with parts of Alabama and Tennessee experiencing their driest weather in over a century, together with a rising number of unprecedented flooding events. In Arizona, and also in parts of Greece and Turkey, summer temperatures can now reach well above 115 degrees. We have seen wildfires sweep repeatedly through large, populated areas of southern California, and it is now clear that the hurricanes that devastated New Orleans and surrounding areas in 2005 were intensified by anomalously high sea temperatures in the Gulf of Mexico and across the South Atlantic.[1]

But the particulars of the weather, and even natural disasters, are of merely fleeting interest to most people. In New Orleans after Hurricane Katrina, activists tended, quite reasonably, to focus more on the substandard condition of the dikes, how they were undermined by over-development of the surrounding wetlands, and the persistent lack of funds to restore public services. Most people paid only passing attention to the correlation between the devastating human consequences of Hurricane Katrina and accelerating global climate disruptions.

This is partly the fault of those who regularly communicate global warming to the mainstream public. Most often, the climate crisis is still framed as a mainly scientific or technical matter. The hazards are severe, but generally uncertain and long-range in nature. The proposed solutions vary from relatively trivial suggestions like changing light bulbs, to disastrous technical fixes like reviving nuclear power, pumping sun-blocking particulates into the atmosphere, or processing the world's grain supplies into automotive fuels. In sharp contrast to, say, the radical anti-nuclear activists of thirty years ago, few are talking about the underlying roots of the problem, much less the need for a sweeping ecological transformation of society.

WHO IS AFFECTED BY GLOBAL WARMING?

SINCE THE FIRST EARTH DAY, way back in 1970, there has been a serious divide between those who view environmental issues as fundamentally social and political, and those who, like regulatory agencies and middle-of-the-road environmental groups, focus entirely on the technical aspects of individual problems and on narrow solutions that preserve the status quo, typically ignoring the larger picture.

As social ecologists have argued since the mid-1960s, however, environmental problems not only have serious human consequences, but are thoroughly social and political in origin.[2] With respect to global warming, this contrast is becoming central to understanding where we are and where we may be headed. An understanding of the science and politics of global warming is increasingly shaping how we understand problems of social justice, or war and peace, as well as how these concerns will play out in the coming decades. A brief look at the science may help illuminate this.

In 2007, the United Nation's Intergovernmental Panel on Climate Change (IPCC) issued their fourth comprehensive review of climate science, saying for the first time that "warming of the climate system is unequivocal" and that rises in global temperature can only be explained with reference to human-induced increases in carbon dioxide and other so-called "greenhouse gases" (Methane, nitrous oxide, and the banned but persistent chlorofluorocarbons (CFCs) used in air conditioners and refrigerators are the other main culprits). For the first time, the statistical confidence level of many of U.N. calculations came in at better than ninety-five percent.[3]

The IPCC documented an unprecedented convergence of findings from hundreds of studies and tens of thousands of distinct data sets in numerous independent fields of inquiry. This feat of scientific data gathering and assessment may have been worthy of a Nobel Science Prize if the panel hadn't already been awarded the coveted Prize for peace, along with Al Gore. Perhaps never before have scientific studies in so many distinct areas of research converged on one disturbing conclusion: not only is the evidence for the role of human activity in altering the earth's climate "unequivocal," but the ecological and human consequences of those alterations are already being felt in countless different ways.

The IPCC's report appeared in three separate volumes published by distinct international working groups, plus a concluding "synthesis report," all released over the course of 2007. Most media coverage focused on the first volume, where the assembled scientists described and evaluated a wide range of future greenhouse gas emission scenarios, their resulting concentration (in parts per million) of atmospheric carbon dioxide, and how many degrees of global warming would likely result from each possible scenario.

Scientists such as NASA's James Hansen—perhaps the most widely censored senior scientist of our time—have convincingly argued that the IPCC greatly underestimated likely sea level rises, along with several other factors that negatively affect human populations. His analyses over the past year have suggested some very alarming conclusions: that a sensible extrapolation from past climate data would suggest a sea level rise of as much as eighty feet if we don't stop burning fossil fuels, and that we've already reached the historic carbon dioxide level beyond which the Antarctic glaciers cannot remain frozen, a level unsurpassed for over thirty-five million years.[4] For Hansen and many others, the question is literally whether or not our earth will continue to resemble the world in which human civilizations have developed; the only way to accomplish this is to leave most of the remaining fossil fuels in the ground. Meanwhile, policy analysts are proposing "acceptable" or "realistic" greenhouse gas levels that are another thirty to fifty percent higher, and even beyond.

What gets lost in all the long-term projections, however, are the ways that chaotic global warming is already affecting people around the world today. The IPCC wrote about this too, in their second volume, specifically addressing the environmental and human consequences of climate change. But scientists and advocates alike would much rather debate parts per million of carbon dioxide than try to address the ways that people's survival is already imperiled by the over-consumption of the world's affluent minority.

Most poor people live in the earth's tropical and subtropical regions. They are already living in a world of increasingly uncertain rainfall, persistent droughts, coastal flooding, loss of wetlands and fisheries, and increasingly scarce fresh water supplies. The IPCC reports that severely increased flooding will most immediately affect residents of the major river deltas of Asia and Africa. Additionally, the one-sixth of the world's population that depends on water from glacial runoff may see a brief increase in the size and volume of their freshwater lakes as glaciers melt, but eventually the loss of the glaciers will become a life-threatening reality for those people as well.[5]

The data points toward a worldwide decrease in crop productivity if global temperatures rise more than five degrees Fahrenheit, although crop yields from rain-fed agriculture could be reduced by half as soon as 2020. In Africa alone, between seventy-five million and 250 million people will be exposed to "increased water stress," according to the IPCC. Agricultural lands in Latin America will be subject to desertification and increasing salt content.

Probably the grimmest tale is contained in the report's chapter on health consequences of climate changes: "[I]ncreases in malnutrition and consequent disorders; increased deaths, disease and injury due to heatwaves, floods, storms, fires and droughts; the increased burden of diarrheal disease; the increased frequency of cardio-respiratory diseases due to higher concentrations of ground-level ozone; and, the altered spatial distribution of some infectious disease vectors," including malaria. There is little doubt that those populations with "high exposure, high sensitivity and/or low adaptive capacity" will bear the greatest burdens; those who contribute the least to the problem of global warming will continue to face the most severe consequences.[6]

The Millennium Ecosystem Assessment, released in 2005, offered a graphic representation of where we are and where we are headed.[7] One page of that report offers a pair of world maps, each with a bar graph superimposed on every continent.[8] The upper map chronicles the number of major floods reported each decade from 1950 to 2000; the lower map displays the number of major wildfires. Everywhere but in Oceania—which is now facing a drought so severe that some major grain growing regions of Australia are no longer able to support any crops—the graphs rise steeply as the decades advance. Over this time period, global temperatures only rose about one degree Fahrenheit; only the most optimistic of the IPCC's projected future scenarios limits further warming during this century to less than three additional degrees. The U.N. Environment Program projected in late 2009 that current policies would lead to a six degree rise by 2100; a study by the British Meteorological Office predicted an astounding seven degree rise by 2060, resulting in worldwide droughts and heat waves, threatening water supplies for half the earth's population, and condemning half of all animal and plant species to extinction.[9]

The biennial U.N. Human Development Report, issued in November of 2007, reported that one out of every nineteen people in the so-called developing world was affected by a climate-related disaster between 2000 and 2004.[10] The figure for people in the wealthiest (OECD) countries was one out of every 1,500. Yet the funds available thus far to various U.N. efforts to help the poorest countries adapt to climate changes ($26 million) is less than one week's worth of flood defense spending in the United Kingdom, and about what the city of Venice spends on its flood gates every two to three weeks. The report estimates that an additional $86 billion will be needed to sustain existing U.N. development assistance and poverty reduction programs in the face of all the various threats attributable to climate change.

From Bangladesh to Darfur, we are already seeing the ways in which increased climate instability is exacerbating conflict and even bloodshed among people. Droughts in East Africa have caused wells to dry up and livestock to perish, fueling inter-ethnic conflicts among the region's pastoral communities.[11] In India, widespread crop failures due to more frequent droughts and catastrophic flooding events has heightened a tragic wave of farmer suicides, which was first brought on by the widespread failure of chemical pesticides and genetically engineered seeds.[12] And this is just the beginning. A 2007 report by the U.K.-based relief organization International Alert compared maps of the world's most politically unstable regions with those most susceptible to serious or extreme effects of climate change, and concluded that forty-six countries, with a total population of 2.7 billion people, are firmly in both categories. The report, entitled "A Climate of Conflict," states:

> Hardest hit by climate change will be people living in poverty, in under-developed and unstable states, under poor governance. The effect of the physical consequences—such as more frequent extreme weather, melting glaciers, and shorter growing seasons—will add to the pressures under which those societies already live. The background of poverty and bad governance means many of these communities both have a low capacity to adapt to climate change and face a high risk of violent conflict.[13]

International Alert's report profiles eight case studies of places in Africa and Asia where climate changes have already caused great stress on people's livelihoods and often exacerbated internal conflicts. The outlook is significantly improved, however, in places where political institutions are relatively stable and accountable to the population. This contrast allows for a somewhat hopeful conclusion, with the authors extolling "the synergies between climate adaptation policies and peacebuilding activities in achieving the shared goal of sustainable development and peace." One specific recommendation is to prioritize efforts to help people adapt to a changing climate, especially where subsistence-based economies contribute very little to global warming but are highly vulnerable to the consequences. Several international non-governmental organizations have already intervened, particularly in Africa, to document and disseminate changes in farming practices that have proven most useful in facilitating adaptation to a changing climate.

Another study, published in the journal *Political Geography* by Rafael Reuveny of Indiana University, examined thirty-eight cases over the past seventy years where populations were forced to migrate due to a combination of environmental (droughts, floods, storms, land degradation, pollution) and other factors.[14] Half of these cases led to violent conflict between the migrating populations and those in the receiving areas. It is clear, states Reuveny, that those who depend the most on the environment to sustain their livelihood, especially in regions where arable land and fresh water are scarce, are most likely to be forced to migrate when conditions are subjected to rapid and unplanned-for change.

Since the Persian Gulf War of the early 1990s, activists have become increasingly aware of the devastating environmental consequences of warfare and also of 'peacetime' military activities. Oil consumption by the U.S. military, for example, approaches fourteen million gallons per day, according to Michael Klare, which is more than is used daily in all of Sweden or Switzerland.[15] The U.S. military is responsible for thousands of toxic waste dumps spread throughout the world. But today, we are in an escalating spiral of warfare and environmental devastation that threatens to spin entirely out of control if we are unable to achieve a different way of organizing the world's affairs. The world's militaries and elites are preparing themselves for the worst; those of us who seek peace and global justice need to come together as never before if those worst case scenarios are to be averted.

It is clear today that the past two centuries of capitalist development—and especially the unprecedented pace of resource consumption during the past sixty years—have created conditions that threaten everyone's future. "There could be no clearer demonstration than climate," says the U.N.'s Human Development Report, "that economic wealth creation is not the same as human progress."[16] Those who have benefited the least from the unsustainable pace of economic growth and expansion since 1950 are facing a future of suffering and dislocation unlike the world has ever seen, unless we can rapidly reverse the patterns of exploitation that many in the global North have simply come to take for granted.

FALSE SOLUTIONS

IN RECENT YEARS, WE HAVE been inundated with a plethora of seductive, but ultimately false solutions to the threat of catastrophic climate changes. First, there is a well-orchestrated political push, from the highest levels of the U.S. government, for a revival of nuclear power. Not only do we still, after fifty years, have no clue what to do with monstrous quantities of highly radioactive nuclear waste, but if human societies do commit the massive capital resources needed to build a new generation of nuclear power plants—at least tripling the present number according to some estimates—there will be literally no funds left to develop truly green, solar-based alternatives, even in the long run.[17]

Further, a significant expansion of nuclear power would expose countless more communities to the legacy of cancer that critical scientists such as Ernest Sternglass have documented, and additional indigenous communities to the even more severe consequences of uranium mining and milling. Indeed, we would soon run out of the relatively accessible uranium ore that now minimizes greenhouse gas emissions from the nuclear fuel production chain, and the energy needed to mine and purify uranium would quickly become an even larger contributor to catastrophic global warming.[18] For the first time since the partial nuclear meltdown at Three Mile Island in central Pennsylvania in 1979, U.S. utilities are considering the construction of new nuclear power plants, thanks to a new round of subsidies promoted by Congressional allies from both major political parties. This expanded nuclear initiative clearly needs to be stopped.

Another false solution to global warming that we read a great deal about are so-called "biofuels" (activists in the Global South use the more appropriate term, "agrofuels," as

these are first and foremost products of global agribusiness).[19] Running our cars on ethanol fermented from corn and diesel fuel made from soybeans and other food crops has
already contributed to the worldwide food shortages that brought starvation and food
riots to Mexico, Egypt, Thailand, Haiti, and at least thirty other countries.[20] The amount
of corn needed to produce the ethanol for one large SUV tank contains enough calories
to feed a hungry person for a year.[21]

Even if the entire U.S. corn crop were to be used for fuel, it would only displace about
twelve percent of current gasoline use, according to University of Minnesota researchers.[22]
The current push for agrofuels has consumed a growing share of U.S. corn—as much as
thirty percent in 2009—and encouraged growers of crops such as wheat and soybeans
to transfer more of their acreage to growing corn. Land in the Amazon and other fragile
regions is now being plowed under to grow soybeans for export, while Brazil's uniquely
biodiverse coastal grasslands are appropriated to grow sugarcane—perhaps the most efficient source of ethanol.[23] Further, two studies released in 2008 show that deforestation
and other changes in land use that go along with agrofuel development clearly make these
fuels net contributors to global warming.[24]

The increasingly popular "biodiesel" alternative can be equally problematic. In contrast to the waste oil from restaurants that is favored by hobbyists, and sunflowers grown
to power small farms, commercial supplies of biodiesel usually come from soybean or
canola fields in the U.S. Midwest, Canada, or the Amazon, where these crops are genetically engineered to withstand large doses of chemical herbicides. Increasingly, biodiesel
comes from the vast monoculture oil palm plantations that have in recent years displaced
more than eighty percent of the native rainforests of Indonesia and Malaysia. As the global
food crisis has escalated, agrofuel proponents have asserted that using food crops for fuel is
only a temporary solution and that we will soon run all of our cars on fuel extracted from
grasses and trees; this dangerous myth is helping to drive a new wave of subsidies to the
U.S. biotechnology industry to develop fast-growing genetically engineered trees.[25]

Third, and perhaps most insidious, we are told that if the world is to make significant reductions in greenhouse gas emissions, the only acceptable way to carry out these
reductions is through the wonders of the so-called "free market." When Al Gore (as Vice
President) went to Kyoto in 1997, he offered that the U.S. would sign on to what soon became the Kyoto Protocol under two conditions: that mandated reductions in greenhouse
gas emissions be far less ambitious than originally proposed, and that any reductions
be implemented through the market-based trading of "rights to pollute" among various companies and countries. Under this "cap-and-trade" model, companies that fail to
meet their quota for emission reductions can readily purchase the difference from another
permit holder that was able to reduce its emissions faster. While economists argue that
this scheme will induce companies to implement the most cost-effective changes as soon
as possible, experience shows that carbon markets are at least as prone to fraud and manipulation as any other financial market. Over a dozen years after the Kyoto Protocol was
signed, most industrialized countries are still struggling to bring down their annual rate of
increase in global warming pollution.[26]

While the U.S. never adopted the Kyoto Protocol, the rest of the world has had to live
with the consequences of Gore's proposals, creating what the British columnist George
Monbiot has aptly termed "an exuberant market in fake emissions cuts."[27] The European
Union's cap-and-trade scheme, for example, has created a huge new subsidy for highly polluting corporations without any demonstrable reduction in pollution. At least European

governments are actively supplementing carbon trading with active public support for energy conservation and alternative energy technologies; only here in the U.S. do solar and wind technologies first have to prove their viability in the so-called "free market"—in marked contrast to ever-increasing subsidies for nuclear power and agrofuels.

Carbon offsets are the other key aspect of the "market" approach to global warming. These investments in nominally emissions-reducing projects in other parts of the world are now a central feature of carbon markets, and an even greater obstacle to real solutions. (They are aptly compared to the "indulgences" that sinners used to buy from the Catholic Church during the Middle Ages.) Larry Lohmann of the U.K.'s CornerHouse research group has demonstrated in detail how carbon offsets are encouraging the conversion of native forests into monoculture tree plantations, lengthening the lifespan of polluting industrial facilities and toxic landfills in Asia and Africa in exchange for only incremental changes in their operations, and ultimately perpetuating the very inequalities that we need to eliminate in order to create a more just and sustainable world.[28] Even if they can occasionally help support beneficial projects, offsets postpone investments in necessary emissions reductions at home and represent a gaping "hole" in any mandated "cap" in carbon dioxide emissions. They are a means for polluting industries to continue "business as usual" at home while contributing marginally, at best, to emission reductions elsewhere.

Trading and offsets will simply not bring us any closer to the zero-emissions future that we know is both necessary and achievable. Nevertheless, markets in greenhouse gas emissions allowances continue to be a central feature of proposed climate legislation in the U.S. and beyond.[29]

WHAT KIND OF MOVEMENT?

THE LAST TIME A POPULAR movement compelled significant changes in U.S. environmental and energy policies was during the late 1970s. In the aftermath of the Organization of the Petroleum Exporting Countries (OPEC) oil embargo, imposed during the 1973 Arab-Israeli war, the nuclear and utility industries adopted a plan to construct more than 300 nuclear power plants in the U.S. by the year 2000. Utility and state officials identified rural communities across the U.S. as potential sites for new nuclear facilities, and the popular response was swift and unanticipated. A militant grassroots anti-nuclear movement united back-to-the-landers and traditional rural dwellers with seasoned urban activists, as well as a new generation of environmentalists who only partially experienced the ferment of the 1960s.

In April of 1977, over 1,400 people were arrested trying to nonviolently occupy a nuclear construction site in the coastal town of Seabrook, New Hampshire.[30] That event helped inspire the emergence of decentralized, grassroots anti-nuclear alliances all across the country, committed to nonviolent direct action, bottom-up forms of internal organization, and a sophisticated understanding of the relationship between technological and social changes. Not only did these groups adopt an uncompromising call for "No Nukes," but many promoted a vision of an entirely new social order, rooted in decentralized, solar-powered communities empowered to decide both their energy future and their political future. If the nuclear state almost inevitably leads to a police state—due to the massive security apparatus necessary to protect hundreds of nuclear plants and radioactive waste dumps all over the country—a solar-based energy system could be the underpinning for a radically decentralized and directly democratic model for society.

This movement was so successful in raising the hazards of nuclear power as a matter of urgent public concern that nuclear projects all across the U.S. began to be canceled. When the nuclear reactor at Three Mile Island near Harrisburg, Pennsylvania partially melted down in March of 1979, it spelled the end of the nuclear expansion. While politicians in Washington are currently doing everything possible to underwrite a revival of nuclear power, it is still the case that no new nuclear plants have been licensed or built in the U.S. since Three Mile Island. The anti-nuclear movement of the late 1970s also spawned the first wave of significant development of solar and wind technologies, aided by substantial federal tax benefits for solar installations, and helped launch a visionary "green cities" movement that captured the imaginations of architects, planners, and ordinary citizens.

The 1970s and early 1980s—before the "Reagan revolution" fully took hold—were relatively hopeful times, and utopian thinking was far more widespread than it is today. Some anti-nuclear activists looked to the emerging outlook of "social ecology," mainly developed by Murray Bookchin, as a new theoretical grounding for a revolutionary ecological politics and philosophy. Social ecology challenges prevailing views about the evolution of social and cultural relationships to non-human nature and explores the roots of domination in the earliest emergence of human social hierarchies.[31] For the activists of that period, Bookchin's insistence that environmental problems are fundamentally social and political in origin encouraged radical responses to ecological concerns, as well as reconstructive visions of a fundamentally transformed society. Similarly, social ecology's emphasis on popular power and direct democracy helped inspire global justice activists during the late 1990s.

Social ecology views capitalism as standing, in Bookchin's words, "in an irreconcilable contradiction with the natural world."[32] Bookchin viewed the myth of humans dominating nature as an outgrowth of emerging relationships of domination in early human societies. Hence, a genuinely transformative ecological movement needs to challenge capitalism, the state, and indeed all forms of hierarchy. While past attempts to 'green' the capitalist marketplace have mainly brought us more 'green' products to buy, and advanced the careers of 'green' advertisers and public relations operatives, today's capitalist false solutions to the climate crisis are bringing the world ever closer to the edge of catastrophe. For social ecologists, the appropriate response is not to indulge in nihilistic visions of the "end of civilization," but rather to redouble our efforts to realize the long-range reconstructive potentialities inherent in a genuinely ecological world-view.

While radically reconstructive social visions are relatively scarce in today's political climate, dissatisfaction with the status quo reaches both widely and deeply among many sectors of the U.S. population. The more people consume, and the deeper they fall into debt, the less satisfied they seem to be with the world of business as usual. While elite discourse and the corporate media continue to be confined by a narrowly circumscribed status quo, poll after poll suggests the potential for a new opening, reaching far beyond the confines of what is now deemed politically "acceptable."

CAMPAIGNING FOR CLIMATE JUSTICE

As with so many other pressing issues of our time, the impetus for a movement that can reach beyond the status quo and meaningfully confront the full consequences of global climate chaos is coming to us mainly from other parts of the world. An emerging global Climate Justice movement is uniting indigenous opponents of biofuel plantations, international carbon trading skeptics, long-time anti-nuclear and global justice activists, and many others. The demand for climate justice was first articulated by Indigenous Environmental Network founder and director Tom Goldtooth in the mid-1990s, further defined in a 1999 Corpwatch report, and formed the basis for a resolution passed at the Second People of Color Environmental Leadership Summit in 2002.[33] The concept gained international attention following a meeting in Durban, South Africa in the fall of 2004 that included representatives of social movements and indigenous peoples organizations based in Brazil, India, Samoa, the U.S., and U.K., as well as South Africa. That gathering drafted the Durban Declaration on Carbon Trading, which has since gained over 300 endorsers from around the world. The Durban Group has helped bring people to the sites of various U.N. meetings to represent those affected by increased resource extraction and the widespread conversion of forests to monoculture plantations, advanced by the North's desire for carbon offsets. The climate justice movement then emerged at the forefront of global civil society debates during the 2007 biennial conference of the U.N.'s Framework Convention on Climate Change in Bali, Indonesia. In discussions following the summit in Bali, where representatives of affected peoples made a strong showing both inside and outside the official proceedings, a more formal worldwide network emerged under the slogan, "Climate Justice Now!"

The movement also rose in prominence during the lead-up to the much-anticipated 2009 U.N. climate summit in Copenhagen. For over a year prior to the Copenhagen meetings, activists concluded that this summit would likely fall far short of what the world needs to prevent unprecedented climate disruptions and pledged a commitment to direct action against the root causes of climate change. In the summer of 2009, activists from more than twenty countries, including several from the Global South, gathered as part of an emerging Climate Justice Action network, and agreed on an ambitious alternative agenda to the increasingly business-dominated deal-making at the U.N. level.

"We cannot trust the market with our future, nor put our faith in unsafe, unproven and unsustainable technologies," their declaration read. "Contrary to those who put their faith in 'green capitalism,' we know that it is impossible to have infinite growth on a finite planet."[34] The statement called for leaving fossil fuels in the ground, popular and community control over production, reducing the North's overconsumption, respecting indigenous and forest peoples' rights, and, notably, reparations for the ecological and climate debts owed by the richest countries to those who are most affected by resource extraction and climate-related disasters. The emerging issue of climate debt became the focus of a day of action during the Copenhagen summit, as part of a full week of militant actions around the summit site, including an attempted occupation of the summit locations to challenge false solutions and rising corporate influence over the U.N. proceedings.

The emerging discourse of climate justice reflects the growing understanding that those most affected by accelerating climate-related disasters around the world are generally the least responsible for causing disruptions in the climate. Thus any movement seeking an adequate response to global climate changes needs to challenge this discrepancy and prioritize the voices of the most affected communities. People throughout the world are simultaneously impacted by accelerating climate chaos and by the emerging false solutions to climate change, including carbon trading and offsets, the destruction of forests to create agrofuel plantations, large-scale hydroelectric developments, and nuclear power. Corporate "solutions" to global warming are expanding commodification and privatization, whether of land, waterways, or the atmosphere itself, largely at the expense of those same affected communities.

In the U.S., the climate justice effort is increasingly led by environmental justice activists, mainly from communities of color that have been resisting daily exposure to chemical toxins and other environmental hazards for more than twenty years. An important two-day conference in New York City in early 2009, organized by West Harlem Environmental Action (WEACT) brought inner-city activists, community and youth organizers, indigenous representatives, and farmworker advocates together with students, environmental lawyers, scientists, public health advocates and government officials to further the environmental justice critique of carbon markets and discuss the relevance of the climate justice framework for communities of color and their allies across the United States.

A physician from Los Angeles at the WEACT conference described carbon trading as yet another means of "redistributing wealth from the poor to the wealthy," and José Bravo of the Just Transition Alliance suggested that "when we put a price on every square inch of air, there are some of us who won't be able to afford to breathe."[35] Many speakers described the emerging climate justice movement as a continuation of the Civil Rights legacy and of the continuing "quest for fairness, equity and justice," to quote the pioneering environmental justice researcher and author Robert Bullard. Others explained how in recent years, the environmental justice movement has broadened its scope to include issues of justice in food, housing, and transportation. Hence, their embrace of the emerging global climate justice agenda is a logical continuation of a vital living legacy.

In the U.S. and around the world, an impressive array of interests is coming together to shape the climate justice agenda. Among these are the opponents of mountaintop removal coal mining, who are repeatedly putting their bodies on the line to expose devastating mining practices that have already destroyed over 500 mountains in southern Appalachia. Rising numbers of people in Appalachian coal-dependent communities are demanding a new economic model that relieves the stranglehold of the coal companies over their communities, protects people's health, and facilitates the phase-out of the most environmentally destructive form of energy production. Indigenous communities, many organized under the umbrella of the Indigenous Environmental Network, are resisting increased mining of coal and uranium in North America and advancing educational initiatives regarding the false solutions to global warming. An emerging youth climate movement is carrying out creative direct actions, not only at coal industry sites, but also at corporate headquarters, industry conferences, and even the offices of corporate-friendly environmental groups such as the Environmental Defense Fund.[36]

Internationally, people from Pacific Island nations, in some cases already losing land and groundwater to rising seas, have been in the forefront of calls for immediate action. The worldwide confederation of peasant movements, Via Campesina, with affiliated groups in more than eighty countries, joined the call for actions at the 2009 U.N. summit, challenging the status of carbon as a newly privatized commodity and arguing that the U.N. climate convention "has failed to radically question the current models of consumption and production based on the illusion of continuous growth."[37] Critical civil society organizations, many working within the framework of Climate Justice Now! continue to challenge the status quo, both inside and outside various U.N. negotiations. Further, hundreds of cities and towns in the U.S. have defied the federal government's twenty years of inaction and committed to substantial, publicly-aided CO_2 reductions of their own. At the local level, people are regenerating local food systems, seeking locally controlled, renewable energy sources, and building solidarity with kindred movements around the world.

In the fall of 2008, U.S. organizations actively working for climate justice both nationally and internationally, including Indigenous Environmental Network, Global Justice Ecology Project, and Rising Tide North America, launched the Mobilization for Climate

Justice (MCJ).[38] The Mobilization was founded to link the climate struggle in the U.S. to the growing international climate justice movement, with an eye toward building for actions around the 2009 U.N. climate summit and beyond. Its objective was to provide a justice-based framework for organizing around climate change that opened space for leadership by representatives of communities in the U.S. that are most impacted by climate change and the fossil fuel industry. The MCJ's initial open letter to potential allies called for "a radical change in direction to put climate justice, ecological integrity and people's rights at the center of international climate negotiations." Another new network, Climate SOS has emerged to expose the myths of the carbon market as promoted in domestic U.S. legislation.[39]

A new movement is emerging, but clearly has a way to go before it can meaningfully counter the dual obstacles of global warming denial on one hand and nominally well-meaning but counterproductive policy measures on the other. This movement is sharply focused on the social justice implications of the global climate crisis, highlighting the voices of those already massively affected by the heating of the earth for which humans have been responsible. It is linked to antiwar efforts, demonstrating how continuing U.S. military adventures, including the wars in Iraq and Afghanistan, are without question the most grotesquely energy-wasting activities on the planet. It is working to expose the myriad false solutions to global warming promoted by the world's elites, including the sub-sidized expansion of nuclear power and agrofuels, and the continued promotion of carbon trading and offsets. Some also advocate specific policy alternatives, including scientifically adequate emissions reductions, a tax on industrial scale carbon dioxide emissions, altered utility and transportation policies, public funds for solar and wind energy, and aggressive reductions in energy consumption throughout the industrialized world.

Still, there is much more to do. We need to envision a lower-consumption world of decentralized, clean energy and politically empowered communities. Like the anti-nuclear activists of thirty years ago, who halted the first wave of nuclear power in the U.S. while articulating an inspiring vision of directly democratic, solar-powered towns and neighborhoods, we need to again dramatize the positive (even utopian) possibilities for a post-petroleum, post-mega-mall world. The technological means already exist for a locally-controlled, solar-based alternative, at the same time that dissatisfaction with today's high consumption/high debt 'American way of life' appears to be at an all time high. Experiments in raising and distributing food more locally are thriving everywhere and enhancing many people's quality of life, and so are a wide variety of experiments in community-controlled renewable energy production.

There is no shortage of feasible technical solutions to ending excessive energy con-sumption and rapidly curtailing the use of fossil fuels. Thirty years ago, energy analyst Amory Lovins began to demonstrate the feasibility of dramatically increased energy effi-ciency. His work over the past three decades has demonstrated in exhaustive detail how we can reduce energy consumption by sixty to eighty percent, and how many of the necessary measures would result in an unambiguous economic gain.[40] New, innovative technologies for saving energy and replacing fossil fuels are announced almost daily.

Today, more than ever, the obstacles are entirely social and political. The underlying problem, of course, is that capitalism aims to maximize profits, not efficiency. Indeed, economists since the nineteenth century have suggested that improvements in the ef-ficiency of resource consumption will most often increase demand and further economic expansion under capitalism.[41] Nonetheless, while efficiency improvements often reduce the costs of production, corporations will generally accept the perhaps higher expense of sustaining existing methods that have proven to keep profits growing. The *New York Times* reported last year that corporations are hesitant to invest in measures to save energy and make their operations more efficient unless they can demonstrate a two year payback—a constraint that is rarely imposed on other investments.[42]

Corporations almost invariably prefer to lay off workers, outsource production, or move factories overseas than to invest in environmentally-meaningful improvements. Further, we now have the most inequitable distribution of wealth since the period just before the Great Depression of the 1930s. The occupation of Iraq cost the U.S. and its allies over $3 trillion over the past five years, according to Nobel economics laureate Joseph Stiglitz.[43] Public funds are squandered on projects and tax measures that benefit the few at the expense of the many, while our society's contribution to climate catastrophe continues to mount.

Global warming can represent a future of deprivation and scarcity for all but the world's wealthiest, or this global emergency can compel us to imagine a radically transformed society—both in the North and the South—where communities of people are newly empowered to remake their own future. The crisis can drive us to break free from a predatory global capitalism that fabulously enriches the top tenth of one percent, while leaving the rest of us scrambling after the crumbs. The reality is too urgent, and the outlook far too bleak, to settle for anything less than a radically new]social and political outlook on ecology. We need a movement that looks beyond the status quo, actualizes the transformative potential of an ecological outlook, and illuminates the urgent necessity to create a dramatically different kind of world.

NOTES

1   National Oceanic and Atmospheric Administration, "State of the Climate, Global Hazards" (August 2005), HTTP://WWW.NCDC.NOAA.GOV/SOTC/INDEX.PHP?REPORT=HAZARDS&YEAR=200 5&MONTH=AUG.

2   The emerging conflict between technocratic environmentalism and social ecology was first explored by social ecologist Murray Bookchin in the 1970s; several of his essays from that period are compiled in his *Toward an Ecological Society* (Montreal: Black Rose Books, 1980).

3   The various IPCC reports, and condensed "Summaries for Policy Makers," can be downloaded from HTTP://WWW.IPCC.CH.

4   Reported in James Hansen, *et al.*, "Climate change and trace gases," *Philosophical Transactions of the Royal Society, Part A,* Vol. 365, pp. 1925–1954 (2007), and James Hansen, *et al.*, "Target Atmospheric CO_2: Where Should Humanity Aim?" (unpublished manuscript), available from HTTP://WWW.COLUMBIA.EDU/~JEH1/2008/TARGETCO2_20080407.PDF.

5   The IPCC's conclusions in this and subsequent paragraphs are from their Working Group II Report, titled "Impacts, Adaptation and Vulnerability," and available from HTTP://WWW.IPCC. CH.

6   IPCC Working Group II Report, 393.

7   World Resources Institute, *Synthesis: Ecosystems and Human Well-Being,* A Report of the Millennium Ecosystem Assessment (Washington, DC: Island Press, 2005).

8   World Resources Institute, 119.

9   Juliet Eilperin, "New Analysis Brings Dire Forecast Of 6.3–Degree Temperature Increase," *Washington Post,* September 25, 2009, at HTTP://WWW.WASHINGTONPOST.COM/WP-DYN/CONTENT/ARTICLE/2009/09/24/AR2009092402602.HTML; David Adam, "Met Office warns of

catastrophic global warming in our lifetimes," *The Guardian*, September 28, 2009, at HTTP://
WWW.GUARDIAN.CO.UK/ENVIRONMENT/2009/SEP/28/MET-OFFICE-STUDY-GLOBAL-WARMING.

10   Human Development Report 2007/2008: Fighting Climate Change: Human Solidarity in a
       Divided World, United Nations Development Program, 2007, 16.

11   See, for example, Ernest Waititu "Drought Spurs Resource Wars," Pulitzer Center for Crisis
       Reporting, reprinted in *The Indypendent* (NYC), No. 119, April 25, 2008.

12   Jim Yardley, "Drought Puts Focus on a Side of India Left Out of Progress," *New York Times*,
       September 5, 2009.

13   Dan Smith and Janani Vivekananda, *A Climate of Conflict: The links between climate change,
       peace and war* (London: International Alert, November 2007), 3.

14   Rafael Reuveny, "Climate change-induced migration and violent conflict, *Political Geography*
       Vol. 26, 656–673, 2007.

15   Michael T. Klare, "The Pentagon vs. Peak Oil: How Wars of the Future May Be Fought Just to
       Run the Machines That Fight Them," at HTTP://WWW.TOMDISPATCH.COM/POST/174810.

16   *U.N. Human Development Report*, 27.

17   For a detailed comparison of the cost of nuclear power to a variety of low-carbon alternatives,
       see Amory B. Lovins and Imran Sheikh, "The Nuclear Illusion," at HTTPS://WWW.RMI.ORG/
       IMAGES/PDFS/ENERGY/E08–01_AMBIONUCLILUSION.PDF.

18   See, for example, Jan Willem Storm van Leeuwen and Philip Smith, *Nuclear Power: The Energy
       Balance*, available from HTTP://WWW.STORMSMITH.NL.

19   See, for example, the Agrofuels Special Issue of *Seedling*, published in Barcelona by the inter-
       national research group GRAIN, July 2007, available from http://GRAIN.ORG.

20   Estimates of how much agrofuel production has contributed to recent increases in global food
       prices range from the U.S. Department of Agriculture's estimate of less than 5 percent, to the
       World Bank's figure of 80 percent. For comprehensive analyses of the global food crisis and
       various activist responses, see "The Crisis in Agriculture and Food: Conflict, Resistance, &
       Renewal," a special issue of *Monthly Review*, July-August 2009.

21   Lester R. Brown, "Supermarkets and Service Stations Now Competing for Grain," Earth
       Policy Institute Update, July 13, 2006, at HTTP://WWW.EARTH-POLICY.ORG/UPDATES/2006/
       UPDATE55.HTM; C. Ford Runge and Benjamin Senauer, "How Biofuels Could Starve the
       Poor," *Foreign Affairs*, Vol. 86, No. 3, 41–53, May/June 2007.

22   Jason Hill, *et al.*, "Environmental, economic, and energetic costs and benefits of biodiesel
       and ethanol biofuels," *Proceedings of the National Academy of Sciences*, Vol. 103 no. 30, 11206
       –11210, July 25, 2006.

23   For an overview, see *Biofuels: Renewable Energy or Environmental Disaster in the Making?* (Lon-
       don: Biofuelwatch, 2006), at HTTP://WWW.BIOFUELWATCH.ORG.UK/BIOFUEL_PAPER.PDF.

24   In some instances, especially under tropical conditions, it can take centuries of agrofuel pro-
       duction to compensate for the carbon dioxide emissions that result from converting forests and
       grasslands to agrofuel production. See Joseph Fargione, *et al.*, "Land Clearing and the Biofuel
       Carbon Debt," *Science* Vol. 319, 1235–1238 February 29, 2008, and Timothy Searchinger, *et
       al.*, "Use of U.S. Croplands for Biofuels Increases Greenhouse Gases Through Emissions from
       Land-Use Change," *Science* Vol. 319, 1238–1240, February 29, 2008, both available online
       from HTTP://WWW.SCIENCEEXPRESS.ORG.

25   See Rachel Smolker, *et al.*, "The True Cost of Agrofuels: Impacts on food, forests, peoples and
       the climate," Global Forest Coalition, 2008, especially Chapter 6, at HTTP://WWW.GLOBAL-
       FORESTCOALITION.ORG/IMG/USERPICS/FILE/PUBLICATIONS/TRUECOSTAGROFUELS.PDF;   for
       continuing updates see http://NOGETREES.ORG.

26 See, for example, Netherlands Environmental Assessment Agency, "Global CO2 emissions: annual increase halves in 2008," at HTTP://WWW.PBL.NL/EN/PUBLICATIONS/2009/GLOBAL-CO2–EMISSIONS-ANNUAL-INCREASE-HALVES-IN-2008.HTML.

27 In George Monbiot's column, "We've been suckered again by the US. So far the Bali deal is worse than Kyoto," *The Guardian*, December 17, 2007.

28 Larry Lohmann, *Carbon Trading: A Critical Conversation on Climate Change, Privatization and Power*, Uppsala, Sweden: Dag Hammarskjold Foundation, 2006, available from HTTP://WWW.THECORNERHOUSE.ORG.UK/SUMMARY.SHTML?X=544225.

29 For a critical overview of current U.S. climate legislation, see Brian Tokar, "Toward Climate Justice: Can we turn back from the abyss?," *Z Magazine*, September 2009, at HTTP://WWW.ZCOMMUNICATIONS.ORG/ZMAG/VIEWARTICLE/22377, and continuing updates at HTTP://CLIMATESOS.ORG.

30 For analysis of the landmark 1977 Seabrook demonstration, written mainly by participants, see *The Clamshell Alliance at 20*, a special issue of *Peacework* (No. 265, July/August 1996), published in Cambridge, MA by the American Friends Service Committee, and available from HTTP://WWW.PEACEWORKMAGAZINE.ORG/PWORK/CLAM1996/DEFAULT2.HTM.

31 For an overview of social ecology see Brian Tokar, "On Bookchin's Social Ecology and its Contributions to Social Movements," *Capitalism, Nature, Socialism*, Volume 19, No. 2, March 2008. An exceptionally comprehensive statement of the outlook of social ecology is Murray Bookchin's classic *The Ecology of Freedom* (Palo Alto, CA: Cheshire Books, 1982).

32 Murray Bookchin. "Reflections: An Overview of the Roots of Social Ecology" in *Harbinger: A Journal of Social Ecology*, Vol. 3, No. 1 (2002), HTTP://WWW.SOCIAL-ECOLOGY.ORG/2002/09/HARBINGER-VOL-3–NO-1–REFLECTIONS-AN-OVERVIEW-OF-THE-ROOTS-OF-SOCIAL-ECOLOGY/ (Accessed January 1, 2010).

33 Kenny Bruno, Joshua Karliner & China Brotsky, *Greenhouse Gangsters vs. Climate Justice* (San Francisco: CorpWatch, 1999), at HTTP://WWW.CORPWATCH.ORG/ARTICLE.PHP?ID=1048.

34 Brian Tokar. "Politics-as-Usual While the Planet Burns" in *Synthesis/Regeneration* 51 (Winter 2010); HTTP://WWW.GREENS.ORG/S-R/51/51–02.HTML.

35 Brian Tokar. "Toward Climate Justice", *Z Magazine*, Vol. 22, No. 9 (September 2009), available at: HTTP://WWW.ZCOMMUNICATIONS.ORG/TOWARD-CLIMATE-JUSTICE-BY-BRIAN-TOKAR.

36 See HTTP://RISINGTIDENORTHAMERICA.ORG.

37 Brian Tokar. "Toward Climate Justice", *Z Magazine*, Vol. 22, No. 9 (September 2009), available at: HTTP://WWW.ZCOMMUNICATIONS.ORG/TOWARD-CLIMATE-JUSTICE-BY-BRIAN-TOKAR.

38 MCJ, See HTTP://ACTFORCLIMATEJUSTICE.ORG.

39 HTTP://CLIMATESOS.ORG.

40 See, for example, Amory Lovins, *et al.*, *Winning the Oil Endgame: Innovation for Profits, Jobs, and Security* (Snowmass, CO: Rocky Mountain Institute, 2005), available from HTTP://WWW.OILENDGAME.COM. Lovins' pitch is unapologetically aimed at those whose primary concern is market profitability; the absence of a more critical political outlook has led to a conspicuous myopia about why his proposals are not more widely adopted.

41 John Bellamy Foster, "The Jeavons Paradox: Environment and Technology Under Capitalism," in *The Ecological Revolution: Making Peace with the Planet* (New York: Monthly Review Books, 2009), 121–128.

42 Matthew L. Wald, "Efficiency, Not Just Alternatives, Is Promoted as an Energy Saver," *New York Times*, May 29, 2007.

43 Joseph Stiglitz and Linda J. Bilmes, *The Three Trillion Dollar War: The True Cost of the Iraq Conflict* (New York: W. W. Norton & Company, 2008).

THE DESIRE TO HEAL:

Harm Intervention in a Landscape of Restorative Justice and Critical Resistance

Stevie Peace | **Team Colors Collective**[1]

KNOWLEDGE OF HARM, MEMORY OF TRAUMA

N NEW ORLEANS IN THE fall of 2006, a man approached me in the late evening, shouted "CHINK!" and bashed my head open with a U-bolt bike lock. I was twenty-three years old at the time. I am often tempted to consider this to be merely a case of Vincent Chin redux, since the circumstances of my assault—a young Asian-American victim, a stranger as the perpetrator, the trappings of a hate crime, the bludgeoning of the head—are remarkably similar, save one difference: Vincent Chin was killed, and I survived. The significance is not lost on me. And yet the more I reflect, the difference between Vincent and me—or Sean Bell, or Sanesha Stewart, to name a few—seems less apparent.[2] If Vincent had lived—in spite of a baseball bat cracking his skull half a dozen times—he would have surely found his resulting 'life' of exceeding trauma, fear, and despair to be questionable, at best. My own recovery, full of these miserable musings, has made me wonder whether dying, as Vincent had, would have been preferable.

That such a large number of us have lived with and survived one or multiple incidents of violence is clear. What is profoundly unclear is what we mean by 'living' or 'surviving' in the aftermath of violence. To *know* that one has suffered harm at the hands of another human being is a terrible knowledge.[3] That one is expected to continue on an uninterrupted trajectory of life in spite of this knowledge is dangerously absurd. Similarly, that one should heal simply from long spans of time, distance, 'comfort' or 'normalcy'—none of which erase the terrible knowledge—is equally bizarre. Yet these expectations have remarkable staying power. After my assault, I moved 1,000 miles away to the relative comfort and normalcy of Minneapolis-St. Paul, living quietly for over a year, out of the belief that these steps would aid my recovery. Yet all it took was an attempted armed robbery in March 2008 to remind me that I have not healed. As I sat on my bed later that night, shaking uncontrollably, seized once again by the possibility of an early, violent death, I realized that I had not even attempted to heal in the first place.

The absence of the individual's desire to heal is not accidental. Those of us who have experienced harm or trauma feel compelled to continue on instead. Surely some of this comes from the uniquely American myth of inevitable progress and our capacity for selective amnesia. Much of the motivation is also avoidance and fear. But the memory of harm is also intimate; it requires coping mechanisms and resilience as much as the identification of harm's roots, whether systemic, historical, or relationship-driven. Struggle, resilience, coping, mourning, avoiding, confronting: we have seen the dynamics of harm unfold throughout history, in all their complexities, transformations, and moments of loss. In the United States, this history is especially laced with traumatic acts: the genocide of American Indians, the killing and enslavement of African-Americans, the systemic rape, lynching, and torture of both groups, the purge of Chinese immigrants in the West and subsequent Asian exclusion laws, the ongoing beatings and killings of striking workers, increased poverty and violence exacted on women, people of color, and queer and trans folk. This list is easy to generate, but even easier to feel; harm is not solely physical, but also takes extraordinary tolls on emotional, economic, mental, and spiritual levels. We find strength and power in the stories of people who have continued on in the thick of misery, those who organize, who maintain joy and fierce determination, who we know have been through *all that* and still live, still sustain. Yet the voices that say "we're alright, we're going to be alright" carry a hollow and anxious undertone. They speak to the memory of trauma, whether they know it or not.

It is difficult to comprehend this memory of trauma. Our history does not let it go, and we also hold fast to it. Our harms gather before our eyes, heavy and forbidding. Once we take it in unflinchingly, questions arise: what are we supposed to do with this? How do we live in the aftermath? All at once, the trauma rushes in, rendering us catatonic. One would be hard-pressed to call this recurring paralysis "living."[4] What interests me, then, is how people refuse paralysis and choose to *engage* harm. For those of us engaged in community organizing and social justice work, the answer is not as straightforward as simply maintaining such commitments, though struggle is crucial to our common refusal of harm's agents: oppression, exploitation, violence, terror. It is one thing to demand an end to harm, and it is quite another to bear the brunt of harm when one's demands are ignored. The work for healing justice is bruising; not all of us survive it. So how do we *intervene* on harm? How do we address it in both long-term organizing and everyday resistance? How do we develop *harm intervention* as part and parcel of our struggles?

HARM PERPETUATION: THE PRISON-INDUSTRIAL COMPLEX AND THE NORMALIZATION OF VIOLENCE

One of the primary difficulties of engaging with harm is that we have largely ceded that work to a state apparatus called the 'criminal justice' system. This unfortunate situation deserves a critical assessment.

The 'criminal justice' system was not designed by us (at least, not *most* of us); it is not 'ours for the taking' either. Its presence extends well beyond the more obvious practitioners and agents of imposition: prisons, jails, detention centers, probation, and police. While these play a crucial role, the system's growth and determination is not to be found only in distinct, 'separate' institutions. The 'criminal justice' system finds a ready fuel in our lives, inseparability rendered through ideology and culture; it is our default. In the event of an assault, robbery, rape, domestic abuse, threat on one's life, community disruption or even *the possibility of harm*, there is but one immediate recourse for intervention presented to us: dial 911, and bring in agents of the state. But one does not simply 'experience' the 'criminal justice' system when one commits harm or is victimized by harm. The system *is* our experience, even when it is not as 'visible' as police cars pulling up after a 911 call. Trying to envision ideas of a 'safe community' or a 'community free of harm' without the system's rendering of it is exceedingly difficult.

Before us is a complex, changing state apparatus that takes many forms: harm dispensation (policing and surveillance, especially of communities of color), harm accentuation (solitary confinement), harm cultivation (the prison boom, the growth of detention centers, and prison privatization), and harm administration (the death penalty). State and capital are plenty harmful in their imposition; the 'criminal justice' system merely exacerbates and cements the devastation. This is a *harm perpetuation system*.

Perpetuation of any kind, of course, cannot happen in the U.S. without profit, material and affective production. It is not a system we are witness to so much as a ' prison industrial complex,' a term first coined by Critical Resistance and widely used today. Its development in the last few decades coincides with the advent of government counterinsurgency tactics, the rollback of civil rights achievements, and the stunningly quick beginnings of the mass incarceration of black men. The focus on black men was particularly deliberate, as jails and prisons became a disciplinary center for a population with enormous rebellious potential, as demonstrated in the riots of the late 1960s; the prospects of additional labor extraction merely sweetened the deal. Today the prison industrial complex is a super-nexus of capitalism, racism, sexism, classism, and homophobia, one that currently boasts over 7.3 million direct 'participants' with an upsettingly diverse portfolio (its fastest growing prison population is women of color). It criminalizes every historically oppressed people in American history, making immense profit off of them as well.

That the U.S. has the largest imprisoned population in the world is due primarily to the enormous growth of prisons to house them, as well as the increased involvement of contracting companies that thrive off of them. Most astonishing is the mirroring of this growth in other oppressive systems and institutions, all exerting increased discipline and control in cooperation with each other. For example, the complex is responsible for the unnerving growth of the 'juvenile justice' system and its infusion into public schools. The development of a "school-to-prison pipeline" is especially evident in California, where the number of prison beds is determined in part by school drop-out rates. Similar disciplinary mechanisms and oppressive policies have made their way into homeless shelters, hospitals, and all aspects of immigration, where monitoring and detention have skyrocketed in the wake of the "War on Terror." The prison industrial complex also serves as a weapon to be deployed against movements and political actions deemed threatening to capital and state, as witnessed in vicious counter-movement assaults following the successful 2006 *¡Sí, Se Puede!* general strikes and uprisings.[5]

The prison industrial complex yields a particularly sobering consequence: the normalization of violence. One could argue that, as the history of the U.S. both domestically and internationally shows, violence has always *been* normal—a base for this country's founding, a launching pad for its growth and rise to power, and a medium for maintaining capitalism and other oppressive systems. And yet there is something disturbing, even suffocating, about where our normalization has turned: not so much who is committing the harm and who is being harmed (groups that have remained fairly steady over time), but rather that the prison industrial complex financially depends on (and thus works toward) *increasing harm unendingly.* As the complex grows more efficient at compounding violence, harm becomes more interwoven into the social fabric, even in communities of resistance. That so many of us on the Left have embraced the slogan "Don't Mourn, Organize!" as our general attitude to harm should give us pause. We might start to seriously challenge the normalization of violence by considering how to mourn *and* organize all at once.

THE LANDSCAPE OF HARM INTERVENTION: TWO WORKS IN PROGRESS

THE STRUGGLE AGAINST OUR HARM perpetuation system and for new inventions of harm engagement is a daunting one, yet there are precedents to look to. The organizing of harm intervention has been addressed previously in a number of historical movements, like women's liberation and Martin Luther King's "Beloved Community"; others, such as the AIDS Coalition to Unleash Power (ACT UP), are less recognizable, but their contributions have been transformative. Recognizing the importance of control of one's body and life, ACT UP centralized this understanding in its development of "harm reduction" practices and addressed health-risking activities such as substance abuse as well as other measures of safety and security, like organizing for affordable housing. These undertakings developed from and became a source of power within queer communities that continues to this day. Movements centered on restoration for severe historical dispossession have made additional forays into the terrain, including groups working for black reparations and indigenous decolonization. These forays have been less successful in building power and generalizing struggle, but they have raised new challenges as their respective peoples have questioned what meaningful 'justice' looks like after centuries of incredible violence. Recently we have seen movements more directly tied to 'crime' and 'criminal justice'; restorative justice projects, prisoners' rights groups, and prison abolition groups are just a few of the pioneers in this arena. Harm intervention has also been applied in groups targeting sexual violence, domestic abuse, and violence towards those exploited on many levels, INCITE! Women of Color Against Violence being the most prominent group among them.[6]

This wide and varied exploration of interventions, as well as its growing thematic presence in organizing efforts, constitutes a landscape of harm interventions, each project unique and prominent, but still separate and autonomous. All are preoccupied with similar political flows and processes that mark much of contemporary organizing— "undoing" (removing sources of oppression) and "becoming" (arriving at new ways of living and organizing our lives). What differentiates these projects from the rest is a guiding recognition: that harm is not just violence or consequence of oppression, but also *a political act,* and healing, therefore, is *political resistance.*

I want to focus on two of these projects and bring them into encounter with one another: Restorative Justice Community Action (RJCA) and Critical Resistance (CR). The selection is deliberate, since they are disparate in myriad ways, and my discussion of them here should illustrate just how uneven and disjointed this landscape is. RJCA developed out of a small number of neighborhood organizations in Minneapolis, Minnesota; CR was born in a conference in Berkeley, California that drew thousands of activists, former prisoners, academics, and community folks. The scope of CR includes numerous chapters across the nation; RJCA still has not left its doorstep in Minnesota, though it now operates in fifty neighborhoods instead of four. But there are similarities between the two: both are nonprofit organizations, both have been at work for over a decade, and both are well-established on the map of harm intervention. I am particularly interested in these two works in progress for another reason: each has deliberately chosen to center their struggles against harm *in relation to and in response to* the prison industrial complex. This warrants some examination into how their work has developed, what it looks like, and what challenges lie ahead.

HARM REPARATION: CHALLENGES IN A PROFESSIONALIZED MOVEMENT

RESTORATIVE JUSTICE COMMUNITY ACTION MAKES its mark on the landscape through *harm reparation*, focusing specifically on the safety, livability, and health of communities. Police and the courts refer citations for "livability offenses" ("victimless crimes" that still have pronounced effects on communities, such as soliciting prostitution, littering, graffiti, urinating in public, and noisy assemblies) to RJCA. The coinciding offenders, should they choose to accept RJCA rather than pay a fine or go to court, are placed in a "community conference," a facilitated circle that includes offenders and members of the community where the offenders were cited. The community conference is an intervention; as the circle proceeds, offenders are held accountable for their actions, community members are able to express how the offenses harm their neighborhood, and all participants work together on how each of the offenders can "make things right," a plan which, if successfully completed, usually results in the dismissal of their cases.

The form of intervention used by RJCA is common to other restorative justice programs. Restorative justice is itself a very old concept, predating the punitive system of 'criminal justice' by many centuries; its premise is simply that 'crime' or 'harm' is a violation of people and relationships, and therefore 'justice' is the righting of wrongs against people, the 'restoring' of relationships. (This is a direct contrast from conventional 'criminal justice,' which holds all 'crimes' to be violations of state and the law). Indigenous peoples throughout the world have practiced restorative justice as their primary means of harm engagement; however, restorative justice's position, application, and growth in the Global North is a new phenomenon, and the relative 'success' of this mass appropriation of indigenous culture deserves close scrutiny. One could talk at length about the various measures of success here—how extensive restorative justice is now compared to earlier, how many people restorative justice impacts, how meaningful the process is, how transformative harm reparation is in individuals' lives. But viewed through the magnifying glass of movements and movement inquiry, a different picture emerges: mass professionalization and its accompanying dangers. These need to be reviewed carefully, for similar predicaments are developing in other movements, and dialogue and responses to the matter have been insufficient.

Compositionally, restorative justice is, at best, a scattered lot. RJCA emerged as an initiative and tool developed by neighborhood associations who desired safer communities.

Neighborhood associations carry a sordid history, traced to the first public housing battles after World War II, black homeownership and white racist backlash, and massive reconfiguration of urban space that entrenched white power and heightened the stark conditions of life for poor and working-class people of color.[7] So the creation of this restorative justice project, unique as it is, moved in predictable ways: the identified 'problem' was "street crime" and its agents; the support sought to address the problem came primarily from the cooperation of state agents like the courts and police; the end goal was a community with strong norms of responsibility, respect, and dignity, though the implicit emphasis—barely concealed in dialogue—was removal of the 'problem people,' that is, people of color, the homeless, poor and working-class folks, renters, and public housing residents. This is, of course, a strikingly counter-revolutionary premise; today, as a nonprofit organization, neighborhood association interests no longer solely run the engine, and nonprofit industry funding schematics, the prison industrial complex, and (to a lesser extent) the communities 'served' have become the preferred fuels.

Minnesota has seen the development of many restorative justice projects. Most of these developed entirely through the Department of Corrections and other state agents, who secured funding, government backing, and institutional support for many programs operated under the arms of the prison industrial complex. Minnesota likely desires to be the 'progressive' 'criminal justice' leader in the nation due to the many restorative justice programs they endorse and fund, so long as these programs are run by a firm hand that has the interests of the larger prison industrial complex in mind. But other groups were (and still are) separate and autonomous by comparison; some formed out of anti-violence organizing and are still firmly rooted in small communities, some operate independently in schools, and some have thrown their lot in with the nonprofit industry as RJCA has.

This proliferation highlights some of the difficulties in genuine movement composition around harm engagement. The terrain may look different elsewhere, but in Minnesota, there is a persistent two-pronged approach to harm reparation: creating a multitude of strong and useful practices, which presumably could make restorative justice alternatives powerful enough to cut into and minimize the 'criminal justice' system's reach; and expanding restorative justice education and training, a foundational 'cultural shift' that communities can draw from to delegitimize the current system and demand new possibilities. Exciting as the aims are, they lack grist, substituting 'practices' for organizing and 'education' for strategy; the goals are lofty but may remain *just* goals. This is the position of RJCA, constrained in part by its nonprofit status; yet this is symptomatic of other nonprofits, who have largely eschewed organizing for something like a politics of access. RJCA would instantly become a risky program should it prioritize organizing. Instead, like so many nonprofits, it goes to great lengths to cooperate with state and capital and is rewarded in kind. For example, while restorative justice is applicable to all experiences of harm, including historical and social injustices, RJCA strategically focuses on 'offenders' (that is, 'criminals') as the source of harm, *not* the prison industrial complex nor other oppressive forces. 'Victims' are thus the ones affected by particular 'offenses' or 'crimes.' This premise was RJCA's primary point of entry into participating in the 'criminal justice' system. Of course, the reality that 'offenders' commit harms that impact 'victims' is not problematic. But the absence of a power analysis is glaring in this acceptance of terminology, definitions, and notions of 'crime' that reify the current system. The same situation arises concerning funding, partnerships, and the relationships formed among staff and volunteers; none of these crucial organizational elements proceed without the green light of acceptance and access. This does not deny RJCA's constructive contributions on the terrain and the many potential individual transformations for those who participate, but the resulting access-based politics must be situated in a problematic light—especially when it is impossible to discern the effect of this access on Minnesota's prison industrial complex, which still runs smoothly.

The other prong, further education, is indicative of another worrisome trend: a shift towards concentrated energy in academia. Education and training done well—through popular education and innovative dialogue, as two examples—can be crucial for building power and assessing necessary strategies and knowledges in furtherance of movement. But restorative justice and the politics of harm reparation have gone in a different direction. Minnesota is lauded for its advancement of the "restorative justice field": academic institutions (the Center for Restorative Justice and Peacemaking at the University of Minnesota-Twin Cities, one of the first of its kind in the nation); conferences and professional trainings done in coordination with projects and programs, both institutional and grassroots (and often spearheaded by the Restorative Justice Planner, another first-of-its-kind staff position in the Department of Corrections); and publication (Living Justice Press, based in St. Paul and focused exclusively on works about restorative justice). The practices of harm reparation are quickly building professors and trainers, whose attention is more easily devoted to gaining expertise and contributing to the academic 'field' than the movement. Thus restorative justice has been increasingly considered a "professional movement," a more accurate moniker that needs to be critically examined.

The place of harm reparation in movement building, as witnessed from RJCA in Minneapolis, is rather grim due to these immense challenges that have yet to be discussed with any serious strategic reflection. But harm reparation need not be written off entirely. Despite its problematic position, RJCA's program has offered up a way for volunteers and participants to become practitioners of harm engagement, and in so doing they have even learned how to resist—in small ways—the confines of a "professional movement." The community conferences that form the brunt of RJCA's restorative justice work have set confines (acceptance of the prison industrial complex among them), but to most people they are very new spaces that are public, open, and brimming with potential, limited as it may be. The dialogue around the particular 'offenses' rarely stays in the parameters of crime; sometimes participants turn to questions of respect and dignity in our relationships with each other, and sometimes they look well beyond the narrow scope of 'crime' and start finding ways to create safe, supportive communities that centralize autonomous harm engagement without turning to the state. The practice of harm reparation is transformative for many, as the possibility of healing becomes tangible in all parts of their lives. Questions emerge as to what that would look like, what form that may take, and whether a project like RJCA is the right form.[8]

HARM REDUCTION: A PRACTICE GOES NATIONAL

CRITICAL RESISTANCE HAS A DIFFERENT political composition. Its primary goal is *harm reduction*, the same practice developed in AIDS activism and now situated against the prison industrial complex. Recognizing that the complex's failure to address harm illustrates its primary role and intent of perpetuating and exacting harm on oppressed peoples, CR demands the abolition of the prison industrial complex. The allusion to "abolition" is intentional, out of a recognition that previous generations had worked to abolish the system of slavery, not reform it. CR's intervention strategy is mostly three-pronged, focusing on "decarceration" (reducing the prison population), ending prison building (reducing the amount of prisons and jails), and alternative practices (reducing reliance on the prison industrial complex, including prisons and policing, by forming more community-based approaches to harm).

This direct response and resistance to an enormous oppressive apparatus like the prison industrial complex is not significantly different from the approach of other social movement organizations. From the perspective of harm intervention, however, the work is exceedingly difficult, yielding few victories and transformations—a marked contrast from the ease of Restorative Justice Community Action's access-based (and subsequently limited) intervention efforts. CR's sheer survival seems the most remarkable feat of their existence. How this has occurred stems in part from their structure as well as their emphasis on radical community organizing. CR is technically a national nonprofit, but its local chapters wage campaigns that are unique to their specific region; CR national staff provide assistance to the chapters' autonomous organizing efforts. So in California, where the prison population is booming, chapters have waged high-level struggles around one of CR's prongs (ending prison building) through a combination of strategic demonstrations, referenda, lobbying, and direct action. CR's longstanding advocacy of prisoner amnesty gained specific importance in New Orleans, where lawsuits, court struggles, and support networks succeeded in releasing individuals who were arrested and jailed without cause in the aftermath of Hurricane Katrina. Since the emphasis is on sustained local efforts, CR eschews national campaigns entirely. CR organizers are adamant that grassroots struggle and local coalition-building would not work in a 'national organization' defined by hierarchical relationships. The experience and wisdom of radical community organizing appears to guide this decision.

CR has a lot more to resist than the prison industrial complex in its organizing, however; there is also the matter of a Left that has, for many years, implicitly supported the 'criminal justice' system by demanding its reforms rather than its collapse. CR's push for re-thinking has not yet generated a Left consensus on abolition, but at least there is a lukewarm reception today, and some groups and organizations have provided their full support. This stems from strategic coalition-building on the part of the different chapters, as they bring the force of a multitude of organizations to bear on an industry that is difficult to shake. The mutual respect and trust built over time has increased CR's reputation and prowess—if not always its analysis and approach—in radical and 'progressive' circles. "I don't feel that we've had to make very many compromises politically in terms of how we do our work," says Rachel Herzing, a CR organizer, speaking to both the prison industrial complex they face as well as the groups they work with. Yet none of this coalition-building is as paramount to CR's organizing of and outreach to voices that are frequently ignored by the state, communities, and many social movements: the prisoners themselves. For Kai Lumumba Barrow, another CR organizer, it is more than a matter of representation: "We see ourselves as accountable to those who are directly impacted by the [prison industrial complex]: prisoners, former prisoners, family members of prisoners, people who are most often policed." Important as this is, accountability to the massive population of those damaged by the prison industrial complex is much easier said than done. It is worth noting that the placement of CR's current chapters has less to do with where the highest density of prisoners and the policed live, and more to do with which activists (some of whom have been through the complex, but many of whom are also more academically trained, white, and wealthier) have the wherewithal to sustain a chapter. This is an un-surprising situation, given the organization's birth in an activist/academic conference, but there remain significant challenges as to how such a set-up can move towards more gener-alized struggle in all working-class and people-of-color communities who know intimately the terror of the prison industrial complex.

CR is similar to RJCA in that it appeals to victims of harm and remains victim-focused, yet CR arrives at different understandings of 'offenders' and 'victims.' What the state considers an offender, CR recognizes as a victim; the distinction comes out of CR's understanding that most 'offenders' are oppressed peoples that the prison industrial com-plex laps up in order to survive and keep growing. CR does not deny that 'offenders' do indeed commit harm, but they are firm in comparing this to the destruction and violence that the prison industrial complex exacts on us every day. CR also questions our defini-tion of 'crime' and 'harm,' not only in terms of the overwhelmingly disproportionate sentencing for certain 'crimes,' but also in terms of whether these definitions sync up with communities' perceptions of harm. These conceptions constitute a refusal of 'criminal justice' system terminology and cultural and ideological processes around basic necessi-ties: what we need to feel safe, how to protect those we love. This contrasts sharply with restorative justice, which in most of its manifestations in the Global North does not refuse the terms that serve the state. Herzing agrees with this assessment, saying, "Restorative justice has been so completely co-opted. [...] We at CR don't use it as a model." There are larger questions, then, as to the role and importance of "alternative practices" in all harm interventions tied to the prison industrial complex. What seems crucial to any such practices—as CR has suggested and RJCA's development has affirmed—is a firm resis-tance to co-optation, for as new alternatives appear in the landscape, the prison industrial complex and other social forces are primed and ready to swoop in and capture, tame, or crush this energy.

These new terms and understandings have made prison abolition an area of relative excitement and inspiration on the Left, but they also incur a risk: the trap of academia. Co-founder Angela Davis and many other professors and theorists have made invalu-able contributions to many fields sorely in need of a re-education on crime and 'criminal justice,' yet they also recognize how easily such a task can drain movement energy. CR chapters partake in education and training through national gatherings every few years, yet they work to resist the academic tendency by keeping the emphasis on dialogue, sharp-ening their analyses and adopting more critical frameworks. Organizer Melissa Burch said these discussions are instrumental for "redefining the problem" of the prison industrial complex: "That kind of intellectual work that has translated into a difference in how people actually organize on the ground is one of the main things that we've worked on and that we've accomplished." Added Barrow: "We're not moving with one set of answers. We're moving with critical questions." The walking-while-asking-questions approach, reminiscent of the Zapatistas, is key to preventing devolution into debilitating avenues, such as the expertise-building scheme of restorative justice.

Overall, CR has carefully developed its political education and organizing strategy, and its continued autonomy both within its chapters and in relation to other organizations (including the prison industrial complex) can sustain the work for years to come. But the struggle will not get any easier. The prison industrial complex got a major boost after 9/11, due to increased consolidation, the advent of homeland security, an upswing in detention centers, and more surveillance and policing, all signs of an encroaching military state. The complex is wising up to CR and the prison abolition movement, finding ways to continue growing in spite of anti-prison campaigns. "They're continuing to build prisons even as we're throwing up more road blocks," noted Herzing. As CR works towards outsmarting and out-organizing their colossal enemy, one might be hesitant to ask where the lines of healing begin in this scheme. Perhaps it comes with successful battles in particular zones, betraying gaps in the prison industrial complex's armor. Perhaps it develops out of the restoring of prisoners back to their families and communities, as well as the restoring of communities after the shroud of heavy policing finally abates. Perhaps the question must wait until we know for sure if the arc of the prison industrial complex can be stalled and reversed, or if it will continue on its long, agonizing, and violent ascent.[9]

WHAT WOULD IT MEAN TO HEAL?

A GREAT AMOUNT OF INTEREST, analysis, and unexpected thoughts have stemmed from the question that preoccupies the Left of today: "What would it mean to win?"[10] The discussion is encouraging; however, it is not the only discussion needed at the moment. What has yet to emerge in larger discourse is serious reflection on what it means to heal.

At the 2007 National Conference on Organized Resistance in Washington, DC, I found space in a packed room to listen to three woman of color organizers speak about their post-Katrina experiences and challenges.[11] All three were from New Orleans; only one had successfully returned. I had spent less than two months back in Minnesota at this point, and only four months had passed since my assault, yet I remained committed to the struggles of the Gulf Coast and was eager to hear any new developments and insights.

Little in the panel discussion seemed earth-shattering to me, until, seemingly out of the blue, panelist Maya Dempster responded to a question regarding the greatest difficulties in her current work:

> There was never a time we had to actually cry over our city. […] We just kept running, kept going, kept going and all of a sudden it was a year had passed and we were still moving, still trying to find housing, still trying to just live. Those things were interrupted greatly. Life has not returned to normal, there is no sense of normalcy. We're still not OK.

Her answer stunned me. It seemed inconceivable to me that, among the daunting and frustrating challenges of post-Katrina recovery, not having time to cry and mourn would be one of them. And yet, in a horrible flash of clarity, I understood it was *the* challenge of the hour. I remembered how I had barely given myself four days of recovery before I was back to 'business as usual.' Though I had survived, I had not reflected on what I had lost. I did not give myself time to mourn. It was a voluntary decision; for Maya and hundreds of thousands of others, there was no decision, and I wondered which situation was more disturbing. That devastation could reach a point where even important care processes like mourning are disrupted sounded truly awful, but that I experienced no such disruption, and was well-equipped with support systems, friends, and tools like writing, yet consciously *chose not to heal*—the reality is amazing, if not frightfully ludicrous. As a society, as a culture, as a community, we do not ask, "What would it mean to heal?" We do not learn to ask a question like that when the time is right, and soon we come to expect that we cannot ask at all. We have nothing to demand; our healing desires are left isolated and quelled. The real danger is that this amounts to a *refusal* to heal, rather than a refusal of harm's perpetuation.

The question of healing has weighed heavily on me for some time now, in all its permutations: "How do I heal? How will I know I am healing? Does healing reach an endpoint? Do I heal simply by living? What if healing is impossible?" It is astonishing that countless spiritual leaders, counselors, artists, writers, and even politicians have contributed a vast compendium of thoughts on the subject, and yet healing remains a cipher: uncertain in notion, even more uncertain in practice. Perhaps, as bell hooks laid out so clearly in *All About Love*, it is time to unpack the cipher and establish a new, multi-faceted, and abruptly high standard for what we want. Love, according to hooks, is not just commitment, intimacy, and trust; it is also community, solidarity. Love is political.[12] So may it be here; perhaps the crux of healing confounds us because we have yet to address its political dimensions, processes, and practices. Catapulting that discussion forward will likely require a shift of the healing 'realm' away from experts and the well-trained and into common dialogues generated from our shared histories.

And then there is the landscape—the harm reduction work of Critical Resistance, the attempts at reparation at the core of restorative justice, other mountains, mesas, and plateaus scattered over the prison industrial complex bedrock that we all dejectedly stand on. As we look out at the full breadth of the horizon, it seems clear that the last thing we desire is an old-fashioned upheaval, the replacing of our 'criminal justice' system with another, reformed, more 'just' system. And where would we stand when our jackhammers have finally decimated the ground? Thinking beyond the metaphor for a moment, would we be willing to tear down *any* oppressive system if we lacked the accountability, trust, and dignity to support us? Movements around the planet are asking this question, trying to envision the elements that will bring forth another world and "another politics."[13] Harm intervention has a place here; it is more than an organized "undoing" of oppressors or a "becoming" of communities. At its heart is *renewal*, a capacity and commitment to restoring what can be restored, mourning what has been lost, engaging what is at stake—all this *in spite of harm*. In doing so, we work with our history instead of being subject to it. We acknowledge harm while developing "desire" for healing. We reckon with trauma while flowing through it into the entirety of our creative potential. That is: *we intervene so that we may live*, in lives rendered of our own power.

Much of what is suggested here is still conjecture. It is just as well; given the autonomy and locality of most harm intervention efforts, the results of such work will doubtless spawn more conjecture, "asking more questions than answering," as Barrow from CR puts it. Of course, the driving question—"What would it mean to heal?"—is not posed in search of an answer, but rather unveils itself in an array of struggles that act on the *desire* to heal. Harm intervention provides structure, context, and clarity to healing, but wherever one positions oneself on the landscape determines, in part, the definition, magnitude, process, and expression of healing. When the building of a detention center is successfully halted, or a New Orleans resident is released from wrongful imprisonment, or an offender apologizes to a victim, the consequences are clearly varied; and yet a similarity exists, subtle, felt but not seen. I am often impatient to see where these tremors lead, yet I also know that with each day I walk, each day I write and sustain, I can also wait. For I have come to understand that resilience looks up and not down, not resigned, but anticipatory. We might worry less about the strength of our patience and consider more the depths of our fortitude. Do we dare to undo, renew, and become our bodies? Our lives? Our entire understanding of organizing? Do we dare to refuse habitual trauma and flow into a different world? Do we dare to substitute, in short, our sturdy, forlorn landscape for something more liberating?

NOTES

1   This article was inspired greatly by the organizing it addresses and the people 'doing the work.' The author would especially like to thank Critical Resistance organizers Melissa Burch, Rachel Herzing, and Kai Lumumba Barrow for lending their time to a phone interview on May 9, 2008, as well as additional follow-up questions; their direct quotes in this article are taken from those communications. The analysis of Restorative Justice Community Action comes from the author's experience as a former staff member for two years. The opinions and statements shared here are the author's alone and do not reflect nor speak for Critical Resistance or Restorative Justice Community Action nor their members.

2   Vincent Chin, a 27-year-old Chinese-American man from Highland Park, Detroit, was killed in June of 1982, outside the club where he was holding his bachelor party. His killers, two white autoworkers who had accused Chin of driving them out of work, were fined and put on probation. The lenient sentence spawned outrage in Asian-American communities nationwide. Sean Bell, a 23-year-old black man from Queens, New York, was killed in November of 2006 just outside a club, *also* where he was holding his bachelor party. Five undercover police officers fired forty-six times at Bell and two others. Three of the officers were charged in the killings and, in April of 2008, found not guilty. Sanesha Stewart, a 25-year-old black trans woman from Bronx, New York, was stabbed to death in February of 2008. The man who killed her claimed a "trans panic" defense—namely that the shock of discovering her gender identity drove him to end her life (despite the fact that the two had been intimate for several months). The trial for her assailant is still pending as of this publication.

3   I use the term "harm" throughout this article; it is a very cautious, yet very deliberate choice. "Harm" certainly does not capture the essence of our unfortunate situation, and naming things for what they are— violence, war, destruction, devastation, annihilation, genocide—is one of our more crucial tasks, in a vocabulary besieged by euphemisms. But unlike this frank terminology, "harm" avoids the reification of trauma; that it is both noun and verb, action and consequence, allows us to engage with "harm" as endpoint, startpoint, and flow, not a frozen state of being. Additionally, terms such as "injury" or "imbalance" are avoided here; though such language is common in the restorative justice and conflict mediation arena, I want to maintain the reality of *infliction*, where one *does* to another. "Harm" carries this connotation, irrespective of its use.

4   The writer James Baldwin is of some use here. He highlights the dangers of reified trauma in his searing criticism of the "protest novel" and the doomed characters these narratives produce, such as Bigger Thomas in Richard Wright's *Native Son*. He argues that the fatalism of the protest novel removes the agency, power, and potential for resistance in the face of immense harm on a societal and cultural scale. See more on this in his book of essays, *Notes of a Native Son* (Boston: Beacon Press, 1955).

5   These statistics and facts on the scope and breadth of the prison industrial complex in the United States are generated by the organization Critical Resistance (HTTP://WWW.CRITICAL-RESISTANCE.ORG). Numbers of those currently imprisoned or otherwise involved in the prison industrial complex are maintained by the U.S. Department of Justice (Bureau of Justice Statistics, HTTP://WWW.OJP.USDOJ.GOV/BJS).

6   On ACT UP and harm reduction, see Ben Shepard, *Queer Political Performance and Protest: Play, Pleasure and Social Movement* (New York: Routledge, 2010). On black reparations, see Martha Biondi, "The Rise of the Reparations Movement," *Radical History Review* 87 (2003), 5–18; National Coalition of Blacks for Reparations in America (N'COBRA), HTTP://WWW. NCOBRA.ORG. On indigenous decolonization, see Angela Cavender Wilson [Waziyatawin], *What Does Justice Look Like? The Struggle for Liberation in Dakota Homeland* (St. Paul: Living Justice Press, 2008). On struggles against sexual violence and racism, see INCITE! Women of Color Against Violence, *The Color of Violence: The INCITE! Anthology* (Cambridge: South End Press, 2006).

7   Thomas Sugrue, *The Origins of the Urban Crisis: Race and Inequality in Postwar Detroit* (Princeton University Press, 1998).

8   More on Restorative Justice Community Action can be found at HTTP://WWW.RJCA-INC.ORG.

9   More on Critical Resistance can be found at HTTP://WWW.CRITICALRESISTANCE.ORG or in their recent publication, *Abolition Now! Ten Years of Strategy and Struggle Against the Prison-Industrial Complex* (Oakland: AK Press, 2008).

10 In June of 2007, Turbulence: Ideas for Movement released their first publication with a freely distributed newspaper titled "What would it mean to win?" See HTTP://WWW.TURBULENCE.ORG. UK or the second edition, Turbulence Collective, *What would it mean to win?* (Oakland: PM Press, 2010).

11 The workshop, "You Can't Kill the Spirit: A Forum with Three Woman Organizers from New Orleans," was presented by the Catalyst Project, a San Francisco Bay Area-based white antiracist center devoted to political education and movement building.

12 bell hooks, *All About Love: New Visions* (New York: Harper, 2001).

13 "Another politics" is further explained by the Zapatistas in "Sixth Declaration of the Lacandon Jungle," *In Motion Magazine* (August 18, 2005), HTTP://WWW.INMOTIONMAGAZINE.COM (accessed January 19, 2010). The crux of this demand is not only the call for a different world that is free from the constraints and violence of state and capital, but also for different ways of living and being in relation to one another.

DIY POLITICS AND QUEER ACTIVISM

Benjamin Shepard

ON OCTOBER 10, 2009, THE President of the United States spoke at a gala dinner for the Human Rights Campaign (HRC). Simultaneously, the office of HRC was vandalized. Those responsible dubbed their gesture an act of "glamdalism." They explained their gesture in a "Communique from the Forgotten":

> The HRC is not a democratic or inclusive institution, especially for the people who they claim to represent. Just like society, the HRC is run by a few wealthy elites who are in bed with corporate sponsors who proliferate militarism, heteronormativity, and capitalist exploitation.[1]

HRC is known for its support of a strict gay political agenda, including militarism (repealing Don't Ask-Don't Tell), marriage (the right of gays to marry), and law-and-order social policies (hate crimes legislation). Queer activists have described this 'holy trinity' of assimilationist gay organizing as a rejection of the movement's roots in anti-capitalism, sexual liberation, and critiques of militarism. Yet, for as long as there has been gay activism, there have been assimilationist-minded gays who have clashed with queers for suggesting there is something bigger and brighter to life than this.

"Queerness," argues L.A. Kauffman, "[is] more a posture of opposition than a simple statement about sexuality. It [is] about principles, not particularities ... queerness is about acknowledging and celebrating difference."[2] While HRC gets press coverage and receives corporate sponsorship, queer activists embrace a do-it-yourself (DIY) approach to activism and queer world-making, which aspires to create a space for difference, democracy, self-determination, and something richer and more glamorous with urban living.

This essay examines recent episodes in the decades-old clash of queer cultures. It considers the struggles of activists to create a more authentic and vibrant image of queer life than the glossy, bland, commercialized image of citizenship offered by groups like HRC. The essay highlights efforts of groups such as Radical Homosexual Agenda, the Sylvia Rivera Law Project, and others in the queer direct action lineage spawned from the AIDS Coalition to Unleash Power (ACT UP) and gay liberation. Further, it explores queer efforts to create an alternate public commons via DIY approaches to community building, including zine making, direct action zaps, music, poetry readings, and storytelling. These efforts speak to a clash of discourses, with identity-based models of politics favored by the HRC in conflict with an identity-bending queer politics that favors a universalizing view of human interaction, based on care, connection and support for social outsiders, as well as a connection to broad struggles for social justice.

THE PROBLEM WITH THE HUMAN RIGHTS CAMPAIGN

I WAS WALKING DOWN SMITH STREET in my Brooklyn neighborhood in the spring of 2009 when a young man with a clipboard stopped to ask me if I was interested in gay rights. Looking around, I noted that we were standing in front of Starbucks, the symbol of urban monoculture; this was the place where these two attractive and coifed young gay men had picked to canvass. I looked up at the mermaid on their logo, remembering the flack Starbucks had taken a few years earlier when they tried to remove her nipples. What was wrong with the logo? activists had asked, accusing the coffee chain of de-sexing the symbol.[3] As I stood there, it occurred to me that HRC was doing the same thing with gay rights. Was I for gays? Sure. But not this agenda.

"You're from HRC?" I asked the young man.

"Yes," he nodded, earnestly.

"But does HRC support gays when they are busted in vice sweeps?"

"No," the man nodded.

"Does HRC protect bath houses when they are getting shut down?"

"No," the man nodded, with the same banal facial expression. He did not get where this was going.

"Then what do you support?"

As if on cue, he started listing the holy trinity.

"There is more to it than that," I argued, and I began to talk about the legacy of Stonewall, the roots of gay liberation in sexual freedom and queer anti-militarism. I was starting to rant at this guy, who continued looking at me earnestly. Fighting these guys is like throwing darts at Jello. I walked off.

I first heard about HRC in the mid-1990s, when they started angling support away from AIDS activism towards their holy trinity of military service, marriage, and hate crimes laws. In 1998, the group famously endorsed Republican Al D'Amato for Senator in New York and held their assimilationist-oriented Millennium March on Washington in 2000, with little to no support from the grassroots.[4] Activists called it "a march without reason." All the while, HRC was pushing support for gay rights with policies such as the Employment Non-Discrimination Act (ENDA), a 2007 bill banning workforce discrimination based on sexual orientation but not gender identity, at the expense of the trans-inclusive Gender Expression Non-Discrimination Act (GENDA). These kinds of battles—between assimilationist gays and queers hoping for more—had become a driving force in queer activism.[5]

Over the years, 'zapping' HRC fundraisers has become something of a yearly ritual for queer activists. According to Joe Kennedy, such actions are best understood as "direct actions which confront oppressors." "The incessant 'zaps' of groups such as Gay Liberation Front and the Gay Activist Alliance forced gay and lesbian concerns onto the public agenda for the first time."[6] Members of the AIDS Coalition to Unleash Power zapped President Clinton when he spoke at an HRC dinner in 1997. In 2004, the anarchist-inspired Queer Fist zapped HRC's fundraising event in New York. ACT UP's co-founder Larry Kramer was on hand with a sign asking, "What have you done with all that money?"

Four years later, New York's Radical Homosexual Agenda (RHA) zapped two more of HRC's fundraisers. I drafted a few notes for one of these actions, under a working draft called "A Few Creepy Things about the HRC (Why queers should be wary of the assimilationist Human Rights Campaign)":

1. *They refuse to defend pleasure.* While the GLBTQ movements are rooted in defense of sexual self-determination, you will never hear the HRC say anything about pleasure. In a world with war, violence, and hatred, many queers rightfully recognize the transformative political possibilities of pleasure. Today, as the New York Department of Health has stirred up hysteria to generate another round of bath house closures, you will not hear the HRC say a thing about the importance of these vital institutions for queers.

2. *They don't defend public sexual culture.* For as long as many can remember, pubs, molly houses, movie theaters, gay bars, baths, and even cruising spots have provided a context for queer possibilities and cultural development. They helped constitute queerness as a way of being in the world. As such, attacks on homosexual venues served as an attack on gay identity. Gay liberation began in the late 1960s with the recognition that official intimidation constituted all too regular a feature of gay and lesbian social life. Liberation meant queers would fight back. Flashpoints included the police raids and ensuing riots at California Hall in San Francisco in 1965 and the Stonewall Inn in New York in 1969. In the end, assaults on queer spaces spurred the call for gay liberation. Yet today, the HRC rarely support the rights of queers to converge in public commons such as the Christopher Street piers, bath houses, and clubs.

3. *While queerness represents difference, HRC represents homogenization. "We are just like you," HRC pleads to straight people.* For HRC, queer sexuality is something to keep quiet about or apologize for. For liberationists, gay sex was something to revel within and create global solidarity around; "Perverts of the world unite!" was a central gay liberation anthem. Liberationists recognized that while many homosexuals claimed they were just like everyone else, dominant culture did not see them that way. Gay liberation, in alliance with women's liberation, created a vision of sexuality as cultural transformation. Autonomy of the body from the state was a central principle of both movements. Both movements questioned basic tenets of family structure and patriarchal authority in America. Over the years, the distance between HRC and these sentiments has only become wider and more pronounced.

4. *They support the logic of crime and punishment, marriage, war, and patriarchy.* In the year after Matthew Shepard's death, queer groups nationwide took positions on recommending or rejecting the death penalty for Matthew Shepard's killers (Log Cabin Republicans for, National Gay and Lesbian Task Force and Lambda against), but

HRC refused to take a position; their spokesman explained that debates over social justice issues were "not germane" to their mission.

5. *They do not represent your interests.* In 1998, the HRC endorsed anti-choice Republican Al D'Amato for the U.S. Senate. The endorsement of a man who had supported Reagan's budget cuts, the repeal of abortion rights, and criminal neglect of the AIDS carnage was an act of profound political amnesia. HRC maintains the 1998 endorsement of Reagan-loving, tax-cutting, anti-queer D'Amato and the 2000 Millennium March were part of a pragmatic strategy designed to see their agenda enacted into law, but the group has few results to show for this strategy. ENDA did not make it through the Senate; the homophobic Defense of Marriage Act was signed into law by their hero, Bill Clinton.

Instead of supporting solidarity among queer people, HRC dumped transgender people from ENDA. Publicly, HRC executive director Joe Solmonese said, "We absolutely do not support, and, in fact, oppose legislation that is not absolutely inclusive."[7] Behind the scenes, Solmonese eliminated trans protections to make the bill more palatable to straight people. Though ENDA failed in the Senate, HRC hailed the bill as a "victory" because they got a majority of House members to support "gay rights." The real victory was that 360 LGBTQ groups—including all national groups except the Log Cabin Republicans and Gay and Lesbian Alliance Against Defamation—opposed ENDA, telling HRC that they could not turn some into second-class citizens so others can get ahead.

Still the HRC pushes its holy trinity. HRC never came close to securing anything resembling justice for people who are gay and in the armed forces, but they accepted the premise of an imperial military. Despite heavy lobbying, they failed to beat the pernicious Knight ballot in California in 2000, codifying exclusive recognition of hetero marriage.[8] Activists are left wondering what HRC has done with their millions of dollars gained from fundraisers in gay communities, while many have argued that HRC is pushing the wrong agenda.

After gay marriage lost in a legal fight in New York—one of many similar defeats—seminal gay historian and activist John D'Emilio penned an essay in which he challenged the logic of shifting the movement away from a critique of patriarchy, marriage, and heteronormative institutions such as the military:

> Please, can we speak the truth? The campaign for same-sex marriage has been an unmitigated disaster. Never in the history of organized queerdom have we seen defeats of this magnitude. The battle to win marriage equality through the courts has done something that no other campaign or issue in our campaign has done: it has created a vast new body of anti-gay laws. Alas, for us, as the anthropologist Gayle Rubin has cogently observed, "Sex laws are notoriously easy to pass.... Once they are on the books, they are extremely difficult to dislodge."[9]

Rather than push heterosexuals to respect queers as different, D'Emilio worried that assimilationist gay groups like HRC embraced a counterproductive strategy, failing to challenge people to integrate lessons and rich examples of queer experiences in their lives. This was what RHA was thinking when it chose to zap HRC.

On February 23, 2008, members of the RHA brought noise, drums, chants, and three-foot-tall pink cardboard middle fingers to greet an HRC fundraiser at the midtown Hilton

Hotel. Others passed out stickers that said "Can't Spell LGBT with HRC" in response to HRC's long-running neglect of trans issues. Inside the fundraiser, two women from RHA disrupted HRC head Solmonese's address, throwing fliers and unfurling their banner reading "Can't Spell LGBT with HRC!" with a pink middle finger. "It's remarkable that HRC celebrates a legacy of protest, yet they are very quick to stamp out dissent when called out for betraying their community," noted one participant after she was escorted out.[10]

For critics such as RHA, the HRC's betrayal of trans people is one of many reasons to reject the group's work. HRC isn't just derailing the needs of the majority of the queer community, as RHA members argued through the zap; they are also narrowing our vision of the potential of queer relationships.

A HISTORIC SPLIT

CONFLICTS BETWEEN ASSIMILATIONIST GROUPS AND more radical groups date back to the earliest days of gay liberation, and even earlier. Queer pioneer Harry Hay was kicked out of the homophile Mattachine Society in the 1950s because of his organizing history with the Communist Party. In the days after the Stonewall rebellion in 1969, activists who wanted to focus exclusively on gay issues broke off from the multi-issue Gay Liberation Front to form the Gay Activist Alliance.[11] The split would ebb and flow but would never quite fade away. By the 1970s, Harry Hay worried that gay culture was so focused on bar culture and intertwined in the day-to-day ins and outs of capitalist social relations that the unique liberationist impulse of past struggles was becoming obscured, if not lost entirely. So he formed the queer group Radical Faeries, who are still active today.[12]

The split between social justice-minded queers who speak out for social and sexual civil liberties and gays who just want to fit in was particularly glaring during the twenty-fifth anniversary of Stonewall in 1994. Many worried that, rather than critique a social system that supports war, patriarchy, and racism, the GLBT movement was increasingly drifting toward a detente with the status quo. Some activists, including Harry Hay, formed their own counter-march to challenge the gay movement's drift away from struggles for sexual freedom and social justice.[13]

If there is one New York activist who has been an eye witness to this split, it is AIDS Coalition to Unleash Power icon Bill Dobbs. A veteran of Michigan's chapter of Gay Liberation Front, ACT UP, Queerwatch, and New York City's SexPanic!, he marched with Harry Hay during Stonewall Twenty-Five, with activists challenging the Millennium March in 2000, with New York's Queer Fist zapping HRC in 2004, and Radical Homosexual Agenda in 2008. When the New York Public Library held an exhibit on the fortieth anniversary of GLF and Stonewall, Dobbs wrote a few observations:[14]

> The cry was Freedom, Gay Power, Lesbian Power, Liberation. Looking through the exhibit, there are very few references to what is now the ubiquitous gay brand, Equality. Equality is an important touchstone, but in a single short word, it has people asking for more of the same. Equality or change? GLF [Gay Liberation Front] stood for radical social change. Equality is the status quo in lavender wrapping, the empty equals sign of Human Rights Campaign. Alas, our collective dreams have shrunk. From sexual outlaws, visionaries, revolutionaries, and

liberationists to the HRC chapter of the Rotary Club in a few decades. How did that happen?

Yet, as Laurie Essig points out, "Queers are still out there—making connections between homophobia and patriarchy and racism and capitalism. They still think that liberation is not serving in an imperialist army or the mimicry of the heterosexual bourgeoisie in marriage." She continues, "You can hate queers and wish they'd shut up, like the HRC probably does. Or you can love queers and wish more of them would glamdalize the dreary world of 'freedom=being like everyone else,' like I do."[15]

Many of today's queers build on the lessons and history of the liberation movement. Peter Tatchell, co-founder of queer direct action group OutRage and former member of the GLF, similarly mused about the meanings of the Stonewall era for his activism.

> Our vision was a new sexual democracy, without homophobia and misogyny. Erotic shame and guilt would be banished, together with socially enforced monogamy and male and female gender roles. There would be sexual freedom and human rights for everyone—queer and straight. Our message was "innovate, don't assimilate." GLF never called for equality. The demand was liberation. We wanted to change society, not conform to it.[16]

Shortly before President Obama was to speak at the HRC's dinner in October 2009 a group called Queerkidssaynotomarriage posted a call for queer activists to expand an agenda beyond marriage toward issues which actually impact their lives.

> It's hard for us to believe what we're hearing these days. Thousands are losing their homes, and gays want a day named after Harvey Milk. The U.S. military is continuing its path of destruction, and gays want to be allowed to fight. Cops are still killing unarmed black men and bashing queers, and gays want more policing. More and more Americans are suffering and dying because they can't get decent healthcare, and gays want weddings. What happened to us? Where have our communities gone? Did gays really sell out that easily?[17]

The critique is not new, yet advocacy for the HRC holy trinity continues to dominate a national GLBT agenda.

During their February 2008 HRC zap, RHA was quick to point out that there are alternatives to the holy trinity. Rather than throw away their dollars to a group which fails to show progress or success on their agenda, queers should support local groups who provide vital services and win real victories, like ACT UP or the Sylvia Rivera Law Project (a trans legal group that I discuss later in this essay). Better yet, if one does not like what HRC does, RHA suggested that queers get together and start a grassroots group to fight for justice or create community. "HRC will keep trying to out-shout us with their money and advertisers," argued RHA.[18] But they never represented authentic queer experience, and they never will. It is up to queers to do that. The DIY spirit the RHA refers to speaks to a vital ethos of queer world-making: more than putting energy into a critique, generations of queer activists have worked to create a richer, more colorful approach to living of their own invention.

DO IT YOURSELF FOR A NEW QUEER WORLD

The idea of just going out and doing it, or as it is popularly expressed in the underground, the do-it-yourself ethic. [...] Doing it yourself is at once a critique of the dominant mode of passive consumer culture and something far more important: the active creation of an alternative culture. DIY is not just complaining about what is, but actually doing something different.

—Stephen Duncombe[19]

THROUGHOUT THE LAST FOUR DECADES, queers have found their way into countless social and cultural movements. Through do-it-yourself culture, activists create different kinds of spaces for democratic engagement through embodied community building. "The DIY movement is about using anything you can get your hands on to shape your own cultural identity, your own version of whatever you think is missing in mainstream culture," writes Amy Spencer.[20] "You can produce your own zine, record an album, publish your own book; the enduring appeal of this movement is that anyone can be an artist or a creator. The point is to get involved." Those involved help create alternate spaces with whatever tools one has. Within such spaces, use is valued over commercial exchange. Participants play with new social realities, creating a space for life, reflection, and pleasure outside of commerce. "DIY as a form of activity creates value outside of capitalism," Ben Holtzman and others explain.[21]

Much of this creativity took shape within a public commons of the movement's own creation. This included bath houses, punk venues, clubs, underground parties, activist groups, organizations, and cultural outlets including publishing houses, a gay press, films, pamphlets, and self-published zines. "The best zines, whatever their subject, do not inhabit a ready-made world; they create one unto themselves," explains zine historian Fred Wright.[22] Queer zines, including *Faggots and Faggotry*, *Diseased Pariah News*, *Faggo-cytosis*, *Outpunk*, *Homocore*, *JD's*, *Swallow Your Pride*, *YELL*, and *Larry-Bob's Holy Titclamps*, have found readership around the world.[23] Larry-Bob explains what makes this form of publishing distinct:

> There is no apostrophe in zine. Zine is not short for magazine. A magazine is a product, a commercial commodity. A zine is a labor of love, producing no profit, and frequently a loss, of time at least. In a magazine, information is just another ingredient, thinly sliced layers to keep the cream filling of advertising from sticking together. Information is the reason a zine exists; everything else, down to the paper it's printed on, is there to convey information.[24]

Building on the sci-fi zines, beat poetry, and homophile newsletters of the 1950s, the underground magazines of the 1960s, the punk zines of the 1970s through 1990s, and the blogs and guerilla news that followed, a movement to create a democratic information exchange built on a similar impulse. Amy Spencer describes this DIY ethos as "the urge to create a new cultural form and transmit it to others on your own terms."[25] Much of this new cultural form began with the simple desire to communicate a message.

Larry-Bob notes that it is important for queers to make their presence known in many communities, not just the ones on the coasts. "Oh, and you're still stuck in your *Outweek* 'everything-ends-at-the-Hudson-river' perspective. What about the fags and dykes stuck in small-town America?"[26] he asks in his zine, proceeding with a challenge to queers:

Disrupt strip-mall fashion shows with do-it yourself glamour. People are ignorant—they don't have any concept of what is humanly possible, and the shock will hopefully kill them. But remember, the primary purpose isn't to shock breeders—who gives a shit about them, anyway—but to wake up potential queers, who may be scared to death of you this week, but will be improvising their own outfits next week. Victory is assured; we'll be the heroes of a generation of queers, by which time we'll also be cynical enough to make a buck off them.[27]

Implicit in the manifesto is a push to create a new, defiant queer public, with a jigger of humor, sarcasm, camp, and "do-it yourself glamour."

The effort to create this queer world took place in many venues and DIY cultural projects. For example, from the 1970s through the 1990s, queers and punks shared this impulse to build their own scene and by extension, a world of their own creation. Queer bands such as the Germs, the Killer Banshees, Bikini Kill, and Pansy Division, as well as the Riot Grrrl and Queercore scenes, helped invent a space for alternate forms and understandings of power, sexuality, and culture.[28] Building on movements extending back to Dada and Emma Goldman's anarchism, these groups helped create a space "to challenge accepted boundaries."[29]

A critique of repressive social mores churned through the mix of passion, bodies, sweat, play, violence, and pathos that characterized the punk scene. "Punk," writes Stephen Duncombe, "was not just a music; it was an attitude, an ethic, and a sense of community." For Duncombe, punk was a music for outsiders. A sociologist by trade, activist, and occasional musician, Duncombe describes the world-making thinking behind the practice of building a punk scene. "Punk's prime ethic is Do-It-Yourself. This value put on self-sufficiency came largely from necessity." Duncombe started his first band in 1980, and through this experience he learned a profound lesson about cultural resistance and resiliency. "DIY ... is an ideal that transcends immediate need. It's an ethic that guides the punk outlook on the world, encompassing not only the logistics of a music scene, but also artistic creation and political action." Music, play, and cultural production serve as a basis for a community of resistance. "The scene is a place where punks can practice DIY most intimately, in constructing a community by and for themselves that offers up a system of values, aspirations, and behaviors in rebellion against those of the mainstream society." From here, punk builds on cultural movements aimed against monoculture, dating back many decades. "The scene gives the support and reinforcement necessary to stand up and against the daily onslaught of the hegemonic culture. It's a safe space to experiment with new ways of being and doing." Within such a movement, activists find support to play and experiment with new practices in living. "It's a place to reinvent yourself. It is a haven in a heartless world.... It allows for the nuances and variations that necessarily arise through the practices of punks doing-it-themselves as they rebel against local powers...."[30]

In their own way, each punk show, zine, poem, film, zap, piece of art, gesture of direct action, and form of guerilla media that followed them helped spread the word about a queer sensibility. Gradually, even academics came to echo this messy message about all things queer. Queer, writes Eve Kosofsky Sedgwick, involves "the open mesh of possibilities, gaps, overlaps, dissonances and resonances, lapses and excesses of meaning [that occur] when the constituent elements of anyone's gender, of anyone's sexuality aren't made (or can't be made) by signifying monolithically...." Here, queer extends into an urban panorama of "drags, clones, leatherfolk … fantasists … feminist men … masturbators … people able to relish, learn from, or identify with such…. Work around 'queer' spins the term outward along dimensions that can't be subsumed under gender and sexuality at all." More than anything, it implies "same-sex sexual object choice, lesbian or gay…. Given the historical and contemporary force of the prohibitions against every same-sex sexual expression, for anyone to disavow those meanings, or to displace them from the term's definitional center, would be to dematerialize any possibility of queerness itself."[31] Queer serves as "the discursive rallying point for younger lesbians and gay men and, in yet other contexts, for lesbian interventions and, in yet other contexts, for bisexuals and straights for whom the term expresses an affiliation with antihomophobic politics," argues Judith Butler. "That it can become such a discursive site whose uses are not fully constrained in advance ought to be safe-guarded not only for the purposes of continuing to democratize queer politics, but also to expose, affirm, and rework the specific historicity of the term."[32]

More than anything, queer was born of a DIY approach to activism. Two decades after the first meetings of ACT UP, one of its founders described the group's DIY ethos:

> You must know, we must never forget, that every single treatment for HIV/AIDS is out there because of gay AIDS activists, led by ACT UP chapters across the country and Project Inform in San Francisco. They did not come from the government. They came because gay people fought like tigers and screaming banshees to get the system that hates us to deliver them to us…. This achievement, the obtaining of these drugs, I believe is the single greatest achievement gay people have accomplished in all of history, and we must be remembered for it. The lesson should be clear. The lesson should be obvious. It should show us what we are capable of achieving when we put our minds and hearts and brains and bodies together and work together, all together, as brothers and sisters and one big family. There is not one person here today who is not capable of being such an activist.[33]

A generation of activists was born of this disposition, including the Church Ladies for Choice, the Lesbian Avengers, Queer Nation, Housing Works, Gay Shame, SexPanic!, OutR\age, Radical Homosexual Agenda, Fed Up Queers, and the list is long of additional groups whose lineage extends back to ACT UP. Each year, different queer groups are born in this milieu where the challenge has been figuring out how to build on this highly creative, abundant approach to activism, community building, and world-making.

FROM STREET TRANS ACTION REVOLUTIONARIES TO SYLVIA RIVERA LAW PROJECT

QUEER DIRECT ACTION GROUPS ARISE in an environment in constant flux. As groups are born, the social environment changes, needing different kinds of tactics and strategies. Today, this includes a need for activists to contend with an assertive anti-activist set of legal structures. When trans direct action group Bash Back! dropped a banner stating "It's Okay To Be Gay! Bash Back!" inside the Mount Hope Church in East Lansing Michigan in 2008, they were following in the tradition of ACT UP's famous 1989 Stop the Church

Action. Unlike ACT UP, they were hit with federal charges for violating the Freedom to Access Clinics Act.[34] When Radical Homosexual Agenda organized a parade to New York City's City Hall without a permit in 2007, one of the organizers was gang-tackled by members of the New York City Police Department. In 2009, a New York activist was arrested in Pittsburgh and had his files confiscated for twittering.[35] Much of the controversy accompanying these actions seems to stem from an awareness that a network of activists have been engaged in a number of defiant and risqué forms of direct action with an explicit queer and anarchist politic. As the years continue, more and more anarchist queer direct action groups face restrictions on their activist practices. Sometimes they are charged with disorderly conduct or violations of the Patriot Act, and sometimes they are preemptively charged before crimes or acts of civil disobedience have even taken place. It is hard to describe these offenses as anything but "thought crimes." Yet the ways these groups respond suggest their queer activism remains a vital contribution to movements for social change.

A case in point is trans activist Dean Spade's response to his arrest during the World Economic Forum (WEF) meeting in New York City in 2002. Spade, a lawyer and veteran of queer direct action organizing, was going to the bathroom in the men's room after a large march during the WEF meeting. It was a freezing day in February, and Spade had been outside all day. When he walked into the men's room at Grand Central Station, a policeman followed. "As I was looking to see what stalls were open, he approached and asked for my ID. I explained that I was in the right bathroom, that I am transgender and I understood the confusion, but I was just going to use the bathroom and leave," Spade wrote in a mass email sent out after the event.[36] The officer continued with questions about why Spade, a trans man, was in the men's room. Two of Spade's friends soon attempted to intervene. All three were arrested and processed separately in three precincts. Spade recounts:

> The most emotionally challenging part for me was the transphobia I encountered from the court attorney who represented me at my arraignment. He came to the cell around noon yesterday (February 3rd, 2002), read the police statement on my court documents, and asked why I was in the "men's" room. I explained that I am transgender and I customarily use "men's" rooms, and that I go by a male name and pronoun. He wrinkled up his face and said with a very dismissive and disapproving attitude, "That is your business. I don't care." He then asked me what my genitalia are. I asked, "Why do you need to know that?"

The lawyer pushed his case, and Spade was left with the degrading feeling of having to provide private information in order to receive basic legal services:

> The attorney took offense to my questioning the relevance of his inquiry about my genitalia, and communicated that if I would not cooperate with him, that was my problem. Because I was unsure about what would happen to me if he would not advocate for me vigorously, and because I feared being given a bail I could not meet, I ultimately suffered the indignity of having to satisfy his curiosity about my genitalia

by explaining it. Even then, he said dismissively about my transgender, "Well, that is your personal business," and left without giving me any information about what would happen in the courtroom. For the next several hours, I was deeply concerned about the quality of representation I would get in the courtroom, and whether I would be released on my own recognizance.

Spade had no idea what was going to happen. "You can't get a good lawyer in this town," Spade thought to himself throughout the morning.[37] Eventually, he went before a judge and was comforted by what greeted him: "Much to my relief, I discovered upon entering the courtroom that it was filled with friends and allies wearing 'Living Trans is Not a Crime' stickers. Having them there, I knew that I would be safe." All charges were ultimately thrown out.

After this experience, Spade reflected on the lessons of what had happened:

> First, I am outraged, of course, by the double-bind in which gender segregation of bathrooms leaves transgender, transsexual, gender variant, and genderqueer people. Like many people, each time I use a public bathroom I face the fact that no matter what choice I make, I may encounter harassment and potential violence and arrest. My level of bathroom anxiety, of course, is increased by the weekend's events. However, I am hopeful that the increased visibility of this problem afforded by the media coverage of the arrests and the organizing we will continue will result in policy changes about bathroom segregation. I hope that this arrest will spark campaigns to provide safe, non-gendered bathroom options for all people in all public spaces. I intend to continue vigorously advocating on this issue.[38]

In the following weeks, Spade started organizing, helped write a zine about the event, *Piss & Vinegar*, distributed by the Anti-Capitalist Tranny Brigade, and helped create a training video called "About Trans Issues." Spade's activism was a clear example of a queer translation of anger into action, a part of the legacy of ACT UP. In the months after his arrest, Spade continued this work, eventually starting a legal clinic for trans people called the Sylvia Rivera Law Project (SRLP). The aim was to create a different kind of organization which rejected a gendered welfare model.[39] Rather than coerce or control those engaged in services—which has often been the case with social services—Spade hoped to create an organization that focused on promoting social change.[40] SRLP explicitly acknowledged the limits of the non-profit industrial complex.[41] Therefore, rather than replicate the co-optation witnessed in many LGBT organizations, SRLP sought to create something more participatory and consumer-driven. To do so, the group established a collective governance model that encouraged leadership by trans people and people of color. Spade argued this could offer a model for emerging queer and trans organizations.[42] Along the way, Spade and company helped link the law project with a number of movement-building questions and strategies. As the organization grew and racked-up wins, they continued to grapple with the inherent challenges of providing services outside of traditional models of organizational development. Rather than reinforce stigma and social control, they asked questions about power, heath, care, and freedom, and invited many to help answer them.

The organization's namesake, Sylvia Rivera, had grappled with such questions for decades. She was the founder of the Street Trans Action Revolutionaries (STAR). At the time of her death, Rivera was referred to as the grand dame of trans activism.[43] I met Rivera when we were both arrested in 1998 during the Matthew Shepard political funeral (a public memorial service that directly connects the politics of oppression to the death of an individual). Throughout the post-action organizing, Rivera talked about her concern for other trans folks who suffered a similar fate as Matthew Shepard but without the headlines.

An icon of the earliest days of gay liberation, Rivera made a striking comeback in the final years of her life, re-forming STAR and organizing a political funeral for Amanda Milan, a trans person killed in New York.[44] Throughout this organizing, Rivera articulated a concern for those whose experiences failed to match the heavily marketed, commercialized image of gay living seen in the gay glossies or represented by Human Rights Campaign in the late 1990s.[45] Rivera's experience as a queer person—who suffered from chemical dependence and bouts of homelessness, in addition to contributing to movements for Gay and Puerto Rican Liberation—never herself conformed to this image of gay life. "One of our main goals now is to destroy the Human Rights Campaign," argued Rivera shortly before she died. "I'm tired of sitting on the back of the bumper. It's not even the back of the bus anymore—it's the back of the bumper. The bitch on wheels is back."[46] Sadly, Rivera would not live long enough to see such a change.

In the months after her death in 2002, several groups formed to continue her agenda. Projects such as Sylvia's Place, a shelter for queer youth in Manhattan, and Sylvia Rivera Law Project bridged a gap between direct action and direct services, harm reduction, and legal advocacy for trans folks, who had to navigate an unforgiving system involving criminal justice, transphobia, and a gendered welfare state. Spade's SRLP led this wave of trans action. Part of their work was to articulate an agenda for trans people not seen in mainstream GLB and "fake T" groups, like HRC, most of whom have neglected trans people. Through aggressive legal advocacy, the project carved out a series of legal victories for trans people. It also helped to articulate a queer politics that extends beyond the limitations of the HRC holy trinity of military service, marriage, and hate crimes.

In 2009, for example, the State Assembly in New York introduced a version of the Gender Expression Non-Discrimination Act (GENDA) which included provisions for hate crimes. In response, SRLP drafted a smart policy statement with a coalition of trans advocacy groups, including New York City's Fabulous Independent and Educated Radicals for Community Empowerment (FIERCE) and the Audre Lorde Project:

> We are excited and heartened by progress on this front, as many of us
> have struggled to end discrimination against trans people for years.
> Unfortunately, the GENDA bill also includes gender identity and
> gender expression as a "protected" category under the NY hate crimes
> statute. We want and deserve legal protection from discrimination in
> the workplace, in housing, and in public accommodations. Transgen-
> der people in New York are frequently fired from jobs; kicked out of
> housing, restaurants, restrooms and hotels; and harassed in schools
> and public institutions. It is essential that we have legal recourse to
> take action when trans people are discriminated against in this way.
> It is also essential that this form of discrimination is publicly declared

unacceptable—in our state, in our society, and across the world. It pains us that we nevertheless cannot support the current GENDA bill, because we cannot and will not support hate crimes legislation.

Rather than serving as much needed protection, the hate crimes provisions in the law would expose trans communities to additional threats, the groups argued:

> If a particular crime is deemed a hate crime by the state, the supposed perpetrator is automatically subject to a higher mandatory minimum sentence. For example, a crime that would carry a sentence of five years can be "enhanced" to eight years. As GENDA is currently written, if passed it would further expand this law, providing additional grounds for penalty enhancement.

> As a nation, we lock up more people per capita than any other country in the world; one in one hundred adults are behind bars in the U.S. Our penalties are harsher and sentences longer than they are anywhere else on the planet, and hate crime laws with sentencing enhancements make them harsher and longer. By supporting longer periods of incarceration and putting a more threatening weapon in the state's hands, this kind of legislation places an enormous amount of faith in our deeply flawed, transphobic, and racist criminal legal system. The application of this increased power and extended punishment is entirely at the discretion of a system riddled with prejudice, institutional bias, economic motives, and corruption. Trans people, people of color, and other marginalized groups are disproportionately incarcerated.

The statement noted that such policies represent a form of bait-and-switch, whereby liberal-leaning politicians can claim legitimacy by backing a policy that appears to address concerns about discrimination, while simultaneously increasing sentence enhancement to justify creating more prisons. The authors continue:

> Hate crime laws foreground a single accused individual as the "cause" of racism, homophobia, transphobia, misogyny, or any number of other oppressive prejudices. They encourage us to lay blame and focus our vengeful hostility on one person instead of paying attention to institutional prejudice that fuels police violence, encourages bureaucratic systems to ignore trans people's needs or actively discriminate against us, and denies our communities health care, identification, and so much more.

> Anything that expands the power of a system that damages our communities so severely is against our long-term and short-term interests. Any legal weapon that's created to make our justice system more harsh and punitive cannot be trusted in the hands of institutions that have shown their prejudices and corruption time and time again. Because of the way this legislation has been turned against the communities they

were intended to protect, we regard "sentence enhancement" hate crime laws as one of the greatest follies of late-20th-century liberal politics.[47]

The statement ended by offering a set of alternative policy solutions. It called for New York to offer substantive protections for gender non-conforming and trans populations without expanding the powers of an already deeply flawed, discriminatory criminal justice system. In many ways, the statement was years in the making.

QUEERING THE HATE CRIMES DISCOURSE

MY PRACTICE-BASED INTRODUCTION TO QUEER direct action came when I was arrested October 19, 1998, during the political funeral for Matthew Shepard.[48] At the time, many queer activists fought the impulse to call for the death sentence for Shepard's murderers. Assimilationist-minded gays called for enhanced punishment with hate crimes legislation, while justice-minded queers called for a different kind of thinking, linked with a message of liberation and social justice.[49] Many rejected the idea of calling for policies that strengthen the criminal justice system. "I don't think we should be increasing the scope of power in that way," explained Bill Dobbs in a radio interview in January of 1999. Dobbs, who opposes the death penalty across the board, explained his position vis-à-vis hate crimes legislation:

> If somebody says, the penalties for murder are inadequate, or for rob-
> bery or sexual assault, I'm willing to listen to that argument. But I
> find troubling some of these arguments that are advanced to support
> hate crime legislation. For example … some of these arguments try
> to highlight some crimes against others, but fail to take into account
> that crimes, in general, are not a good thing. Crimes against people are
> not a good thing. And paradoxically, again, using a Michigan example,
> there the number one agenda item on the gay and lesbian community
> list is hate crime legislation, yet gross indecency there is a felony. And
> I am very concerned that those kinds of sex laws are resulting in pros-
> ecutions that send people away for long periods of prison time, and yet
> we are still, as a community, asking for more law and order when we
> haven't even gotten rid of our own outlaw status.[50]

The year after the Shepard political funeral witnessed a series of iconic actions. In February 1999, Fed Up Queers, who had organized the Shepard political funeral, initiated the first of a wave of over a thousand acts of non-violent civil disobedience after unarmed African immigrant Amadou Diallo was shot by the New York Police Department. A few weeks later, the same cohort helped organize another political funeral when a gay man in Alabama, Billy Jack Gaither, was burnt in a pyre of tires. At the time, queer activists called for an end to a culture of violence, not for enhanced sentences for hate crimes. The following decade included a number of these gruesome attacks and a debate about how best to respond.

This history ran through my mind when I read about the fate of Jorge Steven Lopez Mercado, a gay man beheaded and dismembered in Cidra, Puerto Rico on November 13, 2009. This act was seen as a response to his being gay. "Thousands of New Yorkers Gather for Vigil In Memoriam of Jorge Steven Lopez Mercado, Victim of Hate Crime," read a call for a response listed on Facebook and posted on several queer list serves. "Why must it always come down to hate crimes legislation?" was the question I posted to the RHA list-serv when I read the call.

Upon arriving at the vigil I encountered Bill Dobbs, who argued against the death penalty for Matthew Shepard's killers in 1999. He carried a sign reading "Repeal Hate Crimes," and handed me another sign declaring "Justice Not Vengeance." "I could not agree more," one woman noted when I held up the sign. Dobbs explained the argument against hate crimes to inquirers. Instead of pushing for a lump of flesh, it would be useful, he said, to let the dust settle. Everyone has a visceral response to violence, which has to be acknowledged. But there are other solutions, including laws already on the books, which serve as antidotes to additional law-and-order social policies. Others on hand for the rally talked about alternatives: education, information, changes in social attitudes, and even harm reduction approaches. Society cannot rehabilitate someone, they argued, by enhancing criminal sentences.

But at a later point in the vigil, New York City Councilwoman Christine Quinn stood up to make the case that this was a hate crime. Watching Quinn rally the emotionally raw crowd, I thought about the scene of Peter Lorre rallying himself against a vigilante mob in Fritz Lang's *M*, set in Weimar Era Berlin. With Quinn leading the charge, the crowd seemed to be pushed to vengeance.[51]

Observing these events, New York activist Panama Vicente Alba wrote about Mercado's murder, noting that there were some 811 homicides in Puerto Rico in 2009, mostly related to drugs.[52] "As heinous as the murder of Jorge Steven Mercado is, it is not the first 'hate crime' in Puerto Rico. In spite of this, no one has ever been prosecuted under the Puerto Rico Hate Crimes Statues," argued Alba. "The murder of Jorge Steven Lopez Merdado cries for justice—Puerto Rican justice." He noted, "There are those who are aware of this case and consider calling on the U.S. Justice Department to prosecute this case under Federal Hate Crime Statutes. They include the Death Penalty under its sentencing guidelines. The Death Penalty is a crime against humanity. Colonialism is a crime against humanity." For Alba, a veteran of the Young Lords and National Congress for Puerto Rican Rights, as well as labor and harm reduction movements, his lifetime of activism was about connecting the dots between movements and causes, rather than seeing particular injustices—such as Mercado's murder and other 'hate crimes'—as isolated 'gay issues.' Queer activism functions within a similar ethos, always seeking connections within a broad multi-issue politics.

For a short while in the early 1970s, Sylvia Rivera was also a member of the Young Lords, a group that fought for sovereignty for Puerto Rico and its people transplanted in the United States. What linked this work with her support for gay liberation was an overarching struggle for human freedom. Rivera's work with STAR, Gay Liberation, and the Young Lords helped connect this vision of global solidarity. These were all direct action groups, favoring a DIY approach to creating solutions rather than more jail cells. Throughout the years of her activism, Sylvia Rivera maintained that spirit. She considered the Matthew Shepard political funeral—where she spent the night in jail—one of the best demonstrations she ever attended. Yet she also considered sleeping in the street to protest cutbacks on homeless services—as she did with me in January of 2000—just as important. She understood that no one was free until everyone was free, and lived her life and her politics in support of all oppressed people. The challenge of sex and gender liberation requires building spaces for countless genders and identities on a foundation of sexual freedom, autonomy, and sociality, rather than falling back on oppressive systems like 'criminal justice' as the best our collective imagination can offer.

CONCLUSION

IN OCTOBER 2003, I WAS invited to speak on a panel for the thirtieth anniversary of *Gay Community News* (GCN) at the New York LGBT Community Services Center. The panel was titled, "What Did We Mean by Queer Activism in the 1970s, 80s, and 90s, and What Do We Mean Today?" Each panelist was invited to write a short bio for the event. "Benjamin Shepard never read GCN," mine read. "But he always cruised the obits in the *Bay Area Reporter* in San Francisco as the AIDS health crisis decimated lives from a cross section of outsiders in American life, in ways that forced him and countless others to re-consider just what queer life, activism, and community mean." Speaking to this group of older organizers, I talked about a generation of queer activists staking a path in a different model of organizing, based on something outside of social identity. From the battle for healthcare, HIV housing, and syringe exchange, to the anti-war and global justice movements, I noted that some of the best queer organizers of the era had linked their work with broad-based, social justice-oriented universalizing discourses. Three decades after *GCN*, queer thinking was re-embracing questions the movement first contended with after Stonewall. Some involved rejecting militarism, crime, and punishment; others involved rejecting hard-and-fast social categories in favor of a liberated sexuality for everyone.

Such queer thinking borrowed from ideas ranging from Freud to Foucault, Eve Kosofsky Sedgwick to Patrick Califia. The latter three found strict delineations around sex and identity completely silly; identities blur as do politics. In the early 1990s, Judith Butler beckoned the question:

> Is it possible to maintain and pursue heterosexual identifications and aims within homosexual practice, and homosexual identifications and aims within heterosexual practices? If sexuality is to be disclosed, what will be taken as the true determinant of its meaning: the fantasy structure, the act, the orifice, the energy, the anatomy? And if the practice engages a complex interplay of all of these, which one of these erotic dimensions will come to stand for the sexuality that requires them all?[53]

Here, social and sexual identity becomes far more fluid. Foucault described living in a world which embraced "an infinity of sexualities" rather than binary categorizations. Just as sexual roles can be approached as performative gestures within a continuum of desires, queer politics offers a politics that embraces a multiplicity of approaches to engagement, outside of hard-and-fast identity-based social categories. This is what marks the multi-issue organizing born of Gay Liberation Front.[54]

In this essay, I have highlighted an interplay between discourses, with identity-based models of politics favored by the HRC in conflict with an identity-bending queer politics that favors a universalizing view of human interaction, based on care, connection, and support for social outsiders. Such queer thinking extends through a huge range of issues, from private to very public concerns. It also involves core questions about organizing. At its most ambitious, queer post-identity models open spaces for new kinds of coalitions and modes of organization, offering spaces based in less coercive models of participation. At its worst, these politics occasionally replicate old power dynamics involving insider and outsider status, bias, and favoritism, as Gay Liberation Front experienced after Stonewall. Queer activism is still a work very much in process, often driven by personality clashes and affinities that mark other forms of activism. A review of the interviews in the ACT UP Oral History Project confirms that the group occasionally resembled a high school, with its own cliques and popularity contests. Yet ACT UP's queer message of a broad struggle opened space for countless forms of engagement for a generation of activists.[55] More often than not, good things have come from this ambitious thinking and activism.

In the years after Stonewall, gay liberationists linked their movement with broad-based liberationist movements around the world. Throughout this period, queers argued that queerness offered richer, more colorful approaches to living. They created a public commons, opened bath houses, wrote zines, started gay papers, generated a highly experimental approach to public sexuality, and openly critiqued heteronormative institutions of marriage, militarism and monogamy. Much of this activism was born of a desire to create something bigger and better than this mess of a world, and so looked to Do-It-Yourself approaches to direct action and community organizing. By the 1990s, when assimilationist minded gays pushed away from this agenda, queer activists responded critically, arguing that liberation was a far more compelling option than trying to fit into a flawed system. Others pushed to create alternative groups, counter-publics, public policies, and programs based on reducing harm, creating connection, and rethinking social notions of gender, pleasure, and self-determination. In the years since the 1999 Seattle alter-globalization demonstrations, queer organizers re-linked their struggles with global movements for social change. "Despite the discomforts of the weekend's events, I have hope that much good will come from these arrests," Dean Spade wrote in the zine *Piss & Vinegar* after his arrest at the World Economic Forum.[56] "I think that it is a step forward to have anti-capitalist activists and movements considering transgender issues and participation." Rather than favor one identity or another, much of queer organizing is practiced intersectionally, between movements and organizational cultures, insistent on expanding imaginations and cultivating radical sentiments that so many of us have in common. As the movement churns forward, such activism offers a route toward a richer, more democratic, and more meaningful experience of queer living for everyone.

NOTES

1   Quoted in: Laurie Essig, "Queers Attack Gays and Lesbians. It's about Time. Class Warfare," October 12, 2009, HTTP://TRUESLANT.COM/LAURIEESSIG/2009/10/12/QUEERS-ATTACK-GAYS-AND-LESBIANS-ITS-ABOUT-TIME (accessed November 11, 2009).

2   L.A. Kauffman, "Radical Change: The Left Attacks Identity Politics," *Village Voice*, June 20, 1992: 20.

3   Bill Talen, *What Should I Do If the Reverend Billy Is in My Store?* (New York: Free Press, 2003).

4   For a brief discussion of the march see: Benjamin Shepard, "The Queer/Gay Assimilationist Split: The Suits Vs. the Sluts," *Monthly Review* 53, no. 1.

5   Benjamin Shepard, *Queer Political Performance and Protest: Play, Pleasure and Social Movement* (New York: Routledge, 2009).

6   Joe Kennedy, *Summer of 1977: The Last Hurrah of the Gay Activist Alliance* (Westport, Ct.: PPC Books, 1994).

7   Ethan Jacobs, "ENDA Vote Postponed," *Bay Windows*, October 4, 2007, HTTP://WWW. THETASKFORCE.ORG/TF_IN_NEWS/07_1009/STORIES/25_ENDA_VOTE_POSTPONED.PDF   (accessed January 10, 2010).

8   California Ballot Proposition 22 was supported by 62% of voters in March of 2000. For a critique see: Eric Rofes, "Beyond Patient and Polite: A Call for Direct Action and Civil Disobedience on Behalf of Same-Sex Marriage," in *From ACT UP to the WTO: Urban Protest and Community Building in the Era of Globalization*, eds. Benjamin Shepard and Ronal Hayduk, (New York: Verso, 2002), 150–155.

9   John D'Emilio, "The Marriage Fight is Setting Us Back," *Harvard Lesbian and Gay Review*, November-December 2004, HTTP://WWW.GLREVIEW.COM/ISSUES/13.6/13.6–DEMILIO.PHP (accessed December 2, 2009).

10   RHA, "Action Report: Radical Homosexual Agenda Flips HRC the Bird, Demands Trans Rights," HTTP://WWW.RADICALHOMOSEXUALAGENDA.ORG/HRC2_08.HTML (accessed March 1, 2008).

11   Don Teal, *The Gay Militants* (New York: St. Martins Press, 1995[1971]).

12   Michael A. Bronksi, "The Real (Radical) Harry Hay," *Z Magazine*, HTTP://ZMAGSITE.ZMAG. ORG/DEC2002/BRONSKI1202.HTM (accessed October 16, 2006).

13   Richard Goldstein, *The Attack Queers* (New York: Verso, 2002).

14   William Dobbs, "Re: [RadicalFaeries] resistance; i put the dreams in the dryer," post to "Radical Faeries" (RADICALFAERIES@LISTS.RADICALFAERIES.NET, June 15, 2009).

15   Laurie Essig, "Queers Attack Gays and Lesbians," unpaginated.

16   Peter Tatchell, "Our Lost Radicalism," *The Guardian London*, June 26, 2009, HTTP://WWW. GUARDIAN.CO.UK/COMMENTISFREE/2009/JUN/26/GAY-LGBT- VICTIMHOOD-STONEWALL?COMME NTPAGE=1&COMMENTPOSTED=1 (accessed June 17, 2009).

17   Queerkidssaynottomarriage, "Queer Kids of Queer Parents Against Gay Marriage!: Resist the Gay Marriage Agenda!," Queer Kids of Queer Parents Against Gay Marriage blog, posted October 9, 2009, HTTP://QUEERKIDSSAYNOMARRIAGE.WORDPRESS.COM (accessed October 12, 2009).

18   RHA, "Action Report," unpaginated.

19   Stephen Duncombe, *Notes from the Underground: Zines and the Politics of Alternative Culture* (New York: Verso, 1997), 117.

20   Amy Spencer, *DIY: The Rise of Low-Fi Culture* (London: Marion Boyars Publishers, 2008), 11.

21   Ben Holtzman, Craig Hughes and Kevin Van Meter, "Do it Yourself and the Movement Beyond Capitalism," *Radical Society* 31, no.1 (2006): 7.

22   Quoted in Steven Shukaitis, "[nyc@] Zines & Beyond ABC No Rio," post to "NYC Anarchists" (NYCANARCHISTS@LISTS.RISEUP.NET, October 14 2009).

23   Amy Spencer, *DIY: The Rise of Low-Fi Culture*.

24   Quoted in Shukaitis, 2009

25   Spencer, 2008, 14.

26   Larry-Bob Roberts, "Not Another Queer Manifesto," *Holy Titclamps* 7 1996[1991], HTTP:// WWW.IO.COM/~LARRYBOB/MANI.HTML (accessed November 1 2009).

27   Roberts, 1991.

28   Spencer, 2008; Benjamin Shepard, "Play and World Making: From Gay Liberation to DIY Community Building," in *Seventies Confidential: Hidden Histories from the Sixties' Second Decade*, ed. Dan Berger (New Brunswick, NJ: Rutgers University Press, forthcoming).

29   Spencer, 2008, 42.

30   Stephen Duncombe, "Notes on Punk," unpublished manuscript, undated, in author's possession.

31 Eve Sedgewick, *Tendencies* (Durham, NC.: Duke University Press, 1993), 8.

32 Judith Butler, *Bodies That Matter: On the Discursive Limits of "Sex,"* (New York: Routledge, 1993), 230.

33 Rex Wockner, "LARRY KRAMER'S REMARKS AT DALLAS GAY PRIDE CELEBRATION, SUNDAY, SEPT. 20," *Wockner Wire*, September 21, 2009.

34 David France, "Meet the Fearsome Gay Gangsters of Bash Back!," *Details Magazine*, HTTP:// MEN.STYLE.COM/DETAILS/FEATURES/LANDING?ID=CONTENT_10417 (accessed October 1, 2009).

35 Colin Moynihan, "Arrest Puts Focus on Protesters' Texting," *New York Times*, October 5, 2009, HTTP://WWW.NYTIMES.COM/2009/10/05/NYREGION/05TXT.HTML?BL (accessed December 2, 2009).

36 Dean Spade, "Report back on the WEF," Mass Email, 2002.

37 Dean Spade, interview with author, 2007.

38 Spade, 2002.

39 Mimi Abramowitz, *Regulating the Lives of Women: Social Welfare Policy from Colonial Times to the Present* (Boston: South End Press, 1996).

40 Richard Cloward and Frances Fox-Piven, "Notes Toward a Radical Social Work," in *Radical Social Work*, eds. Roy Bailey and Mike Brake (New York: Pantheon, 1975), vii-xlviii.

41 Incite! Women of Color Against Violence, *The Revolution Will Not Be Funded* (Boston: South End Press, 2007).

42 Rickke Mananzala and Dean Spade, "The Nonprofit Industrial Complex and Trans Resistance," *Sexuality Research and Social Policy* 5, no. 1 (March 2008): 53–71.

43 Benjamin Shepard, "Sylvia and Sylvia's Children: A Battle for a Queer Public Space," in *That's Revolting: Queer Strategies for Resisting Assimilation*, ed. Mattilda AKA Matt Bernstein Sycamore (Brooklyn: Soft Skull Press, 2004), 123–140.

44 Benjamin Shepard, "Amanda Milan and the Rebirth of the Street Trans Action Revolutionaries," in *From ACT UP to the WTO: Urban Protest and Community Building in the Era of Globalization* (New York: Verso, 2002), eds. Benjamin Shepard and Ronal Hayduk, 156–163.

45 Kai Wright, "Queer, Dead and Nobody Cares: Why Two Violent Deaths Produced two Totally Different Reactions," *The Root*, February 26 2008, HTTP://WWW.THEROOT.COM/VIEWS/QUEER-DEAD-AND-NOBODY-CARES (accessed November 10, 2009).

46 Quoted in Michael Bronski, "Sylvia Rivera: 1951–2002: No longer on the back of the bumper," *Z Magazine*, April 2002, HTTP://WWW.ZMAG.ORG/ZMAG/VIEWARTICLE/12693 (accessed January 18, 2010).

47 Sylvia Rivera Law Project, "SRLP announces non-support of the Gender Employment Non-Discrimination Act," April 6 2009, HTTP://SRLP.ORG/NODE/30 (accessed November 1, 2009).

48 Alisa Solomon, "Back to the Streets: Can Radical Gay Organizers Reignite a Movement," *Village Voice*, November 3, 1998, HTTP://WWW.VILLAGEVOICE.COM/1998–11–03/NEWS/BACK-TO-THE-STREETS/1 (accessed November 22, 2009).

49 Goldstein, 2002.

50 Bill Dobbs, "Interview on the Death Penalty," *Subversity* KUCI, 88.9 FM, January 12, 1999, HTTP://KUCI.ORG/~DTSANG/SUBVERSITY/REALAUDIO.HTM (accessed January 6, 2006).

51 Andy Humm, "Slain Puerto Rican Teen Mourned. In New York, hundred mourn death, as vigils held in 20 cities," *Gay City News*, November 27, 2009, HTTP://GAYCITYNEWS.COM/AR-TICLES/2009/11/27/GAY_CITY_NEWS/NEWS/DOC4B0D4BFE21FCD370051081.TXT (accessed January 18, 2010).

52 Panama Vicente Alba, "Vigil for Jorge Steven Mercado/The Struggle against Homophobia/

The quest for Justice in a Colony—Puerto Rico," post to PANAMOGLOBALJUSTICE@LISTS.RI-SEUP.NET, 2009.

53 Judith Butler, "Imitation and Gender Insubordination," *The Lesbian, Gay and Bisexual Studies Reader*, eds. H. Abelove, M. A. Barale, and D. M. Halperin (New York: Routledge), 310.

54 Don Teal, 1971.

55 See oral history interviews with Ann Northrop and Kate Barnhardt in the ACT UP Oral History Project, HTTP://WWW.ACTUPORALHISTORY.ORG.

56 Dean Spade, "Pee Crimes," in Anti-Capitalist Tranny Brigade, *Piss & Vinegar* (New York, 2002).

ART AS INTERVENTION:

A Guide to Today's Radical Art Practices

Julie Perini

I N AN AGE WHERE CLIMATE change makes daily headlines, the current financial crisis has exposed severe economic inequalities, and the inhumane consequences of capitalism have infiltrated almost every corner of world, it appears as though the only sane thing to do is work to halt the progression of catastrophe. Why, then, would anyone make art?

Art plays an important role in *imagining* and *creating*, shared human traits that can connect individuals in collective, generative action. Art can provide dis-alienating experiences for a society desperately in need of healing. Art allows for experimentation with new ways of seeing, being, and relating, as well as opportunities to develop innovative strategies and tools for resistance movements. Art creates accessible points of entry into political discussions, educating and mobilizing people in ways that may be difficult to quantify but nonetheless tangible.

In this article, I present individuals and groups who believe their work aids in the struggles against the prison industrial complex, corporate control of technology, and the isolation engendered by capitalism. Their projects build and model new kinds of relationships. They shy away from the limited identities of 'artist' or 'activist.' Instead, they use creative energy to transform immediate social realities and construct meaningful experiences that happen in the streets, museums and galleries, domestic spaces, and any location where oppressive, authoritarian forces reign.

To declare that there is *a* radical art community in the U.S. would be both misleading and unproductive. Beyond their self-identification with radical politics, as those artists that follow have artistic expression of the real experiences of oppressed and working-class peoples, people of color, and others takes many forms, with divergent histories then self-identified radicals. Those discussed here form loose networks throughout the U.S. and beyond; they borrow freely from the tools and traditions of theater, painting, printmaking, sculpture, dance, music, film, graphic design, engineering, robotics, biotechnology, and other interdisciplinary arts and sciences. All espouse different approaches to the problem of creating tools and situations that will amplify, augment, and render concrete the messages of progressive and radical social movements. I refer to some of the work as "interventionist" because it disrupts or interrupts normal flows of information, capital, and the smooth functioning of other totalizing systems.

As a media artist, I am deeply invested in this interventionist art. I grapple with synthesizing my desire to explore the aesthetic possibilities of moving-image art with my commitment to radical social change and solidarity with movements of the oppressed. This dilemma likely stems from the professionalization of artists in the U.S., as both the art and academic markets require specialization, newness, and easily digestible products. One can be an artist or an activist, but to be both is viewed with suspicion and skepticism. This is also a struggle for the people discussed in this essay, and their work provides important insights as to how to refuse it.

First, I look at the work of highly visible and vocal advocates for social change like The Yes Men, Josh MacPhee and Justseeds Artists' Cooperative, and Dara Greenwald. Next, I address pointed interventions into the corporate-controlled discourses of science and engineering, through discussions with Natalie Jeremijenko and the collective Critical Art Ensemble. I then examine collectives that are primarily interested in creating platforms for discussion, collaboration, and resource exchange, particularly the Center for Urban Pedagogy, 16 Beaver Group, and AREA Chicago. Finally, I highlight the work of Trevor Paglen, an "experimental geographer" who uses mapping techniques to make visible seemingly 'hidden' structures of power. Although exciting new projects emerge daily across the country, I discuss individuals, collectives, and organizations established in their practices for at least five years. The discussion is intended to inspire and intrigue, but also to empower, since it is generative at heart. It is within all of our power to turn ideas into images, actions, and objects—to realize things that often seem possible only to the imagination.

RADICAL ART AND RADICAL ACTIONS

As long as there have been social movements, there have been people doing the important work of translating the messages of movement builders into understandable documents, objects, stories, and events. The art object itself can reach a person in emotional and intuitive ways that thick layers of explanatory text cannot. Take the image of the raised fist, for example: it instantly communicates the values of unity, strength, and power. While originating in radical labor unions such as the Industrial Workers of the World, this symbol has been adopted by a dizzying array of movements. Most notably in the U.S., the black liberation struggles generalized the image to the point where black athletes at the 1968 summer Olympics raised their fists during the American national anthem, bringing black struggles in the U.S. to a international audience. The pink triangle, originally used as a badge in Nazi concentration camps to identify homosexual prisoners, was reclaimed by gay rights activists in the 1970s and placed above the words "Silence=Death" by the AIDS Coalition to Unleash Power (ACT UP) to call attention to the severity of the AIDS crisis. Images like these are both reproducible and mutable. The raised fist and pink triangle are classic examples of the power of artistic production; they are often invoked graphically, on posters and other printed matter, and as a live action, a collective and individual gesture. People who do not think of themselves as artists become involved in creative production through the reproduction of these symbols, developing confidence and skills, and generating new poly-vocal expressions of a movement mission.

IMPOSTURE AS ART: THE YES MEN

THE YES MEN ARE A well-known network of activists born out of the alter-globalization movement, led by Mike Bonanno and Andy Bichlbaum. For over a decade, Bonanno and Bichlbaum have been staging media interventions that expose corporate crimes and argue for humane global economic relations. The two met when mutual friends alerted them to the fact that each was doing similar creative protest work on gender and sexuality. Mike had been responsible for the Barbie Liberation Organization, a media heist that involved the switching of hundreds of voice boxes from talking G.I. Joe and Barbie dolls just in time for Christmas. Andy had had become well-known in Silicon Valley after he programmed a hidden trigger in a Sims game to activate a kissing frenzy of young men in Speedo bathing suits. This meeting of minds has yielded some of the most effective public political stunts since the Yippies rained dollar bills on the New York Stock Exchange in 1967.[1]

The Yes Men consistently exploit codes: the HTML code that composes web sites, the behavioral codes that regulate conduct in the overlapping spheres of corporate media, global business, and federal government, and the graphic and linguistic codes that dictate the appearance of mass media. Anyone can lift the entire HTML code from a website by right-clicking on the page and selecting "View Page Source." Recognizing this, in 1999 the Yes Men mimicked the site of the World Trade Organization (WTO), transferring a copy of the code from www.wto.org to a new domain, www.gatt.org, with a few significant changes. One key change included re-routing the contact email address for information requests to themselves. When organizations began to request their participation at conferences and other meetings, Mike and Andy obliged, delivering outlandish presentations while masquerading as representatives from the WTO. These lectures push the neoliberal logic of the WTO to such an extent that claims such as "slavery is an economically sound business model" do not seem out of the realm of possibility. In fact, elite audiences often have frighteningly nonchalant—or, even more distressing, enthusiastic—reactions to these ideas.

The Yes Men have pulled off numerous other infiltrations exploiting the power of the mimic, what they call "identity correction": "impersonating big-time criminals in order to humiliate them," and targeting people "who put profit ahead of all else."[2] In one of their most well-known stunts from 2004, Andy posed as a representative for Dow Chemical on the BBC, announcing that the company had taken full responsibility for the 1984 Bhopal disaster that resulted in tens of thousands of deaths and planned to compensate victims and make amends. The event garnered international media attention, while Dow suffered a stock loss of two billion dollars on the German Exchange.

Mike and Andy are both articulate, able-bodied, young white men, educated in American colleges. Using the privileges that these facets of their identity afford them, they effectively pass through systems of power, exposing contradictions and injustices from the inside. These interventions are something other than theatrical protest. Mike and Andy (not their legal names) live their work, stepping in and out of their public identities as needed. The Yes Men acknowledge their unearned privilege as members of the dominant social group and perform important ally work, acting as agents of social change rather than agents of repression.

Though the Yes Men's work has functioned in support of various movements, it has not, until recently, been in concert with any specific one. Their efforts to call attention to the disastrous consequences of unchecked capitalism reveal that anti-sweatshop campaigns, movements to halt global warming, and other struggles are inextricably linked. In public lectures and interviews, the Yes Men acknowledge that their work supports the important, difficult work of grassroots community organizing:

> Our work is a small part of a global movement that is interested in derailing the kind of no-holds-barred capitalism that is starving the world's poor and ruining the environment. Our role is a tiny one in that overall movement, where people are engaged in thousands of other approaches to the issues. It is the people doing the social organizing, legal battles, etc. that are doing the real important work, which we are trying to support.[3]

Recently, the Yes Men have been working directly with organizations to promote policy change, such as Code Pink, Gray Panthers, and other activists. In addition to providing tools and encouragement for people who want to become active in their communities and to become more like Yes Men, the Yes Men's websites now contain information about local and global organizations fighting on a variety of fronts, including global poverty, corporate accountability, and climate change.

The Yes Men's form of irreverent public protest has roots in a strong working-class tradition that brings political theater to the public sphere. An early example of such street theater is the *Punch and Judy* show, which originated in Europe in the sixteenth century and continues to be performed across the globe. This puppet show centers on the comical character Punch as he triumphs over the forces of law and order. Bread & Puppet Theater began in New York City and is known for creating enormous puppets used during Vietnam War protests. Currently based in Vermont, Bread & Puppet continues to serve bread during its performances and remains a strong presence on an international stage, protesting American involvement in wars abroad and supporting struggles for self-determination.

Indeed, many artists and art-activists work directly with political campaigns and community organizers, often creating work with the participation of the constituencies they seek to serve. This solidarity results in the communication of specific messages that can be used as popular education tools. Furthermore, the process of creating artworks directly from movements for instrumental purposes often makes artists out of people who had not previously thought of themselves as particularly creative in this way.

COLLECTIVE ART IN SERVICE OF SOCIAL MOVEMENTS

COLLECTIVE ART PRODUCTION, AS OPPOSED to individual artistic output, complicates traditional conceptions of the artist. Collectively creating an artwork disrupts the romantic notion of 'artistic genius': the familiar figure of the artist alone in their studio, waiting for divine inspiration to flow through their body and onto a blank canvas. Who is the distinct genius if the *all* residents of a particular block paint a mural on an abandoned building? What does the market do when there is no singular personality to commodify? Just as artist collectives have sprung up frequently throughout history, the U.S. in recent years has seen many artists working together in various formations. These groups sometimes share authorship of specific pieces and usually share resources like supplies, information, and even food and shelter.

Even a brief survey of these artists would be too long to enumerate, but a few representatives of this phenomenon include the Beehive Design Collective (based in Maine, with members located throughout the U.S. and Mexico), Temporary Services (Chicago), Art and Revolution (California), and Justseeds Artists' Cooperative (U.S. and Mexico). Bees from the Beehive Collective buzz all over North America, leading educational workshops and creating collaboratively designed posters and murals for communities and campaigns. Their work is anti-copyright, anonymous, and created in close conversation with the people who will use the graphics. David Solnit has been involved with mass movements in the United States for almost three decades, incorporating art and theater—particularly puppets—into his work. In the late 1990s, he helped found Art and Revolution, a network of street theater practitioners and art collectives whose aim is create new forms of resistance that incorporate art and theater into movements. Temporary Services is a collaborative endeavor among three artists in Illinois, which has made an impact on the cultural life of Chicago by creating community-based projects, including experimental exhibition spaces and collectively authored publications.

Justseeds Artists' Cooperative is a group of twenty-five artist-workers throughout the U.S. and Mexico who cooperatively maintain a web presence, which functions both as a marketplace for their work and as a site for information exchange and community building. The artists of Justseeds create affordable artworks that are reproducible, lacking an 'original' object: silkscreen prints, block prints, stencils, zines, and other multiples. These works often depict figures and events from radical and under-represented histories, or address themes like anarchism, the environment, labor, anti-racism, and gender liberation. Justseeds artists often collaborate to generate calendars and poster series.

In addition to generating income from the sale of postcards, calendars, and limited edition prints, Justseeds provides a context for critical discussions about art and activism. Many Justseeds artists are also involved in ongoing projects, including the God Bless Graffiti Coalition, a loose network of artists combating anti-graffiti trends, and GhostBikes.org, a site that documents the creation of Ghost Bike memorials by local communities. Ghost bikes are bikes painted white and locked to urban locations where cyclists have lost their lives or been the victims of traffic accidents.

One example of collective creative action in solidarity with movement organizers is the *Voices from the Outside: Justseeds Prison Portfolio Project*, which effectively complements prison abolition work (such as that done by Critical Resistance). This portfolio brought together the work of twenty artists and one collective from North America, each of whom created a print that addressed the prison industrial complex or its abolition. These portfolios were bundled with a CD containing high-resolution images of the prints, and were distributed to prison organizing groups, who then used the posters and images in their own organizing and campaign work.

Another notable project by Justseeds co-founder Josh MacPhee is the book *Reproduce & Revolt!*, edited with artist Favianna Rodriguez. Filled with over 600 royalty-free illustrations from around the world, the book is designed for use by individuals involved with social justice movements. Rodriguez is active in Oakland, California as an artist and community organizer. Well-known for her bold political posters, she is a printmaker, digital artist, and educator who proclaims, "I am in the business of education and liberation. My subjects are Black, Latino, Asian, and Native communities that have been ignored and smashed by this government."[4] She is the co-founder of the East Side Arts Alliance, an organization devoted to training young people in the tradition of muralism. Rodriguez continues a long tradition of political poster making, one that remains important for all national and international grassroots struggles.

Some of the recent history of political poster making is documented in the ambitious exhibition, *Signs of Change: Social Movement Cultures 1960s to Now*, organized by Josh MacPhee and artist Dara Greenwald in 2008. This exhibition surveys artwork from more than forty-years of international movement building, including anti-Apartheid work in Africa and the civil rights movement in the U.S. This important exhibition explores histories of oppressed peoples through artworks created by the movement makers themselves. The exhibition contains over 800 posters, photographs, videos, and other works that have been generated concurrent with movements for social justice. Greenwald explains:

> One of the hopes of doing *Signs of Change* was to share moments with other artists when people used creativity to mobilize for social transformation, to show social movement history through the lens of culture and not primarily through the lens of individual artistic production. We also wanted to show activists, who might not see art as a serious political activity, that there are historical examples of artistic production being integral and important to movements and movement success. We found that movements themselves can become cultural producers in which the mobilizations inspire new kinds of creativity. In the examples we looked at, the art and media coming out of social movements was often anonymously and collectively produced.[5]

Signs of Change is one of many recent artist projects that reanimates radical histories. With MacPhee and artist Olivia Robinson, Greenwald has begun a project called *Spectres of Liberty*, an ongoing series of public projects about the history of the movement to abolish slavery in the U.S. The group has created one public project, *The Ghost of the Liberty Street Church*, which consisted of a life-sized inflatable church occupying the site of the former Liberty Street Church in Troy, New York. The space is currently a parking lot; through posters, video projections, sound, and other media, the group sought to bring to life the history of what had been a central location for anti-slavery organizing. Greenwald has extensive knowledge of historical and contemporary trends in radical art production and the relationship between cultural production and social movements:

> Unfortunately, in the neoliberal system we live in, it is so hard to make a living and find support for our art that a kind of careerism, competition, marketing and branding of the self seems necessary. This can be at odds with participating in social movements. Although we are all complicit in the logic of the market, we still must strive to resist and transform it if we are laying claim to doing work for social change. This is no easy task.[6]

Greenwald elaborates on these ideas in her essay, "The Process is in the Streets: Challenging Media America," which surveys the history of video collectives in the U.S. in the

1970s and 1980s.[7] Like Justseeds, these collectives accounted for the economic conditions behind the production of cultural objects and media, by pooling equipment that at the time was unaffordable to most individuals. Media collectives like upstate New York's Videofreex, though not explicitly 'political,' were unquestionably anti-authoritarian and experimental in their collective structure. Artists today can look back to this time to see a moment when the process of creating art, particularly media art, successfully transformed social relationships.

Other critical art interventions speak to a tradition of exploring identity. African American conceptual artist Adrian Piper's street antics from 1960s and 1970s continue to influence later generations. With her *Mythic Being* series, Piper donned a mustache and men's clothing and walked the streets of New York City in order to experience first-hand public attitudes toward black men. William Pope.L, calling himself "The Friendliest Black Artist in America," carries out similar critical street performances today. His project, *The Black Factory*, is a large truck that travels to public places and gathers "black things" from participants (objects that speak to them of blackness) which are then pulverized and turned into new objects. Coco Fusco is a Cuban-American interdisciplinary artist whose work in multimedia and performance explores women and society, war, politics, in addition to race. She and Mexican-born performance artist Guillermo Gomez-Peña collaborated on *Couple in a Cage* in 1993, a social experiment and traveling exhibition where they exhibited themselves as caged American Indians from an imaginary island, complete with feathered headdresses and 'native garb.' While they had intended to create a commentary on colonialism and objectification of indigenous peoples, to their surprise, many spectators believed that the two artists actually were "savages from a faraway land."

MEDIA, TECHNOLOGY, AND INTERVENTIONS

LIKE STREET ARTISTS RECLAIMING COMMON space to widen its latitude of acceptable use, media artists have always trespassed onto the largely privatized turf of technology. The history of media art is one of innovative artists and technologists collaborating, sharing resources, and blurring the boundary between scientific research and art production. Technology is one of the most mystified areas of our culture, fetishized as extremely difficult and complex, something only specialists and those with access to adequate resources—like corporations—can understand and develop. The artists described in this section prove that amateurs, hobbyists, and collectives can co-produce knowledge and engage in "contestational" scientific inquiry.[8] Technology can provide us with more than disposable gadgets and gizmos; it can create tools that reverse the alienating effects of capital, aid activists in their work, and increase our understanding of the natural and social worlds.

For the past ten years, the Institute for Applied Autonomy has been developing technologies specifically for use by activists. Calling their practice "contestational robotics," this collective produced *GraffitiWriter*, a robot that spray paints subversive messages in public locations, and *StreetWriter*, a van equipped with a computerized system that also paints subversive messages, but on a much larger scale. In 2009, Nike appropriated the latter project for use during the Tour de France, much to the dismay of its original collective of inventors. Years before the Nike scandal, artist Cat Mazza, who also maintains a blog that provides information about anti-sweatshop campaigns and the history of organized labor, had combined the low-tech art of knitting with the high-tech art of software design to create the *Nike Blanket Petition*, a fourteen-foot wide blanket combining hundreds of knit squares by individuals from forty countries, created to protest Nike's use of sweatshop labor. This simple object—a large hand-knit blanket featuring the Nike logo— powerfully communicates the message of global, collective solidarity with sweatshop laborers.

Paul Vanouse originally studied painting, but soon began to investigate what he has termed "emerging media."[9] Emerging media are technologies and processes that have hitherto been unexplored by artists, including such new fields as genetic experimentation. Vanouse's works playfully and critically interrogate current popular scientific issues, particularly those around the scientific construction of race. *The Relative Velocity Inscription Device* is a live experiment and installation that takes DNA samples from four members of a multiracial family, literally racing them against one another in a genetic separation gel. The winner of the race is different each time, a result that flies in the face of early twentieth century eugenics theories. Instead, the experiment encourages viewers to examine their own conceptions of racial identity. Another artist, Brooke Singer, often works with the collective Preemptive Media, using new media to create projects that address environmental and social issues. Their collaborative projects include *Purpool*, a social networking site designed to promote and facilitate carpooling, and *Swipe*, a project that allows participants to find out what kind of data is being collected about them each time their driver's license is swiped and pooled into a database.

Many of the artists listed above are continuing an interventionist approach to technology that the collective Critical Art Ensemble (CAE) has been engaged in for over two decades. CAE is a name that has become synonymous with tactical media, a practice the collective describes as "situational, ephemeral, and self-terminating." Tactical media "encourages the use of any media that will engage a particular sociopolitical context in order to create molecular interventions and semiotic shocks that contribute to the negation of the rising intensity of authoritarian culture."[10] Tactical media derives its name from an influential passage from philosopher Michel de Certeau's *The Practice of Everyday Life*, where he distinguishes between strategies used by structures of power and tactics used by individuals to carve out autonomous space within these same structures. Artists have responded positively to de Certeau's description of the tactic, eager to utilize the concept: "The space of a tactic is the space of the other. [...] In short, a tactic is an art of the weak."[11]

Founding CAE member Steve Kurtz describes his outlook on contemporary art interventionist practices:

> How are people doing these kinds of interventions? It is not going to be through a dropout culture, and it is going to be through people who are trying to construct new kinds of social relationships, new kinds of relationships to the commodity, new kinds of relationships to information, new kinds of relationships to technology. That's what the best interventionists do now. They create new relationships; that's the creative practice and that is how we can somehow relate it to art in some way.[12]

CAE's practice is process-oriented and performance-based. Their projects explore the intersections among technology, critical theory, and radical politics. Working in public, educational, academic, and art contexts, their work has, for the past few years, focused on demystifying the modern biotech industry by developing participatory performance experiences for audiences. *Free Range Grain* typifies their method of inquiry and presentation: a mobile microbiology lab allows audience members to perform tests on food they bring from home to determine whether or not the food contains common genetic modifications. CAE often works directly with community organizers and other times as an outside operation. Kurtz explains:

> CAE has always tried to strike a balance between autonomy and alliance. On one hand we need to be free to move when we see a concrete opening, or to explore possibilities that could fail. On the other hand, we feel compelled to support progressive causes. CAE is a cultural research wing off the main body of collected progressive movements—we have points of conjunction, but are still a part unto ourselves.[13]

Natalie Jeremijenko is another defiant artist/engineer whose work tirelessly imagines and develops new ways for humans to understand, relate to, and connect with the natural environment. Her public experiments focus on creating methods for the participatory production of knowledge about the natural world, as well as the development of technologies that enable social change and promote critical dialogue.

Since 1991, when Jeremijenko established the Bureau of Inverse Technology, she has been committed to using machines to address the needs of an increasingly alienated, mediated society. Her projects include *HowStuffisMade*, a collectively produced encyclopedia providing information about the manufacturing, environmental costs, and labor conditions behind the creation of products. With her *Feral Robot Dogs* project, she organized workshops and other public events that provided support for hacking into robotic dog toys and reprogramming them to sniff out environmental waste in communities. Inverting the logic and typical structure of a zoo, her *OOZ* projects describe a variety of technological interfaces that facilitate human interaction with natural systems and encourage meaningful interactions between humans and non-humans.

Responding to current environmental justice movements and drawing upon the history of the 1970s feminist art movement, Jeremijenko's most recent project is the *Environmental Health Clinic*, a clinic that works with clients to prescribe plans of action that will address their environmental health concerns. Clients work with Jeremijenko at the *Clinic* to generate processes and devices that will improve local air quality or stimulate food production. She refers to the protocols she develops with clients as "lifestyle experiments":

> At the *Environmental Health Clinic*, in addition to the prescriptions and protocols I've been developing, it is also facilitating these different lifestyle experiments. There are a number of bio-monitoring protocols I've developed and coded. The clinic has a website and people blog on their 'medical records' and share information. The clinic works as a context over which we can take very specific, locally optimized protocols and start to generalize and figure out what to do. Initiatives such as efforts to recycle, urban agriculture, or recycling grey water are happening already. I think the role of the artist is to produce it in a way that is demonstrable, in a way that makes these ideas accessible.

In the arts, it's an endemic practice that comes out of 1970s feminist practices that used the domestic sphere as the realm of representation. These are small experiments with one's own lifestyle where you have control, a high standard of evidence, you know when it works and when it fails, and yet it's demonstrative and not just symbolic. So these lifestyle experiments, in the tradition of Thoreau's lifestyle experiment of Walden Pond, are about figuring out how to re-imagine relationships to natural systems, not through consumption, but through taking the lifestyles over which we have agency and changing them.[14]

EXPERIMENTS WITH COMMUNITY BUILDING AND CREATING PLATFORMS FOR DISCUSSION

JEREMIJENKO'S WORK WITH "LIFESTYLE EXPERIMENTS" links to other cultural work similarly focused on ways of living. In addition to generating images, stories, technologies, and other items useful for resistant culture, cultural workers can offer movement builders new ways to conceive of social relationships, pedagogical practices, and communication. Not tethered to particular political positions and free of the need to produce tangible results, artists often use their autonomy to experiment with new ways of living, relating, and communicating. Below I describe several groups whose purpose is to create situations or platforms in which other people can exercise creativity, or to stimulate critical thought and community dialogue. These groups create subtle interventions; they destabilize norms and disrupt structures of power by posing questions and broadening access to creative and critical practices.

The Journal of Aesthetics & Protest is a print and online publication that reports on the activities of a wide variety of cultural workers and thinkers in the U.S. and abroad. The Journal is a valuable resource for people looking to learn about the intersections of contemporary social theory, critical art production, activist practices, and other global struggles. AREA Chicago is another hub for people working in art, research, education, and activism. AREA engages in many projects, including a biannual publication and an accompanying events series, as well as maintaining an informative website about political and cultural work concerning local social justice issues, such as prisons, gentrification, and food systems. Dan Tucker, one of the main organizers of AREA Chicago, discusses how movements can better utilize cultural strategies:

Art practices bring a highly experimental approach to how and why things can be organized that goes far beyond aesthetic strategies. Artists embedded within social movements have the greatest potential to push the conceptual boundaries of what we mean by "community," "solidarity," "revolution," "grassroots," "utopia," and "struggle"—to name a few of the often narrowly defined frameworks which categorize the subcultures of contemporary Left politics.[15]

In New York City, 16 Beaver Group exists as a loose coalition of artists, activists, and curators who regularly gather at 16 Beaver Street in lower Manhattan. It began as a reading group in 1999 and has evolved to include film screenings, walks, lunches, workshops, and other types of events. Rent from the studio spaces on the same floor as the communal space covers the cost of maintaining the common areas that function as event spaces. As their website describes, "16 Beaver is the address of a space initiated/run by artists to create and maintain an ongoing platform for the presentation, production, and discussion of a variety of artistic/cultural/economic/political projects. It is the point of many departures/arrivals."[16] Filmmaker and activist Paige Sarlin, a longtime member and organizer of 16 Beaver Group, speaks about their activities:

> Having some knowledge of the history of the organized Left in the United States, it has always struck me that there is an absence of space for sustained political education and training in movements. 16 Beaver addresses this need, but unlike movements that are tied to a sense of urgency and necessity for action, 16 Beaver provides a space for self-organized research and inquiry that is really flexible. We have been teaching each other for ten years and the curriculum keeps changing as different people become involved. We have developed an ethic of conversation that responds to particular ideas, events, questions and concerns. As a result, we have built a shared interest in what makes conversation useful, working together to make discussion productive but not tied to finding a solution. That's not to say that we don't all grapple with searching for solutions or projects or actions to take. But we don't see our discussion and presentation practice as needing to be over-determined by that sort of urgency or necessity.
>
> To a great degree, this is an alternative holding space for both politics and aesthetics. "Politics and aesthetics" in the sense that it's a space that has been teaching people how to be in the world as feeling, thinking beings, as people who are able to live and build relationships with others at the same time that they are building movements which are aimed at changing conditions and structures, addressing issues and problems within the economic and social world.[17]

She also discusses the need for systemic change in the U.S. and how initiatives like 16 Beaver Group can contribute to the growth of inclusive social systems:

> What does it really mean to build a broad-based mass movement? We need a profoundly diverse broad-based mass movement in order to enact structural change and not reform. We need to learn to coexist with differences. This is the difference between a united front and popular front. We all know how transformative it is to be part of a movement socially; you become more confident because you understand you're not the only one who thinks and feels the way you do. That's an important part of movement building. But everyone is so overextended and isolated. Artists can do more than just inspire people; artists can model other ways of living your life, offer different ways to relate to other people other than in the instrumental, urgent way that the neoliberal capitalist society requires and forces on us. We can attempt a more humane way of life.

Also engaged in this transformative work is The Center for Urban Pedagogy (CUP), an organizing body that creates projects to investigate, understand, and educate New York

City dwellers about their built environments. Much of their work involves pairing skilled artists and researchers with school groups and urban neighborhoods that typically lack funding for community art, often reaching communities of recent immigrants and people of color. CUP facilitates this co-production of knowledge about particular urban issues and oversees the creation of educational tools such as videos, comics, pamphlets, posters, exhibitions, or a combination of these forms. Their ongoing series of fold-out posters, *Making Policy Public*, pairs innovative graphic designers with policy advocates to make complex policy issues accessible to everyday people. Another project, *Garbage Problems*, was a collaborative endeavor between CUP and students from City-As-School. When Fresh Kills landfill closed in 2001, New York needed to devise new methods of waste disposal. The students and CUP members involved with *Garbage Problems* investigated garbage infrastructure and produced educational posters, a video, and a speculative design for reuse of the landfill. This fusion of research, design, and community involvement characterizes CUP's inquiry-based approach to local social justice activism. Rosten Woo, one of CUP's founders and its former executive director, discussed his experiences and CUP's development over the past several years:

> CUP works as a connecting vehicle, a platform for cooperation. The act of collaboration and creation of a tangible product is uniquely powerful and able to forge connections between people with really different approaches and ways of working, from activists to high school teachers, to bureaucrats, to graphic designers. One of the really wonderful things about our early exhibition projects was that we were able to collect work from all these different kinds of folks into one space and forge spatial or conceptual connections that way, and then at the openings, because we had involved so many people and they wanted to see their work, we would get these big crowds from very different communities, and so the exhibition space could be a place where personal connections could also be formed. Over time, our focus shifted away from doing exhibition work and towards making works that were more easily distributable. There is definitely a particular kind of magic that happens when you use a space to gather material and people, but a year's worth of work could disappear after a couple of months at an exhibition, whereas a DVD or a publication could be utilized by people for years, and in multiple cities at once, etc. So the challenge is to find ways of maintaining the excitement, momentum, and sense of shared purpose that an exhibition project generates, but also find ways to kind of bottle and distribute the fruits of that work.[18]

Because of their emphasis on urban exploration, projects by the Center for Urban Pedagogy often find themselves included in exhibitions about geography, space, place, and the practice of map-making. This allows CUP's work to extend beyond their immediate intended audience and impact other communities.

CREATIVE CARTOGRAPHY

MAPS ALLOW US TO VISUALIZE our relationships to space, power, resources, and social formations. In recent years, creative cartography has become an increasingly popular way to make often invisible information visible. This interdisciplinary practice often brings together people working in community building, design, geography, environmental issues, art, and sociology.[19]

Artist and geographer Trevor Paglen coined the term "Experimental Geography." Much of his work focuses on researching secret government operations and representing these networks of invisible power through photography and book projects, and by leading group expeditions to view clandestine military activity. He has mapped information about locations of the CIA's extraordinary rendition program and other covert activities, and created photography projects about classified American reconnaissance satellites orbiting the earth. In a recent article in the popular art magazine *Art Forum*, he commented on this latter project, called *The Other Night Sky*. He writes:

> If, as was the case with the landscape photographers of the past, the production of symbolic order goes hand in hand with the exertion of control—if, that is, we can only control things by first naming or imaging them—then developing a lexicon of the other night sky might be a step toward reclaiming the violence flowing through it.[20]

Others use maps as tools for the participatory production of knowledge about social life. AREA Chicago's *People's Atlas* is a multi-city mapping initiative, collecting blank city maps that participants have filled in with information about diverse areas of knowledge and human experience. Maps made in Chicago include "The Streets I Walk Down," "Neighborhoods by Income," and "Iraq Veterans Against the War." Maps, with their portability and flexibility, are important artistic tools for representing and communicating complex information, and they can aid in many grassroots struggles.

ACTIVE IMAGINATIONS AND ACTIVE PARTICIPANTS

EVERY PRACTITIONER DISCUSSED IN THIS essay is concerned with imagining and practicing new kinds of relationships. Steve Kurtz noted this when he said that today's interventionists are going to be people who construct "new kinds of social relationships, new kinds of relationships to the commodity, new kinds of relationships to information, new kinds of relationships to technology."[21] From collectively authored community murals to the development of contestational technologies, the work of the artists discussed here show numerous ways to conceive of and implement new social relations and practices in everyday life; there are countless more to explore.

Radical and interventionist art resonates with other cultural practices occurring throughout the U.S. both now and in the past, a rich area for inquiry. For example, there are numerous interventionist practices that specifically explore social relationships through the lenses of gender, race, sexuality, and class; the work of Adrian Piper, William Pope L., Coco Fusco, Guillermo Gomez-Peña are just some areas to explore for divergent and different histories. Additionally, the use of art and community-building practices in public murals, graffiti, community gardens, and traditional crafts are other avenues of exploration. While these critical interventions deserve further inquiry and contextualization as radical art practices working alongside liberationist movements, there are neighboring traditions and rich histories that should not be excluded from our understanding of the role of arts in radical change and community building.

There are also lingering questions as to how radical artists move from simply being in solidarity with working-class- and people of color-led movements to seeing themselves contextualized within a larger patchwork of practices. Specifically, artists who are members of privileged social groups do not always take responsibility for learning how oppression manifests in everyday life. Artists, to be critical and useful, must make themselves vulnerable, ask questions, and do the work of being an ally in the struggle against all forms of oppression. The Beehive Collective's method of "cross-pollination" is one of the most important and useful strategies among creative communities for building new social relations. It is a simple idea, though not often deployed by cultural workers: testing one's ideas by running them by people from communities other than one's own. In their own words:

> The Beehive prefers to gain its knowledge of issues as directly from the source as possible, by conducting interviews with those being directly affected, or organizers that are specialists on the issues. We research each topic of our graphics campaigns thoroughly, including visits to botanical societies for photos of the specific species of animals and plants we convey, and have our ideas and facts critiqued by many people before they hatch and get shouted to the world. Filtering the information for subtle racist assumptions, cultural appropriation, and myopic North American perspectives through critique from people of color and those directly affected by the issues being discussed is an important step in our collaboration process. [22]

Of course, many people would hesitate to call themselves creative in the multitudinous ways mentioned here. Yet most everyone would agree that every human being possesses an imagination. We use it each time we perform mundane tasks or plan future events. Our imagination allows us to link our private experiences to broader collective struggles, social institutions, and our society's position in history. Artists are simply people who activate their imaginations regularly and mindfully, to the point where it becomes a reflex and a way of seeing, thinking, and acting creatively; this, too, is a strategy to build new forms of social relations. The imagination is not an untroubled space, for it is here that assumptions about what is and is not possible collide. This alternate reality is a rehearsal space, a laboratory, and a place to become acquainted with uncertainty. It is here that active imaginations, combined with active participation, become critical tools for co-creating social systems that benefit everyone.

NOTES

1   The Youth International Party, whose members were known as Yippies, was an American youth-oriented radical organization formed in the late 1960s, known for its use of street theater and political pranks.

2   From the Yes Men website, HTTP://WWW.THEYESMEN.ORG.

3   C. Ondine Chavoya, "The Yes Men," in *The Interventionists: Users' Manual for the Creative Disruption of Everyday Life*, eds. Nato Thompson and Gregory Sholette (Cambridge: MIT Press, 2004), 106.

4   From Favianna Rodriguez's website, HTTP://WWW.FAVIANNA.COM. (accessed January 20, 2010).

5   Dara Greenwald, interview with the author, October 14, 2009.

6   Dara Greenwald, interview (2009).

7   Dara Greenwald, "The Process is in the Street: Challenging Media America," in *Realizing the Impossible: Art Against Authority*, eds. Josh MacPhee and Erik Reuland (Oakland: AK Press, 2007), 168–179.

8   Critical Art Ensemble describes the concept of "contestational biology" in their book, *The Molecular Invasion* (Brooklyn: Autonomedia, 2002). Contestational biology is the radical appropriation of knowledge systems to create new biochemical fronts that can be engaged to disrupt profits. "Contestational" is a term that cultural workers use to describe other critical art practices including "contestational robotics" and "contestational geography."

9   Conversation with Paul Vanouse (2009); HTTP://WWW.CONTRIB.ANDREW.CMU.EDU/~PV28/

10 C. Ondine Chavoya, "Critical Art Ensemble," in *The Interventionists: Users' Manual for the Creative Disruption of Everyday Life*, eds. Nato Thompson and Gregory Sholette (Cambridge: MIT Press, 2004), 117.

11 Michel de Certeau, *The Practice of Everyday Life* (Berkeley: University of California Press, 1984), 37.

12 Steve Kurtz, interview with the author, Buffalo, NY, September 6, 2009.

13 Steve Kurtz, email interview with the author, November 27, 2009.

14 Natalie Jeremijenko, interview with the author, New York, NY, October 4, 2009.

15 Dan Tucker, email response to general survey, November 3, 2009.

16 16 Beaver Group, HTTP://WWW.16BEAVERGROUP.ORG. (accessed January 20, 2010).

17 Paige Sarlin, interview with the author, October 10, 2009.

18 Rosten Woo, interview with the author, October 11, 2009.

19 In the U.S., a useful place to begin to learn about this work is through *An Atlas of Radical Cartography*, edited by Lize Mogel and Alexis Bhagat, a collection of ten maps and ten essays about social issues.

20 Trevor Paglen, "1000 Words," *Art Forum* (March 2009), 228.

21 Steve Kurtz, interview with the author, Buffalo, NY, September 6, 2009.

22 From the Beehive Collective website, HTTP://WWW.BEEHIVECOLLECTIVE.ORG (accessed January 20, 2010).

WHISTLING INTO THE TYPHOON:

A Radical Inquiry Into Autonomous Media

Dorothy Kidd

INTRODUCTION

THE INVITATION TO JOIN WITH others "in the middle of a whirlwind" reminds me of an earlier moment in a tradition of radical inquiry. Documenting eighteenth and nineteenth-century working-class organization, radical English historian E.P. Thompson wrote that reviewing the "alternative needs, expectations and codes" may renew our sense of the range of possibilities, and "prepare us for a time when both capitalist and state communist needs and expectations may decompose, and human nature be made into a new form. This is perhaps to whistle into a typhoon." In 1992, a year after those words were published, Zapatista Subcomandante Marcos spoke prophetically of two winds, one from above (neoliberalism) and one from below (anti-capitalist/globalization struggle): "From the clash of these two winds the storm will be born, its time has arrived. Now the wind from above rules, but the wind from below is coming."[1]

Self-organized, creative production has a long history in proletarian contests with capitalist development, as E.P. Thompson and a handful of others have pointed out.[2] Documenting the struggles of insurgent communicators, in the same period as described by Marcos, Nick Dyer-Witheford and I teased out an autonomist analysis of the communications commons and media enclosures. "Our new commonwealth ... is the creation of a 'communications commons' a counter-project against capital's attempts to 'enclose' the immaterial territories of airwaves, bandwidths and cyberspaces in the same way it once enclosed the collective lands of the rural commons."[3] Then, in 1999, a new cycle started in Seattle with the founding of the global Independent Media Center (IMC) Network, amidst the organizing against the World Trade Organization.

In this article, I use the vantage point of the IMC's tenth anniversary to discuss contemporary struggles over media power in the United States. In the spirit of this collection of essays, it *is not prescriptive, nor comprehensive;* instead, it *is a call for a* larger radical inquiry. I am interested in analyzing moments of movement and counter-movement throughout all the circuits of the global communications system. My focus is on the affirmation of autonomous media power in three different dimensions: the means (infrastructure) of mass communications, the social relations of cultural production, and the symbolic meanings. I draw on Raymond Williams' useful idea to describe the concurrent and overlapping development of cycles of radical media, and analyze the interplay between 'dominant,' 'residual,' and 'emergent' forms of commercial media, the alternative media and social justice communications, and social media networks.

THE INDYMEDIA CENTER: A NEW COMPOSITION

DURING THE 1999 PROTESTS AGAINST the World Trade Organization (WTO) in Seattle, the power of the first Independent Media Center (IMC) took the dominant media, neoliberal capitalism, and academic scholars by surprise. Cooperatively running a storefront center and sharing a computer server, they broke through the dominant media's gate-keepers, and those of the non-governmental organization spokespeople, with direct reporting from participants of the counter movements. They circulated a multitude of perspectives from the protesters themselves about the impact of the trade deals, and more importantly, began to circulate a critique of the neoliberal agenda. Countering Margaret Thatcher's claim that "there is no alternative" to free-market capitalism, and modeling the direct action of the streets, the IMC demonstrated a new genre of do-it-yourself (DIY) media.

The story of the global IMC network is well-known among activist circles, international journalists, and some academics. It grew virally via the global justice movement, re-combining into 150 autonomously-controlled centers around the world, via a shared DNA of social organization, collective knowledge, norms of governance, and linked computer mainframes. Less familiar was the concurrent emergence of media hubs and hacker labs, at almost all the World and regional Social Forums, which shared similar norms of collective experimentation, knowledge creation, and media representation. The resultant social and political networks morphed into many other organizations; however, the link between 'self-directed' autonomous media and global justice is now taken for granted.

The global IMC represented a qualitative shift in the scope and scale of media power. Until then, alternative media had been limited by small-scale production, shut out from most of the capitalist circuits of distribution, and divided internally by the craft logics of capitalist industry (print, radio, public access television, video, and music). The IMC represented a leap beyond the monopoly control of production of corporate media. It was a recomposition of media makers, bringing together open source software hackers and technicians, alternative media and independent video producers, punks, and social justice communicators. All of these groups had developed, in part, through the mass appropriation of sophisticated digital tools of production and circulation, and earlier collective experiments in their use.

It was also no accident that the IMC was born in the home of Microsoft, then the dominant corporate player in the rapidly growing sector of information capitalism. Many in the new class of computer knowledge workers operated with vehemence against Microsoft in particular, demonstrating collective principles antithetical to proprietary ideas of intellectual property. Their gift to the IMC was the "open publishing" software which allowed anyone with access to the Web, anywhere in the world, to upload and download any kind of digital media content for global distribution. En masse, the IMC centers started circulating counter-hegemonic content in forms that prefigured podcasting and blogging. This development was a significant blow against neoliberal logic, which was furiously attempting to fence off access to and privatize the content of the internet.

Two other constitutive elements, alternative media makers and social justice communicators, formed a communications network in response to the developing neoliberal agenda.[4] This was made famous when the Zapatistas, with minimal communications capacity, utilized the "electronic fabric of struggle" to bring world attention to their resistance to the North American Free Trade Agreement and the Mexican Army, but the roots went back at least a decade.[5] Forged in Latin America, Asia, and Africa, in struggles against structural adjustment programs, activists used their own autonomous media, and some of the same circuits of communications as global capital, to exchange programming and participate in solidarity actions and transnational mobilization. By the major economic crisis in Asia in 1998, the South Korean labor and student movements had developed sophisticated, on-the-spot web-based reporting, which they then circulated back via huge monitors to people demonstrating in the streets against neoliberalism.

BE THE MEDIA

MARKET CONTROL OF THE CIRCUITS and media products had been a controversial policy demand of the U.S. Government since the end of World War II, when it lost its claim to make culture a tradable commodity in the precursor treaty to the WTO, the General Agreement on Tariffs and Trade. After a fierce round of debates ending in the early 1980s, all the countries in the United Nations—with the exception of the U.S., the United Kingdom, and Honduras—called for a New World Information Communications Order. Stinging from that round, the U.S. began imposing a market strategy on media products through intellectual property agreements and bilateral trade agreements. The WTO summit in Seattle was to be a test case to try to move back to global agreements. It was not to be.

Formed from the three constitutive networks of global social justice movements, alternative media, and free/open software creators, the Seattle IMC helped circulate the message about the cancellation of the World Trade Organization talks far and wide. The global IMC then grew very quickly, first as convergence centers countering the WTO and other neoliberal institutions, and then in 150 autonomous controlled centers across the world, as the threat of a good idea took hold. The resultant global IMC rivaled commercial popular news organizations in scale, reach, and potential comprehensiveness.[6] Here was a new model of social production that challenged the practices and codes of representation of professional journalists in multiple ways. The IMC demonstrated the power of a multi-media approach, presenting photos, text, radio, and video content, all on the same site. Open publishing removed the gate-keepers of the dominant media, as well as the mediation of NGO spokespeople. Instead, the IMC presented an idea of truth-making based on a variety of framings through active witnesses and eyewitness reporting from correspondents in protests, communities, and movements. The IMC challenged the professional doctrine of 'objectivity' that U.S. journalists had established in the 1920s through the adaptation of 'scientific rationalism,' partly as a response to state propaganda.[7] Audiences were addressed as co-participants in the production of information for political action and engagement rather than as targets of commercial messages.

If the global IMC network prefigured other social justice media networks, it also led to a quick reaction from old and new U.S. information capitalists. During this period, the older dominant media were urging enclosure of the internet through harsh new regimes of intellectual property; in the U.S., they mounted attacks on individual peer-to-peer users through suits and legislation like the Digital Millennium Copyright Act. Globally, they supported the U.S. government inserting U.S.-styled intellectual property agreements within world and bilateral free trade agreements. In Silicon Valley and other centers of capital, they decided to appropriate the radical designs of internet infrastructure, relations of production, and the software of the IMC and others. Social network media did not arise, as James Hamilton notes, "through industry research and development, but through the commercialization of grassroots developments within transnational digital systems."[8] The emergence of the business model Web 2.0 followed the same historical pattern of technological development in the U.S. seen in the early days of radio and the internet, when technologies developed by grassroots actors—in the spirit of global participatory connection—were then harvested as engines of new capitalist growth.[9]

By 2005, the global IMC network began to slow almost as quickly as it had grown. Many of the sites imploded, as the end of highly visible international protests halted recruitment. Local teams were less able to sustain the long hours of unpaid work, or to overcome differences of political perspective, gender, race, and class. In addition, the IMC began to be eclipsed as the platform of protest in many countries, and other sites like Slashdot, Kuro5hin, and Plastic stepped up.

The IMC's harnessing of the tremendous power of digital and global social justice networks shrunk many of the production and distribution barriers of earlier alternative media, but by no means eliminated them. Telephone lines, computers, internet access, expertise, and wages (most importantly) remain as unequally distributed between rich and poor communities in the U.S. as between rich and poor countries. As English media critic James Curran has noted, the move to digital media production does not vaporize capital needs, but just transfers them "directly to the receiver, who pays for the computer and the connection charge," or by society in public libraries or other public access centers.[10] The global IMC was only able to maintain its independence from capitalist media through the volunteer labor of younger middle- and professional- class activists and students, as well as the donation of server space and production equipment. Although weakened as an institution, the Indymedia meme of 'DIY direct action media' circulated among the emerging web of internet-based news projects and networks.

SOCIAL JUSTICE MEDIA

THE CLOSURE OF SPACE IN the dominant media, which helped prompt groups to form the Independent Media Center, had also affected other groups on the front line of neo-liberal attacks (i.e. labor, anti-poverty, immigrant, and prisoners' rights organizations).[11] Recognizing this, as well as the limits of the protest cycle of the global justice movement, some local IMC centers connected with ongoing community struggles. One of the San Francisco Bay Area IMCs initially started as a collaborative media project by organizers from housing, anti-poverty, and prison campaigns. In Urbana-Champaign, Illinois, grassroots labor activists were the instigators, and the local IMC has since created a Community Media and Arts Center, with a free monthly paper, new community radio station, stage, production studios, art studios, library, and meeting spaces. In New York City, Philadelphia, and Los Angeles, IMC crews formed broader community-based media organizations, which train, produce, and circulate the direct representation of organizers from a number of different campaigns and neighborhoods.

A recent survey of 100 grassroots community organizations confirmed that they use a combination of residual, emerging, and dominant media to mobilize and get their messages out.[12] Although broadcast television has been eclipsed for the younger people who have migrated to the web, as well as the upper/middle-class who pay for cable and satellite TV, the majority of working class Americans still rely on commercial broadcast TV for important information; a Pew Research poll in September 2009 found that 71% of Americans say they get most of their national and international news from television.[13] The crisis of declining markets and advertisers has upped the ante and led to an increased reliance on cheap sensationalism to attract viewers. It is no accident, then, that broadcast news is the locus of many attacks on immigrant communities, Arab-Americans and Latinos in particular. In self-defense, many organizations, such as the National Network for Immigrant and Refugee Rights, have developed a complex of their own news media, as well as strategic campaigns to influence the corporate media.[14] In 2009, the National Capital Immigrant Coalition and the Fair Immigration Reform Movement supported the successful campaign calling for the resignation of Lou Dobbs from CNN.[15]

Many organizations also use community radio and public access television, much of which was developed by older generations of grassroots political networks. For example, the Latino community radio network Radio Bilingüe was founded in 1976 by young Mexican-Americans in support of organizing efforts in the agricultural fields and urban barrios of the San Joaquin Valley. During the mass mobilizations of 2006 and 2007 against proposed anti-immigration legislation in Congress, the network, which now stretches across the U.S. and into Mexico, provided eyewitness reports, extensive call-ins, and analysis.[16] Networks such as Radio Bilingüe are especially important in smaller urban centers and rural areas, which have fewer resources for information and media making. Xochitl Bervara, originally from the Bay area, hadn't realized the importance of community radio and public access TV until she moved to Louisiana, where she works with Families and Friends of Louisiana's Incarcerated Children (FFLIC); she believes that "it's an important source of civic information, especially because of literacy rates."[17]

Social justice groups have also developed alternative media as a tool for community building and as part of the articulation and circulation of their own self-directed expertise, social identities, and analyses. Twenty years ago, a group of San Francisco homeless people and social service workers formed the Coalition on Homelessness to counter the Reagan administration's version of structural adjustment programs: the massive social service cuts and off-loading of programs to state and municipal governments. As news about poor people almost disappeared from the national press, the Coalition faced a very difficult time getting positive coverage in the *San Francisco Chronicle*, whose editorials supported commercial development and whose advertising base was in the real estate industry and large downtown merchants.

They started *Streetsheet*, a monthly tabloid in English and Spanish. *Streetsheet* opposed gentrification, supported campaigns for affordable housing, living wage employment, accessible health care, and educational opportunities, and gave updates on public events and political demonstrations. They framed housing as a systemic and national problem, as a *collective* need, and homelessness as a *human rights* abuse. Their human rights-styled campaigns defended the rights of those prosecuted for 'quality of life' crimes, pressured the city to investigate assaults against poor people as hate crimes, and lobbied for improvements in shelters as well as better support (including language services) of immigrants. In December 2009, when commercial newspaper circulation in San Francisco was in a rapid period of decline, *Streetsheet* doubled their frequency to twice-a-month, circulating 32,000 copies monthly, 1,200 by mail, 1,000 to shelters, and the remaining copies for sale on the street.[18]

In 1996, the Coalition helped start the North American Street Newspapers Association, and later joined the International Network of Street Papers. *Streetsheet*, like many of the North American street newspapers, was developed as a media-making venture for the perspectives of poor people, and as a way to contribute to the income of vendors who sell it on the street. The Coalition provides regular reports from poor people participating in work groups, who help produce the street paper as well as a newer web version. However, most of the news reporting is produced by staff.

In another example from a decade ago, two local homeless women in San Francisco started a DIY project, the Poor News Network. They describe themselves as "a multi-media access project of *Poor Magazine*, dedicated to reframing the news, issues and solutions from low and no income communities, with a perspective usually not heard or seen within the mainstream media."[19] They train "poverty scholars" in investigative journalism, photo-journalism, multi-media, and broadcasting, yielding regular reports from campaigns against the criminalization of youth, poor, indigenous people, and most recently, undocumented immigrants, as well as larger mobilizations to redistribute resources. Poor News co-founder Tiny, a.k.a. Lisa Gray-Garcia, has always used media tactically, creating short-term artistic performances and media events to defend tenants and homeless people, and to intervene in municipal debates about development in San Francisco and Oakland. For Tiny, "media organizing" means using the media as the root of a political campaign. "Media can be so harmful to low and no-income communities, and it is therefore so vital to keep our truths out there…. We're not an island unto ourselves."[20] Thus, they complement their own DIY media with efforts to reach out to other constituencies via commercial media and other alternative media.

DIY social justice projects like Poor News have taken media power into their own hands. They provide an expressive space to question dominant knowledges, as well as develop, assemble, and share alternative "scholarship" and creativity. In this process, they create new forms of individual identity, social identity, and political agency. They also provide space for more established media-makers who earn their living in the dominant commercial spaces, as in the recent visit of hip-hop artist M1 of Dead Prez to the *Poor Magazine* Community Newsroom, where he spoke to community members about the implications of the Black Panthers.[21]

Finally, upon recognizing the importance of communications to their projects of social change, and experiencing first-hand the exclusion of their views, many groups have become involved in campaigning for a redistribution of communications resources— sometimes called 'media justice' politics. They are fighting for a wider array of communications rights and for redistribution of communications resources. They are especially concerned that the legacy monopoly companies, such as AT&T and Comcast, still control access to the internet by refusing to build lines in poor or rural communities, pricing people out of the market, and controlling online behavior (i.e. shutting down peer-to-peer users). Accordingly, they are calling for universal broadband and net neutrality.[22]

A NEW GENERATION OF SOCIAL MEDIA

In California, younger activists have been using the newest generation of social networks in a cycle of struggles that extends from the mass mobilizations against attacks on immigrants in 2006–2007, to organizing against homophobia in the schools and racism in the gay marriage campaign in 2008, to the current wave of student protests against funding cuts on college campuses.[23] They use the productive capacity of digital communications and the internet to produce music, photos, and videos, which they then circulate via social networking sites such as Facebook, Youtube, and Twitter. Unlike the earlier generation of left media, they are not absorbed with countering the arguments of dominant powers. Much like the IMC, they not only bypass the dominant media representation of their struggles, but also the codes of representation. Operating within their own autonomous frames of reference, they inventively use all kinds of cultural expression—from hip-hop to dance and performance—to connect and mobilize among and across communities of resistance. In this new cycle, they build even more from the inside out, from their own rich affective domains, rather than from a reaction to the dominant logics and codes of meaning. Their use of social networks is part of the creation of new horizontal social and political relations, and "the production of an alternative symbolic economy and its expansion of the number of contenders that may participate in the normative debate."[24]

Using social networks, they have stepped beyond the control of the traditional leaders, from the Left to the union movement to the LGBT movement. Documenting a national protest in Canada, Judy Rebick noted how a new set of younger leaders were able to step up because of the "decentralization, the low level of entry," which allowed "individuals without organizational or institutional support to organize in a new way."[25] Elsewhere, a group of five young activists in Los Angeles were more circumspect about the use of social media networks. Andres Ruiz, a student at a south Los Angeles community college said, "A lot of the time we become so dependent on the internet that we become detached from the community, and [from] that one-on-one dialogue that we would have with community members. The internet has its positives, and it has its negatives […] and you have to kind of keep a balance between the two…. If you want to reach out to the older generation, you know, a lot of them, they're not facebookers, they're not on myspace." They remained concerned with the need to use all the digital and on-the-ground forms of communications to bridge the continuing social and political divides of generation, racism, sexism, and homophobia within their own communities, other communities of color, and white communities.[26]

This development signals a sea change, as millions of producer-users circulate a wide range of content, including investigative journalism, news commentary and analysis, satire, and musical and cultural commentary. On a mass level, it expresses a revolt against the monopoly control of the media giants over the means of communications, a general disregard for the attempts to commodify production, and the fencing of cultural work behind digital gates of private property. It also expresses a profound revolt against gatekeeping professionals as arbiters of quality.

ABSORPTION AND INCORPORATION OF THE ALTERNATIVE

THE VIRAL SUCCESS OF THESE autonomous practices in social and social justice media networks has driven internet-based corporations to figure out how to best enclose and commodify the productive labor. The greatest competition is amidst the commercial social networks, used routinely by organizers all over the world. However, the flipside of the power, scope, and scale of these inter-connected systems of digital communications is that they also make the marshaling and disciplining of labor, the heart of capitalist accumulation, considerably easier. When audiences produce content for free by uploading photos or posting links, or when they provide detailed information about their social and cultural tastes, it is immediately aggregated and leveraged into advertising directed to them individually, or as content to marshal their social networks, producing profits for large corporations such as Google and Yahoo.

Digital social networks are also much easier to survey and manipulate. Christian Fuchs reminds us that autonomous space from capital and state power does not automatically exist, it must be struggled for. He argues that the new composition of the "produser" (producer-user) is not automatically participatory democracy, but a total commodification of human creativity, an understanding shared by many of the techies associated with the Independent Media Center and other sectors of the open source movement.[27] At the tenth anniversary of the IMC in Los Angeles in December 2009, these techies called for more collaboration between technologists across the global IMC movement and progressive technology organizations to continue contesting the enclosure and control of public space by corporate and government powers—through campaigning for open technology standards, software, and open publishing policies—and to defend against the use of the Digital Millennium Copyright Act to intimidate progressive providers and interrupt service for free speech and fair use content.[28] Like the social justice organizations, they recognize the importance of protecting the commons of digital communications from corporate control.

There are huge stakes in the current contest over the control of the means of communications. The crisis is partly economic, with the U.S. commercial model in crisis, with daily reports of massive layoffs, declining advertising revenues, shut-downs of legacy news outlets, and audiences retreating from the commercial news. It has also deeply affected public trust; the U.S. public's approval ratings of press accuracy and fairness are at their lowest in two decades.[29] It is within this context of declining commercial media dominance that the current trend towards corporate and foundation funded experiments with "citizen's" media (with an emphasis on the individual citizen) must be seen.[30] This trend, of course, was built on three decades of alternative media's collective appropriation of information and communication tools for social change.

Most of the dominant commercial news services now incorporate user-generated content in the form of eyewitness and personal testimony, and audience response applications. Some smaller publications even encourage this corps of citizens to become advertising sales people, who help to syndicate or franchise concepts and content, or license citizen journalism software.[31] The unpaid labor of citizens reduces costs as well as acting to discipline the remaining journalists and media workers. It also serves, as Atton and Hamilton point out, to neutralize radical alternative journalism and recuperate its value for marketing and control.[32] User-generated content builds a more durable brand loyalty with audiences; it helps reassemble audiences for new kinds of products, especially in the local urban neighborhoods, which the nationally oriented media has abandoned.

Citizens often receive training, but it is according to standardized formats, fitting existing industry requirements. In addition, the only content that is incorporated is the most superficial vox pop, and not the politically engaged, reflexive philosophy or counter-hegemonic point of view.[33] Unchallenged is the corporate professional control of content design, editing, and distribution.

Finally, the contest over the incorporation of radical forms of autonomous media is ongoing outside the commercial media space, in the wider social factory of communications. As James Hamilton documents, the greatest portion of grant money from foundations and governments continues to go to major public broadcasters, professional organizations and trade groups, and universities. In the last decade, during the period of rapid do-it-yourself media growth, foundations began to fund media projects "with appropriate professional, reformist credentials" that "begin to take on such a form as a result of the need to gain support."[34] In 2009, foundations, most notably the Knight Foundation, and university journalism programs, such as UC Berkeley, began to roll out a new set of hyperlocal news experiments in citizen's media, based on a combination of unpaid student and citizen labor. Many of these projects are providing better local news, representing communities and perspectives that have been missing from the dominant commercial news. They help to challenge the traditional gate-keepers of information, and reinforce a more "liquid" notion of both journalism and citizenship, in which news is produced by both professionals and amateurs, in the recognition of the urgent necessity of a collective intelligence for our global survival.[35] However, as with the commercial crowd-sourcing, the goals of these projects are much narrower than that of radical media; their aim is to enlist individuals and not social justice organizations, nor politically engaged perspectives. Just as troubling, they are supplanting some of the earlier media attempts to keep funding, direction, and control of production autonomous from the commercial media and the government. Nowadays, many of these previously radical organizations have eliminated some kinds of political content in favor of promoting 'individual' expression that is easier to fund.

THE FUTURE

HERE I HAVE TEASED OUT the lines of a more general radical inquiry of autonomist communications. Drawing on the method first laid out by the Zerowork collective in 1975, I have sought to describe the development and direction of these communications, analyzing the composition of the producers—and especially the new unities—in relation to the composition of capital.[36] This is but one contribution; many more questions remain.

Ten years after Seattle, the meme of the Independent Media Center has already had a major impact on media power. The global corporate giants still dominate the mediascape and page views of the web; nevertheless, their absolute monopoly of the means of producing media, their factory-like production process, and the indisputable link between content and commercials has all been shaken up. The IMC and other notable grassroots experiments in local and globally networked political communication have challenged the hegemony of the U.S. corporate news media, at a time when their confidence level among the public is at an all-time low. Although access for the majority of the world's people is still severely circumscribed, and low in some poorer neighborhoods of the U.S., the impact of the IMC's model of autonomous media has been considerable. Millions of people all over the world produce and circulate do-it-yourself media, on a global scale and outside of the bonds of the commercial system. Millions more seek information from sources not governed by the commercial or professional logics.

If we have moved to a new phase of media production, have we shifted to a new paradigm of what Raymond Williams called "direct autonomous composition"? The global IMC network suggested in abstract form another vision, of a network of networks, linking autonomous production centers. This new model of more participatory production is now in competition, with moves to re-professionalize both social media and social justice media. There is pressure for groups in all of these fields to narrow their approaches and limit their goals of long-lasting change, similarly to what other movements have characterized as "NGO-ization."[37]

Many groups continue to support autonomous communications activities that challenge corporate monopoly control and are centered on collective projects of popular education, mobilization, and action-based media circulation of media. However, many are moving away from those focuses, to projects of individual 'voice.' More technically adept and professionalized groups are moving "toward policy-focused activities, issue specialization, and resource concentration," much like the trend toward "NGO-ization."[38]

These interlinked contests will only intensify as control over communications becomes ever more important for global capital, national governments, and all the rest of us. We are in the midst of the storm between global multimedia business networks attempting to exploit the labor of producers in the new social factory, and the commoners who are trying to keep open the collective mechanisms of expression, the commonwealth of knowledge.

I am reminded of an earlier period of transformation, when the powerful workers' struggles in the industrial factory contributed to major changes in the game plan of industrial capital. Their collective drive for wages became the engine of growth during the Fordist period. Will the current mass demand for autonomous media be incorporated as the new engine of growth was for post-Fordist capital? We need further inquiry to address those questions posed by Marcos and Thompson that began this essay, to know which wind rules, and whether the whistle will finally be heard.

NOTES

1   E.P. Thompson, *Customs in Common* (New York: The New Press, 1993), 11; Subcommandante Marcos, "Chiapas: The Southeast in Two Winds A Storm and a Prophecy," HTTP:// FLAG.BLACKENED.NET/REVOLT/MEXICO/EZLN/MARCOS_SE_2_WIND.HTML (accessed January 29, 2010).

2   Raymond Williams, "Radical and/or Respectable.," in R. Boston (ed.) *The Press We Deserve* (London: Routledge & Kegan Paul, 1970), 14–26; John Downing, *Radical Media: The Political Experience of Alternative Communication* (Boston: South End Press, 1983); James Hamilton, "Remaking Media Participation in Early Modern England," *Journalism: Theory, Practice, Criticism* 4, no. 3: 293–313; Jesús Martin-Barbero, *Communication, Culture and Hegemony—From the Media to Mediations* (London: Sage Publications, 1993).

3   For an analysis of the use of radical radio in the Americas of the twentieth century, see: Dorothy Kidd, *Talking the Walk: The Media Enclosures and the Communications Commons* (Doctoral Dissertation, Simon Fraser University, 1998).

4   Dorothy Kidd, "Carnival to Commons," in Eddie Yuen, Daniel Burton-Rose, and Geroge Katsiaficas (eds.) *Confronting Capitalism: Dispatches from a Global Movement* (New York: Soft Skull Press, 2004), 328–338.

5   Harry Cleaver, "Computer-Linked Social Movements and the Global Threat to Capitalism," July, 1999, HTTP://WWW.ECO.UTEXAS.EDU/FACSTAFF/CLEAVER/POLNET.HTML (accessed May 12, 2002).

6   Chris Atton and James Hamilton, *Alternative Journalism* (Thousand Oaks, CA: Sage, 2008).

7   Atton and Hamilton, *Alternative Journalism*, 85.

8   James Hamilton, *Democratic Communications: Formations, Projects, Possibilities* (Lanham, MD: Lexington Books, 2009).

9   Kidd, *Talking the Walk*, 328–338.

10   Atton and Hamilton, *Alternative Journalism*, 39.

11   Dorothy Kidd and Bernadette Barker-Plummer, "Neither Silent nor Invisible: Anti-Poverty Communication in the San Francisco Bay Area," *Development in Practice* 19 (2009): 4–5, 479–490.

12   Dharma Dailey, "A Field Report: Media Justice through the Eyes of Local Organizers" (New York: The Media Justice Fund of the Funding Exchange, 2009).

13   Reported on September 13, 2009. "Press Accuracy Rating Hits Two Decade Low. Pew Research Center," HTTP://PEOPLE-PRESS.ORG/REPORT/543/ (accessed March 6, 2010).

14   National Network for Immigrant and Refugee Rights publishes a regular news digest bulletin called Network News, as well as posting regular news releases for the media on their web-site HTTP://WWW.NNIRR.ORG/NEWS/INDEX.PHP?OP=LIST&MAXITEMS=10&TYPE=8&START=2.

15   For more on the Lou Dobbs protests, see Susan Carroll, "Immigrant Advocates protest Lou Dobbs," HTTP://BLOGS.CHRON.COM/IMMIGRATION/ARCHIVES/2009/05/IMMIGRANT_ADVOC. HTML (accessed March 6, 2010).

16   Graciela León Orozco, "Radio as a Mobilization Tool in Latino Communities," HTTP:// MEDIARESEARCHHUB.SSRC.ORG/GRANTS/FUNDED-PROJECTS/RADIO-AS-A-MOBILIZATION-TOOL-IN-LATINO-COMMUNITIES/RADIO-AS-A-MOBILIZATION-TOOL-IN-LATINO-COMMUNITIES (accessed 2008).

17   Quoted in Dharma Dailey, "A Field Report," 8.

18   *Streetsheet*, December 15–31, 2009, 2.

19   Information on Poor Magazine can be found at: HTTP://WWW.POORMAGAZINE.ORG/

20   Tiny Gray-Garcia, interview with author, February 15, 2006.

21   "*M1* Speaking with Migrant, Poverty, Disability and Indigenous SKolahs at POOR Magazine," HTTP://WWW.POORMAGAZINE.ORG/INDEX.CFM?LI=NEWS&STORY=2367 (accessed January 2010).

22   Dailey, "A Field Report."

23   "Sojourner Truth" KPFK-Pacifica, January 20, 2010, HTTP://ARCHIVE.KPFK.ORG/PARCHIVE/ MP3/KPFK_100120_070030SOJOURNER.MP3 (accessed January 20, 2010).

24   Michael Strangelove, *Empire of Mind: Digital Piracy and the Anti-capitalist Movement* (Toronto: University of Toronto Press, 2005), 218–219.

25   Judy Rebick, "Tens of thousands protest democracy erosion in Canada," blog post to Judy Rebick's blog, January 24, 2010, HTTP://WWW.ZMAG.ORG/BLOG/VIEW/4174 (accessed January, 2010).

26   KPFK-Pacifica, "Sojourner Truth."

27   Christian Fuchs, "Information and Communication Technologies and Society: A Contribution to the Critique of the Political Economy of the Internet," *European Journal of Communication* 24 (2009): 69–87.

28   Mallory Knodel, "LA IMC 10th Anniversary—Technology Workshop," post to Los Angeles Indymedia, November 28, 2009, HTTP://LA.INDYMEDIA.ORG/NEWS/2009/11/232781.PHP (accessed January 16, 2010).

29 See the Pew Report of September 13, 2009.

30 Clemencia Rodríguez, *Fissures in the Mediascape: An International Study of Citizens' Media* (Creskill, NJ: Hampton Press, 2001).

31 Atton and Hamilton, *Alternative Journalism*, 68.

32 Atton and Hamilton, *Alternative Journalism*, 67.

33 Atton and Hamilton, *Alternative Journalism*, 140.

34 Hamilton, *Democratic Communications*, 109.

35 Mark Deuze, "The Changing Context of News Work: Liquid Journalism and Monitorial Citizenship," *International Journal of Communication* 2 (2008), 848–865.

36 Unsigned, "Introduction," in Zerowork Collective, *Zerowork: Political Materials 1* (Brooklyn: Zerowork, 1975), 1–6.

37 Sonia E. Alvarez, "Advocating Feminism: The Latin American NGO 'Boom,'" Dialogo Solidaridad Global Solidarity Dialogue, March 2, 1998, HTTP://WWW.ANTENNA.NL/~WATERMAN/ ALAVAREZ2.HTML (accessed 5/31/2002). Currently available at HTTP://WWW.MTHOLYOKE.EDU/ ACAD/LATINAMERICAN/ADVOCATING_FEMINISM.HTML.

38 Alvarez, "Advocating Feminism."

GETTING TO KNOW YOUR CITY AND THE SOCIAL MOVEMENTS THAT CALL IT HOME:

The Hybrid Networking and Documentary Work of AREA Chicago

Daniel Tucker

INTRODUCTION

THIS TEXT OUTLINES A METHODOLOGY for researching localized social movements as a means of analyzing their history, effectiveness, and ability to strategically participate or intervene in politics. I use insights gained from AREA Chicago—a publication founded in 2005 that has compiled a print/online archive based on interviews with over 300 Chicago activists, cultural producers, and organizers—to offer up a proposal for a broad-based pan-leftist approach that can help avoid classic sectarianism yet still ask challenging questions and produce forward-moving analysis.[1]

In this essay, I outline AREA Chicago's long-term and locally situated method of 'movement mapping.' The text should be relevant to anyone hoping to strategically contribute to the development of a robust and critically reflexive Left movement, which can advance the absolutely necessary goal of replacing the logics that govern our lives with systems that promote a long-term healthy balance between living things and the earth, where people have equal access to resources, and where movement is determined not by brute force, but by creative collective process.

AREA Chicago began at a moment when Chicago, in a manner similar to many other places, experienced a break in its typical flurry of social, political, and cultural community organizing. That break may have been characterized by exhaustion due to very hectic, yet largely ineffective, anti-war and economic justice activism of the late 1990s and early 2000s. The source of this lull was multi-faceted, but to an engaged participant, it was plain to see. At the same time, there were burgeoning networks of people working at the intersections of art, research, education, and activism, in ways that did not fit into the rigidly defined conceptions of community organizing, social justice, and authentic struggle that had characterized previous moments. This hybrid work encompassed organizations such as the Department of Space and Land Reclamation, Pilot TV, non-exploitative collaborations between academics and neighborhood groups, Neighborhood Writing Alliance, Feel Tanks (as opposed to Think Tanks), Mess Halls, Freedom Schools, Social Justice Curriculum Fairs, Chances Dances, Iraq Veterans Against the War (IVAW) and its Operation First Casualty action, and a plethora of new reading groups and post-sectarian political education projects. These activities happened parallel to (but often disconnected from) the tried-and-true peace vigils, community arts classes, youth media literacy programs, labor unions, neighborhood coalitions, temporary affinity groups, and other short-lived as well as institutionalized community centers that had previously characterized the city and its social movements. These practices—new and old, experimental and tested, consistent and temporary—had to find each other and build new connections if their work was ever going to amount to something more. Often separated by vast geographic, cultural, and generational divides, these different ways of working needed to both co-exist as well as find common ground. We created AREA Chicago as a device to make visible the disparate practices to one another, to create a common ground, and to critically frame the present moment in a way that would challenge groups to feel compelled to see one another as potential allies in times that require unconventional alliances.

We were inspired by the local work mentioned above, but also by international projects such as What is To Be Done? (Russia), Sarai (India), Colectivo Situaciones (Argentina), What, How and For Whom? (Croatia), Copenhagen Free University (Denmark), the Center for Urban Pedagogy (U.S.), the Right to the City Alliance (U.S.), INCITE! (U.S.), and numerous other regional and international efforts.

GETTING TO KNOW YOUR CITY

THE CITIES WE LIVE IN are always expanding, contracting, and changing. People have compared cities to living organisms (living, breathing), microcosms (reflecting and reproducing the world in which they exist), and parasites (sucking the resources of the regions on their periphery), as well as to independent nations (having their own rules and identities distinct from the world around them), markets (where people are merely buyers and sellers), and command-and-control centers (where networks of people, wealth, and resources are organized and manipulated from a safe and distanced vantage-point). These metaphors are frameworks for understanding what cities are, why they exist, how they work, and where they are going.

AREA is based in one particular city: Chicago. The project is organized by an advisory group of twenty people working in various social justice, educational, and cultural projects throughout the city. One approach we have used to examine the city is a 'conceptual limiting' strategy, which is borrowed from literary traditions; if you limit and focus the framework to a specific area or topic, then you can more fully explore that area and navigate complex ideas through that lens. Some people might try to explore contemporary capitalism through the lens of culture (i.e. soccer), or commodities (i.e. tea), or perhaps though a particular movement (i.e. socialism). In our work, a place—Chicago—is the lens through which we view the complexities of an increasingly mobile and always violent capitalism. This mobility influences the places people live, how often they move, the jobs they can have (and for how long), and how they relate to their neighbors and surroundings. This affects the kind of politics and culture that emerge in a place at a particular time, and we focus on this as our magazine's subject matter.

Soon after we started the AREA Chicago project in 2005, a feature article appeared in the magazine *The Economist* hailing Chicago as a "post-industrial success story":

> This is a city buzzing with life, humming with prosperity, sparkling with new buildings, new sculptures, new parks, and generally exuding vitality. The Loop, the central area defined by a ring of overhead railway tracks, has not gone the way of so many other big cities' business districts—soulless by day and deserted at night. It bustles with shoppers as well as office workers. Students live there. So, increasingly, do gays, young couples, and older ones whose children have grown up and fled the nest. Farther north, and south, old warehouses and factories have become home to artists, professionals, and trendy young families. Not far to the east, locals and tourists alike throng Michigan Avenue's Magnificent Mile, a stretch of shops as swanky as any to be found on Fifth Avenue in New York or Rodeo Drive in Beverly Hills. Chicago is undoubtedly back.
>
> Back, that is, from what many feared would be the scrap heap. In 1980, when *The Economist* last published a survey of Chicago, it found a city whose "facade of downtown prosperity masked a creaking political machine, the erosion of its economic base, and some of the most serious racial problems in America...."[2]

This declaration was curious, as it very clearly conflicted significantly with our own experiences and observations. One of the questions that informed the development of AREA as an activist research project was a slight re-framing:"*Is* Chicago a post-industrial success story?"

It is difficult to assess the validity of "success stories" in our contemporary cities. In an era of place-marketing and of cities competing among each other for everything, from tourists, to Olympic Games, to corporate re-locations, seeing through the public relations haze of what constitutes success can be tricky. In an era of urban real-estate 'renewals' amidst housing bubble bursts, wading through the public relations muck of simultaneous mortgage crisis and neighborhood renaissance can make 'success' seem like an abstraction.

In order to provide critical perspectives of our city's success narrative, AREA printed a series of articles dealing with the flip-side of Chicago's supposed success. From AREA #1:

The new world order is coming to roost in Chicago with a vengeance. Increasingly the city is defined by neoliberalism, the global policies of transnational capital that make the market and individual self-interest primary in every sphere of economic and social life. On every side we see the elimination of the public interest and public control— from privatization (and corporatization) of parks (Millennium Park), schools (Renaissance 2010), and bus shelters to the elimination of public housing. Corporate and finance capital in collaboration with the Daley administration are reconstructing the city to serve their interests. Their agenda grows out of changing relations between cities and the global economy and the emergence of gentrification as a pivotal force in urban economies.[3]

From AREA #2:

One day I decided I wanted to eat something healthy, and I thought greens would be perfect because they were healthy for cleaning negative particles out of my body. So I started on a horrible journey from one store to the next, about eight stores to be exact. I went from California and Jackson past Pulaski and Madison. I was getting very angry. I couldn't understand why there weren't any fresh vegetables in these stores. Was it because it was a predominantly Black area, or was it because the community didn't care enough to demand that the stores supply the essential goods they needed? I couldn't believe it.[4]

From AREA #4:

After a four-year, $7 million investigation, special prosecutors have released their findings on police torture in Chicago, and the results are familiar. Once again, former Commander Jon Burge and the white police officers under him—who, in the words of the *Chicago Tribune*, "for two decades coerced dozens of confessions with fists, kicks, radiator burns, guns to the mouth, bags over the head, and electric shock to the genitals"—are walking away scot-free from their crimes.[5]

From AREA #6:

I have lived in Chicago since 1979. My family was a part of the exodus that followed the steel plant closings in Buffalo, and we arrived here when I was seven. I grew up in Logan Square and have spent most of my life on the Near Northwest Side. There have been two major sea changes in the landscape of Chicago since my childhood, which parallels the era of the deepest deprivation and disinvestment in the history of the city. One is the rise of the Latino community, in numbers, in community development, in aspiration, creativity, and political power. The second is the gutting of the inner city and its replacement with an amnesiac, upscale consumer paradise for outsiders with money. What has changed the least in Chicago is this state of control by a cohort of elite gangsters known as The Machine, who are desperately trying to buy out the first change and raking in buckets of cash over the second. I hate how we betray the best of our histories and our communities, which I love to death.[6]

While cities are not the end all/be all of contemporary capitalism, they are strategic places to focus our energies because of the dense accumulation of contradictions within them. As Nik Theodore states in AREA #6:

> [C]ities (including their suburban peripheries) have become increasingly important geographical targets and institutional laboratories for a variety of neoliberal policy experiments, from place-marketing and local boosterism, enterprise zones, tax abatements, urban development corporations, and public-private partnerships to workfare policies, property redevelopment schemes, new strategies of social control, policing and surveillance, and a host of other institutional modifications within the local state apparatus. The overarching goal of such experiments is to mobilize city space as an arena both for market-oriented economic growth and for elite consumption practices.

> Indeed, we must understand this function of cities in the more diffuse and international manifestations of uneven development and capitalist exploitation. Cities are home to nearly half of the world's population, and our existence in them plays a significant role in their reproduction.[7]

Since its inception, AREA has coordinated *Notes for a People's Atlas of Chicago*, a project intended to highlight people's role in the production of the city in their daily lives. Blank maps are circulated at our public events, through workshops, at curriculum fairs for public school teachers, and through drop-boxes at local community centers. They are accompanied by a call for mapping to anyone and everyone:

> What should I put on my map?

> You are encouraged to map out sites that are significant to you as someone who lives, works and plays in this city. You can map out sites of past or current political struggles, lost histories, cultural spaces, environmental devastation, personal histories, real estate speculation, social movements of the past, places of formal/informal education, sites of gang violence, where to get the best coffee, places where tourists do not go, the periphery of the city, proposals for alternative uses of public space, distribution of wealth, anything. You are encouraged to combine, intersect, contrast, flip upside down themes or topics of your maps. You are encouraged to map out personal histories and points of interests as well as what else they relate to, why are these points important, and to whom are they important to?

Why maps? Because maps are a visual tool for sharing information with others. Because they can be produced by many people and combined together to tell stories about complex relationships. Because maps are never finished and only tell part of a story that can constantly be expanded upon. Because power exists in space, struggle exists in space, and we exist in space. Because we cannot know where we are going if we do not know where we are from.

The project, like many which utilize maps and visual information methods, engages people across literacy levels and larger cultural barriers. Simply presenting the blank map, with an invitation to express a person's knowledge and impressions of this place they live, work, and play in everyday, gives voice and meaning to the statement by Nik Theodore above: that we play a significant role in the reproduction of our city every day. In what direction we push that role is the next subject to explore.

GETTING TO KNOW THE LEFT IN YOUR CITY

ONCE THE CONTEXT IS THOROUGHLY understood—or is at least on its way to being understood—it is time to get to know the social actors and engaged citizens, both subjects of the city and its dynamics. There are many kinds of practices that could be considered as social movements that operate in a progressive Left tradition. There are many strands, many stripes, many projects, and many approaches. The deeper one looks, the more fragmented they will appear. It can be difficult to map them or get an image of what these dedicated people and organizations are doing and in what directions they are traveling. Yet such a map is essential for any strategic effort. This map, and the process of making it, can furnish an understanding of the full spectrum of actors and enable the mapmakers to assess the most effective sites for intervention and engagement.

If this seems a bit abstract, an illustration can assist here. Imagine a field, and then think about a political or social question relevant to your background. Think about the variety of social and political actors working around that question that share similar goals. Then think about the larger 'group of groups' that share more loosely related goals. The pool gets bigger. Maybe the labor union in town has one tactic they use to work towards that goal. Perhaps there are some non-profits that do some combination of reform and community organizing around that goal. There are also politicians working from within the system to try and get to that place too, who are influenced and pushed along the way by these other actors. These are the obvious characters in this story, the social actors who inhabit the field and who care urgently about the matter. Then there are self-organized groups, there are artists making culture that directly addresses the issue at hand, there are teachers who integrate the questions into their classroom work, and there are community groups that conduct popular education to try to understand how this issue is playing out in their hyper-local context. One could take this scenario further and identify more folks and organizations occupying places on the field.

An essential first step towards a variety of strategic and long-term goals is developing the capacity to assess the spectrum of interrelated practices attempting to achieve similar outcomes using different tactics and methodologies. First, it helps in building strategic alliances that bring visibility to the issue and maximize the limited resources available to do the work (that is, avoiding redundancy). Secondly, it assists in identifying weak points where unity and collaboration across many different groups may be difficult, or where the movement is most susceptible to external disruption. Third, it helps to interpret the potential for currently existing groups to achieve their stated end-goals. Finally, it provides a vantage point for beginning a complex and critical evaluation of the efficacy of different ideas, actions, and forms of organization. It is a first step, though it is not a simple solution to resolving historical disputes, economic differences, or cultural tensions. It is also not an argument for an abstract 'multitude;' rather, it is an argument for an honest assessment of the actually existing Left and the ideas and actions it produces.

We have used this methodology in the creation of our thematic magazines and events in order to enable the incredible diversity of people and groups who are invested in an issue to present their ideas together in a shared space.

Our methodology is quite simple: What is a pressing or challenging question in the city? What are people doing or not doing about it? Once that is identified, then a call for participation is circulated, and people from local networks associated with art, research, education, and activism formulate a response. That response is edited, designed, printed, and then circulated back out to the networks from which it came.

We've asked the following question in our publications:

> What kind of infrastructure of services and resources do we need when our welfare state is in disrepair and being increasingly privatized? (AREA #1: *Private Parties and Public Services*)

> What kind of food policy can we create to make sure that people of the city are healthy enough to pursue organization? (AREA #2: *After Winter Comes Spring—A Look at Local Food Systems*)

> What are the things we mean and want when we say 'we'? What are critical approaches to the commonplace political concept of solidarity? (AREA #3: *Solidarities*)

> In contexts where more and more Chicagoans are entrapped in the expanding industry of mass incarceration, how can meaningful, visionary, and practical changes to the criminal justice system occur? (AREA #4: *No Justice, No Peace*)

> What is the role of education and pedagogy in strengthening social movements? (AREA #5: *How We Learn*)

> How do experimental policies turn the city into a social and economic laboratory? (AREA #6: *City as Lab*)

> What kinds of logics and strategies do contemporary social movements inherit from their predecessors, especially the New Left and Counter-Culture Left of the late 1960s/early 1970s? (AREA #7: *68/08—On the Legacy of 1968 in Chicago*)

What connections can be made between ongoing struggles for economic justice and those conflicts which are arising out of the current economic recession? (AREA #8: *Everybody's Got Money Issues*)

Can our urban-centered politics and culture become more connected with those places on the geographic periphery, and more generally, can our narrow-minded culture and politics be influenced by ideas and people who are on the margins? (AREA #9: *Peripheral Vision—Chicago From the Outside In*)

What infrastructures and institutions from the past do we need to maintain or rethink, and how can we critically create the new ones to support our work? (AREA #10: *Community Infrastructures and Institutions*)

Through this approach of asking questions about the city, how it works, and where it is going, we have been able to learn a great deal. By soliciting the reflections of our city's activists and organizers, AREA Chicago has pieced together a map of the local Left. While it is incomplete and always evolving, we can better understand where local groups and initiatives are situated and where they might be going. These social and political actors are who and what we have to work with. So it is not merely a pluralist project to get everyone together and work towards the lowest common denominator without debate or conflict; it is simply what we must understand in order to consider what directions we can feasibly move towards that can unite our idealism with the currently available material reality. The Left in its current composition is going to provide the basis and history for future forms of thought and social organization. So let's get to know each other and learn each other's history and desires. What we are still working on—and what we are always challenged by—is how to create a feedback mechanism that allows the final publication and events to serve as a starting point for larger strategic efforts.

COMPOSITION: FRAGMENTATION

WE ARE FLAILING IN THESE times. There is no compass, no rhyme or reason for what we do; it's like shooting in the wind. Anxiety explodes as we wonder if we are being effective or getting anything done, and this should not be the case. There is much to do and much to think about. There is much to be angry about and much to be excited about.

We are living in a historical moment when two things are happening regularly enough that we should be learning from them. The first is that our resistance is commodified: it is depoliticized, packaged, and sold back to us; sometimes we don't even know that it happens. The second of these is that we are encouraged to work locally and marginally, while often starting our own organizations to accomplish massive undertakings. Solidarity has become an agreement of 'you do your thing, and I'll do mine, and if we write our names on each others' fliers, then we are bound.' This is ineffective. We are too weak and too marginal to constantly be starting our own splinter groups and initiatives without a strategic assessment of our role in the broader Left and the commodification of resistance. There are a handful of sweeping generalizations I use as the basis of my understanding of the current composition of Left and progressive social and political work in the United

States. In order to get a generalized image of this complicated mess, it is absolutely necessary to step back and consider these major factors.

To understand the contemporary U.S. Left, one must consider two state-sponsored power plays, the first of which were the state disruption and counter-intelligence campaigns that decimated Left organizations. Most relevant to our time is the 1950s-era Red Scare, which was followed by the infiltration, assassination, imprisonment, and sabotage campaigns begun in the 1960s and extending well into the 1980s; these were directed mostly at various New Left, Nationalist, and anti-imperialist organizations. There are histories of state counter-intelligence and 'red-baiting' that precede this and that have followed since, but these two periods effectively destroyed much of the organizational infrastructure of the Left in the United States.

Secondly, the gradual dissolution of state-sponsored welfare programs that had stabilized economic growth in the U.S. following the Great Depression (with significant growth occurring directly following World War II) has also had a tremendous impact on the work of leftists in this country. This restructuring of state priorities and policies has meant that many of the gains won by previous generations of progressive social movements and reformers were swept away. On a more basic level, the gutting of welfare infrastructure has brought us to the point where the state doesn't do much for the majority of citizens, beyond keeping citizens on a short leash with their increased security and surveillance methods and imprisoning several million people in the process.

In turn, the people who cared about the livelihood of their neighbors—people who in previous generations might have been a part of Leftist labor unions or political parties—had to pick up the pieces. This means that agencies, groups, non-governmental organizations, collectives, websites, and magazines—the potential organizational infrastructure of a Left social movement—started doing the work that was previously paid for and, even if only partially, implemented by the State. The movements became service providers because that is what people needed. While this built on the informal role that people already played in helping their neighbors through a commitment to community, as well as the work of reformers like the Hull House, Settlement House, and neighborhood churches, this era signaled dramatic transformations in how people accessed basic resources. Through an absorption of this work—previously done informally—into what has been called "the non-profit industrial complex," much of the political potency was stifled out of groups aiming to combine service and politics, as their work would come to be watched and, in many cases, contracted out by the government.[8]

COMPOSITION: SOCIAL NETWORKING AS ORGANIZING

ONE MUST ALSO CONSIDER CONTEMPORARY organizing tendencies that, combined with the aforementioned state disruptions, contribute to our collective marginalization: heavy reliance on rhetoric over strategy.

Today online social-networking is considered sufficient as a form of organizing and solidarity. As a result of being strapped for resources, we 'organize' via commodified forms of social networking such as online media platforms like Friendster, Myspace and Facebook. This 'narrowcasting' is more affordable, but if we really care about the ideas we are engaging in, then we can find a way to saturate the visual landscape with our messages and visions. This will provide points of entry for those who are compelled by the ideas but outside of the narrowcast distribution systems.

While many instances of work towards and demands for solidarity are vacuous, there are just as many that really do challenge us to consider what it means to be in solidarity with one another. It is over-reliance on rhetoric as the overarching definition of the *practice* of solidarity that obscures and hinders new insights into the concept's meaning.

In this confusing landscape of infinite online networking potential concurrent with a fragmented social reality, it is an imperative challenge to consider how we can find meaningful community and solidarity to support our long-term work.

RE-COMPOSITION: A DIFFERENT "WE"?

IN ITS NEARLY FIVE YEARS of existence, AREA's impact is as difficult to assess as much of our work. We have created a methodology for roving the city and attempting to be city-wide in our approach. Nearly all of our events have taken place in unique locations, creating a process of discovery and celebration that shows people the special hubs of culture and politics in the city that they might not have otherwise known about. The same practice takes place in our publication, with an ongoing effort to bring new people into the project as authors or interview subjects—oftentimes people with lots to say, but without very much experience expressing what they do outside of the constraints of fifteen-second media blips or the fluffy language of grant applications.

While there has undoubtedly been some apprehension on the part of groups and organizations to contribute to the publication or participate in events, our slow-building process of demonstrated patience and commitment has convinced people from most sectors of our relevance. The first two years were certainly more reliant on the informal social networks of the key organizers, while in years since, contributions from people who had previously not engaged with us have increased significantly. We have certainly struggled to find ongoing engagement with people, especially more professionalized activists as well as organizers of color, despite our occasional successes in bringing them to the table. Some groups confused by our non-explicit ideological approach have still found value in our potential to convene unexpected and diverse collaborators. A Marxist reading group, the Chicago Political Workshop, even went so far as to propose that they take the eclectic contributions of the eighth issue of AREA Chicago and write an "afterword" that responded to the texts and made proposals for how greater coherence could be cultivated between the diverse and divergent practices. This was an instance of integrating critique into the project itself in a constructive manner, putting the critique and the objects of critique—the practices discussed in our publication—in direct conversation with each other. The group has since developed a reading group inspired by AREA, which illustrates one of our objectives, to inspire critical self-education while not necessarily having to own or control all of the outcomes of our work.

Over the years, we have successfully illustrated and documented the existing and potential networks of our city, creating a common ground for anarchist farmers, social justice educators, hard-line Marxist academics, teenage slam poets, socially-engaged artists, social workers, and more. The process we now have to embark on is to move that network into a new phase of cohesion. We cannot just celebrate our differences by laying them out on the page, or by staging events that bring disparate voices together in symbolic unity. Our networks must move into a phase of community, a new "we," in order to forge the trust, understanding, and commitment that will move us to a better world.

NOTES

1   The AREA Chicago database can be found online at HTTP://AREACHICAGO.ORG/P/AUTHORS/ (accessed January 29, 2010).

2   John Grimmond, "A Success Story," *The Economist*, March 16, 2006.

3   Pauline Lipman, "Whose City is it Anyways?" in AREA 1, "Private Parties and Public Services," 2005, available online at: HTTP://WWW.LEARNINGSITE.INFO/NEOTRASHING.PDF (accessed January 29, 2010).

4   Nancy Thomas, "Looking For Greens," in AREA 2, "After Winter Comes Spring—A Look at Local Food Systems" 2006, available online at: HTTP://WWW.AREACHICAGO.ORG/P/ISSUES/ISSUE-2/LOOKING-FOR-GREENS (accessed January 29, 2010).

5   Julien Ball, "The $7 Million Whitewash," in AREA 4, "No Justice, No Peace," 2007, available online at: HTTP://WWW.AREACHICAGO.ORG/P/ISSUES/ISSUE-4/SEVEN-MILLION-DOLLAR-WHITE-WASH (accessed January 29, 2010).

6   Jesse Mumm, "City Wide Interview about What Has Changed and What Has Stayed The Same," AREA 6, "City as Lab," 2008, available online at: HTTP://WWW.AREACHICAGO.ORG/P/ISSUES/CITY-AS-LAB/CITYWIDE-INTERVIEW (accessed January 29, 2010).

7   Jamie Peck, Neil Brenner, Nik Theodore, "City as Policy Lab," in AREA 6, "City as Lab," 2008, available online at HTTP://WWW.AREACHICAGO.ORG/P/ISSUES/CITY-AS-LAB/CITY-POLICY-LAB (accessed January 29, 2010).

8   The notion of the "non-profit industrial complex" is explored in: INCITE! Women of Color Against Violence (eds.), *The Revolution Will Not Be Funded: Beyond the Non-Profit Industrial Complex* (Boston: South End Press, 2007).

THEORETICAL ANALYSES

SECTION SUMMARY

Harry Cleaver, whose article "Uses of an Earthquake" influenced the politics and title of this collection, once stated to us that political theory and political concepts are simply abstractions from concrete reality. He suggested that the test of such theorization is not the act of abstraction *per se*, but rather the accuracy and usefulness of the concept to explain, amplify, communicate, and create encounters. The explorations of the previous sections suggest concepts that complicate and expand our understanding of the composition of radical movements. Here we find questions of power: power of the working class in relation to and against the technical composition of capital, as well as the neoliberal state's processes of enclosure and a burgeoning society of control.

One way to begin assessing these theoretical questions is through knowledge, communication, and encounter. Two of our contributors explore these areas here. The first looks at categories of understanding and how they translate struggles taking place in particular locales, in a general circulation of knowledges. The second examines means by which knowledges are shared. These different forms and uses of knowledge-sharing enrich and complicate our understanding of the struggle against capital and empire.

As part of this understanding, this section includes a pair of contributions that explore the current economic crisis. By describing three elements of the crisis—food, energy, and work—and exploring the financialization of capital and the university, these contributions look at the crisis in terms of its effect on working class composition.

Couched in the current crisis is the continued process of capitalist enclosures, necessitating a political project of recreating the commons. One of our contributors argues that any discussion of the common must include a reorganization of gendered work, as well as centralizing the question of our own reproduction in organizing. Another contributor approaches the commons through the act of commoning in creating popular sovereignty, identifying historical structures conceived as weapons against tyranny.

Our final chapter in this section seeks to address many of the themes contained throughout this collection, calling for "radical patience and the need to construct meaningful communities, rather than just spectacular actions, self-referential identities, and creating more 'activists.'"

Maribel Casas-Cortes and Sebastian Cobarrubias offer a translation of struggles across the Atlantic in **"Transatlantic Translations: Detectives and Researchers for the Revolution(s)."** From the university triangle of Durham, North Carolina to the squatter neighborhoods of Madrid, Spain, they begin mapping circulating knowledges. They offer a trilogy of translations, where concepts, theories, ideas, and ways of acting politically are challenged and interrogated with the purpose of improving practice on the ground.

In a cooperative format of co-interviewing entitled **"Organizing Encounters and Generating Events,"** theorist Michael Hardt and "community center" El Kilombo Intergaláctico explore Hardt's theoretical work with Antonio Negri—particularly, their concept of 'empire'—and move into the current constructions of capitalism. They offer insights into new forms of political organizing that conclude with a dual theory of encounter: event-encounter and community-encounter. Returning to this notion in 2010, they examine new challenges and moments of rupture for movements in the Obama era.

Brian Marks describes some of the paths that have brought us into the current economic crisis in his chapter **"Living in a Whirlwind: The Food/Work/Energy Crisis of 2008–09."** Marks argues that this crisis, and crisis in general, is a form of planning or strategy for capital in its fictitious (securities, bonds, stocks, debts, futures, and derivatives) and primitive (accumulation) forms. He describes how wealth is transferred from billions of workers into the sectors of energy and food, locating refusals of the working class that are disrupting the deployment of the food/work/energy crisis.

In his chapter **"Notes on the Financial Crisis: From Meltdown to Deep Freeze,"** George Caffentzis discusses the recent financial crisis as a development arising from international class struggles. He analyzes capitalist strategies of financialization as mechanisms to protect sectors of capital while undermining and attacking workers' struggles. Caffentzis ties this context of financialization into the growth of the Chinese economy, the victories of Chinese proletarian struggles, the crisis of neoliberalism, and the implications of multibillion dollar corporate bailouts.

In response to capital's insistent need to subjugate all life to the market, the concept of the commons has gained new importance. Reflecting on what is common, Silvia Federici draws our attention to the continued gendered nature of reproductive labor. In **"Feminism and the Politics of the Commons In an Era of Primitive Accumulation,"** she argues that any meaningful revolutionary movement and engagement with the politics of the common needs to centralize self-reproduction, which in turn requires a re-centering of reproductive labor, social reproduction, and care work.

The power of common people prior to political constitution is an area rich in historical and theoretical exploration. In **"Pallas and 'The People's Business',"** historian Peter Linebaugh examines the commons and the act of commoning in current and historical forms. Linebaugh describes the jury as a weapon against terror, a crucial communing practice at a time when popular sovereignty was resurgent. Today, when the market endlessly surges into our everyday lives and the state shores up against resistance, we may find tools from this history to inform our struggles.

Chris Carlsson addresses the difficulties of contemporary activism in **"Radical Patience: Feeling Effective Over the Long Haul."** Through a contextualization of the mass mobilizations of recent years, Carlsson calls for checking the Activist-identity and living a life based in pleasure, fulfillment, and resistance. He suggests that a healthier take on activism—one that takes our personal desires and needs for community into account— will be more successful in building movements and avoiding burn-out.

These final reflections lend grist to *Uses of a Whirlwind*; our project seeks to prod further in this direction, raising questions as to what is necessary for building and sustaining movements in the United States at the present moment.

TRANSATLANTIC TRANSLATIONS:

Detectives and Researchers for the Revolution(s)

Maribel Casas-Cortes & Sebastian Cobarrubias |
Producciones Translocales

TEN YEARS INTO THE MILLENNIUM and where are we? The promise of a growing coordination of global resistance disappeared with the dusts of war, domestic rollbacks, and
multilateral trade agreements in the United States. The 2008 U.S. elections and victory
of Barack Obama has presented special challenges for social movements; this may be the
first time in decades that U.S. social movements have had to deal with a national political
power that adopts and co-opts their rhetoric for ends as contradictory as debt relief and
bank bailouts, ending the Iraq War and escalating the Afghan War. The collapse of the
global economy has also brought on a whole new set of challenges.

In this same time period, we can see movements of different stripes growing, involving
new sectors and populations. The millennium that for many young movement activists
started with the hope brought by the mythical Battle in Seattle has not completely lost its
promise of alternative futures. New struggles have emerged to challenge assumptions of
where revolt happens and what it looks like.

As Producciones Translocales, we have spent the past decade on both sides of the Atlantic, feet firmly grounded in movements in the U.S. and Spain, translating texts from
movements around the world. In this essay, we use a trilogy of these translations to reinvent
categories of struggle that are often taken for granted. The first translation—"Smashing
Categories of Privilege"—problematizes categories commonly used among U.S. social
movements, raising the possibility and need for a "non-categorical politics." The second
translation, entitled "Conocimiento en Movimiento: Research Riots and Mapping Revolutions," discusses militant research and cartography, two techniques we find useful for

both avoiding frozen categories and responding to actual situations. The final translation, "Queering our Categories of Struggle," returns to the discussion of categories with a focus on the concept of "precarity." It calls for a politics that questions and adjusts its categories to the complex realities movements face, thus allowing for the emergence of more horizontal alliances and networks of mutual solidarity.

SMASHING CATEGORIES OF PRIVILEGE

CATEGORIES USUALLY WORK IN DUALIST, essentialist terms: class (working/middle), race (black/white), sexuality (homo/hetero). They are used to share a common understanding of certain issues; categories work, in the sense that they communicate, generate emotions, and mobilize. Yet they also carry the risk of simplification, reducing the actual diversity and richness of entities that fall within these delineations. What happens when these categories are insufficient or inaccurate? Here we engage with some of these categories, problematize them, and flesh out the costs and benefits of their use.

Privilege: Does White Skin Trouble the Revolution?

The critique of privilege has been an important achievement for acknowledging structural relations of power in the everyday practices of participants in social movements. U.S. social movements are quite unique in working on the question of privilege, exploring how class, race, sexual orientation, ethnic background, or ways of talking carry certain unwritten rights. The critique of privilege is an inheritance from the struggles of the 1960s and 1970s, especially the explosion of "diversity" seen in black liberation, black feminism, Chicano/a movements, Indian/Indigenous movements, queer struggle, or functional diversity/handicapped movements. Confronting diversity forced many activists to rethink how they understood oppression in the broader society as a whole, as well as how they would confront oppressive practices within movements.

Many movements practice critiques of privilege to avoid reproducing oppressive dynamics in their own groups and to expand political participation to those excluded from certain forms of activism by work schedules, family situations, and linguistic difficulties. They do so in a variety of ways: for example, examining how "white skin privilege" works in visible and invisible ways, paying attention to process in meetings and workshops so that normally silenced voices have a chance to participate, organizing daycare in order to facilitate the participation of parents, and not smoking in meetings.

But the critique of privilege also has pitfalls. Focusing on the 'unprivileged' can lead to activist forms of 'profiling,' a search for 'authentic' subjects of struggle and oppression. People categorized as privileged often find it more acceptable to "fight for others" than start from the problems of their own conditions. Without this, they may have to play the victim in order to justify to the world that they are genuinely oppressed. Thus the category of privilege can limit the potential activities or alliances of social movements, or dismiss those that already exist. We offer two stories as illustrations of these limitations.

An activist from Central Europe arrived in the U.S. and quickly became active in the founding of a new anti-authoritarian collective in New York City. The group began with promise and enthusiasm but quickly became bogged down in the question of privilege. Most or all of the members felt that they were privileged in some way, which hampered the types of activism they could do. The group had to wait for "authentically oppressed" membership and eventually collapsed, partly because of the weight of this problem. Our

European activist was shocked. While the critique of privilege made sense, the idea of waiting and doing nothing rather than struggling from that privilege seemed pointless.

Two friends of ours, active members in the Baltimore-based United Workers Association, attended an anti-racist workshop during the 2003 mobilizations against the Free Trade Area of the Americas in Miami. The workshop partly focused on white skin privilege and how this works its way into our activism and our lives. One of those two individuals would be categorized as white, and therefore privileged in the context of the workshop. However, he was also homeless, drifting in and out of day-labor centers and shelters. Though the workshop facilitator was very competent overall, they could not step out of the category of white skin privilege that grounded their analysis. Our friend certainly did experience white skin privilege in some ways, but hammering it home did not make sense to do, and instead created a divide where there could have been a linkage.

Class: We Are All "Middle Class"

Despite visible class differences and some of the highest rates of inequality in the Global North, people in the U.S.—including movement activists—are still clumsy at talking about class. The problems with the category of class are related to the critique of privilege, as well as the contradictory attitudes towards the term "middle class" here in the U.S. In movement circles, there is a general aversion to anything associated with middle class; the category is superficially applied to certain activities/jobs/shopping habits without digging any deeper. Yet "middle class" is an integral part of the national identity, used to designate almost anyone above homelessness and below the Rockefellers.

The "middle class" label thus precludes the expansion of many struggles and possibilities of coalitions-alliances. Many jobs that are typically associated with the working class, such as automobile manufacturing, command far larger salaries and greater job security than university and service economy labor, categorized as "middle class." Organizing efforts have begun in these realms—such as the Industrial Workers of World's Starbucks campaign, or the newly formed Adjunct and Teaching Assistant unions—but the category of "middle class" remains largely unassailable. Some discussions have broken through the veneer of middle class myth since the subprime loan crisis, as we have learned that the status markers of middle-class consumption are built on dangerous and unstable debt mechanisms: home loans, car loans, credit cards, and student loans.[1]

What is most striking is that "middle class" in the U.S. is considered "working class" elsewhere. In Spain, students, doctors, teachers, translators, and programmers are considered working class. Certain styles of dress and attitude might be considered bourgeois, but they do not fundamentally change a person or render their concerns irrelevant. People agree on defending certain services as rights—health care, education, quality public transportation—and understand these as class issues. In the U.S., however, "class" often refers to consumption patterns, rather than inherited wealth or ownership of the means of production. It is difficult to understand who the bourgeois upper class is in today's economy, but it would be more relevant and useful to clarify political differences between individuals coming together in coalition, rather than noting which individuals eat white bread, bagels, or croissants.

University: A Privileged Bubble?

University movements in the U.S. seem to be plagued by this understanding of privilege. Some impressive and necessary mobilizations have taken place on campuses in recent years: anti-war organizing, anti-sweatshop activism, and student/labor solidarity. In order to subvert the current conditions in the university, something else may be needed: struggles around its own population. The emergence of Teaching Assistant and Adjunct organizing, the 2008 occupations at New School in New York City, the recent University of California walkouts and strikes, and budget cut protests in many parts of the country are throwing the university itself into question. Until recently, the fights to stop tuition hikes, rising student debt, federal and state cutbacks in student aid, and the marketization of student life and campuses have been widespread, but often with limited success. It is assumed that the "middle classes" go to university, or folks who will become "middle class"—not "grassroots," "community-based," or "working-class" people; hence, the university is not worth defending.

Many U.S. student movements still mobilize from a discourse of being "privileged." From this standpoint, one's only options are to 'help' others or show solidarity 'for' them, ignoring the fact that socio-economic changes affect *everybody*, including oneself. The irony, of course, is that failing to defend accessible education, low tuition, autonomous spaces of learning, and public funding for research leads to a more stratified and exclusionary higher education system.

When we began graduate studies at a university located in the jungles of the U.S. South, we were very frustrated at the perceived isolation of the ghettoized U.S. academy. But after conversations with others, we realized that this isolation was reinforced by the myth of the "ivory tower": the university was displaced from the 'real' world as well as 'real' activism. This common spatial understanding of the university as an untouched entity erases the multiple socio-economic roles universities hold beyond formal education, including employment and flexible labor markets, the knowledge economy and corporate research, defense contracts and recruiting, finance capitalism (through loans, university endowments, and investments), and gentrification.

The university is not only connected to the 'outside' world; the 'real' world also exists inside the university. There is a need, then, to destabilize the university from within. This is the focus of a new wave of university struggles that target the university system as an "edu-factory," organizing as knowledge workers or precarious people to transform higher education. In addition, the university contributes to the production and reproduction of the same neoliberal world (e.g. notions of individual merit, private property, and competition) that many are fighting off from the 'outside.' Thus, political action within the university is crucial for exploring the shortcomings and possibilities at one of the most powerful points where the system is being reproduced.

Activist and Organizer

Another category worth questioning is that of "activist" and "organizer." While often worn (implicitly or explicitly) as a badge of pride, these identities can also become an exclusive club, discouraging many interested people from organizing. Ask anyone who has had to change "activist scenes," contexts, or countries, and they can share stories of many limits of openly coded activist circles: streams of acronyms, less-than-explicit cultural codes, rigid views of appropriate behavior, and feelings of superiority. These faults are common among any group of folks that work together for lengthy periods of time, but we would do well to check them, lest we fall prey to becoming subcultures instead of movements.

This attitude of exclusivity can often lead to an implicit or explicit "professionalization" of activism, where many people feel certain organizing work is beyond them and better delegated to others more suited for the job. This can be linked to current criticisms of the non-profit industrial complex and the selection of organizations to fund. Movements begin to internalize this elitism; many of us have experienced or participated in insiders' clubs of 'organizers' that are steadfast in their self-importance. But we do not have to be members of a 501(c)3 to see this aspect of activist culture which has permeated many sectors: 'union organizers,' non-governmental organization 'staffers,' even 'key anarchist folks.' We wonder if it is possible to stop basing movement building on 'organizers' and 'activists,' and instead 'activate' different parts of the social fabric that we already inhabit.[2]

CONOCIMIENTO EN MOVIMIENTO: RESEARCH RIOTS AND MAPPING REVOLUTIONS

WE HAVE SEEN IN THE U.S. a tendency not to reflect on what has been done in actions, campaigns, and movements. These reflections could potentially provide tools for organizing efforts and recuperate genealogies of movement struggles. How do we learn and build on our successes and failures in order to advance our causes? How do we share those lessons with others? Often, even simple things like keeping track of a collective's activities and sharing its history with others are left by the wayside in the daily grind of activist work. Movement participants in the U.S. have a strong foundation to build from here, but it is all too often forgotten and minimized.

Here we examine some experiments in Europe, Latin America, and the U.S. that encourage more systematic reflection, record keeping, and other activities related to knowledge production, from militant research initiatives to the proliferation of autonomous universities. We examine the politics of taking our own 'knowledges' seriously, as we share, exchange, compile, and improve them. Struggles are opening up the possibility to speak more forcefully, without representational or expert-based politics. They can develop alliances in a reciprocal way, recognizing people as geo-politically positioned and embedded in a certain place. In that sense, positioned knowledge implies situated organizing. In contrast, *fixed* categories work abstractly, building notions inattentive to concrete histories and specific knowledges; they act like imported 'brands.' We argue for a non-categorical politics, engaging in a more specific, caring, and place-based organizing.

Madrid: We Are the Experts

On a Sunday afternoon in downtown Madrid, around forty women packed a large, cozy room at Eskalera Karakola, a women's social center. There are posters from actions on the wall, a big window to the street, and a coffee table filled with hot drinks and snacks. It was the beginning of one of the monthly workshops on "imagining a revolt by domestic workers," organized by the *Agencia de Asuntos Precarios* (Agency for Precarious Affairs) and *Servicio Doméstico Activo* (Active Domestic Service) throughout 2008 and 2009.

During the round of introductions, some domestic workers new to the workshops expressed their interest in talking to lawyers, asking if the organizing groups were legal consultancies. One Precarios participant, a freelance translator, replied:

> Well, not really, there are institutions to offer that kind of legal information. La Agencia is a way to create tools of self defense, to face certain unfair and challenging situations at your workplace and beyond. [...]

The principle is to depart from our own experiences as real experts on our own situations […] who else is going to know better what is our problem?

An adjunct professor at several universities explained:

This is a space to share those knowledges to form a common knowledge, useful for many of us. […] That's the goal of today's encounter: to narrate and share our own concrete expertise, in this case, what to do in certain cases, what to avoid … things that a lawyer would be unable to know.

A domestic worker from the Caribbean continued:

Exactly, the experience and knowledge on domestic work is not owned by them, but by ourselves […] in order to improve the conditions of this sector, the organizing has to come from ourselves, arranging informal encounters during our everyday lives, encounters that involve a lot of storytelling since we have a lot of dramatic stories to share, as well as music and dance. […] Then we can devote some time and energy to those other spaces that claim to represent us, but our participation on those would already depart from a solid strengthening of our connections, arguments, and building of a common voice.

This emphasis on knowledge production by movements themselves speaks to the potential for self empowerment, post-representation, and effective organizing.

U.S.: Knowledge is Power

This episode resonates with traditions of popular education that are quite well established in the U.S. Popular education movements in the U.S. have been inspired by Latin American thinkers such us Paulo Freire and traditions such as Pedagogy of Liberation and Participatory Action Research; both traditions are based in the credo "knowledge is power." Projects like the Highlander Center in rural Tennessee, known for its important work on popular education for Civil Rights, have been outstanding examples of action research and critical pedagogy. Founded in 1932 as a school for labor movement leaders, the Highlander Center was in its third decade when it turned its focus to the Civil Rights movement. The Civil Rights struggle provided many important contributions to traditions of activist pedagogy, from the Citizenship Schools and activist training of Highlander, to the Mississippi Freedom Schools, which led to anti-authoritarian notions of teaching such as the Free School movement and the Afro-American Radical Pedagogy of bell hooks.

Another important lineage in this genealogy is the teaching of American philosopher and pedagogue John Dewey, who wrote *Democracy and Education* in 1916. The first Dewey schools were founded in the 1930s; Highlander is an echo of them. Dewey's principle of "knowing-doing-being," which contrasted with conventional notions of knowledge, helped to politicize knowledge-making. His pragmatism questioned the neutrality of science and insisted on the practical uses of research. Knowing was not about looking for an abstract representation of reality, but engaging in world-making. This perspective had an empowering influence on the processes of community organizing of the 1950s. Research strengthened the movement of social workers to develop more effective strategies and actions by and for affected communities.

A radically different way of politicizing knowledge-making in the U.S. has been developed by the feminist movement. At theoretical and practical levels, feminists developed strong critiques to the mainstream notion of 'objectivity' as abstract, neutral, and bodiless. Instead they proposed a different kind of epistemology, based on a person's situated experience.[3] Sandra Harding's notion of "strong objectivity" and Donna Haraway's idea of "situated knowledge" were key contributions that traveled far beyond the walls of academia.[4] Feminist epistemologies paralleled the formation of consciousness-raising groups, born out of the radical feminist movement in the late 1960s. Both trends are considered antecedents of the current wave of militant or activist research.[5]

Since their inception, women's consciousness-raising groups proposed that women would become experts in their own oppression, building theory from personal and intimate experience instead of the filter of previous ideologies. These groups were pejoratively labeled as "meetings for tea and cookies," "gossip sessions," or "gatherings of witches." They were the target of many accusations, especially of being therapeutic rather than 'political.' "The personal is political" was coined in response to these criticisms, affirmatively and defiantly questioning what counts as 'political.'[6]

There is also the unprecedented example of AIDS Coalition to Unleash Power (ACT UP). Born out of the turmoil in the 1980s against the stigmatization of AIDS, ACT UP was one of the first struggles to openly engage the question of expert knowledge, challenging medical authority to be more democratic and less driven by pharmaceutical interests. The movement invested in learning medical jargon and arguments in order to discuss on the same plane as 'experts' and successfully ask for feasible demands. The impressive amount of medical research, translation to more colloquial language, and publication and distribution of information speak to the power of engaging and producing expert scientific knowledge. ACT UP is based on the saying "Knowledge is Power," though this time closer to the notion of 'power' developed by the French philosopher Michel Foucault.[7] While Brazilian pedagogue Paulo Freire emphasized the empowering force of knowing more and better about one's own conditions, Foucault pushes the notion of 'power' further, as a force able to constitute reality. This force includes the powers that construct the world through the instrument of dominant scientific knowledge.[8]

According to Foucault, much of reality is maintained through "regimes of truth." These regimes are made real through discourse—very often scientific or other expert discourses—to produce "truth-effects." Truth-effects define and shape what we see, experience, and think, what we can say and do, as well as what is outside the realm of comprehension.[9] In effect, our knowledge of the world as well as how we understand 'truth' and 'reality' both enable and constrain our actions in the world. Thus, in order to fight back against the truth-effects of the scientific discourse on AIDS (which began describing it as an incurable illness to be socially excluded), movements had to invest in understanding particular scientific discourses, intervene in them, and hijack them from within, in order to create another (and improved) reality surrounding the experience of AIDS.

Research Riots

Many contemporary autonomous collectives engaged in the practice of activist research work from the understanding that, through the research process, movements produce knowledges, and thus power, and somehow, reality. In the words of Precarias a la Deriva, "Militant research is that process of re-appropriation of our own capacity of world-making, which [...] questions, problematizes and pushes *the real* through a series of concrete procedures."[10]

Today's militant research initiatives illustrate many approaches to the production of knowledge. Some efforts treat such production subtly, letting it act upon concrete organizing practices; others take on the process in more explicit and systematic ways, by registering mechanisms and developing research questions, hypotheses, and projects of inquiry. This research component aims to have a better understanding of people's particular conditions, thus boosting tactics and organizational strategies.

A conscious practice of activist research is inseparable from action. Separation results in "dead books" that might look interesting, but as one participant of Precarias puts it, they "are not alive and unable to produce communicative resonances." Research is thus conceived not as something apart from, but rather embedded in concrete struggle. In the words of one Precarias participant in January 2007:

> The goal of the research is simply to improve our knowledge about ourselves and our knowledge about each other. Many of us come from activist backgrounds that are very enclosed; you just hang out with your similar ones, and live through categories and codes of struggle you inherited from others. Everything, from clothing to your own vocabulary, from the places you live and go, speaks of a certain type: the activist, the squatter. [...] There is a problem of ghetto-identity that does not allow you to cross trajectories with different people but your own. Research was a tool to open up, to start knowing more about those others that we spoke about from a discursive level, but without actual or everyday encounters.[11]

Conceiving and conducting research in this way does not imply a formalized project with a rigorous research plan. The plan comes *a posteriori*, in the process of writing and putting the pieces together; only then do the results start to look more coherent. Research here is an open-ended process, open to improvisation and encounters. This understanding stems from traditions of action-research and auto-inquiry, including the idea of simultaneous thinking and acting, or what the Zapatistas call "asking while walking;" research is a process of searching for tools, putting together cartographies, registering our own steps.

The first activist group we encountered that directly embraced research as a constituent trait in their struggle was Colectivo Situaciones in Buenos Aires. This small collective of independent researchers works in collaboration with different sectors of the Argentinean civil society, from HIJOS, the sons and daughters of the "disappeared," to the *piqueteros*, formed by unemployed workers organizing community-based micro-enterprises, known for picketing and blockading roads. The kind of relationship that Situaciones envisions with these groups is based on a firm premise that the research is part of the struggle: "Situaciones aims to work as an 'internal' reading of struggles, and not as an 'objective' description. The point is to compose situational knowledges able to accompany and strengthen the emergence of new values superior to those of capitalism."[12]

One of the methodologies used by Situaciones is the co-production of workshops, where collective members and particular social movement participants focus on a shared problem. After identifying a pressing issue, that problem becomes the 'third object' to be analyzed by all the participants during a series of workshops. This methodology tries to articulate a subject-to-subject relationship, by both parties sharing their knowledges and listening to each other in order to generate a series of analyses, hypotheses, and proposals. These are usually documented in texts that are published (often in "just-in-time" or "on-demand" fashion) in accessible publishing houses, which are then distributed among grassroots groups and others. The latest project of Situaciones is an inquiry about recent changes in labor patterns, done in collaboration with call center workers. They insist that social struggles themselves generate research questions and hypotheses that we must address through our experiences, eschewing inherited ideas in favor of producing updated analyses in cooperation. They propose an understanding of militant research:

> Processing what you are living through. Working with others, working with texts. [...] Overcoming the stupidity that distinguishes researchers from researched. Understanding every experience as a living being that dialogues with another, in the present tense, or looking towards the past and the future.

What does knowledge become when it renounces the comfort of "critical distance" with regards to the 'object,' when it refuses each and every "evenly balanced evaluation" and adopts a point of view based in struggles? How is the ability to research experienced when it becomes part of the experience of life, when it has the potential to create? What happens when the discussion is no longer about "who is who?": who is on the inside and who on the outside, who 'thinks' and who 'acts,' who has the right to speak and who lets others speak on their behalf? When the question of 'who is who?' is no longer policed, a new possibility emerges: producing together.[13]

Observatorio Metropolitano[14]

In response to the candidacy of Madrid for the Olympic Games, a group formed to study this 'event' and the consequential restructuring of Madrid. The project soon surpassed that initial focus, examining larger questions of how global processes are transforming the city. After a series of self-education seminars and the formation of working groups, the research project ended with a series of public presentations by the collective Observatorio Metropolitano. The result is a 700–page book entitled *Madrid: La Suma de Todos?*, one of the first serious engagements with the contemporary transformations in Madrid. The book has been circulating among community centers since 2008, a tool for action targeting many unexplored or misunderstood problems of the city.

Most of the work by Observatorio Metropolitano involves a macro-analysis with solidified historical and descriptive data in order to understand global political-economic processes. These analyses constitute great political tools. Presented as objective portraits, findings are easier to communicate and circulate. Institutional actors as well as public opinion are called into question through means such as court cases, mainstream media, and mass campaigns. Normally, this research leans toward empirical, filled with statistics and a sociological bent. Examples of this kind of research by social movements, such as watchdog projects, are numerous and actually quite successful in their campaigns.

However, the macro approach carries a risk: the possibility of generating a *paralyzing* kind of knowledge. By providing such overarching presentations of macro socio-economic processes, a strong sense of inevitability seems to be inscribed in those producing and receiving the information. What kind of political agencies arise from this research approach? On the one hand, the data provides indispensable and strategic utensils to put together political campaigns supported by empirical arguments; on the other hand, the macroscopic view loses sight of individualized everyday reality, conveying a sense of impotence.

Precarias a la Deriva: Researching the Commons

Other research strategies can address this risk. By attending to the microscopic elements of everyday life, research can connect directly with people's experiences, allowing for mutual recognition and the discovery of previously unthinkable combinations and possibilities. When the Situationists described the city through their unconventional wanderings, they broke the monolithic rhythm of "metro-boulot-dodo" (subway-work-sleep). Their findings suggested other forms of inhabiting the city, provoking the reinventions of the individual and creating a new/other sense of collectivity. Research methodologies that acknowledge the limits of the observer (or better yet, embrace the incompleteness of the data) can facilitate other kinds of political possibilities. Imagination-fueled politics thus involves processes of re-subjectification, generation of solidarities with others, mutual resonances, collective imaginations, and ultimately, organized interventions. One example can be found in Laboratorio de Trabajadoras, a project that became Precarias a la Deriva, and is now the Agency of Precarious Affairs.

For Precarias, finding collective ways of struggle was one of their main challenges, especially considering that women who shared common experiences of precarity were also employed in very different types of work with different social statuses: university professors, sex workers, translators, and domestic servants. In order to search for commonalities, they needed research methodologies that would fit their circumstances and be relevant enough to provoke conflict. Looking for a procedure that could capture their mobile, open-ended, and contingent everyday lives, they found inspiration in the Situationist technique of 'drifting.' By wandering in the city, allowing for encounters, conversations, interaction, and micro-events to guide their urban itineraries, Situationist researchers produced a psycho-geography based on haphazard coincidences. Of course, this approach is appropriate for a "bourgeois male individual without commitments," and not necessarily a *precaria*. Instead of an exotic itinerary, the Precarias' version of drifting consists of a situated and intended trajectory through the everyday life itineraries of the different participants.[15]

While Situationists create unexpected spatial situations generating realities worth exploring, Precarias' method pursues an intentional model of the drift, where spaces normally perceived as unconnected are linked. Everyday itineraries become the leading line to follow, making underground realities visible. This mode of the drift is attentive to the spatial-temporal continuum that they experience as women under the new labor conditions, contributing a methodology which could be understood as a feminist version of drifting, a 'dérive à la femme.' This innovative methodology generates a political-economic analysis that is informed by current theoretical trends. Alternating between a variety of theoretical sources and actual lived experience, participants develop a situated investigation about the material conditions held in common, as well as radical differences.[16] These feminist drifts act as circuits, articulating fragmented spaces and experimental tours to re-imagining what is 'political' as collective interventions in everyday life. They produce participatory cartographies of their collective itineraries, where 'field research' is a temporary expedition into singular experiences.[17] Precarias' project searches for commonalities *and* fosters singularities; this tension is maintained, as they look for ways to articulate "lo común singular" (the singular in common).[18] They aim to cross-fertilize collective action among radically different specificities.

THE MAPPING REVOLUTION

CONTINUING THIS TRANSLATION OF RESEARCH/KNOWLEDGE practices, we want to emphasize the importance of one particular form for our time: map-making. Many of us frequently use GoogleMaps or MapQuest; newspapers and television broadcasts make extensive use of colorful maps of weather, traffic, and the latest U.S. bombing sites. The Department of Defense has recently developed a special Geo-Spatial Intelligence Division to focus on map-making.

A wave of cartographic practices is spreading among various social movements throughout the world, as they re-appropriate the tools of the age. These mapping projects help us navigate the shifting territories of globalization. In the cases we have seen in Spain, this is applied to the European Union, the new European border regime, and other macro-transformations. This resonates with Fredric Jameson's call to initiate a project of "global cognitive mapping" in order to reorient subjects in a postmodern world.[19] Yet beyond this initial "way-finding" role, there are other reasons for using cartography:

> Because power, impotence, and resistance take place in space and assume specific forms within it, maps can lend a spatial perspective to [our] political analysis.
> —An Architektur

> It is time to draw new maps, maps of resistance that can be used to attack the visible and invisible fences and walls, to tear them down or sail around them quietly, to hollow them out and to undermine them.
> —NoLager

> Even though the map is not the territory, to make maps is to organize one's self to new connections and to be able to transform the material and immaterial conditions in which we find ourselves immersed. It isn't the territory, but it definitely produces territory.
> —Cartografias Tácticas[20]

With this in mind, activist mappings serve as organizing nodes rather than just navigational tools. They suggest new connections and relations that aid in not only re-conceiving the territory, but also recreating it. Thus, a subversive map of a border helps to create a subversive border. Maps can be understood as agents that help assemble distinct subjects into new joint processes, a form of radical *bricolage*.

Otra Málaga: Socialized Research

In 2004, the Social Forum of Málaga was going to take place. The entire Spanish state was emerging from a period of high-level mobilizations, including the anti-European Union campaign of 2002, large movements against ecological disasters and an educational reform bill, and the anti-war movement. 2004 was also a year of general elections. Many changes were occurring at the local level, including major construction for the tourist sector, the growth of services industries, and a rapid influx of immigration. The Social Forum aimed to direct anxiety about these transformations into local interventions, beyond just a series of interesting workshops and panels.

An in-depth mapping project began forming, combining a process of Participatory Action Research with different movements and local struggles to remap the territory. The goal of the project was to understand the connections between the different transformations—ecological, economic, and demographic—and use these understandings as tools to build connections between the often isolated experiences of self-organization occurring in each of these spheres. The result included a book, a map, and a DVD. The map shows different processes happening simultaneously, exposing the links between these processes: land speculation, tourist infrastructure, the growth of temporary labor, and the ways new migrants are channeled into certain jobs and areas. The project intensified relations, opening up collectives to work with each other and mixing disparate populations. This process strengthened the social fabric of the movement in Málaga and beyond.

Cartographies of the Straits of Gibraltar: Mapping Flows

A map of the Straits was made by a wide network of people based in Andalusia, Spain, and areas of northern Morocco. This network of activist hackers, artists, and architects created a map that rethinks the border between Spain and North Africa. Instead of accepting the border as a fixed entity, constraining bodies and movement, this map conveys border relationships, including "geographies of empire" (capital flows, police networks, and jurisdiction) and "geographies of the multitude" (migrant-flows and social networks).[21] The map ignores the geopolitical and epistemological borders that have been naturalized by the dividing line of the sea; instead, a particular flow is followed across the Mediterranean, between Spain and Morocco, Europe and Africa. Human flows of migrants or police agents and capital flows of the Moroccan government's foreign debt repayments, immigrant remittances to family members, or European corporate investment (i.e. factory relocation) are constantly in flux. Cell phone and internet coverage span the Straits of Gibraltar, facilitating denser nodes of contact and coordination between social movements on both sides. The resulting map does not reproduce the border as a space of separation, but invokes it as a site of connection and reciprocal flows that traverse the Mediterranean.[22]

3Cs: Cartographies of the Knowledge Machine

Through our experience with the Counter-Cartographies Collective (3Cs) in Chapel Hill, we found an unexpected attraction to maps. We brainstormed reasons that explain its growing use among social movements: mapping, as compared to writing, is non-textual and non-grammatical, so a reader is not forced to follow a linear thought pattern; maps are easier to produce in a participatory and collective manner; maps can act as excellent tools for teach-ins and workshops; and maps never need to be considered 'finished,' as they are constantly open to interaction and re-appropriation by the reader.[23] In 2006, 3Cs distributed University DisOrientation Guides to the students, faculty, and staff at the University of North Carolina (UNC), which included many maps. The 3Cs collective compiled a large quantity of complex information on the university—rarely accessed and considered unattractive—and put it all into a large pocket-map. One side displays a variety of diagrams and maps, presenting the university as a factory, a functioning body; and a machine producing one's view of the world. The opposite side situates UNC as a historical site of activism, providing tools, contacts, and concepts to re-inhabit, intervene in, and subvert the university.

The process of investigating and mapping the academic territory opened the possibility of rethinking the university in challenging and empowering ways. 3Cs wanted to emphasize the major socio-economic role played by the university, especially in the case of UNC, located at the apex of the Research Triangle Park, one of the largest science research parks in the U.S. In the fall of 2009, 3Cs printed its second DisOrientation Guide. This guide delves deeper into many of the same themes as the first guide, but also makes an effort to find commonalities with other university-based struggles.[24] In early 2010, 3Cs is planning a small-scale intervention on campus, where the salaries of different employees of the university will be displayed in large posters in different university buildings. This will be the first action of a long-term and multi-sector campaign to rethink the university as a space of conflict, highly invested in economic and political questions. These interventions seek to destabilize old notions of the university, reclaiming education in search of autonomy and liberation within the university itself.

QUEERING OUR CATEGORIES OF STRUGGLE

So, WHAT EXAMPLES OF NON-CATEGORICAL politics have resulted from research and mapping experiments? We will briefly mention one instance of how this rethinking of our categories through processes of inquiry has led to more flexible understandings and tools for contemporary struggle: the queered notion of precarity.

Challenging the Monolithic Idealized Working Class: What About Precarious People?

Movements across the Atlantic do not always operate with the duality of 'privileged' and 'oppressed,' as constructed in the U.S.; some are actively trying to articulate more flexible identities of struggle, seeking affinities and facilitating alliances. This is the case of many movements working on "precarity" in the European Union. Precarity involves living and working conditions associated with several factors, including current labor transformations (increases in temporary contracts, loss of labor protections, and day-labor), neoliberal approaches to social services, and the real estate market's effects on access to housing.[25] A diverse array of people fit under this broad category: including domestic workers, tenants, teaching assistants, and immigrant families. Despite the differences and asymmetries among the populations, certain common experiences are being identified, allowing the coming together of struggles and mobilizations, each person or group departing from their own singularity and meeting in common shared struggle. Instead of accepting a series of atomized struggles of strategies that may not work (and that new identities may not fit into), precarity has become a struggle where the search for something in common does not homogenize conditions, respecting the singularity of each situation and perspective. This queered category is largely the result of processes of self-inquiry, cartographies, activist research and reflection, and the sharing of histories and stories of struggles. The following call suggests how movements are engaging the question of precarity:

Since the end of the 19th century, on May First we celebrate Labor Day.

Are those of us who care for dependent members of our families and don't get paid for it workers? Are those of us with functional diversity/handicap (physical-mental-intellectual) and who don't even have the recognized right to lead an autonomous/independent life workers? What about those of us who sell pirated compact discs in the street as the only way to earn a living while laws condemn us to second-tier citizenship as the 'undocumented' workers? Are those of us employed in domestic work whose labor regime legalizes a situation of de facto slavery—workers? Are those of us who translate, teach classes, do research—but our 'work life' doesn't count for the archives of the state because we work under the table and we don't chip into Social Security—workers? Are any of us for whom 'mileurismo' (term used for those that make 1000 euros a month), decent housing, and labor rights are unreachable dreams because we make pizzas, hamburgers, or conduct surveys, but we've never had a contract for more than two or three months—workers?

The only thing we're sure about is that we're not those types of 'workers' that the big labor union confederations refer to and claim to represent on the 1st of May. But then what are we? What do we have in common? Can we join forces and dreams for change from such different legal, labor, and life situations?[26]

This call for a MayDay picnic in 2008 by the Agencia de Asuntos Precarios / Precarias a la Deriva captures the feel of precarity and how it results from a process of questioning our own situations and movements. We are faced with changing conditions of labor, new sectors, and new populations. New tools and languages are needed that speak to the multiple conditions many people are encountering. Precarity has arrived as a way to speak about worsening conditions within the same idealized image of a working class that encompasses most everyone in the country. Different groups explore how to link new struggles that were not founded on the subject of the factory or miner (such as the unemployed, migrants, temporary workers, domestic workers, free software developers, interns), without trying to homogenize such diverse populations. What is new (and what is not new) about these situations? Can they be coordinated or thought about together?

Precarity is not meant to be a 'perfect' concept; rather it is unfixed and mobile, avoiding a frozen ideal of the "precariat." It seeks to understand a trend occurring in many places with many populations stretching beyond the workplace, into questions of social services, public and private spaces, and housework. The looseness of the category can be its weakness, but it also reflects the inspiration of the global resistance movements and their attempts to link disparate struggles, as well as a deeper understanding of class and class struggle that goes beyond the gates of the workplace. The ways of engaging and re-appropriating the concept of precarity is demonstrated by the quantity of different movements related to it: housing movements, migrants' struggles, university fights, and copy-left claims.[27]

The introduction of precarity as a new concept from which to think, live, and fight among certain European movements has opened up the possibility of politicizing current conditions and fragmented lives, generating a common language and building another kind of subjectivity. We do not wish to make it bigger than it is: current concrete organizing efforts—such as the emergent *Oficinas de Derechos Sociales* (Offices for Social Rights)—are promising, but are still very small. Precarity is also not widely used in the U.S., where communities face different kind of oppressions and wage different types of struggle, organizing less as 'workers' and more around other conditions of exclusion. There are efforts in the U.S. at day labor organizing, experiments with non-union forms, and horizontal, empowering forms of organization. But it is impossible to link these struggles as long as they are framed as "solidarity *for*," between the seemingly secure and the very oppressed. The challenge is recognizing the specificities of ghetto struggles and labor struggles to create true affinity, identifying common problems, common dreams, and common tactics. Precarity, or perhaps another *queer* concept for the U.S., could help overcome this challenge.

Experiments in activist research might help in the pursuit of a non-categorical politics, in order to avoid the pitfalls of fixity and reductionism. Specifically, queering our categories with experiential understandings of our surroundings could provide a different way to look and act upon our worlds and envision alternatives. In order to be effective and imaginative in this process, engaging militant research experiments can be of much use. When we get stuck organizing alliances that cannot grow into mutual solidarity, when we are faced with grave multi-sector issues that people won't move on, and when we are not even sure what to protest or how to do so, then it is time to retrace our steps and start building counter-knowledges as launching points for organizing.

One thing we know for sure is that police forces, expansive multinational corporations, think-tanks, and militaries all engage in their own forms of knowledge production.[28] These actors have internalized the "knowledge is power" adage, approaching the recording, producing, and funding of knowledge with remarkable seriousness. The activist research and cartography examples mentioned here take seriously the idea of infusing the entire research process with movement politics in both outlook and methodology, including participatory, anti-authoritarian, inclusive, multiple-perspective, and specific knowledge.[29] The focus is on how movements grow—or get stuck repeating strategies that do not work—and how to build long-term movements that are not simply knee-jerk reactions. We yearn for movements that outlive collectives *and* activists. This is why we call for a non-categorical politics: a continuous process of queering, mixing up, adjusting, tinkering, and hacking our ways of engaging the world.

NOTES

1   Barbara Ehrenreich, *Bait and Switch: The (Futile) Pursuit of the American Dream* (New York: Holt Paperbacks, 2006).

2   One piece that explores this—entitled "Give Up Activism"—was issued following the June 1999 Carnival Against Capitalism in England. Anonymous, "Give Up Activism" in *Do or Die*, #9 (1999), available at: HTTP://WWW.ECO-ACTION.ORG/DOD/NO9/ACTIVISM.HTM (accessed April 22, 2010).

3   Linda Alcoff and Elizabeth Potter (eds.), *Feminist Epistemologies* (New York: Routledge, 1993); Maria Puig de la Bellacasa, "Think We Must. Politiques Feministes et Constructions de Savoirs," unpublished doctoral dissertation (Université Libre de Bruxelles, 2005).

4   Sandra Harding, *Whose Science? Whose Knowledge?* (Ithaca: Cornell University Press, 1991);

Donna Haraway, "Situated Knowledges: The Science Question in Feminism and the Privilege of Partial Perspective," *Feminist Studies* 14 (1988): 575–99.

5   For a detailed description of feminist consciousness rising and other genealogies of certain current activist research experiences, see Marta Malo, "Introduction to Common Notions," *Transform* (web journal special issue on militant research), 2004. HTTP://TRANSFORM.EIPCP.NET/TRANSVERSAL/0406/MALO/EN (accessed January 15, 2010).

6   Malo, "Common Notions."

7   See article about Foucault, Knowledge and ACT UP Paris and the French AIDS movement: Philippe Mangeot, "Sida, angles d'attaque," *Vacarme* 29 (2004), HTTP://WWW.VACARME.ORG/ARTICLE456.HTML (in French).

8   Michel Foucault, *Power/Knowledge: Selected Interviews & Other Writings 1972–1977*, ed. Colin Gordon (New York: Pantheon Books, 1980); Paulo Freire, *Pedagogy of the Oppressed*, translated by Myra Bergman Ramos (New York: The Continuum Publishing Corporation, 1987).

9   This thesis is further developed in Michel Foucault, *The History of Sexuality*, "Volume I: An Introduction," translated by R. Hurley (New York: Vintage Books, 1978).

10   Precarias a la Deriva, "A la deriva por los circuitos de la precariedad femenina" (Madrid: Traficantes de Sueños, 2004), 92.

11   Precarias a la Deriva meeting (2007).

12   Colectivo Situaciones and MTD-Solano, "Hipotesis 891: Mas alla de los Piquetes" (Buenos Aires: Ediciones de Mano en Mano, 2001).

13   Colectivo Situaciones, "Something More on Research Militancy: Footnotes on Procedures and (In)Decisions," in *Constituent Imagination: Militant Investigations, Collective Theorizations*, eds. Stephen Shukaitis, David Graeber, and Erika Biddle (Oakland: AK Press, 2007).

14   Loosely translated as Metropolitan Center.

15   Precarias a la Deriva (2004), 26.

16   For example, an undocumented domestic worker and a freelance journalist are flexible, temporary, part-time, and self-employed workers, but there are huge differences in terms of social status, salary, rights, and risks.

17   See cartographic representations of their drifts in Precarias a la Deriva (2004).

18   Precarias a la Deriva (2004), 47.

19   Fredric Jameson, *Postmodernism, or the Cultural Logic of Late Capitalism* (Durham: Duke University Press, 1991).

20   Car_tac, "Taller de Cartografias Tacticas, Fadaiat 2005," in *Colectivo Fadai'at: Libertad de Movimiento+Libertad de Conocimiento* (Málaga: Imagraf Impresiones, 2006), 157. In Spanish and also available in English and Arabic in the same publication.

21   Jose Perez de Lama, "Geografías de_la_multitud_[conectada]" (2003) at HTTP://HACKITECTURA.NET/OSFAVELADOS/TXTS/SCI_FI_GEOGRAPHIES.HTML (last accessed January 15, 2010).

22   Pilar Monsell and Jose Perez de Lama, "Indymedia Etrecho," in *Colectivo Fadai'at: Libertad de Movimiento+Libertad de Conocimiento* (Malaga: Imagraf Impresiones, 2006), 138. In Spanish and also available in English and Arabic in the same publication.

23   For a deeper engagement with the practice of activist mapping, see Sebastian Cobarrubias, "Mapping Machines: Activist Cartographies of the Labor and Border Lands of Europe," unpublished dissertation (University of North Carolina at Chapel Hill, 2009).

24   This guide can be found online at HTTP://WWW.COUNTERCARTOGRAPHIES.ORG/PROJECTS-MAINMENU-27/14–REMAPPING-THE-UNIVERSITY/69–DISORIENTATION-DE.

25   For English material on this emerging concept of precarity mobilizing struggles in several European countries, see "Precarity Explained to Kids," HTTP://WWW.JOURNALOFAESTHETICSANDPROTEST.

ORG/4/AVIV.HTML (accessed January 15, 2010); and "Precarious Lexicon," HTTP://WWW.SIN-DOMINIO.NET/KARAKOLA/PRECARIAS/LEXICON.HTM (accessed January 15, 2010); Nate Holdren in "Understanding Precarity," HTTP://PRECARIOUSUNDERSTANDINGS.BLOGSOME.COM (accessed January 15, 2010); and Stevphen Shukaitis, *Imaginal Machines* (New York: Minor Compositions, 2009),165–189; Maribel Casas-Cortes, "Social Movements as Sites of Knowledge Production: Precarious Work, the Fate of Care and Activist Research in a Globalizing Spain," unpublished dissertation (University of North Carolina at Chapel Hill, 2009).

26 Agencia de Asuntos Precarios, email communication (April 2008). In Spanish, translated into English by the authors.

27 There is an ongoing project called the Precarity MAP that puts together cartography of the different struggles around precarity in Europe. See Maribel Casas-Cortes (2009), "Precariedad: A Cartography of a Concept," 321–422.
Copy-left licenses are anti-copy-right licenses. They allow for different forms of free re-usage and distribution; one of the most well-known is Creative Commons.

28 See *Networks and Netwars. The Future of Terror, Crime, and Militancy*, eds. John Arquilla and David Ronfeldt, HTTP://WWW.RAND.ORG/PUBS/MONOGRAPH_REPORTS/MR1382/ (accessed January 15, 2010). See chapters 4 and 7 in particular.

29 For an engagement with activist research as a form of anti-authoritarian politics, see Maribel Casas-Cortes (2009), "Investigacion Militante: The Cultural Politics of Activist Research," 104–229.

ORGANIZING ENCOUNTERS AND GENERATING EVENTS

El Kilombo Intergaláctico & Michael Hardt in Conversation

The conversation from which "Organizing Encounters and Generating Events" was produced took place in the spring of 2008 before the convention protests and election. A postscript was added during the winter of 2010.

LESSONS IN EMPIRE

El Kilombo: *So much has been said about the concept of Empire since the publication of your book with Toni Negri. How would you summarize the importance of this concept for political action today?*

Michael Hardt: One of the problems some people seemed to have with the concept of Empire was that it poses a difficulty for organizing. In other words, it seems that the notion that the emerging global order is organized not by a single imperialist state, or even by a small group of dominant nation states, but rather by a wide network of collaborating powers, including the dominant nation states of course, but also major corporations, supranational institutions, non-governmental organizations (NGOs), etc.— that hypothesis of Empire, that there was no single center to global power, seems, from a certain perspective, to make organizing and protest impossible. In other words, you can protest, but there is nobody home. Now, already the globalization movements from the late 1990s and early 2000s were addressing this new situation. In fact, the way I see the various examples of summit-hopping from that period as trying to articulate that theory of Empire: they recognized that it's not just the U.S. that's in control of global order (if you did think that, you should be protesting in front of the White House every week), but rather the protests were an attempt to identify the new enemy through a of series of experimentations: with the International Monetary Fund (IMF) and the World Bank, the G-8, the Free Trade Area of the Americas, that these were all revealing nodes in the network of the new global command. The problem, of course, that everyone realized at the time and that is even more pressing today is summit-hopping is only organized around these events and doesn't leave us with anything else. Today when we're faced once again with confronting the new global order, which is not simply dictated by the U.S. or by the White House, we have to address this problem again: of how to organize when the powers we're facing are multiple and dispersed. And how to do it in such a way that leaves us with lasting organizations.

EK: *From our perspective, the first thing that the discussion around the notion of Empire has accomplished is to bring us back to the very basic idea that there is no struggle against capitalism as such, that one must always take time to define the parameters of what the struggle is today. You must always begin by conducting a survey of sorts to understand what's happening now so that we can act accordingly; it's never enough to simply denounce capitalism and its relation to imperialism as if these phenomena and their relations were timeless.*

MH: I agree that we can't just reject capital as such at an abstract level, that we have to recognize or invent concrete instances for resistance and struggle. But how does having to think about Empire force you or allow you to recognize the concrete situation?

EK: *For example, the given-ness of inter-imperialist competition, or imperialism as the functioning parameters of capitalism were for a long time a simple given. But today we have to go back, and the concept of Empire gives us the capacity to at least open the discussion and say, if we're not dealing with that situation, what is the situation that we're dealing with today? It helps us to remember that we must always keep asking this question.*

MH: It's not the nature of what we're calling Empire that forces this; it's the notion that you have to rethink constantly the conditions of capital, and therefore the conditions of struggle. So whether you agree with our notion of Empire or not, maybe that part doesn't matter, its just having to recognize that in capitalist relations and command something is new.

EK: *Although it matters in the sense that reanalyzing the conditions and the tactics of struggle require a new analysis. So we were using the example of imperialism, where we still have anti-imperialist struggles because some motions, some particular gestures, look like imperialist gestures, but in fact are not. This is where the conceptual innovation makes quite a difference.*

MH: Right. If you're fighting against an old form of enemies, you risk not only being ineffective but even reinforcing them.

EK: *Exactly. We also feel that the concept of Empire has had a second positive effect on the U.S. political scene; political agency in U.S.-based activism has tended to be displaced onto subjects in the "third world." The concept of Empire, this massive dispersal of capitalist networks which exceeds any given nation-state, forces us to question this displacement and instead attempt to place ourselves at the center, or at least within possibilities for political action, to imagine ourselves both as subjects of capitalist impositions as well as agents of possible change. It really puts* *an end to that bad habit of displacing our agency.*

MH: To add to that, I wonder if it is the same thing to say that what we have to recognize is that the need for activism in the U.S. is becoming more like the need for activism elsewhere, so in that way too, U.S. exceptionalism is also coming to an end. Part of the exceptionalism was manifested by those practices of a politics of guilt and displacement, making our political actions not about us but only about people elsewhere.

PROTEST AND REVOLUTION

EK: *This recognition is important in determining the possibilities and limitations for protest politics in the U.S., such as the upcoming demonstrations against the Republican and Democratic National Conventions this summer. For us, it is first important to clarify what these protest events should not be about. We need to disinvest from making demands toward political parties and the State, because the problems we are facing run much deeper than the party system—which from our perspective is now a product of media simulation and the spectacularization of politics. In that sense, we shouldn't be waging protest as a plea or appeal to these parties, or as an appeal to the media. It is through media spectacle that the politics of the politicians is legitimated: through the circulation of images, the polling of 'public opinion,' political partnerships with civil society, and the permission and even encouragement of "dissent" which supposedly signals a healthy democracy. The imagery of public protest in and of itself doesn't challenge this schema, but can in fact play an integral role in this game of simulation that has replaced representation (as limited as this concept already is) as the substance of electoral politics.*

This shouldn't suggest, however, that there is nothing to be gained through the organization of these protests. If the focus is not outward and upward—aimed at the politicians, the parties, the media—but is oriented inward, for and among those of us struggling against capitalism in a multiplicity of ways, these gatherings can become productive spaces of encounter. By this we mean the meeting and exchanging of struggles, getting to know people, projects, and organizations with which we might otherwise never connect. Yet these extraordinary encounters in and of themselves are not sufficient for establishing an alternative to our current situation. The space of protest is a temporary one, and the type of encounter it can provide is all too brief. However, it would be a mistake to falsely oppose the brevity of such encounters with the constancy of organizations. A careful examination of these protests will always show the prior existence of extensive organization, while all organizational efforts necessarily come about through a series of unplanned encounters. Therefore, rather than oppose these phenomena or fix them into a model of supercession (i.e., from protest to organization), what we need is a politics that opens each to the other in a constant relation of mutual regeneration—as the continuous articulation, embodiment, and renewal of our own collective political desires. The potential of the events planned for the summer lies exactly in the opportunity to enact this other kind of politics.

MH: I am little worried about cutting off the notion of revolt… I agree with making primary the encounters of the process of organization, but that doesn't prohibit, functioning secondarily, making demands on the state, demands on the Democratic Party, demanding a living wage from the city, or calling on any number of political powers, even organizing our own spectacles for the media. What present organizing is moving against is a *primacy* of spectacle and a *primacy* of demands, and even a *primacy* of indignation. It doesn't seem to me the right way to think about it to refuse those, but rather subordinating those to the organizing practice.

EK: *We believe that what is needed is a form of organizational force independent of those structures. We're not saying "never spectacle and never demands" in a transcendental way, but only that we think at this particular moment, participating in the spectacle empties all meaning from the act, and requires that you evacuate any other platform to stand on. We're discussing the relation between a movement and its demands of state institutions, and in short what we're trying to get at is that in order to be able to have this discussion we have to build a movement first.*

MH: But what the spectacle is, is really just allowing people to see in the dominant media that some of us don't agree—that we don't agree with the electoral process, that we don't agree with the party platform, etc. Even when that objection isn't given any content by the media, but just appears as people who are against, I still think it can have great effect.

It might seem like I'm contradicting myself, to first propose this idea of Empire, and then to advocate making these kinds of demands on the political powers and the U.S. government, but that's exactly how I think we need to act in this context, without believing that they are sovereign powers, without believing that they can determine their own fate, we still have to constantly make demands on them, in particular to open more spaces for ourselves to act autonomously. So I agree with you on the priority of organizational relationships, but I think that we could maintain a secondary mission also, of expressing our indignation and rage and hatred of the powers that be. I'm only worried that your exclusive focus on organization might cut off those necessary functions.

EK: *Just to clarify, we're not trying to avoid discussion with these institutions or these parties for the sake of revolutionary purity. That would be ridiculous. But we still need to have a discussion about the effectivity of political action towards reform. So we have to constantly question the effectivity of the way demands are posed and the tie of organizational structure to those forms of demands. For example, the effective provision of education by the autonomous communities of Chiapas has had way more of an impact on Mexican national policy on education than if the Zapatistas had gone to the national government and made demands that there should be educational reform because in a way, the national government is then forced to attempt to oc-cupy that issue by addressing the underlying demand. Or, another example, the Black Panther Party here in the U.S. didn't say, "we want a national breakfast program;" instead, they built a breakfast program that fed tens of thousand of children. J. Edgar Hoover identified these programs as the greatest weapon in the hands of the Panthers and subsequently the federal government stepped in to create free breakfast programs in public schools. The same thing took place with the Panthers' sickle cell anemia project.*

MH: So it is more a question of what forms of organization are best for gaining reforms, the effectiveness of political action in that sense because, after all, any real reforms are ori-ented toward revolution. In Italy recently, some of the most successful political activity has been really broad, "multitudinous" organizing campaigns against large public works which are bad for the environment and bad for the local residents, and then most recently the most inspiring struggle has been against the expansion of a U.S. military base in Vicenza. And I would say the actual object of these struggles—stopping the expansion of the base for instance—is itself important, but it turns out to be secondarily important compared to the lasting organization that's been built in Vicenza, of the different groups that came together that hadn't been working together before but discovered new possibilities for organization. So I wouldn't say that stopping the base doesn't matter; it's important, even if it is secondary to the connections and the new forms of organization that have emerged and the construction of a model for organizing that is being repeated elsewhere.

EK: *So, in a way, we're back to where we began, saying that that these protests are important to the extent that they provide us all a base for constructing encounters and new organizational forms. But it still might be useful for us to distinguish the effectiveness of achieving reforms from the goal or intent of reform; so if we establish an autonomous institution, and that causes a certain response or some kind of reform, then it has been an effective action, but reform was never the goal. So it is still important from our perspective to maintain a distinction between organizations that set out for reforms, and organizations that achieve reforms.*

MH: You can tell the difference between the two by the fact that in that in the first model, once the reform is achieved, everybody goes home and never sees each other again, while in the other model, the achievement of the reform is just one step in a much larger process that continues on.

EK: *Absolutely, and nobody should deny the importance of achieving those reforms, so in a way we're saying the same thing; and for us, what is most urgent right now is building the organizational power that gives us the power to force useful reforms.*

A NEW CYCLE OF STRUGGLE: EVENT AND ENCOUNTER

MH: At this point then, it might be helpful to situate the challenges for organizing today in the context of the recent cycle of struggles that have now come to an end. It seems to me that we lived through an incredibly productive and innovative cycle of struggles that lasted from the mid-1990s until about 2003, which was oriented toward questions of globalization, especially in North America and Europe, and the power of it was precisely its diversity in organization and in agendas. In other words, it was not required that the movements unify under a single leadership or support even a common agenda. Rather the strength was precisely in the networks of groups, organized autonomously, cooperating together. But throughout that period, everyone in the movements recognized at least two limitations. One limitation was primarily geographical, which was that the movements in North America and Europe were oriented towards global issues but never managed, despite numerous attempts, to adequately extend outside of the Global North. The second limitation was that organizations were centered on protest and therefore oriented toward a kind of summit-hopping, and therefore there was a lack of an institutionalization of movements. That movement came to a kind of forced end with the war on terror and the need to combat the second Bush administration, but these movements—anti-war, anti-Bush, in 2003 and 2004—though of course necessary, destroyed the multiplicity of the organizing of the previous era because, by necessity it seemed, they required a single central agenda, and a unified organizational technique; and partly as a consequence, all the excitement and innovation dropped out of the movements. Today we're at the beginning of a third cycle of struggles that in some ways can pick up where the globalization protest movements left off, but maybe now we're in a position to address its limitations better. Last summer's events at the G-8 summit in Germany near Rostock were a good start. Maybe the Republican National Convention (RNC) and Democratic National Convention (DNC) events can continue this.

EK: *Perhaps one place we might want to begin this discussion of moving toward a new cycle of struggle is what we referred to above as the necessary interplay, or mutual regeneration, of protest and organization. From our perspective, this would provide a way for the new cycle of struggles to move beyond a certain impasse that has formed within the alter-globalization movements—between on the one hand, organizational models that tout effectivity but don't allow for difference, and on the other, the randomness of encounters that don't allow for the development and consistency of new collective habits.*

In El Kilombo, we feel that moving beyond this impasse implies the construction of permanent spaces of encounter, where no single subject (immigrant, student, industrial worker) is believed to be the principal agent of change, but rather where encounters across subjective positions allows for the creation of new collective habits. That is, this form of organization is capable not only of acting to provide for basic needs, but also of producing itself as a new collective subject (a community). In contrast to the vacuous "grassroots" rhetoric used by non-profits, we have to be careful to note here that community never pre-exists this process of self-constitution and creating a community is not simply the process of recognizing people as they are, but rather acting collectively on who we want to become. Therefore, we need to reclaim this capacity for ourselves, to generate and sustain community, to exercise power collectively, to realize projects of autonomy and self-determination. We need the organizational consistency and structure to deal with real-life problems and be open to new desires, so we can move beyond the politics of the politicians and the paralyzing spectacle. If we look at the Latin American movements, for example, it becomes clear that only the ones that have been able to make this leap toward what you call "institutionalization" have remained vibrant and effective, and they have in many ways avoided the pitfalls that have tended to trap us here in the North.

MH: I love the way you use the notion of encounter, and it seems to me you're actually talking about two theories of encounter. There is one notion of encounter that functions in the event; in other words, at a protest movement there are new connections that are made that open up towards the future and towards different kinds of organizing; let's call this the 'event encounter.' Then there's another kind of encounter you're talking about which has to do with continuity and what I think of as the construction of institutions. So this is an encounter that's repeatable, and this kind of encounter makes clear how your notion of community is different from the traditional notion of community. I think you're right to find the idea of community creepy, and this notion of the encounter allows you to draw it away from these organic, fixed, identitarian, even familial notions, and allows you to bring community back to the common. What this second kind of encounter is about is a kind of institution of the common, in a way drawing out or developing our common powers that we find through our repeated engagement with each other.

EK: *Shifting to this second kind of encounter seems to be a particularly difficult task now because within Empire politics has been de-linked from a specific mode of spatialized power—the nation-state—and as such, we are struggling to define the new parameters for the practice of politics and organization. We need a new map for understanding the territorial and spatial dimensions of power, a cartography that allows us to see how empire functions as an extremely spatially intense form of exploitation. The struggle to remove the producers of metropolitan forms of cooperation is most literally a struggle to displace them to the periphery of global cities, leaving behind remnants of their collective habits and practices for the enjoyment of others. We would like to be really concrete about this: we believe this is exactly what the issue* *of gentrification and the current foreclosure crisis are actually about. In the United States, this has taken the form of the largest transfer of wealth from families of color to banks, brokers, and investment firms in history, specifically, $164 billion—$213 billion over the past eight years. This scrambling of the geography has made it difficult to remember that all political practice necessitates spatialization, and therefore requires a struggle over territory.*

Having said that, we have to recognize that although the struggle for territory is necessary, it is never sufficient. The aim of our struggle is not simply the control of territory, but rather the effective deployment of space as the necessary conduit for the production of collective habits which make possible a whole series of new social relations. (Perhaps rather than territory, it would make more sense to talk about "habitat.") Therefore, in reality there is no such thing as a struggle against gentrification; there can only be the defense and organizing of territory as a tactical move in the struggle to dismantle Empire.

MH: So, on the one hand we were talking about the importance of the event, such as the protest event, when we make new connections and expand our networks—an extensive development—and now, on the other hand, you are emphasizing the need to create lasting institutions, like El Kilombo, through a kind of intensive development.

EK: *Yes, because we're dealing with two kind of events—first is the question of unexpected events, and then there is the question of trying to appropriate the means of producing/precipitating events.*

MH: The second kind of encounter, though, the intense repeated engagement with each other, I don't know if I'd want to call it an event.

EK: *Don't you think that the production of difference that would create the common is an event?*

MH: Well, does it happen once or does it happen everyday, continually in our interaction with each other? What do you consider the "event" of El Kilombo? It seems counterintuitive to talk about habituation as event.

EK: *By habituation, though, we don't mean repetition. So it is habituation yes, but the habituation of encounter—the habituation of innovation.*

MH: So one is a punctual dividing line of before and after, and then the other identifies the event with creativity and making that isn't temporally isolated but is a duration, a procession of instances or a constant process of creation. So the question might be, why call it an event anymore?

EK: *Because that highlights the innovation involved in it—despite the fact that it happens everyday, it is new every time. The event of Kilombo is the territory that becomes inhabited and habitual. But we should also be very clear about this point; we're not talking about localism or turning inward, but creating a collective body and terrain that allows us to act with and in relation to others. It gives us the means to act and interact more effectively and more cooperatively, not just within and among ourselves but in relation to other communities—opening, in fact, more surfaces of struggle, not fewer. This is why we need practices and habits and collective ways of inhabiting our territory that keep it open to more and more connections.*

MH: And that brings us back to what can be useful in the RNC and DNC actions later this summer, not only to show our dissent but also for the opportunity to open up and make more connections with other singularities. That is an extensive work that complements the intensive work of inhabiting the territory, as you say.

Holding together these two kinds of encounter, these two kinds of events, may be one way of thinking how we can take this new cycle of struggles beyond the limitations of the previous ones.

2010 POSTSCRIPT

MH: Our conversation took place just before the Republican and Democratic National Conventions and now, a year after Obama's election, some of the points we made seem ever more urgent. In particular, the fate of the electoral mobilization for Obama highlights the need for movements to create autonomous institutions and lasting encounters. As many have noted, the remarkable Obama electoral mobilization drew in several ways from the movements, appropriating the "Sí, Se Puede" slogan from the May 2006 immigration protests, pulling in the anti-war movements, engaging a wide spectrum of anti-racist movements and institutions, and so forth. The election was indeed an extraordinarily significant event, in my view, but the big question after the November victory was whether this mobilization would transform into a movement and continue moving forward or whether everyone would de-mobilize, like tired troops after a war, go home, and "let Obama do his work," trusting in the structures of representation. Well, it is clear that, at least so far, the electoral mobilization has not proven to be a lasting encounter.

EK: *In order to analyze the potential for encounter with regards to the last election, we would like to first take a step back and state that for El Kilombo, the election of Barack Obama presents a deeply ambivalent situation that poses both tremendous dangers and obstacles as well as an intensely heightened awareness of the necessity for a deep transformation of our society. To begin with, the danger presented for social movements consists of the powerful draw of the near total "spectacularization of politics" and the near impotence (at this moment) for social movements to act within this realm. If we were to accept a very simple definition of power as "the capacity to define phenomena and make them act in a desired fashion" (per Huey Newton), we cannot avoid the conclusion that the realm of "the politics of the politicians" is an arena of diminishing if not completely non-existent returns for those interested in democratizing our society. Rather, it is an arena increasingly dominated by enormous corporate and political monopolies, by the logic of advertising rather than that of principle, and by the persona of the commodity-individual exchange and promoted therein rather than by political orientation. Yet the circulation of this spectacle as a completely vacuous and therefore infinitely interpretable discourse, supported by its polling and preference databases, has the pernicious effect of appearing to allow for the participation in and even the determination of the political process by people and organizations independent of the political sphere proper and those acting from "above." That is, it increasingly appears as though this process was in fact determined from "below," or even as if it constituted a social movement in and of itself. It is extremely doubtful that under these conditions an encounter in a strict sense has or can take place.*

MH: It's interesting how you pose the spectacle in inverse relation to the encounter. Where there is spectacle, there can be no encounter, and, I suppose, conversely, the creation of encounters destroys the spectacle. This seems to me an extension of conventional notions of political representation and, too, the critique of representation: representation claims both to connect and to separate, that is to link the representatives to the represented, making them accountable to a certain extent and at certain times, but also to create a gap that separates the representatives, giving them a limited independence. At least that's the claim conventionally associated with political representation. Well, on the one hand, your notion of the 'spectacularization' of politics tips the balance of such a relation, minimizing the connection and maximizing the separation of representatives from the represented. And, on the other, the logic of encounter refuses entirely the separation implied by representation itself. So would it be right to say that regarding the Obama camp, you see in this year a movement from encounter to spectacle, that is, from the promise of encounter during the election campaign to realization of spectacle in the Obama government?

EK: *We feel that whether the Obama camp ever constituted an encounter is exactly the question that needs to be brought to the forefront. For us, the Obama campaign, Advertising Age's "2008 marketer of the year," is a paradigmatic case of the spectacularization of politics and its devastating consequences for social change. Toward the end of the Bush II years, and after the post 9/11 fear and paranoia harnessed by that administration began to wear off, there appeared to be a deep skepticism within the U.S. public toward the entirety of the political process. Given this skepticism, it is no surprise that the Obama campaign attempted to depict Barack Obama as the consummate "outsider" with the credentials of a "community organizer" from South Chicago who stood for "hope" and "change." Necessary for this depiction was what sociologist and rocker Angel Luis Lara has termed the "vampirization" of existing social movements, a process which has included Obama's use of prophetic oratory closely associated with the Black radical tradition as exemplified by Martin Luther King Jr. (that "preacher from Atlanta" to whom Obama frequently alludes but never names), Malcolm X, and his own (now disowned) pastor, Jeremiah Wright.*

In addition, this "vampirization" is also exemplified by Obama's appropriation of the social force generated by the migrant protests of the spring of 2006 (which included the largest single day protest in the history of the United States on May 1, 2006) through the (mis)translation, total decontextualization, and transformation of this movement's motto, "¡Si se puede!" into Obama's campaign slogan and into what he has alternatively referred to as "that American creed": "Yes, we can!" It is important to take note of how the agent of repression identified by the migrant movement as their object of protest (i.e. that polity called the United States of America) in Obama's hands becomes the originating subject of the statement of protest ("America"). "¡Si se puede!" is not an "American" creed as brand-Obama would like us to believe; it is rather the creed of those who today are brutally kept in the shadows and refused by "America." Yet, this sleight of hand performs the dual function of appropriating the social force created by the migrant movement while simultaneously delinking that force from political principle. It is a paradigmatic example of the centrality of "induced" opposition in the contemporary "politics of the politicians"—an opposition reduced to the circulation of free floating signifiers carefully detached from the social struggles that originated them. Given this dependence on the social movements, the power of spectacle should not be thought of as some massive conspiracy from above. Rather, as Raúl Zibechi has theorized in the rather disparate context of Argentina, this spectacle is the name for that place where the strategies of the capitalist relation, the "politics of the politicians," and the impasse of social movements meet in a particularly skewed relation of force. (The impasse of social movements should be thought of in relation to our own incapacity to fully discern the radical difference between visibility and power.)[1]

Thus, in order to better understand the "vampirization" of the social movements it could be said that if there was an encounter within the Obama camp, it was one premised, despite outward appearances, on the hierarchical subjugation of key elements of that relation, and is therefore an encounter based on sad passions rather than joyful affects. That is, it is difficult to conceive that it constitutes an encounter at all.

MH: I think it's important to keep in mind, even though it is not our primary concern here, that this spectacular form of rule as you describe it is not really advantageous for the Obama administration either. It is quite clear, as we have both said, that the Obama administration has not made space for or encouraged the movements. On the contrary, the governing strategy seems thus far to have been to quiet the movements and seek a national political consensus by appealing to the center and the right, negotiating with pharmaceutical and health insurance industries, for instance, in an effort to gain support for health care reform. That strategy of mediation has clearly not worked and, in fact, while quieting the movements on the Left, the government has opened the space for some very strange, sometimes crazy outbursts on the Right which often adopt, at least in appearance, the tactics of the Left. It seems to me that sooner or later the Obama administration will need the reactivated power of the movements to push its agenda forward. This is part of what I think of as a shift from government to governance. Conventional practices of government and strategies of sovereignty, in other words, which attempt to construct a stable center of rule, are no longer possible. Governance, in contrast, is more like surfing, unmoored from sovereign rule and forced constantly to ride the waves of a wide variety of forces and inputs. My point in this context is that governance is only possible with the movements, feeding off their power.

EK: *We couldn't agree more that the shift from sovereign rule to governance is exactly what is at stake in the Obama administration. Yet, we see no democratic tendency within that shift in and of itself; we see, rather, the necessity to adequate our strategy to the parameters of a new battlefield. We feel we must raise the question of whether the Obama administration constitutes a form of governance fully within the neoliberal capitalist paradigm, and thus that it is therefore still up to us to think of what a communist governance for our times might look like. It may sound paradoxical, but couldn't we say that the Obama campaign and administration constitute a form of governance if not exactly from above then certainly for above, and that the task of constituting a governance from below and for below is yet to come? For us it is important to take note that, unlike many of his 'progressive' supporters who firmly believed that they were participating in a progressive political 'movement,' Barack Obama has demonstrated himself to be acutely aware (as were his funders from finance, investment, and real estate) of the fact that his appeal is rather distant from political principal and instead lies squarely in the realm of a power made possible by the spectacular. As he has himself stated, "My treatment of the issues is often partial and incomplete," so that, in effect, "I serve as a blank screen, upon which people of vastly different political stripes [can] project their own views."[2] Given this situation and the overall subordination of the circulation of the spectacle to the stability and long term goals of contemporary capitalism, it can be no surprise that brand-Obama's "change" seems so uncomfortably similar to George W. Bush's status quo: the extreme exacerbation of inequality through the largest wealth transfer in the history of the United States (a wealth transfer that has disproportionately affected Blacks and Latinos), the continuation of the war in Iraq, the expansion of the war in Afghanistan into Pakistan, the obliteration of habeas corpus, the privatization of* *the public school system, the complete neutralization of the demand for universal healthcare, the continued existence of torture bases at Guantanamo and elsewhere, the expansion of military force throughout Latin America, the refusal to abandon the policy of secret detentions, the growth of the logic and presence of policing in the U.S. and the outrageous explosion of incarceration (again, disproportionately affecting the Black and Latino population), and... oh yeah, we almost forgot! Not a single word about a migratory amnesty for those who gave Obama his campaign slogan, but rather an expansion of the repressive deportation apparatus through the extended reach of '287(g).' From this perspective there can be little doubt that brand-Obama, its uncritical 'progressive' supporters, and the politics which they "re-present" constitute a direct obstacle to the radical transformation of our society. Given these effects, we are tempted to go so far as to say that both Bush II and brand-Obama constitute different moments within the unfolding of a much larger process of neoliberal spectacularity composed of self-reinforcing counter-images of "fear" and "hope." In this regard, the Spinozian analysis of encounter seems particularly useful. It is Spinoza who reminds us that both "hope" and "fear" are inextricable emotions that have no significance without the other: both arise as mere reactions to pain and therefore hinder our capacity to think and act (with hope constituting a sad-joyful passion and fear simply a sad passion) and thus to sustain active encounters.*

MH: Perhaps because of (or despite) the fact that the Obama election has not meant "change," at least so far, the movements find themselves in a kind of impasse or double-bind. During the eight years of the Bush government, the oppositional stance of the movements was unproblematic, at least at a conceptual level. It was not always clear what tactics would be most effective, but there was no question what and who we were against. With respect to the Obama administration, though, the movements need to invent a new approach and a new direction. On the one hand, Obama is not Bush and simple opposition is no longer adequate, especially when attacks on the government from the Right are increasingly intense. On the other hand, merely supporting the Obama team and trusting that they will represent us clearly won't get us far. The pressure will build on this impasse, for instance, over the war in Afghanistan, where U.S. military involvement seems likely to continue if not increase. The anti-war movements will have to reactivate, but with a new stance. Impasses like this, although on the surface seem to be defined by stasis or even paralysis, instead often constitute periods of great conceptual creativity. The movements need to invent a mode of operation that is neither simple opposition nor support but rather creates a lasting and autonomous force that can push and interact with the government.

It's interesting to think back again to when we were discussing these issues earlier. In the summer of 2008, at the time of the Democratic and Republican electoral Conventions, the need for and the direction of protest was clear. In the first year of the Obama government, there has been a feeling of disorientation, at least among certain sectors of the movements. But, as I said, such moments of impasse or even disorientation are not necessarily bad or unproductive. In fact, now is when reorientation and the invention of new directions can really take place.

EK: *We tend to agree on this last point, and, having laid out our position in the previous paragraphs, we want to insist that it is in no way meant to be a critique of Barack Obama. Such a critique would reduce our contemporary problem to the crisis of a given political representative when in fact we believe that it is at this very juncture, exactly after the heightened expectations* for "change" raised by the Obama campaign, that it is most obvious that we are today experiencing a crisis of the entire system of representational politics, of representativity. Thus, in our view, both those who would read the above lines and accuse us of playing into the strategy of the right wing by criticizing Obama as well as those that now dedicate endless pages to a critique of Obama share what is, in our eyes, a flawed premise: that it is in the arena of the given system of political representation and its legitimation through the electoral apparatus that "power," and therefore the future of the left, resides. Both positions fail to harness the massively raised expectations surrounding the election of Barack Obama in order to move us from an analysis centered around the crisis of representatives (Obama is better than Bush or alternatively, Obama is no better than Bush) toward actually coming to grips with the crisis of representativity and the urgent necessity of an alternative beyond it. In other words, neither position has recognized that it is not that we did not want the election of Barack Obama, but rather that we want and desperately need more than that election could ever provide. From our point of view, these expectations can only be met today by acting from (a different) power, a power that we simply do not have in the realm of the spectacle but which unquestionably exists beyond that realm (an insight that we owe to the many non-parliamentary movements of the 1960s and 1970s and of which we are constantly reminded by figures like Grace Lee Boggs). For El Kilombo then, the order of the day for the left (if one can be said to exist) is to pull the plug on the spectacle, to definitively alter the given relations of force between the strategies of capital, the "politics of the politicians," and the impasse of social movements in favor of the social movements themselves by building on the power of autonomy. As that excess of power that exists in our favor between the power of the spectacle and our own power to act beyond representation, autonomy cannot belong to the capitalist relation or the "politics of the politicians," but must be built through the establishment of a worldwide network for generalized convivial self-governance in which, as Malcolm would say, "everything that is done for us, is done by us!"

In our experience, such a network may arise from two key actions that we feel are inextricable and mutually reinforcing (therefore, we list them in no particular order). First, we need to directly challenge the State's monopoly on the provision of services (food, clothes, and shelter) which perhaps even more than violence keeps us at the mercy of the existing system of political representation, the extension of credit by the financial sector, and the unequal relations of force which they preserve. That is, we must first intervene beyond representation at the level of direct provision so as to allow ourselves a space to disengage from what in another discourse we might refer to as the reproduction of the existing relations of production. Second, we must understand that this intervention must go beyond mere survival through the provision of "things," as these are simply preconditions to a larger goal: the constitution of a new social fabric where new relations both to the earth and to each other are made possible. We might say then that this second task is the formation of an "ecology" of affects (equally beyond representation) which give us certain criteria for the selection of desires that in turn allow us to produce encounters based on joy and solidarity, beyond the sadness and social wasteland produced within the realm of the spectacle. This is an ecology which is absolutely necessary if we are to definitively move beyond what we believe is quickly becoming an increasingly devastating and desperate global dialectic between "hope" and "fear," a dialectic whose moment of synthesis can only be the event of our annihilation.

MH: This brings us back to the notion of two kinds of encounter and two kinds of event, but now the order is reversed. Earlier we were talking about how the specific and limited event-encounter at the actions surrounding the RNC and DNC could open up the possibility for the type of lasting, habituated encounters that involve the construction of territory, the creation of institutions, and the practices of autonomy. Now, it seems to me, in our discussion we are starting from this second notion of event-encounter, which serves, in part, as an antidote to spectacularlized politics and its regimes of representation, and recognizing the need to create or precipitate an event-encounter as rupture to break through the impasse and push forward the process. In the end, these two kinds of event and encounter are never very distant from each other, but neither are they the same thing. They are linked instead as poles of a relay in a movement that shuttles back and forth to open new possibilities.

NOTES

1   For more on this impasse, see "The Arts of Living in Common," HTTP://WWW.ELKILOMBO. ORG/THE-ARTS-OF-LIVING-IN-COMMON/.

2   Barack Obama, *The Audacity of Hope: Thoughts on Reclaiming the American Dream* (New York: Vintage, 2008).

LIVING IN A WHIRLWIND:

The Food/Energy/Work Crisis of 2008–09

Brian Marks

WE ARE LIVING IN A whirlwind. Like Dorothy in *The Wizard of Oz* looking out the window in the midst of a tornado, the past two years have seen daily economic life take on unfamiliar and bizarre forms, transforming the mundane into the unknown and alarming. Like Dorothy's schoolteacher transformed into a witch, things made monstrous spin around us—a world in which rice needs armed guards, money vanishes overnight to return shrunk by half the next morning on a red-eye from Dubai, cars eat food, people eat oil, and no one ever gets full. It all seems to be happening so fast and from one hundred places at once. To paraphrase Marx, rather than melting into air, all that was apparently solid has now been flung up into the air, and we are all along for the ride.

A WHIRLWIND TOUR OF THE GLOBAL CRISIS

THIS IS NOT THE FIRST time that the crisis of 2008 has been referred to as a "whirlwind." As the food crisis exploded in the spring of that year, the World Food Programme (WFP) announced that the world faces "a perfect storm" and a "silent tsunami" of hunger.[1] El Salvador's president claimed, "This scandalous storm might become a hurricane that could upset not only our economies but also the stability of our countries."[2] In Vietnam, one of many nations struck by a major inflationary shock accompanying the financial, food, and energy crises, newspapers reported the struggles of living in a "price storm."

World leaders were right to be worried. According to the Food and Agriculture Organization (FAO), the urban poor in dozens of countries in the Global South revolted against rising food prices in early and mid-2008.[3] Huge crowds of people demonstrated, blocked highways, ransacked food stores, and fought with police in major cities across the Global South.

State responses to explosions caused by food price hikes often took the form of repression, but this hardly contained the conflict. News of struggles over food circulated globally as fast as prices rose and virally through the mass media. Police raided television stations in Senegal that reported on food riots, in an attempt to prevent the circulation of images of the violence to other places where the tactics could be copied.[4] The scale and power of mobilizations have compelled some governments to reduce the price of food, largely by re-imposing subsidies and tariffs eliminated on the advice of foreign governments and banks. While the food riots were a sign of desperation and panic on the part of their participants, they were also a sign of those governments' weakness against the masses of urban poor to maintain the fiscal austerity measures they have implemented, under the guidance of the International Monetary Fund and other international financial institutions, since the 1980s.

Food-exporting countries were not immune to the crisis either. In Argentina, long-standing traditions of cattle and grain production were pushed aside for the monoculture of genetically-modified soybeans for export. Since the collapse of the Argentine economy in 2001, the largely urban population has suffered a decline in income and living standards; absurdly, widespread hunger has reappeared in a country that is one of the world's largest food producers. The 2008 food and energy shocks deepened these hardships, while the reformist Kirchner government sought to provide more aid to the urban majority by increasing the tax on soy exports, which at the time enjoyed a boom in prices and production. Soy production in the Southern cone of Latin America largely profits domestic oligarchs and international agribusiness, and big players in Argentina's soy industry were crucial backers of resistance to the tax that saw farmers blockading the highways into the capital city in February and March 2008, causing severe food shortages.[5] Yet most involved in the blockades were small farmers, who saw the tax as a last straw that would break their ability to survive.[6] Many rural farmers regard soy as a last refuge of viable production; they see the money from this tax going to Buenos Aires and not their rural provinces.

Meanwhile, oil companies and agribusiness continued to make even bigger money. In the first quarter of 2008 alone, Shell made a profit of $9.08 billion (a 25% increase); for BP, it was $7.62 billion (up 63%). Among the major food and grain multinationals, Cargill's 2007 profits were $2.3 billion (up 36% from 2006); ADM, $2.2 billion (up 67%); ConAgra, $764 million (up 30%); and Bunge, $738 million (up 49%).[7] In the late 2000s, high energy prices caused huge capital surpluses to pile up in oil exporting nations. In 2006 'petrodollars' made up about a third of net global capital outflows, and the oil money in the Persian Gulf countries' foreign investment holdings equaled $2 trillion.[8]

In Europe and North America, the food/energy crisis of 2008 was overshadowed by the near-simultaneous arrival of the financial and housing market crises, but still struck at many people's incomes and engendered notable, if largely ignored, resistance. Transport sector workers were among the most visible in the U.S. in confronting the Whirlwind (as were transport workers in other nations).[9] This includes a few in highly strategic workplace actions, like the West Coast dockworkers' union (the International Longshore and Warehouse Union) that shut down all Pacific Coast ports for May Day 2008, and the far more diffuse (but numerous) independent long-haul 18–wheeler truckers who bear rising energy costs more directly than any other sector of the American working class.

On April Fool's Day 2008, truckers coordinated their trucks into a diesel-powered Critical Mass on the nation's freeways, snarling traffic in several cities and disrupting business at ports by driving slowly and blocking lanes.[10] In April, there were slow-downs at the ports of Tampa, Florida and Savannah, Georgia, rallies at state capitols, and a national rally in Washington that included not just long-haul rigs, but also dump truck drivers from Washington, DC.[11] Word spread through websites, CB radio, and public gatherings, like those that a short-lived group called Truckers and Citizens United (TCU) held at truck stops around the country.[12] Truckers' tactics, using their means of production and the public highways to disrupt commodity circulation, were hard to counter.

The truckers' leaders expressed an understanding of their power to disrupt the economy—"If all the truckers decide to shut this country down, there's going to be nothing they can do about it"—and their interest in circulating the refusal of energy price hikes throughout the working class: "It's about everybody—the homeowners, the construction workers, the elderly people who can't afford their heating bills…. This is not the action of the truck drivers, but of the people."[13] TCU comprised an interesting mix of nationalist responses (meeting with politicians, boycotting Middle East oil) and radical responses (organizing a May Day drive-through of Manhattan with the Industrial Workers of the World) to the energy crisis. Demands included minimum rates sufficient to cover their costs, as well as:

- Immediate stoppage to the subsidies being given to big oil.
- A reduction in tax credits being given to big business.
- No selling out of Interstates to foreign countries like the Indiana toll road.
- Stop the NAFTA [North American Free Trade Agreement] Super Highway project … which will destroy the quality of this great nation.[14]

Somebody must have gotten nervous about this trajectory, because the permit for the truckers' May Day rally was canceled shortly before the action was to take place. Similar to the anti-nuclear movement in the 1970s, the resistance of a specific population to energy price hikes has the potential to circulate that refusal throughout the working class, remain isolated, or be co-opted by some aspect of capital and the state. Truckers have a very different class composition than the No Nukes movement, which was composed largely of rural New Englanders, particularly ex-urban intellectuals. In the case of No Nukes, its principal weakness was the lack of appeal to broader working class refusals of energy price hikes in the cities, opting instead for visions of solar employment and labor-intensive farm work.[15] That was not the issue here. The positions of the truckers in 2008 were generated out of their own everyday experiences, not by intellectual 'leaders,' and were decidedly Left Populist, more Huey Long than Glenn Beck. This illustrates how fickle ideological commitments can be, and how 'anti-big government' sentiment often barely conceals an equally strong 'anti-big business' undercurrent that Right commentators constantly downplay.[16]

As much as transportation workers represented a narrow but sharp edge of the American working class, class struggles in the U.S. hardly countered crises that hammered down incomes and standards of living for millions of Americans. One part of the world where such struggles were more effective in defending against the Whirlwind is East Asia.

The booming export-oriented economies of East Asia were not spared the Whirlwind or its aggravating effects on struggles. In China, Vietnam, India, and elsewhere, rampant inflation ate into factory workers' incomes. Waves of wildcat strikes erupted, many of them violent. In China, approximately 127,000 'mass incidents'—from riots and arson of police headquarters to petitioning and strikes—broke out in 2008, up 50% from an already huge number in 2004, challenging the authority of the state as well as the social stability and low labor costs transnational capital had come to expect from this new 'workshop of the world.' A similar trend occurred in Vietnam, where major industrial belts were paralyzed for weeks due to strikes in the garment, shipbuilding, and seafood sectors over unpaid wages, overtime, and working conditions. In both countries, the official unions and Party bureaucracies were almost completely impotent in containing workers made militant by rising costs of living.[17] However defensive and isolated these struggles may be in their specific manifestations, major concessions were made in many cases—so many that their collective effect was to drive the global circulation of inflation through the rising price of Asian manufacturing exports. It is unclear to what degree global capital or the global working class bore these costs; they were tossed among subcontractors in China, parent companies in Korea or Japan, retailers in the U.S. or Europe, and all the people who work or shop at these places. Wherever this inflationary hot-potato finally landed, industrial workers in East Asia were able to partially push the price spike off their backs and onto their employers through these struggles.[18]

While the forces behind this storm had been brewing and building for years, they accelerated in 2008 as the contagion of crisis infected every facet of life. Seemingly unrelated economic sectors and trends appeared to fuse together under the heat of crisis in a myriad of surprising and disturbing tele-connections and short-circuits. Images of nodding oil well heads and gas flares blurred with corn fields and grain silos, until it became increasingly impossible to know which was which. Bread lines in Cairo and Dakar jostled with the crowded floor of the Chicago Mercantile and New York Stock Exchange. A skyrocketing trend line could easily have been the rate of inflation in China, the number of home foreclosures in Arizona, the rice prices in Bangkok, or the soaring cost of a barrel of oil that seemed to cast its shadow over all. From the energy and food price spikes at the beginning of the year, to the food riots of April and May, to the financial panics of the fall and winter, the crisis proliferated like a political-economic pandemic across the world.

THE POLITICAL ECONOMY OF THE FOOD/ENERGY/WORK CRISIS

A CRISIS IS NEVER MERELY a matter of catastrophes and the responses that attempt to halt them and fix their damage. Crisis is also a form of planning or strategy. This is not to imply conspiracies or behind-the-scenes string-pulling, nor does it diminish the role of droughts, crop failures, real shortages of oil relative to demand, world population growth, or other factors in the contemporary crises. Crisis is strategic, because the way crises arise and are managed—which solutions are chosen and which are ignored—are not obvious or inevitable, but rather reflect the power and interests of the social, economic, and political forces involved.

We live in a world deeply marked by working-class struggles against capital for control over labor and the conditions under which it is performed. Capital is a political-economic system that derives profit from the unpaid and underpaid labor of the working class. The contemporary financial, food, and energy crises are all components of the struggle between the working class and capital.

How are food and energy implicated in class struggle? How are they implicated in each other? First, food and energy comprise a large part of the cost of getting us in shape to work on a daily, yearly, and lifelong basis, the 'reproduction of labor-power,' and thus society.[19] The gasoline we use to get to work, basic utilities, food we purchase, and a great deal of unwaged labor make up much of the cost of living and raising new workers. The cost of these articles is thus a crucial determinant of the cost to produce more labor-power and, consequently, of wages. Second, energy is productively consumed in almost every point of the production process. Energy is capital as pure motion and force, standing in for labor-power, multiplying the productivity of labor while shrinking the labor's share in the total value of production—what is known as relative surplus value.

When energy and food prices rapidly increase, they affect the distribution of surplus value between workers' wages, capital's profits, and rents to those who control resources.

The circulation of higher prices throughout the economy brings a greater overall rate of inflation and a widening divergence between money prices and the real value of commodities. This divergence of prices and values has very uneven sectoral effects. Rentiers such as food traders, land owners, and distributors of energy commodities gain a greater unearned share of the total social production, to the deficit of both capital and labor.[20]

Prices diverge from values not only under crisis conditions; this occurs normally in the capitalist economy, under the name "transformation of values into prices." It is accomplished through the transfer of value from the labor-intensive sectors—employing many workers and little machinery, physical plant, and raw materials, including energy—towards the capital-intensive ones, where labor is a tiny fraction of total investment.[21] Capital-intensive or 'high organic composition' industries produce little surplus value on their own; there is little labor present to produce that value. On the other hand, 'low organic composition' industries produce high rates of surplus.[22] It is through the circulation of commodities in the market that the rate of profit is generalized across all economic sectors. Prices of commodities from 'high' industries sell above their real value; commodities from 'low' sectors sell below their value. In effect, the highly capital-intensive industries suck up the high profits from the labor-intensive ones, making for an overall average rate of profit.[23] It is no coincidence that highly strategic energy, agribusiness (in the developed countries at least), and financial industries are among the most capital-intensive of all sectors, while the 'sweatshop' industries producing cheap consumer goods in the Global South and the 'flexibilized' and undocumented retailing and construction sectors in the North are among the most labor-intensive.

The effect of the crisis is to expand the difference between the high and low organic composition sectors of the economy, the 'squeezing' of the low sector caused by the divergence between prices and values. This concentrates economic power in the hands of finance and energy transnationals while intensifying exploitation of labor in low sectors, dispersing that exploitation more thoroughly in all facets of life. While the money is sweated from every pore of society through gas pumps, grocery aisles, and electric bills, it is being reinvested at the opposite end of the spectrum—in highly capital-intensive energy production like deep-sea oil and gas, nuclear power, as well as heavily subsidized biofuels, tar sands, and other forms of 'alternative' energy—or to shore up the tottering financial system. It's also appropriated by national states, in part to support those two objectives.

The most immediately visible outcome of the food/energy crisis is the effect on the cost of living. Workers' real incomes decline if costs of living rise more rapidly than wages. While this can instigate workers' struggles for higher wages to keep up with inflation, a more likely outcome is the erosion of the purchasing power of the wage, falling living standards, and the non-reproduction of labor-power. This can take the form of increasing debts, foreclosures, and erosion of savings in the U.S.; across much of the Global South, it looks like increasing hunger, deprivation, and death, forcing people off land into cities or abroad in search of work. Non-reproduction of labor-power goes hand in hand with the two previously mentioned consequences of the food/energy crisis, in that the surplus siphoned off to rents and high organic composition capital is, almost literally, the skin off the backs of the working class, as well as significant fractions of small business and labor-intensive industry. As in the so-called 'primitive accumulation' of capital, capital accumulation is accomplished in the present crisis through looting already-produced wealth, not production. In this sense, we cannot speak of capital in the Whirlwind as the 'expanded reproduction' of value, but as the cannibalistic looting of value from non-capitalist sectors—the reproduction of labor-power, the consumption fund derived from wages, accumulated savings, direct production for use, forms of wealth embodied in land and other fixed assets, and less strategically placed fractions of capital—by the 'commanding heights' of the energy and financial sectors.[24]

In a particularly perverse outcome, as profit opportunities in the stock and real estate markets declined, a great deal of finance capital was injected into the commodities market, which inflated food and energy prices an estimated additional 10–20%. Investments in commodities tripled from 2001 to 2008.[25] Here we see the pinnacle of the Whirlwind's logic—transforming food not only into energy, but into finance capital.

The financialization of food particularly harmed Mexico. Through NAFTA and government policies, Mexico opened itself to unlimited imports of maize, its staple food. Consolidation in the grain trading, tortilla manufacture, and grocery retail sectors followed, gaining greater market shares for transnational and national companies. The apparent manipulation of the market by these companies and a complacent or complicit government caused corn prices to jump 50% in three months in 2007, even though harvests were good and international prices stable.[26] In 2008, a rice crisis developed bearing many of the same marks, but affecting many more people.

In coastal industrial centers of China, where some 40% of an assembly worker's income goes to food, double-digit monthly increases in food prices in 2007–2008 meant that workers could no longer afford to live on their salary. Compounding this problem was widespread adulteration of ingredients by Chinese food companies, like the melamine-in-milk scare that killed many children. Chinese workers could afford to 'eat,' if that is the appropriate word, by unknowingly eating fictitious food. Melamine, the chemical at the heart of the biggest Chinese food scandal, is a plastic ingredient derived from petroleum; when added to milk, it boosts the apparent protein content, allowing watered-down milk to appear normal.[27] Ironically, and in keeping with the alchemical genius of the Whirlwind, people were, in effect, eating oil. Such are the creative frontiers of the non-reproduction of labor-power.

The food and energy crises are further interlinked because the price of food is, in large part, the price of energy. The cost of tractors, roto-tillers, water pumps, fertilizers, pesticides, and transport are generally a reflection of the cost of oil. With the development of bio-fuels, the circle is completed; energy can be conjured out of food as easily as food from energy, making the price of oil that much more of a global lever commanding the cost of living.

Food and energy hikes are the compulsion of work and the direct looting of workers' wealth by capital. Food riots, energy strikes, debt boycotts, demands for subsidies and wage increases, as well as autonomous production and distribution of energy, food, and credit are forms of worker refusal of this forced labor and pillaging. What is at stake is not just food, energy, or credit as such, but what lies behind them and all commodities: the struggle between labor and capital over social production. For these reasons, and because the commodities in crisis are the very raw materials for making labor-power, the present crisis is, at heart, a *work crisis*.

That is why I refer to the contemporary situation as the food/energy/work crisis, or simply, the Whirlwind—a simpler term that captures how these simultaneous crises have fused together into something larger, throwing all before it into confusion.

THE WHIRLWIND AND CLASS COMPOSITION

THE WHIRLWIND DOES NOT SIGNAL capital's unparalleled power, but rather the fact that it is in deep trouble. The entire structure of financialized capitalism remains vulnerable, despite bailouts implemented in late 2008, to a catastrophic devaluation akin to the Great Depression. In the U.S., public and private debt has increased seven-fold in the past quarter-century to more than triple the annual Gross Domestic Product, and is expected to expand at a faster pace over the next decade.[28] Other financial bubbles around the world have imploded regularly, from Eastern European and Icelandic banking sectors to the mirage of Persian Gulf real estate booms. Only massive lending and currency devaluation in China continues that country's overheated expansion; ballooning U.S. debt finances the country's tepid recovery while the dollar falls and crisis investments, like gold, continue to rise. The food and energy crises emerged at the inflection point between boom and bust, and although they were associated with the turbulence of those few months and years, they have not disappeared, and have only somewhat subsided. The number of hungry people worldwide remains at the level that provoked the riots of 2008. Energy prices, which fell dramatically in late 2008, have rebounded substantially and may go even higher. The crisis is far from over.[29]

It was not strength but desperation that compelled the Whirlwind. These crises are highly dangerous strategies of accumulation, because they directly challenge people's living standards (or their ability to live at all). The global coordination of energy and food prices and their circulation through almost every corner store, gas station, and kitchen on earth circulated resistance almost as efficiently, leading to the rapid recomposition of working class struggles globally around food and energy costs.

The class composition of the working class encompasses its diversity—including the division of labor between sectors, between waged and unwaged workers, differences of nationality, gender, age, sexuality, and legality, among others—and the degree of unity and power it is capable of exercising vis-à-vis capital. What people have in common is not the work they do, their normative politics, or their consciousness, but that they work and struggle against capital's appropriation of that work. To say the global working class partially recomposed itself—that is, strengthened its power—inside the Whirlwind doesn't mean everyone is receiving orders from a vanguard or following a common program. It means that struggles, in their varied and multiple forms, are taking on a more unified aspect that translates into greater working class power.

The Whirlwind has incurred various forms of resistance around the world. Capital and the state have, to varying degrees, been able to co-opt, repress, or make concessions to these struggles. Sometimes the crisis has aggravated contradictions among sections of the working class—between food and energy producers and consumers, or between country and city. In this sense, crisis has furthered the decomposition of the working class. Where struggles against the crisis have accomplished increasing concordance of action across a widening diversity of the class, the effect has been class recomposition.

Capital first brought on the Whirlwind to save itself by imposing crisis on the global working class.[30] We lack ruby slippers to whisk us back to different times, before it carried us aloft. But if this tornado has flung the house of humanity up into the sky, we also possess the power to land that house squarely on capital's head.[31]

THE FOOD/ENERGY/WORK CRISIS, THE 1970S/80S CRISIS, AND THE NEOLIBERAL INTERIM

IN MANY WAYS, WE'VE BEEN here before—specifically, during the energy crisis of 1973–1982 and its accompanying food crisis, although the causal factors are not the same.[32] The main impetus of the last energy crisis was neither an Arab oil embargo nor inherent 'limits to growth,' as is often argued. Rather, working-class wage, welfare, and development offensives dried up profits and threatened capitalist control of production. Energy crisis, then as now, is a symptom of a crisis in accumulation and a means of overcoming it by 'recycling' value back into capital through higher prices, but it was deployed in the 1970s oil shocks in a very different context. Energy prices acted to undermine centers of worker militancy in assembly-line industries and inner cities, for example the de-industrialization of the 'Rust Belt' and the federal government's refusal to bail out New York City during its fiscal crisis in the 1970s.

Another result was the concentration of capital into higher organic composition sectors—especially energy and information technology—and its geographic shift to the Sun Belt and Global South, seeking to counter the wage offensive and restore profits by re-centering accumulation on new industries and more compliant workers elsewhere. Energy prices fell sharply during the 1980s as capital shifted to a strategy of financialization, deregulation, and more aggressive globalization that led up to the current global financial crisis.[33]

The greatest growth in the American economy since the end of the last energy crisis has been in finance. Since the 1970s, the finance industry has introduced hedge funds, credit default swaps, sub-prime mortgages, and so on. These new kinds of securities deliver high returns but also bring unpredictable risks. Indeed, they have become so complex that the heads of the banks selling and buying them apparently don't know how they work.[34] These new kinds of instruments reflect the ongoing 'financialization' of capital—the ever-greater gulf between ballooning investment in fictitious capital and stagnating real long-term economic growth.[35] The devaluation of all this funny money has been a long time coming; the current devaluation spread first from the paper values held by mortgage lenders to their banking partners, then to major international investment houses whose assets evaporated overnight. The stability of the entire global financial system came into question, provoking massive bailouts around the world.

The median real wage of American workers held steady during the energy crisis years. However, from around 1980 through the 2000–2007 'Bush boom' years preceding the current crises, median U.S. wages actually fell in terms of real value. The restructuring of the American working class gutted the manufacturing sector and boosted retail, construction, and technology, reflecting the growing capital-intensivity and internationalization of production on one end of the organic composition spectrum, and the development of new 'pink-collar' and casualized labor-intensive sectors on the other.

So it seemed that capital had definitively won the class war, overcoming all barriers to its global circulation and restructuring every locality in its image. Yet at the peak of the boom in the mid-2000s, as the storm clouds of the Whirlwind were gathering, there was a marked increase in struggles worldwide. The upsurge was led by young, precarious workers that occupied the basement floors of the global accumulation pyramid. They used the tight labor markets of the boom period to accelerate their demands. Their struggles would carry forward into the 2008–2009 crisis.

STRUGGLES IN THE RUN-UP TO THE WHIRLWIND

CONSIDER THE ACTIONS OF U.S. undocumented workers, high school students, and independent truck drivers in 2005–06. In 2005, the Sensenbrenner immigration bill looked like it was going to become law; this bill would have intensified the precariousness of undocumented workers in the U.S., who were gaining power in access to public services, workers' rights, and bargaining power in the period of the housing boom. In 2006, apparently from nowhere and spreading through networks of local organizers, radio stations, and word of mouth, the 'sleeping giant' appeared on the streets of cities where marches of any size, never mind general work stoppages, are hardly normal: 100,000 in Phoenix, more than 300,000 in Dallas. The mega-marches drew huge crowds of people across immigrant communities and beyond. The movement jumped into the high schools, where tens of thousands abandoned classes to join marches or start their own, angry about the dead-end of education for undocumented teenagers and, more generally, to escape temporarily from an education that is, by and large, the imposition of unwaged labor preparing people for a lifetime of imposed waged labor. One element of the Great Strike of 2006 was the shutdown of the Los Angeles port on May 1st by short haul *trocquervs* over soaring diesel prices, flat wages, and immigration raids. The strike was a continuation of *trocquero* wildcats in the two previous years at major ports.[36]

In the U.S., the mega-marches spread from L.A. to become a national movement, and from adult blue-collar working class to high school students, but remained isolated from more stably-employed and legal parts of American class composition, many of whom saw their falling wages and growing indebtedness as the fault of immigrant workers. The slogan "No work—no school—no selling—no buying" and its infectious spread compelled the government to back down from the Sensenbrenner bill, but the movement was unable to transpose its defensive victory onto objectives like amnesty and citizenship for undocumented people. The role of transportation workers in the movement parallels truckers' actions in 2008, but the hostility of the majority of U.S. truckers to Mexican transport workers over the NAFTA-imposed entry of Mexican trucks to U.S. highways means class composition in the potentially powerful transport sector remains divided and weakened.

East Asia became the global manufacturing center in the capitalist expansion between the energy crisis of the 1970s and the present crisis. Accumulation centered on the circuit between U.S. finance and Asian consumer goods exports. The foundations of this trans-Pacific circuit included cheap food and energy, thereby reducing costs of industrial production and reproduction of labor-power. An expensive dollar fueled a consumption and debt boom in the U.S.; this debt was bought up by those same East Asian states that supplied the exports, completing the circuit.

U.S. debt financed new highways, hotels, and industrial parks in Asia, while the primitive accumulation of land, labor, and resources discounted the cost of reproducing laborers and the means of production. In recent decades, approximately 120 million Chinese people moved from the countryside to join the floating population of industrial workers. This was due to widening income inequality between urban and rural areas as well as the combined burdens of low agricultural prices, high taxes, and land confiscation faced by farmers.[37]

It seemed this circuit would go on forever, but in 2006, we started to hear about the Chinese 'labor shortage.'[38] This might seem contradictory: a labor shortage in the world's most populous country, with millions of people pouring off of farms and out of downsized state enterprises every year. *Business Week* translated the enigma, arguing that the problem is that "managers can no longer simply provide eight-to-a-room dorms and expect laborers to toil 12 hours a day, seven days a week." Labor shortage, decoded, is a weakening of capitalist command over the labor force. It is the refusal of Chinese workers to bear the dispossession that drives migration to the cities and coastal provinces, as well as the barracks housing and poor food awaiting them upon arrival.

One factor in this refusal is the resistance by farmers and workers to what might be called 'primitive accumulation with Chinese characteristics'—unpaid wages, land seizures, sacking of state-owned enterprise workers through privatization, police harassment of informal-sector workers, and recent increases in transport costs. The Chinese government estimated that there were 74,000 mass incidents in 2004, a four-fold increase from a decade before.[39] In order to counter these refusals and rebellions, new subsidies were extended to farmers, which had the effect of slowing down rural-to-urban migration. This shrinking reserve army of new laborers made it harder to check the growing wage struggles of workers in the boom years when labor markets were in workers' favor.

Chinese workers face a major obstacle to generalizing their struggles. Any autonomous organization of workers results in police repression. However, for their employers, these small scale actions compounded into an attack on their profit margins waged on a nationwide scale. Employers have also been unable to translate rising wages into productivity increases to recover their profitability, leading multinationals to seek even lower wages in inland China, Vietnam, and Indonesia.[40]

But even as capital runs from the 'People's Republic' of China to the 'Socialist Republic' of Vietnam, it is finding an equally hostile reception to sub-survival wages. Wildcat strikes have followed manufacturers seeking low labor costs and a 'China+1' site to offset their dependence on that country. Before the full onslaught of the present crisis, a nationwide strike surge in 2007 and rising inflation pushed the Vietnamese government to raise the minimum wage by 12% overall and 25% in the foreign-owned, export-oriented sector.[41] As the food/energy crisis of 2008 hit, the wildcat strike movement was well-established, showing its ability to push back against the inflationary erosion of buying power of industrial workers' wages.

Globally, the mid-2000s saw the revolt of young, marginalized workers in major cities. From France in late 2005 came the wave of arson and rioting instigated by young, under- or illegally employed immigrant workers—first surrounding Paris, then throughout the country. The next summer saw the revolt of high school and university students against the CPE law that would further casualize their work and drive down pay for jobs that already offered no advancement or decent standard of living. The CPE law was scrapped following the occupation of a great many schools, and several huge demonstrations and strikes across the country that enjoyed popular support, unlike the 2005 riots that largely provoked fear and concern among most people (encouraged by the state and media).

There were major strike actions elsewhere in these years, like the wildcat strike waves that struck the garment sector of Bangladesh in May 2006.[42] The Greek cycle of struggles that exploded in 2008 was initiated in 2006 by an attempted university reform to orient education to the job market, cut scholarships and other supports, and end the sanctuary status of the universities from the police. This led to a huge mobilization of students, the occupation of two-thirds of university departments, and the postponement of the reforms.[43]

Latin America in 2006 saw the expansion of a 'Bolivarian Crescent' into Bolivia and Ecuador, the 'ungovernability' of Southern Mexico, and the evolution of 'dual power' in Venezuela.[44] In Venezuela, both the opposition and the state capitalist *Boli-burgesia* (Bolivarian bourgeoisie) is being contested, sometimes outside of legal and institutional structures and sometimes within them, by those same masses of precariously waged people who initiated riots against the International Monetary Fund in 1989, launching a cycle of struggles that brought Chavez into power and reinstated him after the 2002 coup attempt.

What we can learn from the wave of revolt that circled the world at mid-decade is that the struggles against the crisis of 2008 were shaped by prior movements that transpired as the 2000s boom overheated. Those struggles left their mark on the Whirlwind and resistance to it. Many of the same demographic groups (the young and the precariously waged) that waged offensive struggles in 2005–06 were at the forefront of defensive struggles in 2008–09. Where class recomposition developed most strongly during the boom, as in East Asia, workers were more capable of defending themselves in the bust, and where class decomposition was more pronounced, as in the U.S., struggles against the food/energy crisis were more isolated and less successful.

AFTER THE STORM

IT'S UNCLEAR WHERE ALL OF this activity is heading. This food/energy crisis is not just the farcical remix of a 1970s disco-beat of tragedy. Nor will reciting the 'capitalist crisis leads to inter-imperialist rivalry leads to global war leads to revolution' mantra demystify events any more than it can animate Lenin's taxidermied body. What is sure is that wherever the Whirlwind leaves us, it will be a confusing and disorienting landscape that will have to be carefully assessed. The tools of class composition analysis and militant research, some of which are modeled in this volume, are a good place to begin mapping class composition and plotting a course towards recomposition.[45]

The varied geography of the global working class and its struggles in the Whirlwind have already shaped what may come next. The Chinese proletariat's recent explosiveness scared that country's rulers into throwing considerable sums of money at problems of unemployment, rural poverty, and corruption. Now, in 2010, the Chinese economy is growing rapidly on a shaky scaffolding of credit drawn down from foreign exchange reserves that may pop like other bubbles have in recent years, likely bringing a new wave of revolt and instability to China and decapitating any Asia-led recovery from the crisis.[46]

Greece, the site of the greatest anti-capitalist revolt of 2008—where massive property destruction was inflicted on posh department stores, banks, and government buildings following the police murder of a youth—has in 2009 seen the occupation of hundreds of high schools and universities across the country by students and other young people protesting the neoliberal gutting of education and work. This situation is compounded by the government's massive foreign debts to pay for a state bureaucracy, as well as transfer payments that barely contain further explosions by greater swathes of the Greek populace. If the Greek debt bubble of $200 billion defaults, the country may move into a situation of ungovernability and dual power with the potential for profound political change: perhaps the spread of the movement to other EU countries, or perhaps its isolation, repression, and austerity.

The most prominent class recomposition among Americans in 2009 has been the Right regrouping of white, middle-aged, small business and independent workers and their attempted folding into electoral politics by the Republican Party. The failure of the Left to communicate with or organize these (nominally) culturally conservative but potentially economically populist people will mean the deepening of class decomposition in the U.S. along racial and geographic lines, as well as the channeling and negation of working class energies away from economic struggles. Movements of public university and high school students against budget cuts and tuition hikes saw some significant mobilizations in 2009, especially in California. Yet it is unclear how those movements will act following the imposition of cuts, or if they can make linkages across and among campuses, or if they will connect up with other movements, such as the immigrant rights movement of 2006 that also developed power in the high schools and posed access to higher education as one of its issues.

If we can imagine the recomposition of the global working class within the swirling eddies of the Whirlwind or the calm of its aftermath, we might find a North American trucker (either the redneck or *trocquero* variety), meeting up with a factory worker from Ho Chi Minh City, sharing a cup of tea with an African street vendor. While none lack brains, courage, or a heart, each of their struggles lacks something which the others can contribute. In their encounter within the circuits of the crisis, they possess the power to transform themselves, and in so doing, transform our world. We must all start walking from where we find ourselves, though, in order to make the path to each other while walking it.[47]

NOTES

1   World Food Programme, "WFP says high food prices are a silent tsunami, affecting every continent,"April 22, 2008, HTTP://WWW.WFP.ORG/ENGLISH/?MODULEID=137&KEY=2820; Julian Borger, "Feed The World? We Are Fighting a Losing Battle, UN Admits," *The Guardian (UK)*, February 26, 2008, HTTP://WWW.GUARDIAN.CO.UK/ENVIRONMENT/2008/FEB/26/FOOD. UNITEDNATIONS.

2   Marc Lacey, "Across Globe, Empty Bellies Bring Rising Anger," *New York Times*, April 18, 2008.

3   Thalif Deen, "Global Hot Spots of Hunger Set to Explode," *Inter Press Service*, April 15, 2008.

4   Lacey, "Across Globe, Empty Bellies."

5   For more on soy production in the Southern Cone of Latin America, see the website La Soja Mata (Soybeans Kill): HTTP://WWW.LASOJAMATA.ORG.

6   Maria Trigona, "Argentina's Soy Storm: Tensions Rising Among Farmers," *Upside Down World*, April 28, 2008, HTTP://UPSIDEDOWNWORLD.ORG/MAIN/CONTENT/VIEW/1253/1.

7   Julia Werdigier, "Record Profits Reported for BP and Shell," *New York Times*, April 30, 2008; Steven Weisman, "Oil Producers See the World and Buy It Up," *New York Times*, November 28, 2007.

8   GRAIN, "Making a Killing from Hunger," April 28, 2008, HTTP://WWW.GRAIN.ORG/ARTICLES/?ID=39.

9   Mneesha Gellman and Josh Dankoff, "Rising Fuel Costs Provoke Transportation Strike in Nicaragua," *Upside Down World*, May 12, 2008; Reuters, "Fuel Protests Spread, China to Increase Prices," *New York Times*, June 19, 2008.

10 Barbara Ehrenreich, "Truckers Hit the Brakes," *The Nation*, April 8, 2008.

11 Clarissa Kell-Holland, "Demands for Action on Fuel Prices Gain Momentum," *Land Line Magazine*, April 7, 2008, HTTP://WWW.LANDLINEMAG.COM/TODAYS_NEWS/DAILY/2008/APR08/040708/040708–01.HTM.

12 Barbara Ehrenreich. "Truckers Take Their Case to the Capitol," *The Nation*, April 29, 2008.

13 Ehrenreich, "Truckers Hit the Brakes."

14 Frederick Schaffner, "Truckers and citizens united—goals," HTTP://WWW.THEAMERICANDRIVER.COM/FILES/WP/LONG_TERM_GOALS.HTML (accessed May 5, 2008).

15 Midnight Notes Collective, "Strange Victories," Midnight Notes Collective eds.,1979, HTTP://WWW.MIDNIGHTNOTES.ORG/PDFSTRANGVICO.PDF; Midnight Notes Collective, "No Future Notes: the Work/Energy Crisis & The Anti-Nuclear movement," Midnight Notes eds., 1980, HTTP://WWW.MIDNIGHTNOTES.ORG/WORKENERGYNOFUTURE.HTML.

16 The Left scarcely picks up on this undercurrent due to urbane and shallow cultural biases against fractions of the American working class in the Midwest, South, and Mountain West.

17 Ian Johnson, "China Sees Protest Surge by Workers," *Wall Street Journal*, July 10, 2009; China Labour Bulletin, "Going it Alone: The Workers' Movement in China (2007–2008)," HTTP://WWW.CLB.ORG.HK/EN/NODE/100507 (July 9, 2009); Human Rights Watch, "Not yet a Workers' Paradise: Vietnam's Suppression of the Independent Workers' Movement" (New York: Human Rights Watch, 2009).

18 Keith Bradsher, "Inflation in Asia Begins to Sting U.S. Consumers," *New York Times*, April 8, 2008; Keith Bradsher, "Booming China Suddenly Worries That a Showdown Is Taking Hold," *New York Times*, August 5, 2008.

19 Katharyne Mitchell, Sallie Marston, and Cindi Katz, eds., *Life's Work: Geographies of Social Reproduction* (Oxford: Wiley-Blackwell, 2004).

20 Renfrew Christie, "Why Does Capital Need Energy?" and Mohssen Massarrat, "The Energy Crisis: The Struggle for the Redistribution of Surplus Profit from Oil" in *Oil and Class Struggle*, eds. Petter Nore and Terisa Turner, (London: Zed Press, 1980), 10–25, 26–68.

21 Karl Marx, *Capital: Volume Three* (London: Penguin Classics, 1991), 241–301.

22 David Rigby, "The Existence, Significance, and Persistence of Profit Rate Differentials," *Economic Geography* 3, no. 67(1991): 210–222; Gerard Dumenil and Dominique Levy, "The Profit Rate: Where and How Much did it Fall? Did it Recover? (USA 1948–2000)," *Review of Radical Political Economics*, no. 34 (2002): 437–461.

23 George Caffentzis, "The Work-Energy Crisis and the Apocalypse," in *Midnight Oil: Work, Energy, War, 1973–1992*, eds. Midnight Notes Collective (Boston: Autonomedia, 1992), 215–271 is the inspiration for this analysis.

24 For a more thorough explanation of non-capitalist economic sectors in the contemporary world economy, see J.K. Gibson-Graham, *A Post-Capitalist Politics* (Minneapolis: University of Minnesota Press, 2006), 53–100.

25 Diana Henriques, "Commodities: Latest Boom, Plentiful Risk," *New York Times*, March 20, 2008.

26 Ana de Ita, "Fourteen Years of NAFTA and the Tortilla Crisis," Americas Program and Center for International Policy, January 10, 2008, HTTP://AMERICAS.IRC-ONLINE.ORG/AM/4879.

27 Associated Press, "China's 'Out of Control' Dairy System Led to Abuse," September 23, 2008; David Barboza, "China's Dairy Farmers Say They Are Victims," *New York Times*, October 4, 2008.

28 Kevin Phillips, *Bad Money: Reckless Finance, Failed Politics, and the Global Crisis of American Capitalism* (New York: Viking, 2008).

29 Neil MacFarquhar, "Food Experts Worry as World Population and Hunger Grow," *New York Times*, October 22, 2009; Tom Raum, "Guess who Pays? Rising U.S. Debt may be Next Crisis," *Associated Press*, July 5, 2009; Andy Xie, "Insight: Is China due a reality check?," *Financial Times*, October 15, 2009; Javier Hernandez, "Stirred by a Weakening Dollar, Markets Rise," *New York Times*, November 12, 2009.

30 This act was not conceived in some smoke-filled, monocular-viewed room but, like most things in history, was birthed of the convergence of social forces and a bit of chance, as partially narrated here.

31 'Humanity' here should be understood as the breadth of global class composition in the fullness of its diversity, in possession of dignity, and against neoliberalism, as explained in The Zapatistas, *Zapatista Encuentro: Documents from the Encounter for Humanity and against Neoliberalism* (New York: Seven Stories Press, 1998).

32 Harry Cleaver, "Food, Famine, and the International Crisis," 1977, available online at: HTTP://WWW.LIBCOM.ORG/FILES/FOOD_FAMINE_INT_CRISIS.PDF.

33 Midnight Notes Collective, *Midnight Oil: Work, Energy, War, 1973–1992*, eds. Midnight Notes Collective (Brooklyn: Autonomedia, 1992).

34   David Leonhardt, "Can't Grasp Credit Crisis? Join the Club," *New York Times*, March 19, 2008.

35   Harry Shutt, *The Trouble with Capitalism: An Inquiry into the Causes of Global Economic Failure* (London: Zed Books, 1998).

36   Chris Kutalik, "As Immigrants Strike, Truckers Shut Down Nation's Largest Port on May Day," *Counterpunch*. June 2, 2006, HTTP://WWW.COUNTERPUNCH.ORG/KUTALIK06022006.HTML.

37   Ching Kwan Lee and Mark Selden, "China's Durable Inequality: Legacies of Revolution and Pitfalls of Reform," *Japan Focus*, January 24th, 2007, via *Znet*, HTTP://WWW.ZCOMMUNICA-TIONS.ORG/ZNET/VIEWARTICLE/2227.

38   David Barboza, "Shortage of Cheap Labor in China," *International Herald Tribune*, April 3, 2006; Dexter Roberts, "How Rising Wages Are Changing The Game In China," *Business Week*, March 27, 2006.

39   John Gulick, "Insurgent Chinese Workers and Peasants: The 'Weak Link' in Capitalist Globalization and U.S. Imperialism," in Eddie Yuen, Daniel Burton-Rose, and George Katsiaficas eds. *Confronting Capitalism: Dispatches from a Global Movement* (Brooklyn: Soft Skull Press, 2004), 292–306; Libcom.org, "20,000 Farmers and Workers Riot in China," March 12, 2007, HTTP://LIBCOM.ORG/NEWS/20–000–FARMER-WORKERS-RIOT-CHINA-12032007.

40   Keith Bradsher, "Investors Seek Asian Options to Costly China," *New York Times*, June 18, 2008.

41   Jeff Ballinger, "Squeezed Vietnamese Workers Strike Back," *Counterpunch*, April 16, 2008, HTTP://WWW.COUNTERPUNCH.ORG/BALLINGER04162008.HTML.

42   Wildcat, "Another paradise lost: Strikes and riots in the Export Zones of Vietnam and Bangladesh," *Prol-Position News* 6, 2006, HTTP://WWW.PROL-POSITION.NET/NL/2006/06/VIETNAM.

43   TPTG, "Greek student movement: A brief outline of the student movement in Greece, June 2006," *Prol-Position* #7 (2006), HTTP://WWW.PROL-POSITION.NET/NL/2006/07/GREEK.

44   George Ciccariello-Maher, "Dual Power in the Venezuelan Revolution," *Monthly Review* 59, no. 4, (2007): 42–56; Caiman del Barrio, "Tropical Waterfight: the Struggle for Basic Services in Caracas, Venezuela," Libcom.org, October 28, 2009, HTTP://LIBCOM.ORG/BLOG/TROPICAL-WATERFIGHT-STRUGGLE-BASIC-SERVICES-CARACAS-VENEZUELA-28102009.

45   In another recent article I sketch out the history and geography of autonomist Marxism in relation to the present crisis, giving more context on these methodologies, their origins, and capitalist crisis past and present. See: Brian Marks, "Autonomist Marxist Theory and Practice in the Current Crisis," *ACME: An International E-journal for Critical Geographies*, 2002, 9, no. 2.

46   David Harvey, "Why the U.S. Stimulus Package is Bound To Fail," blog post, February 2009, HTTP://DAVIDHARVEY.ORG/2009/02/WHY-THE-US-STIMULUS-PACKAGE-IS-BOUND-TO-FAIL/; Ian Johnson, "China Sees Protest Surge by Workers," *Wall Street Journal* July 10, 2009; Paul Krugman, "Chinese New Year," *New York Times*, January 1, 2010.

47   Paraphrasing: Myles Horton and Paolo Friere, *We Make the Road by Walking: Conversations on Education and Social Change*, eds. Brenda Bell, John Gaventa, and John Peters (Philadelphia: Temple University Press, 1990); and the Zapatista slogan "Walking, We ask Questions" as mentioned in: *Notes from Nowhere, We are Everywhere: The Irrestistible Rise of Global Anti-capitalism* (London: Verso, 2003).

NOTES ON THE FINANCIAL CRISIS:

From Meltdown to Deep Freeze

George Caffentzis[1]

T HESE NOTES WERE INSPIRED BY the political-financial crisis (often called the "Wall Street Meltdown") in September of 2008, when many U.S. financial corporations were, in effect, nationalized—some temporarily, some to this day—in response to the bankruptcy of several major investment and commercial banks. They were also prompted by the fact that, for a year after the "meltdown," there has been remarkably little political activity in the streets, union halls, or retirement communities of the U.S. demanding a resolution of the crisis in favor of the millions who are losing wages, houses, and pensions.

There are many ways of explaining this deep freeze. But one factor might be that money and the financial sector of capitalism that deals directly with it have been inherently opaque to working class political analysis and action for more than a century. (Although workers are often obsessed by money or the lack thereof, the last time there occurred a self-conscious working class debate on a national level concerning the money form was the 1896 election, when the fate of money hung on "a cross of gold.") Ironically, the time lag between capital's large-scale financial action and the proletarian response is increasing in this era, when financial information and transactions circulate at light speed. This lag gives a sense of the sluggishness of contemporary class struggle.

The purpose of these notes is to present a way of understanding this crisis as developing out of class struggles taking place in the U.S. and internationally in the last decade. I believe this can be useful, for if class struggles had the power to create the crisis, then understanding them might guide us to the path that would lead out of the crisis with more class power. This maxim is not mine alone, of course. It has constituted the web of continuity of the political projects my comrades and I have been weaving since the early 1970s, especially in the journal *Zerowork* and later with the Midnight Notes Collective.

These notes also constitute a methodological experiment. I want to see how far the interpretation of the Marxian categories of value, surplus value, profit, interest, and rent that my comrades and I have developed over the last forty years can be used to understand the present crisis. At the moment, most methodological experiments emerging from anti-capitalist mental labs tend to stretch Marx's basic categories beyond their elastic limit: declaring the end of value, identifying finance and industrial capital, or conflating rent and profit.[2] I am assuming here the continued functioning of Marx's categories and distinctions in contemporary capitalism, including the transformation of surplus value into profit, interest, and rent (although I, too, do some "stretching" of these categories).

I recognize that these notes might look like dry stuff from the outside, but I have three things to say about their style. First, the contents of this analysis—however dry—concern the fates of millions of people, including ourselves. Secondly, the pace of this analysis is deliberate; I walk one step at a time, slowing down the speed of thought concerning this crisis in order to combat the artificial acceleration it has been imbued with. Third, I neither take on an 'apocalyptic' tone nor open up a sweeping historical perspective—however tempting these rhetorical options are in crisis situations—because I do not pretend to anticipate the contours of the struggle to come.

1. FINANCIAL CRISES ARE DIFFICULT to understand from the point of view of average class politics, for the standard Marxist model of class struggle to this day is still the factory, farm, and office, where the workers' labor power is bought—through the payment of a wage—by capitalist firms and put to work, along with machines and other inputs, to produce a product that is sold for a profit. Workers are worked harder, longer, more dangerously, and more 'productively' in order to make a larger profit. They respond to this work regime by a combination of means, from compliance, to a thousand-and-one ways of passive resistance, to strikes and factory takeovers, while capitalists devise strategies to resist this resistance. This struggle can take a myriad of forms, sometimes involving the most refined application of social and psychological sciences, and sometimes the most brutal forms of assassination and torture, but the factory-office-farm model is categorically straightforward: waged workers resist exploitation and capitalists resist their resistance, with profits and wages most often moving inversely. It is apparently simple, but it can become complex because in struggle, there are many deceits and tricks each side plays on each other as well as on observers, both present and future.

When it comes to money and the financial corporations that operate with it—banks, mortgage loan corporations, hedge funds, and other money market firms—this model of class struggle does not seem to operate. Why? There are at least four primary reasons.

First, money is quite a different 'product' than physical things such as cars, services like massages, or paradigms like software programs. Money is a bit mysterious. Words that combine the philosophical and necromantic like "magical," "abstract," "fetishistic," and "universal" are often used to describe money, immediately giving the impression that, compared to other commodities, the usual rules do not apply. For example, money is a unique kind of commodity that exchanges with all other commodities, a role that no other commodity plays. By calling money a "commodity," I do not mean that it is a physical thing, as it was during the era of precious metal coinage that stretched from Lydia (in contemporary Turkey) in the seventh century B.C. to the twentieth century A.D. But contemporary money is exchanged by the hundreds of billions of dollars a day, it is bought and sold, it is loaned, and it accumulates. Since it walks and talks like a commodity, for our purposes, it *is* a commodity.

Second, while industrial firms require the production and sale of a non-monetary commodity in order to 'make money,' financial firms make 'money from money.' They seem to operate in an abstract realm without a spatial location, or, if they do locate in a huge metropolis like New York or London, they make the city itself abstract.[3] This adds to the weirdness of the financial firms that, during the history of capitalism, have always attracted both fascination and hostility from other capitalists and workers. "We work so hard for our money," the workers and industrial capitalists say—with different meanings of work, of course—while they imagine the money-people literally creating money by some nefarious scheme or other.

Third, the financial capitalists claim a different form of income than other capitalists and workers: interest. When it comes to making money, they make it in the form of interest on loans to capitalists, who pay interest out of 'their' profits, and workers, who pay interest out of 'their' wages. In other words, the value financial firms 'make' through money lending is created 'elsewhere' by those who work for non-financial capitalists. The workers of the financial firms themselves may be exploited—being forced to work long hours and getting paid in worthless stock bonuses—but the income that the firms' owners receive does not derive from these employees' efforts in producing a product. Its value comes from the profits and wages of those who received loans, who are, in most cases, not their employees.

Where does the 'right' to earn interest come from? How is it determined? These kinds of questions haunt our understanding of financial firms, since it appears that in a society where work is the source of value, interest appears to be a "creation out of nothing"!

There are two aspects of capitalism that should be remembered at this juncture. First, it is a system of continual transformations and conversions, so that at the end of a cycle, there is no direct connection between the creation of surplus value and its appearance. Secondly, surplus value is an un-owned creation of the system; it is only when it is transformed into profit, interest, and rent that it appears as a value that is owned by individuals or firms. It is one of the great ironies of history that capitalism—the moral system of greed and "mine-ness"—is actually founded on the creation of a common pool of value that is shared by those most protective of private property.[4] This aspect of capitalism is now being recognized in the work on the "embeddedness" of the economy in relations of trust and in the importance of "social capital."[5]

The fourth difficulty in the typical class struggle scenario is that 'financialization' adds a new twist to the story. Financialization is a term with multiple meanings that is now used to mark the fact that, in this historical period, finance capital has played new roles in addition to its traditional one. This change has been widely recognized in the Left—from the *Monthly Review* perspective, which baptizes this period as one of "Monopoly-Finance Capital," to the autonomist Marxist views of Antonio Negri, Michael Hardt, and Christian Marrazi, all of whom have different emphases.[6] One thing is certain: financial capital firms are no longer serving just their traditional functions of pooling together money capital and either lending it to corporations, or giving investors an alternative short-term road to profit when the average rate of profit begins to decline in the industrial production.

What are these new functions, and what are their sources? Some see this novelty as part of an increasing immateriality of contemporary capitalism, where the 'money of the mind' begins to substitute for both money and the mind. However, I trace this novelty to the need for a new tool of control, once structural adjustment programs (SAPs) operated by state and international agencies like the International Monetary Fund and World Bank, as well as war, reach their limits.

The emergence of financialization indicates that capitalists have found a way to get their problems solved through the invention of new roles for money. As with so much else in capitalist society, financialization is a process that takes a different form when directed to workers or to capitalists: (a) financialization provides protection to investors through hedge funds and derivatives, indicating that the level of uncertainty has increased due to the higher level of resistance; (b) financialization allows for aggressive war against governments by monetary means; (c) financialization undermines workers' struggles. It describes a situation where capital is able to move freely from country to country, hence intimidating governments, and even more importantly, putting struggles on their knees. This can be seen in South Korea during the 'Asian financial crisis' in the mid-1990s, when the South Korean workers' struggle was halted in its tracks by the financial crisis that engulfed them.[7] Financialization is also a process that eases the creation of bubbles, driving up the prices of vital commodities like food and oil, which could also be used to stop people's struggles. What SAPs and war do not accomplish, financialization can, by enhancing some of their most destructive results. And, as billions of people have learned to their chagrin, it is very hard to fight the consequences of monetary flows since they operate outside of state control and the national territory.

2. ON EACH OF THESE counts then, financial firms do not fit into the factory-office-farm model of class struggle. There undoubtedly is a form of struggle that financial firms, in their nature, are involved in, that has an ancient origin: the struggle of debtor versus creditor. For when a firm lends out money to a person or firm, the debtor makes a promise to repay this loan with interest at some time in the future. The failure to do so in ancient times often led to slavery or mutilation, such as the famous "pound of flesh" the creditor was allowed to cut from the body of the defaulting debtor. In contemporary capitalism, besides criminal sanctions in the most egregious cases, default on loans leads to bankruptcy for capitalist firms and liens on the property and future income for workers. This debtor-creditor struggle differs from the wage struggle in many regards—it is temporal, as workers usually get paid after their work is over, while the debtor gets the loan money before repaying the loan.

There is clearly a struggle going on in the U.S. today concerning money and finance, but how best to understand it? Workers versus capitalists, debtors versus creditors, or some new way? What are the political demands that are being voiced in this crisis? After all, the struggle is about how the social surplus, which in communal societies was to be shared, is distributed.

3. TO ANSWER THESE QUESTIONS, we must get back to the basics and how they apply to contemporary capitalism. Before examining the "bailout" legislation, however, let us look to the elements of capitalism that are involved: F, the financial sector; I, the industrial sector, which includes all the information/computation firms, since they exploit material workers in order to produce "immaterial commodities;" and W, the working class.

Are the next few years going to be the epoch-making ones we have expected would come? That will depend on whether those 'in' W, the working class, are ready to struggle against their subordination.

Also, we must remember that the act of assigning a "W" to represent the working class does not magically unify this class. W's referent has a complex class composition that is continually in transformation.[8] It has a *technical composition*, a *sociological composition*, and a *political composition*, and these do not neatly fit into each other. For example, the most powerful and technologically advanced sectors of the working class might be at a particular moment politically the least aggressive, while those workers on the lowest levels of technology might be the most demanding and effective.

Moreover, the working class is profoundly divided by the wage itself. Some workers get higher wages than others, and a large part of the working class is unwaged. These unwaged workers in a money economy are often subordinated to their wage-earning fellows. These divisions and hierarchies appear as racism, sexism, and many of the other sources of class weakness. Most importantly, we need to recognize that the workers involved in this crisis story are not simply those in the territorial United States.

Given these elements, we will have to look at the relations and struggles between F and I (the finance sector and industrial sector); F and W (the finance sector and the working class); and, of course, W and I (the working class and the industrial sector). Thus there is an intra-class and well as an inter-class struggle: one between wages and profits and wages and interest, but also one between profits and interest. The entrance of wages into the class equation concerning finance is very important because there has been a profound shift in the twentieth century concerning our notion of interest.[9] In the nineteenth century and before, waged workers were never important direct players in the financial world since they had almost no property that could be used as collateral to take out loans from financial institutions and they had almost no savings to be used as deposits in banks. As Marx writes, "Interest is a relationship between two capitalists, not between capitalist and worker."[10] In fact, the many mutual aid and credit union organizations that sprang up in the nineteenth century were due to the fact that banks and other financial institutions considered themselves as having solely capitalists (large and small) as their customers or that workers were too suspicious to hand over their hard-earned savings into the hands of financial capital. This is no longer the case. Consequently, when we speak of financial crisis in the twenty-first century, we must speak of inter-class conflict as well as conflict between factions of capital.

4. WHAT IS THE SOURCE of the financial crisis and the "bailout"? At first, it appears like every other financial crisis in history: the inability of debtors to pay back old loans and the inability of financial firms to make new loans. Instead of money creating money out of nothing, we now have money creating nothing.

But this way of looking at it is almost tautological. For another explanation, we should examine the class relations. There are at least three reasons for this crisis: the condition of the U.S. working class, the globalization of financial flows, and the phenomenon of financialization.

The ignition of the current crisis in the financial sector has much to do with working-class homeowners instead of capitalists not being able to sell their production for a profit large enough to pay the interest on their loans, which was the usual origin of a crisis scenario in the nineteenth century. In this case, workers' wages were not large enough to pay the interest and principal on the loans they took out to purchase their homes. Indeed, there was a bout of real wage stagnation at the very moment when the housing market was booming and housing prices bubbled. So, the inability to sustain a successful wage struggle in the U.S. of the twenty-first century is at the heart of the present financial crisis. *Of course, if such a struggle were successful, an altogether different kind of crisis would have resulted.*

The second aspect of the crisis is the restriction in the flow of new investment funds into the U.S. financial system. It was vast flows of capital into the financial sector, especially from China, that led U.S. financial firms to offer mortgages and extend credit to U.S. capitalists and workers. Here the word "flow" is important, for as long as there is new capital coming into the sector, "bad" loans can be "rolled over" and payments delayed without any serious problems. However, when there are significant constraints in these flows, the mechanisms of deferral cannot be used, and loans are defaulted on while new loans cannot be transacted.

China was the major—though not the only—source of restriction of flows into the U.S. for two reasons. First, the recent reduction of the growth rate of the Chinese economy indicates that there has been a decline in the average rate of profit in China. Secondly, Chinese workers have recently been able to dramatically increase their wages and better their working conditions. This has lead to increased Chinese investment within China itself and the cultivation of the domestic market in government planning. These trends have negatively affected the flows of Chinese foreign investment into the financial sector of the United States. Thus, China's sovereign wealth fund has refused to come to U.S. capitalism's rescue. These factors have been part of the reason why the U.S. government has to make up for the shortfall.[11]

Thus we see how the mortgage crisis in the U.S. is the effect of at least two proletariats: first, the U.S. proletariat's inability to increase wages—there have been almost no strikes of significance in the U.S. in the last few years—and workers' use of credit and equity to satisfy their subsistence needs, which traditionally was the attribute of rentiers; and second, the Chinese proletariat's success, through thousands of strikes and protests, in increasing wages and forcing more investment in its social reproduction.

5. GIVEN THESE CAUSES ROOTED in class struggle, let us examine the "bailout" legislation as a set of "deals" between different elements of contemporary capitalism, coordinated by the state. By a "deal" I mean something like a tacit agreement between two enemies that sometimes appears in, but often underlies, the official legislative formulation of a social contract.[12] We use this language to indicate that the concept of a social contract is too formal and "peaceful" a structure to capture the often unspoken aspects of these agreements that are dependent on the state of power relations and grow out of a protracted and open-ended struggle. Antagonists can agree on the rules of the struggle until the rules become the object of struggle: this is the first axiom of "agonology," the study of struggles.

Let us take each of these sectors and examine the deal that is being offered by the state to them in outline:

F (THE FINANCIAL SECTOR): THIS sector must agree to government-imposed open-ended restrictions on their freedom of action and government regulation of their money capital movements. It also agrees to at least temporary nationalization of certain branches of the industry. In exchange it will get a large-scale 'socialization' of debt losses across the board (not just in so-called subprime mortgage loans). Implicitly, there is an assumption that this socialization will not be adversarial; the personnel involved in choosing the debts to be purchased by the government will not look out only for the government's interest. The Obama administration has definitely lived up to this part of the deal with the appointment of and support for Larry Summers and Tim Geithner.

I (INDUSTRIAL SECTOR): THIS SECTOR must agree to support the 'rescue' of the financial sector in exchange for a government guarantee of a continuous access to credit—the end of the 'credit crunch'—and an implicit indication that the principle "too big to crash," used to judge which firms in the financial sector would be "bailed out," would also be applied to this sector.

Of course, the distinction between these two sectors is not clear superficially, for many industrial firms have financial subsidiaries and many financial firms are invested in industrial corporations. Moreover, the accounting category used to describe accumulation in both sectors is the same: profit. According to these semantics, banks make profits as do car companies (or, at least, they hope to) even though they have a different relation to the surplus value produced throughout the system.

W (THE WORKING CLASS): OUR class must agree to a dramatic wage decrease, either through debt-inspired inflation and exchange rate devaluation, or the theft of the Social Security fund, or both, in exchange for a return to relatively full employment, relatively quickly— with the nature of the "relatively" a matter to be determined by struggle.

The configuration of the relations between *F*, *I*, *W* in the immediate future is described below:

F-I (*the relation between interest and profit, and financial and industrial capitalists*): This coming period will repose the 'eternal conflict' between the financial sector (and its claim to interest) and the industrial sector (and their claim to 'the profits of enterprise') after a period of hegemony of the financial sector. Economic rhetoric will be filled with snide remarks about pure money magicians and rocket scientists who land their projectiles in teacups and the need for 'real' investments, especially in the energy sector.

F-W (*the relation between wages and interest or working class and financial capitalists*): The coming period will be, on the one side—in the face of a tremendous downward pressure on wages—replete with moralistic and largely ineffectual demands for debt cancellation or abatement and, on the other side, draconian sanctions for breaking loan agreements, for falling behind the mortgage schedule, and for sending money to cover the credit card statement *too late*. This prediction has already been confirmed by the "bail out the homeowner" laws that were passed in the last two years, which have assisted a risible number of people facing foreclosure.

I-W (*the relation between wages and profits, and between workers and industrial capital*): The Bush Administration's "ownership" society begins to look quaint in the Obama era. As a consequence, the efforts by workers to regain their previous levels of income will no longer rely on finding a 'financial' exodus—through stock ownership or house purchasing—and will have to confront capital directly around wage struggle, broadly conceived. By "wage struggle" I do not only mean pickets around the factory gate. I include the struggle to have the power not to have to sell one's labor power and to have increasing control of the means of production and subsistence. For much of the history of the working class, this power to be able to refuse work has been rooted in the existence of common property resources or "commons" that people could access independent of their status as wage workers. Thus, in my view, "wage struggle" includes the power to preserve old commons and to create new ones.[13]

All classes and sectors, however, agree that much of the ideology and some of the practice of neoliberalism will be turned into relics. 'Government' is now trumping 'governance' on all levels of the economy (not, of course, that the state was ever aiming to wither away, as some postmodern thinkers were led to believe during the last decade). Just as developments after 9/11—such as the invasions of Afghanistan and Iraq—showed, the center-less and "flat" world of globalization was more an advertising gimmick than a reality. Similarly, the return of the surveillance state with the "war on terrorism" showed that the internet was no field of open communication. So, too, events in September and early October 2008 have shown that the era of the symbolic, future-centered economy operating at light speed has reached its limits in a meteor shower of falling stock prices, bankrupt investment houses, foreclosed homes, and tent cities.

It is also clear that the bailout deal is only as strong as the results it produces. There is no guarantee that either buying up hundreds of billion of dollars of 'toxic' loans will be adequate to 'restore' confidence in the financial sector, or that the credit flows will resume to the extent that will make an economic 'upturn' possible, or that there will be a return to historically normal levels of employment after a period of 'turbulence.' Moreover, some parts of the system might eventually reject the deal previously accepted when confronted with demands that were merely implicit in the initial offering. For example, how will workers respond to a demand that the Social Security fund be invested in stocks, after just seeing the latest of a series of stock market crashes? Will the financial sector 'masters of the universe' balk if they are regulated too stringently? Will a 'collapse' of neoliberalism lead to a more powerful anti-capitalist movement in the U.S. or perhaps something resembling what we would call "fascism"? These are the kinds of questions that will be central to understanding the class politics of the crisis of neoliberalism.

6. CRITICS OF NEOLIBERAL GLOBALIZATION might take a moment to gloat about the destiny of its antagonist—but only for a moment, since the consequences of this "bailout" are momentous and need to be considered carefully from the point of view of the state and from the point of view of the proletariat.

The great debate with China that the U.S. government was engaged in for more than a decade—concerning the role of the state in capitalism—has been won by the Chinese, at least for this round. This is an important strategic outcome of the "bailout" and is often referred to when the international fall-out of the crisis is discussed. The bailout is an ideological blow of major proportions. How can the U.S. government seriously push financial de-regulation at the very moment when it is practicing the exact opposite policy? It is true that consistency is not to be expected in the world of power. After all, the U.S. government has been preaching the abolition of agricultural subsidies to the governments of Africa at the very moment when it has substantially increased subsidies to its own farmers! But there are limits to political hypocrisy, and, moreover, the governments like China's that the U.S. is preaching financial de-regulation to are exactly those which have the capacity to resist its embrace.

On the contrary, the Chinese model of strong state control of the financial sector and the exchange rate has proven the winner in this period, not only over the Russian transition from Communism to Capitalism, but now, apparently, in the U.S. transition from a 'straight, no chase' doctrinaire neoliberalism to a form of neoliberalism Plan B (or Financial Socialism for the Sake of the Market). But this victory also has consequences for the development of a full political economy. What will the re-entrance of the state into the micro-organization of the economy mean for the whole system? Neoliberalism has been a political and a cultural paradigm as well as an economic one. It will require much research to anticipate how these areas of life will be affected by its collapse. How would a Chinese-like economic model bleed into U.S. politics and culture?

Finally, can the U.S. working class inspire world society out of this crisis of neoliberalism? The electronic assault on the politicians in Washington via the internet and the telephone system that led to the first defeat of the bailout bill in September 2008 gave many around the world some hope, but it was not followed by a more sustained resistance and was subsequently defeated in one week. On the basis of the wavering political response to the Bush Administration's 'blitz,' then, the immediate answer must be "no." Right-wing talk radio patter and left-wing internet petitions were ultimately weak tokens in this particular struggle. Indeed, by taking 'subprime' mortgages as the origin of the crisis, the working class demands for reliable housing and income security have been branded to be systematically 'toxic' to the credit system (to use the reigning metaphor of our day). The blockage of the credit route out of long-term wage stagnation will have major strategic consequences. Since capital will not allow the U.S. working class to be a class of rentiers—living off the ever increasing value of their stocks and the equity on their homes—workers must return to the hard terrain of the wage struggle, in the widest sense, in the coming era, however unpropitious it appears.

Are there any indications that the "deep freeze" of struggle that generated these notes is thawing? One sign is to be found in the renaissance of the student movement in California in the fall of 2009. After all, one of the most important "deals" with the working class in the neoliberal era has centered on university education. A tremendous wage premium existed for those who were able to graduate from the university, especially for those enrolled in the relatively cheaper public universities, compared to proletarians who only managed to graduate high school. The huge student loan business thrived exactly on this wage gap.[14] One aspect of this crisis has been its use by government officials and capitalists to attack this deal by dramatically increasing tuition fees in public universities and equally dramatically reducing government financial support.

In response to this "last fair deal going down," as Robert Johnson used to sing—that is, to this widely recognized end of the 'public university' ladder to a higher wage—young proletarians, especially in the University of California system, are finally organizing mass resistance. The fate of this resistance in the "edu-factories" in the coming months will tell us much about the power relations at the end-of-crisis moment of this cycle, perhaps more than the coming struggles in the 'real' factories, farms, and offices. If so, it would constitute an important shift in the physiognomy of class struggle in the United States.

NOTES

1   I learned much from Harry Cleaver's careful analysis of an earlier version of this text, to which he kindly sent his comments in the fall of 2008. Thanks, Harry. I also want to thank Silvia Federici for her help in the formulation of the remarks on financialization. Of course, neither Harry nor Silvia are responsible for the final product. This essay was written in Portland, Maine between October 12, 2008 and December 18, 2009.

2   Christian Marazzi, *Capital and Language: From the New Economy to The War Economy* (Cambridge, MA: MIT Press/Semiotext(e), 2008).

3   Georg Simmel, *The Philosophy of Money*, second ed. (London: Routledge, 2002), 503–505.

4   Karl Marx, *Capital: Vol III* (London: Penguin Books, 1981), 270.

5   Francis Fukuyama, *Trust: The Social Virtues and the Creation of Prosperity* (New York: The Free Press, 1995).

6   John Bellamy Foster and Robert McChesney, "Finance Capital and the Paradox of Accumulation," *Monthly Review* 61, no. 5 (October 2009): 1–20; Michael Hardt and Antonio Negri, *Multitude: War and Democracy in the Age of Empire* (New York: Penguin, 2004); Christian Marrazi, *Capital and Language* (New York: Semiotext(e), 2008).

7   Midnight Notes Collective (eds.), *One No, Many Yeses* (Brooklyn: Autonomedia, 1997).

8   Midnight Notes Collective (eds.), *Midnight Oil: Work, Energy, War* (Brooklyn: Autonomedia, 1992).

9   This is one reason why Marx's work in *Capital Vol. III* is of only limited assistance, while at the same time tremendously needed in this period. The third volume of *Capital* is where Marx attempts to trace the transfers of value that are continually taking place "behind the backs" of both workers and most capitalists and makes for the hellish sense of capitalism's invisible invulnerability.

10 Karl Marx, *Capital Vol III*, 506.

11 Midnight Notes and Friends, *Promissory Notes: From Crisis to Commons* (Brooklyn: Autonomedia, 2009); Niall Ferguson, *The Ascent of Money: A Financial History of the World* (London: Penguin Books, 2008), 338–339.

12 p.m., *bolo bolo* (Brooklyn: Autonomedia, 1985); Midnight Notes Collective (eds.), "Outlaw Notes," *Midnight Notes* 8, 1985.

13 See for example Silvia Federici, *Caliban and the Witch: Women, the Body and Primitive Accumulation* (Brooklyn: Autonomedia, 2004); Chris Carlsson, *Nowtopia: How Pirate Programmers, Outlaw Bicyclists, and Vacant-lot Gardeners are Inventing the Future Today* (Oakland: AK Press, 2008); Peter Linebaugh, *The Magna Carta Manifesto: Liberties and Commons for All* (New York: Penguin, 2007); Massimo De Angelis, *The Beginning of History: Value Struggles and Global Capital* (London: Pluto Press, 2007).

14 Jeffrey Williams, "The Pedagogy of Debt," in *Towards a Global Autonomous University: Cognitive Labor, the Production of Knowledge, and Exodus from the Education Factory*, eds. Edu-Factory Collective (Brooklyn, NY: Autonomedia, 2009).

FEMINISM AND THE POLITICS OF THE COMMONS IN AN ERA OF PRIMITIVE ACCUMULATION

Silvia Federici

Our perspective is that of the planet's commoners: human beings with bodies, needs, desires, whose most essential tradition is of cooperation in the making and maintenance of life; and yet have had to do so under conditions of suffering and separation from one another, from nature and from the common wealth we have created through generations.
—The Emergency Exit Collective[1]

The way in which women's subsistence work and the contribution of the commons to the concrete survival of local people are both made invisible through the idealizing of them are not only similar but have common roots.... In a way, women are treated like commons and commons are treated like women.
—Maria Mies and Veronika Bennholdt-Thomsen[2]

Reproduction precedes social production. Touch the women, touch the rock.
—Peter Linebaugh[3]

INTRODUCTION: WHY COMMONS

A<small>T LEAST SINCE THE</small> Z<small>APATISTAS</small>' takeover of the *zócalo* in San Cristóbal de las Casas on December 31, 1993 to protest legislation dissolving the *ejidal* lands of Mexico, the concept of 'the commons' has been gaining popularity among the radical left, internationally and in the United States, appearing as a basis for convergence among anarchists, Marxists, socialists, ecologists, and eco-feminists.[4]

There are important reasons why this apparently archaic idea has come to the center of political discussion in contemporary social movements, of which two in particular stand out. On one side is the demise of the statist model of revolution that for decades had sapped the efforts of radical movements to build an alternative to capitalism. On the other, the neoliberal attempt to subordinate every form of life and knowledge to the logic of the market has heightened our awareness of the danger of living in a world in which we no longer have access to seas, trees, animals, and our fellow beings except through the cash-nexus. The "new enclosures" have also made visible a world of communal properties and relations that many had believed to be extinct or had not valued until threatened with privatization.[5] Ironically, the new enclosures have demonstrated not only that the common has not vanished, but also that new forms of social cooperation are constantly being produced, including in areas of life where none previously existed, such as the internet.

The idea of the common/s, in this context, has offered a logical and historical alternative to both State and Private Property, the State and the Market, enabling us to reject the fiction that they are mutually exclusive and exhaustive of our political possibilities. It has also served an ideological function as a unifying concept prefiguring the cooperative society that the radical left is striving to create. Nevertheless, ambiguities as well as significant differences exist in the interpretations of this concept, which we need to clarify if we want the principle of the commons to translate into a coherent political project.[6]

What, for example, constitutes a common? Examples abound. We have land, water, air commons, and digital commons; our acquired entitlements (e.g., social security pensions) are often described as commons, and so are languages, libraries, and the collective products of past cultures. But from the viewpoint of devising an anti-capitalist strategy, are all these commons on the same level? Are they all compatible? And how can we ensure that they do not project a unity that remains to be constructed? Finally, should we speak of 'commons' in the plural, or "the common" as autonomist Marxists propose we do, this concept designating in their view the form of production in the post-Fordist era?

With these questions in mind, in this essay, I examine the politics of the commons from a feminist perspective where "feminist" refers to a standpoint shaped by the struggle against sexual discrimination and over reproductive work, which, to paraphrase Linebaugh's comment above, is the rock upon which society is built and by which every model of social organization must be tested. This intervention is necessary, in my view, to better define this politics and clarify the conditions under which the principle of the common/s can become the foundation of an anti-capitalist program. Two concerns make these tasks especially important.

GLOBAL COMMONS, WORLD BANK COMMONS

F<small>IRST, SINCE AT LEAST THE</small> early 1990s, the language of the commons has been appropriated by the World Bank and the United Nations and put at the service of privatization. Under the guise of protecting biodiversity and conserving global commons, the Bank has turned rain forests into ecological reserves and has expelled the populations that for centuries had drawn their sustenance from them, while making them available to people who can pay for them, for instance, through eco-tourism.[7] For its part, the United Nations has revised the international law governing access to the oceans in ways that enabled governments to consolidate the use of seawaters in fewer hands, again in the name of preserving the common heritage of mankind.[8]

The World Bank and the U.N. are not alone in their adaptation of the idea of the commons to market interests. Responding to different motivations, a re-valorization of the commons has become trendy among mainstream economists and capitalist planners; witness the growing academic literature on the subject and its cognates: social capital, gift economies, altruism. Witness also the official recognition of this trend through the conferral of the Nobel Prize for Economics in 2009 to the leading voice in this field, the political scientist Elinor Ostrom.[9]

Development planners and policymakers have discovered that, under proper conditions, a collective management of natural resources can be more efficient and less prone to conflict than privatization, and commons can be made to produce very well for the market.[10] They have also recognized that, carried to the extreme, the commodification of social relations has self-defeating consequences. The extension of the commodity form to every corner of the social factory, which neoliberalism has promoted, is an ideal limit for capitalist ideologues, but it is a project not only unrealizable but undesirable from the viewpoint of long-term reproduction of the capitalist system. Capitalist accumulation is structurally dependent on the free appropriation of immense quantities of labor and resources that must appear as externalities to the market, like the unpaid domestic work that women have provided, upon which employers have relied for the reproduction of the workforce.

It is no accident, then, that long before the Wall Street meltdown in 2008, a variety of economists and social theorists warned that the marketization of all spheres of life is detrimental to the market's well-functioning, for markets too, the argument goes, depend on the existence of non-monetary relations like confidence, trust, and gift giving.[11] In brief, capital is learning about the virtues of the common good. Even *The Economist*, the organ of capitalist free-market economics for more than 150 years, cautiously joined the chorus. "The economics of the new commons," the journal wrote, "is still in its infancy. It is too soon to be confident about its hypotheses. But it may yet prove a useful way of thinking about problems, such as managing the internet, intellectual property or international pollution, on which policymakers need all the help they can get."[12]

We must be very careful, then, not to craft the discourse on the commons in such a way as to allow a crisis-ridden capitalist class to revive itself, posturing, for instance, as the environmental guardian of the planet.

WHAT COMMONS?

A SECOND CONCERN IS THAT, while international institutions have learned to make commons functional to the market, how commons can become the foundation of a non-capitalist economy is a question still unanswered. From Peter Linebaugh's work, especially *The Magna Carta Manifesto*, we have learned that commons have been the thread that has connected the history of the class struggle into our time, and indeed the fight for the commons is all around us.[13] Mainers are fighting to preserve their fisheries and waters;

residents of Appalachia are organizing to save their mountains threatened by strip mining; open source and free software movements are opposing the commodification of knowledge and opening new spaces for communications and cooperation. We also have the many invisible commoning activities and communities that people are creating in North America, which Chris Carlsson has described in his book *Nowtopia*.[14] As Carlsson shows, much creativity is invested in the production of "virtual commons" and forms of sociality that thrive under the radar of the money/market economy.

Most important has been the creation of urban gardens, which had started to spread across the country in the 1980s and 1990s, thanks mostly to the initiatives of immigrant communities from Africa, the Caribbean, or the South of the United States. Their significance cannot be overestimated. Urban gardens have opened the way to a 're-urbanization' process that is indispensable if we are to regain control over our food production, regenerate our environment and provide for our subsistence. The gardens are far more than a source of food security: they are centers of sociality, knowledge production, and cultural and intergenerational exchange. As Margarita Fernandez has written of urban gardens in New York, they "strengthen community cohesion" as places where people come together not just to work the land, but to play cards, hold weddings, and have baby showers or birthday parties.[15] Some have partner relationships with local schools whereby children engage in environmental education after school. Not least, gardens are "a medium for the transport and encounter of diverse cultural practices" so that African vegetables and farming practices, for example, mix with those of the Caribbean.

Still, the most significant feature of urban gardens is that they produce for neighborhood consumption, rather than for commercial purposes. This distinguishes them from other reproductive commons that either produce for the market, like the fisheries of Maine's Lobster Coast, or those that are bought on the market, like the land trusts that preserve open spaces.[16] The problem, however, is that urban gardens have remained a spontaneous grassroots initiative and there have been few attempts by movements in the U.S. to expand their presence and to make access to land a key terrain of struggle. More generally, the left has not posed the question of how to bring together the many proliferating commons being defended, developed, and fought for to form a cohesive whole to provide a foundation for a new mode of production.

An exception is the theory proposed by Antonio Negri and Michael Hardt in *Empire*, *Multitude*, and recently *Commonwealth*, which argues that a society built on the principle of "the common" is *already evolving* from the informatization and "cognitivization" of production. According to this theory, as production presumably becomes production of knowledge, culture, and subjectivity, organized through the internet, a common space and common wealth are created that escape the problem of defining rules of inclusion or exclusion. For access and use multiply the resources available on the net rather than subtracting from them, thus signifying the possibility of a society built on abundance— the only remaining hurdle confronting the "multitude" being how to prevent the capitalist "capture" of the wealth produced.

The appeal of this theory is that it does not separate the formation of "the common" from the organization of work and production but sees it immanent to it. Its limit is that its picture of the common absolutizes the work of a minority possessing skills not available to most of the world population, that it ignores that this work produces commodities for the market, and that it overlooks the fact that online communication/production materially depends on economic activities—mining, microchip, and rare earth production—that, as presently organized, are extremely destructive, both socially and ecologically.[17] Moreover, with its emphasis on knowledge and information, this theory skirts the question of the reproduction of everyday life. This is true, however, of the discourse on the commons as a whole, which is mostly concerned with the formal preconditions for the existence of commons and less with the material requirements for the construction of a commons-based economy enabling us to resist dependence on wage labor and subordination to capitalist relations.

WOMEN AND THE COMMONS

IT IS IN THIS CONTEXT that a feminist perspective on the commons is important. It begins with the realization that, as the primary subjects of reproductive work, historically and in our time, women have depended on access to communal natural resources more than men and have been most penalized by their privatization and most committed to their defense. As I wrote in *Caliban and the Witch*, in the first phase of capitalist development, women were at the forefront of the struggle against land enclosures in both England and the 'New World,' and they were the staunchest defenders of the communal cultures that European colonization attempted to destroy. In Peru, when the Spanish *conquistadores* took control of their villages, women fled to the high mountains where they recreated forms of collective life that have survived to this day. Not surprisingly, the sixteenth and seventeenth centuries saw the most violent attack on women in the history of the world: the persecution of women as witches. Today, in the face of a new process of Primitive Accumulation, women are the main social force standing in the way of a complete commercialization of nature, supporting a non-capitalist use of land and a subsistence-oriented agriculture. Women are the subsistence farmers of the world. In Africa, they produce 80% of the food people consume, despite the attempts made by the World Bank and other agencies to convince them to divert their activities to cash-cropping. In the face of rising food prices in the 1990s, in many African towns, they have appropriated plots in public lands and planted corn, beans, cassava "along roadsides … in parks, along rail-lines," changing the urban landscape of African cities and breaking down the separation between town and country in the process.[18] In India, the Philippines, and across Latin America, women have replanted trees in degraded forests, joined hands to chase away loggers, made blockades against mining operations and the construction of dams, and led the revolt against the privatization of water.[19]

The other side of women's struggle for direct access to means of reproduction has been the formation across the Third World, from Cambodia to Senegal, of credit associations that function as money commons.[20] Differently named, the *tontines* (as they are called in parts of Africa) are autonomous, self-managed, women-made banking systems that provide cash to individuals or groups that have no access to banks, working purely on a basis of trust. In this, they are completely different from the microcredit systems promoted by the World Bank, which function on a basis of mutual policing and shame, reaching the extreme (e.g., in Niger) of posting pictures of the women who fail to repay the loans in public places so that some have been driven to suicide.[21]

Women have also led the effort to collectivize reproductive labor both as a means to economize the cost of reproduction and to protect each other from poverty, state violence, and the violence of individual men. An outstanding example is the *ollas communes* (common cooking pots) that women in Chile and Peru set up in the 1980s when, due to stiff inflation, they could no longer afford to shop alone.[22] Like land reclamation, or the formation of *tontines*, these practices are the expression of a world where communal bonds are still strong. It would be a mistake, however, to consider them something pre-political, 'natural,' or simply a product of 'tradition.'

After repeated phases of colonization, nature and customs no longer exist in any part of the world, except where people have struggled to preserve them and reinvent them. Thus, as Podlashuc has noted in his article "Saving Women: Saving the Commons," grass-root women's communalism today is the production of a new reality; it shapes a collective identity, it constitutes a counter-power in the home and the community, and it opens a process of self-valorization and self-determination from which there is much to learn.

The first lesson we can gain from these struggles is that the 'commoning' of the material means of reproduction is the primary mechanism by which a collective interest and mutual bonds are created. It is also the first line of resistance to a life of enslavement and the condition for the construction of autonomous spaces undermining from within the hold that capitalism has on our lives. Undoubtedly the experiences I described are models that cannot be transplanted. For us in North America, the reclamation and commoning of the means of reproduction must necessarily take different forms. But an added benefit is that by pooling our resources and re-appropriating the wealth that we have produced, we can begin to de-link our reproduction from the commodity flows that, through the world market, are responsible for the dispossession of so many people in other parts of the world. We can begin to disentangle our livelihood not only from the world market but also from the war machine and prison system on which the U.S. economy now depends. Not last, we can move beyond the abstract solidarity that so often characterizes relations in the movement, which limits our commitment and our capacity to endure, as well as limits the risks we are willing to take.

In a country where private property is defended by the largest arsenal of weaponry in the world and where three centuries of slavery have produced profound divisions in the social body, the recreation of the common/s appears as a formidable task that could only be accomplished through a long-term process of experimentation, coalition building and reparations. But though this task may now seem more difficult than passing through the eye of a needle, it is also the only possibility we have for widening the space of our autonomy and refusing to accept that our reproduction occurs at the expense of the world's other commoners and commons.

FEMINIST RECONSTRUCTIONS

WHAT THIS TASK ENTAILS IS powerfully expressed by Maria Mies when she points out that the production of commons requires first a profound transformation in our everyday life in order to recombine what the social division of labor in capitalism has separated. For the distancing of production from reproduction and consumption leads us to ignore the conditions under which what we eat, wear, or work with have been produced, their social and environmental cost, and the fate of the population on whom our waste is unloaded.[23] In other words, we need to overcome the state of irresponsibility concerning the consequences of our actions that results from the destructive ways in which the social division of labor is organized in capitalism; short of that, the production of our life inevitably becomes a production of death for others. As Mies points out, globalization has worsened this crisis, widening the distances between what is produced and what is consumed, thereby intensifying, despite the appearance of an increased global interconnectedness, our blindness to the blood in the food we eat, the petroleum we use, the clothes we wear, and the computers we communicate with.[24]

Overcoming this state of oblivion is where a feminist perspective teaches us to start in our reconstruction of the commons. No common is possible unless we refuse to base our life and our reproduction on the suffering of others, unless we refuse to see ourselves as separate from them. Indeed, if commoning has any meaning, it must be the production of ourselves as a common subject. This is how we must understand the slogan "no commons without community." But 'community' is not intended as a gated reality, a grouping of people joined by exclusive interests separating them from others, as with community formed on the basis of religion or ethnicity, but rather as a quality of relations, a principle of cooperation and responsibility to each other, the earth, the forests, the seas, and the animals.

Certainly, the achievement of such community, like the collectivization of our everyday work of reproduction, can only be a beginning. It is no substitute for broader anti-privatization campaigns and the reclamation of our common wealth. But it is an essential part of our education for collective governance and recognition of history as a collective project, which is perhaps the main casualty of the neoliberal era of capitalism.

On this account, we too must include in our political agenda the communalization of housework, reviving that rich feminist tradition that we have in the U.S. that stretches from the utopian socialist experiments of the mid-nineteenth century to the attempts that 'materialist feminists' made from the late nineteenth century to the early twentieth century, to reorganize and socialize domestic work (and thereby the home and the neighborhood) through collective housekeeping—efforts that continued until the 1920s when the Red Scare put an end to them.[25] These practices and, most importantly, the ability of past feminists to look at reproductive labor as an important sphere of human activity, not to be negated but to be revolutionized, must be revisited and re-valorized.

One crucial reason for creating collective forms of living is that the reproduction of human beings is the most labor-intensive work on earth which, to a very large extent, is work that is irreducible to mechanization. We cannot mechanize childcare, care for the ill, or the psychological work necessary to reintegrate our physical and emotional balance. Despite the efforts that futuristic industrialists are making, we cannot robotize care except at a terrible cost for the people involved. No one will accept 'nursebots' as caregivers, especially for children and the ill. Shared responsibility and cooperative work not given at the cost of the health of the providers are the only guarantees of proper care. For centuries, the reproduction of human beings has been a collective process. It has been the work of extended families and communities on which people could rely, especially in proletarian neighborhoods, even when they lived alone so that old age (for example) was not accompanied by the desolate loneliness and dependence which so many of our elderly suffer. It is only with the advent of capitalism that reproduction has been completely privatized, a process that is now carried to a degree that it destroys our lives. This trend must be reversed, and the present time is propitious for such a project.

As the capitalist crisis destroys the basic elements of reproduction for millions of people across the world, including those in the U.S., the reconstruction of our everyday life is a possibility and a necessity. Like strikes, social/economic crises break the discipline of wage work, forcing new forms of sociality upon us. This is what occurred during the Great Depression, which produced a movement of hobos who turned the freight trains into their commons in pursuit of freedom in mobility and nomadism.[26] At the intersections of railroad lines they organized *hobo jungles* that, with their self-governance rules and solidarity, pre-figured the communist world in which many of their residents believed.[27]

However, but for a few Boxcar Berthas, this was predominantly a masculine world, a fraternity of men, and in the long term it could not be sustained.[28] Once the economic crisis and the second World War came to an end, the hobos were domesticated by the two great engines of labor power fixation: the family and the house. Mindful of the threat of working class recomposition during the Depression, American capital excelled in its application of the principle that has characterized the organization of economic life: cooperation at the point of production, separation and atomization at the point of reproduction. The atomized, serialized family house that Levittown provided, compounded by the car, its umbilical appendix, not only sedentarized the worker, but also put an end to the type of autonomous workers' commons that hobo jungles had represented.[29]

Today, as millions of Americans' houses and cars are being repossessed, as foreclosures, evictions, and massive loss of employment are again breaking down the pillars of the capitalist discipline of work, new common grounds are again taking shape, like the tent cities that are sprawling from coast to coast. This time, however, it is women who must build the new commons so that they do not remain transient spaces, "temporary autonomous zones," but become the foundation of new forms of social reproduction. If the house is the *oikos* on which economy is built, then it is women, historically the house workers and house prisoners, who must take the initiative to reclaim the house as a center of collective life, one traversed by multiple people and forms of cooperation, providing safety without isolation and fixation, allowing for the sharing and circulation of community possessions, and, above all, providing the foundation for collective forms of reproduction. As has already been suggested, we can draw inspiration for this project from the programs of the nineteenth century materialist feminists who, convinced that the home was an important "spatial component of the oppression of women," organized communal kitchens, cooperative households calling for workers' control of reproduction.[30]

These objectives are crucial at present. Breaking down the isolation of life in a private home is not only a precondition for meeting our most basic needs and increasing our power with regard to employers and the state. As Massimo de Angelis has reminded us, it is also a protection from ecological disaster. For there can be no doubt about the destructive consequences of the "un-economic" multiplication of reproductive assets and self-enclosed dwellings that we now call our homes—dissipating warmth into the atmosphere during the winter, exposed to unmitigated heat in the summer. Most importantly, we cannot build an alternative society and a strong self-reproducing movement unless we redefine our reproduction in a more cooperative way and put an end to the separation between the personal and the political, and political activism and the reproduction of everyday life.

It remains to be clarified that assigning women this task of commoning/collectivizing reproduction is not to concede to a naturalistic conception of femininity. Understandably, many feminists view this possibility as a fate worse than death. It is deeply sculpted in our collective consciousness that women have been designated as men's common, a natural source of wealth and services to be as freely appropriated by them as the capitalists have appropriated the wealth of nature. But to paraphrase Dolores Hayden, the reorganization of reproductive work, and therefore the reorganization of the structure of housing and public space, is not a question of identity; it is a question of labor and, we can add, also a question of power and safety against interpersonal violence, as the women of the Landless People's Movement in Brazil have found.[31]

Arguing that women should take the lead in the collectivization of reproductive work and housing is not to naturalize housework as a female vocation. It is refusing to obliterate the collective experiences, knowledge, and struggles that women have accumulated concerning reproductive work whose history has been an essential part of our resistance to capitalism. Reconnecting with this history is a crucial step for women and men today both for undoing the gendered architecture of our lives and for reconstructing our homes and lives as commons

NOTES

1   The Emergency Exit Collective, *The Great Eight Masters and the Six Billion Commoners* (Bristol: May Day, 2008).

2   Marie Mies and Veronika Bennholdt-Thomsen, *The Subsistence Perspective: Beyond the Globalized Economy* (London: Zed Books, 1999).

3   Peter Linebaugh, *The Magna Carta Manifesto: Liberty and Commons for All* (Berkeley: University of California Press, 2008).

4   A key source on the politics of the commons and its theoretical foundations is the UK-based electronic journal *The Commoner*, now entering its ninth year of publication, HTTP://www. COMMONER.ORG.UK.

5   A case in point is the struggle that is taking place in many communities in Maine against Nestlé's appropriation of Maine waters to bottle Portland Spring. Nestlé's theft has made people aware of the vital importance of these waters and the supporting aquifers and has truly constituted them as a common (*Food and Water Watch Fact Sheet*, July 2009). Food and Water Watch is a (self-described) "non-profit organization that works to ensure clean water and safe food in the United States and around the world."

6   An excellent site for current debates on the commons is the recently published issue of the UK journal *Turbulence: Ideas For Movement* (December 5, 2009), HTTP:// TURBULENCE.ORG.UK.

7   For more on this subject, see the important article "Who Pays for the Kyoto Protocol?" by Ana Isla, in which the author describes how the conservation of biodiversity has provided the World Bank and other international agencies with the pretext to enclose rain forests on the grounds that they represent "carbon sinks" and "oxygen generators." In *Eco-Sufficiency and Global Justice: Women Write Political Ecology*, ed. by Ariel Salleh (New York and London: Macmillan Palgrave, 2009).

8   The United Nations Convention on the Law of the Sea, passed in November 1994, establishes a 200–mile offshore limit, defining an Exclusive Economic Zone in which nations can exploit, manage, and protect resources from fisheries to natural gas. It also regulates deep-sea mining and the use of resulting profit. On the development of the concept of the "common heritage of mankind" in United Nations debate see Susan J. Buck, *The Global Commons: An Introduction* (Washington: Island Press, 2008).

9   As described by Wikipedia, Ostrom's work focuses on common pool resources and "emphasizes how humans interact with ecosystems to maintain long-term sustainable resource yields." *Wikipedia*, January 9, 2010, p.1.

10 For more on this topic, see Calestous Juma and J.B. Ojwang eds., *In Land We Trust* (London: Zed Books, 1996), an early treatise on the effectiveness of communal property relations in the context of capitalist development and efforts.

11 David Bollier, *Silent Theft: The Private Plunder of Our Common Wealth*. (New York and London: Routledge, 2002), 36–39.

12 *The Economist*, July 31, 2008.

13 Linebaugh, 2008.

14 Chris Carlsson, *Nowtopia: How Pirate Programmers, Outlaw Bicyclists, and Vacant-lot Gardeners are Inventing the Future Today* (Oakland: AK Press, 2008).

15 See Margarita Fernandez, "Cultivating Community, Food and Empowerment," project course paper, unpublished manuscript, 2003, 23–6. An early, important work on urban gardens is Bill Weinberg and Peter Lamborn Wilson eds., *Avant Gardening: Ecological Struggle in the City & the World* (Brooklyn: Autonomedia, 1999).

16 However, the fishing commons of Maine are presently threatened with a new privatization policy that is justified in the name of preservation and ironically labeled "catch shares." This is a system, already applied in Canada and Alaska, whereby local governments set a limit on the amount or fish that can be caught and allocate individual shares on the basis of the amount of fishing done in the past. This system has proven to be disastrous for small, independent fishermen who are soon forced to sell their share to the highest bidders. Protest against its implementation is now mounting in the fishing communities of Maine. See "Catch Shares or Share-Croppers?" *Fishermen's Voice*, Vol. 14, No.12, December 2009.

17 It has been calculated, for example, that 33,000 liters of water and between fifteen and nineteen tons of material are required just to produce a personal computer. See Saral Sarkar, *Eco-Socialism or Eco-Capitalism?: A Critical Analysis of Humanity's Fundamental Choices* (London: Zed Books, 1999), 126. Elizabeth Dias cites claims made by Global Witness—an organization campaigning to prevent resource related conflicts—to the effect that the trade in the minerals at the heart of the electronic industry feeds the civil war in the Democratic Republic of Congo. See HTTP://WWW.TIME./COM/TIME/WORLD/ARTICLE/0,8599,1912594,00.HTML.

18 Donald B. Freeman, "Survival Strategy or Business Training Ground? The Significance of Urban Agriculture For the Advancement of Women in African Cities," *African Studies Review*, Vol.36, N.3 (December 1993), 1–22.

19 See Vandana Shiva, *Staying Alive: Women, Ecology, and Development* (London: Zed Books, 1989), 102–117, and *Ecology and the Politics of Survival: Conflicts Over Natural Resources in India* (New Delhi/London: Sage Publications, 1991), 274.

20 See Leo Podlashuc, "Saving Women, Saving the Commons," in Salleh, ed., 2009.

21 I owe this information to Ousseina Alidou, Director of the Center for African Studies of Rutgers University.

22 See Jo Fisher, *Out of the Shadows: Women, Resistance and Politics in South America* (London: Latin American Bureau, 1993), and Carol Andreas, *When Women Rebel: The Rise of Popular Feminism in Peru* (Westport, CT: Lawrence Hill & Company, 1985).

23 Mies, 1999.

24 Mies, 1999.

25 See Dolores Hayden, *The Grand Domestic Revolution* (Cambridge, MA: MIT Press, 1981), and *Redesigning the American Dream: The Future of Housing, Work and Family Life* (New York: Norton and Company, 1986).

26 See George Caffentzis, "Three Temporal Dimensions of Class Struggle," paper presented at ISA Annual Meeting (San Diego, CA, March 2006).

27 See Nels Anderson, *On Hobos and Homelessness* (Chicago: The University of Chicago Press, 1998); Todd De Pastino, *Citizen Hobo* (Chicago: The University of Chicago Press, 2003); and Caffentzis, 2006.

28 *Boxcar Bertha* (1972) is Martin Scorsese's adaptation of Ben Reitman's *Sister of the Road*, "the fictionalized autobiography of radical and transient Bertha Thompson." (Wikipedia)

29 Hayden, 1986.
30 Hayden, 1981.
31 Hayden, 1986, 230. I am reminded here of the experience of the women members of the Landless People's Movement of Brazil (the MST) who, after their communities won the right to maintain the land that they had occupied, insisted that the new houses be built to form one compound so that they could continue to communalize their housework, wash together, cook together, take turns with men as they had done in the course of the struggle, and be ready to run to give each other support when abused by men.

PALLAS AND "THE PEOPLE'S BUSINESS"

Peter Linebaugh

IN PARIS DURING THE FRENCH Revolution, the neighborhoods organized themselves by forty-eight different *sections*, and the *section* became the basis of the people's power at the grass-roots. In Russia after 1905, the grass-roots organized themselves in soviets, and these then became the basis of power in 1917. In England during the Puritan Revolution of the seventeenth century, the people gathered together in congregations. Political theorists call this 'constituent power'; it is the power of the common people prior to making a political constitution. Not long after the conclusions of such upheavals in England, the authorities passed the Riot Act of 1714 in an attempt to limit such unpredictable, unauthorized public gatherings of people to less than twelve. Thereafter, apart from sport and the jury, any crowd whose size exceeded a dozen was basically a licensed affair of which the Church-and-King mob was the classic example.

A Guyanese fresh-fruit drink seller expressed this popular sovereignty in action very clearly when some years ago we marched through the public farmer's market in Toledo, Ohio, in a noisy demonstration on behalf of Mumia Abu-Jamal. "What right have you to be here?" demanded an irate stall-holder, and our newly-found mango drink friend answered, "the People's business" and smiled. There was a touch of irony in his expression as he uttered these words which arose from memories of struggle in Guyana whence he summoned up this bit of rhetoric. It stirred something in us as well, for in a twinkling we clamored on top of some vegetable crates for a little marketplace oratory to denounce racism and capital punishment by means of class analysis. A small crowd began to gather, but between the hostility of two or three nasty merchants and the police, ever grateful for something to do, the "People's business" could not go much further that day. Future meetings were held in friendly churches: R.S.V.P., as Tom McGrath used to say, inviting you to the "Ramshackle Socialist Victory Party."

The clerical pulpit and the politician's rostrum had emerged as places of discussion in the Democratic Party presidential nomination process in 2008. Few expect that these are places of the transaction of "the People's business," as they are the locations of indirect democracy, at best. The corporate media are the "ugly mirrors" which the anthropologist and direct action activist David Graeber has described as the means to make us believe that we're incapable of self-government.[1] Hollywood, television, and even school textbooks confirm the danger of direct democracy as "mob rule." Rebecca Solnit has described how self-government is the natural response of communities hit by disaster, which the Government actually distrusts and often destroys.[2]

Graeber asks, "Is it possible for those trying to develop decentralized forms of consensus-based direct democracy to reclaim the world? If so, how will we ever convince the majority of people in the world that 'democracy' has nothing to do with electing representatives?"[3] He refers to remarkable convergences of practice in recent years: Dutch squatters, anti-eviction activists in South Africa, Zapatista communities, unemployed *piqueteros* of Argentina. He sees in these a project of recuperation, finding democratic process without the coercive mechanism of the state, where it is not an ideological project but part of the habitus of the movement. He has a broad range of examples: Swedish *ting*, native American councils, African village assemblies. Each of us can make a list; I'd certainly add the Popular Assembly of the Peoples of Oaxaca, or APPO, and of course the entire experience of the Zapatistas who raised the International of Hope against the International of Terror.[4] The latter began a process of re-membering our indigenous history as our shield and buckler against the dis-membering of neoliberalism.

There is a contradiction between the coercive mechanism of the state and the procedures of listening to everyone and building agreement. This is the contradiction that was exposed in the 1968 Democratic convention in Chicago when the Mayor Daley's infamous 'blue meanies' went haywire, pummeling young people, activists, delegates, and reporters alike. Since then, each component has become more sophisticated, the democrats more concerned with process, the delegates hidden behind the police, the law, and the state, which now has the media totally prone, embedded, and tucked in. Together they produce ugly mirrors. The conflict between police and street activists has developed rapidly since then—with gas, razor wire, temporary lock-ups, bicycles, cell-phones, and video cameras altering the techniques of contest—while the political essence remains the same: direct democracy versus indirect representation (so vastly corrupted).

The strengths of direct action include: affinity group structure, consensus process, innovative popular education techniques, radical critique of capitalism, and the formation of Indymedia networks. At Seattle, trainings were held on nonviolent direct action, medical support, puppet building, theater skills, legal rights, the spoken word, music and dance, and techniques such as banner drops and body blockades. Tactical teams and strategy circles were formed. High importance was placed on direct democracy, or the experience of consensus building even in the street intersections with state violence imminent. Naomi Klein called it "hub-and-spoke organization;" others likened it to a spider's web, or to a many-headed Hydra, or to a school of fish. The strengths were indeed startling, and the shortcomings all stemmed from the absence of a community base.[5] Despite this shortcoming, David Graeber concludes that democratic improvisation arises when "diverse sorts of people with different traditions and experiences are obliged to figure out some way to deal with one another."[6]

These experiences, these experiments, were severely curtailed by 9/11 and the subsequent measures of the 'national security state' or dictatorship: the impatient disregard of habeas corpus, the arrogant organization of command, the shameless advocacy of pre-emptive war, the bombastic proclamation of endless war, the leering defense of torture, the triage of entire cities, the pretense of delivering constitutions to others while destroying them at home, the foreclosure of shelter, the privatization of water, the *défrichement* of forest, the planning of starvation, the devalorisation of work, the malign neglect of the imprisoned, the elevation of intellectual ruffians to the judiciary, the deliberate diffusion of fear and trembling throughout society, the base falsehoods against the Four Freedoms, and the transformation of the national border from a gateway of freedom to a portcullis of fear.

MAGNA CARTA OFFERED THE JURY AS THE LAST DEFENSE AGAINST TYRANNY

IT SO HAPPENED THAT ON December 3, 2007, the publisher sent me a copy of my book, *The Magna Carta Manifesto: Liberties and Commons for All*, in which I sought in an ancient portal to find an emergency exit from our dire and barricaded times. Chapter 39 of Magna Carta—"No free man shall be seized or imprisoned ... except by the lawful judgment of his peers or by the law of the land"—is often quoted, and sometimes carved in stone at courthouses. A key perhaps to the door of mutual aid and direct democracy can be teased from the term "peers," often better translated as "equals." Certainly they express a countervailing power to the King.

You see it in the architecture of the court room: one axis has the judge and the prosecutor at ends of a pole (both agents of the State), and the opposite axis has the defendant and jury facing each other. The antagonism can be described in various ways, as the State versus citizens, as the rulers against the ruled, even as the well-paid versus the poorly paid, sometimes as outsiders versus neighbors. Edward Thompson explains, "The jury box is where the people come into the court: the judge watches them and the jury watches back. A jury is the place where the bargain is struck [between the state and the people]. The jury attends in judgment, not only upon the accused, but also upon the justice and humanity of the Law."[7]

I quoted only part of Chapter 39 of Magna Carta, omitting what is signified by the three dots. Here is what is left out by that ellipsis: "No free man shall be seized or imprisoned, or stripped of his rights or possessions, or outlawed, or exiled, or deprived of his standing in any other way, nor will we proceed with force against him, or send others to do so, except by the lawful judgment of his peers or by the law of the land." More than imprisonment is protected in these clauses. The realm of material production is implied here too, because standing or status, possessions, and rights may be construed to refer to subsistence.

Bear with me a moment. We can relate Chapter 39 to Chapter 7, which provides the widow with her reasonable estovers in the common. Or, if we examine the little charter, the Charter of the Forest—an inseparable companion to Magna Carta—then we find that this principle of neighborhood is stated in the first chapter, "all forests ... shall be viewed by good and lawfull men." The rangers, the walkers, the foresters, the verderors held swanimote courts. They watch the vert and venison, they're guardians of the "greenhue." Freeman are not to enclose the forest, or arable ground, nor annoy the neighbors. The jury and jury-like progenitors were essential to the process of subsistence commoning. From the court leet in England to the panchayat in the Indian village, the local jury combined functions of the administration of justice and economic resource allocation.

The jury makes us think "small"—we cannot be grand theorizers. The jury forces us to think "local"—we cannot be universalists, we belong to a neighborhood. The jury forces us to think "slow"—consensus can take a long time to build. The jury is random but chosen by lot, one of the oldest methods used to choose individuals for disagreeable tasks. The jury is anonymous, and it is collective. The jury is a consciousness-raising group. Jury deliberation is not a balancing of interests, as in possessive individualism, but a means of asserting communality and constituting subjectivities.

The jury was dear to Edward Thompson, the peacenik and influential social historian. He wrote, "The jury is a very ancient creature…. It is also a very odd beast…. It is less an institution than a practice."[8] Thompson sees it as theater, playing to a public out of doors; he sees it as a lay presence conferring legitimacy to authority. The mysteries of law must be broken down into lay language. It must appear rational and humane. As a practice, it is a place where the fingers remember the melodies when the mind may have forgotten.

We think of the jury as rendering verdicts in criminal cases, 'Guilty' or 'Not Guilty.' In its origins it adjudicated other kinds of disputes, especially concerning the commons, or the usufructs of the land. This entailed issues of both production and consumption. The option of the jury trial was 'putting oneself on one's country,' to use the medieval expression, and it was still a technical formulation at the time of industrialization—to put oneself on the country. That our language plays tricks on our thinking is illustrated by the double meanings of the word 'country'—as the place where things grow like trees, grains, vegetables and such, or as the entity of political sovereignty.

What about industrialization, you may ask? How could a jury supervise it? What about shop-floor democracy? Or the results of self-activity? Here consensus is built at lunch-time, or at the neighboring pub or bar. It is a way of cutting through red-tape, bringing the grievance process into the hands of the victimized, its importance after World War II clearly outlined by auto-worker James Boggs in *The American Revolution*, during the 1960s and early 1970s; in Bill Watson's article "Counter-Planning on the Shop-Floor"; or Huw Beynon's *Working for Ford*.[9] Here one 'puts oneself on one's shopfloor' so to speak. In other words, you submit to the judgment of your peers, a judgment which adheres to habit, local mores, usages, or custom, in addition to law. As Alexis de Tocqueville wrote, "Laws are always unstable unless they are founded upon the customs of a nation: customs are the only durable and resisting power in a people."[10]

Edward Thompson defended the jury with that savage irony he learned from Swift: "The quaint archaic notion that anyone—randomly selected—might be able to perform a human-sized office or role." He continued, "Only a crank could possibly suggest such a direct exercise of democracy today."[11] We have a few of these cranks now, and we need many more.

Let's see… there was the court leet. And then there was the swanimote court. There was the jury of matrons. The court leet, or sometimes simply "the leet," was a manorial court and a precursor of the modern jury. Court leet could present tenants for a wide range of offenses. It took a "view of the frankpledge," or ensured that every man over twelve years of age was in frankpledge; it enforced the assizes of bread and beer.[12] It could find facts and declare the custom of the region. Frankpledge was the system by which every member of a tithing was answerable for the good conduct of, or the damage done by, any one of the other members. Frankpledge was thus a system of both mutual aid and mutual responsibility. All men over the age of twelve belonged to it; the "view of frank-pledge" resembled an assembly.

It might be helpful to mention a few examples of the judgments of court leet. "The jurors present that Alan Rushpiller, John Kiggel, William Godloke habitually collect bittern eggs and export them out of the fen to the great destruction ... [&c.]," or that "William Fisher sold 500 of sedge outside the commune," or, "that the Brethren of the Hospital [of St. John] have pastured their sheep in autumn before the gleaners against the by-law and that the said Brethren keep two dogs which run into the lord's warren which give rise to suspicion."

Here is Thompson again, with his fine rhetorical irony. "It is an old story of a certain inconvenience in our legal system. Time and again, when judges and law officers, mounted on high horses, have been riding at breakneck speed towards some convenient despotism, those shadowy figures—not particularly good nor especially true—have risen from the bushes beside the highway and flung a gate across their path. They are known to historians as the Gang of Twelve."[13]

The Coroner's jury is yet another kind and it has defied the police function of the state, famously in the Calthorp Street affair of 1833. Calthorp Street is in Clerkenwell, a venerable working-class district of London. At the coroner's inquest, the jury returned a verdict of justifiable homicide upon the body of police constable Culley who died from wounds caused by a knife during a demonstration of the National Union of the Working Classes. William Lovett had drafted its declaration two years earlier. After stating that labor is the source of wealth, its first four principles were:

1. All property (honestly acquired) to be sacred and inviolable.
2. That all men are born equally freed, and have certain natural and inalienable rights.
3. That all governments ought to be founded on those rights; and all laws instituted for the common benefit in the protection and security of all the people: and not for the particular emolument or advantage of any single man, family, or set of men.
4. That all hereditary distinctions of birth are unnatural, and opposed to the equal rights of man; and therefore ought to be abolished.

The newly established London metropolitan police force (1829) was anxious to demonstrate its usefulness to the established powers and by all accounts acted with brutal ferocity against the small demonstration, blocking all exits and then, without further ado, unmercifully beating men, women, children, bystanders, and vendors, as well as the few members of the National Union of the Working Classes who were gathered around an American flag! The jury composed of craftsmen and shopkeepers found

> ... a verdict of justifiable homicide on these grounds—that no Riot Act was read, nor any proclamation advising the people to disperse: that the Government did not take the proper precautions to prevent the meeting from assembling; and that the conduct of the police was ferocious, brutal and unprovoked by the people; and we moreover, express our anxious hope that the Government will, in future, take better precautions to prevent the recurrence of such disgraceful transactions in the Metropolis.

The Coroner endeavored to dissuade the jury of this verdict, but the jury argued back, sticking to its finding. Their opinions were not uniform, the foremen said—"there have been conflicting opinions among us"—yet this was "the conscientious verdict of us all."

Let us add to this de Tocqueville's stress on the educational function of the jury:

> The jury contributes powerfully to form the judgment and to increase the natural intelligence of a people; and this, in my opinion, is its

greatest advantage. It may be regarded as a gratuitous public school, ever open, in which every juror learns his rights, enters into daily communication with the most learned and enlightened members of the upper classes, and becomes practically acquainted with the laws, which are brought within the reach of his capacity by the efforts of the bar, the advice of the judge, and even the passions of the parties. I think that the practical intelligence and political good sense of the Americans are mainly attributable to the long use that they have made of the jury in civil causes.[14]

If the criminal trial jury dates back almost 800 years as a check on the King, it dates 350 years as a check on the judges. Let us take the case of Free-Born John Lilburne, who in 1653 referred to "his honorable Jury, and said they were the keepers of the Liberties of England; and will make it appear that the Jury are Judges of Law as well as of the Fact." He closed his defense, "You judges sit there, being no more, if the jury please, but ciphers to pronounce the sentence, or their clerks to say Amen." This puts the judge in his/her place.

In 1670, William Penn gathered a crowd speaking truth to Power in Gracechurch Street, London. Power imprisoned him for it. At his trial, one of the jurors, Bushel, refused to convict him of a crime. The judge said of the hold-out, "I will cut his nose," but lost on appeal. Horne Tooke, Thomas Hardy, and John Thelwall were acquitted of sedition in 1794, and their jurors were feasted and toasted all over town, their independence commemorated in tokens and medals. In O'Coigley's case (1798) one of the prospective jurors shook his fist at the Irishman cursing him as a damned rascal, but the judge did not determine that such blatant partiality or "unindifferency" was grounds for dismissal, and O'Coigley hanged whilst defiantly and pointedly peeling an orange. The parodist, William Hone, was acquitted in 1817, which was also the year of trial for treason of the workers who led the Pentridge Rising. A spy wrote the Home Office of Thomas Bacon, an old Jacobin, "Old Bacon has been telling the prisoners they are not tried by their Peers but by men of property." William Cuffay, a son of a slave, black tailor and English Chartist leader in 1848 was transported to Australia despite his protest that the "jurors were not his equals as he was a journey-man mechanic."

It is always a fight to determine who is a peer and who is an equal. Pauli Murray led the struggle to prevent discrimination against women on the jury pools. If the modern jury is mainly middle-aged, middle-class, and middle-minded, to paraphrase Lord Devlin, it need not remain that way. The wise defense attorney serves 'the Gang of Twelve' with all due respect. In a society so driven between rich and poor, the concept of an 'equal' is fairly foreign in the court room.

After the French Revolution was defeated, Henry Kissinger's favorite period of history commenced: the conservative reaction, a period of Church, King, and Banks. Such destruction! Such slavery! So in 1816, interest in the jury resumed, as we find in Jefferson, de Tocqueville, and Shelley. It preoccupied Thomas Jefferson after he left public life. "Divide the counties into wards," he wrote. These were "elementary republics" or "little republics" in which the voice and vigor of the whole people could be directly expressed.[15] In 1835 Alexis de Tocqueville said of the American jury that it "places the real direction of society in the hands of the governed."[16] He continued, "The jury system as it is understood in America appears to me to be as direct and as extreme a consequence of the sovereignty of the people as universal suffrage."

De Tocqueville wrote:

The institution of the jury may be aristocratic or democratic, according to the class from which the jurors are taken; but it always preserves its republican character, in that it places the real direction of society in the hands of the governed, or of a portion of the governed, and not in that of the government. Force is never more than a transient element of success, and after force comes the notion of right. A government able to reach its enemies only upon a field of battle would soon be destroyed. The true sanction of political laws is to be found in penal legislation; and if that sanction is wanting, the law will sooner or later lose its cogency. He who punishes the criminal is therefore the real master of society. Now, the institution of the jury raises the people itself, or at least a class of citizens, to the bench of judges.[17]

De Tocqueville also observed that "If an oppressive law were passed, liberty would still be protected by the mode of executing that law; the majority cannot descend to the details and what may be called the puerilities of administrative tyranny."[18]

In 1820, P.B. Shelley started to write an essay called "A System of Government by Juries"—maybe the word "system" deterred him from finishing—but we have a fragment which begins, "Government, as it now subsists, is perhaps an engine at once the most expensive and inartificial that could have been devised as a remedy for the imperfections of society. Immense masses of the product of labour are committed to the discretion of certain individuals for the purpose of executing its intentions, or interpreting its meaning. These have not been consumed, but wasted in the principal part of the past history of political society."[19]

Something about Shelley's prose causes you to stop and think. For him too, he began to think and then stopped, hence the fragment. There are just three sentences here. In that first sentence, government is compared to a machine, a telling comparison in his age when various machines were introduced in order to destroy the apprenticeship system, the living wage of textile workers, the careful and autonomous domestic rhythms of work, and the standards of production. Comparing government to machinery, he implies that government too did much the same—dumbing down the children, introducing starvation wages, speeding-up production under industrial work-discipline, and beginning the production of shoddy. The powerful critic of the period was Captain Ludd. What does he mean by "inartificial"? It means not in accordance with artistic principles, rude and clumsy, not produced by constructive skill or technical art.

The second sentence refers to taxation and surplus value. The word labor at that time in the discourse of political economy stood for money or the entire of social production as we saw in the declaration of the National Union of the Working Classes. The mass of surplus value was at the command of a single class of capitalists. Then with the third sentence, he proposes that we understand that all political history suffered from the identical expropriation by the state. This is part of the tremendous anarchist daring, the profound radicalism, of Shelley.

Shelley exiled himself from England, once to Ireland another time to Switzerland and Italy where he heard in horror of the Peterloo massacre of the artisans, the women workers, and the children who were meeting to hear a speech by the orator Henry Hunt advocating Parliamentary reform. Perhaps his piece on the jury was a fragment because Shelley wondered about direct democracy while the movement for democratic representation (indirect) was being slaughtered. Shelley wrote the fragment on the jury while intensely thinking of political reform. He wrote about poets: "They are the priests of an unapprehended inspiration, the mirrors of gigantic shadows which futurity casts upon the present; the words which express what they conceive not; the trumpet which sings to battle and feels not what it inspires; the influence which is moved not, but moves. Poets and philosophers are the unacknowledged legislators off the world."[20] His fragment on the jury was thinking about something he could not yet name.

In the eighteenth century, Blackstone said that the jury was the palladium of liberty. Junius disagreed: he said free speech was the palladium of liberty. Habeas corpus was also a strong contender for the prize. But what is it exactly? We are talking about the goddess here. When Ilus founded Troy he prayed to Athene who threw down from heaven a palladium. The palladium was an image of a woman with a spear in one hand, the distaff and spindle in the other, and the aegis wrapped around her breast. Athene named it after her dead Libyan playmate, Pallas. Pallas was African; she helps us understand "black Athena." You dig far enough and you'll find yourself back with the Mother Continent. Touch the woman, touch the rock. "Preserve the Goddess who fell from the sky, and you will preserve your city," said Apollo. Thus, the palladium is that upon which the safety and health of the nation/city depends. Liberty: Africa: the Jury. The palladium is a wreck.

Well, almost. On the very same day that *Magna Carta Manifesto* came back from the publisher, I left the public gallery of the trial of Dr. Catherine Wilkerson in Ann Arbor, Michigan, having heard the verdict. The eloquent defense lawyer, "Buck" Davis, had rested the case urging the jury to reject the prosecution's case. She had come to the aid of a man knocked down and knocked out by police as he was expelled from a meeting where he had been holding a sign protesting war from Iraq to Iran.

Buck Davis defended her on the grounds that in detaining Dr. Wilkerson by wrenching her arm in a hammer lock behind her back, exacerbating a pre-existing shoulder rotator cuff condition, the officer was restraining her speech. The first amendment was violated, said he, and he called it "the criminalization of speech." But what was the speech? There were two kinds: the speech of a doctor to a paramedic advising proper medical treatment, and the speech of a university crowd opposing the arguments of nuclear war against Iran.

The behavior of all these men-in-uniform was consistent with a disturbing national trend, the policing of public lectures. Certainly this was the overall context of the arrests, brutalities, mistakes, and malpractice of the uniformed personnel. The police officers of the municipality, in circumstances allied with the fire department, with the private armed forces of the university, and with the private paramedics, actually superseded the human authority, recognized throughout the world over perhaps two millennia, of a physician in her act of administering life-preserving instructions.

The prosecutor preserves order, the academic transmits truth, the physician provides health. We have well-developed and time-tested habits of mind, protocols of action, and courtesies of respect to assure that these goals are sought harmoniously, as together they comprise, if not utopia, then an actual community. When these habits, protocols, and courtesies are upset, corruption ensues to our entire *habitus*. If the punitive impulse supersedes the educational impulse, or, even worse, if the punitive impulse supersedes the medical impulse, another balance in a community already at war is destroyed.

Recall the origins of the Red Cross which arose to alleviate human suffering in the midst of the slaughter of battle. In 1859 Henry Dunant witnessed 40,000 dead, dying and wounded strewn moaning and twitching on the field of battle of Solferino. He and the local population cared for the wounded without discrimination. The soldier lay down his arms, the healer picked up the stretcher. Each is trained to the respective task. When the cry of pain is uttered, it is time for the guardians of public order to restrain the punitive impulse and to let the doctor do her ancient task, heal the wounded.

It is the one easiest to grasp, of course, by dint of constant repetition. Neighborhood, or human solidarity, is more difficult to grasp, yet it is what we yearn for and fight for. The substance of the speech is what is contested. In one case it may be opposition to preemptive war, in another it may be the right of return, in a third opposition to nuclear bombs, and in this case the provision of medical care.

Buck Davis defended Dr. Wilkerson against the "criminalization of speech" and "the criminalization of medical treatment," the content of the struggle and the substance of the speech. May the police stop the provision of medical treatment to an injured man? Which is to prevail, the principle of healing or the principle of coercion? Which is paramount, the law of force or the principles of diagnostics and therapeutics? When the weak, the injured, the powerless, the aggrieved begin to find strength in their numbers, to find health for injuries in the kindness of strangers, to find redress for grievances in the mutualism of 'one for all and all for one,' then the patriarchal rule of Caesar is threatened. For statesmen, no condition is worse.

In the Roman Empire, Samaria was considered a place of iniquity. Samaritans still live in Nablus and Jaffa. Once it was the capital of an Assyrian province. Samaritan and Jew hated one another, an apparent assumption of the parable described in Luke 10:30–7. "What is the law?" the lawyer asked the carpenter's son of Nazareth, whose terse answer, "to love your neighbor as yourself," only brought another question from the wily lawyer, "And who is my neighbor?" The Legislator of Man replied by telling the story of the man robbed, beaten, and left half dead by the wayside. A priest passed by and did nothing. A Levite similarly passed to the other side of the road. A Samaritan came along and was moved to pity, so bandaged the wounds, bathed them with oil and wine, lifted him onto his animal, and brought him to an inn for care, giving the innkeeper two silver pieces promising more on his return. The story tells us both *who* is a neighbor and *what* is a neighbor.

From Dr. James Parkinson to Dr. Che Guevara to Dr. Benjamin Spock, physicians have understood that the health of the individual is inseparable from the health of society. If society is dependent on exploitation (slavery, wage-slavery, "the poor are always with you"), then ill health becomes inevitable, and some even argue that it is necessary as a stick to beat the healthy just as unemployment beats down wages. The public health movement arose to oppose that view. The criminalization of medical treatment that was brutally attempted in Ann Arbor was thus part of the privatization of health care generally and the devaluation of the class of people who work or who must be ready to work, men, seniors, women, children, immigrants.

There is thus a link between the jurors and the physician. The link between Dr. Catherine Wilkerson and the jurors sitting opposite her express a profound relation of neighborhood on the one hand and healing on the other, neither depending on police, law, or judge. This is why the jury returned a verdict of not guilty, and the puerility of administrative tyranny was properly chastised.

Can the jury become, as it once was, a means of commoning? Can we finish the thinking which Shelley began? Can we restore our palladium from the inhuman wreckage of privatization by participatory democracy and prefigurative politics?

NOTES

1   David Graeber, *Possibilities: Essays on Hierarchy, Rebellion and Desire* (Oakland: AK Press, 2007).

2   Rebecca Solnit, *A Paradise Built in Hell: The Extraordinary Communities That Arise in Disaster* (New York: Viking, 2009).

3   Graeber, 2007.

4   Gustavo Esteva and Madhu Suri Prakash, *Grassroots Post-Modernism: Remaking the Soil of Cultures* (London & New York: Zed Books, 1998).

5   Naomi Klein, "The Vision Thing," in *Confronting Capitalism: Dispatches from a Global Movement*, eds. Eddie Yuen, Daniel Burton-Rose, and George Katsiaficas (Brooklyn: Soft Skull Press, 2004).

6   Graeber, 2007: 356.

7   E.P. Thompson, "In Defense of the Jury," *Persons & Polemics* (Merlin Press: London, 1994).

8   E.P. Thompson, "The State versus its 'Enemies'," *Writing by Candlelight* (London: Merlin Press, 1980).

9   James Boggs, *The American Revolution: Pages from a Negro Worker's Notebook* (New York: Monthly Review Press, 1963); Bill Watson, "Counter-Planning on the Shop-Floor" *Radical America* (May-June 1971); and Huw Beynon, *Working for Ford* (London: Penguin, 1984).

10 Alexis de Tocqueville, *Democracy in America*, translated by Gerald Bevan (Penguin: London, 2003).

11 Thompson, 1980.

12 John W. Cairn and Grant McLeod (eds.), "The Dearest Birth Right of the People of England," *The Jury in the History of the Common Law* (Portland, Oregon: Hart, 2002), 66.

13 E.P. Thompson, "The State versus its 'Enemies'," 107.

14 Tocqueville, 2003.

15 Hannah Arendt, *On Revolution* (Viking: New York, 1965).

16 Tocqueville, 2003, Book 1, Chapter 16.

17 Tocqueville, 2003, Book 1, Chapter 16.

18 Tocqueville, 2003, Book 1, Chapter 16.

19 P.B. Shelley, *A Philosophical Review of Reform* (written in 1820) in David Lee Clark (ed.), *Shelley's Prose* (University of New Mexico Press: 1966).

20 Shelley, 1966.

RADICAL PATIENCE:

Feeling Effective over the Long Haul

Chris Carlsson

MAYBE THERE IS A LIFE cycle of political activism. Whatever our age, we all have experienced that vigorous radicalism of youth as well as the slow diminishing of rage that accompanies the passing of time. Some of us stoke those rages and keep the fires burning for much longer, but even if we do, there is usually a moment of truth where some kind of accommodation with the world as it is must be made—or we go mad, maybe even to the point of suicide. Sometimes that life cycle runs in reverse: we go through life for a time, even entering middle age or later only beginning to smolder, before bursting into a deep anger at the injustice and stupidity that dominates life.

Radical movements lose adherents as steadily as they are joined by new ones. Fallen heroes and martyrs, many lost to their own hands or bad habits, fill the roster of radical activism. As troubling as these losses are, countless other people abandon their politics as they age, growing more conservative with passing years, giving up youthful idealism, ultimately dropping dreams of a more just, equitable, and pleasurable life for all.

If revolution is a shifting target—perhaps better understood as a process than a destination—how do we keep ourselves going in the face of inevitable disappointments? What makes life worth living in a mad world? How does political action feed us and bolster our stamina rather than sap our morale and leave us feeling used up?

Many of us find solace in our relationships, families, and sometimes our communities. But how do we address larger social questions from within our individual lives? Don't we have to alter systems that are much larger than our local or particular conditions? How do we shift the 'imperatives' of growth and industrial production to reflect a biologically harmonious, ecologically sane orientation to life on earth? Shopping conscientiously is not going to do it. Growing our own food, riding our bicycles, and making our own media and art are not going to do it either, at least not by themselves.

Individual responses might be where we find our starting point, but our efforts gain political traction when they shape (and are shaped by) a shared experience. To be sure, there is a shared experience that shapes us all, one that is rarely named in polite company:

class. Class is a complex concept, and this essay is not a treatise on it. But a basic understanding of class is needed to make sense of the world we're in and especially to figure out possibilities for its meaningful transformation.

If you are not pushing a shopping cart down the street looking for cans and bottles, or riding in your Lear Jet to your next golfing vacation in a tropical paradise, you probably think you are middle class. In the U.S., nearly everyone believes they are in the 'middle class.' Whether anyone wants to admit it, the majority of us are working class. Every day, for whatever the price (wage), we find ways to exchange our working lives for money. At the heart of this exchange is the alienation of our creative capacity to shape the world—to decide what is worth doing, how to do it, and with whom. Instead we are hired, where we must do as we are told. Perhaps we are even encouraged to help increase profits by making *suggestions* to improve efficiency. To keep this elaborate rat wheel of dumb work going, countless people now work ten- to twelve-hour days in increasing isolation, driving to and fro, worrying about bills, traffic, love and family, war, pollution, and community. A constant flux of new neighbors, new co-workers, and new cities make it more difficult to build trusting relationships because few people know each other for very long at a given workplace or in many neighborhoods.

Luckily, there is a history to this condition. Life has not always been like this, where it takes five emails and four phone calls to find a time to have a coffee with a friend. We are living through an enormous speed-up of life produced by the accelerating control of society by the logic of capitalism. To perpetuate and extend that control, work processes are continuously revised. New technologies are introduced, more measuring and surveillance is applied, and sometimes factories and offices have to move from one part of the world to another. The result is a fragmented, geographically dispersed, and deskilled workforce, tied together by global shipping, logistics, and communications systems.

This particular design of modern production and distribution is a moment in an unheralded class struggle. Four decades ago, a crash in U.S. profitability led to a number of profound reorganizations of global rules and expectations. In retrospect, we lump it all together under the rubric of 'globalization': free markets and free trade, reduced state budgets, open foreign investment and capital flows; but also thirty years of falling or stagnant income, widespread civil wars and ethnic fratricide, and tight restrictions on human migration (even though there are more people moving across borders these days than ever before). Those global changes were designed in no small part to break up and weaken the working classes that were impeding profitability through their own autonomous actions in the late 1960s and early 1970s.

ON CLASS COMPOSITION[1]

CAPITAL IS A RELATIONSHIP OF social power that warps human relations to its perverse logic but which faces persistent resistance. Seeking to overcome blockages to profitability and continued capital accumulation, capitalists redesign labor processes, integrate new machinery, move factories overseas or across the country, and use state power to enforce their interests legally and militarily. People resist these forces in their normal daily lives by carving out spaces of autonomy in which they act concertedly outside—and often against—capital's attempts to commodify their activities. Capital inexorably seeks to colonize all such spaces and relationships and reintegrate them into the market logic of buying and selling.

Since capital's counterattack began in the mid-1970s, the working class has been systematically altered, or "decomposed." By the late 1960s, movements across the planet had pushed not only for shortened working hours and increased pay but had also, and more crucially, begun contesting the very definitions of life and work and the reasons why we live the way we do. The oil shock of 1973–74 was the first loud response of the world capitalist elite, afraid of losing its power and determined to rein in an unruly working class.[2] Historic wage highs were reached in the early 1970s in the U.S. and elsewhere. Since that time, working hours have been radically intensified and in the 1990s absolutely lengthened, while wages in real dollars have remained constant or diminished. In the early twenty-first century, in spite of an economy four times larger than it was in 1980 (as measured by the terribly inaccurate and misleading Gross Domestic Product [GDP]), we are working more hours per year and working much harder to sustain a life that has not improved![3] Most people are just glad to have work and income in a world where 'falling' is perceived as a real possibility, where one does not have to look beyond the next street corner to see how abject life can be if you do not stay in the good graces of ever-more demanding employers.

Abdication to the initiative of capital has led to the mind-numbing expansion of useless work while social needs are neglected and creative capacities left dormant. People are richly rewarded to create advertising, to invent new 'financial instruments,' to design 'anti-personnel' bombs, to analyze ways to increase credit card use (debt). This same society will not spend meaningful resources on early childhood education, and it starves public schools of the most basic resources. Public subsidies pour into agribusiness and oil company coffers while urban gardens are bulldozed to make way for box stores and warehouses, and organic farmers have to sell their unsubsidized products at higher prices. Basic needs are going unmet for millions. Worse, urgent efforts at long-term and medium-term planning to adapt to the increasingly visible collapse of natural systems are rejected out of ideological blindness. But individual human ingenuity is flowing in spite of government and corporate obstacles. People who work for solutions to the social and ecological crises of our time supersede the role of simple laborers in order to plan and carry out incredible amounts of necessary (if frequently unpaid) work.

"Class composition" frames the ebb and flow of social movements that erupt and subside in relation to the dynamics of economic expansion and contraction, but it is not narrowly determined by that relationship. The complexity of daily life can lead at times to atomization, political fragmentation, or depoliticization, and at other times can create common sensibilities or unified political responses. In order to overturn fatalism and unleash our potential to live consciously and collaboratively, it is fruitful to study the social conditions under which life is reproduced and how those relationships and institutions that shape our lives are understood. Some radicals have challenged or reinvigorated the standard definitions that have come down from earlier political movements. One of the freshest analysts is John Holloway, who breaks with the nearly religious adherence to a glorified concept of the working class. He has written, "Capitalism is the ever renewed generation of class, the ever renewed class-ification of people."

> We do not struggle *as* working class, we struggle *against* being working class, against being classified…. There is nothing good about being members of the working class, about being ordered, commanded, separated from our product and our process of production. Struggle

arises not from the fact that we are working class but from the fact that we-are-and-are-not working class, that we exist against-and-beyond being working class, that they try to order and command us but we do not want to be ordered and commanded, that they try to separate us from our product and our producing and our humanity and our selves and we do not want to be separated from all that. In this sense, working-class identity is not something "good" to be treasured, but something "bad," something to be fought against, something that is fought against, something that is constantly at issue. The working class cannot emancipate itself in so far as it is working class. It is only in so far as we *are not* working class that the question of emancipation can even be posed.... The working class does not stand outside capital: on the contrary it is capital that defines it (us) as working class. Labor stands opposed to capital, but it is an internal opposition. It is only as far as labor is something *more than* labor, the worker *more than* a seller of labor power, that the issue of revolution can even be posed.[4]

Precisely because so many people find their work lives inadequate, incomplete, degrading, pointless, stupid, and oppressive, they form identities, communities, and meaning outside of paid work, in spaces where they *are not* working class. It is in these activities that people who are reduced on the job to 'mere workers' become fully human, fully engaged with their capacities to create, to shape, to invent, to cooperate without compulsion, to bring consciously to life relations, objects, and activities of their own choice.

The decomposition of the working class imposed by three decades of global crisis and restructuring has isolated most people and broken the transmission belts of class and community memory, at least in North America. Such a severe fragmentation stands in the way of the human need for community, solidarity, and cooperation. For the most part, the glue that holds human society together seems to be commerce, but countless invisible daily interactions precede commerce, without which the economy could not exist. From having a conversation, to watching a child, to helping someone lift an object or make a choice, daily life is the pre-existing raw material that capital seeks to exploit.

The steady 'mining' of daily life—of the capacities and increasingly the knowledge of people who sell their labor—feeds the expansion of new kinds of products. People, left to their own devices, learn, think, mature, and invent. This makes them more productive workers, who can give greater skills and knowledge to capital when employed as wage-labor. This underscores one paradox lying at the heart of the technological advancement: when human labor is supplanted by machines, humans are free to work less and pursue their own interests, but activities individuals pursue often bolster their usefulness to capital when they are employed. Moreover, capital seeps into every nook and cranny of life and creates new work as fast as it reduces the human labor needed in previous systems. In her book *Network Culture*, author Tiziana Terranova describes how this restructured capitalism has annexed more and more of our "free time":

> ... the paradox of immaterial labor in the age of general intellect, is that the production of value increasingly takes place in what was supposed to be "liberated time" and in "free action," in as much as at least in late capitalist societies, this liberated, intensive time is the force that

drives innovation in the information economy… in a sense, we might
say that productivity starts before one even goes to work and cannot be
measured according to traditional criteria.[5]

Instead of a steady reduction of working time, capital brings a vast intensification and expansion of work, such that we are now enduring one of the greatest 'speed-ups' in human history (alongside one of the sharpest accelerations of wealth polarization). Modern capitalism spends enormous resources selling products as replacements for human interaction, portraying commodities as superior alternatives. But technological mediation is unsustainable—not just in ecological terms (though it is that too), but crucially, in social terms. Human beings want to congregate, socialize, party, discuss and debate, share and cooperate. It may be the most powerful drive we have.

As businesses are spending ever more money advertising endless rivers of New Stuff, increasing numbers of people are turning away. Still at the margins of modern life for now, many individuals and communities are making new ways to live together based on engagement with a range of ecologically informed technologies. These initiatives do not just promise to reinvent our relationships with transportation, food, energy, art, and culture, but underpin a deeper challenge to how we frame knowledge and truth. Out of these emergent convivial communities, which are largely grounded in unpaid practical work, a gradual reversal of the extreme atomization of modern life is beginning.

Capital does co-opt, but not everything that we do in our free time is (or could possibly be) immediately co-opted by capital. In the context of a global ecological crisis, a crisis of the commons that is already centuries old, and the increasingly urgent necessity of shifting how we choose what work is done and how to do it, a new kind of class consciousness is taking shape. This new class consciousness escapes the boundaries that have been erected around the concept over the last two centuries.

THE PROBLEM OF POLITICS

THE TASKS BEFORE US ARE daunting. Climate change is well underway, and in response, many are organizing to put the brakes on industrial systems whose pollution is accelerating the breakdown of climate predictability. But there is a disconnection between, on one hand, efforts to reinvent our daily lives on a new basis, and on the other hand, the out-of-control capitalist system and its main actors, corporations and governments. Bridging that gap is the challenge of our time. Many people are already busy with the kinds of everyday life changes we need to reduce human pressure on climate and ecosystems, and to reinvent urban life. But these activities taken individually or in aggregate do not seem to impact politics or economics in any serious way. In other words, our urgent, arduous, and creative efforts are politically invisible and have no political voice when it comes to shaping the future of human society.

This is partly because the old ways of organizing have been forgotten or, in some cases, rejected. Leaving behind centralized, quasi-authoritarian social forms like trade unions and political parties is an act of self-liberation. But in the resulting space, we have not found new ways to organize ourselves to contest power. The 'ad-hocracies' that came together to challenge the World Trade Organization (WTO), the International Monetary Fund, the G-8, and the G-20 have depended too much on people who have the wherewithal to travel long distances and sleep on couches and floors. This is usually a young, somewhat affluent crowd, and though they may live without much overt wealth, they usually are not desperately poor. The alter-globalistas have comprised the majority of protesters in the decade since the 1999 WTO protests in Seattle. I don't intend to criticize the demographics of those people who have been involved; it is not entirely their fault if large numbers of other people have not joined their protests and demonstrations. But they (we) do bear some responsibility for the narrowness of the culture of protest, as well as many of its self-conceptions, behaviors, and, frankly, consumer tastes—none of which are easy to embrace if you're not already 'in the church.'

Political actions rooted in daily life, rather than in spectacular protest, are more elusive nowadays. Strikes have lost their power, except in the public sector or education contexts where the bureaucracies, hospitals, and schools cannot be moved offshore. Demonstrations are ignored or ridiculed, rendered invisible or absurd. Participating in traditional political demonstrations often feels like an exercise in impotence, being herded by self-appointed monitors, barked at by overheated orators who specialize in tired clichés, and subsumed in a mass with which we can barely identify. (It is also true that even the dullest demonstration to a jaded participant can be a life-changing experience for a newcomer. Therein lies some of the lasting attraction of the form, which otherwise seems moribund).

When politics appears in public, it shows up as dueling advertising campaigns *masquerading* as politics. Most of us have a palpable hunger to take part in history, to act and to be effective. But when we bring excluded questions, hidden populations, and forgotten problems to the public arena—during an election campaign, for example—we are pushed aside as annoyances or attacked as threats.

During national elections, the actors are pre-cast, the scripts already written, and history is staged as pre-regurgitation. What is a dissenter to do? Locked in protest pens at summits and conventions, barked at by 'official speakers,' entertained by 'radical' millionaire musicians, is it our historic role to be a faceless mass, to cheer on cue, to march where and when we are 'allowed,' hoping against hope that our clever home-made sign will skitter behind the reporter's thirty-second TV spot on 'the protest'? Surely we can do better. It must be possible to shatter the glittering chimeras of pseudo-democracy and finally resurrect something approaching a genuine public politics.

The shrinking boundaries of protest and politics have already turned generations of thoughtful Americans away from participating in their irrelevance. But it does not end with that. The pre-defined rules of political engagement have successfully depoliticized a majority of the population, forcing the reinvention of opposition and political/historic agency on new terms. Exploring the fissures of modern life, probing for weak spots in the ruling order, uncovering resources in our daily lives that are practically invisible until we stop to look, finding the real politics of everyday life—these are vague descriptions of a necessary reorientation that can rapidly and dramatically re-engage us as actors in our own drama, as makers of our own histories.

One characteristic of the empty politics on display in national elections is how much the real issues of daily life are systematically ignored: what work is being done, by whom, to what end, under whose control? How can cities be reinvented to radically reduce energy use, improve human communities, feed everyone fresh and tasty food, guarantee basic sanitation and health care to all? How do we redesign our transit systems so that we don't slaughter 50,000 people a year (and treat that murderousness as 'natural' as the weather)? Can climate change and global warming be addressed locally through de-paving, urban agriculture, and aquaculture, as well as an urgent commitment to a flourishing biodiversity to complement our under-nourished cultural diversity? How can we democratize decisions, socially and politically, that shape our technological choices?

Democracy is a hollow ritual. It is at the same time a radical expectation! We want to democratize our lives, not just in electoral rituals, but to profoundly alter the rhythm of life so that each and every one of us has a real say over the conditions of our lives. It is not a matter of better leaders getting elected, but reorganizing how we decide life itself should be arranged. But 'politics' has been severed from our day-to-day lives.

In our role as producers, as economic actors, we are expected to negotiate the price of our labor as 'free individuals' or, in some societies, together in unions. But the idea that we should contribute our efforts to social prosperity and share the products of those collective efforts as an extension of our democratic lives is considered absurd. If we want to 'act' and effect change, we are left to 'vote with our wallets' and buy the 'right' products. What about deciding what products should even exist? How should they be produced? What ecological consequences are socially acceptable and which are not? Which technologies facilitate the general welfare, including ecological health, and which are impossibly in conflict with those goals? There are so many basic questions rendered invisible and meaningless by this hollow democracy we are living every day.

Changing the frame of reference for political thinking is a key long-term, even life-long task for making radical change not only plausible but, crucially, *desirable*. For protesters and dissenters in our mad world, a difficult but urgent challenge is to convince people who do not already share our views to come along. But dissent revels in its outsider status, its angry self-righteousness. It can inspire those who are already upset, already at the cusp of refusal and revolt. But what about those who are unhappy, unclear on the causes of their woes, and basically afraid that 'change' will make things worse? Today's radicals are awful at speaking across this divide. If we can't overcome our sense of superiority long enough to actually converse with people who are not already like us, then we will not know how to describe the world we are fighting for. Will it be better than this one? Sure, of course. But how? How will life be better for most people in a post-capitalist, ecologically sane world?

On our path, problems are addressed instead of ignored, while individual skills and tastes are welcomed and encouraged instead of stifled and defeated. Life for everyone improves greatly while planetary ecological health shapes our deeper vision of wealth. Rather than a mindless social system dedicated to an absurd measurement called 'growth,' we propose a different way of understanding well-being. We seek a relatively stable, comfortable life for everyone on earth, based on generalized abundance, less work, and a regenerative approach to physical and social resources. Put very simply, let's not waste and destroy the foundation of life and call it economic health!

Revolution can seem an empty goal without a real engagement on the ground with daily lives *as they are*. To that end, spectacular protests at national conventions or international summits can become unmoored and attract only a self-referential set of subcultures. To be sure, those of us in these 'choirs' need to keep dialoguing with each other in addition to widening our scope to welcome people with other agendas and experiences. Experiments in tactics and self-organization at convergence centers, guerrilla gardens, mass bike rides, and even familiar marches and picket lines are all important parts of maintaining and growing a culture of opposition.

But let's admit that 'activist identity' is not an attractive role model. Activists are not prefiguring the New Man (or Woman)! But they are separating from an oppressive and

maladapted society, making consumer choices (or refusals) that demonstrate a more ethical and ecological lifestyle. Often they are also producing new communities as they find
new ways to reproduce life outside of what is considered 'normal.'

Not everyone wants to join though, and this causes some to dismiss these activist experiments and enclaves as self-marginalizing. To some extent, that is true. Folks who have
chosen to live 'off the grid' as much as possible have different aesthetics and tastes than
folks who live in suburbs and work in offices all day. They distance themselves from the
behaviors and products that they abhor, but those same behaviors and products are often
at the heart of 'mainstream culture,' from wage-labor to TV and video games, to hot dogs
and hamburgers. Insofar as their critique remains hitched to anti-consumerism, the self-
marginalization is reinforced and worsened.

But if the critique begins to propose and enact new ways of doing things or providing
for the general well-being, then something new is potentially afoot. It is precisely in the
community food gardens, the mass bike rides, the tinkering and experimenting going
on in alternative energy and fuels, free software, and many other avenues where we see
quotidian examples of this new kind of production. By producing goods from recycled
materials, or that use much less energy or water, and by doing it in ways that escape the
narrow bounds of capital and wage-labor, these activities can be seen as pre-figurative
moments where today's workers (broadly understood) are deciding and carrying out their
own activities, under their own control, and often for the sake of ecological health.

These kinds of activities are historically rooted too. Our amnesiac culture promotes a
disconnection between the culture of Now and the long histories that got us here. If we
better understand those histories and see our choices as rooted in a social context that is
historically defined, we often have better choices and make better decisions going forward.
Community food gardens, for example, depend on knowledge developed by millions of
gardeners and urban farmers who provided 40% of the country's fresh produce by the end
of World War II from their "Victory Gardens." Bicycling activism depends in part on an
ever-growing mountain of discarded machines and parts, and a growing desertion from
the rat wheel of car ownership and debt. But the tactics that have spread the culture, from
Critical Mass to social and political protest rides, have roots stretching back more than a
century to the Good Roads movement of the 1890s. New political and social networks
have used online tools to facilitate their growth and densification, rediscovering a web of
human relations in the virtual ether of the internet.

Learning from the *piqueteros* in Argentina and Bolivia who clogged the vital arteries of
modern society by blockading roads, we can turn our attention to the vulnerable *flows* on
which modern society depends, rather than the static spectacles designed to absorb and
demoralize oppositional energies. Learning from radical reform groups like the Ontario
Coalition Against Poverty, who combine direct action with demands for improved social
safety nets and benefits, points us towards practical goals with tactics that reinforce and
expand communities who can act together.[6]

Ultimately, our ability to persist over the long haul, facing certain disappointments
and defeats amidst our successes, depends on the pleasure we take from living our lives to
the fullest. Avoiding the cycle of frenzied overwork and burnout in favor of a convivial life
of good friends, good food, and full enjoyment is a *political responsibility!* We *can* change
the world, and our everyday behaviors *do make a difference*. But we cannot subordinate
our own pleasure of living to urgent political agendas—no matter how vital they might
sound. Our enjoyment is a much more subversive force than our anger, as is our dignity.

This is not to say that anger is not a well-established motivator. Few revolutionary movements, or even resistance movements, have lacked their angry partisans, and that anger has fueled heroic acts and surprising turns of history. But our practice of mirthful enjoyment is the crucial resource fueling our ability to actually create and develop new ways to organize life in the shell of the old ways. A deep enjoyment of living gives us the resilience to continue in the face of adversity and also puts into immediate practice some of the goals towards which our political efforts are striving. We cannot subordinate our lives to an unknown future and must live as fully as we can now, knowing that our satisfactions sustain us, demonstrate what is possible, and give hope to many others.

But I do not mean to reduce this to a Manichean opposition between anger and pleasure. Dignity is a driving motivation for people in every corner of the world, and is often an even more powerful foundation on which to build a life that can sustain itself over the long haul. A friend recently told me this story:

> Over a decade ago, there was a fantastic interview with a couple of South African militants forced into exile to avoid being killed during the reign of apartheid. They were asked, "During all those long, darkest years of apartheid, how did you keep going in the face of so much defeat? How did you stay hopeful?" They both laughed, "Hope. We never had hope! It was so bleak. We saw hope as completely irrelevant. What kept us going was our dignity. We knew what we were doing was our best response, regardless of whether it was effective. We did what we knew we should do. It was based on realizing our fundamental dignity as a human being. It was what made our lives worth living."

Radical patience takes many forms. It does not mean frivolously self-indulgent behavior while the world burns, but it also does not mean endless worry, stress, and sacrifice. It does not mean waiting around for others to change things, but it does mean recognizing that history moves in fits and starts—sometimes your own work is part of a lurch forward (or sideways), but much more often, our political activities accrete slowly across time and space, giving others self-confidence and strength to carry on far from our immediate view. Keeping our inner fires burning steadily requires a good sense of history—fantasies of sudden, overwhelming change are fundamentally religious beliefs. Real change, deep and lasting, takes mutual aid and cooperation on a scale few of us can imagine and almost none of us have experienced. We catch glimpses of it when we come together in large-scale protests, when for a fleeting time we feel the solidarity and visionary excitement that set us on fire in the first place.

It is in our daily lives that we can find real solidarity, which in turn can provide interesting combinations of security and satisfaction. Social experiences rooted in solidarity, sharing, and new-found trust are self-generating. The more you participate, the more you can extend this logic to newcomers and old acquaintances alike. Radical patience is one of the resources we cultivate to withstand the inevitable failures and disappointments of our grand plans to remake life. It allows us to be resilient, flexible, thoughtful, and innovative. Radical patience lets us stay in the game, do what we can, accept our limits without seeing them as fixed or permanent, and emerge day after day to push against the world of stupid work, war, and ecological destruction. The sky might be falling, but radical politics requires confidence, humor, and steadfastness. Hand-wringing despair, guilt-tripping, and

sacrificial politics are the enemies of a revolution worth fighting for. Pleasure and cooperation are their own reward and can nurture basic human dignity along with the seeds of
revolt. We have to be patient with ourselves and our friends, family, and neighbors, while
not giving in to inactivity, spectacle, or despair. Even in the times when it does not go
where we want it to, history is a ride to be fully enjoyed.

NOTES

1   This discussion of class composition is taken from my book *Nowtopia: How Pirate Program-
    mers, Outlaw Bicyclists, and Vacant-Lot Gardeners are Inventing the Future Today* (Oakland: AK
    Press, 2008).

2   For a full analysis of the price of oil in combating working class militancy, first in the so-
    called First World, then turning the attack to the oil-producing workers themselves later, see:
    Midnight Notes Collective (eds.), *Midnight Oil: Work, Energy, War, 1973–1992* (Brooklyn:
    Autonomedia, 1992).

3   For example, the Gross Domestic Product "grows" when a person gets into a car accident,
    leading to the consumption of emergency services, follow-up medical services, a new car or
    repair to the old one, etc. GDP measures the movement of monetary value, regardless of
    whether or not it is a negative expenditure, worthless, or actually making life worse (think mili-
    tary production). Many alternative systems to measure the quality of life have been designed
    (the Genuine Progress Indicator being one, HTTP://WWW.RPROGRESS.ORG/PROJECTS/GPI/), but
    none have yet supplanted the pernicious GDP.

4   John Holloway, *Change the World Without Taking Power* (London: Pluto Press, 2002),
    142–45.

5   Tiziana Terranova, *Network Culture: Politics for the Information Age* (Ann Arbor, MI: Pluto
    Press, 2004), 30–31.

6   More on the Ontario Coalition Against Poverty can be found at HTTP://WWW.OCAP.CA.

INTERVIEWS

SECTION SUMMARY

THE WINDS THAT CIRCULATE THROUGH the United States and across the planet often need reminders of the ground they are blowing over; this also holds true for Team Colors, as we attempt to situate this book amongst current struggles. We thus conclude this collection with three interviews of movement elders. As historians, organizers, and theorists in their own right, Robin D.G. Kelley, Ashanti Alston, and Grace Lee Boggs have been engaged in decades of cumulative struggle; in their words we seek both history and lessons.

Historian and scholar Robin D.G. Kelley brings forward an analysis that develops from the urgent questions faced in contemporary struggles for social justice. In **"Challenging Power and Creating New Spaces of Possibility: A Discussion with Robin D.G.**

Kelley," he discusses the political trajectories that challenged and clarified his understandings of change, noting the importance of everyday resistance, political education, and historical memory within movements. Kelley argues for a renewed emphasis on reflection, projection, and imagination in struggle, sustained with practices of integrity and daily politics of desire.

Ashanti Omowali Alston draws from his experiences in the Black Power movement and the challenges posed by a wide range of struggles and methodologies, as he illustrates his becoming-revolutionary process in **"We Can Begin to Take Back Our Lives: A Discussion with Ashanti Omowali Alston."** Ashanti delineates the contributions of many movements, noting the importance of community work and confronting histories of privilege and oppression. He suggests that we will have to do whatever is necessary to resist oppressive forces if we are to create new worlds and lives.

Philosopher and activist Grace Lee Boggs has been instrumental in evolving our understandings of revolution in the United States. In **"The Power Within Us to Create the World Anew: A Discussion with Grace Lee Boggs,"** Grace reflects on her early involvement in political organizing, the connections she sees across the history of struggle, and the necessity of transformation, divisions, and complexities. She sees new questions and 'answers' emerging in places as wide-ranging as Copenhagen and Montgomery, and in projects as disparate as urban agriculture and healing work.

Thus this collection ends with an appropriate reminder: that the myriad organizations, strategies, theories, and histories circulating within today's whirlwinds illustrate our capacity for ushering in new worlds and ways of living, fueled by "the power within us to begin anew." It is up to readers to discern the uses of these whirlwinds in amplifying, improving, and furthering the struggles of our everyday lives.

CHALLENGING POWER AND CREATING NEW SPACES FOR POSSIBILITY:

A Discussion with Robin D.G. Kelley

Benjamin Holtzman[1]

Robin D.G. Kelley has been called "the preeminent historian of black popular culture writing today." His works include Hammer and Hoe: Alabama Communists During the Great Depression *(University of North Carolina, 1990) and* Race Rebels: Culture, Politics and the Black Working Class *(Free Press, 2004), among numerous other books and articles. Kelley's historical analyses have consistently offered brilliant insight into past political and cultural realities and have just as often provided critical political lessons for today's radicals. In this interview, Kelley discusses his politicization, the connections between social struggle and historical study, everyday resistance, the turn-of-the-century alter-globalization protests in the U.S., and, finally, the election of Barack Obama.*

Benjamin Holtzman: *Growing up, what was your introduction to politics and political engagement?*

Robin D.G. Kelley: I grew up in New York, my young years right up in the Harlem/Washington Heights area. My mother was a single parent whose politics were informed by her spiritual convictions. She was a member of the Self-Realization Fellowship. Paramahansa

Yogananda. Back in the 1960s, everyone was reading *Autobiography of a Yogi*, which wasn't political, but it informed a kind of bohemian, collectivist politics and a concern with the public. With my mother, she was always involved in school issues. In the middle to late 1960s, the main issues were overcrowded schools, community control. These were issues that were dear to my mother. She was a role model. Then, moving to the West Coast, it was more of the same. Makani Themba, who is the Founding Director of the Praxis Project, she's my big sister, so she was a role model as well in terms of her high school and college activism, mainly around issues of race. Like a lot of young African Americans— especially growing up in New York City, where the Black Panther Party had a presence and had a free breakfast program in our area, where Black Nationalism was in the fabric of social life—you just can't help it; race becomes the dominant factor. It was not until I got to college, and then listening to my sister, that we began to move towards Marxist/Leninist politics. That led both of us to join the Communist Workers Party. To go from the All-African People's Revolutionary Party to the Communist Workers Party made sense in the early 1980s. It may not make sense to young people today. That was really the beginning of it. It's still evolving.

BH: *How do you think your background and upbringing contributed to your political beliefs and positioning and the types of activities that you've been involved with over the years?*

RDGK: I guess there are three things. One, growing up in a low-income, oppressed community of people, every day you witness grassroots, community-based organizing. We didn't see much labor union organizing. We didn't see much national organizing. We saw local, grassroots, community-based organizing, where women, who were friends with my mother, who lived up on 157th street, would be fighting the landlords on a day-to-day basis. They would be out there protesting the conditions of the schools, the failure to pick up the trash, the basic survival issues. Number two, growing up in New York and later in Los Angeles, political education was important. It wasn't enough to take battle by battle, issue by issue. We also witnessed street corner speakers and soapbox speakers who would speak to a crowd for two hours at a time about issues, like why we need reparations. This is like 1969, '70', '71. Issues like, why we need to support the Chinese revolution and why we need to support the struggles of African peoples worldwide. So suddenly, what appears to be a world dominated politically by local issues then connects with the globe. Most of those speakers weren't talking about landlords. They really were talking about what was happening across the Pacific, or the Atlantic, or in the Caribbean. The third thing, in terms of my own upbringing, had to do with my mother's household. My mother never cursed. She never raised her voice. She never really showed anger. She showed enormous empathy for people, and care and love of other people. She would bring strangers into the house who didn't have a place to stay. Her politics were driven not by a hatred of the man or a hatred of power, but by a love for humanity. And that was spiritual for her. Her religion demanded that she treat human beings as if they're her family and that she love everybody. She practiced it to this day. You ask my mother, "Is that politics?" She'd say, "No, not really." And yet it is politics, very much as a political practice.

BH: *I suspect you might continue on some of those themes with this question. One thing that is striking about your work is the tremendous sense of optimism you have about the future— that today's political activities really can led to significant change and that greater freedom* *and liberation really may not be too far off in the future. Where did this optimism come from, and how have you retained it so well in your outlook, especially during periods of low political mobilization?*

RDGK: You know what, that's a *good* question. It doesn't come from any abstract sense of hope. Nor does it come from any sense of denial about the political realities that confront us and the extent of power and how it works. It comes out of being a historian. There are so many historical examples of seemingly impossible circumstances in which we had these revolutionary transformations. The period I always turn back to is the period of the end of slavery and Reconstruction. W.E.B. Du Bois' masterpiece, *Black Reconstruction*, I think is the most important political text I've ever read in my life. What he shows is what happens when enslaved people have this vision of what society ought to look like: what the public sphere should look like, how to govern, how to reconstruct social lives around schools, churches, the right to vote, reconstructing families. You have in a matter of less than a decade a moment where people who were enslaved go to suddenly passing legislation in the states of South Carolina and Mississippi and places like that, calling for land reform, implementing free universal public education. There's been nothing like it. We had more black senators in those days than today. No one in 1864 thought, "This is what's going to happen in 1869." In the so-called Civil Rights movement or human rights movement in 1951, no one thought that Jim Crow would actually be toppled. It's hard to see what's possible. It's hard to see the future. It's easy to look in hindsight. I think our problem is that when we look in hindsight, we tend to focus on the failures and losses and the intransigence of power. If our expectation is that you can challenge power and create space for new possibilities, then we have millions of examples of that.

BH: *I want to keep talking about history for a little bit. I understand that when you first began to study history seriously—not just as an undergraduate, but even in graduate school—that you did so not with the intention of becoming a historian, but to "attempt to solve a series of political problems."[2] Can you discuss how "political problems" led you to pursuing historical research?*

RDGK: At the time, I was literally caught between a very classic debate or struggle of living between a black nationalism/Third World nationalism/anti-colonial position versus emphasis on class struggle and proletarian revolution. So, I'm reading everything I can read on the subject, from the Russian and Chinese revolutions to African and Caribbean to the United States, and I'm trying to figure out what's the best path forward for someone who, at the time, identified as a Communist in the United States. That's why I decided to write my dissertation on the Communist Party in a place that did not have traditions of Marxism/Leninism and did have a black majority.[3] That was my lesson. I learned a lot about how people bring their own cultures and traditions to movements. I learned a lot about the dynamics between race and class and, in particular, the challenge—always the challenge—to mobilize white working people in support of anti-racism. I went there thinking, "I'm going to study black history." I learned more about white working-class consciousness and building solidarity—and what that means and the cost of that—than I did about the black liberation movement. It was very helpful to me. Each one of the texts that I ended up publishing grew out of the political questions of the day. They didn't grow out of trying to make a contribution to scholarship. In fact, to this day, I've never written a book, *ever*, with the mindset of, "Here's a gap in the scholarship, I really want to fill it." I'm not interested in that.

BH: *In your experience, how great of a sense of history do you think those involved in current U.S. political movements have? Do you think that history is underutilized as a tool or form of knowledge amongst those engaged in political activities today?*

RDGK: I'm afraid to generalize too much because I think that there are some organizations and movements in which history is essential. In the Labor/Community Strategy Center in Los Angeles, they're constantly studying history. The Miami Workers Center, a great activist center, they're always thinking about historical issues. I think that it's on peoples' minds. I also think that we as so-called "professional historians" have not done as good a job of looking at things that really matter. I include myself in that. There are some movements that are studied over and over again. How many takes on Garveyism can you really have? How many books on the Civil Rights movement can you really have? But what happened in Detroit in the 1970s and '80s is extremely important for understanding history; it's just not on the agenda. Moreover, I think that we place so much emphasis on studying the history of social movements, successes, and failures, and we probably need to spend more time looking at the reproduction of power and how things work. What are the weaknesses in a system? How are decisions made? Something as basic as the history of Katrina. So much of the story is about grassroots organizing on the ground. But a good part of the story is about the recent history of corruption and business as usual for the Bush administration. I think the more that stuff is exposed and the more we trace the relationships between those corporations and slumlords and gentrification, then we start to realize that the communities that are falling apart are not falling apart by accident; they're connected to public policy. I think how they're connected is something we need to know more about. I hope future historians deal with these questions of power more directly.

BH: *Do you mean specifically that historians who have focused on social movements have not engaged enough with what is happening on a policy level or the interactions between the two, and instead focus too much on the grassroots efforts?*

RDGK: Well, I'm being self-critical. I don't want to attack or criticize everybody. What I've come to realize is that a lot of people involved in social movements want history that's inspiring: successes, strategy. But with strategy comes understanding how power works, where it lies. Even something like an electoral strategy at a local level is actually useful. Greensboro, North Carolina is really a great example of what happens when a group of radicals decide, "You know what, we'll calculate: we could actually take over the city council." What's so radical about that, taking over the city council? They essentially pass a living wage bill at the municipal level, which raises wages significantly. They wage a battle against Kmart. They have a platform now. In some cities, that's not going to work. In other cities, it does work. We need to understand just how power operates. Even for those people in the university who say, "Where do these investments go?" What's the relationship between university endowments and, say, the prison industrial complex? Expose those things. I love when I tell my students, "Your project now is to study the university from the top down and follow the money." I think the more that you follow the money, it will change the way you talk about strategy. Because then you can actually hit up certain soft spots or expose certain things that are not meant to be exposed.

BH: *I want to hopefully go back to some of those issues, but for now I want to talk about some of your earlier work, specifically* Race Rebels. *One of the arguments you make in that book is that, in order to really understand some of the most dynamic forms of resistance and struggle, we need to look beyond "trade union pronouncements, political institutions, and organized social movements."⁴ When one looks at history through the lens of everyday resistance, what type of picture emerges?*

RDGK: Well, before I answer that question, I would add that part of my argument—the part that often gets left out, for the record—is that when we do look at those everyday forms of resistance, it makes the organizing work more effective because part of what it reveals is a set of desires. What are people really struggling over? What are the things that are affecting them directly? What are they fighting over? Sometimes, if you have a national union without a local perspective, or you have an industry-wide perspective that's not really rooted in the particular needs of the workers themselves, they may miss the fact that you have pregnant women having miscarriages. It may not be their issue. Their issue may be, "We just want you to have higher wages." Everyday forms of resistance are supposed to be diagnostic, to reveal the underlying tensions of where they lay. So, having said that, the question is, what do we do with that information?

BH: *When we look at history through the lens of everyday resistance—since I think that's a pretty uncommon way of looking at history—what type of picture emerges?*

RDGK: On the one hand, you find residents of various communities and people working in certain enterprises who are not satisfied with their situations. There's a wonderful book by Rick Fantasia, called *Cultures of Solidarity*, where he says, "Here's a bunch of surveys being done on whether or not workers are satisfied."⁵ The surveys are done in like, 1945, and everyone's saying, "I'm satisfied with my job, I like my job." Yet, a year later, there are wildcat strikes everywhere. What's the connection? Part of what he's revealing—and part of what my work tried to do—is to say that the picture that emerges is one of dissatisfaction, one of storm in the midst of calm. One in which people—even when it does not seem like it's possible—can be mobilized.

On the other hand, it also reveals a certain fear in the power of the dominant ideology to basically shut down any organizing work. It's a lot easier to pilfer from the job, and maybe safer, than to ever sign a union card. You know you're going to lose your job over that. If there are ways to survive, or to get something, or to get back at the boss without having to jeopardize your job or your reputation, then that's even easier. The irony is that we can make too much about the everyday forms of resistance because it's really diagnostic more than anything else. This is not the basis for a revolutionary movement. But what it does do is tell us that these are human beings: they are alive, they have a conscious, they have feelings and sensibilities, they have desires, and we have to read those and read them really carefully, because that's how you become effective organizers—knowing what those desires are.

BH: *All these forms of everyday resistance—from workplace slowdowns and sabotage, to cultural activities like humor, graffiti, music—why do you think so many of these forms of activity have been overlooked or misinterpreted in so much historical writing?*

RDGK: I don't mention this in the book because I read it after the fact: Cedric Robinson, his very first book was called *Terms of Order*. I had to go back and re-read it because it's brilliant. What he says is that one of the problems with historical materialism, with empiricism, with virtually every single model of understanding—political theory, structuralism, historical theory, any kind of social phenomenon—has been based on the myth of a certain kind of logic: that social life operates under a certain set of logics, that there's order. In fact, so much of political activity is chaotic. In other words, the order that we impose on it is an academic or theoretical imposition. Part of the reason why we miss these things is because as scholars, as thinkers, we presume this order and we try to find it through structures. You begin with structures. So, what is the structure? The structure is capital, then the structure is the labor union, then the structure is civic organization, the structure is the political process itself, elected officials, and you go through the structures, and you look through the historical moments of tension and movement. If they exist between the cracks, you're not going to see them. Or you're going to see them and say, "Well, this doesn't really mean anything." Or you see them, and if you can't trace back that individual to one of the structures that makes sense in your narrative, then they're not going to exist in your story. If we throw out the terms of order and begin to see where people are in their daily lives, and watch their behavior, and try to make sense of the choices that they're making—including the choice not to join an organization—then we're going to see more. It's not even a new idea because all the serious organizers do that. They don't go to organizations; they build organizations. They build organizations around the people who are not organized. In their own narratives of why they want to join or how they're trying to recruit you, they start to learn about each other. They start to learn about the things that they feel in common. The things that they feel are so individual and isolated and atomized suddenly become part of a collective experience. I think the best of Marx understood that—socialized production, labor and alienation.

BH: *I think part of that, too, is that people who have studied history have generally devalued activity that hasn't taken place in an organized fashion. I think you have certainly touched on some of the reasons why, but I think on a simpler level, most people who look at political activity that is going on today or yesterday do not focus on what is not taking place in institutional channels or in an organized fashion. In any case, you also argue that recognizing these acts is not only critical for understanding "the political history of oppressed people," but also for how they "have a cumulative effect on power relations."[6] Can you discuss this point?*

RDGK: They sometimes erode power. Again, all of this is situational. The terms of order is also a myth of order, and the myth of order is fundamental for the maintenance of order. In other words, where there's a slave regime, they have to convince everyone around them—and themselves—that there's no revolt going on. It reaches the point of writing off active resistance as acts of ignorance or Sambo-like behavior. They're not going to take all these acts of opposition, even if they're organized resistance, for that matter, and acknowledge them and say, "See, we're in crisis." Like what George Bush said about some of the biggest demonstrations against the war—against any war, at any point in history: he called them "focus groups." It produces a sort of common sense: this is not what real Americans are doing, this is a handful of renegades. Eventually, if it gets out of hand, they have to respond. They respond sometimes by changing the terms: improving conditions, offering the bone, reform. Or just shutting down, violence, capital flight. There are all kinds of ways to respond. It's not always good. Sometimes, acts of resistance—though not intended—can have a deleterious effect. For example, if a job site becomes unruly, and governing becomes difficult, and the option of capital flight is always there, they'll leave.

This brings us back to a really important issue: everyday forms of resistance—all these daily actions—don't really mean much without some sort of ideological intervention, political education. In other words, people learn a lot in process. They learn about what the weaknesses are in the system, but they're not learning about whether or not they want another system, or what's wrong with that system. They may just see it as their personal problem. That's why all these forms of activities have to be followed up with political education. How does the system work? How does the state of Mississippi work? Why are so many people in prison? How come wages aren't going up, but CEO bonuses keep going up? Why is that? What are the answers to those questions? Those answers don't come out of everyday forms of resistance. They come out of political engagement and conversation and information.

BH: *Historically speaking, what do you see as some of the more successful models of political education really taking hold, where we see that type of everyday resistance already taking place and furthered to the next level?*

RDGK: There's probably dozens, but one is the Mississippi Freedom Schools. What they decided to do was reach young people whose parents were too afraid to participate in voter registration campaigns and that sort of thing. They said, "We're going to build a whole curriculum around social justice. And we're going to take what you know best—what you think you know—and that is the state of Mississippi, and we're going to study it. First assignment: you're going to make a list of the kind of world you live in. Second assignment: what kind of world do you want to live in?" To take something even more specific, the Freedom School teachers would say, "Make a list of all the things that black people have. What do they possess? And what are all the things that white people have? And of both of those groups, what things would you retain if you had a choice to rebuild your society?" Or have a mock debate about state expenditures, things like that, to be able to really investigate the world you live in and expose why so many black people are poor, why poor whites are not necessarily on their side or don't act like they are. What would it mean to have the right to vote? What impact would it have on your lives? That generation went on to really transform Southern politics. Those kids became adults very soon. And they were the ones who ended up continuing the legacy of the Civil Rights movement.

For more contemporary examples, I always point to the Labor/Community Strategy Center, where they're doing political education all the time. And one really good example I should give is when they were organizing the Bus Riders Union, and they were doing political theater on the buses, and getting people to not pay their fare in demand for a seat. It occurred to them that one of their biggest stumbling blocks was the bus drivers because the bus drivers were like, "Well, you're coming and disrupting my bus." And they realized, "We need to organize the bus drivers. We need the bus drivers to know what this campaign is about, number one. And number two, we need to support the bus drivers union." Suddenly, in no time, the bus drivers became supporters of the Bus Riders Union. The union was pushing for a no seat/no fare campaign, and when the bus was full, the bus drivers put their hand over the meter and said, "You don't pay today, because there's no seat." And to me, that's tremendous education.

BH: *You spoke about the recent anti-war protests, but going back a few years further, the 1999 protests in Seattle and the subsequent summit protests are often used as a turning point in narratives of recent radical history. Yet so much of the energy from those protests seems to have waned. What do you think the mass protests of the late 1990s and early 2000s in the U.S. did or did not accomplish?*

RDGK: If the goal was to disrupt the summits and to bring attention to globalization and its negative impacts on the world, I think it succeeded. It did disrupt; it didn't stop capital. I think the idea was to bring international attention and shut down certain events. What I don't know if it did, which it should have done, was really educate people on what impact globalization has had on ordinary people. What's so sad about living in the United States is that it's a very narcissistic culture. And so for some people, if they don't believe that you're talking about them, they just don't care. You could tell them every day that half the world doesn't have clean drinking water or half the world makes less than a dollar a day; it doesn't mean jack, which is sad. There was a time when it did mean something. But if you say, "You don't have health care right now because of this," or "You're paying enormous prices for food because of globalization," then a certain kind of self-interest kicks in. Will it mobilize people? I don't know. But I think most people just don't know the connections, and activists are trying to compete with a discourse of globalization that says it's the end-all, it's proof that we've reached the end of history, everything is great. We've finally achieved something fantastic, because you can get any fruit you want at any time of the year. Isn't that great? Globalization?

The one campaign that I thought did a pretty good job was the Nike campaign. That was a difficult campaign, because it was divided. Some activists said, "Don't boycott Nike, it will shut down these shops where people are living on slave wages and don't have any other options, so basically what we have to do is put pressure on Nike." I think it made a difference. Those campaigns were sustained, they were propaganda, they were deeply educational, and they constantly exposed connections that hit home, whether it's the shoes on your feet or the food that you eat. I think those kinds of campaigns could work in the big protests if they become teach-ins, where you come away saying, "Wow, I didn't know that and now I'm mad."

BH: *If not literally at the event, then in generally raising awareness and providing a way of speaking about those issues, that normally does not get into the discourse at all.*

RDGK: Right. I could be wrong, but I think of these events as international political theater, to project out to the world that it's not business as usual. And they project out typically to the non-American world, both in the Global South and the Liberal West, that there are American activists living in the belly of the beast who refuse to accept the terms. I think it's a very powerful message, and I think it generates support and mobilizes people. Sort of like all those peace activists in Israel who are risking their lives, that sort of thing. It's a huge thing to stand up like that, for people to see it. That's why it is sort of a one-shot deal in some ways. But it has to be sustained, always in the media, and not waiting for the next big event.

BH: *In* Freedom Dreams, *you note that "progressive social movements do not simply produce statistics and narratives of oppression; rather, the best ones do what great poetry always does:*

transport us to another place, compel us to relive horrors and, more importantly, enable us to imagine a new society"[7] What role do you see imagination playing in contemporary radical organizing? Where do you see the most innovation on this level—the most exciting prospects and the most useful dreams?

RDGK: A lot of that comes out of my experiences talking to and working with various community-based and grassroots organizations. It's in those sorts of spaces—protected spaces, enclosed spaces—and not so much in the streets themselves that people are able to articulate why they're in it, what they're fighting for. The Strategy center, the Miami Workers Center. I just met with a group there, mostly older black people—Haitians, Cuban Americans, African Americans—who are developing a very clear sense of what kind of society they want to build. I've had many conversations with Sista II Sista, a group that's based right here in Brooklyn, and with Domestic Workers United. It's in those places that people, young and old, can articulate why they're fighting. In the case of Sista II Sista, they're probably the most visionary because they're creating these cooperatives of not just young women, but older women as well, where they're doing collective child-care, where they're training people as child-care providers to make money, pulling their resources together, trying to find different ways to live together as a community, putting forward what their socialist life might look like. What you're talking about is how you reconstruct relationships as a parent to your child, as a partner to your partner, your neighbor. How can you interact with your neighbor differently? How do you share what you have? How do you participate politically in a different manner, where your discourse is no longer private but public? How do you do those things? If you can find those liberated zones, where people can practice that, that's where it's the most visionary, because there's no turning back then.

This goes back to the idea of the commons. Peter Linebaugh has written one of the most important books out there today, which is the *Magna Carta Manifesto*.[8] It's all about the struggle for the commons, the return to the commons, globally. One of the things that he points out—which E.P. Thompson and others pointed out as well—is that you never had to ask permission to chop down wood in the forest, or to cultivate something, or to graze your cattle or your sheep. It was just part of the collective. But then, struggle ensued through enclosure and through expropriation, to make sure people did not have access to things. The things that we had once accepted as common—common courtesy, common practice—are taken away. If you also take away the memory of that, then people aren't willing to fight for it. But if you return the memory, people will fight. Why do we have to pay for health care? Why do we have to pay so much money for food? Why is housing ridiculously expensive? And who's really making the money? Why don't the people who have been displaced by Katrina have a right to return? How did their land get seized—even if they did not own it? It was their property in the sense that they occupied it. How did the land get seized and turned into high-priced condominiums? It's about the return of the commons. That demand itself is one of the most visionary demands you can possibly make right now. It's not a pipe dream. It's saying, "This is the obligation of society to provide these things for us." It's not a hand-out or a gift.

BH: *You have also written that "once we strip radical social movements down to their bare essence and understand the collective desires of people in motion, freedom and love lay at the very heart of the matter."[9] I think this is absolutely right, but many folks I know struggle to retain* *a sense of dreaming and love in their day-to-day work and lives for a better world. How can we preserve these aspects in our work and lives when the struggle for change can be so difficult and frustrating?*

RDGK: I don't know! I really don't know. But I have an idea. The important thing to begin with is an acknowledgment that people—and it doesn't matter who you are, what you look like, how old you are, color of skin, any of that—anyone who is committed to social justice is suddenly at war. You're beaten down immediately. You cannot fight for social justice without being beaten down because we live in a country where you actually have to fight for social justice. It's not taken for granted. I mean, why do you have to fight for it? Why can't it just be something that everyone enjoys? But that's not the case. Therefore, how do you sustain a sense of purpose, love, commitment, a desire and expectation for freedom, when you are thrown into an army? It's like fighting a war every day. You're watching people, your comrades, older and younger, fall by the wayside every day, over some basic stuff. Well, this is where the question of the spiritual comes in. What my mother taught me was that spirituality is not exogenous. It's not something from the outside that penetrates you, like the Holy Ghost. It's not something that you try to find or some kind of embodiment. It's nothing. Glass is just glass. Floor is just floor. But it is what St. Thomas Aquinas—I never thought I'd quote St. Thomas Aquinas—said about faith: you have to believe that, even if you lose and destroy the process, you are doing the will of this greater spirit. Let's say this spirit is not a god or anything, but the spirit is the spirit of Marx. The spirit of Rosa Luxemburg. You're committed to a higher principle. Everything you do has to embody that principle. People look at you, the way you behave, the way you treat other people, the way you challenge power. You hold onto the principle because that gives you an ethical and moral center. When you go to bed at night, you know that you're not compromising, that you're not selling out, that you're doing what is correct and right. It's funny; again, I'm not a religious person at all, but that stuff is in the Bible. Jesus asks the question, I forget to who, Paul or somebody, one of those biblical things: you walk down a road and you see somebody hungry, what do you do? What do you ask that person? How do you respond to that? And we've got to figure out a way to be able to walk that walk, knowing that you're not going to "win" in the traditional sense of the word, but that every day that you can help someone, or change a life, or make a dent, you are winning.

But it also means being smart about it, because if you see social activism as a kind of stewardship, then you've got to take care of yourself. You've got to find time to rest. You've got to find time to protect yourself. And you've got to stay out of the state's clutches. I don't think there's anything romantic about always being arrested. If you're being arrested as a symbolic gesture to mess up business as usual, that's cool. But there comes a point where you've got to be able to attend to the living of social justice. Transforming your life and the lives of others is much more powerful than having to always get into a fight with the police.

BH: *Marx made the argument that revolution is necessary both to overthrow the ruling class and for the "class overthrowing it [to] rid … itself of all the muck of ages and become fitted to found society anew."[10] Can you discuss your feelings on the importance of revolution today?*

RDGK: It is a hard question, because what is revolution? I think there are generations of people who think of revolution literally as the violent overthrow of a class. I don't necessarily believe that's always the case. Even in cases of clear-cut revolutions, like the French Revolution, it literally *wasn't* the violent overthrow of a class. The bourgeoisie came to power on the backs of working-class violence. Even that doesn't quite fit.

So, what is revolution? Revolution is a fundamental change in the status quo, however that change comes about. In the past fifty years, I think we've actually had revolutions. They're not the revolutions that we chose. I think that the move from the so-called Great Society to extreme *laissez-faire* capitalism was a revolution. A significant revolution took place—for the worse. That's not to say that the Great Society was so great, but something revolutionary happened in the fundamental nature of social relations, of power, of the economy. Can we have a revolution? I think yes. What will it look like? I don't really know, but the revolution I just referred to is an example of a kind of muck of society being thrown off, what was once common sense: that you need to help all poor people no matter what, that you don't have such a thing as a deserving/undeserving poor, that social welfare is a fundamental human right, that racism is unacceptable. The muck of 60s radicalism, that's good muck. We lost that. So, how do you build a revolutionary movement that could throw off the current muck? I don't know how to do that, but it's fundamental. It's fundamental that the common sense of this age is destroyed. The biggest muck I think we have is the muck of a) a consumer culture, which is so prevalent that it just shuts down any other discourse, and b) a kind of blind patriotism, which is incredibly dangerous because with a blind patriotism comes a justification for war, for shutting down any forms of dissent, and not just for shutting it down, but for those people who are observers to not say anything about it. It generates a culture of fear and terror like we've never had before, under the name of fighting terrorism. I think all of that needs to be overthrown for freedom. You don't overthrow that, and it's going to be hard to go forward.

POSTSCRIPT ON OBAMA, DECEMBER 2009

BH: *What does Obama's election tell us about people's desires?*

RDGK: Of course, it's hard to lump together all the different constituencies and communities who united to elect President Obama, but I think the most urgent desire was a deep opposition to Cheney/Bush and the disastrous eight years of their reign. So many people were tired of war, the creeping police state, generalized fear of the so-called terror threat, and an economy that gave more and more to the rich at the expense of the poor. However, I don't want to suggest that Obama's election was a reaction, a negation of a terrible moment. I do think it symbolized a new way forward, or rather, a desire for a new way forward. For some, this means the end to a cynical politics of self-interest, and instead a politics of empathy, the creation of a caring culture that lifts the bottom and even restores the welfare state, which also eroded under Clinton. For others, for better or worse, his election marked the end of race and/or racism. Suddenly, no one had to feel guilty, we no longer had to talk about it, no angst over things like affirmative action. For still others, it was a victory for working people, for unions that had been so battered under Bush, for women's rights under attack for so long by the Right, for subjugated groups like people of color, LGBT, and disabled, for an intelligent approach to saving the environment. It was the forgotten—if not suppressed—Rainbow Coalition, come back to life—sans Jesse Jackson. Of course, it doesn't seem like any of these desires will reach fulfillment.

BH: *Does his campaign and presidency tell us something about today's social movements, or anything about the co-optation of social movements?*

RDGK: Absolutely. For one thing, the tone of the campaign at its best is, in some ways, a far cry from Obama's approach to governing. On the other hand, he did reveal himself along the way: his focus on Afghanistan as the "right" war to fight; his bending over backward, or I should say forward, in order to attract as many Republicans as possible; the way he often berated poor black folks for their bad behavior, and never spoke directly about significant policy initiatives that might end the grinding poverty and police oppression and substandard housing in the inner cities of the United States. Still, his message of hope was compelling, and it allowed aggrieved groups to write their desires onto this rhetoric.

On the question of his impact on social movements or even how we think about social movements: I do think Obama has been thoroughly de-coupled from the social movements that laid the basis for his election. And he's partly to blame, but he's not the only one. Everyone around him knew that using the energy and organization of progressive social movements while maintaining his distance was the way to win the election. Consequently, in the popular discourse, there is almost no acknowledgment or understanding of why social movements even matter or how change is made. President Obama has been turned into a kind of savior who descended on to the world stage, transcendent of race and other fetters of identity, a transformational force upon whose shoulders the future of the nation and the free world rests. The Great Man theory of history has come back with a vengeance, as Obama's rise has encouraged endless comparisons with past presidents—Abraham Lincoln, Franklin Roosevelt, John F. Kennedy, Lyndon B. Johnson, even Ronald Reagan. The result has been the evisceration of social movements as a force for change. Many of my own students now believe that change comes only from intelligent, benign, almost divine leadership, not social movements.

Of course, anyone who pays attention to American politics knows that many of the social justice movements that put him in office have felt betrayed by his actions, often in pursuit of an illusory bi-partisanship. The Nobel Peace Prize winner is preparing to send more troops to Afghanistan, is reluctant to reverse Bush policies of extraordinary rendition or refuse terror suspects a trial, backed a watered-down healthcare reform bill. The list goes on. Of course, he also faces the worst economic crisis since the Great Depression and intractable House and Senate Republicans, and he's but ten months into his first term.

My point, of course, is that where President Obama moves will depend on how he's pushed. Were Abe Lincoln able to preserve the Union and contain slavery without war, he would have done so. Had the enslaved worked loyally for the Confederacy, defending their masters rather than running toward Union lines, there may not have been a Confiscation Act, an Emancipation Proclamation, a Northern victory. What would Lincoln have done without abolitionists—white and black?

I do think that as Obama continues to blunder—either on the advice of generals, or out of some ambition to be "presidential," or some bogus understanding of pragmatism defined as gathering information and making allegedly "non-ideological" decisions, or just plain hawkishness or stupidity—the abolitionists will come out in large numbers. There is no alternative.

NOTES

1   This interview originally took place on April 21, 2008 in New York City and was published as part of *In the Middle of a Whirlwind: 2008 Convention Protests, Movement and Movements*. Subsequently, Kelley provided his insights to additional questions in December of 2009. This interview was conducted and transcribed by Benjamin Holtzman.

2   Robin D.G. Kelley with Jeffrey J. Williams, "History and Hope: An Interview with Robin D.G. Kelley," *minnesota review* 58–60, 2003: 94.

3   Eventually published as Robin D.G. Kelley, *Hammer and Hoe: Alabama Communists During the Great Depression* (Chapel Hill: University of North Carolina Press, 1990).

4   Robin D.G. Kelley, *Race Rebels: Culture, Politics, and the Black Working Class* (New York: The Free Press, 2004), 3–4.

5   Rick Fantasia, *Cultures of Solidarity: Consciousness, Action, and Contemporary American Workers* (Berkeley: University of California Press, 1989).

6   Robin D.G. Kelley, *Race Rebels*, 8.

7   Robin D.G. Kelley, *Freedom Dreams: The Black Radical Imagination* (Boston: Beacon Press, 2002), 9.

8   Peter Linebaugh, *The Magna Carta Manifesto: Liberties and Commons for All* (Berkeley: University of California Press, 2008).

9   Robin D.G. Kelley, *Freedom Dreams*, 12.

10   Karl Marx and Frederick Engels, *The German Ideology: Parts 1 & III*, ed. R. Pascal (New York: International Publishers, 1966[1947]), 69.

WE CAN BEGIN TO TAKE BACK OUR LIVES:

A Discussion with Ashanti Omowali Alston

Team Colors Collective

Ashanti Omowali Alston—"anarchist panther," community organizer, political prisoner, and renowned activist—has for the past thirty years represented a thoughtful and rich revolutionary politics, blending traditions as he engages with the world around him. Here Alston maps out in detail his personal revolutionary-becoming through various influential strands of the Black Power movement of the 1960s and 1970s. He continues by exploring the current difficulties within movements and offers tools from many methodologies and theories, historical lessons, and successful organizing work in specific localities in the United States and further afield, such as the Zapatistas in southeastern Mexico. Using his vast array of movement knowledges, Ashanti offers a pointed understanding of the dire stakes in struggle today, arguing passionately for the importance of challenging the Left, radicals, and anarchists of all stripes to start moving seriously to the creation of a new world, one where our self-determination and everyday lives are central.

This interview with Alston occurred in 2008 and was conducted and transcribed by Team Colors Collective.

Team Colors: *To begin, could you speak about some of your early life experiences and how they have affected you?*

Ashanti Alston: I'm from Plainfield, New Jersey, and I was born in 1954. I come out of a Baptist and Hebrew family. There was a split in the church at one point, so my family was basically Hebrews, they didn't call themselves Jews. My father and others decided that they wanted to be Baptists, so my father and his family became Baptist. But my mother's side is still Hebrew. So I come from that background, and I still got both in me. My father was a Baptist minister, he was helping people and I really admired him. My family always would be helping people.

So the 1960s came along, and I'm seeing the Civil Rights movement, and I'm curious. I was already struggling to understand Malcolm X when the 1967 rebellions happened in Plainfield.[1] People took over the community. That was profound. It was profound to see the National Guard come in with troops and tanks, and they took it back over kind of brutal. That was my entry. I wanted to be one of them black revolutionaries. After that I was reading everything I could.

I wasn't a great reader, and I was struggling with Malcolm X's autobiography. But the more I struggled through Malcolm X, the more I understood. I flipped from page to page. I didn't read it cover to cover. I got little bits here and there. And at the same time here's Plainfield, here's the news, here's what's going on in Africa, and the anti-Vietnam war stuff. So we found ourselves in junior high school fighting for Black History—there was no Black History. There was two junior high schools in my hometown, and at both schools, the black students left and marched down to City Hall and demanded Black History. By the next school year we had it. So Black Power had us trying to understand self-determination, how to implement Black Power in the schools. Winning Black History was the first sweet taste of that.

By 1969–70, me and my best friend David started finding out about the Black Panther Party, and we wanted to know more about them. We all respected Martin Luther King and the Civil Rights movement, but that non-violent resistance, we couldn't get with it. So something more aggressive was for us. I mean, Black Power was aggressive, but the Black Panther Party was openly saying, "We're arming ourselves; we're going to do all this, but we're going to do this with arms." We wanted to find out more. So we would go travel to Newark, Jersey City, and New York to the different chapters, talk to people, pick up papers. Sometimes they would let us attend political education classes. When it became more frequent, they'd let us sell papers. Then when we had enough folks that we thought we could do a chapter, they actually helped us start a chapter. It was a whole process though, it wasn't simple. They had to work with us.

At a certain point, from junior year in high school going into senior year, we had an office, a storefront, a free clothing program, we had helped tenants organize against land-lords, we was on the streets every night in the most crime-ridden areas of Plainfield's black community and in the high schools doing party work. There was a black student union in the high school. So we was pretty effective. But then this cop gets killed, and they tried to pin that cop on me and David, as we were the main organizers of the Plainfield Black Panther Party. From there it was being in jail for 14 months; the last four months was the trial. Our lawyers showed the typical frame-up stuff and actually convinced an all-white jury that we were innocent, and they acquitted us. But all during that time, our mindset was, "We wasn't scared." We were prepared. Because we knew what happened to Huey Newton, we knew what happened to Fred Hampton just two years before.[2] Panthers were getting framed in other places, so we knew it could happen to us too.

This was in 1971; we got out fourteen months later in 1972. When we got acquitted, the police was making threats, so our families wanted us out of Plainfield. I went down south to Greensboro, North Carolina, and David went to Rochester, New York. I stayed down there for six months, and then I'm back. And then we're re-organizing the chapter. But at the same time we had lost a lot of members; Newark, Jersey City, New York chapters lost a lot of members. At some point there was Panthers who were also Black Liberation Army (BLA) members who were facing the death penalty in California, but they was locked up in New York accused of a San Francisco police department ambush.[3] So I was approached to become a part of the BLA, specifically to get them out before they were shipped back to California.

So I'm nineteen. My girlfriend, who was also a member of the Panther Party in my hometown, she was pregnant. I had a lot of thinking to do. I want to be around for this child, I'm getting ready to be a daddy, but I was still feeling like we could make this revolution happen. It was clear that movements in general were on the decline; the FBI (Federal Bureau of Investigation) was doing their job, and we were losing support, people were backing away from us. But we felt, too, from what we understood of guerrilla warfare, that the guerrillas can help bring that movement back. We could help to fortify them chapters that were still functioning, from underground. Bring other people back if we could bring up the spirit of people.

At some point, I came back to them and said, "I'm ready to join," and I brought one of my younger comrades with me. So here we are getting integrated into the BLA, but at that time we're still doing above-ground work and underground work. For me, it was helping to keep the Harlem office open, making sure the breakfast program is running, keeping the office functioning, and then also doing the work in my hometown. But as the underground cell got more into our work, then it was mainly doing more underground, trying to prepare to get these folks out of the Manhattan House of Detention—the Tombs.[4]

So we had a couple of plans. None of them worked, but we tried. We had word that there was a tunnel that led up under the Manhattan House of Detention. So we went to the area, lifted the manhole cover; there was no tunnel. It was the wee hours in the morning and some John Q. Citizen saw these black folks down there and called the police. So while one of the members was coming up out of the sewer, here the police come and arrest us. They don't quite know who we are yet, or what we're up to. When they do find out, we were front page news; they called us 'the sewer rats.' They called us BLA sympathizers, and they thought we was trying to get into the Department of Corrections building, where they have all the prison files in upstate New York. But the only thing they could really charge us with was tampering with city property. So they had us in Rikers Island,[5] then let us out on our own recognizance, and eventually dropped the charges. We went right back to work; we had to figure another way to get them out.

Everyday we were allowed to bring them food. After they was brought from court, we would bring a bag of food, we gave it to the guard, they checked the food and passed it over to the prisoners. So everyday we'd sign the log sheet, take the food, have a little chit-chat. But on this particular day, we had already figured out we would have to go in with an acetylene torch and cut a hole in this wall where the visiting room is—a solid metal wall with a glass window. So on the day that we went in to pass over the food, we opened up our bag like we was going to let them examine it, but we pulled out our weapons. We locked the guards up in the bathroom, went to the visiting room floor and commenced the cutting. I was the one who was cutting, but I wasn't an experienced cutter. There was about two inches to go, and I couldn't cut no more. We just had to look at them behind the walls and say, "We gotta go." If we had been successful, we would have had four BLA soldiers out, and probably all the other prisoners who was out for visits at that time too. But as easy as it was for us to go in and do it, it was as easy to get out of there. So we planned it pretty good.

The thing we had going for us was their arrogance of power. They would have never thought some black folks would dare to come up in there and attack in the inside of their fortress. We knew we had that. So after that we're fully underground; this was in 1974.

During the course of a bank expropriation in New Haven, Connecticut, there was a shootout, and three of us were captured. So that's when we got time, around 1975. I ended up doing a little over eleven years, and once I got out, I ended up doing ten months for a parole violation. I guess that's the beginning—it's like, I learned through practice. We was young and inexperienced, but we also understood that we gonna learn as we go. We knew we didn't have to wait for everything to be perfect. You don't have to have the theory perfect before you act; the theory will change as you go, and you will learn more instead of just sitting back theorizing. For me, that was some of the most important stuff I learned in the Panther Party: you don't have to wait.

TC: *So by 1974 and 1975, mass movements are waning. Around that time, the New York City fiscal crisis is starting as well. You were directly involved in militant organizing at a time when mass movements were waning and the City was going into crisis, which meant that things in New York were really tough. What was your experience around that—and the decomposition of that movement—coming from a revolutionary standpoint?*

AA: It was not only that I remember, but it was also when the oil prices shot up from the Arab nations' oil embargo. I remember that so clear. But for us too, because our support base was not there anymore, it meant we had to do a lot more expropriations. We had to have money for places that we were living, for food and transportation. Those sources that we generally had were drying up.

All around, you see that people are really suffering. I was just going through old issues of the *New York Times*, and there was this one article dealing with the BLA. The police had come across this house in Brooklyn that was probably a pad, and it had a lot of weapons in it. They got wind of it, raided it, and got the weapons. It was interesting that the person who wrote the article interviewed people in the neighborhood. A lot of people in the neighborhood were saying that the newspapers were going to blame it on the BLA anyhow. But people were saying, "They may blame it on the Black Liberation Army, but look at what's going on." And they was talking about no jobs, all this other stuff. And that they could make that connection with what the BLA was trying to do. I remember so much of that, times where it felt like the community was backing us.

They backed the Black Panther Party; the BLA was a little harder because we wasn't just defensive anymore, now we're going on the offensive. When the police was getting hit for shooting people in our community, people did understand; if they heard about these bank expropriations, people did understand. Even though it was at the end of a movement, I think people still had enough feeling of community and struggle to put some context to it. Even when the community was going through some struggles, they didn't just dismiss the Panther Party or BLA even though this was 1973–74, and it was rough. The community was going through a lot. It was probably a high point in bank expropriations in general, not just the BLA. Everybody seemed to have been hitting the banks, doing stickups because it called for something.

TC: *On an emotional level, what was it like to be involved in militant activity while larger movements were waning?*

AA: Knowing that we were suffering? I think we knew things was falling apart after the death of George Jackson in August, 1971.[6] A lot of the Left didn't support us anyhow. Weather Underground folks did, folks that were in that tendency within the Students for a Democratic Society (SDS), the Nationalist groups.[7] We always had critical support for the Panthers because of the fact that we were dedicated to the black community. But damn, man, it was like, with the arrests, shoot-outs, the media constantly bombarding the community with, "We're thugs, we're murderers"—it had some effect. People was buying into that stuff, obviously. But some of the stuff that the FBI and the local police were doing, who knew? We said we knew, but the reliance on mass media was still there. It was like this ideological battle we was losing, and that was a big part of our support drying up. And when the police was coming in the community and looking for us, they would terrorize a whole neighborhood. When they was looking for Assata,[8] it wasn't just one person. If it was a housing project, they're gonna make everyone in that project pay. So the thing would be, "See what the Panthers are causing, see what the BLA is bringing down on us?" All of that was happening.

From 1972 to 1976, we suffered a lot of losses from people being captured, killed or shut down in other ways; a lot of people just had to split or lay low. There was so much chaos and paranoia. The "Split" (in the Black Panther Party), I think, played a big part in terms of who you could trust. After the Split, you didn't know anymore if you could go to former comrades and say, "We need this, we need that."[9]

It was a rough period. It put a lot of tension on our relationships. I remember one time we were getting low on monies. The men wanted to get some wine, and there was one sister in particular, with real strong feminist politics, who was like, "Y'all can't do that." And we talked her down and did it anyhow, because we wanted to loosen up. It did create tension within our group that these things was happening—whenever it was uncertain if we had everything in place, our machismo would make us still do it anyway. That's when we made some real mistakes and people got captured, hurt, killed. I think a lot of it was pressure of a movement that was on decline from local police, FBI, and then us, just not knowing how to deal with our internal relationships, really getting shaky. They were really deteriorating. We still had the spirit, but it was more out of, "We have to do this because we're getting ready to fail if we don't." At some point you've gotta say, "Hey, it's different, something is happening, maybe we all need to step back." But for a lot of us, to step back meant cowardice, so we didn't. And then things happened, and then that movement falls, and then a lot of us are in prison.

When I went to prison in 1974, I'm joining a whole bunch of other political prisoners, and everybody's trying to figure out how to keep this going, how to reorganize from within the prison, and get the forces on the street to reorganize. Because I think being in prison was the first time that we was physically taken out of the situation, not by choice. But still, it's a chance to reflect. So people are trying to work it, people are trying to figure out what happened, where did we go wrong? What should we have been doing? So all through that, from 1974 to the early 1980s, it was all about trying to reorganize the BLA, on the street and in other ways. But there was no more movement; there was no more mass-connected or community-connected movement anymore. We had to watch that from the prisons.

TC: *One thing you have written that we find interesting is: "Either you respect people's ca-*
pacities to think for themselves, to govern themselves, to creatively devise their own best ways
to make decisions, to be accountable, to relate, problem-solve, break down isolation and
commune in a thousand different ways ... OR: you dis-respect them. You dis-respect ALL of
us." If people have the capacity to govern themselves and make their own decisions, what role
does the idea that people have to think a certain way or attain a certain consciousness have
in movement building?

AA: I think that when people interact around whatever their issues are and really share
and dialog, there is the possibility to create a common page of understanding, a common
page of action too. But people need to understand that it's happening in other communities around other issues, and they are already forming their own page of understanding
and action. So we've gotta accept that there are going to be differences, and even with
our differences, still be on some page together, like, "We know that we can't be free with
this empire over us." Can we figure out some way to respect each other's uniqueness, each
other's autonomous desire to create something better for the situation that we're in?

The consciousness thing is gonna be different. So the Panther Party comes into the
scene in the 1960s, they're Black nationalists. In their struggles, the Panther ideology is
changing because it's interacting with other readings and experiences: reading from Mao
and traveling to Cuba or China or Africa and checking out movements and seeing what
moves them, seeing their ideological motivations, integrating these stories and information. At some point, we started calling ourselves the vanguard. But, it was also a broad
range of people motivated and inspired by Panthers, from poor white folks in the Ap-
palachians, to Chicanos, to Puerto Ricans, to folks from other countries. The good thing
about it was that everyone was developing this Panther-type activity but from their own
ground. But then comes the Revolutionary People's Constitutional Convention, where
all the groups are supposed to come together to theoretically rewrite the constitution for
this new society, and everybody's supposed to be contributing. But because the Panthers
called it, and they had the vanguard mentality, the Panthers had too much control in it.
The women's groups, the White Panthers Party, the SDS, and all these other people are
bringing their contributions, but the Panthers are pushing for too much control. So every
group has their consciousness, but why's this one group trying to dominate the thing?
Because we'd convinced ourselves that we had the right analysis, that this revolution can't
happen unless we are in the leadership.[10]

But today, I look at how the Zapatistas are trying to do this, saying, "Well, let's just
try to create that space." A space where different consciousnesses can come from different places, and we can figure out the dialog, how to create a way forward that respects us
all and the different worlds that we come from. For me, that's such a better way to go.
Whether one is a small geographical community, or tied to their ethnicity, or dealing with
a lifestyle, we should just be open to come together and see how we can do this in a different kind of way. That's the challenge.

TC: *Do you think that the contemporary anarchist scene suffers from some of this ideological*
'correct-line' approach?

AA: I think there's some of it in the anarchist movement. For me it always comes up with
the nationalism. I was just reading an article in the latest *Fifth Estate*, and the writer was

talking about nationalism, and he used a real foul word with it. I was like, "Goddamn, I'm a nationalist, however you understand that. If you want to know what I mean by it, let's talk. So that you see that I'm not talking about creating no nation-state." It hasn't ever really meant that for black people and a lot of other folks. It has been a way for people who have been oppressed by a racist system to take their lives in their own hands, to create self-determination and autonomy.

So with me, even in the anarchist movement, even when you start dealing with nationalism or sovereignty or Puerto Rican independence, or even Chicanos who are fighting for what they see as the liberation of Aztlan,[11] it ain't for you to see whether that fits some old category. You really need some dialogue so that you can see what it is they are fighting for. You've got the Lakota, or at least certain factions in the Lakota, who have called for secession.[12] Instead of saying, "Oh man, I can't deal with this, more division," you need to take a step back and find out, "What do they mean?" You need to see that this is a struggle for their survival, still an anti-neoliberal, anti-imperial struggle that you need to support, and it does not have to fit some preconceived set of categories you've got.

TC: *One thing we thought was remarkable about you was your mix of revolutionary traditions: your dedication to classical anarchism, Black nationalism, post-anarchism, and Marxism. In a movement that seems increasingly ideologically based, how do you find your positions in relation to these individual traditions?*

AA: Even with the word ideology, I don't use it, 'cause I see ideology as coming out of having a set of answers for something. So for me and my anarchism, I don't think it's classical; I don't call myself an anarcho-communist or none of the others. There's definitely anarchism that's open to changing realities. Anarcho-communists have good points about certain things, primitivists have good points about certain things. They don't get along, but I get something from both of them. I like some aspects of anarcho-individualism and Tolstoy's spiritualism.

There's certain things from Marxism that I like, but I'm not on the working class as being the ones that we've gotta organize, and I'm not on their historical materialism where communism evolves. I don't want their solutions when it goes into the historical or political because it did very poorly with race, with sex, with environmental issues. That's okay, 'cause in the Panther Party we were never taught to look at Marx like he was the shit. I learned early that I don't have to take the whole Marxist picture. Some of it does work, and I think there are great ideas, but they are ideas and they don't necessarily have to unfold according to Western streams of scientific thinking, or that things *have* to unfold according to the iron law of history. I take what I can from it, and from workers, and anarcho-communism and syndicalists.

I don't want to be in that category that says, "This is that magical class that's going to bring about change." It may come from all kinds of different places. It may come from the universities, the black community, the reservations; it may come from all of them rather than some pre-ordained class. We have to figure out how to create a world where it's possible for all different people to be who they are, to have a world where everyone fits.

TC: *You have helped to bridge a predominantly white anarchist movement, a Zapatista support movement, and an anti-prison movement, which is predominantly of color. How have you seen your position as an organizer and communicator between these movements?*

AA: I think that it seems like my role is bridging more with the white anarchist communities. I also want to bridge anarchist ideas and practices into my own black community and into the academic world of radical academics who really want to play a big part in our struggle. That's my desire. But of all the groups, the anarchist mindset is still open to understanding all the different oppressions; they're not stuck on a notion that it's just the system out there and you have to change the system. Anarchists, I think, understand power more than others, so there's potential there. Already, anarchists will deal with movements that silence queers and folks of color; they'll even deal with ageism, ableism.

When I'm getting involved with Andy Stepanian and Daniel McGowan and Warcry and others,[13] it means I'm broadening my own understanding of the movements, and at the same time I'm constantly thinking, "How can I bring them movements into my community?" Also encouraging them to not just stay in their community movement, but also constantly figure out how to get that message going into other communities so that they're not insular.

And when we start talking about how we have centered everything around us as human beings, I think that's great shit. Animal liberation is a hell of a thing, to say, "Look at what we have done as human beings, and look at how we have become the center of everything." This is challenging us to do a re-evaluation: "How do we get in this position? What does it mean for us to stay in it? What might it mean to change the relationship we have to all living things?" And this goes for the Earth First! folks, too. It seems like common sense that we figure out how to love this earth that we're part of, but then a movement comes along and says, "We're not doing that well, we need to figure out how to save this planet." So for me, it's constantly figuring how my vision of revolution can get enriched. I'm taking in this stuff like de-centering *man*, de-centering *human* being, having a whole new relationship to all living things on this planet and where we are in the universe. The indigenous folks have been saying this for generations; some have been living close to the earth forever. They have got some lessons for us to learn. So I want my community to understand that this ain't just white folks doing this; this is folks all over the world, from all different lifestyles, saying, "Yo, we gotta stop!" We have to stop the machinery, even if it's the machinery inside of us. And then figure out how to hook up with others of like mind and like heart and organize in a massive way to stop the machinery and save this planet, let alone our individual lives. For me, that's the potential of the anarchist movement and why I'm going to stay with it. I just want that movement to figure out more ways to be relevant to the broader communities.

TC: *What lessons can be shared between the movements you are talking about, especially during a time when the anarchist movement does not seem to be engaged in substantial local organizing efforts?*

AA: I always encourage folks to get involved with the local. The thing I miss most about the Black Panther Party is the local organizing. At first they would walk us through stuff —"This is study groups, this is how we organize, this is how we rap in the community selling newspapers." But then they would leave, and it was on us to do the work. When we started really doing the work, you're scared, even a little intimidated. But then you start talking, and people start asking you questions, like, "My landlord, he won't fix this, and other people in the building have the same problem." Then you have to learn tenant organizing so that you can show them. The effect is so great. You can share something with people in your community, and they trust you. You don't even realize how they're looking at you—like, "I'm proud of you, young person." It's really heavy stuff. Then you're joining anti-war protests and encounters with the police, and people in the community see that you ain't even scared of them. You're in the toughest areas—here's the hustlers, the pushers, the stickup kids, and you can even relate to them. And they respect you, 'cause they see you there every day or every night, doing your thing, selling your paper, and there's the Nation of Islam and the other groups, and everyone has respect 'cause they know that you're part of this movement.

When you read about the early Civil Rights movement, that's what they were doing too. It was around voting and other issues, but for white folks and Northern blacks, going down to the south was a whole new experience. You had to go with a certain mindset, you had to be humble. But if the people see you enough, that you're coming from that place of humility, they're gonna respect you. A lot of them white folks that went down there, they was accepted into the community. A lot of the Northern blacks and even Northern Puerto Ricans and others were accepted, because they worked with them day to day, eating the same way people ate, dressing the same way people dressed. A certain level of respect happened that allowed them to work together down there.

Even with the anarchists, you've gotta do some local work. Even if it's not your community, begin to interact, go into dialog. You've got some information, you've got some things to share? Well, so do they. And in the dialog, you see some points where you can begin to work together. It's a tough struggle, but I think people respect honesty, they respect integrity. They wanna feel like you a genuine person, that you ain't trying to be someone you're not. They can accept you as long as you are there consistently, and you're demonstrating that you really are there in the struggle, that you're gonna help any way you can. You've gotta be dedicated and pull your life into this. You can't just do it and then move somewhere else when it's no longer in season.

TC: *Do you see the anarchist movement moving into that direction?*

AA: I see certain efforts. I don't think it's enough. Like here in New York, I think that there are certain groups like New York Metro Alliance of Anarchists, the Industrial Workers of the World, and 123 Space that, as far as I understand, are doing some community work. Anarchist People Of Color is not there yet; we're still trying to figure it out.[14] Once you start figuring it out, you got to integrate, you have to start putting your life into that community where you're at. Each one of us is part of two, three, four different communities. You're not just one community; you're a community where you live, a community that's your ethnic group or spiritual group, a community that's your activist group. You got to learn to work all of those communities and really start this networking process, where so many connections are being made, where you actually becoming aware of your creative power.

Nothing beats community work. Nothing beats putting your life into something, knowing you're going to change in the process too. Don't think that you're not gonna change. Zapatista Subcomandante Marcos and them learned that. They were university people, going to create a Marxist-Leninist-Maoist revolution with the peasants in southeast Mexico. But they got humbled by the people of that area and had to learn to accept that their ideas may have some relevance, but so do the Mayan people's ideas. You may even see how your ideas came about because they had their basis in the destruction of a lot of Mayan culture and communities, when the Spaniards came in with their highfalutin ideas. Now the Mayans are like, "We got ours too. We can sit down as equals at the table. Not with you thinking you're giving us something."[15] I think anarchists, when we talk about direct democracy and 'horizontalism,' a different way to relate to planetary life, we are going to find a lot of people who agree, but maybe not putting it in the same language. There you've got a basis for the dialog, to start working on these issues together. You don't have to water down what you say, but you need to find a way to communicate to them in an honest and understandable way. Which ain't talking down to them. Maybe you've got to look at that like, "I just got so caught up in a language that opened up so many doors for me that I lost my ability to just talk."

TC: *What limitations do you see within movements in the United States as they work on this engagement?*

AA: I see the biggest limitations being around our fear of grappling with race, gender, and class. I think it's the thing in the U.S. history of struggles that has kept us divided, and I think it's the most difficult thing for us to confront and work through. If we can do better on that, we could propel forward, but those are the messy things. It's our fear of dealing with the messy things that holds us back. We can really work this out if we put it on the table. We don't have to know exactly how it's going to turn out. Like the Zapatistas: figure it out as we go. Ask questions.

I think that people are also afraid of consequences. I mean, I come out of the Black Panther Party. I am convinced that we're not going to change this world or bring down this empire unless, like Malcolm X says, it's gonna be by any means necessary. That expression means that we have to understand that this is a murderous system. It will kill its own mama. I mean look what happened to Brad Will.[16] I don't care that it was in Mexico; it's still part of this neoliberal power grid. It will kill. It will lock up, it will frame, it will drive people insane. We have to have in our minds that this is war.

Sometimes we're going to have to fight. I believe that we should be preparing an underground all the time. Why do we wait for fascism to drive us under? Why do we wait? I don't think that we wait. There should be something *now* for those communities who feel the need to develop an armed movement. Whether it's the Lakota or whether it's the black community or the Puerto Rican independence movement—how do we support the different struggles that diversely attack? Some groups are going to decide they want to implement armed struggle; we should have something, something that we're working on all the time. Because the law is against us. There are those who are going to use the law, but we should have a way to keep people out of the grip of the monster. We'll help people disappear, we'll get you somewhere, there's doctors, people who know how to make ID's. There's some money here for you, go! We have to be clear that this is not a nice struggle. It can't be won through legality. We can use legalities, but it can't be won that way.

TC: *Do you think that the Left has the ability to take that on as an accepted notion?*

AA: I think the Left is going to fight it. I think it challenges the Left in terms of how comfortable the Left has gotten. The Left and the Right are part of the same system. We have to figure out how to go beyond. A lot of people in the Left are caught up in doing things with a certain legality. It doesn't make sense to me that you call yourself a revolutionary and you won't even jaywalk. Or if you're hungry, you won't even steal. Or you won't support somebody else who has to or feels the need to. I want to deal with people who aren't even a part of the Left. A lot of those people are ready to struggle to survive, and maybe take it beyond survival.

But the system is not going to let people withdraw to the point where it threatens how the system functions. Even to withdraw, it's going to come after you. Is your idea spreading? Are other people trying to withdraw? I live everyday with the thought that one day they going to come after me. Being an enemy of the state, the state is going to send someone after me, whether it be an official employee or a reactionary from unofficial gangs. When we become effective, they're coming for us. They keep tabs. We can be very naïve about them staying on us. When they was coming for people as a result of the Green Scare,[17] a lot of them was kind of naïve. When the state gets you, they going to put the pressure on. They're gonna make it seem like everyone is pointing the finger at you, then you'll start running your mouth about everybody else. Then it's another slew of people getting ready to be political prisoners, which is what the system wants. And they ain't going to stop with discouraging people, they will kill people. Fred Hampton is classic, but he wasn't the only one. So many Native Americans was just disappeared. You are really putting your life on the line when you become a revolutionary. I think that we have to take the struggle more seriously, 'cause when we don't, it's a block in terms of what we do, what we are willing to do.

TC: *How can the community work you have been involved in—the Panthers, Critical Resistance, the Jericho Amnesty Movement[18]—be used to critique the problems you have addressed?*

AA: Figuring out how to get involved with community struggles—that's still number one. I would love for groups to begin to put the issue of political prisoners on their agendas in a prominent way. The issue of political prisoners forces people to think about what this struggle is about. These are the people who made the sacrifices back in the 1960s and 1970s. What does it mean that they're locked up there and we pay them no attention as we still struggle to make changes in the United States? I think to connect with them brings needed history; it brings stories that people need to know. When you connect with the political prisoner, you're saying you are honoring the dreamers of the past, whose dreams you've taken on now, and you're honoring the future, because you're saying that we can't move with real integrity unless we're working for their freedom. In the Mumia case,[19] I always say, "I don't care whether Mumia killed that cop or not. He belongs to us, he's our freedom fighter. Free him." So the facts point to his innocence; if it works in the interim to say 'new trial', okay, but let's be clear, that's just for the interim. It's *their* judicial system! They have no right to have him. He's ours. *We are at war.*

If we ever get to the point where we can bring the powers that be to the table, this should be the first thing we put on the table. Just like with the anti-apartheid movement: "Free Nelson and the rest of them first. Then we can sit down and talk."[20] I think it's a way for us to deepen our understanding of our struggle, to deepen the commitment, and to honor those from the generation before. In a sense it's like reconnecting on that intergenerational thing. With the Zapatistas, every generation is in their struggle. It's not just young people, it's whole communities. We need to have that intra-generational connection. We need to honor those who laid it down before us. Especially those who are still alive but in these dungeons. We need to let the system know that they are on the front of our minds. We want them out.

TC: *Looking at the current movement composition within the anti-prison struggle, Zapatista support, environmental justice movement, and anarchism, can you describe the current potential and problems that you see in those movements?*

AA: That's a huge question. Anti-prison struggles. There's an abolitionist understanding about a lot of them. We are envisioning a world without prisons. That used to be the banner written on Critical Resistance: "Once there were no prisons; that time shall come again."[21] We ain't just talking about reforming prisons or cutting down on them. We're trying to figure out a society where we don't have prisons at all. We understand the class nature, we understand how brutal they are, how anti-human they are. Let's figure out what kind of world we want.

The Zapatistas are trying to create a world; they don't call themselves the anarchist movement, but they do so much that's anarchistic. Some people were a little upset when they found out the Zapatistas set up these houses, so when somebody's drunk and out of control, they may just take this person and just lock them up in a house. Some people said, "Oh look, they're not what I thought, they're not anarchists. They're using a prison-like system." But for the Zapatistas, they're trying to figure it out. They're not saying, "This is going to be a main feature in the society we're trying to create." They're trying to figure it out, and this is what they're going to do right now. Even with the little jail they have, transformative justice and restorative justice are concepts they obviously deal with. They trying to find ways to not just confine people, but bring balance, bring Mayan forms of justice to Western forms. If a member of the community harms or even kills someone, they're not going to bring them to the police; they're not even arresting them. They are going to sit them parties down and try to figure out how to bring balance or reparations back to the community that has been harmed. The family's representatives and the community's representatives get together. So if you harmed this person's family's ability to produce for themselves, you may be required to produce for the other person's family 'til they figure something out. That they are even experimenting with this means they are not just trying to do things from the old way, from the old oppressive system. So it has particular interest for me as an anarchist. They are posing questions that have always been hard for us.

The other thing is in terms of the environmental. We gotta figure out, what is environmental justice when it's related to a community that is predominately of color? What's environmental racism? How does one bring justice to that type of situation? Here in Harlem, we got a lot of environmental racism, from where they dump garbage to oil spills to the air pollution to the automobile congestion and gas, the high levels of asthma and stuff. How would that be resolved in the interest of the people that live there? It poses some questions. We're a pretty complex society. We can't operate as if communities are insular and they can just make decisions as if they're not connected to all these other structures. It makes us think about it. You don't have to have it all together, but when it gets on the table, you can be sure that people have given it a lot of thought, people who are involved in the day-to-day anti-environmental racism struggles, who are doing these forms of organizing.

The job is not as difficult as I think we believe it is. We have all the knowledge to create another world, if only we could be convinced of it. I used to go to the Institute for Social Ecology, I would sit in on some of classes. Some of the classes would take students outside to learn about herbs that we would just think of as weeds.[22] I'm amazed at how the students know so much about these plants that grow right in our neighborhood that can be used for medicinal purposes or for food. They just learn this from being a part of the Institute for Social Ecology. There's people we know who do alternative healing in the community. There's people we know who know all about climate change and the atmosphere. They're not experts; they're damn smart activists. We just need to convince ourselves that we know this. We're practicing this stuff every time we experiment.

TC: *So the new society erupts in the process?*

AA: Yes! That's the way it happens. We're not alone in this; we know that people are doing this all around the world. The U'wa people[23] and all these other groups, that's what they're doing, they're snatching their lives out of neoliberalism. We also doing it in our ways in this technologically advanced urban society called the United States. We just need to do more of that interconnected work. We need to realize that we probably have the power to change the world tomorrow; we can begin to take back our lives.

NOTES

1   See Thomas Sugrue and Andrew Goodman, "Plainfield Burning: Black Rebellion in the Suburban North," *Journal of Urban History*, vol. 33 (May 2007): 568–601. The 1967 Plainfield Riots/Rebellions were one of hundreds of black uprisings that occurred that year, the most well-known of which happened in Newark, New Jersey and Detroit, Michigan. The Plainfield rebellions lasted for nearly a week and included a raid on a local arms factory.

2   Huey P. Newton was co-founder of the Black Panther Party. In 1968, he was falsely accused of murdering a police officer in Oakland, California and subsequently imprisoned until the California Appellate Court reversed his conviction in 1970. Fred Hampton was deputy chairman of the Party. Chicago police raided his apartment in 1969 while he was sleeping and murdered him; all involved officers were later exonerated of any crime. Both incidents were coordinated by the Federal Bureau of Investigation's Counter Intelligence Program (COINTELPRO) and contributed significantly to the Black Panther Party's decline.

3   The group was known at the time as the New York Five.

4   The Manhattan House of Detention was one of the more notorious jails due to its corruption and squalid conditions. Shortly after the attack on the Tombs that Ashanti Alston describes here, the jail was closed, razed, and replaced with a new jail that opened in 1990.

5   Rikers Island has been used as New York City's jail facility since 1884. As of this publication, it is one of the largest penal colonies in the world.

6   George Jackson became a Black Panther while serving time in prison; his book of letters, *Soledad Brother*, made him one of the most internationally recognized prison activists, as he documented his communication with Angela Davis and his brother Jonathan, who was eventually killed during a 1970 hostage-taking attempt to demand George's release. Jackson was murdered by prison guards in 1971, an event that sparked the Attica Prison Uprising mere weeks afterward.

7   The Weather Underground and Students for a Democratic Society were some of the very few mostly white groups on the Left that continuously and prominently struggled in support of the Black Panther Party and the Black Liberation Army.

8   Assata Shakur was one of the most prominent female members of the Black Panther Party and Black Liberation Army. After a 1973 shootout in New Jersey, Shakur was convicted of first-degree murder and subsequently incarcerated; yet in 1979, three BLA members successfully

organized her escape. She currently lives in Cuba under political asylum. Her 1987 book, *Assata: An Autobiography*, brought her additional prominence, especially in academia. Her work and writings have inspired prison abolition groups such as Critical Resistance.

9   The "Newton-Cleaver Split," fueled by COINTELPRO and internal disagreements, proved ruinous for the Black Panther Party. Huey Newton, already paranoid and engaged in other member purges, expelled well-known member Eldridge Cleaver, Minister of Information, for projecting a more confrontational vision for the party. Cleaver went on to lead the Black Liberation Army.

10   See Mumia Abu-Jamal, *We Want Freedom: A Life in the Black Panther Party* (Boston: South End Press, 2004) for a detailed account. The Revolutionary People's Constitutional Convention (RPCC) gathered over 6,000 people in Philadelphia in 1970. Many Party members consider the RPCC a failure on several levels.

11   The Chicano independence movement of the 1960s and 1970s offered the concept of Aztlan as the lands north of Mexico that were stolen by the United States as a result of the Mexican-American War. Aztlan thus carried great symbolic importance in the struggle as a claim to land.

12   The Lakota people, mostly situated in the Midwest of the U.S., have a long history of sovereignty struggle. Contemporary secession demands by the Lakota are situated in a larger strategy and vision of decolonization. See Angela Cavender Wilson [Waziyatawin], *What Does Justice Look Like? The Struggle for Liberation in Dakota Homeland* (St. Paul: Living Justice Press, 2008) for one account.

13   Andy Stepanian is one of the SHAC 7, a group of animal rights activists who were convicted in 2006 and served three years for acts of terrorism associated with SHAC's campaign against Huntingdon Life Sciences. Daniel McGowan is an environmental justice activist who entered into a non-cooperation plea agreement on charges of conspiracy and arson in 2006 for actions claimed by the Earth Liberation Front; he began serving a seven-year sentence in July of 2007. Warcry is an environmental and anarchist activist who was a prominent supporter of Jeff 'Free' Luers. Luers was also convicted of arson in a widely recognized 2000 action where three SUV's were burned and was released in December of 2009 after serving nine and a half years in jail.

14   New York Metro Alliance of Anarchists and 123 Space are both based in New York City; the Industrial Workers of the World and Anarchist People of Color are national. All are anarchist/radical organizations; the 123 Space is an anarchist/radical community center.

15   Subcomandante Marcos is the de facto spokesperson for the Zapatista Army of National Liberation, located in Chiapas, Mexico.

16   Brad Will was a journalist for New York City's Indymedia. He was shot and killed in 2006 as he was reporting on the uprising and occupation of Oaxaca by the Popular Assembly of the Peoples of Oaxaca. There is significant evidence that Will was murdered by counterrevolutionary agents.

17   The "Green Scare" describes the current wave of repression and criminalization targeting the radical environmentalist movement, utilizing similar tactics during the Red Scare of the 1950s. The most comprehensive and current site for information on the Green Scare is "Green is the New Red," at HTTP://WWW.GREENISTHENEWRED.COM.

18   The Jericho Movement is a national organization that works for amnesty and freedom of all political prisoners and prisoners of war in the U.S. The group formed out of a national march and demonstration in support of political prisoner Jalil Muntaqim. They can be found at HTTP://WWW.THEJERICHOMOVEMENT.COM.

19   Mumia Abu-Jamal is a former member of the Black Panther Party and current inmate on

Death Row after being convicted for murder in 1981. His status as a political prisoner has gained international attention and continues to fuel campaigns and organizing for his release.

20 The anti-apartheid movement, which organized massive political and economic resistance to South Africa's racist apartheid system of governance, was one of the few sustained and successful movements in the U.S. and abroad during a time of massive movement decline. The campaign centered specifically on political prisoner Nelson Mandela and demanded his freedom.

21 Critical Resistance is a national prison abolition organization that formed after a 1998 conference in Berkeley, California entitled "Critical Resistance to the Prison-Industrial Complex." The group is credited with identifying the "prison industrial complex" and shifting discourse on the Left to more abolitionist visions of criminal justice. Their exact quote referenced by Ashanti Alston in this interview: "One day there were no prisons. That day shall come again." See HTTP://WWW.CRITICALRESISTANCE.ORG.

22 The Institute for Social Ecology is a radical educational institution based in Vermont, with a thirty-year history of anarchist and ecological politics.

23 The U'wa are an indigenous people of Colombia who number 7,000–8,000 at the time of this publication. They gained international recognition through their fourteen-year-long successful struggle against oil companies Royal Dutch Shell and Occidental Petroleum, who sought to drill on their lands. Their tactics included roadblocks, a coordinated social strike, and a mass suicide threat should the oil extraction project commence. After they forced the oil companies to withdraw from their land in 2002, they stated, "We want to continue being crazy if it means we can continue to exist on our dear mother earth." See Notes from Nowhere Collective, *We Are Everywhere* (London & New York: Verso, 2003): 118.

THE POWER WITHIN US TO CREATE THE WORLD ANEW:

A Discussion with Grace Lee Boggs

Stevie Peace | **Team Colors Collective**

Out of an incredible movement history, bound up with individuals like C.L.R. James and Malcolm X as well as organizations from the Black Panthers to Detroit Summer, Grace Lee Boggs has emerged as one of the foremost political thinkers and philosophers in the United States. Now 94 years old and still committed to activism and new conversations in Detroit, her home of over fifty years, Grace shares in this interview some of the most important insights she has gleaned throughout her life. She discusses the tangible connections between her personal and political experiences, expounding on the importance of theory in movement building, the recognition of our constantly changing reality, and the historical examples of sea changes in the struggle, as new questions and divisions have challenged us to not only think differently, but to also understand how we know. Grace suggests that the present moment can be a tremendous opportunity for evolving our humanity—a task that requires a full assessment of the damage done by oppressive forces, a commitment towards healing and "growing our souls," and an imagination stemming from new stories and new relations that we create.

This interview was conducted and transcribed by Stevie Peace of Team Colors Collective on December 11, 2009. Additionally, Grace participated in the editing process and provided important footnotes and citations. Both participants also benefited from the assistance and guidance of Matthew Birkhold, a New York-based theorist and educator/writer.

Stevie Peace: *Grace, what kind of introduction did you have to politics growing up?*

Grace Lee Boggs: My introduction to politics has been very personal. I emphasize and acknowledge that because most radicals tend to deny that their personal histories have anything to do with their political views. They like to believe that their views are universal, true for everybody, and for all time. I used to believe that.

But over the years, I have learned how much my politics has been influenced by my being born female; to a mother who never learned how to read and write because there were no schools for women in her little Chinese village; who didn't know her father and as a child stole food from the ancestors' graves. I think a lot of that had to do with my politics as they have developed.

Understanding how much the personal and the political are inseparable has been one of the most important philosophical contributions of the women's movement.

SP: *How have the political leaps that you have made throughout your life been related to your personal leaps, if they have at all?*

GLB: I have a *lot* of examples. After I got my PhD in philosophy in 1940, there was no chance of my getting a university job as a philosophy professor. In those days, even department stores would come right out and say, "We don't hire Orientals." And so I went to Chicago, where George Herbert Mead, the man on whom I had done my dissertation, had taught, and got a part-time job in the University of Chicago Philosophy Library for ten dollars a week. That wasn't very much money even though in those days, a lot of people weren't making much more than $500 or $1000 dollars a year. So I was very lucky to find a woman down the street from the university who was willing to let me live in her basement, rent-free. The only drawback was that in order to get into the basement, I had to face down rats in the alley.

That made me very rodent-conscious. So I found a tenants' group in the city which was fighting rat- and mice-infested housing and joined the group.

That is how I got in touch with the black community and came into contact with the March on Washington (MOW) movement, which A. Philip Randolph had organized in 1941 to demand jobs for blacks in the defense industries. Without even actually marching on Washington, the MOW movement aroused so much interest and support in the black community that President Franklin D. Roosevelt was forced to issue Executive Order 8802, banning discrimination in defense industry hiring. I was so inspired by the power of the movement that I decided to become a movement activist.

That is how my personal problems brought me to politics. I think that's true of a whole lot of us, much more than we are ready to acknowledge.

SP: *It sounds like you are talking about this notion that, instead of people arriving at a politics that is 'out there' to be involved in, more often people arrive at it from their own personal position.*

GLB: The important thing is acknowledging the connection between the personal and the political because it is acknowledging how much subject and object are interconnected. It's a very female epistemology or way of knowing, as contrasted to the more masculine claim that what you're saying or thinking has universal validity.

SP: *You wrote and published your autobiography in 1998. How did writing your autobiography influence your emphasis on reflection, and how did reflecting on your personal life changes provide insight into how your politics has changed over time?*

GLB: How I came to write my autobiography is interesting in itself. I didn't really understand this until a linguist—whom I had never met, but who had decided to study my rhetoric—came to me recently and asked, "How and when did your rhetoric begin to change?" It was only then, in conversation with her, that I realized that how I wrote and spoke began to change after Jimmy died in 1993. Jimmy and I had been married for forty years, and during that time, I depended a lot on his ideas, both because he was black and I was not and because those forty years were a period during which black struggles were really at the center of the country's struggles.[1]

After Jimmy died in 1993, I found myself on my own but still thinking about Jimmy's role in the movement more than mine. So I wrote to a publisher I knew, and I asked if she would like to publish the biography of Jimmy that someone wanted to write. To my surprise, she replied that she would prefer to publish an autobiography by *me*. I hadn't believed that I had anything to contribute! But as I started writing *Living for Change*,[2] and as I went back and reflected on my own personal development, I realized that, like everybody else, I had arrived at where I was because *I had come from some place.* I had thought that my personal struggles were just part of my own life; I didn't realize they were social/political struggles.

SP: *How had you thought previously about where people come from and how important that is in the development of one's politics?*

GLB: I was very much more theoretical and objective in my thinking. I thought that being political demanded—*required*—that you not be too introspective or personal. And I think a lot of people, and especially men, still believe that.

I emphasize this because I believe that epistemology—how we know—is extremely important and has been ignored for too long in radical politics. My study of Hegel[3] and my reflections on the movement over these years have helped me to understand that it's not only reality that is changing all the time, but that "how we think" must be constantly changing. In the radical movement, the main emphasis has been on *practice*. Marx's point in his *Theses on Feuerbach*—"Philosophers only contemplate reality; our task is to change it"[4]—has become so fixed in the minds of radicals, and in the practice of radicals, that they *look down* on thinking. But we have to be constantly on guard against getting stuck in old notions.

SP: *Has that been a recent development, or has that been the situation for radicals for a long time?*

GLB: It has been my experience since I became part of the radical movement in the early 1940s, and it's still my experience when I talk to people who are proudly 'leftist.' They don't like to examine their own thinking. Maybe because most of them come to the movement as intellectuals, they are determined to avoid being called intellectuals instead of activists. So they're not willing to examine how we think, and they turn into ideologues, stuck in old calcified ideas.

SP: *When and why do new theories and new ways of thinking emerge, and why is this important to activism today?*

GLB: New ways of thinking are important because the world has changed so much. I feel very fortunate that I've lived for so long because I have some idea of the world in which Marx wrote in the nineteenth century—my professors in college in the 1930s had gone to college in the lifetimes of Marx and Darwin—and I know that world is long gone. I also have a pretty good idea of how revolutions took place in the early part of the twentieth century and the enormous impact that those revolutions have had on how radicals thought and still think about revolution.

I have a pretty good sense of how the world began to change after World War II and after the splitting of the atom. I often recall Einstein's statement that "the splitting of the atom has changed everything but the human mind, and thus we drift toward catastrophe." That's why he insisted that "imagination is more important than knowledge." I think most of us are not sufficiently conscious of how much the world has changed since the middle of the twentieth century.

SP: *These kinds of new theories and new ways of thinking that enhance people's ideas of change—where do they come from? Do they come from movements and the knowledge they produce? Do they come from others?*

GLB: It's difficult to tell how the changes actually take place. But I think that prior to the splitting of the atom, radical thinking focused on the oppressed struggling against the oppressor. There were only victims and villains in the scenario. But when the atom was split, *we* became part of the problem. *We* became responsible for how the world has developed. So we had to recognize our complicity and thus acknowledge our responsibility for creating our unsustainable society.

The turning point in movement history was the Montgomery Bus Boycott. Instead of just struggling against the Montgomery Bus Lines for their absolutely inexcusable treatment of black passengers, the blacks in Alabama who decided to boycott the Montgomery buses (for more than a year!) began to act as models of the new kind of human beings we need to become in the twenty-first century.

Women were very important in triggering and organizing the Montgomery boycott. It was not only Rosa Parks, who has become an icon for her refusal to give up her seat, but women like Jo Ann Robinson, a university professor who helped organize the boycott,[5] and Mother Pollard, the old black woman who, when asked if she was tired from so many weeks of walking instead of busing, replied, "My feet's tired, but my soul is rested." Together, a number of different people, including Martin Luther King Jr., created something new.

Most of the struggles that took place in the 1960s and thereafter—the anti-war struggles, the women's struggles, the ecological struggles—were inspired by the Montgomery Bus Boycott. It introduced something new into the world: the concept of two-sided transformation. To change the world, we must not only transform the system. We must transform ourselves.

SP: *Would you say that movements today have inherited those new questions of human transformation, of what is possible in human life?*

GLB: I don't think enough people have. I don't think we have even begun to internalize that concept, especially in our response to 9/11. But I think that at the Battle of Seattle in 1999, people began to understand something new. It was not only the World Trade Organization, not only those huge structures that have been created by corporate globalization that we have to replace. Especially with the climate crisis, we have to begin changing ourselves radically.

That's the challenge of the twenty-first century. What's going on now at Copenhagen is making that clear.[6] At Copenhagen there are many activists both from 'developing' and 'developed' countries saying, "The main question is how you/we in the Global North live." We in the North are responsible for global emissions that now threaten all life on Earth. We have to begin living differently so that others can simply live.

SP: *So what is happening at Copenhagen is the raising of those larger questions. But you were saying we had not addressed that in our relationship to 9/11; why do you suppose that is?*

GLB: I was at a women's forum the week of 9/11. An older woman with her four-year-old grandson in her arms spoke up and said that, watching the attack on the World Trade Centers on 9/11, he had asked a very simple question: "Why do they hate us so?" We've not yet asked that question of ourselves. It was really sad the other night to hear Obama at West Point,[7] mouthing those myths about how we represent freedom and that it is our duty to bring it to the world. We still believe in that myth of our exceptionalism, that we are the ones who can save the world even though we're an empire with a hundred military bases all over the world. It was very sad.

Fortunately, more people are starting to question this. For example, Andrew Bacevich, a retired colonel, Vietnam War veteran, and Boston University professor of history and international relations, is currently being invited to share his views on many talk shows. He's the author of *The Limits of Power: The End of American Exceptionalism.*[8]

SP: *I agree that the myth of exceptionalism still runs strong; a big part of Obama's 2008 presidential campaign success came from trumpeting that tone. It was not too far removed from Reagan and his "morning in America." What does that say about Obama? Or more importantly, what does that say about the Left in the U.S.?*

GLB: In the last year, Obama's support has steadily declined with his bailout of the bankers, his compromises on health care reform, and his latest decision to send additional troops to Afghanistan. This is disappointing, but it also provides us with the opportunity for serious reflection and discussion. Why, as President, has Obama become the capable and self-satisfied manager of problems? Why is he no longer the visionary for which people—especially young people—campaigned? It is a learning process through what Hegel, reflecting on his experience of the French Revolution, called the "labor, patience, and suffering of the negative."

What do we do now? Do we campaign for a president with more radical or progressive solutions, like Dennis Kucinich or Ralph Nader? Or do we start looking elsewhere for leadership, to people at the grassroots, to be and to make the change in ourselves and in all our institutions?

SP: *That brings us back to that notion you had mentioned earlier, of two-sided transformation and what we will need personally to re-conceive and re-think the kind of world we want to have. But it seems like we cannot confine this to what we in the U.S. want, important as that is; it seems that two-sided transformation must be planetary.*

GLB: I think that the people of the United States are probably the most backward people on Earth. Europeans, while they still have a long way to go, are more advanced than we are because they have suffered two World Wars on their territory. Because they have experienced so many losses of life through war, they have become more peace-loving. The American people haven't even thought about what it means to be peace-loving, either abroad or in our communities at home. We have not even begun to understand how much we are responsible for the number of deaths that take place on the African continent. We have not begun to look at ourselves in the mirror. I think that the inability of the American people to look in the mirror is one of the most tragic episodes in world history and the evolution of humanity. We need to recognize that we are at a very special time on the clock of the world when we need to make a huge leap forward in what it means to be a human being, not only for our own survival, but for the survival of the earth and for the survival of all living things on earth.

SP: *How do these processes—a national "looking in the mirror"—happen? I understand the notion, but maybe you could provide an example to clarify. Does it happen nationally? Is it more local, or from person to person? What do your experiences tell you?*

GLB: When Kennedy was killed in 1963, Malcolm X warned that "the chickens have come home to roost." A few years later, in his 1967 anti-Vietnam war speech, Martin Luther King Jr. warned that our country is on the wrong side of the world revolution. In his 1976 'malaise' speech, President Carter tried to alert the American people to the consequences of our over-consumption.

We still need to ask ourselves and discuss with our families and friends why 9/11 happened. When these discussions finally get under way, we will begin to understand that, essentially, the World Trade Center and the Pentagon were attacked because we haven't heeded all these warnings.

SP: *But this also comes from a much longer history we are complicit in—colonization, genocide, slavery; the list is endless. I think the larger question, though, is how do we create change from this position, and how do we engage people accordingly.*

GLB: I think the thing that we have to do is probe more deeply, to understand the link between our passion for economic growth and slavery. We talk about enslaving people as if it were only a question of racism. It was not just racism. In the seventeenth and eighteenth centuries, this country's rapid economic growth depended on having many more people doing the work. That's why we enslaved blacks. And it depended on getting more land. That's why we exterminated so many Native Americans.

That fundamental contradiction—of dehumanizing ourselves by degrading others for the sake of rapid economic growth—was built into the founding of this country. We still don't recognize the extent to which rapid economic growth and slavery have been linked together in our history.

We have to rediscover our past as it really was. Until then, we cannot recognize that a revolution in the United States will be unlike all previous revolutions. Instead of getting more, the next American Revolution means giving things up because so many of our comforts and conveniences have been bought at the expense of the earth and other people. That's a very different way of looking at revolution, which Jimmy explained in his chapter on dialectics and revolution, in *Revolution and Evolution in the Twentieth Century*.[9] The next American Revolution is for the purpose of recovering our humanity, restoring our humanity. Advancing another stage on the evolutionary road of humanity requires that we Americans start giving up things. Despite the physical suffering from the economic meltdown and the climate crisis, these have a positive side, because they force us to face that reality of our past and our challenge for the future.

SP: *You mentioned that whatever revolution is to come has to be unlike others that have come before. Could you speak more to what that means to you, in terms of the old ways of organizing and the new ways we will need to see?*

GLB: I think a lot of people are still organizing to get *more*. I'm not saying that when people are hungry and homeless, you should not organize to get food stamps or to have a roof over your head. What I am saying is that in this period, we need to be organizing ourselves, at the same time, to live differently. We have to begin living more simply so that others can simply live, for the sake of all living things, including ourselves.

SP: *How do you see those questions developing in Detroit?*

GLB: I think that Detroit is very fortunate, in the sense that, having once been the symbol of the miracle of industrialization, and then becoming the symbol of the devastation of deindustrialization, we find more people willing to begin anew, even *forced* to begin anew.

To me, one of the most amazing things about Detroit is the rapid growth of the urban agricultural movement. I remember when it started. Back in the early 1980s, the "Gardening Angels"—mainly Gerald Hairston and African American women who had been born and raised in the South—looked around them at all the vacant lots and decided they could be used for community gardens. They said very openly that these gardens could not only grow food for our bodies, but could also give our young people the sense of process that they cannot get in an urban environment. This combination of material need and psychological need was what created the community gardening movement in Detroit. That's why it has grown so rapidly.

I remember when the Detroit Agriculture Network was established. We used to sponsor a garden tour every August so that people could visit the gardens. In the beginning, we only needed one bus, seating forty-two people. We would complete the tour in maybe an hour, an hour and a half. However, in the last few years, so many community gardens have been planted—there are now over 800!—that we need as many as *six* buses, and several *hours* for the tour. And still, people can only see a few of the gardens. Some buses go to the east side, and some to the west side. And the community gardeners now hold quarterly meetings during the year so that they can share experiences and resources. So gardening becomes a way of building community. It's an example of how something new can emerge out of crisis and out of disaster,

SP: *It sounds like this particular struggle builds community, but also helps to build power as well.*

GLB: The idea of power is a very complicated concept. What do you mean by power?

SP: *In this case, I think power is the control and ability to act in the ways that we wish to live our lives.*

GLB: Have you ever thought that talking about power in terms of control is a very masculine way of talking about power?

SP: *Well, how do you conceive of power?*

GLB: I think that as a result of the women's movement, we are able to think less of control and more of the power within us to create the world anew. In other words, we are able to think more about empowering people and people empowering themselves. The whole concept of revolution has been undergoing a seismic shift. In the first half of the 20th century, when the Russian Revolution was the model of revolution, radicals thought of revolution as seizing or grasping power from those in power so that we, rather than they, would be in control. But at the beginning of the 1960s, the idea of power began to divide into two: between the idea of power as control and the idea of power as empowerment.

SP: *So there were new conceptions of power that were contesting older conceptions of power.*

GLB: Right. To me, one of the most important things is to recognize how one is constantly dividing into two. For example, we are now at the point of recognizing that the more the black middle class has succeeded in integrating into and gaining access to the system, the more blacks at the bottom are suffering. One has divided into two. At the same time that an African American has achieved the pinnacle of power—election to the Oval Office— we are also faced with the fact that the conditions for blacks and other have-nots at the bottom continue to deteriorate. So we have to get rid of kid gloves in examining and critiquing Obama.

SP: *Could you enumerate more clearly what "one dividing into two" means in terms of how we re-think these political questions?*

GLB: There are many examples of one dividing into two. For example, there was the Grassroots Leadership Conference in November 1963. As Malcolm began finding the personal conduct of Mr. Muhammad increasingly unacceptable, he also began to question black political unity. The high point of the Grassroots Leadership conference, which Jimmy chaired, was the distinction Malcolm made between "house Negroes" and "field Negroes." That was one dividing into two.[10]

I also recall how the Detroit Black Power movement developed in the 1960s. While most people saw the movement as a struggle for access to positions at City Hall and in the state legislature, some of us began to think of power in terms of the majority black population at the grassroots creating a new kind of life, a new kind of living to address the questions of deindustrialization.

We also need to give more thought to the split that was emerging at the height of Black Panther Party prominence, between those Black Panthers committed to violent confrontations with the 'pigs' and those creating community-building breakfast programs, especially some of the women. Detroiter Ron Scott, one of those community builders, has remained in the community, and is now leading the struggle to transform the "war zones" of our inner cities into "peace zones." So one is dividing into two all the time, in every struggle.

SP: *Can you describe how that process of division is necessary in how movements mature?*

GLB: I have arrived at this understanding mainly because I have been part of so many movements over so many years. I joined the radical movement when the Russian Revolution was still fresh in people's minds and radicals and progressives were struggling over whether the Soviet Union was still a workers' state. During the Depression, if you were on a college campus in New York and you weren't some kind of radical, Communist, Socialist, or Trotskyist, you were considered brain-dead—and you probably were. There was still some of that around when I worked with C.L.R. James in New York in the 1940s. But reality shifted again come World War II. Roosevelt had taken us into the war because there was no other way for him to create jobs; all his New Deal programs still left millions unemployed. So in the course of World War II, we became a nation that depended on the military-industrial complex for jobs, and during the mid-century years, that complex became a growing reality in the United States.

At the same time, World War II introduced new production technology—high-tech automation—that was eliminating millions of people from work, *reducing* the work force rather than expanding it, as Marx had anticipated. So we had to go beyond the thinking of Marx. It's the constant changing of reality that forces us to begin thinking differently. You don't begin thinking differently just because it would be nice to think differently.

SP: *You think differently because the conditions change.*

GLB: Yes. Reality is constantly changing.

SP: *I am wondering if you could speak more about changes in labor and industry and how they are raising new challenges and questions for us in terms of how we struggle.*

GLB: I think that one of the most fundamental questions facing us is how to begin 'working' rather than 'laboring.' Post-industrial production has created the opportunity and necessity to begin thinking seriously about this distinction. In the book *Expanding the Boundaries of Transformative Learning*,[11] there is an article by Brian Milani which talks about how jobs have changed over the last hundred years. In Marx's time in the nineteenth century, people had to labor so hard and were so exhausted from their jobs that they couldn't think for themselves and needed radical parties. But gradually, as a result of workers' struggles, the hours of work have been reduced, and work itself has become much more relational, not just occupied with the production of material things.

In their new book, *Commonwealth*,[12] Michael Hardt and Antonio Negri write that production has become "bio-political." In other words, it produces subjectivities—new subjective relations, new commonalities—as well as material things. There have been tremendous transformations in production that not only make it possible for us to com-municate 24/7, but also enable us to think much more subjectively about what kind of human beings we want and need to be and what kind of society we want and need to create. So work can become ennobling and life-giving, rather than just something done for a paycheck. For example, when you look at the growing number of health workers, you realize how relational they are to their clients. They produce charts and measurements, but the charts and measurements are only a minor part of what they produce. What is pro-duced, hopefully, is a mutual social relationship—something that in the words of Hardt and Negri is "bio-political." This new stage of "bio-political" production is what should be at the core of health care reform in our time—not changing health insurance.

SP: *As you have talked about previously, we have seen immense cultural changes since World War II. Materialism, mass consumption, suburbanization—we could list many of these forc-es. They have had many devastating and damaging consequences: the prison industry, crack cocaine, deindustrialization. Where do the questions of health—on mental, emotional, and spiritual levels—enter into our struggles and our theory-making, and in our relationships?*

GLB: I remember when violence and crime began to explode in the wake of the urban rebellions of the 1960s. It forced us to begin thinking more programmatically about what it means for young people who can no longer look forward to the kinds of jobs their parents had, jobs which enabled them to raise a family, buy a house and a car. All of a sud-den, these young people were faced with the prospect of not being of any use. So a lot of them turned to drugs, burglary, and other petty crimes. But all the power structure could conceive of was a military response, the "War on Drugs," which meant a war on young people. They could not see that a historic change had happened in the whole productive process, something that required us to think of people not just as laborers forced to work for a paycheck, but as *human beings* who need to be of use. There is a marvelous poem by Marge Piercy, that I quote very often, called "To Be of Use."[13] It ends with these two lines: "The pitcher yearns for water to carry/The person for work that is real."

We didn't take seriously enough the reality that automation had made millions of young people superfluous or expendable, which means that we are challenged to re-con-ceptualize the whole meaning of what it means to be a human being. The person yearns for work that is real; therefore, we have to re-conceptualize work. It was because we didn't re-conceptualize work that we now have so many people on drugs, two million people in prison and many millions of ex-cons.

Malcolm was an ex-con who was able to begin transforming himself and to keep trans-forming himself until the day that he was killed. Because Malcolm's transformation from a hustler and a convict is so much a part of my experience and the movement of the 1960s, I see the potential in other ex-cons to build on his legacy and undertake healing themselves and others. What I see happening at this point is that some ex-cons like Yusef Shakur are coming back into their neighborhoods and trying to give back. During the Martin Luther King weekend in January 2010, Yusef's group, Urban Network, and Detroit-City of Hope are hosting an event to explore how we can heal ourselves, our families, and our commu-nities in order to "bring the neighbor back into our 'hoods'."

SP: *What is the importance of healing in both personal and political work, especially in regard to relationships?*

GLB: I think that healing begins by recognizing how damaged we have become, how in the last thirty to forty years the American people have experienced a sharp decline in our humanity. Most Americans, including members of our families with whom we get together only or mainly on holidays, are living lives of quiet desperation. They are bitter and angry because the American Dream of never-ending upward mobility which we have been living has become a nightmare. This bitterness and anger are fueling the counter-revolution. We must be ready to listen to their stories and help them face the truth which they know but have been evading, that we have come to the end of the rainbow. If we listen patiently enough, we can help people discover their compassion, which is the way to create community. In other words, we should view the emergence of the "teabaggers" as both a danger and an opportunity to help "we the American people" transform ourselves by rediscovering our humanity.[14]

Most people do not realize that, until we consciously explore and embrace another philosophy, the way we think and act is still based on the philosophy of the society we live in—a racist, materialist, militarist, selfish, capitalist society. Seventy years ago, I wrote my dissertation on George Herbert Mead, the "Philosopher of the Social," because I was drawn to his philosophy, that we create ourselves in and through communication with others—a very different philosophy from the dominant one in our society. In retrospect, I suspect that it was this idea which prepared me to leave the ivory tower of the university, become involved with the 1941 MOW movement, and out of that movement experience, decide to become a movement activist.

For an introduction to this new philosophy, I recommend reading the novels and essays of Charles Johnson, who studied the phenomenologists to obtain his PhD in philosophy before becoming a university professor and novelist. In "The End of the Black American Narrative," Johnson explains that, with the emergence of Oprah Winfrey, Colin Powell, and Barack Obama, we have come to the end of the American narrative of blacks as victims.[15] So we need a new, much more complex story to help us discover the kind of organizing we need to do in this period.

Johnson provides one such narrative in his 1990 award-winning book *Middle Passage*, which is the drama of how a ship's crew undergoes apocalyptic catastrophes from which a handful emerges transformed. *Middle Passage* is Melville's Moby Dick for our time. The Pequod, a whaler, has become the Republic, a slave ship; Captain Ahab has become Captain Falcon; Ishmael has become Rutherford Calhoun, a newly-emancipated African American.[16] A few years later, Johnson re-discovered Martin Luther King, which inspired him to write the novel *Dreamer* as well as articles on the significance of King's concept of Love and community.[17]

In the 1990s, as we struggled with growing violence in Detroit, I also re-discovered Martin Luther King. I had identified much more with Malcolm in the 1960s and had viewed King's non-violence as somewhat naïve. But decades later, I began studying King's life and speeches, especially his 1967 anti-Vietnam war speech calling for a radical revolution in values against racism, materialism, and militarism. I was delighted to discover that Hegel had been King's favorite philosopher. I also learned that after Watts erupted in 1965, King realized that he had not paid enough attention to urban youth, so he moved to Chicago to connect with them. In one of his last speeches, King said that what young people in our "dying cities" need are direct action projects that provide them with opportunities to change both their surroundings and themselves. Out of our own experiences and struggles, we in Detroit came to the same conclusion. So in 1992, we founded Detroit

Summer, an intergenerational, multicultural youth program to rebuild, redefine, and re-spirit Detroit from the ground up.[18] And I began talking and writing more about King.[19] In 2004 I became part of the Beloved Communities Initiative, which has been identifying and reporting on the very diverse groups who are creating forms of "beloved community" all around the country.[20]

These are the alternatives that some people are creating in response to the materialism and militarism that now dominate our culture. Looking at the kind of human beings we have become, they are asking, "How is it that we have become so dehumanized, and what do we have to do to re-humanize ourselves?" It's a wonderful opportunity to look at evolution and revolution in a very different way. I think often of Ardipithecus, the woman who emerged four and a half million years ago in Africa and whose fossil remains have been discovered and reconstituted. I see a kind of humanity in Ardi's face that is not present in Lucy's, who anthropologists believe emerged a million years later. I think that is because today's paleontologists, reconstructing Ardi for our day and age, think about evolution not only in anatomical terms, but in human/psychological/spiritual terms. What looks out from Ardi's eyes as they've reconstructed her is a very spiritual human being.

SP: *What does your own process of healing and spiritual development look like, especially after many losses and splits that have happened in your life?*

GLB: It was only a few years ago, in 2003, that I made a speech called "These Are the Times to Grow Our Souls" to an artists and activists convention in Flint. For most of my life, I *never* would have used the word 'soul,' because I thought of 'soul' only as a sort of substance, as a thing. But once I began to understand how we are undergoing what Martin Luther King called a "spiritual death,"[21] I started to recognize that growing our souls means acting differently, based on radically different values. We need to recognize and begin acting from the power within us to create the world anew. We need to view the world not just with our bodies or minds, but with our hearts, and to be creating ways of acting from our hearts, from caring. We have to stop thinking of ourselves as Descartes[22] did in the seventeenth century and Scientific Rationalists have done since—that is, only as physical bodies and rational, calculating minds.

SP: *Just about six months from now, your city will be hosting the next U.S. Social Forum and who knows how many other developments to come. What excites you the most about the present moment, and what are you looking forward to on the horizon?*

GLB: Yesterday I had a very interesting visit with a young woman from Chicago. We only talked for about an hour; it was the first time we met. She told me that her mother, who is an artist, warned her very early on never to let her 'schooling' interfere with her *education*. She also said that she gave up on Obama when he appointed Arne Duncan as Secretary of Education because she knew how he had acted in Chicago.[23]

It's just amazing to me how young people, like this woman—who's only eighteen!—have arrived through their own experiences at such insights. Almost every week, someone like that shows up at the Boggs Center. That doesn't mean that everyone else is like this young woman. But we have to stop thinking in terms of 'everybody' or 'masses' so much, and recognize that the leaders we've been looking for are here, among the people that we meet. Human beings are not like schools of fish, all shifting direction at the same time.

There are people constantly emerging who are seeing the world anew and can help the rest of us see it anew. A young woman of eighteen, coming out of Chicago, can give us another lens to look at the larger reality. That's what leaders do.

SP: *It sounds like that is a source of hope for you.*

GLB: We call the very loose network of grassroots groups that is emerging here "Detroit—City of Hope." I think that Detroit embodies a lot of hope. The national and international media had been conditioned to think that Detroit was hopeless, that it was the end of the world. And yet, in the last few months, I've watched a big change taking place. Reporters and filmmakers come to Detroit and find hope in small things, as we have. They discover that we don't need huge buildings to give us hope. In fact, it's the huge abandoned buildings that signal the end of one epoch and provide us with the opportunity to begin a new one.

SP: *Seeing the world anew seems very much tied into creativity and vision, as you had mentioned with Einstein's quote that "Imagination is more important than knowledge." How are you seeing creativity manifest among the leaders we have been looking for?*

GLB: I believe that movement builders have not thought enough about that statement by Einstein, which is essentially about epistemology. When he made the statement, Einstein was at the point in his own life when his contributions to the knowledge so prized by institutions and Western civilization had resulted in his being complicit in the bombing of Hiroshima and Nagasaki. So he warned that knowledge only informs us of the past, of what has already happened, whereas imagination opens our hearts and minds to the future, to what is possible, to what it is within our power to create. I have never forgotten the placards of French youth calling for "L'Imagination au Pouvoir" during the May-June 1968 revolt.[24] At the time, Jimmy and I were in Paris on our way back to the United States after a week of speaking engagements in Italy, followed by another week of discussions with exiled Ghanaian President Kwame Nkrumah in Guinea. These placards profoundly influenced the conversations in Maine which we began with Lyman and Freddy Paine soon after our return.[25]

We have to understand that the closer you get to the corridors of power, to the Oval Office and Congress, the more you become a prisoner of the past. The closer you get to the marginalized, the grassroots and the groundlings, the greater your incentive to think imaginatively and 'outside the box.'

SP: *So much of what you have touched on here is about the challenges facing 'we' as Americans, or 'we' as human beings, but as you have noted, thinking on those lines does not necessarily mean thinking of what 'masses' will have to do. You have spoken and written a lot about a quote from Margaret Wheatley: "Rather than worry about critical mass, our work is to foster critical connections."[26] What does this mean to you, and what might it mean to us as we work towards change?*

GLB: This quote has helped me realize how most radicals are still stuck in Newton's quantitative way of knowing. That way of knowing was crucial to beginning the industrial revolution, but that was 300 years ago. Like our leaders in Washington, today's radicals remain obsessed with size and mass. So they are still trying to mobilize masses or large numbers to gain enough force to take power from those in power. On the other hand, a quantum view, as Wheatley explains, enables us to think less about mass and organize more organically and locally, in terms of critical connections.

For example, it was only after the Montgomery Bus boycott of 1955–56, followed by the sit-in of four students at the Greensboro Woolworth's in 1960, and by small numbers of Freedom Riders defying segregated transportation in 1961, that we began to recognize the enormous power that a few committed visionaries have within them to change the world. All the great humanizing movements of the 1960s were inspired by a relatively small number of people.

We need to learn from that experience, although we should be wary of trying to repeat it today, because we are at a new place. At this time in the evolution of the human race, especially in the United States, organizing begins with quiet listening to the stories of others, so that our individual selves become interconnected, overcoming our solipsism and self-centeredness and, instead, becoming each other, and discovering within us the power to create the world anew.

NOTES

1   James Boggs (Jimmy), a black autoworker from Alabama, met Grace through the Third Layer School of the Johnson-Forest Tendency, formed with Raya Dunayevskaya and C.L.R. James after a series of splits in various Workers Parties, and is widely regarded today as one of the most important contributors to autonomist Marxist thought in the U.S. Jimmy and Grace were tireless in their discussions and organizing in Detroit, starting in the Black Power movement and extending in many directions since. Jimmy in particular is known for one of his many writings, *The American Revolution: Pages from a Negro Worker's Notebook* (New York: Monthly Review Press, 1963), which was recently re-issued with a new introduction by Grace and commentaries by six other Detroit activists.

2   Grace Lee Boggs, *Living for Change: An Autobiography* (Minneapolis: University of Minnesota Press, 1998).

3   Georg Wilhelm Friedrich Hegel (1770–1831) was one of the foremost German philosophers, known particularly for his examinations of the interconnectedness of subject and object in our understanding of knowledge and epistemology.

4   The *Theses on Feuerbach* were written by Marx in 1845 and published in 1888 after his death. His notes are focused on critiques of Young Hegelian philosophers like Ludwig Feuerbach. The concluding statement is translated thus: "Philosophers have hitherto only interpreted the world in various ways; the point is to change it." See Frederick Engels, *Ludwig Feuerbach and the End of Classical German Philosophy*, with appendix "Theses on Feuerbach" by Karl Marx (Peking: Foreign Languages Press, 1976), translated from the German edition of 1888.

5   Jo Ann Robinson was head of the Women's Political Council, originally formed as a civic organization for professional African American women. The Women's Political Council was the first group to officially call for the boycott of the Montgomery buses following Rosa Parks' arrest.

6   The United Nations Climate Change Conference was held in Copenhagen from December 7 through December 18 of 2009. Over 1,000 climate change activists were arrested in actions planned during the event. The conference ended in disarray, yielding an accord that is not legally binding, nor capable of enforcing commitments made by various nations to reduce carbon dioxide emissions.

7   President Barack Obama announced at West Point in December 2009 the escalation of the war in Afghanistan, including the deployment of 30,000 additional troops to the area.

8   Andrew Bacevich, *The Limits of Power: The End of American Exceptionalism* (New York: Macmillan, 2008).

9   James Boggs and Grace Lee Boggs, *Revolution and Evolution in the Twentieth Century* (New York: Monthly Review Press, 1974). The book was reprinted again in 2008 with a new introduction written by Grace.

10 Grace discusses this incident more thoroughly in *Living for Change*, 128–9.

11 Bruce Milani, "From Opposition to Alternatives: Postindustrial Potentials and Transformative Learning," in *Expanding the Boundaries of Transformative Learning: Essays on Theory and Praxis*, eds. Edmund O'Sullivan, Amish Morrell, and Mary Ann O'Connor, 47–58 (New York: Palgrave, 2002).

12 Michael Hardt and Antonio Negri, *Commonwealth* (Boston: Belknap Press, 2009).

13 Marge Piercy, *To Be of Use: Poems by Marge Piercy* (New York, Doubleday: 1973).

14 The "Tea Party" movement emerged in early 2009, a New Right formulation of communities and individuals alarmed by increased government spending in the economic crisis, in addition to a plethora of other issues. Though frequently disjointed, targeted for cooptation, and in a state of general disarray at the time of this publication, this movement illustrates a serious commitment to organizing a New Right base that deserves further attention.

15 Charles Johnson, "The End of the Black American Narrative," *The American Scholar*, vol. 7, #3 (Summer 2008): 43–58.

16 Johnson, *Middle Passage* (New York: Scribner, 1990).

17 Johnson, *Dreamer: A Novel* (New York: Scribner, 1999).

18 More on Detroit Summer can be found at HTTP://WWW.DETROITSUMMER.ORG.

19 Examples include "From Marx to Malcolm and Martin," *The Other Side* (Jan-Feb. 2003); "Recapture MLK's Radical Revolutionary Spirit: Create Cities and Communities Of Hope," talk given at Eastern Michigan University, January 15, 2007; "Let's talk about Malcolm and Martin," talk given at the Brecht Forum, May 4, 2007. A recorded copy of these speeches as well as others given by Grace from 1990 to 2009 is available at the Boggs Center in Detroit.

20 More on Beloved Communities Initiative can be found at HTTP://WWW.BELOVEDCOMMUNITIESNET.ORG.

21 From Martin Luther King's speech, "Beyond Vietnam: A Time to Break Silence," April 4, 1967: "A nation that continues year after year to spend more money on military defense than on programs of social uplift is approaching spiritual death."

22 Rene Descartes (1596–1650) is considered the "Father of Modern Philosophy." His ideas were a key influence in the development of scientific—and eventually political—rationalism.

23 Henry Giroux and Kenneth Saltman, "Obama's Betrayal of Public Education? Arne Duncan and the Corporate Model of Schooling" (TruthOut, Dec. 17, 2008): HTTP://WWW.TRUTHOUT.ORG/121708R. Arne Duncan previously served as CEO of Chicago Public Schools. "Duncan ... presided over the implementation and expansion of an agenda that militarized and corporatized the third largest school system in the nation, one that is about 90 percent poor and nonwhite. Under Duncan, Chicago took the lead in creating public schools run as military academies, vastly expanded draconian student expulsions, instituted sweeping surveillance practices, advocated a growing police presence in the schools, arbitrarily shut down entire schools and fired entire school staffs."

24 "L'Imagination au Pouvoir" translates to "All Power to the Imagination" or "Let Imagination Rule." For additional context and analysis, see George Katsiaficas, *The Imagination of the New Left* (Boston: South End Press, 1987).

25 See Grace Lee Boggs, James Boggs, Freddy Paine, and Lyman Paine, *Conversations in Maine: Exploring our Nation's Future* (Boston: South End Press, 1978). Grace discusses these conversations further, as well as her and Jimmy's travels and meetings with Nkrumah, in *Living for Change*.

26 Margaret Wheatley, *Leadership and the New Science: Discovering Order in a Chaotic World* (San Francisco: Berrett-Koehler, 2001).

BIOGRAPHIES

Team Colors Collective (Conor Cash, Craig Hughes, Stevie Peace, Kevin Van Meter, and friends) is a collective engaged in militant research to provide strategic analysis for the intervention into everyday life. Our purpose is to explore questions of everyday resistance, mutual aid, the imposition of work, social reproduction, class composition, community participation, movement building, and the commons by creating engaging workshops and producing provocative written documents and articles. Currently, Team Colors operates in the United States with members based in the Mid-Atlantic Region, Midwest, Northwest, and Southwest. Our approach has developed out of our involvement in community organizing projects, community dialogs, and resistance activities for more than a decade.

Craig Hughes (editor) is an anarchist and independent researcher who lives in New York. Hughes is a member of the Executive Committee of the East Timor and Indonesia Action Network and has been involved in numerous organizing efforts since he became involved in punk and radical politics during the 1990s. He holds master's degrees in History and Social Work and Community Organizing, for which he has to pay back a very large amount of money in loans.

Stevie Peace (editor and contributor) is a writer and organizer from Shoreview, Minnesota. Peace first met Team Colors in 2005 through his work at the Common Ground Health Clinic in New Orleans; he joined the collective in 2008. He has conducted several workshops and presentations on racism and sexual violence, the prison industrial complex, and harm and healing, and his writings have been published in several zines. On the side, he's amassing a plethora of words and networks for a narrative mapping project of radical Asian America. He lives in Minneapolis/St. Paul.

Kevin Van Meter (editor) is an organizer and researcher originally from Long Island and currently based in Portland, Oregon. Van Meter appears, along with Benjamin Holtzman and Craig Hughes, in the AK Press collection *Constituent Imagination: Militant Investigation, Collective Theorization*, with an article titled "DIY and the Movement Beyond Capitalism." He has also written for a variety of radical publications and zines. Van Meter is finishing a master's degree in Political Science at the City University of New York Graduate Center, focusing on current political theory, everyday resistance, and social movements.

Ashanti Omowali Alston (interviewed) is a revolutionary, speaker, writer, organizer, and motivator. Ashanti is one of the few former members of the Black Panther Party who self-describes as an anarchist within the Black Liberation Movement. He is also a former Black Liberation Army political prisoner. He is currently co-chair of the National Jericho Movement to free U.S. political prisoners and a member of the Malcolm X Grassroots Movement-New York City. On top of all that, he is an Elder-in-training and a grandfather of a small 'nation.'

Grace Lee Boggs (interviewed) was born in 1915 to Chinese immigrant parents in Providence, Rhode Island. After receiving her PhD, she worked from 1942 to 1952 with West Indian Marxist C.L.R. James in New York. In 1953 she moved to Detroit and married James Boggs, African American autoworker, activist, and writer. After his death in 1993, she co-founded the Boggs Center to Nurture Community Leadership. Besides many awards for community activism, Grace has been named a Doctor of Humane Letters by the College of Wooster, 2004; Kalamazoo College, 2007; and the University of Michigan, 2009. Her autobiography, *Living for Change*, was published by University of Minnesota Press in 1998.

George Caffentzis is a member of the Midnight Notes Collective and has edited with the Collective two books published by Autonomedia: *Midnight Oil: Work, Energy War, 1973–1992* (1992) and *Auroras of the Zapatistas: Local and Global Struggles of the Fourth World War* (1998).

Chris Carlsson, director of the multimedia history project Shaping San Francisco, is a writer, publisher, editor, and community organizer. For the last thirty years, his activities have focused on horizontal communications, organic communities, and public space. Carlsson was one of the founders, editors, and frequent contributors to the San Francisco magazine *Processed World*; he also helped launch the monthly bike-ins known as Critical Mass that have spread to five continents and over 300 cities. Carlsson has edited four books and published a novel, *After the Deluge* (Full Enjoyment Books, 2004). His most recent work is *Nowtopia* (AK Press, 2008).

Maribel Casas-Cortes & Sebastian Cobarrubias | Producciones Translocales are a trans-Atlantic collaboration/couple/family between Maribel Casas-Cortes and Sebastian Cobarrubias (and Gabriel, their young child). They have been involved in political work with a variety of collectives, such as the Chicago Direct Action Network, the Coalition of Immokalee Workers, the Mexico Solidarity Network, and La Agencia de Asuntos Precarios. They are currently PhD candidates in Anthropology and Geography, respectively, at the University of North Carolina, Chapel Hill, where they participated in the Social Movements Working Group and co-founded the Counter Cartographies Collective (3Cs). Producciones Translocales have written about the 3Cs' experience in the edited volume on militant research, *Constituent Imagination* (AK Press, 2007), and in *Brumaria*. Their work has also appeared in the *Atlas of Radical Cartography* and *Activist Research Newsletter*.

City Life/Vida Urbana, founded in 1973, is a grassroots radical community organization in Boston. It is multi-issue but has focused especially on fighting forced displacement. Currently, City Life is leading a campaign against evictions after foreclosure. This successful effort continues City Life's historic strategy of "shield and sword," or legal defense and public protest. Through a series of dramatic eviction blockades, City Life has limited post-foreclosure evictions and gotten back people's homes at much less than loan value. City Life's organizing model is avowedly radical, seeking to respond effectively to immediate problems in a way that builds a movement for fundamental change.

Direct Action to Stop the War is a radical anti-war organization based in the San Francisco Bay Area.

John Duda is an activist-scholar who lives in Baltimore, Maryland and is currently researching the history of the concept of self-organization. A founder of the wildly successful Red Emma's project, John co-organized the City from Below conference, which took place in Baltimore in 2008, and brought together intellectuals and community organizers from around the world for a weekend of intensive debate and networking. He teaches cultural studies at Towson University, and is a doctoral candidate in intellectual history at the Humanities Center at Johns Hopkins University.

Roxanne Dunbar-Ortiz grew up in rural Oklahoma, where her paternal grandfather had been an organizer for the Industrial Workers of the World. She is a writer, historian, teacher, and long-time leftist organizer, beginning in the 1960s. She recently retired as a professor in the Department of Ethnic Studies at California State University, East Bay, and currently lives in San Francisco. She is the author of numerous books and articles on indigenous peoples, including *Indians of the Americas: Human Rights and Self-Determination* and *Roots of Resistance: History of Land Tenure in New Mexico*, as well as a historical memoir trilogy of *Red Dirt: Growing Up Okie*, *Outlaw Woman*, and *Blood on the Border*.

Silvia Federici is a scholar and an activist; she teaches Philosophy and Women's Studies at several American universities and at the University of Port Harcourt (Nigeria). Federici has been active in the feminist movement, the movement against the death penalty, and the anti-globalization movement. In 1972 she was a co-founder of the International Feminist Collective; from 1973 to 1977, she was active in the international campaign for Wages for Housework and a founder of the New York Wages for Housework Committee. Federici's authored works in English include *Caliban and the Witch: Women, the Body and Primitive Accumulation* (Autonomedia, 2004), and the following edited collections: *African Visions: Literary Images, Political Change and Social Struggle in Contemporary Africa* (Praeger, 2000), *A Thousand Flowers: Social Struggles Against Structural Adjustment in African Universities* (Africa World Press, 2000), and *Enduring Western Civilization: The Construction of the Concept of the West and Its 'Others'* (Praeger, 1995).

Harmony Goldberg | Right to the City Alliance and National Domestic Workers Alliance is a founding director of the movement-based political education center SOUL (the School Of Unity and Liberation) and has been a long-time supporter of radical and Left community-based organizations. Goldberg is currently a Resource Ally of the Right to the City Alliance and a supporter of the National Domestic Workers Alliance. Harmony is also a PhD student in Cultural Anthropology at the City University of New York Graduate Center, and she provides political education support for grassroots organizations around the country.

Andrej Grubacic is an anarchist dissident and historian who has written prolifically on anarchism and the history of the Balkans. Following the collapse of Yugoslavia, Grubacic was based in Belgrade, before leaving his position as assistant lecturer of History at the University of Belgrade due to tensions relating to his political activism. He relocated to the Fernand Braudel Center at State University of New York-Binghamton in the United States, where he taught in the Sociology department. His most recent book, *Wobblies and Zapatistas: Conversations on Anarchism, Marxism and Radical History* (PM Press, 2008), *was written* with Staughton Lynd.

Michael Hardt teaches in the Literature Program at Duke University; he is co-author with Antonio Negri of *Empire* (Harvard University Press, 2001), *Multitude* (Penguin, 2005) and *Commonwealth* (Harvard University Press, 2009).

Ben Holtzman's work has appeared in *Clamor Magazine, Journal of Popular Music Studies, Left History, Maximumrocknroll, Popular Music and Society, Radical Society*, and the collection *Constituent Imagination* (AK Press, 2007). He is the editor of *Sick: A Compilation Zine on Physical Illness* and co-director/editor of the documentary *Between Resistance and Community: The Long Island Do It Yourself (DIY) Punk Scene*. After many years working as an academic book editor in New York City, he is now a PhD student in History at Brown University.

The **Journal of Aesthetics & Protest Press** forwards change by focusing on how art, media, activism, and rhetoric function effectively in this neo-liberal age. Based in Los Angeles, they collectively run a DIY press and distributor. Their journal of the same name is an almost annual release, publishing since 2000. They see their projects as generous and rigorous possibilities, filling vacuums left after the de-funding of smaller institutions, the corporatization of knowledge production, and the ensuing commodification and spectacularization of discourse. They sculpt projects, linking knowledge to specific contexts that spark situations for community-based creation. Current collective members include Marc Herbst, Robby Herbst, and Christina Ulke.

Malav Kanuga | Bluestockings Bookstore and Activist Center is a member of the workers' collective that operates Bluestockings Bookstore in New York City. He is also a movement-researcher, organizer, and doctoral student and teacher in the City University of New York system.

Marina Karides | U.S. Social Forum (USSF) Documentation Committee is a professor of Sociology at Florida Atlantic University; she serves as the Sociologists Without Borders representative to the USSF National Planning Committee and is coordinator for World Social Forum participation in several U.S. academic associations. She is currently representing Sociologists for Women in Society on the Gender Justice Working Group for the 2010 USSF. Along with articles and chapters on the social forum process, she has co-authored with eleven scholar-activists the volume *Global Democracy and the World Social Forums*, and edited (with Judith Blau) *The World and US Social Forums: A Better World is Possible and Necessary* (Brill Academic Publishers, 2008). As part of the USSF Documentation Committee, she has edited a volume of activists' voices, entitled *The USSF: Perspectives of Movement.*

Robin D.G. Kelley (interviewed) is a professor of American Studies and Ethnicity at the University of Southern California. His books include *Thelonious Monk: The Life and Times of an American Original* (2009); *Freedom Dreams: The Black Radical Imagination* (2002); and *Race Rebels: Culture, Politics, and the Black Working Class* (1994). His essays have appeared in several anthologies and journals, including *The Nation*, *Monthly Review*, *The Voice Literary Supplement*, *New York Times Magazine*, *Rolling Stone*, *Color Lines*, *Code Magazine*, *Utne Reader*, *Lenox Avenue*, *African Studies Review*, *Journal of American History*, *New Labor Forum*, and *Souls*.

Dorothy Kidd started using video with housing and other social struggles in Toronto in the early 1970s. Since then, she has worked with aboriginal broadcasters in northern Canada, community radio and feminist publications in Vancouver, and most recently, the first Indymedia centers in San Francisco. Now teaching at the University of San Francisco, her research focuses on documenting and circulating struggles around communication in North America and internationally, using political economy and autonomist Marxist frameworks as well as radical ethnography. Her writing on media enclosures and communications commons has circulated widely.

El Kilombo Intergaláctico is a social center and community organization based in Durham, North Carolina.

Peter Linebaugh is a professor of History at the University of Toledo. He is the author of *The London Hanged: Crime and Civil Society in the Eighteenth Century* (Verso, 2006) and co-author (with Marcus Rediker) of *Many-Headed Hydra: The Hidden History of the Revolutionary Atlantic* (Verso, 2002). His most recent book is titled *The Magna Carta Manifesto: Liberties and Commons for All* (University of California Press, 2008).

Brian Marks is a geographer originally from Louisiana. His current work on the globalization of the seafood industry in the Mississippi and Mekong Deltas involves the household economies of producers, changes in land use and ecology, and the political economy of international commodity chains. His intention is to foster cooperation between shrimp producers to achieve fair prices and greater power in the industry. He is also co-author of the forthcoming book *The New Deal in Reverse*, which discusses the development of public schools, hospitals, and housing in New Orleans, as well as neoliberalism and the destruction of those public services after Hurricane Katrina.

John Peck | Family Farm Defenders grew up on a 260–acre farm in central Minnesota; he has a B.A. in Economics from Reed College and a PhD in Land Resources from University of Wisconsin-Madison. Peck attended the 1992 Earth Summit in Rio de Janeiro as a student activist and has also participated in protests against the World Trade Organization in Seattle, the World Bank/International Monetary Fund in Washington DC, and the Free Trade Area of the Americas in Quebec and Miami. For the past six years, Peck has been the executive director of Family Farm Defenders, a national grassroots organization with members overseas and in all fifty states.

Julie Perini is an artist and educator working in time-based media, including video, film, and live events. For the past several years she has split her time between Portland, Oregon and the Rust Belt cities of Buffalo, New York and Erie, Pennsylvania. She teaches media production and film studies at art schools, universities, and community centers. She has been involved with collaborative initiatives that promote independent media, community cultural production, and radical social change. Her recent manifesto on "Relational Filmmaking" was included in *INCITE! The Journal of Experimental Media and Radical Aesthetics*, edited by Brett Kashmere.

Picture the Homeless is a grassroots organization based in New York City, founded and led by homeless people. They work to change existing policies as well as challenge the root causes of homelessness. Their strategies include base-building organizing, direct action, know-your-rights education, and changing media stereotypes. Their campaigns have challenged the flaws of shelters and social services, pursued economic justice for subsistence workers, and won dignity for those who die while homeless. Currently, their housing campaign fights for truly affordable housing for all, while their civil rights campaign takes on criminalization and police harassment.

Roadblock Earth First! is a radical environmental organization and campaign to stop the Interstate 69/North American Free Trade Agreement super-highway. They are associated with the larger Earth First! movement and are based in Indiana.

Betty Garman Robinson is a long-time community organizer. She worked with the Student Nonviolent Coordinating Committee from 1964–66 as a staff member in Mississippi and the national office in Atlanta. In the 1970s she moved to Baltimore to do rank-and-file labor organizing. Later, while raising her two daughters in Baltimore, she worked in public health research. She returned to community organizing in 1997 as the Lead Organizer for Citizens' Planning and Housing Association. Robinson was awarded an Open Society Institute Community Fellowship in 2003 to connect Baltimore organizers across issues and constituencies, and to popularize the history of social justice organizing in the city. A strong ally of grassroots organizing groups in Baltimore, she works closely with the Baltimore Algebra Project and the United Workers.

Basav Sen is a community activist and writer in Washington, DC; he is active in struggles for a just global economy, immigrants' rights, and housing justice.

Benjamin Shepard, PhD, is Assistant Professor of Human Services at City Tech/City University of New York. He is the author/editor of five books and many articles and essays. His books include *From ACT UP to the WTO: Urban Protest and Community Building in the Era of Globalization* (Verso, 2002) and most recently *Queer Political Performance and Protest and Play* (Routledge, 2009). Shepard has done organizing work with ACT UP, SexPanic!, Reclaim the Streets/New York, CitiWide Harm Reduction, Housing Works, the More Gardens Coalition, and the Times Up! Bike Lane Liberation Front and Garden Working Group.

The **Starbucks Workers Union** is a grassroots organization of over 300 current and former employees at the world's largest coffee chain, united for secure work hours, a living wage, and respect on the job. The union has members around the world fighting for systemic change at the company and remedying individual grievances with management. They are affiliated with the Industrial Workers of the World, a global union open to all working people.

The **Student/Farmworker Alliance** is a national network of students and youth organizing with farmworkers to eliminate sweatshop conditions and modern-day slavery in the fields. They work mainly in partnership with the Coalition of Immokalee Workers. Their chapter was written by current and former staff and Steering Committee members.

Take Back the Land is an American organization based in Miami, Florida devoted to re-housing homeless people in foreclosed houses. Take Back the Land was formed in October 2006 to build the Umoja Village Shantytown on a plot of unoccupied land, to protest gentrification and a lack of low-income housing in Miami.

Brian Tokar is a long-time activist and author and serves as the current Director of the Institute for Social Ecology, based in Plainfield, Vermont. His books include *Earth for Sale*, *Redesigning Life?* and the forthcoming collection (co-edited with Fred Magdoff) *Crisis in Food and Agriculture: Conflict, Resistance and Renewal* (Monthly Review Press). Tokar has been acclaimed as a leading critical voice for ecological activism since the 1980s and lectures widely on environmental issues and popular movements.

Daniel Tucker | AREA Chicago works as an organizer and documenter, focusing primarily on space, place, and the cultural and social movements that define them. Since 2005 he has worked on the journal AREA Chicago: Art/Research/Education/Activism, which releases issues on various themes related to culture and politics in Chicago and hosts associated events. In 2008 he co-organized an interview project with 100 politically engaged artists living in Chicago, Los Angeles, New York City, Baltimore, and New Orleans for the public art organization Creative Time. Most recently, he co-authored a book of interviews and photo essays of activist farmers throughout the U.S., to be released on Chronicle books in the fall of 2010.

The **United Workers** is a multiracial and bilingual poor people's economic human rights organization of over 1,000 members. Founded in 2002 by homeless day laborers in an abandoned firehouse-turned-homeless shelter, the United Workers organizes around transformative human rights values with a focus on the leadership development of low-wage workers; the goal is to build a movement led by the poor that is capable of ending poverty. In 2008, after a three-year campaign that resulted in securing living wages for stadium workers at Camden Yards, the United Workers declared Baltimore's Inner Harbor a "Human Rights Zone." Inner Harbor workers are calling on Harbor developers to enter into a binding economic human rights agreement to ensure the human right to work with dignity, healthcare, and education for all Harbor workers.

Kristine Virsis | Justseeds Artists' Cooperative is a printmaker currently living and working in New York. Her silkscreen prints, which begin as intricate paper cuts and stencils, deal with the personal end of the political spectrum: creativity, self-sufficiency, nostalgia, and mental health and resiliency. Her hand-pulled prints are produced in large or unlimited editions in order to keep them affordable. She is part of the Justseeds Artists' Cooperative, a group of artists and activists involved in local struggles around public space, political repression, socially engaged street art, and political printmaking.

BIBLIOGRAPHY

Abramowitz, Mimi. *Regulating the Lives of Women: Social Welfare Policy from Colonial Times to the Present*. Boston: South End Press, 1996.

Abu-Jamal, Mumia. *We Want Freedom: A Life in the Black Panther Party*. Boston: South End Press, 2004.

ACT UP Oral History Project. HTTP://WWW.ACTUPORALHISTORY.ORG.

Adam, David. "Met Office warns of catastrophic global warming in our lifetimes," *The Guardian*, September 28, 2009.

Adamy, Janet. "At Starbucks, A Tall Order For New Cuts, Store Closures." *Wall Street Journal*, January 29, 2009.

Agamben, Giorgio. *The Coming Community*. Minneapolis, MN: University of Minnesota Press, 1993.

——. *Homo Sacer: Sovereign Power and Bare Life*. Stanford: Stanford University Press, 1998.

Alcoff, Linda and Elizabeth Potter, eds. *Feminist Epistemologies*. New York: Routledge, 1993.

al-Fadhily, Ali and Dahr Jamail. "Iraq: Corruption eats into food rations," *Inter Press Service* (May 3, 2008).

Alvarez, Sonia E. "Advocating Feminism: The Latin American NGO 'Boom'," Dialogo Solidaridad /Global Solidarity Dialogue (March 2, 1998).

American Friends Service Committee. "The Clamshell Alliance at 20," Special Issue, *Peacework*, No. 265 (July/August 1996).

Andreas, Carol. *When Women Rebel: The Rise of Popular Feminism in Peru*. Westport, CT: Lawrence Hill & Company, 1985.

Anderson, Nels. *On Hobos and Homelessness*. Chicago: The University of Chicago Press, 1998.

Arendt, Hannah. *On Revolution*. Viking: New York, 1965.

Arquilla, John and David Ronfeldt, eds. *Networks and Netwars. The Future of Terror, Crime, and Militancy*. Rand Corporation; available at HTTP://WWW.RAND.ORG/PUBS/MONOGRAPH_REPORTS/ MR1382/ (accessed January 15, 2010).

Atton, Chris and James Hamilton. *Alternative Journalism*. Thousand Oaks, CA: Sage, 2008.

Bacevich, Andrew. *The Limits of Power: The End of American Exceptionalism*. New York: Macmillan, 2008.

Baldi, Guido. "Theses on Mass Worker and Social Capital," *Radical America*, Vol. 6, No. 1 (1972): 3–21.

Baldwin, James. *Notes of a Native Son*. Boston: Beacon Press, 1955.

_____. *The Fire Next Time.* New York: Dial Press, 1963.

Ball, Julien. "The $7 Million Whitewash," AREA 4: *No Justice, No Peace*, (2007).

Ballinger, Jeff. "Squeezed Vietnamese workers strike back," *Counterpunch* (April 16, 2008); available at HTTP://WWW.COUNTERPUNCH.ORG/BALLINGER04162008.HTML (accessed January 30, 2010).

Barboza, David. "Shortage of cheap labor in China," *International Herald Tribune* (April 3, 2006).

_____. "China's dairy farmers say they are victims," *New York Times* (October 4, 2008).

Barry, Casper and Paul Wellstone. *Powerline: The First Battle of America's Energy War.* Minneapolis: University of Minnesota Press, 2003.

Beinin, Joel and Hossam el-Hamalawy. "Egyptian textile workers confront the new economic order," *Middle East Report* Online (March 25, 2007); available at HTTP://WWW.MERIP.ORG/MERO/MERO032507.HTML (accessed January 30, 2010).

Berry, Wendell. *The Unsettling of America: Culture and Agriculture.* San Francisco: Sierra Club Books, 1977.

Biondi, Martha. "The Rise of the Reparations Movement," *Radical History Review* 87 (2003): 5–18.

Biofuelwatch. *Biofuels: Renewable Energy or Environmental Disaster in the Making?*, London: Biofuelwatch, 2006.

Boggs, Grace Lee. "From Marx to Malcolm and Martin," *The Other Side* (January-February 2003).

_____. "Let's talk about Malcolm and Martin," Talk given at the Brecht Forum, New York, NY (May 4, 2007).

_____. *Living for Change: An Autobiography.* Minneapolis: University of Minnesota Press, 1998.

_____. "Recapture MLK's Radical Revolutionary Spirit: Create Cities and Communities Of Hope," Talk given at Eastern Michigan University (January 15, 2007).

_____, James Boggs, Freddy Paine, and Lyman Paine. *Conversations in Maine: Exploring our Nation's Future.* Boston: South End Press, 1978.

Boggs, James. *The American Revolution: Pages from a Negro Worker's Notebook.* New York: Monthly Review Press, 1963.

_____, and Grace Lee Boggs. *Revolution and Evolution in the Twentieth Century.* New York: Monthly Review Press, 1974.

Bollier, David. *Silent Theft: The Private Plunder of Our Common Wealth.* London: Routledge, 2002.

Bookchin, Murray. *Toward an Ecological Society.* Montreal: Black Rose Books, 1980; Oakland: AK Press, 2005.

_____. "Reflections: An Overview of the Roots of Social Ecology," *Harbinger: A Journal of Social Ecology*, Vol. 3, No. 1 (2002); available at: HTTP://WWW.SOCIAL-ECOLOGY.ORG/2002/09/HARBINGER-VOL-3–NO-1–REFLECTIONS-AN-OVERVIEW-OF-THE-ROOTS-OF-SOCIAL-ECOLOGY/ (accessed January 1, 2010).

_____. *The Ecology of Freedom.* Palo Alto, CA: Cheshire Books, 1982; Oakland: AK Press, 2005.

Borger, Julian. "Feed The World? We Are Fighting a Losing Battle, UN Admits," *The Guardian* (February 26, 2008).

Bowley, Graham and Catherine Rampell. "In wake of Dubai, trying to predict the next blowup," *New York Times* (December 1, 2009).

Bradsher, Keith. "Inflation in Asia Begins to Sting U.S. Consumers," *New York Times* (April 8th, 2008).

_____. "Investors seek Asian options to costly China," *New York Times* (June 18, 2008).

_____. "Booming China suddenly worries that a showdown is taking hold," *New York Times* (August 5, 2008).

_____. "China Seeks to Slow Rapid Growth of Lending," *New York Times* (November 24, 2009).

Bronski, Michael. "Sylvia Rivera: 1951–2002," *Z Magazine*, (April 2002).

_____. "The Real (Radical) Harry Hay," *Z Magazine*, (December 2002).

Brown, Lester R. "Supermarkets and Service Stations Now Competing for Grain," *Earth Policy Institute Update* (July 13, 2006).

Bruno, Kenny, Joshua Karliner and China Brotsky, "Greenhouse Gangsters vs. Climate Justice," *CorpWatch* (1999); available at: HTTP://WWW.CORPWATCH.ORG/ARTICLE.PHP?ID=1048 (accessed January 30, 2010).

Buck, Susan J. *The Global Commons. An Introduction.* Washington: Island Press, 1998.

Butler, Judith. *Bodies That Matter: On the Discursive Limits of "Sex".* New York: Routledge, 1993.

_____. "Imitation and Gender Insubordination," In *The Lesbian, Gay and Bisexual Studies Reader*, 307–320, Edited by H. Abelove, M A. Barale, and D. M. Halperin. New York: Routledge, 1993.

Caffentzis, George. "Globalization, The Crisis of Neoliberalism and the Question of the Commons," Paper presented to the *First Conference of the Global Justice Center*, San Miguel d' Allende, Mexico (July 2004).

_____. "Three Temporal Dimensions of Class Struggle," Paper presented at *ISA Annual Meeting*, San Diego, CA (March 2006).

Cairn, John W. and Grant McLeod, eds. "The Dearest Birth Right of the People of England," *The Jury in the History of the Common Law.* Portland, OR: Hart, 2002.

Carlsson, Chris. *Nowtopia: How Pirate Programmers, Outlaw Bicyclists and Vacant-Lot Gardeners are Inventing the Future Today.* Oakland: AK Press, 2008.

Carmona, Pablo, Tomás Herreros, Raúl Sánchez Cedillo, Nicolás Sguiglia, "Social Centers: monsters and political machines for a new generation of movement institutions," *Transversal* (April 2008).

Casas-Cortes, Maribel. *Social Movements as Sites of Knowledge Production: Precarious Work, the Fate of Care and Activist Research in a Globalizing Spain.* Unpublished Doctoral Dissertation, University of North Carolina at Chapel Hill (2009).

Cash, Conor. "Decomposition and Suburban Space," *Affinities* 3, "The New Cooperativism" (Forthcoming 2010).

Catedra Experimental Sobre Produccion de Subjetividad. "From Knowledge of Self-Management to the Self-Management of Knowledge," *Transversal* (May 2005).

Cedillo, Raúl Sánchez. "Towards New Political Creations: Movements, Institutions, New Militancy," *Transversal* (May 2007).

Center for Food Safety. *Monsanto Versus U.S. Farmers.* Washington, DC: Center for Food Safety, 2005.

Ciccariello-Maher, George. "Dual power in the Venezuelan revolution," *Monthly Review* 59, No. 4, (2007): 42–56.

Cleaver, Harry. "Food, famine, and the international crisis", *Zerowork: Political Materials* 2 (1977).

_____. "Uses of an Earthquake," *Midnight Notes* 9 (1988).

_____. "Kropotkin, Self-Valorization, and the Crisis of Marxism," *Anarchist Studies*, Vol. 2, No. 2 (Autumn 1994).

_____. "Computer-Linked Social Movements and the Global Threat to Capitalism" (July 1999); available at: HTTP://WWW.ECO.UTEXAS.EDU/FACSTAFF/CLEAVER/POLNET.HTML (accessed January 31, 2010).

_____. *Reading Capital Politically.* Oakland: AK Press, 2000.

Cloward, Richard and Francis Fox Piven. "Notes Toward a Radical Social Work," *Radical Social*

Work, Edited by Roy Bailey and Mike Brake. New York: Pantheon, 1975.

Cobarrubias, Sebastian. *Mapping Machines: Activist Cartographies of the Labor and Border Lands of Europe*. Unpublished PhD Dissertation, University of North Carolina at Chapel Hill (2009).

Colectivo Situaciones. "On the Researcher-Militant," Translated by Sebastian Touza. *Transform* (2003).

_____, and MTD-Solano. *Hipotesis 891: Más allá de los Piquetes*. Buenos Aires: Ediciones de Mano en Mano, 2001 (In Spanish).

Collins, Patricia Hill. *Black Feminist Thought*. Sydney: Allyn and Unwin, Ltd., 1990.

Combahee River Collective. "Combahee River Collective Statement," In *Home Girls: A Black Feminist Anthology*, Barbara Smith, ed. New York: Kitchen Table Women of Color Press, 1983.

"The Crisis in Agriculture and Food: Conflict, Resistance, and Renewal," Special Issue, *Monthly Review* (July-August 2009).

Critical Art Ensemble. *The Molecular Invasion*. Brooklyn: Autonomedia, 2002.

The CR10 Publications Collective. *Abolition Now! Ten Years of Strategy and Struggle Against the Prison-Industrial Complex*. Oakland: AK Press, 2008.

Dailey, Dharma. "A Field Report: Media Justice through the Eyes of Local Organizers." New York: The Media Justice Fund of the Funding Exchange, 2009.

Dalla Costa, Mariarosa and Selma James. *The Power of Women and the Subversion of the Community*. Brighton, UK: Falling Walls Press, 1972.

De Angelis, Massimo. *The Beginning of History: Value Struggles and Global Capital*. London: Pluto Press, 2007.

_____. "The Commons and Social Justice," Unpublished manuscript (2009).

de Certeau, Michel. *The Practice of Everyday Life*. Berkeley: University of California Press, 1984.

de Ita, Ana. "Fourteen Years of NAFTA and the Tortilla Crisis," *Americas Program and Center for International Policy* (January 10, 2008); available at: HTTP://AMERICAS.IRC-ONLINE.ORG/AM/4879 (accessed January 30, 2010).

de la Merced, Michael J. "Starbucks Announces It Will Close 600 Stores." *New York Times*, July 2, 2008.

Deleuze, Gilles. *Negotiations, 1972–1990*. New York: Columbia University Press, 1995.

_____, and Félix Guattari. *A Thousand Plateaus*. Minneapolis, MN: University of Minnesota Press, 1987.

Demac, Donna and Philip Mattera. "Developing and Underdeveloping New York," *Zerowork* 2 (Fall 1977).

D'Emilio, John. "The Marriage Fight is Setting Us Back," *Harvard Lesbian and Gay Review* (November-December 2004).

Democracy Now!, "Stockton, California City Reverses Water Privatization it Passed Over Widepsread Local Opposition" (August 1, 2007); available at: HTTP://WWW.DEMOCRACYNOW. ORG/2007/8/1/STOCKTON_CALIFORNIA_CITY_COUNCIL_REVERSES_WATER.

De Pastino, Todd. *Citizen Hobo*. Chicago: The University of Chicago Press, 2003.

Desmarais, Annette. *La Via Campesina: Globalization and the Power of Peasants*. London: Pluto Press, 2007.

de Tocqueville, Alexis. *Democracy in America*. Translated by Gerald Bevan. Penquin: London, 2003.

Deuze, Mark. "The Changing Context of News Work: Liquid Journalism and Monitorial Citizenship." *International Journal of Communication* 2 (2008): 848–865.

Dobbs, William. "Interview on the Death Penalty," on *Subversity*, KUCI 88.9 FM, (January, 12 1999).

Dumenil, Gerard and Dominique Levy. "The profit rate: where and how much did it fall? Did it recover? (USA 1948–2000)," *Review of Radical Political Economics*, No. 34 (2002): 437–461.

Duncombe, Steven. *Notes from the Underground: Zines and the Politics of Alternative Culture*. New York: Verso, 1997.

_____. *Notes on Punk*. Unpublished Manuscript, Undated.

Dyer-Witheford, Nick. *Cyber-Marx: Cycles and Circuits of Struggle in High Technology Capitalism*. Champaign, IL: University of Illinois Press, 1999.

_____. "For a Compositional Analysis of the Multitude," *Subverting the Present*. Edited by Werner Bonefeld. Brooklyn: Autonomedia, 2007.

The Ecologist. Whose Commons, Whose Future: Reclaiming the Commons. Philadelphia: New Society Publishers with Earthscan, 1993.

The Economist. "Why it still pays to study medieval English landholding and Sahelian nomadism" (July 31, 2008); available at HTTP://WWW.ECONOMIST.COM/FINANCEPRINTERFRIENDLY. CFM?STORY_ID=11848182 (accessed January 31, 2010).

Ehrenreich, Barbara. "Truckers Hit the Brakes," *The Nation* (April 8, 2008).

_____. "Truckers Take Their Case to the Capitol," *The Nation* (April 29, 2008).

_____. *Bait and Switch: The (Futile) Pursuit of the American Dream*. New York: Holt Paperbacks, 2006.

Eilperin, Juliet. "New Analysis Brings Dire Forecast Of 6.3-Degree Temperature Increase," *Washington Post* (September 25, 2009).

El Kilombo Intergaláctico. "The Arts of Living in Common," (February 19, 2009); available at: HTTP://WWW.ELKILOMBO.ORG/THE-ARTS-OF-LIVING-IN-COMMON/ (accessed January 31, 2010).

The Emergency Exit Collective. "The Great Eight Masters and the Six Billion Commoners," May Day Statement, Bristol (2008).

Emory, Ed. "No Politics without Inquiry! A Proposal for a Class Composition Inquiry Project 1996–7," *Common Sense*, No. 18 (December 1995).

Engels, Frederick. *Ludwig Feuerbach and the End of Classical German Philosophy*. Includes appendix "Theses on Feuerbach" by Karl Marx. Peking: Foreign Languages Press, 1976.

Enke, Anne. *Finding the Movement*. Durham: Duke University Press, 2007.

Essig, Laurie. "Queers Attack Gays and Lesbians. Its about Time," *Class Warfare*. (October 12, 2009).

Esteva, Gustavo and Madhu Suri Prakash. *Grassroots Post-Modernism: Remaking the Soil of Cultures*. Zed Books: London and New York, 1998.

ETC Group: Action Group on Erosion, Technology, and Concentration. *Who Will Feed Us?: Questions for the Food and Climate Crisis*. Ottawa: ETC Group, 2009.

Fantasia, Rick. *Cultures of Solidarity: Consciousness, Action, and Contemporary American Workers*. Berkeley: University of California Press, 1989.

Fargione, Joseph and et al., "Land Clearing and the Biofuel Carbon Debt," *Science*, Vol. 319 (February 29, 2008): 1235–1238.

Federici, Silvia. "Women, Globalization, and the International Women's Movement," *Canadian Journal of Development Studies*, Vol. XXII (2001): 1025–1036.

_____. *Caliban and the Witch: Women, The Body, and Accumulation*. Brooklyn: Autonomedia, 2004.

_____. "Women, Land Struggles and Globalization: An International Perspective," *Journal of Asian and African Studies*, Vol. 39, Issue 1/2 (January-March 2004).

_____. "Witch-Hunting, Globalization and Feminist Solidarity in Africa Today," *Journal of*

International Women's Studies with WAGADU, Special Issue: Women's Gender Activism in Africa, Vol. 10, No. 1 (October 2008).

_____. "Women, Land Struggles, and the Reconstruction of the Commons," Unpublished Manuscript (2008).

Ferguson, Niall. *The Ascent of Money: A Financial History of the World*. London: Penguin, 2008.

Fernandez, Margarita. "Cultivating Community, Food, and Empowerment: Urban Gardens in New York City," Project Course Paper (2003).

Fisher, Jo. *Out of the Shadows: Women, Resistance and Politics in South America*. London: Latin American Bureau, 1993.

Food and Water Watch. *The Poisoned Fruit of American Trade Policy: Produce Imports Overwhelm American Farmers and Consumers*. San Francisco, CA: Food and Water Watch, 2008

Foster, John Bellamy and Robert McChesney. "Monopoly-Finance Capital and the Paradox of Accumulation," *Monthly Review*, Vol. 61, No. 5 (October 2009), 1–20.

_____. "The Jeavons Paradox: Environment and Technology Under Capitalism," *The Ecological Revolution: Making Peace with the Planet*, 121–128. New York: Monthly Review Books, 2009.

Foucault, Michel. *Power/Knowledge: Selected Interviews and Other Writings, 1972–1977*. New York: Pantheon Books, 1980.

_____. *The History of Sexuality. An Introduction Volume One*. New York: Random House, 1978; New York: Penguin Books, 1984.

France, David. "Meet the Fearsome Gay Gangsters of Bash Back!," *Details Magazine* (2009).

Freeman, Donald B. "Survival Strategy or Business Training Ground? The Significance of Urban Agriculture For the Advancement of Women in African Cities," *African Studies Review*, Vol. 36, No. 3 (December 1993): 1–22.

Freire, Paulo. *Pedagogy of the Oppressed*, Translated by Myra Bergman Ramos. New York: The Continuum Publishing Corporation, 1987.

Fuchs, Christian. "Information and Communication Technologies and Society: A Contribution to the Critique of the Political Economy of the Internet," *European Journal of Communication* 24 (2009): 69–87.

Fukuyama, Francis. *Trust: The Social Virtues and the Creation of Prosperity*. New York: The Free Press, 1995.

Garofoli, Joe and Jim Herron Zamora. "S.F police play catch-up; Protesters roam in small, swift groups to stall city traffic," *San Francisco Chronicle*, March 21, 2003.

Gellman, Mneesha and Josh Dankoff. "Rising fuel costs provoke transportation strike in Nicaragua," *Upside Down World* (May 12th, 2008); available at HTTP://UPSIDEDOWNWORLD.ORG/MAIN/CONTENT/VIEW/1279/1/ (accessed January 30, 2010).

Gibson-Graham, J.K. *A Post-Capitalist Politics*. Minneapolis: University of Minnesota Press, 2006.

Gilbert, Melissa Kesler and Catherine Sameh. "Building Feminist Educational Alliances in an Urban Community," *Teaching Feminist Activism: Strategies from the Field*, 185–206. Edited by Nancy A. Naples and Karen Bojar. New York: Routledge, 2002.

Giroux, Henry and Kenneth Saltman. "Obama's Betrayal of Public Education? Arne Duncan and the Corporate Model of Schooling," *TruthOut* (Dec. 17, 2008).

Goldstein, Richard. *The Attack Queers*. New York: Verso, 2002.

Graeber, David. *Possibilities: Essays on Hierarchy, Rebellion and Desire*. AK Press: Oakland, 2007.

GRAIN. *Seedling*, Agrofuels Special Issue (July 2007).

_____. "Making a killing from hunger," (April 28th, 2008); HTTP://WWW.GRAIN.ORG/ARTICLES/?ID=39 (accessed January 30, 2010).

Graves, Robert. *The Greek Myths*, 2 Volumes. London: Penguin, 1955.

Greenwald, Dara. "The Process is in the Street: Challenging Media America," *Realizing the Impossible: Art Against Authority*, 168–179. Josh MacPhee and Erik Reuland, eds. Oakland: AK Press, 2007.

Grimmond, John. "A Success Story," *The Economist* (March 16, 2006).

Hamilton, Todd and Nate Holden. "Compositional Power," *Turbulence: Ideas for Movement*, June 2007: 20–21.

Hansen, James and et al., "Climate Change and Trace Gases," Philosophical Transactions of the Royal Society, Part A, Vol. 365 (2007).

_____. "Target Atmospheric CO2: Where Should Humanity Aim?," Unpublished Manuscript.

Harding, Sandra. *Whose Science? Whose Knowledge?* Ithaca, NY: Cornell University Press, 1991.

Hardt, Michael and Antonio Negri. *Empire.* Cambridge: Harvard University Press, 2000.

_____. *Multitude: War and Democracy in the Age of Empire.* New York, Penguin, 2004.

_____. *Commonwealth.* Boston: Belknap Press, 2009.

Hamilton, James. *Democratic Communications: Formations, Projects, Possibilities.* Lanham, MD: Lexington Books, 2009.

Haraway, Donna. "Situated Knowledges: The Science Question in Feminism and the Privilege of Partial Perspective," *Feminist Studies* 14, (1988): 575–99.

Hartmann, Thom. "American Rebellions," *Yes Magazine* (May 2004).

Harvey, David. *Brief History of Neoliberalism.* Oxford: Oxford University Press, 2007.

_____. "Why the U.S. Stimulus Package is Bound To Fail," (February 2009); HTTP://DAVIDHARVEY.ORG/2009/02/WHY-THE-US-STIMULUS-PACKAGE-IS-BOUND-TO-FAIL/ (accessed January 30, 2010).

Hayden, Dolores. *The Grand Domestic Revolution.* Cambridge, MA: MIT Press, 1981.

_____. *Redesigning the American Dream: The Future of Housing, Work and Family Life.* New York: Norton and Company, 1986.

Helena, Paul and et al. *Agriculture and Climate Change: Real Problems, False Solutions: Preliminary Report by Group de Reflexion Rural, Biofuelwatch, EcoNexus and NOAH—Friends of the Earth Denmark.* Bonn: 2009.

Henriques, Diana. "Commodities: Latest Boom, Plentiful Risk," *New York Times* (March 20, 2008).

Hernandez, Javier. "Stirred by a Weakening Dollar, Markets Rise," *New York Times* (November 12, 2009).

Hill, Jason and et al., "Environmental, economic, and energetic costs and benefits of biodiesel and ethanol biofuels," Proceedings of the National Academy of Sciences, Vol. 103, No. 30 (July 25, 2006): 11206–11210.

Holloway, John. *Change the World Without Taking Power: The Meaning of Revolution Today.* London: Pluto Press, 2002.

Holtzman, Benjamin, Craig Hughes, and Kevin Van Meter. "Do It Yourself and the Movement Beyond Capitalism," *Constituent Imagination: Militant Investigation // Collective Theorization*, Edited by Stevphen Shukaitis, David Graeber with Erika Biddle. Oakland: AK Press, 2007; Originally Published in *Radical Society* 31 (2006): 7–20.

hooks, bell. *All About Love: New Visions.* New York: Harper, 2001.

Horton, Myles and Paulo Freire. *We make the road by walking: Conversations on Education and Social Change*, Edited by Brenda Bell, John Gaventa, and John Peters. Philadelphia: Temple University Press, 1990.

Human Development Report 2007/2008. *Fighting Climate Change: Human Solidarity in a Divided World.* United Nations Development Program (2007).

Humm, Andy. "Puerto Rican Teen Mourned. In New York, hundred mourn death, as vigils held in 20 cities," *Gay City News* (November, 25 2009).

Huntington, Samuel. "The United States," *The Crisis of Democracy: Report on the Governability of Democracies to the Trilateral Commission*, 59–118. Michel Crozier, Samuel Huntington, and Joji Watanuki, eds. New York: New York University Press, 1975.

Incite! Women of Color Against Violence. *The Revolution Will Not Be Funded: Beyond the Non-profit Industrial Complex.* Boston: South End Press, 2007.

Isla, Ana. "Enclosure and Microenterprise as Sustainable Development: The Case of the Canada-Costa Rico Debt-for-Nature Investment," *Canadian Journal of Development Studies*, Vol. XXII (2001): 935–943.

_____. "Conservation as Enclosure: Sustainable Development and Biopiracy in Costa Rica: An Ecofeminist Perspective," Unpublished manuscript (2006).

_____. "Who pays for the Kyoto Protocol?," *Eco-Sufficiency and Global Justice*. Ariel Salleh, ed. New York and London: Macmillan Palgrave, 2009.

Jameson, Fredric. *Postmodernism or, the Cultural logic of Late Capitalism.* Durham: Duke University Press, 1991.

Jehl, Douglas. "As Cities Move to Privatize Water, Atlanta Steps Back," *New York Times* (February 2, 2003).

Jezzabell, "Toward Stronger Communities and Direct Action," *Earth First! Journal*, Vol. 29, Issue 1 (Samhain/Yule 2008).

Johnson, Charles. *Dreamer: A Novel.* New York: Scribner, 1999.

_____. "The End of the Black American Narrative," *The American Scholar*, Vol. 77, No. 3 (Summer 2008): 43–58.

_____. *Middle Passage.* New York: Scribner, 1990.

Johnson, Ian. "China sees protest surge by workers," *Wall Street Journal* (July 10, 2009).

Juma, Calestous and J.B. Ojwang, eds. *In Land We Trust. Environment, Private Property and Constitutional Change.* London: Zed Books, 1996.

Katsiaficas, George. *The Imagination of the New Left.* Boston: South End Press, 1987.

KPFK-Pacifica. "Sojourner Truth," (January 20, 2010); available at: HTTP://ARCHIVE.KPFK.ORG/PARCHIVE/MP3/KPFK_100120_070030SOJOURNER.MP3 (accessed January 31, 2010).

Kauffman, L.A. "Radical Change: The Left Attacks Identity Politics," *Village Voice* (June 30, 1992).

Kell-Holland, Clarissa. "Demands for action on fuel prices gain momentum," *Land Line Magazine* (April 7, 2008); available at: HTTP://WWW.LANDLINEMAG.COM/TODAYS_NEWS/DAILY/2008/APR08/040708/040708–01.HTM (accessed January 30, 2010).

Kelley, Robin D.G. *Hammer and Hoe: Alabama Communists During the Great Depression.* Chapel Hill: University of North Carolina Press, 1990.

_____. *Freedom Dreams: The Black Radical Imagination.* Boston: Beacon Press, 2002.

_____. *Race Rebels: Culture, Politics, and the Black Working Class.* New York: The Free Press, 2004.

_____, and Jeffrey J. Williams. "History and Hope: An Interview with Robin D.G. Kelley," *minnesota review* (2003): 58–60.

Kennedy, J. *Summer of 1977: The Last Hurrah of the Gay Activists Alliance.* Westport, CT: PPC Books, 1994.

Kidd, Dorothy "Carnival to Commons," *Confronting Capitalism: Dispatches from a Global Movement*, 328–338. Edited by Eddie Yuen, Daniel Burton-Rose and George Katsiaficas. New York: Soft Skull Press, 2004.

_____, and Bernadette Barker-Plummer. "Neither Silent nor Invisible: Anti-Poverty Communication in the San Francisco Bay Area," *Development in Practice* 19 (2009).

King, Martin Luther. "Beyond Vietnam: A Time to Break Silence," Speech delivered on April 4, 1967 at Riverside Church, New York, NY.

Klein, Naomi. *The Shock Doctrine: The Rise of Disaster Capitalism*. New York: Picador, 2007.

Knodel, Mallory. "LA IMC 10th Anniversary—Technology Workshop," Post to *Los Angeles Indymedia* (November 28, 2009); available at: HTTP://LA.INDYMEDIA.ORG/NEWS/2009/11/232781. PHP (accessed January 31, 2010).

Krugman, Paul. "Chinese New Year," *New York Times* (January 1, 2010).

Kutalik, Chris. "As Immigrants Strike, Truckers Shut Down Nation's Largest Port on May Day," *Counterpunch* (June 2, 2006); available at: HTTP://WWW.COUNTERPUNCH.ORG/KUTA-LIK06022006.HTML (accessed January 30, 2010).

Lacey, Anita. "Forging Spaces of Liberty," *Constituent Imaginations: Militant Investigations, Collective Theorization*. Edited by Stevphen Shukaitis and David Graeber, with Erika Biddle. Oakland: AK Press, 2007.

Lacey, Marc. "Across Globe, Empty Bellies Bring Rising Anger," *New York Times* (April 18th, 2008).

Lee, Ching Kwan and Mark Selden. "China's Durable Inequality: Legacies of Revolution and Pitfalls of Reform," *Japan Focus* (January 24th, 2007).

Lefebvre, Henri. *Production of Space*. Oxford: Blackwell, 1992.

_____. "The Right to the City," *Writings on Cities by Henri Lefebvre*. Edited by Eleanor Kofman and Elizabeth Lebas. Cambridge: Blackwell Publishing, 1996.

Leonhardt, David. "Can't Grasp Credit Crisis? Join the Club," *New York Times* (March 19, 2008).

_____. "For Many, a Boom that Wasn't," *New York Times* (April 9, 2008).

Lichten, Eric. *Class, Power and Austerity: The New York City Fiscal Crisis*. New York: Bergin and Garvey, 1986.

Linebaugh, Peter. *The Magna Carta Manifesto: Liberties and Commons For All*. Berkeley: University of California Press, 2007.

Lipman, Pauline. "Who's City is it Anyways?" AREA 1, "Private Parties and Public Services," (2005).

Lohmann, Larry. "Carbon Trading: A Critical Conversation on Climate Change, Privatization and Power," Uppsala, Sweden: Dag Hammarskjold Foundation, 2006.

Lovins, Amory et al., "Winning the Oil Endgame: Innovation for Profits, Jobs, and Security," *Rocky Mountain Institute* (2005); available at HTTP://WWW.OILENDGAME.COM (accessed January 31, 2010).

Lummis, C. Douglas. *Radical Democracy*. Cornell University Press: Ithaca, 1996.

Lynd, Staughton. *Solidarity Unionism: Rebuilding the Labor Movement from Below*. Chicago: Charles H. Kerr Publishing, 1992.

M1 of Dead Prez. "Speaking wit Migrant, Poverty, Disability and Indigenous SKolahs at POOR Magazine," (October 27, 2009); available at: HTTP://WWW.POORMAGAZINE.ORG/INDEX. CFM?LI=NEWS&STORY=2367 (accessed January 31, 2010).

MacFarquhar, Neil. "Food Experts Worry as World Population and Hunger Grow," *New York Times* (October 22, 2009).

Malo, Marta. "Common Notions, Part 1: Workers-Inquiry, Co-Research, Consciousness-Raising" and "Common Notions, Part 2: Institutional Analysis, Participatory Action-Research, Militant Research," *Nociones Communes*. Traficantes de Sueños: Madrid, 2004 (Spanish Original); *Transversal* (April 2004 and August 2006 Respectively, English Translation).

Mananzala, Rickke and Dean Spade. "The Nonprofit Industrial Complex and Trans Resistance," *Sexuality Research and Social Policy* (March 5, 2008).

Mangeot, Philippe. "Sida, angles d'attaque," *Vacarme* 29 (2004); available at: HTTP://WWW.VAC-ARME.ORG/ARTICLE456.HTML (accessed January 31, 2010, In French).

Marazzi, Christian. *Capital and Language: From the New Economy to The War Economy.* Cambridge, MA: MIT Press/Semiotext(e), 2008.

Marcos, Subcomandante Insurgente. "Chiapas: The Southeast in Two Winds A Storm and a Prophecy," Communiqué (January 27, 1994; Originally Written August 1992); available at: HTTP://FLAG.BLACKENED.NET/REVOLT/MEXICO/EZLN/MARCOS_SE_2_WIND.HTML (accessed January 31, 2010).

_____, and The Zapatistas. *Zapatista Encuentro: Documents from the Encounter for Humanity and against Neoliberalism.* New York: Seven Stories Press, 1998.

Marks, Brian. "Autonomist Marxist theory and practice in the current crisis," *ACME: An international E-journal for Critical Geographies* 9, No. 2 (Forthcoming 2010).

Marx, Karl. *Capital Volume Three.* London: Penguin Classics, 1991.

_____. *Economic and Philosophic Manuscripts of 1844.* New York: International, 1966.

McKay, George. *DIY Culture.* Verso: London, 1998.

Midnight Notes Collective. "Strange Victories," *Midnight Notes* 1 (1979).

_____. "No Future Notes: the Work/Energy Crisis and the Anti-Nuclear Movement," *Midnight Notes* 2 (1980).

_____. "Outlaw Notes," *Midnight Notes* 8 (1985).

_____. *Midnight Oil: Work, Energy, War, 1973–1992.* Brooklyn: Autonomedia, 1992.

_____. "One No, Many Yeses," *Midnight Notes* 12 (1998).

_____, and Friends. *Promissory Notes: From Crisis to Commons.* Brooklyn: Autonomedia, 2009.

Mies, Maria. Patriarchies *and Accumulation on a World Scale: Women in the International Division of Labor.* London, UK: Zed Books, 1986.

_____, and Veronika Bennholdt-Thomsen. *The Subsistence Perspective: Beyond the Globalized Economy.* London: Zed Books, 1999.

_____. "Defending, Reclaiming, and Reinventing the Commons," *The Subsistence Perspective: Beyond the Globalized Economy.* London: Zed Books, 1999; Reprinted in *Canadian Journal of Development Studies*, Vol. XXII, (2001): 997–1024.

Milani, Bruce. "From Opposition to· Alternatives: Postindustrial Potentials and Transformative Learning," *Expanding the Boundaries of Transformative Learning: Essays on Theory and Praxis,* 47–58. Edited by Edmund O'Sullivan, Amish Morrell, and Mary Ann O'Connor. New York: Palgrave, 2002.

"Millions join global anti-war protests." BBC News online. February 17, 2003. HTTP://NEWS.BBC.CO.UK/2/HI/EUROPE/2765215.STM.

Mohanty, Chandra Talpade. *Feminism Without Borders: Decolonizing Theory, Practicing Solidarity.* Durham, NC: Duke University, 2003.

Monbiot, George. "We've been suckered again by the US. So far the Bali deal is worse than Kyoto," Column, *The Guardian,* (December 17, 2007).

Monsell, Pilar and Jose Perez de Lama. "Indymedia Etrecho," *Colectivo Fadai'at: Libertad de Movimiento+Libertad de Conocimiento.* Málaga: Imagraf Impresiones, 2006. (In Spanish; available in English and Arabic in the same publication)

Moynihan, Colin. "Arrest Puts Focus on Protesters' Texting," *New York Times* (October 5, 2009).

Mumm, Jesse. "City Wide Interview about What Has Changed and What Has Stayed The Same," AREA 6, "City as Lab," (2008).

Murray, Pauli. *Song in a Weary Throat: An American Pilgrimage.* New York: Harper 1987.

Nore, Peter and Terisa Turner, eds. *Oil and Class Struggle.* London: Zed Press, 1980.

Notes from Nowhere Collective, eds. *We Are Everywhere*. London and New York: Verso, 2003.

Olivera, Oscar in collaboration with Tom Lewis. ¡*Cochabamba! Water War in Bolivia*. Cambridge, MA: South End Press, 2004.

Olsen, Joel. "Between Infoshops and Insurrection U.S. Anarchism, Movement Building, and the Racial Order," *Contemporary Anarchist Studies*. Edited by Randall Amster, Luis Fernandez, et al. New York: Routledge, 2009.

Onosak, Junko R. *Feminist Revolution in Literacy: Women's Bookstores in the United States*. New York: Routledge, 2006.

Orozco, Graciela León. "Radio as a Mobilization Tool in Latino Communities," *Media Research Hub*; available at: HTTP://MEDIARESEARCHHUB.SSRC.ORG/GRANTS/FUNDED-PROJECTS/RADIO-AS-A-MOBILIZATION-TOOL-IN-LATINO-COMMUNITIES/RADIO-AS-A-MOBILIZATION-TOOL-IN-LATINO-COMMUNITIES (accessed January 31, 2010).

Osterweil, Michal and Graeme Chesters. "Global Uprisings: Towards a Politics of the Artisan." *Constituent Imagination: Militant Investigations, Collective Theorization*, 253–262. Edited by Stevphen Shukaitis and David Graeber, with Erika Biddle. Oakland, CA: AK Press, 2007.

Ostrom, Elinor. *Governing the Commons. The Evolution of Institutions for Collective Action*. Cambridge: Cambridge University Press, 1990.

Peck, Jamie, Neil Brenner, and Nik Theodore. "City as Policy Lab," AREA 6, "City as Lab," (2008).

Peck, John. "Via Campesina Confronts the Global Agrofuel Industrial Complex." *Z Magazine* (January 2009).

Pew Report. "Press Accuracy Rating Hits Two Decade Low," September 13, 2009. Last accessed March 6, 2010. HTTP://PEOPLE-PRESS.ORG/REPORT/543/

Phillips, Kevin. *Bad Money: Reckless finance, failed politics, and the global crisis of American capitalism*. New York: Viking, 2008.

Piercy, Marge. *To Be of Use: Poems by Marge Piercy*. New York, Doubleday: 1973.

Pimbert, Michael. *Towards Food Sovereignty: Reclaiming Autonomous Food Systems*. London: International Institute for Environment and Development, 2008.

p.m., *bolo bolo*. Brooklyn: Autonomedia, 1985.

Podlashuc, Leo. "Saving Women: Saving the Commons," *Eco-Sufficiency and Global Justice*, Ariel Salleh, ed. New York, London: Macmillan Palgrave, 2009.

Polanyi, Karl. *The Great Transformation: The Political and Economic Origins of our Time*. Boston: Beacon Press, 1957.

Pollan, Michael. *In Defense of Food: An Eater's Manifesto*. New York: Penguin, 2008.

Precarias a la Dervia. *A la deriva por los circuitos de la precariedad femenina*. Madrid: Traficantes de Sueños, 2004 (In Spanish).

Raum, Tom. "Guess who pays? Rising U.S. debt may be next crisis," *Associated Press* (July 5, 2009).

Read, Jason. *The Micro-Politics of Capital*. Albany, NY: SUNY Press, 2003.

Rebick, Judy. "Tens of thousands protest democracy erosion in Canada," Blog (January 24, 2010); available at: HTTP://WWW.ZMAG.ORG/BLOG/VIEW/4174 (accessed January 31, 2010).

Reitman, Ben. *Sister of the Road: The Autobiography of Boxcar Bertha*. Oakland: AK Press, 2002.

Reuveny, Rafael. "Climate change-induced migration and violent conflict," *Political Geography*, Vol. 26 (2007): 656–673.

Reyes, Oscar. "What is Wrong With Carbon Trading," *Carbon Trade Watch, A Project of the Transnational Institute*. Netherlands (2009); available at: HTTP://WWW.CARBONTRADEWATCH.ORG/ (accessed January 31, 2010).

Rice, Andrew. "Agro-Imperialism," *New York Times Magazine* (November 2009).

Rigby, David "The existence, significance, and persistence of profit rate differentials," *Economic Geography*, No. 67, Issue 3 (1991): 210–222.

Roadblock EF!. "Roundup of Actions Against I-69," *Earth First! Journal*, Vol. 28, Issue 6 (Mabon 2008).

Roberts, Dexter. "How Rising Wages Are Changing The Game In China," *Business Week* (March 27, 2006).

Rodríguez, Clemencia. *Fissures in the Mediascape: An International Study of Citizens' Media.* Creskill, NJ: Hampton Press, 2001.

Roggero, Gigi and Alberto de Nicola, "Eight Theses of University, Hierarchization and Institutions of the Common," *Edu-Factory* (January 2008); available at : HTTP://WWW.EDU-FACTORY.ORG (accessed January 31, 2010).

Runge, C. Ford and Benjamin Senauer. "How Biofuels Could Starve the Poor," *Foreign Affairs*, Vol. 86, No. 3 (May/June 2007): 41–53.

Salevurakis, John and Sahar Abdel-Haleim. "Bread subsidies in Egypt: Choosing social stability or fiscal responsibility," *Review of Radical Political Economics* 40, No. 1, (2008): 35–49.

Salleh, Ariel, ed. *Eco-Sufficiency and Global Justice: Women Write Political Ecology.* New York, London: Macmillan Palgrave, 2009.

Sassen, Saskia. *The Global City: New York, London, Tokyo.* Princeton: Princeton University Press, 1991.

_____. *Eco-Socialism or Eco-Capitalism?: A Critical Analysis of Humanity's Fundamental Choices.* London: Zed Books, 1999.

Schaffner, Frederick. "Truckers and citizens united—goals," *Truckers and Citizens United* (May 5th, 2008); available at: HTTP://WWW.THEAMERICANDRIVER.COM/FILES/WP/LONG_TERM_GOALS. HTML (accessed January 30, 2010).

Searchinger, Timothy and et al., "Use of U.S. Croplands for Biofuels Increases Greenhouse Gases Through Emissions from Land-Use Change," *Science*, Vol. 319 (February 29, 2008): 1238–1240.

Sedgewick, Eve Kosofsky. *Tendencies.* Durham, N.C.: Duke University Press, 1993.

Shepard, Benjamin. "Amanda Milan and the Rebirth of the Street Trans Action Revolutionaries," *From ACT UP to the WTO: Urban Protest and Community Building in the Era of Globalization.* Edited by Benjamin Shepard and Ronald Hayduk. New York: Verso, 2002.

_____. "Sylvia and Sylvia's Children." *That's Revolting: Queer Strategies for Resisting Assimilation.* Edited by Mattilda AKA Matt Bernstein Sycamore. Brooklyn: Soft Skull Press, 2004.

_____. *Queer Political Performance and Protest: Play, Pleasure and Social Movement.* New York: Routledge, 2009.

_____. "Play and World Making: From Gay Liberation to DIY Community Building," *Seventies Confidential: Hidden Histories from the Sixties' Second Decade.* Edited by Dan Berger. New Brunswick, NJ: Rutgers University Press, Forthcoming.

Shepard, Daniel and Anuradha Mittal. *The Great Land Grab: Rush for World's Farmland Threatens Food Security for the Poor.* Oakland: The Oakland Institute, 2009.

Shelley, Percy Bysshe. "A Philosophical Review of Reform," *Shelley's Prose.* David Lee Clark, ed. Albuquerque, NM: University of New Mexico Press, 1966.

Shiva, Vandana. *Staying Alive: Women, Ecology and Development.* London: Zed Books, 1989.

_____. *Ecology and The Politics of Survival: Conflicts Over Natural Resources in India.* New Delhi / London: Sage Publications, 1991.

_____. *Earth Democracy: Justice, Sustainability, and Peace.* Cambridge, MA: South End Press, 2005.

Shukaitis, Stevphen. *Imaginal Machines.* New York: Minor Compositions / Autonomedia, 2009.

_____, and David Graeber, with Erika Biddle. *Constituent Imagination: Militant Investigation, Collective Theorization.* Oakland: AK Press, 2007.

Shutt, Harry. *The trouble with capitalism: An enquiry into the causes of global economic failure.* London: Zed Books, 1998.

Simmel, Georg. *The Philosophy of Money*, 2nd ed. London: Routledge, 2002.

Simone, Adbou Maliq. *For the City Yet to Come.* Chapel Hill: Duke University Press, 2004.

Smith, Andrea. *Conquest: Sexual Violence and American Indian Genocide.* Cambridge: South End Press, 2005.

Smith, Dan and Janani Vivekananda, "A Climate of Conflict: The links between climate change, peace and war." London: International Alert, November 2007.

Smith, Neil. *Uneven Development: Nature, Capital and the Production of Space.* Athens: University of Georgia, 1984.

Smolker, Rachel and et al., "The True Cost of Agrofuels: Impacts on food, forests, peoples and the climate," Global Forest Coalition (2008); available at HTTP://WWW.GLOBALFORESTCOALITION. ORG/IMG/USERPICS/FILE/PUBLICATIONS/TRUECOSTAGROFUELS.PDF.

Smyth, D.J., G. Briscoe, and J. M. Samuels, "The variability of industry profit rates," *Applied Economics*, No. 1 (1969): 137–149.

Solnit, Rebecca. *A Paradise Built in Hell: The Extraordinary Communities that Arise in Disaster.* New York: Viking, 2009.

Solomon, Alisa. "Back to the Streets: Can Radical Gay Organizers Reignite a Movement," *Village Voice* (November 3, 1998).

Spade, Dean. "Pee Crimes," *Piss & Vinegar. A Zine by the Anti-Capitalist Tranny Brigade* (2002).

Spencer, Amy. *DIY: The Rise of Low-Fi Culture*, 2nd ed. London: Marion Boyars Publishers, 2008.

Stiglitz, Joseph and Linda J. Bilmes. *The Three Trillion Dollar War: The True Cost of the Iraq Conflict.* New York: W. W. Norton & Company, 2008.

Stimpson, Catharine. *Where the Meanings Are: Feminism and Cultural Spaces.* New York: Routledge, 1989.

Strangelove, Michael. *Empire of Mind: Digital Piracy and the Anti-capitalist Movement.* Toronto: University of Toronto Press, 2005.

Sugrue, Thomas. *The Origins of the Urban Crisis: Race and Inequality in Postwar Detroit.* Princeton: Princeton University Press, 1998.

Sugrue, Thomas and Andrew Goodman. "Plainfield Burning: Black Rebellion in the Suburban North," *Journal of Urban History*, Vol. 33 (May 2007): 568–601.

Sylvia Rivera Law Project. "SRLP announces non-support of the Gender Employment Non-Discrimination Act," (April 6, 2009); available at: HTTP://SRLP.ORG/NODE/301 (accessed November 1, 2009).

Tatchell, Peter. "Our Lost Radicalism," *The Guardian* London (June 26, 2009); available at: HTTP:// WWW.GUARDIAN.CO.UK/COMMENTISFREE/2009/JUN/26/GAY-LGBT-VICTIMHOOD-STONEWALL?C OMMENTPAGE=1&COMMENTPOSTED=1 (accessed June 17, 2009).

Teal, Don. *The Gay Militants.* New York: St. Martins Press, 1995.

Team Colors Collective, eds. *In the Middle of a Whirlwind: 2008 Convention Protests, Movement, and Movements.* Online Journal. Los Angeles: The Journal of Aesthetics and Protest Press, 2008; available at: HTTP://WWW.INTHEMIDDLEOFAWHIRLWIND.INFO (accessed January 31, 2010).

_____. "Of Whirlwinds and Wind Chimes (or ways of listening): Movement Building and Militant Research in the United States," *The Commoner* (February 4, 2009); available at: HTTP://WWW. COMMONER.ORG.UK/?P=76 (accessed January 31, 2010).

_____. "To Show the Fire and the Tenderness: Self-Reproducing Movements and Struggles In, Around, and Against the Current Economic Crisis in the United States," *Indypendent Reader* 12 (Spring / Summer 2009); available at: HTTP://INDYREADER.ORG/CONTENT/TO-SHOW-FIRE-AND-TEN-DERNESS-BY-TEAMS-COLORS-COLLECTIVE-CONOR-CASH-CRAIG-HUGHES-STEVIE-PEACE- (accessed January 31, 2010).

_____. "Abandoning the Chorus: Checking Ourselves a Decade Since Seattle," *Groundswell Journal* 1, (February 2010).

_____. "Radical Community Organizing to Make a Revolution Possible," (Forthcoming 2010); available at: HTTP://WWW.WARMACHINES.INFO.

Terranova, Tiziana. *Network Culture: Politics for the Information Age*. London and Ann Arbor, MI: Pluto Press, 2004.

Thalif, Deen. "Global hot spots of hunger set to explode," *Inter Press Service* (April 15th, 2008).

Thoburn, Nicholas. *Deleuze, Marx and Politics*. New York: Routledge, 2003.

Thomas, Nancy. "Looking For Greens," AREA 2, "After Winter Comes Spring—A Look at Local Food Systems," (2006).

Thompson, E.P. "The State versus its 'Enemies'," *Writing by Candlelight*. Merlin Press: London, 1980.

——. *Customs in Common Studies in Traditional Popular Culture*. New York: The New Press, 1993.

——. "In Defense of the Jury," *Persons & Polemics*. Merlin Press: London, 1994.

Thompson, Nato and Gregory Sholette, eds. *The Interventionists: Users' Manual for the Creative Disruption of Everyday Life*. Cambridge, MA: MIT Press, 2004.

Tokar, Brian. "On Bookchin's Social Ecology and its Contributions to Social Movements," *Capitalism, Nature, Socialism*, Volume 19, No. 2 (March 2008).

——. "Toward Climate Justice: Can we turn back from the abyss?," *Z Magazine*, September 2009; available at HTTP://WWW.ZCOMMUNICATIONS.ORG/ZMAG/VIEWARTICLE/22377 (accessed January 30, 2010).

Toret, Javier y Nicolas Sguiglia. "Cartografiando el exceso, frontera y trabajo en los caminos del movimiento," *Colectivo Fadai'at: Libertad de Movimiento+Libertad de Conocimiento*. Málaga: Imagraf Impresiones, 2006. (In Spanish; available in English and Arabic in the same publication)

TPTG, "Greek student movement: A brief outline of the student movement in Greece, June 2006," *Prol-Position* 7 (2006); HTTP://WWW.PROL-POSITION.NET/NL/2006/07/GREEK (accessed January 30, 2010).

Trigona, Maria. "Argentina's Soy Storm: Tensions rising among farmers," *Upside Down World* (April 28th, 2008); available at HTTP://UPSIDEDOWNWORLD.ORG/MAIN/CONTENT/VIEW/1253/1/ (accessed January 30, 2010).

Turbulence, "What Would It Mean to Win?" *Turbulence: Ideas for Movement* (May 2007); available at: HTTP://WWW.TURBULENCE.ORG.UK (accessed January 31, 2010).

Uctum, Merih and Sandra Viana, "Decline in the US profit rate: a sectoral analysis," *Applied Economics*, No. 31 (1999): 1641–1652.

Ugwumba, Chidozie. "Freeloading Bankers: How the Global Economy's Rulemakers Thrive on Subsidies from an Impoverished and Disenfranchised City," *50 Years is Enough Network*; available at: HTTP://WWW.50YEARS.ORG/ISSUES/TAXTHEBANK/REPORT.HTML (accessed January 31, 2010).

United Nations Population Fund. "State of the World Population 2007: Unleashing the Potential of Urban Growth"; available at: HTTP://WWW.UNFPA.ORG/SWP/2007/ENGLISH/INTRODUCTION.HTML (accessed January 30, 2010).

United States Department of Justice. Bureau of Justice Statistics. HTTP://WWW.OJP.USDOJ.GOV/BJS.

vanden Heuvel, Katrina. "In the Trenches and Fighting Slavery." Article for online blog *Editor's Cut*, December 28, 2008; available at: HTTP://WWW.THENATION.COM/BLOGS/EDCUT/391546/IN_THE_TRENCHES_AND_FIGHTING_SLAVERY.

van Leeuwen, Jan Willem Storm and Philip Smith. "Nuclear Power: The Energy Balance"; available at HTTP://WWW.STORMSMITH.NL (accessed January 30, 2010).

Virno, Paolo. *Grammar of the Multitude*. New York: Semiotext(e), 2004.

Voichita Nachescu. "Radical Feminism and the Nation: History and Space in the Political Imagination of Second-Wave Feminism," *Journal for the Study of Radicalism*, Vol. 3, No. 1 (2009): 29–59.

Vradis, Antonios. "Infoshops," *The International Encyclopedia of Revolution and Protest*, Edited by Immanuel Ness. Malden, MA and Ames, IA: Blackwell, 2009.

Waititu, Ernest. "Drought Spurs Resource Wars," Pulitzer Center for Crisis Reporting, Reprinted in *The Indypendent*, No. 119 (April 25, 2008).

Wald, Matthew L. "Efficiency, Not Just Alternatives, Is Promoted as an Energy Saver," *New York Times* (May 29, 2007).

Waziyatawin. *What Does Justice Look Like? The Struggle for Liberation in Dakota Homeland*. St. Paul: Living Justice Press, 2008.

WDSU News. "Nagin Nixes Water Privatization, Appoints New Director" (August 18, 2004); available at: HTTP://WWW.WDSU.COM/NEWS/3664128/DETAIL.HTML (accessed January 31, 2010).

Wheatley, Margaret. *Leadership and the New Science: Discovering Order in a Chaotic World*. San Francisco: Berrett-Koehler, 2001.

Williams, Jeffrey. "The Pedagogy of Debt," *Towards a Global Autonomous University: Cognitive Labor, the Production of Knowledge, and Exodus from the Education Factory*. Edited by Edu-Factory Collective. Brooklyn: Autonomedia, 2009.

Weisman, Steven. "Oil Producers See the World and Buy It Up," *New York Times* (November 28, 2007).

Werdigier, Julia. "Record Profits Reported for BP and Shell," *New York Times* (April 30, 2008).

Wheatley, Margaret. *Leadership and the New Science: Discovering Order in a Chaotic World*. San Francisco: Berrett-Koehler, 2001.

Wilson, Peter Lamborn and Bill Weinberg. *Avant Gardening: Ecological Struggle in the City & the World*. Brooklyn: Autonomedia, 1999.

World Food Programme. "WFP says high food prices are a silent tsunami, affecting every continent," *World Food Programme* (April 22, 2008); available at: HTTP://WWW.WFP.ORG/ENGLISH/?MODULEID=137&KEY=2820 (accessed January 30, 2010).

World Resources Institute. *Synthesis: Ecosystems and Human Well-Being, A Report of the Millennium Ecosystem Assessment*. Washington, DC: Island Press, 2005.

Wright, Kai. "Queer, Dead and Nobody Cares," *The Root* (February 26, 2008); available at: HTTP://WWW.THEROOT.COM (accessed November 10, 2009).

Wright, Steve. *Storming Heaven: Class Composition and Struggle in Italian Autonomia*. London: Pluto, 2002.

Xie, Andy. "Insight: Is China due a reality check?," *Financial Times* (October 15, 2009).

Yaffe, Deborah. "Feminism in Principle and in Practice: Everywomans Books," *Atlantis: A Women's Studies Journal*, Special Issue, *Connecting Practices, Doing Theory* 21.1 (Fall 1996): 154–157.

Yardley, Jim. "Drought Puts Focus on a Side of India Left Out of Progress," *New York Times* (September 5, 2009).

Yuen, Eddie, Daniel Burton-Rose, and George Katsiaficas, eds. *Confronting Capitalism: Dispatches from a Global Movement*. Brooklyn: Soft Skull Press, 2004.

The Zapatista Army of National Liberation. "Sixth Declaration of the Lacandon Jungle," *In Motion Magazine* (August 18, 2005).

Zerowork Collective. *Zerowork: Political Materials* 1 (1975).

——. *Zerowork: Political Materials* 2 (1977).

INDEX

Wind(s) from below:
Radical Community Organizing to Make a Revolution Possible

Team Colors Collective

In "**Wind(s) from below: Radical Community Organizing to Make a Revolution Possible**," we address current organizing in the U.S. in context of the class decomposition of recent decades. Following the years of fire we find ourselves circulating through winds and whirlwinds, which are struggling to intensify and connect amongst historically-specific forms of repression, infusion and capitulation. Through an inquiry into and analysis of contemporary social struggles, we argue that the social field is populated with a rich set of organizational possibilities, all of which are potential and becoming. We argue for a renewed emphasis on radical community organizing that challenges the non-profit industrial complex, the self-imposed limitations of activist identity, professionalized organizing, the limitations of the Alinsky model and urban-centrism. In their place we seek to amplify struggles that form through the substance of our own lives and our own reproduction, continuing into creating concrete mechanisms and procedures, and ending with the importance of becoming-other and becoming-revolutionary to build movements. It is through these movements that we build a new world, one in which many worlds fit.

Team Colors
warmachines.info

Eberhardt Press
eberhardtpress.org

May 2010 | 84 Pages | $6.00 | ISBN: 978-0-9778392-1-6
Published by Team Colors in Association with Eberhardt Press.
Available for Sale and Distribution from AK Press & Microcosm Publishing.

AK PRESS
EDINBURGH · OAKLAND · BALTIMORE

AK Press
akpress.org

Microcosm Publishing
microcosmpublishing.com

Support AK Press!

AK Press is one of the world's largest and most productive
anarchist publishing houses. We're
entirely worker-run and demo-
cratically managed. We operate
without a corporate structure—no
boss, no managers, no bullshit. We
publish close to twenty books every
year, and distribute thousands of
other titles published by other likeminded independent presses from
around the globe.

The Friends of AK program is a
way that you can directly contribute to the continued existence
of AK Press, and ensure that we're able to keep publishing great
books just like this one! Friends pay a minimum of $25 per month,
for a minimum three month period, into our publishing account.
In return, Friends automatically receive (for the duration of their
membership), as they appear, one free copy of every new AK
Press title. They're also entitled to a 20% discount on everything
featured in the AK Press Distribution catalog and on the website, on any and every order. You or your organization can even
sponsor an entire book if you should so choose!

There's great stuff in the works—so sign up now to become a
Friend of AK Press, and let the presses roll!

Won't you be our friend? Email friendsofak@akpress.org for
more info, or visit the Friends of AK Press website:
http://www.akpress.org/programs/friendsofak